미국 중·고등학교 유학 및 SAT/ACT 필수 영단어

Ted Chung's

The
Bodacious Book
of
Voluminous
Vocabulary

* 방대한 양의 단어가 수록된 대단한 책 *

HERMONHOUSE

📝 서문

안녕하세요, Ted쌤 정태훈입니다.

제 온라인 강의 질문 게시판에 심심치 않게 이런 질문이 올라옵니다. "SAT/ACT를 잘 보려면 단어를 몇 개나 알아야 하나요?" 아쉽게도 이 질문에 대한 명확한 답이 없습니다. SAT 출제기관인 College Board에서 지정한 단어 목록이란 건 없거든요. 그래서 저는 이렇게 대답합니다.

"많이 알면 알수록 좋다." 사실입니다.

어휘력이 곧 실력이거든요. 특히나 SAT/ACT Reading Section에서는… 그래서 상대적으로 미국에서 조기유학 생활을 하지 않았거나 미국계 중고등학교의 커리큘럼을 이수하지 못한 채로 SAT/ACT를 응시한 학생 중에는 본인의 이러한 약점을 막강한 어휘력을 갖춤으로써 극복하는 경우를 가끔 보았습니다.

사실 SAT 선생님들끼리도 이렇게 얘기합니다. "Reading Section은 단어 싸움이다." 단어를 많이 알수록 저절로 해결되는 것들이 많습니다. 단어는 많이 아는 것이 무조건 장땡입니다.

또, 이런 질문도 많이 올라옵니다. "선생님 강의에 나오는 단어만 다 알면 SAT/ACT에서 고득점 받나요?" 이 질문은 다행히 명확한 답이 있습니다. "받을 수 있다. 단, 정말로 학생이 이 단어들을 다 아는 경우에만, 안다고 착각하는 경우가 아니고…"

대부분의 경우 우리는 어떤 단어를 여러 번 보았다거나, 발음이 익숙하다거나, 여러 가지 뜻 중에 한두 가지를 안다고 해서 그 단어를 "안다"고 생각하는데, 그건 "착각"입니다. SAT/ACT에서 요구하는 수준은, 그 단어의 정확한 사전적인 의미, 문장에 어떻게 쓰였는지, 어떤 동의어가 있는지 뿐만 아니라, 특히 의미가 여러 개인 경우 일반적인 의미가 아닌, 즉 사전을 찾으면 첫 번째, 두 번째로 나오는 의미가 아닌, 여섯 번째, 일곱 번째의 의미도 다 알고 있어야 문제를 맞출 수 있는 수준입니다.

예를 들면 charge라는 단어가 있습니다. 이 단어는 이제 한국어에서도 흔히들 많이 쓰죠? "그거 얼마 차지(charge)하던가요?" 다시 말해 "그거 얼마 내라고 하던가요?", "어떤 금액을 요구하던가요?"의 뜻이지요. 그런데 SAT 문장에는 이런 게 나옵니다. "She is his charge." 이 문장은 어떻게 해석될까요? "그녀는 그의 가격이다?", "그녀는 그의 금액요구다"? 해석이 이상하지요? 이 문장의 뜻을 이해하려면 charge라는 얼핏 보기에 익숙한 단어의 여러 가지 뜻 중 "책임져야 하는 사람"이 있다는 걸 알아야 합니다. 그러면 문장이 금방 해석되지요. "그녀는 그가 책임져야 할 사람이다." 이제 이해가 되지요?

너무나 많은 경우에 학생들이 자기가 charge라는 단어의 일반적인 의미를 알기 때문에 그 단어를 안다고 착각합니다. 그런데 SAT/ACT에서는 그렇게 호락호락하게 문제가 나오지 않습니다. 오히려 일반적인 단어 뜻만 알고 있는 학생들이 속아서 고를 만한 보기를 함정으로 문제에 넣지요. 호기롭게 찍고 그 문제가 맞았다고 생각하는 학생 중에서 나중에 낭패를 보는 학생이 한두 명이 아닙니다.

그러면 어떻게 해야 정말로 어떤 단어를 "알 수 있을까요?"

지금의 기성세대가 써왔던 방법-하루에 단어 200개씩 외운다, 한 단어와 정의를 50번씩 반복해서 쓴다 등등의 방법-으로는 불가능합니다. 저는 단어를 습득하는 것은 사람을 사귀는 것과 비슷하다고 생각합니다. 얼굴을 자주 보고, 자주 만나고, 대화도 많이 해보고, 같이 많은 시간을 보내야 하는 겁니다. 그렇기 때문에 단어 공부를 할 때는 단순히 뜻만 외우는 것이 아니라 그 단어가 문장에서 어떻게 쓰였는지 예문도 보고, 동의어는 어떤 것이 있는지 묶어서 암기도 하고, 연습 문제를 통해서 복습도 하고, 이 단어의 명사형이나 동사형은 어떻게 생겼는지 같이 보기도 하고…. 이처럼 한 단어를 여러 번 반복해서 보고 또 봐야 마침내 머릿속에 각인됩니다.

이 책에서는 여러분들이 최대한의 효과를 볼 수 있도록 단어마다 영문의 의미, 동의어, 예문, 발음기호 그리고 반대어, 명사형, 형용사형이나 동사형 등을 포함해 하나의 단어를 다각도로 접근하여 가급적 반복해서 접할 수 있도록 집필하였습니다. 명심해 두기 바랍니다. 한 번 외웠다고 그 단어가 확실히 자기 것이 되지는 않습니다. 반드시 여러 번 봐야 합니다.

Series 1은 Founding Documents and Great American Conversations에서 발췌한 단어들로 이 뤄졌습니다. 몇 년 전 SAT가 개정되면서 출제기관인 College Board가 향후 모든 시험에 이 토픽에서 지문을 출제하겠다고 발표를 했는데, 여기서 Founding Documents는, 미국의 건국 전 독립운동과 독립전쟁에 관련된, 건국 후 국가체계 설립과 관련된 문서, 글, 혹은 연설, 그리고 Great American Conversations는 그 이후 미국이 대국으로 성장하는 과정에서 역사적 분기점마다 큰 영향을 미친 문서, 글, 혹은 연설 등을 말합니다. 여러분들이 잘 알고 있는 미국 독립선언문, 미국 헌법전문, 미국 개국공신들의 글, 연설, 그리고 역대 미국 대통령들의 취임사, 흑인 노예해방운동가와 여성 인권운동가들의 글, 연설 등이 여기에 포함됩니다.

이 토픽의 문서는 특히 17~19세기에 쓰여진 것들이 많아, 마치 현대 한국인들이 조선 시대의 고문을 이해하지 못하는 것처럼 미국에서 영어를 모국어로 쓰는 사람들도 이 당시의 문장에 대한 공부를 별도로 하지 않으면 어려워하는 내용들입니다. 따라서, 일상적인 학교생활이나 영어 공부에서 자연스럽게 만날 수 있는 영역이 아니기 때문에 의도적으로 단어 공부를 따로 하는 것이 중요합니다. 또한 이런 문서는 SAT/ACT뿐만 아니라 일반적인 고등학교 커리큘럼에서 반드시 만나는 것들이라 단어 공부를 해 두면 GPA에도 도움이 되는 이점이 있습니다.

그리고 말미에 철자나 발음이 비슷하여 착각하기 쉬운 단어들, 중의적인 의미로 자주 쓰이는 단어들을 별도로 정리하였습니다.

Series 2는 저자가 2006년부터 SAT/ACT 강의를 하면서 모은 실제시험, College Board에서 공개한 실제시험 및 Kaplan, Princeton Review나 Barron's 같은 저명한 출판사의 SAT/ACT 교재에 출판된 Practice Test까지 모두 약 150개 이상의 Test에 수록된 지문에서 필수 단어를 발췌하고 정리한 것입니다.

이 정도의 분량을 모두 검토하고 단어를 발췌하여 동의어 정리, 예문까지 작문하는 노력은 학생 개개인이 하기에는 불가능한 작업입니다. 그러므로 그 어떤 시험도 준비할 때 반드시 기출 문제를 풀어 봐야 하듯이, Series 2의 단어들도 SAT/ACT 기출 단어라고 생각하고 반복 학습을 하시기 바랍니다.

끝으로, Series 1과 2에는 몇몇 중복되는 단어들이 있습니다. 이는 각기 다른 지문에서 반복적으로 출제된 단어들 즉, 시험에 출제빈도가 높은 단어들이므로 앞에서 본 거라고 가볍게 여기지 말고 중복해서 다시 한번 공부하시기 바랍니다. 두 Series의 난이도는 비슷하게 조정했습니다. 가급적 시간을 갖고 순서대로 반복해서 여러 번 공부할 것을 추천합니다.

마지막으로 이 책을 출간하는 데 도움을 준 모든 분들께 감사의 말을 전합니다.

정태훈 (Ted Chung) 드림

집필 취지 및 교재의 특징/구성

이 책은 Ted Chung 선생님이 시중에 출판되는 전문 SAT/ACT Vocabulary 교재의 수준과 실제 SAT/ACT CR Section의 지문에서 요구하는 수준 간에 상당한 차이가 있음을 감지하고 집필한, SAT/ACT 고득점을 희망하는 학생의 어휘력 증대를 위한 맞춤형 교재입니다.

이 책은 다음과 같은 특징이 있습니다.

1) Series 1은 미국의 SAT 출제기관인 College Board에서 출제를 예고한 지문이자 미국 고등 교과과정에도 포함된 미국의 Founding Documents와 the Great American Conversations 중 핵심 문서에서 SAT 수준의 단어를 발췌하였습니다.

2) Series 2는 지난 15년 이상 공식적으로 공개된 SAT/ACT 실제 시험, 저자가 개인적으로 취합한 SAT/ACT 실제 시험, 그리고 전문 출판사가 시판 중인 SAT/ACT 교재의 연습 시험 Reading Comprehension 지문에서 핵심 단어를 발췌하였습니다.

3) 모든 단어의 정의를 영어로 표기하여 단순히 한국어 정의를 암기하는 공부법의 맹점을 보완하였습니다.

4) 단어당 동의어를 최대한 제공, 정의가 같은 단어 여러 개를 한꺼번에 학습하여 단시간에 많은 단어를 습득할 수 있도록 하였습니다.

5) 해당 단어를 이용한 예문(sample sentence)을 포함하여 해당 단어가 실제 문장에서 어떻게 사용되는지 보여주어 빠른 이해를 돕고 효과적인 암기가 가능하도록 하였습니다.

6) 각 단어의 발음기호를 추가하여 소리 내어 읽으며 공부할 수 있도록 하였습니다.

7) 각 강의당 연습문제, 그리고 5강마다 종합연습문제를 제공하여 학생이 해당 단어의 의미를 여러 번 확인할 수 있게 하였습니다.

이 책에 수록된 단어의 수준은 SAT/ACT에서 요구하는 수준에서 더 나아가 미국에서의 성공적인 대학생활을 영위할 수 있기 위해 각 대학들이 권장하는 Collegiate Level Vocabulary의 수준에 맞춰져 있기 때문에 SAT/ACT 준비 및 미국대학에서의 공부 준비를 위한 가장 적합한 단어 교재입니다.

Series 1 & 2 교재는 다음과 같이 구성되어 있습니다.

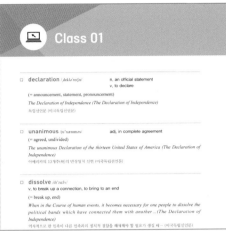

Class 01

□ **declaration** /ˌdekləˈreɪʃn/   n, an official statement
    v, to declare

(= announcement, statement, pronouncement)

The Declaration of Independence (The Declaration of Independence)

독립선언문 (미국독립선언문)

□ **unanimous** /juˈnænɪməs/   adj, in complete agreement

(= agreed, undivided)

The unanimous Declaration of the thirteen United States of America (The Declaration of Independence)

아메리카의 13개주(州)의 만장일치 선언 (미국독립선언문)

□ **dissolve** /dɪˈzɑːlv/

v, to break up a connection, to bring to an end

(= break up, end)

When in the Course of human events, it becomes necessary for one people to dissolve the political bands which have connected them with another ...(The Declaration of Independence)

역사적으로 한 민족이 다른 민족과의 정치적 결합을 해체해야 할 필요가 생길 때...(미국독립선언문)

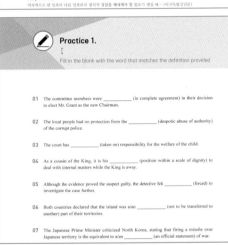

Practice 1.

Fill in the blank with the word that matches the definition provided

01 The committee members were _____ (in complete agreement) in their decision to elect Mr. Grant as the new Chairman.

02 The local people had no protection from the _____ (despotic abuse of authority) of the corrupt police.

03 The court has _____ (taken on) responsibility for the welfare of the child.

04 As a cousin of the King, it is his _____ (position within a scale of dignity) to deal with internal matters while the King is away.

05 Although the evidence proved the suspect guilty, the detective felt _____ (forced) to investigate the case further.

06 Both countries declared that the island was a/an _____ (not to be transferred to another) part of their territories.

07 The Japanese Prime Minister criticized North Korea, stating that firing a missile over Japanese territory is the equivalent to a/an _____ (an official statement) of war.

Class 06 ———— EXERCISE

Find the correct word which can replace the bold phrase in the following sentences. Change the word form appropriately to fit the sentence, if necessary

formidable, conjure, unanimous, station, unalienable, abolish, disposed, assent, pressing, abdicate, perfidy, subsist, latent, prohibit, faculty

01 The General was known as an honorable man, and so no one could have imagined that he would commit _____.

02 At this moment of national crisis, the President _____ his countrymen to stay strong and not to lose hope.

03 The Board of Directors rejected the proposal by a _____ decision.

04 The Duke and Duchess opposed their daughter's wish to marry a commoner, saying that they will not allow her to marry under her _____.

05 Although women's right to vote seems to be _____ now, it has barely been 100 years since this right has been guaranteed by the constitution.

1. 단어강의 Class

- 각 Class마다 표제어 20여 개 영문 정의 및 발음 기호
- 각 표제어마다 중급에서 SAT 수준의 동의어 5개까지 제공
- 각 표제어마다 예문 제공
- 각 강의마다 단어를 Review 할 수 있는 Practice 문제들을 따로 구성
- 교재 공란에 단어를 테스트할 수 있음

2. Review Test: 5개 Class마다 배치함

- 5개 Class마다 5개 Class 전체를 Review 할 수 있는 종합 Review Test 배치(표제어는 물론 동의어까지 포함한 테스트)
- 각 Class별 Review 테스트와는 별개로 한 번 종합 Test를 통해서 자연스럽게 복습이 될 수 있도록 구성
- Class별 연습문제와 상이한 문제 유형으로 다각도로 학생의 어휘력을 테스트할 수 있는 기회를 제공

▶ Series 1 & 2에 수록된 단어를 전부 습득할 경우 약 3,500~4,000개의 단어를 커버하게 됩니다. 반복 단어는 출제 빈도수가 높은 단어로 의도적으로 반복 삽입하였습니다.

차례 ⟶ Series 1-Core

차례 ⟶ Series 2-Real

Ted Chung
유학/SAT/ACT 필수 Vocabulary

| The Bodacious Book of |

Voluminous Vocabulary

Series 1-Core

(from Founding Documents and
Great American Conversations)

Class 01

☐ **declaration** /ˌdekləˈreɪʃn/ n. an official statement

v. to declare

(= announcement, statement, pronouncement)

The Declaration of Independence (The Declaration of Independence)

독립선언문 (미국독립선언문)

☐ **unanimous** /juˈnænɪməs/ adj. in complete agreement

(= agreed, undivided)

The unanimous Declaration of the thirteen United States of America (The Declaration of Independence)

아메리카의 13개주(州)의 만장일치 선언 (미국독립선언문)

☐ **dissolve** /dɪˈzɑːlv/

v. to break up a connection, to bring to an end

(= break up, end)

When in the Course of human events, it becomes necessary for one people to dissolve the political bands which have connected them with another…(The Declaration of Independence)

역사적으로 한 민족이 다른 민족과의 정치적 결합을 해체해야 할 필요가 생길 때… (미국독립선언문)

☐ **assume** /əˈsuːm/ v. to take upon oneself

(= seize, to take on)

..and to assume among the powers of the earth, the separate and equal station to which the Laws of Nature and of Nature's God entitle them…(The Declaration of Independence)

…세계의 여러 국가들 사이에서 자연의 법과 자연의 신이 부여한 독립과 평등의 지위를 차지하는…
(미국독립선언문)

□ **station** /ˈsteɪʃn/   n. the position within a scale of dignity(지위)

(= rank, class)

..and to assume among the powers of the earth, the separate and equal station to which the Laws of Nature and of Nature's God entitle them...(The Declaration of Independence)

⋯세계의 여러 국가들 사이에서 자연의 법과 자연의 신이 부여한 독립과 평등의 지위를 차지하는⋯ (미국독립선언문)

□ **impel** /ɪmˈpel/   v. to compel

(= compel, force, drive)

...a decent respect to the opinions of mankind requires that they should declare the causes which impel them to the separation. (The Declaration of Independence)

⋯인류의 신념에 대한 예의가 왜 (우리가) 독립을 할 수밖에 없는지 밝히게 한다. (미국독립선언문)

□ **endow** /ɪnˈdaʊ/   v. to furnish with some talent or quality

(= award, bestow, provide)

We hold these truths to be self-evident, that all men are created equal, that they are endowed by their Creator with certain unalienable Rights, (The Declaration of Independence)

다음과 같은 사실을 자명한 진리로 받아들인다. 즉, 모든 사람은 평등하게 태어났고, 창조주로부터 거부할 수 없는 권리를 부여받았다는 것 (미국독립선언문)

□ **unalienable** /ʌnˈeɪlɪənəbl/   adj. not to be transferred to another

(= inalienable, absolute, incontrovertible)

We hold these truths to be self-evident, that all men are created equal, that they are endowed by their Creator with certain unalienable Rights, (The Declaration of Independence)

다음과 같은 사실을 자명한 진리로 받아들인다. 즉, 모든 사람은 평등하게 태어났고, 창조주로부터 거부할 수 없는 권리를 부여받았다는 것 (미국독립선언문)

□ **institute** /ˈɪnstɪtuːt/   v. to establish

(= establish, set up)

That to secure these rights, Governments are instituted among Men.. (The Declaration of Independence)

이 권리를 확보하기 위하여 인류는 정부를 조직하며, (미국독립선언문)

☐ **alter** /ˈɔːltər/   v. to change

(= modify, amend, correct)

That whenever any Form of Government becomes destructive of these ends, it is the Right of the People to alter or to abolish it, (The Declaration of Independence)

어떠한 형태의 정부이던 이러한 목적을 파괴할 때는 국민이 그 정부 형태를 변경하던지 폐지하는 권리를 가지며 (미국독립선언문)

☐ **abolish** /əˈbɑːlɪʃ/   v. to get rid of

(= eliminate, put an end to, eradicate)

That whenever any Form of Government becomes destructive of these ends, it is the Right of the People to alter or to abolish it, (The Declaration of Independence)

어떠한 형태의 정부이던 이러한 목적을 파괴할 때는 국민이 그 정부 형태를 변경하던지 폐지하는 권리를 가지며 (미국독립선언문)

☐ **prudence** /ˈpruːdns/   n. caution with regard to practical matters

(= carefulness, discretion, good sense)

Prudence, indeed, will dictate that Governments long established should not be changed for light and transient causes (The Declaration of Independence)

오랜 역사를 가진 정부들이 가볍고 덧없는 이유로 변경되지 않도록 신중해야 할 것이고 (미국독립선언문)

☐ **transien** /ˈtrænʃnt/   adj. lasting only a short time

(= fleeting, ephemeral, evanescent)

Prudence, indeed, will dictate that Governments long established should not be changed for light and transient causes (The Declaration of Independence)

오랜 역사를 가진 정부들이 가볍고 덧없는 이유로 변경되지 않도록 신중해야 할 것이고 (미국독립선언문)

☐ **disposed** /dɪˈspəʊzd/   adj. having an inclination

(= inclined, willing, predisposed)

and accordingly all experience has shown, that mankind are more disposed to suffer, while evils are sufferable (The Declaration of Independence)

그리고 모든 경험으로 비춰보아 인간은 악패를 참을 수 있을 때까지 참는 경향이 있다는 것 (미국독립선언문)

□ **sufferable** /sʌˈfərəbl/　　　　adj. able to endure

(= endurable, manageable, tolerable)

and accordingly all experience has shown, that mankind are more disposed to suffer, while evils are sufferable (The Declaration of Independence)

그리고 모든 경험으로 비춰보아 인간은 악패를 참을 수 있을 때까지 참는 경향이 있다는 것 (미국독립선언문)

□ **usurpation** /ˌjuːzɜːrˈpeɪʃn/　　　　n. wrongful or illegal encroachment

(= infringement, seizure, encroachment)

But when a long train of abuses and usurpations evinces a design to reduce them under absolute Despotism (The Declaration of Independence)

그러나 오랫동안 계속된 학대와 착취가 그들을 완전한 전제주의의 예속하에 두고자 하는 의도가 있다는 걸 보여줄 때 (미국독립선언문)

□ **despotism** /ˈdespətɪzəm/　　　　n. the exercise of absolute government

(= dictatorship, totalitarianism)

But when a long train of abuses and usurpations evinces a design to reduce them under absolute Despotism (The Declaration of Independence)

그러나 오랫동안 계속된 학대와 착취가 그들을 완전한 전제주의의 예속하에 두고자 하는 의도가 있다는 걸 보여줄 때 (미국독립선언문)

□ **constrain** /kənˈstreɪn/　　　　v. to compel or force

(= compel, force, oblige, pressure)

..and such is now the necessity which constrains them to alter their former Systems of Government. (The Declaration of Independence)

…그리고 그들에게 이제 정부의 형태를 바꾸도록 강요하는 것이 필요한 이유가 이것이다. (미국독립선언문)

☐ **tyranny** /ˈtɪrəni/   n. despotic abuse of authority

(= oppression, dictatorship, autocracy)

n. tyrant: an oppressor, a dictator

The history of the present King of Great Britain is a history of repeated injuries and usurpations, all having in direct object the establishment of an absolute Tyranny over these States.. (The Declaration of Independence)

영국 국왕의 역사는 반복되는 악행과 착취의 역사이며 그 목적은 이 땅에 완전한 전제정치를 설립하고자 하는 것이다.(미국독립선언문)

☐ **candid** /ˈkændɪd/   adj. of the truth

(= truthful, honest)

To prove this, let Facts be submitted to a candid world. (The Declaration of Independence)

이 사실을 밝히기 위해 공정한 세계에 다음의 사실을 밝힌다. (미국독립선언문)

☐ **assent** /əˈsent/   n. consent

(= acquiescence, concurrence, sanction)

He has refused his Assent to Laws, the most wholesome and necessary for the public good. (The Declaration of Independence)

그는 공익을 위해 대단히 유익하고, 필요한 법을 설립하는 것에 동의하지 않았다. (미국독립선언문)

Practice 1.

Fill in the blank with the word that matches the definition provided

01 The committee members were _____ (in complete agreement) in their decision to elect Mr. Grant as the new Chairman.

02 The local people had no protection from the _____ (despotic abuse of authority) of the corrupt police.

03 The court has _____ (taken on) responsibility for the welfare of the child.

04 As a cousin of the King, it is his _____ (position within a scale of dignity) to deal with internal matters while the King is away.

05 Although the evidence proved the suspect guilty, the detective felt _____ (forced) to investigate the case further.

06 Both countries declared that the island was a/an _____ (not to be transferred to another) part of their territories.

07 The Japanese Prime Minister criticized North Korea, stating that firing a missile over Japanese territory is the equivalent to a/an _____ (an official statement) of war.

08 When testifying in court, one must always be _____ (truthful).

09 The company's organizational structure has not been _____ (changed, modified) for 20 years.

10 In these unpredictable times, _____ (caution with regard to practical matters) is the best policy.

11 The police chief announced that he will _____ (establish) a task force to investigate the case.

12 Many people protest the government's new decision to expand the screening of personal information as a/an _____ (illegal encroachment) of privacy.

13 Jewish mothers are famous for trying to _____ (force or compel) their children to marry.

14 Father advised me that youth is _____ (lasting only a short time), so I should enjoy it.

15 Janet felt _____ (having an inclination) to agree with anything Kevin says because he is her brother.

Class 02

☐ **wholesome** /ˈhəʊlsəm/   adj. beneficial to general well-being

(= healthy, nourishing, moral)

He has refused his Assent to Laws, the most wholesome and necessary for the public good.
(The Declaration of Independence)
그는 공익을 위해 대단히 유익하고, 필요한 법을 설립하는 것에 동의하지 않았다. (미국독립선언문)

☐ **pressing** /ˈpresɪŋ/   adj. urgent

(= vital, imperative, serious)

He has forbidden his governors to pass laws of immediate and pressing importance (The
Declaration of Independence)
그는 그의 총독들에게 긴급하게 요구되는 법률의 시행을 금지하였다. (미국독립선언문)

☐ **suspend** /səˈspend/   v. to hold or keep undetermined

(= defer, delay, postpone, shelve)

..unless (these laws are) suspended in their operation till his Assent should be obtained..
(The Declaration of Independence)
…그의 동의를 얻기 전까지 그런 법들이 시행되지 못하도록… (미국독립선언문)

☐ **utterly** /ˈʌtərli/   adv. completely

(= absolutely, totally, outright)

.. he has utterly neglected to attend to (these laws) (The Declaration of Independence)
..그는 그러한 법들을 철저히 묵살하였다. (미국독립선언문)

☐ **accommodation** /əˌkɑːməˈdeɪʃn/   n. readiness to aid

(= adaptation, adjustment)

He has refused to pass other Laws for the accommodation of large districts of people, (The Declaration of Independence)

그는 많은 사람들이 거주하는 지역에 필요한 법제정을 거부하였다. (미국독립선언문)

□ **relinquish** /rɪˈlɪŋkwɪʃ/   v. to give up

(= surrender, abandon, resign)

He has refused to pass other Laws for the accommodation of large districts of people, unless those people would relinquish the right of Representation in the Legislature, (The Declaration of Independence)

그는 많은 사람들이 거주하는 지역에서 입법기관에 대의원을 파견할 권리를 포기하게 만들기 위해 많은 사람들이 거주하는 지역에 필요한 법제정을 거부하였다. (미국독립선언문)

□ **inestimable** /ɪnˈestɪməbl/   adj. unable to estimate

(= incalculable, immeasurable, enormous)

..unless those people would relinquish the right of Representation in the Legislature, a right inestimable to them and formidable to tyrants only... (The Declaration of Independence)

…가치를 매길 수 없을 정도로 중요하며 폭군들만이 무서워할 권리인 입법기관에 대의원을 파견할 권리를 그 지역의 사람들이 포기하게 만들기 위해… (미국독립선언문)

□ **formidable** /ˈfɔːrmɪdəbl/   adj. causing fear

(= impressive, awe-inspiring, astounding)

..unless those people would relinquish the right of Representation in the Legislature, a right inestimable to them and formidable to tyrants only... (The Declaration of Independence)

…가치를 매길 수 없을 정도로 중요하며 폭군들만이 무서워할 권리인 입법기관에 대의원을 파견할 권리를 그 지역의 사람들이 포기하게 만들기 위해… (미국독립선언문)

□ **depository** /dɪˈpɑːzɪtɔːri/

n. a place where something is deposited or stored

(= store, reserve, stock)

He has called together legislative bodies at places unusual, uncomfortable, and distant from the depository of their public Records.. (The Declaration of Independence)

그는 공문서 보관소로부터 유별나고 멀고 불편한 곳에 입법기관을 소집하였고.. (미국독립선언문)

☐ **fatigue** /fə'tiːg/   v. to cause someone to be tired

(= exhaust, tire, enervate)

n. fatigue: low energy, tiredness

..for the sole purpose of fatiguing (legislative bodies) into compliance with his measures.. (The Declaration of Independence)

···순전히 입법기관들을 피곤하게 만들어 그의 정책에 복종하게끔 만들기 위하여.. (미국독립선언문)

☐ **compliance** /kəm'plaɪəns/   n. obedience or cooperation

(= obedience, acquiescence, submission)

..for the sole purpose of fatiguing (legislative bodies) into compliance with his measures.. (The Declaration of Independence)

···순전히 입법기관들을 피곤하게 만들어 그의 정책에 복종하게끔 만들기 위하여.. (미국독립선언문)

☐ **dissolution** /ˌdɪsə'luːʃn/   n. the act of dissolving

(= disbanding, termination, ending)

He has refused for a long time, after such dissolutions, to cause (other Houses of Representations) to be elected.. (The Declaration of Independence)

그는 의회를 해산한 후 오랫동안 새로운 의회가 선출되기를 거부하였고.. (미국 독립선언문)

☐ **annihilation** /əˌnaɪə'leɪʃn/   n. total destruction

(= obliteration, extinction, extermination)

He has refused for a long time, after such dissolutions, to cause others to be elected; whereby the Legislative powers, incapable of Annihilation, have returned to the People at large for their exercise.. (The Declaration of Independence)

그는 의회를 해산한 후 오랫동안 새로운 의회가 선출되기를 거부하였고, 그러나 입법권이 완전이 없어질 수는 없으므로 다시 일반에게 돌아와 행사가 되기는 하지만.. (미국 독립선언문)

☐ **at large**   idiom. in general

(= in general, as a whole)

He has refused for a long time, after such dissolutions, to cause others to be elected; whereby the Legislative powers, incapable of Annihilation, have returned to the People at large for their exercise.. (The Declaration of Independence)

그는 의회를 해산한 후 오랫동안 새로운 의회가 선출되기를 거부하였고, 그러나 입법권이 완전이 없어질 수는 없으므로 다시 일반에게 돌아와 행사가 되기는 하지만.. (미국 독립선언문)

☐ **convulsion** /kənˈvʌlʃn/   n. violent disturbance

(= shaking, seizure, spasm)

...the State remaining in the meantime exposed to all the dangers of invasion from without, and convulsions within.. (The Declaration of Independence)

..그 기간동안 식민지는 외부로부터 침략 위험 및 내부의 격렬한 소요에 노출이 되었으며.. (미국독립선언문)

☐ **hither** /ˈhɪðər/   adv. toward this place

(= to here, this way)

..refusing to pass others to encourage (foreigners) migrations hither, and raising the conditions of new Appropriations of Lands.. (The Declaration of Independence)

..외국인들이 이곳으로 이민오기를 장려하는 법을 제정하기를 거부하며, 또한 새로이 토지를 취득하는데 어려운 조건을 부여하고.. (미국독립선언문)

☐ **appropriation** /əˌprəʊpriˈeɪʃn/

n. the grant of money for some special purpose

(= assumption)

..refusing to pass others to encourage (foreigners) migrations hither, and raising the conditions of new Appropriations of Lands.. (The Declaration of Independence)

..외국인들이 이곳으로 이민오기를 장려하는 법을 제정하기를 거부하며, 또한 새로이 토지를 취득하는데 어려운 조건을 부여하고.. (미국독립선언문)

☐ **obstruct** /əbˈstrʌkt/   v. to block with an obstacle

(= block, barricade, hinder)

He has obstructed the Administration of Justice, by refusing his Assent to Laws for establishing Judiciary powers. (The Declaration of Independence)

그는 사법권을 수립하는 법의 제정을 거부하여 사법행정을 방해하였다. (미국독립선언문)

☐ **judiciary** /dʒuˈdɪʃieri/   adj. related to the judicial branch of a country

(= bench, courts)

He has obstructed the Administration of Justice, by refusing his Assent to Laws for establishing Judiciary powers. (The Declaration of Independence)

그는 사법권을 수립하는 법의 제정을 거부하여 사법행정을 방해하였다. (미국독립선언문)

☐ **tenure** /ˈtenjər/   n. a duration of holding office

(= tenancy, term, duration, period)

He has made Judges dependent on his Will alone, for the tenure of their offices, and the amount and payment of their salaries. (The Declaration of Independence)

그는 법관들의 임기, 임금의 액수 및 지불과 관련하여 오로지 자신의 뜻에만 따르도록 하였다. (미국독립선언문)

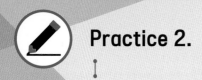

Practice 2.

Fill in the blank with the word that matches the definition provided

01 I was up against a/an _____ (causing fear) opponent, but I believed that I could beat him, if I only played as well as I did in practice.

02 Some people say that a single five-year _____ (duration of holding office) for Superintendent of Schools is too short to institute any meaningful policies.

03 The store announced that it will _____ (to hold or postpone) the sales of the product until further notice.

04 The manager told the workers that they could leave if there were no _____ (urgent) matters.

05 Dr. Oppenheimer warned that the continued competition among developed countries to develop more and more destructive weapons can lead to the _____ (total destruction) of human kind.

06 Foreign companies working in Korea must ensure full _____ (obedience or cooperation) with Korean laws.

07 The Church, where Leonardo Da Vinci's famous mural "The Last Supper" is located, was used as a/an _____ (place for storage) for ammunition during World War II.

08 The news broadcasted that the hurricane caused _____ (unable to measure) damage along its path.

09 Our view of the sunrise was _____ (blocked with an obstacle) by the thick clouds gathered over the horizon.

10   The food served at the school cafeteria may not be fancy, but it is very _____ (healthy).

11   In this country, the _____ (act of dissolving) of a company takes longer than the establishment of it.

12   The city government granted a/an _____ (the grant of money for a special purpose) of U$10 million to install escalators in all subway stations.

13   The scandal caused the entire country to have a/an _____ (violent disturbance).

14   Many politicians do not understand what the opinion of the public _____ (in general) is.

15   When the President was proven to have committed a crime, he was forced to _____ (to give up) his authority to the Vice President immediately.

Class 03

☐ **swarm** /swɔːrm/

n. a great number of insects/people/things in motion

(= horde, crowd, mass, mob)

He has erected a multitude of New Offices, and sent hither swarms of Officers to harass our people. (The Declaration of Independence)
그는 새로운 관직을 여럿 만들고 관료를 무리로 보내 우리를 괴롭혔다. (미국독립선언문)

☐ **abolish** /əˈbɑːlɪʃ/　　　　　　　v. to get rid of

(= eliminate, stop, eradicate)

For abolishing the free System of English Laws in a neighboring Province.. (The Declaration of Independence)
이웃하는 지역에 영국법 체계를 없앴고... (미국독립선언문)

☐ **charter** /ˈtʃɑːrtər/

n. a document, issued by the British King, outlining the conditions under which the American colonies are organized, and defending their rights and privileges

(= contract, deed, approval, commission)

For taking away our Charters, abolishing our most valuable Laws, and altering fundamentally the Forms of our Governments (The Declaration of Independence)
우리의 허가증을 빼앗고, 우리의 가장 소중한 법을 폐지하며, 우리의 정부형태를 근본적으로 바꾸었고.. (미국독립선언문)

☐ **abdicate** /ˈæbdɪkeɪt/　　　　　　v. to voluntarily give up authority

(= renounce, relinquish, resign)

He has abdicated Government here, by declaring us out of his Protection and waging War against us. (The Declaration of Independence)
우리를 그의 보호 밖에 두고 우리를 향해 전쟁을 도발하여 이곳의 정부를 해산시키고.. (미국독립선언문)

☐ **plunder** /ˈplʌndər/   v. to take wrongfully

(= loot, steal, pillage)

He has plundered our seas, ravaged our Coasts, burnt our towns, and destroyed the lives of our people. (The Declaration of Independence)

우리의 바다를 약탈하고, 우리의 해안을 크게 파괴하고, 우리의 도시를 불태우고, 우리 식민들의 삶을 파괴하였다. (미국독립선언문)

☐ **ravage** /ˈrævɪdʒ/   v. to cause extreme damage to

(= devastate, destroy, ransack)

He has plundered our seas, ravaged our Coasts, burnt our towns, and destroyed the lives of our people. (The Declaration of Independence)

우리의 바다를 약탈하고, 우리의 해안을 크게 파괴하고, 우리의 도시를 불태우고, 우리 식민들의 삶을 파괴하였다. (미국독립선언문)

☐ **mercenary** /ˈmɜːrsəneri/   n. a soldier who fights for anyone for money

(= soldier)

He is at this time transporting large Armies of foreign Mercenaries to complete the works of death, (The Declaration of Independence)

살해의 작업을 완수하기 위해 많은 수의 용병을 지금 이곳으로 이동시키고 있으며..(미국독립선언문)

☐ **perfidy** /ˈpɜːrfədi/   n. deliberate breach of faith or trust

(= treachery, deceit, betrayal)

..already begun with circumstances of cruelty and perfidy scarcely paralleled in the most barbarous ages.. (The Declaration of Independence)

역사상 가장 야만적인 시대에도 흔히 볼 수 없었던 잔혹스러움과 배신의 상황을 시작하였고…
(미국독립선언문)

☐ **constrain** /kənˈstreɪn/   v. to make excessive demands upon

(= force, demand)

He has constrained our fellow citizens taken captive on the high Seas to bear arms against their country.. (The Declaration of Independence)

해상에서 납치된 우리의 동료 국민들에게 그들의 조국을 향해 무기를 들도록 하였고.. (미국독립선언문)

□ **brethren** /ˈbreðrən/   n. comrades

(= comrades, brothers, colleagues)

to become the executioners of their friends and Brethren.. (The Declaration of Independence)

그들의 친구와 형제의 처형자가 되게 하고.. (미국독립선언문)

□ **insurrection** /ˌɪnsəˈrekʃn/   n. resistance against civil authority

(= insurgence, rebellion, revolt)

He has excited domestic insurrections amongst us.. (The Declaration of Independence)

내란을 선동하였고.. (독립선언문)

□ **petition** /pəˈtɪʃn/   v. to address a formal complaint to

(= repeal, implore, plead, solicit)

In every stage of these Oppressions We have petitioned for Redress in the most humble terms.. (The Declaration of Independence)

이러한 탄압의 모든 단계에서 우리는 가장 겸손한 조건으로 우리의 불만사항이 시정되기를 청원하였고.. (미국독립선언문)

□ **unwarrantable** /ʌ`nwɔ´ːrəntəbl/   adj. unjustifiable

(= inexcusable, indefensible, deplorable)

We have warned (our British brethren) from time to time of attempts by their legislature to extend an unwarrantable jurisdiction over us.. (The Declaration of Independence)

우리는 (영국 형제들에게) 간간히 그들의 입법부에서 우리에게 정당화 될 수 없는 법적 구속권을 가지려고 한다고 경고하였다. (미국독립선언문)

□ **appeal** /əˈpiːl/   v. to ask for sympathy

(= plead, entreat)

We have appealed to (our British brethren) native justice and magnanimity. (The Declaration of Independence)

우리는 (영국 형제들에게) 그들만의 타고난 정의와 관대함을 간청하였다. (미국독립선언문)

□ **magnanimity** /ˌmægnəˈnɪməti/   n. extreme generosity

(= benevolence, kindness, fairness)

We have appealed to (our British brethren) native justice and magnanimity.. (The Declaration of Independence)

우리는 (영국 형제들에게) 그들만의 타고난 정의와 관대함을 간청하였다. (미국독립선언문)

□ **conjure** /ˈkɑːndʒər/   v. to appeal to solemnly

(= plead, entreat)

..we have conjured (our British brethren) by the ties of our common kindred to disavow these usurpations.. (The Declaration of Independence)

..우리는 (영국 형제들에게) 우리가 같은 피를 나눈 사실을 상기시키며 이러한 침탈을 거부해주기를 (탄원하였고).. (미국독립선언문)

□ **consanguinity** /ˌkɑːnsænˈgwɪnəti/   n. close connection

(= kinship, connection)

They too have been deaf to the voice of justice and of consanguinity.. (The Declaration of Independence)

그들 역시 정의와 혈연의 목소리에 귀기울이지 않았다.. (미국독립선언문)

□ **acquiesce** /ˌækwiˈes/   v. to agree

(= comply, accept, consent, concur)

We must, therefore, acquiesce in the necessity, which denounces our Separation, and hold them, as we hold the rest of mankind, Enemies in War, in Peace Friends.. (The Declaration of Independence)

우리는, 그러므로, (영국과) 갈라서야 하는 필요성에 동의하며 모든 인류를 대하듯이 그들도 전쟁시에는 적으로, 평화시에는 친구로 받아들일 수 밖에 없다. (미국독립서언문)

□ **rectitude** /ˈrektɪtuːd/   n. correctness

(= righteousness, morality, decency)

..appealing to the Supreme Judge of the world for the rectitude of our intentions.. (The Declaration of Independence)

..세계의 최고 심판관에게 우리의 정당함을 호소하며... (미국독립선언문)

□ **to levy war**   to start a war

..as Free and Independent States, they have full Power to levy war.. (The Declaration of Independence)

..자유독립국가로서 전쟁을 치를 권리..(미국독립선언문)

□ **divine** /dɪˈvaɪn/   adj. of God

(= godly, heavenly)

And for the support of this Declaration, with a firm reliance on the protection of divine Providence, we mutually pledge to each other our Lives, our Fortunes and our sacred Honor.. (The Declaration of Independence)

그리고 이 선언문을 지지하기 위하여, 하느님의 가호를 굳게 믿으며 서로에게 우리의 생명과 재산과 신성한 명예를 걸기로 다짐한다. (미국독립선언문)

□ **Providence** /ˈprɑːvɪdəns/   n. God

(= God)

And for the support of this Declaration, with a firm reliance on the protection of divine Providence, we mutually pledge to each other our Lives, our Fortunes and our sacred Honor.. (The Declaration of Independence)

그리고 이 선언문을 지지하기 위하여, 하느님의 가호를 굳게 믿으며 서로에게 우리의 생명과 재산과 신성한 명예를 걸기로 다짐한다. (미국독립선언문)

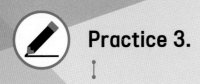

Practice 3.

Fill in the blank with the word that matches the definition provided

01 I did not _____ (agree) to the decision: it was too petty for me to agree to.

02 We couldn't get close to the hive because a/an _____ (a great number of insects flying) of bees was buzzing around it.

03 Many social leaders_____ (asked for sympathy) to the public to remain calm.

04 Many people find it strange that the death penalty has not been _____(terminated) in many U.S. states.

04 When the witness wouldn't talk to the police, they tried to _____ (compel or force) him to talk by threatening to put him under arrest.

06 The man is an example of moral _____ (moral correctness).

07 Solomon prayed to God for _____ (of God) help.

08 During the civil war, our people were forced to fight our own _____ (brothers).

09 King Edward III of England is known as the Romantic King: he _____ (gave up authority) his throne to marry the woman he loved – an American woman, who had been married once before.

10 In medieval wars, once a castle was taken, the troops of the winning army were allowed to _____ (pillage or steal from) the city within it for three nights.

11 Several shops were _____ (cause extreme damage to) overnight by thieves.

12   Surprisingly, the instinctively suspicious Stalin never imagined that Hitler would commit _____ (betrayal) after their secret non-aggression pact in 1941.

13   The protesters were accused of trying to stage a/an _____ (rebellion).

14   The unreasonable guest continued to make _____ (unjustified) requests.

☐ **tranquility** /træŋˈkwɪləti/   n. peacefulness

(= serenity, calmness, peace)

We the People of the United States, in Order to form a more perfect Union, establish Justice, insure domestic Tranquility, provide for the common defense.. (the U.S. Constitution)

우리 미국의 국민들은, 더욱 완벽한 연방을 설립하고, 정의를 실현하며, 국내 평화를 보장하고, 공동의 방위를 제공하기 위하여.. (미국헌법)

☐ **welfare** /ˈwelfer/   n. wellbeing

(= wellbeing, happiness, safety)

..promote the general welfare, and secure the Blessings of Liberty to ourselves and our Posterity.. (the U.S. Constitution)

..공공의 복지를 증진하고, 우리와 우리 후손들에게 자유의 축복을 확보해 주기 위해.. (미국 헌법)

☐ **posterity** /pɑːˈsterəti/   n. future generations

(= successors, descendants, heirs)

..promote the general welfare, and secure the Blessings of Liberty to ourselves and our Posterity.. (the U.S. Constitution)

..공공의 복지를 증진하고, 우리와 우리 후손들에게 자유의 축복을 확보해 주기 위해.. (미국헌법)

☐ **ordain** /ɔːrˈdeɪn/   v. to enact by law

(= establish, decree, proclaim)

..do ordain and establish this Constitution for the United States of America. (the U.S. Constitution)

다음과 같이 미국의 헌법을 법으로 제정하고 공표한다. (미국헌법)

☐ **vest** /vest/   v. to place power in the control of

(= bestow, confer, entrust)

All legislative Powers herein granted shall be vested in a Congress of the United States (the U.S. Constitution)

(헌법에 보장되는) 모든 입법권은 미국의 상원에 부여된다. (미국헌법)

☐ **apportion** /əˈpɔːrʃn/   v. to distribute proportionally

(= allocate, allot, distribute)

Representatives and direct taxes will be apportioned among the several states which may be included in this union. (the U.S. Constitution)

이 연방에 포함되는 주(州)에 대의원(의 수)와 직접세(의 징수)가 적절히 분배된다. (미국헌법).

☐ **preamble** /ˈpriːæmbl/   n. introductory statement

(= preface, beginning, prelude)

The Preamble of the Bill of Rights (Bill of rights)

권리장전의 전문 (권리장전)

☐ **beneficent** /bɪˈnefɪsnt/   adj. causing good to be done

(= charitable, beneficial)

And as extending the ground of public confidence in the Government, will best ensure the beneficent ends of (the Government's) institution. (Bill of rights)

정부에 대한 국민의 믿음을 확대하며, 정부기관의 유익한 목표를 가장 잘 보장할 것이다. (권리장전)

☐ **concur** /kənˈkɜːr/   v. to express agreement

(= agree, assent, accept, acquiesce)

Resolved by the Senate and House of Representatives of the United States of America, in Congress assembled, two thirds of both Houses concurring, that the following Articles be proposed…(Bill of rights)

미국의 상원과 하원에 의해 의결되고, 상원에 소집되며, 양원의 2/3 이상이 동의하여, 다음과 같은 조항들이 건의되고… (권리장전)

□ **ratify** /ˈrætɪfaɪ/   v. to confirm by expressing approval

(= approve, sanction, indorse)

..when ratified by three fourths of the said Legislatures, to be valid to all intents and purposes, as part of the said Constitution.. (Bill of rights)

상기한 입법기간의 3/4가 비준에 동의할 경우, 모든 경우와 목적에 유효하며, 상기한 헌법의 일부가 된다. (권리장전)

□ **prohibit** /prəˈhɪbɪt/   v. to not allow

(= forbid, ban, exclude, veto)

Congress shall make no law respecting an establishment of religion, or prohibiting the free exercise thereof.. (Bill of rights)

상원은 종교의 설립이나 자유로운 종교활동을 금지하는 그 어떤 법도 제정하지 못하며.. (권리장전)

□ **abridge** /əˈbrɪdʒ/   v. to shorten

(= edit, condense, curtail)

...or abridging the freedom of speech, or of the press.. (Bill of rights)

...혹은 언어의 자유 혹은 출판의 자유를 축약하는.. (권리장전)

□ **infringe** /ɪnˈfrɪndʒ/   v. to encroach on

(= invade, overstep, interfere)

A well regulated Militia, being necessary to the security of a free State, the right of the people to keep and bear Arms, shall not be infringed. (Bill of rights)

자유국가의 안전을 위해 반드시 필요한 잘 통제된 민병대를 조직하거나 국민이 무기를 소지할 자유는 억압되지 못한다. (권리장전)

□ **quarter** /ˈkwɔːrtər/   v. to lodge

(= accommodate, lodge, house)

No Soldier shall, in time of peace be quartered in any house, without the consent of the Owner.. (Bill of rights)

어떤 군사도 평화시에 집주인의 동의 없이 그의 집에 주둔할 수 없다.. (권리장전)

☐ **indictment** /ɪnˈdaɪtmənt/   n. formal accusation

(= condemnation, accusation, prosecution)

No person shall be held to answer for a capital, or otherwise infamous crime, unless on a presentment or indictment of a Grand Jury.. (Bill of rights)

대배심의 제시나 기소 없이 누구도 금전적 손해나 악명높은 범죄에 대한 책임을 지지 않는다. (권리장전)

☐ **impartial** /ɪmˈpɑːrʃl/   adj. neutral

(= unbiased, fair, independent)

In all criminal prosecutions, the accused shall enjoy the right to a speedy and public trial, by an impartial jury.. (Bill of rights)

범죄의 소추 중에 피의자는 중립적인 배심원이 판결하는 빠르고 공개된 재판을 받을 권리가 있다. (권리장전)

☐ **enumeration** /ɪˌnuːməˈreɪʃn/   n. a list

(= listing, inventory)

The enumeration in the Constitution, of certain rights, shall not be construed to deny or disparage others retained by the people.. (Bill of rights)

헌법에 제시된 특정한 권리들의 목록이 국민들이 영위하는 다른 권리들을 거부하거나 폄하할 수 없다. (권리장전)

☐ **faction** /ˈfækʃn/

n. a group of people that hold the same political beliefs

(= party, section, circle, bloc)

Among the numerous advantages promised by a well constructed Union, none deserves to be more accurately developed than its tendency to break and control the violence of faction. (“Federalist Papers”)

올바르게 구성된 연방이 보장하는 다수의 장점 중에 파벌이 폭력을 행사하는 것을 억제하거나 조정하는 것 만큼 정확하게 개발되어야 하는 것은 없다. (연방주의자 논집)

☐ **propensity** /prəˈpensəti/   n. a tendency

(= predilection, inclination, bent, penchant)

The friend of popular governments never finds himself so much alarmed for their character and fate, as when he contemplates their propensity to this dangerous vice. ("Federalist Papers")

민간정부가 이런 부도덕함으로 기우는 성향을 보일 때만큼 그 정부를 지지하는 사람이 그 정부의 성격과 운명에 대해 놀라워 할 때가 없다. (연방주의자 논집)

......

☐ **vice** /vaɪs/   n. an evil habit

(= immorality, depravity, wickedness, sin)

The friend of popular governments never finds himself so much alarmed for their character and fate, as when he contemplates their propensity to this dangerous vice. ("Federalist Papers")

민간정부가 이런 부도덕함으로 기우는 성향을 보일 때만큼 그 정부를 지지하는 사람이 그 정부의 성격과 운명에 대해 놀라워 할 때가 없다. (연방주의자 논집)

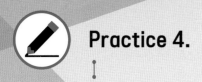

Practice 4.

Fill in the blank with the word that matches the definition provided

01 I do not _____ (to express agreement) with the opinion that foreign immigrants are to blame for the domestic unemployment problem.

02 The treaty was _____ (to confirm by expressing approval) by all member countries of the United Nations.

03 It is _____ (to not allowed) to hunt animals in this park from September to May.

04 The professor told Francis that his report was too long and that he should _____ (to shorten its length) it.

05 The lying politician faces _____ (formal accusation) for perjury.

06 I find it difficult to believe that his judgement was_____ (neutral and unbiased).

07 At the end of a debate, each candidate must conduct a candid _____ (a list) of the gains and losses of his performance.

08 Stanley Park is located just minutes away from Vancouver's bustling downtown and is a place where people can enjoy nature's _____ (peacefulness) to the fullest.

09 People are sick of politicians who bow before the voters when they need votes, but soon forget that their jobs are to improve the _____ (well-being) of those who voted for them.

10 At the site of the former Auschwitz Concentration Camp, now stands the Auschwitz-Birkenau State Museum, erected as a reminder to _____ (future generations) of the horrible war crimes that happened there during World War II.

11 Most bees have the _____ (a tendency) to be attracted by the color yellow.

12 Drinking and smoking are the two most common _____ (evil habits) of modern people.

13 In most democratic countries, the ability to make supreme legal judgement is _____ (to place power in the control if) in the Supreme Court.

14 There were five of us and only four sandwiches, so everyone was anxious that I _____ (to distribute evenly) the sandwiches fairly.

15 When Mr. Thatcher was a boy, his family was so poor that they had to accept _____ (causing good to be done) assistance to the needy.

16 The reporter _____ (to encroach on) upon the candidate's privacy by asking about his personal finances.

17 The refugees were _____ (to lodge or accommodate) in makeshift huts for the time being.

☐ **perish** /ˈperɪʃ/   v. to die, to rot

(= expire, decease, succumb)

The instability, injustice, and confusion introduced into the public councils, have, in truth, been the mortal diseases under which popular governments have everywhere perished.. ("Federalist Papers")

의회에서 발생하는 불안정, 부당성과 혼란이, 사실, 다른 곳에서 민간 정부를 실패하게 만든 불치병이었다. (연방주의자 논집)

☐ **adversary** /ˈædvərseri/   n. enemy

(= opponent, challenger, rival)

..as they continue to be the favorite and fruitful topics from which the adversaries to liberty derive their most specious declamations.. ("Federalist Papers")

..그것들은 계속해서 자유를 반대하는 사람들이 가장 겉으로만 번지르르한 연설들을 할 때 사용하는 최애의 생산적인 토픽들로 사용되며.. (연방주의자 논집)

☐ **specious** /ˈspiːʃəs/   adj. pleasing to the eye but deceptive

(= hollow, erroneous, inaccurate, fallacious)

..as they continue to be the favorite and fruitful topics from which the adversaries to liberty derive their most specious declamations.. ("Federalist Papers")

..그것들은 계속해서 자유를 반대하는 사람들이 가장 겉으로만 번지르르한 연설들을 할 때 사용하는 최애의 생산적인 토픽들로 사용되며.. (연방주의자 논집)

☐ **declamation** /ˌdeklə'meɪʃn/   n. formal speech

(= recitative, narrative)

..as they continue to be the favorite and fruitful topics from which the adversaries to liberty derive their most specious declamations.. ("Federalist Papers")

..그것들은 계속해서 자유를 반대하는 사람들이 가장 겉으로만 번지르르한 연설들을 할 때 사용하는 최애의 생산적인 토픽들로 사용되며.. (연방주의자 논집)

☐ **unwarrantable** /ʌ`nwɔ´:rəntəbl/   adj. unforgiveable

(= uncalled-for, inexcusable, deplorable, reprehensible)

..but it would be an unwarrantable partiality, ("Federalist Papers")

..그러나 그것은 정당화 할 수 없는 편파가 될 것이고.. (연방주의자 논집)

☐ **contend** /kən'tend/   v. to argue

(= declare, maintain, assert, insist)

..to contend that (the improvements made by the American constitution) have as effectually obviated the danger on this side, as was wished and expected.. ("Federalist Papers")

..(미국의 헌법 도입으로 개선된 것들이) 바라고 기대한 만큼 이 방면에서의 위험을 예상하고 예방했다고 주장하는 것이.. (연방주의자 논집)

☐ **obviate** /'ɑ:bvieɪt/   v. to anticipate and prevent

(= remove, avoid, preclude, avert, hinder)

..to contend that (the improvements made by the American constitution) have as effectually obviated the danger on this side, as was wished and expected.. ("Federalist Papers")

..(미국의 헌법 도입으로 개선된 것들이) 바라고 기대한 만큼 이 방면에서의 위험을 예상하고 예방했다고 주장하는 것이.. (연방주의자 논집)

☐ **overbearing** /ˌəʊvər'berɪŋ/   adj. rudely arrogant

(= haughty, domineering, imperious, pompous)

..that measures are too often decided, not according to the rules of justice and the rights of the minor party, but by the superior force of an interested and overbearing majority.. ("Federalist Papers")

..지나치게 많은 경우에 정의로운 규칙과 소수당의 권리에 의하지 않고 이해관계가 더 크고 강압적인 다수의 우월한 힘에 의해 조처들이 결정된다는 것.. (연방주의자 논집)

☐ **actuate** /'æktʃueɪt/   v. to incite into action

(= activate, motivate, stimulate)

..who are united and actuated by some common impulse of passion, ("Federalist Papers")

..공동의 열정으로 인해 연합되고 행동을 하게 되는.. (연방주의자 논집)

□ **adverse** /əd'vɜːrs/   adj. opposed to

(= contrary, hostile, antagonistic, confrontational)

..adverse to the rights of other citizens, or to the permanent and aggregate interests of the community.. ("Federalist Papers")

..타 국민의 권리에 반대하거나 공동사회의 지속적이고 누적된 이해관계에 반대하는..(연방주의자 논집)

□ **mischief** /'mɪstʃɪf/   n. cause of harm

(= disruption, injury, malice, damage)

There are two methods of curing the mischiefs of faction: the one, by removing its causes; the other, by controlling its effects. ("Federalist Papers")

파벌의 폐해를 치료하는 두 가지 방법이 있다: 첫째는 그 원인을 제거하는 것이고, 다음은 그 영향을 조정하는 것이다. (연방주의자 논집)

□ **folly** /'fɑːli/   n. foolishness

(= idiocy, imprudence, recklessness, irrationality)

But it could not be less folly to abolish liberty, which is essential to political life.. ("Federalist Papers")

그러나 정치적 생명을 위해 반드시 필요한 자유를 폐지하는 것 만큼 아둔한 것일 순 없다. .(연방주의자 논집)

□ **impart** /ɪm'pɑːrt/   v. to give

(= convey, expose, communicate, disclose)

But it could not be less folly to abolish liberty, which is essential to political life, because it nourishes faction, than it would be to wish the annihilation of air, which is essential to animal life, because it imparts to fire its destructive agency ("Federalist Papers")

그러나 정치적 생명을 위해 반드시 필요한 자유를 폐지하는 것 만큼 아둔한 것이다. 왜냐하면 그것은 파벌이 생기는 것을 조장하는 것이며, 그렇다면 마치 동물이 생명을 영위하는 데 필요한 공기를, 공기가 불을 더 잘 타게 만들어 파괴적이다는 이유로 없애자라고 주장하는 것과 같은 일이기 때문이다..(연방주의자 논집)

☐ **fallible** /ˈfæləbl/   adj. liable to be erroneous

(= imperfect, unsound, mortal)

As long as the reason of man continues fallible ("Federalist Papers")

인간의 사고가 완벽하지 않은 한..(연방주의자 논집)

☐ **subsist** /səbˈsɪst/   v. to continue in existence

(= exist, survive, live)

As long as the connection subsists between his reason and his self-love, his opinions and his passions will have a reciprocal influence on each other; ("Federalist Papers")

그의 사고와 자애(自愛) 간에 관계가 존재하는 한, 그의 의견과 열정은 상호간에 영향을 주고 받을 것이다; (연방주의자 논집)

☐ **reciprocal** /rɪˈsɪprəkl/   adj. corresponding

(= matching, equivalent, equal, communal)

As long as the connection subsists between his reason and his self-love, his opinions and his passions will have a reciprocal influence on each other; ("Federalist Papers")

그의 사고와 자애(自愛) 간에 관계가 존재하는 한, 그의 의견과 열정은 상호간에 영향을 주고 받을 것이다; (연방주의자 논집)

☐ **faculty** /ˈfæklti/   n. a natural ability

(= facility, ability, aptitude, endowment)

The diversity in the faculties of men, from which the rights of property originate, is not less an insuperable obstacle to a uniformity of interests. ("Federalist Papers")

인간의 본능의 다양함에 기본을 둔 재산권은 이해관계의 획일성을 추구하는데 극복하기 덜 어려운 장애물이 아니다.(연방주의자 논집)

☐ **insuperable** /ɪnˈsuːpərəbl/   adj. undefeatable

(= insurmountable, unbeatable, overwhelming, undefeatable)

The diversity in the faculties of men, from which the rights of property originate, is not less an insuperable obstacle to a uniformity of interests. ("Federalist Papers")

인간의 본능의 다양함에 기본을 둔 재산권은 이해관계의 획일성을 추구하는데 극복하기 덜 어려운 장애물이 아니다. (연방주의자 논집).

□ **proprietor** /prə'praɪətər/   n. an owner of property or a business

(= owner, manager, landowner, landlord)

and from the influence of these on the sentiments and views of the respective proprietors, ensues a division of the society into different interests and parties. ("Federalist Papers")

그리고 이러한 것들이 사업주, 토지주의 심리와 의견에 미치는 영향이, 사회가 서로 다른 이해관계와 파벌들로 나뉘게끔 한다. (연방주의자 논집)

□ **latent** /'leɪtnt/   adj. present but not visible

(= dormant, hidden, embryonic, underlying)

The latent causes of faction are thus sown in the nature of man.. ("Federalist Papers")

파벌이 생기는 잠재적 원인이 인간의 본성에 내재되어 있다..(연방주의자 논집)

Practice 5.

Fill in the blank with the word that matches the definition provided

01 That the President declared his support for the candidate does not _____ (to anticipate and prevent) the need to verify the candidate's credentials.

02 Fifteen years after I graduated from high school, Mrs. Beecham still remembers me for the _____ (cause of harm) I caused in her chemistry class.

03 I am _____ (opposed) to using underhanded methods to achieve my goals.

04 The area is so poor that some residents _____ (to continue to survive) on one meal a day.

05 He has sent me a fine present on my birthday, so I feel I must make a _____ (equivalent, corresponding) gesture on his.

06 Father called it a/an _____ (foolishness) when I quit my secure job to start my own business.

07 Many people _____ (died) in the massive hurricane that hit the coast last weekend.

08 The two men have bickered and argued for years, but they are not really _____ (enemies) of each other.

09 Racism in the United States never went away; it is only _____ (present but invisible)

10 The professor looked right through Geoff's _____ (pleasing to the eye only) excuses.

11 Many people think that the government's spending years trying to solve the unemploy-ment problem with nothing to show for it is _____ (unforgivable).

12 I must _____ (argue) that your explanation is illogical.

13 My great grandfather is 94 years old, but all his physical and mental _____ (natural abilities) are still intact.

14 Do not think you can treat David in such a/an _____ (rudely arrogant) way, just because he is your subordinate.

15 Their cooperation was _____ (incited into action) by their common desire to defeat Harry.

Find the correct word which can replace the bold phrase in the following sentences. Change the word form appropriately to fit the sentence, if necessary

formidable, conjure, unanimous, station, unalienable, abolish, disposed, assent, pressing, abdicate, perfidy, subsist, latent, prohibit, faculty

01 The General was known as an honorable man, and so no one could have imagined that he would commit _____.

02 At this moment of national crisis, the President _____ his countrymen to stay strong and not to lose hope.

03 The Board of Directors rejected the proposal by a _____ decision.

04 The Duke and Duchess opposed their daughter's wish to marry a commoner, saying that they will not allow her to marry under her _____.

05 Although women's right to vote seems to be _____ now, it has barely been 100 years since this right has been guaranteed by the constitution.

06 Although the death penalty has been _____ in many countries, it is still legal in 31 states of America.

07 Although Dr. Blaire has operated his clinic for over 50 years, he is not yet _____ to the idea of retiring.

08 If you wish to join in the expedition, you must hand in a written _____ signed by your legal guardian.

09 We wasted almost all our meeting time discussing trivial matters and didn't get to resolve any of the _____ issues

10 Edward VIII decided to voluntarily _____ in order to marry a divorced American woman.

11 As adults, we find that many children's stories are _____ with biting satire of human behavior.

12 As a devout Buddhist, I am _____ from drinking alcohol or eating meat.

13 A close relationship between business people and politicians has always _____.

14 For a man in his 90s, Mr. Davis' _____ are surprisingly intact; he still works as a taxi driver for a living.

15 In their first match, Robert was an easy opponent for James. Three years later, Robert has become such a _____ rival that James will have to battle hard to win this match.

Find the correct word which can replace the bold phrase in the following sentences. Change the word form appropriately to fit the sentence, if necessary

posterity, apportion, tranquility, perish, annihilation, tenure, abolish, infringe, propensity, magnanimity, obviate, acquiesce, adverse, folly, ravage

16 Based on the range of illegal activities committed by the culprit, it must be assumed that his bosses, although probably didn't order such actions, at least _____ to them.

17 Many people believe that the problem of climate change must be solved now, or else our _____ will suffer gravely for our inaction.

18 When Mr. Harrison died, his assets were not _____ to his children but donated to charity.

19 The reason for increased cases of attacks from wild animals is that man continues to _____ on their natural habitats.

20 Kevin's _____ to enjoy sweets is the main impetus for him to become a chocolatier.

21 Many political prisoners _____ in the Siberian gulags between the 1920s and 1940s under Stalin's regime of terror.

22 Email has _____ the need for businesses to purchase traditional communications equipment such as facsimile machines or telex machines.

23 The first Western settlers of North America had to endure _____ conditions: disease, harsh weather and hostile natives were just some of the hardships they faced.

24 When Henrietta tried to persuade her son-in-law to become a Christian, her husband reminded her of the _____ of trying to enforce religion on others.

25 It is ridiculous to expect _____ from someone you have publicly disgraced.

26 If a nuclear war were to happen today, it would mean the _____ of mankind.

27 In Korea, the President serves a single term with a _____ of five years.

28 Ironically, slavery still existed in some African countries even after it was _____ in the U.S.

29 Two typhoons _____ huge parts of the country, killing several, displacing thousands and causing millions of dollars of damages.

30 When his wife took their three kids with her to his in-laws' for a few days, Dave enjoyed the rare _____ of being alone for the first time in years.

Select the pair of words that most nearly expresses the same relationship

31 adversary: ally
    A. impartial: biased
    B. welfare: safety
    C. providence: God
    D. brethren: comrades

32 ravage: restore
    A. convulsion: seizure
    B. fatigue: tire
    C. obstruct: clear
    D. suspend: shelve

33 wholesome: healthy
    A. sufferable: intolerable
    B. honest: candid
    C. ephemeral: everlasting
    D. prudence: carelessness

34 institute: establish
    A. alter: stop
    B. prudence: arrogance
    C. despotic: magnanimous
    D. impel: drive

35 relinquish: maintain
    A. compliance: disobedience
    B. insurrection: mercenary
    C. swarm: horde
    D. plunder: pillage

36 perfidy: loyalty
    A. consanguinity: kinship
    B. disagree: acquiesce
    C. tranquility: serenity
    D. children: posterity

37 charitable: malicious
   A. concur: agree
   B. prohibit: forbid
   C. curtail: abridge
   D. disapprove: ratify

38 quarter: house
   A. partial: neutral
   B. faction: party
   C. vice: enumeration
   D. specious: accurate

39 infallible: perfect
   A. reciprocal: matching
   B. compose: excite
   C. proprietor: employee
   D. dormant: underlying

40 impart: withhold
   A. idiocy: foolishness
   B. indictment: accusation
   C. kind: overbearing
   D. infringe: interfere

Choose the word that isn't a synonym

41 incontrovertible – fleeting – transient

42 disposed – inclined – candid

43 adaptation – concurrence – consent

44 treachery – rectitude – correctness

45 wickedness – vice – bloc

46 inaccurate – pompous – erroneous

47 impart – convey – actuate

48 reciprocal – dormant – underlying

49 dissolve – depend – disperse

50 depository – accommodation – stock

51 appropriation – termination – dissolution

52 ransack – implore – petition

53 proclaim – ordain – entreat

54 bestow – renounce – confer

55 abridge – condense – overstep

56 enumeration – indictment – prosecution

57 entrust – approve – ratify

58 duration – tenure – judiciary

59 deed – loot – charter

60 force – strain – relinquish

61 revolt – benevolence – insurgence

62 rank – pronouncement – station

63 bestow – endow – assume

64 alter – force – amend

65 discretion – oppression – tyranny

Class 07

☐ **zeal** /ziːl/   n. enthusiastic energy

(= eagerness, fanaticism, fervor, ardor)

A zeal for different opinions concerning religion.. ("Federalist Papers")

종교와 관련된 다양한 의견을 향한 열정..(연방주의자 논집)

☐ **speculation** /ˌspekjuˈleɪʃn/   n. guessing

(= conjecture, assumption, theory, supposition)

..as well of speculation as of practice.. ("Federalist Papers")

..행동 및 추측과 관련하여..(연방주의자 논집)

☐ **pre-eminence** /ˌpriːˈeminəns/   n. the state of being above others

(= supremacy, ascendancy, domination, eminence)

..an attachment to different leaders ambitiously contending for pre-eminence and power.. ("Federalist Papers")

우월한 위치와 권력을 차지하기 위해 야망있게 싸우는 서로 다른 지도자들에 대한 애착..(연방주의자 논집)

☐ **inflame** /ɪnˈfleɪm/   v. to cause anger

(= arouse, provoke, agitate, ignite)

..inflamed them with mutual animosity, and rendered them much more disposed to vex and oppress each other than to co-operate for their common good.. ("Federalist Papers")

상호간의 악감정으로 인해 분노하고, 공동의 이익을 위해 협조하기보다는 서로 짜증나게 만들고 억압하는 성향이 있게 만든.. (연방주의자 논집)

☐ **animosity** /ˌæniˈmɑːsəti/   n. ill feeling

(= hostility, loathing, acrimony, enmity)

..inflamed them with mutual animosity, and rendered them much more disposed to vex and oppress each other than to co-operate for their common good.. ("Federalist Papers")

상호간의 악감정으로 인해 분노하고, 공동의 이익을 위해 협조하기보다는 서로 짜증나게 만들고 억압하는 성향이 있게 만든.. (연방주의자 논집)

☐ **vex** /veks/   v. to irritate

(= annoy, aggravate, exacerbate, incense, rile)

..inflamed them with mutual animosity, and rendered them much more disposed to vex and oppress each other than to co-operate for their common good.. ("Federalist Papers")

상호간의 악감정으로 인해 분노하고, 공동의 이익을 위해 협조하기보다는 서로 짜증나게 만들고 억압하는 성향이 있게 만든.. (연방주의자 논집)

☐ **frivolous** /ˈfrɪvələs/   adj. lacking seriousness

(= thoughtless, trivial, vain, inconsequential)

..where no substantial occasion presents itself, the most frivolous and fanciful distinctions have been sufficient to kindle their unfriendly passions and excite their most violent conflicts. ("Federalist Papers")

..어떠한 결정적인 사건이 발생하지 않는 이상, 가장 하찮고 공상적인 차이가 그들의 적대적인 열정과 가장 폭력적인 갈등을 부추기게 된다. (연방주의자 논집)

☐ **creditor** /ˈkredɪtər/   n. someone to whom money is due

(= lender)

Those who are creditors, and those who are debtors, fall under a like discrimination.. ("Federalist Papers")

채권자들이나 채무자들이나 다 같은 부류로 나뉘어진다.. (연방주의자 논집)

☐ **debtors** /ˈdetər/   n. someone who owes money

(= borrower)

Those who are creditors, and those who are debtors, fall under a like discrimination.. ("Federalist Papers")

채권자들이나 채무자들이나 다 같은 부류로 나뉘어진다.. (연방주의자 논집)

☐ **mercantile** /ˈmɜːrkənti:l/   adj. commercial

(= merchant, commercial, trade)

A landed interest, a manufacturing interest, a mercantile interest, a moneyed interest, with many lesser interests, grow up of necessity in civilized nations.. ("Federalist Papers")

문명국가 내에서 지주들, 생산자들, 상인들, 금융업자들, 그리고 많은 상대적으로 작은 규모의 이해관계들이 필요에 의해 발생한다. (연방주의자 논집)

☐ **bias** /ˈbaɪəs/   v. to unfairly influence

(= prejudice, sway, distort, predispose, prepossess)

No man is allowed to be a judge in his own cause, because his interest would certainly bias his judgment, and corrupt his integrity. ("Federalist Papers")

그 어떤 사람도 자신의 의도를 스스로 판결할 수 없다, 왜냐하면 그의 이해관계가 그가 편견을 가지게 할 것이고 그의 도덕성을 타락시킬 것이다. (연방주의자 논집)

☐ **integrity** /ɪnˈtegrəti/   n. soundness of moral character

(= honesty, honor, veracity, uprightness)

No man is allowed to be a judge in his own cause, because his interest would certainly bias his judgment, and corrupt his integrity. ("Federalist Papers")

그 어떤 사람도 자신의 의도를 스스로 판결할 수 없다, 왜냐하면 그의 이해관계가 그에게 편견을 가지게 할 것이고 그의 도덕성을 타락시킬 것이다. (연방주의자 논집)

☐ **apportionment** /əˈpɔːrʃnmənt/   n. the act of distributing proportionately

(= distribution, allotment, sharing)

The apportionment of taxes on the various descriptions of property is an act which seems to require the most exact impartiality.. ("Federalist Papers")

다양한 종류의 재산에 부과하는 세금의 분배가 가장 중립성을 요구하는 작업이다. (연방주의자 논집)

☐ **impartiality** /ˌɪmˌpɑːrʃiˈæləti/   n. the state of being neutral

(= neutrality, fairness, objectivity, nonalignment

The apportionment of taxes on the various descriptions of property is an act which seems to require the most exact impartiality.. ("Federalist Papers")

다양한 종류의 재산에 부과하는 세금의 분배가 가장 중립성을 요구하는 작업이다. (연방주의자 논집)

□ **enlightened** /ɪnˈlaɪtnd/

adj. free from ignorance, prejudice or superstition

(= edified, educated, open-minded, progressive)

It is in vain to say that enlightened statesmen will be able to adjust these clashing interests, and render them all subservient to the public good. ("Federalist Papers")

개화된 정치인들이 이러한 이해관계의 충돌을 해소시키고 공공의 이익의 아래 두게끔 할 것이라고 말하는 것은 의미가 없다. (연방주의자 논집)

□ **subservient** /səbˈsɜːrviənt/   adj. acting in a subordinate capacity

(= submissive, obedient, acquiescent, servile, compliant)

It is in vain to say that enlightened statesmen will be able to adjust these clashing interests, and render them all subservient to the public good. ("Federalist Papers")

개화된 정치인들이 이러한 이해관계의 충돌을 해소시키고 공공의 이익의 아래 두게끔 할 것이라고 말하는 것은 의미가 없다. (연방주의자 논집)

□ **helm** /helm/   n. a post of control

(= controls, rudder, wheel)

Enlightened statesmen will not always be at the helm. ("Federalist Papers")

개화된 정치인이 항상 조정칸에 있지 않을 것이다. (연방주의자 논집)

□ **prevail** /prɪˈveɪl/   v. to be superior

(= triumph, predominate, conquer)

..which will rarely prevail over the immediate interest which one party may find in disregarding the rights of another.. ("Federalist Papers")

..한 개의 당이 다른당의 권리를 무시함으로 생기는 단기간의 이득에 우선하는 일은 드물 것이고.. (연방주의자 논집)

□ **inference** /ˈɪnfərəns/   n. reasoning from premise to conclusion

(= implication, extrapolation, interpretation, corollary)

The inference to which we are brought is, that the causes of faction cannot be removed, and that relief is only to be sought in the means of controlling its effects. ("Federalist Papers")

우리가 도달하는 추론은, 파벌을 조장하는 원인을 제거하기는 불가하고, 오직 그 파벌의 영향을 조절하는 것만이 우리에게 안심을 제공한다는 것이다. (연방주의자 논집)

☐ **convulse** /kənˈvʌls/   v. to shake

(= tremble, shudder, agitate, quiver)

..it may convulse the society.. ("Federalist Papers")

..사회에 동요를 일으킬 수 있고… (연방주의자 논집)

Practice 7.

Fill in the blank with the word that matches the definition provided

01 The two men argue about everything, but there is no real _____ (ill feeling) between them.

02 She is neither rich nor well educated, but she always behaves with total _____ (soundness of moral character)

03 The parties have been in dispute for years because the original sales contract did not define the _____ (the act of distributing proportionately) of the land clearly.

04 The police reported that they had gathered enough evidence to make a reasonable _____ (reasoning from premise to conclusion) as to what exactly happened at the scene of the crime.

05 His mother warned Michael, that if he continues to answer _____ (not seriously) to her questions, he will be in big trouble.

06 He has talent, but he lacks the _____ (enthusiastic energy) to be a truly great musician.

07 There is no evidence that Gary committed any crime: the accusations are all based on _____ (guessing).

08 The artist attributes his _____ (state of being above others) to a little talent, good teaching and a lot of practice.

09 I did not mean to _____ (cause anger) her, but for some reason she became angry at my questions.

10 Most people are too _____ (free from ignorance) to believe in such superstitions.

11 Having been a butler for 40 years, Mr. Ustinov can't seem to quit his _____ (acting in a subordinate capacity) manners.

12 This company is like a ship with no one at the _____ (a post of control)

13 At the beginning of the war, each side was sure that it would _____ (to triumph)

14 In the Renaissance Age, Venice was one of the biggest _____ (commercial) ports in the Mediterranean region.

15 His experience of having been bitten by a German shepherd _____ (unfairly influences) Henry against all dogs.

☐ **desideratum** /dɪˌzɪdəˈrɑːtəm/   n. something lacked and wanted

Let me add that it is the great desideratum by which this form of government can be rescued from the opprobrium under which it has so long labored.. ("Federalist Papers")

그것은 이러한 형태의 정부가 오랫동안 시달려 온 맹비난으로부터 구조해 주는 필요물이라는 것을 말하고 싶다. (연반주의자 논집)

☐ **attainable** /əˈteɪnəbl/   adj. capable of being accomplished

(= possible, manageable, within reach)

By what means is this object attainable? ("Federalist Papers")

이 목적은 어떤 방법으로 달성이 가능한가? (연방주의자 논집)

☐ **efficacy** /ˈefɪkəsi/   n. effectiveness

(= efficiency, usefulness, ability, value)

..and lose their efficacy in proportion to the number combined together.. ("Federalist Papers")

..그리고 그들의 통합된 숫자와 비례하여 그 효과가 절감되며.. (연방주의자 논집)

☐ **inducement** /ɪnˈduːsmənt/   n. something that motivates

(= stimulus, incentive, enticement, lure)

..and there is nothing to check the inducements to sacrifice the weaker party or an obnoxious individual..("Federalist Papers")

그리고 상대적으로 약한 정당이나 무례하게 구는 개인을 희생하고 싶은 동기를 통제할 수단이 없고.. (연방주의자 논집)

☐ **obnoxious** /əbˈnɑːkʃəs/   adj. highly objectionable or offensive

(= loathsome, abhorrent, repugnant, intolerable)

..and there is nothing to check the inducements to sacrifice the weaker party or an obnoxious individual..("Federalist Papers")

그리고 상대적으로 약한 정당이나 무례하게 구는 개인을 희생하고 싶은 동기를 통제할 수단이 없고.. (연방주의자 논집)

☐ **spectacle** /ˈspektəkl/   n. anything presented to view

(= display, manifestation, exhibition, phenomenon)

Hence it is that such democracies have ever been spectacles of turbulence and contention.. ("Federalist Papers")

그러므로 이러한 민주주의들은 항상 동요와 논쟁의 볼거리가 되었다는 것이다. (연방주의자 논집)

☐ **patronize** /ˈpeɪtrənaɪz/   v. to support

(= support, back up, stand by)

Theoretic politicians, who have patronized this species of government, have erroneously supposed that ("Federalist Papers")

이러한 종류의 정부를 지지하는 이론적인 정치가들이 잘못 추측하고 있는 것이.. (연방주의자 논집)

☐ **assimilate** /əˈsɪməleɪt/   v. to incorporate as one's own

(= integrate, adapt, espouse, conform)

..have erroneously supposed that by reducing mankind to a perfect equality in their political rights, they would be perfectly equalized and assimilated in their possessions.. ("Federalist Papers")

인간의 정치적 권리를 완전히 평등하게 만들면, 그들의 재산규모 역시 완전히 동등해지고 그들의 재산에 완전히 동화될 것으로 잘못 추측하고 있으며.. (연방주의자 논집)

☐ **medium** /ˈmiːdiəm/   n. something intermediate in nature or degree

(= vehicle, channel, mode, avenue)

..by passing them through the medium of a chosen body of citizens.. ("Federalist Papers")

..그들을 국민으로 구성된 집단이 선택한 매개체에 통과시키면.. (연방주의자 논집)

☐ **discern** /dɪˈsɜːrn/   v. to distinguish

(= determine, recognize, perceive, fathom)

..whose wisdom may best discern the true interest of their country.. ("Federalist Papers")

..그들의 지혜가 그들의 국가의 이득을 가장 잘 식별한다면.. (연방주의자 논집)

☐ **consonant** /ˈkɑːnsənənt/   adj. in agreement with

(= consistent, compatible, harmonious)

Under such a regulation, it may well happen that the public voice will be more consonant to the public good.. ("Federalist Papers")

그러한 규정하에서 어쩌면 대중의 목소리가 대중의 이익에 더 조화롭게 공명할 것이고.. (연방주의자 논집)

☐ **invert** /ɪnˈvɜːrt/   v. to turn upside down

(= overturn, upend, capsize, upset)

On the other hand, the effect may be inverted. ("Federalist Papers")

다른 한 편으로, 그 효과가 뒤집어질 수도 있다.

☐ **factious** /ˈfækʃəs/   adj. pertaining to faction

(= divisive, sectarian, schismatic, discordant)

Men of factious tempers…. or of sinister designs, may, by intrigue, first obtain the suffrages, and then betray the interests, of the people. ("Federalist Papers")

파벌을 구성하고자 하는 성향이 있는, 혹은 사악한 의도를 가진 사람들은… 음모를 통해 먼저 투표권을 쟁취하고 그 이후 대중의 이익을 배반한다. (연반주의자 논집)

☐ **intrigue** /ɪnˈtriːg/   n. use of deceit

(= conspiracy, deception, stratagem, machinations)

Men of factious tempers…. or of sinister designs, may, by intrigue, first obtain the suffrages, and then betray the interests, of the people. ("Federalist Papers")

파벌을 구성하고자 하는 성향이 있는, 혹은 사악한 의도를 가진 사람들은… 음모를 통해 먼저 투표권을 쟁취하고 그 이후 대중의 이익을 배반한다. (연방주의자 논집)

□ **suffrage** /ˈsʌfrɪdʒ/   n. the right to vote

(= voting right, ballot)

Men of factious tempers…. or of sinister designs, may, by intrigue, first obtain the suffrages, and then betray the interests, of the people. ("Federalist Papers")

파벌을 구성하고자 하는 성향이 있는, 혹은 사악한 의도를 가진 사람들은… 음모를 통해 먼저 투표권을 쟁취하고 그 이후 대중의 이익을 배반한다. (연방주의자 논집)

□ **cabal** /kəˈbæl/   n. a small group of secret plotters

(= faction, clique, group, gang)

..in order to guard against the cabals of a few.. ("Federalist Papers")

..소수 당파의 횡포를 막기 위해.. (연방주의자 논집)

□ **constituent** /kənˈstɪtʃuənt/   n. a person with a voting right

(= voter, citizen)

..the number of representatives in the two cases not being in proportion to that of the two constituents.. ("Federalist Papers")

..이 두 가지 경우에 대의원의 숫자와 투표권자의 숫자가 정비례하지 않는.. (연방주의자 논집)

□ **diffusive** /difjúːsiv/   adj. spreading in all directions

(= dispersive, disseminative)

..and the suffrages of the people being more free, will be more likely to center in men who possess the most attractive merit and the most diffusive and established characters. ("Federalist Papers")

..그리고 국민의 투표권이 더욱 자유로와진다면 매력적인 장점을 가지고 다방면으로 인정받는 성격을 가진 사람들에게 표가 집중될 경향이 있다. (연방주의자 논집)

□ **render** /ˈrendər/   v. to cause to be

(= make, leave)

By enlarging too much the number of electors, you render the representatives too little acquainted with all their local circumstances and lesser interests.. ("Federalist Papers")

선거인의 숫자를 지나치게 늘리면, 대의원들이 그들 지역의 고유한 상황 및 상대적으로 덜 중요한 이해관계에 대해 알 수 없게 만들며..(연방주의자 논집)

☐ **impediment** /ɪmˈpedɪmənt/　　　　　n. something that acts as a barrier

(= impairment, disorder, inhibition, weakness)

Besides other impediments, it may be remarked that, where there is a consciousness of unjust or dishonorable purposes, communication is always checked.. ("*Federalist Papers*")

다른 장애물과 별도로, 정의롭지 않거나 명예롭지 않은 목적이 있는 곳에는 의사소통이 항상 확인된다고 말할 수 있고.. (연방주의자 논집)

Fill in the blank with the word that matches the definition provided

01   The bakery on the corner has been open for 60 years, and my grandmother has _____ (supported) it since she married my grandfather 55 years ago.

02   The government has come up with no practical _____ (motivation) for young couples to increase the birth rate.

03   After his _____ (highly offensive) behavior at the gathering, Jake was never asked to join another one.

04   It was clear that the reason Mr. Grover was fired was due to the _____ (use of deceit) against him.

05   Forty years after he immigrated to the United States, Mr. Kim still hasn't been totally _____ (incorporated as one's own) into American society.

06   In less than a decade, the smart phone has become the widest used _____ something that intermediates) of communication in the world.

07   I had never seen the "Lighting of the Christmas Tree" ceremony in Rockefeller Center before: It was truly a/an impressive _____ (something presented to view).

08   Mr. Dover's trained eye can _____ (tell apart) which bills are real and which are counterfeit.

09   My father's actions were always _____ (in agreement) to his moral principles.

10   I do not trust alternative medicines: their _____ (effectiveness) has not been proven scientifically.

11 It turned out that the candidate that was leading the polls received less than 30% of votes from his _____ (persons with voting rights).

12 Stories of good behavior are _____ (spreading in all direction): they spread very far very quickly.

13 Many people were _____ (caused to be) homeless by the devastating hurricane.

14 The on-going political bickering is a real _____ (something that acts as a barrier) to the nation's economic growth.

15 The stunt pilot _____ (turned upside down) his plane only 30 feet above the ground.

16 _____ (pertaining to factions) sentiments usually surface when national rivalries are triggered.

□ **requisite** /ˈrekwɪzɪt/ adj. needed

(= necessary, obligatory, mandatory, essential)

It will not be denied that the representation of the Union will be most likely to possess these requisite endowments. ("Federalist Papers")

연방의 대변자들이 이러한 필수적인 재능을 갖출거라는 건 거부할 수 없다. (연방주의자 논집)

□ **endowment** /ɪnˈdaʊmənt/ n. natural talents or character

(= talent, ability, aptitude, faculty)

It will not be denied that the representation of the Union will be most likely to possess these requisite endowments. ("Federalist Papers")

연방의 대변자들이 이러한 필수적인 재능을 갖출거라는 건 거부할 수 없다. (연방주의자 논집)

□ **expedient** /ɪkˈspiːdiənt/ n. a means to accomplish something

(= measure, device, maneuver)

To what expedient, then, shall we finally resort, for maintaining in practice the necessary partition of power among the several departments, as laid down in the Constitution? ("Federalist Papers")

그럼 헌법에 규정된 각기 다른 정부기관의 권력을 지속적으로 적절히 분배하기 위해 우리는 결국 어떤 방편을 이용해야 하는가? (연장주의자 논집)

□ **contrive** /kənˈtraɪv/ v. to plan with ingenuity

(= engineer, plan, scheme, machinate, design)

..by so contriving the interior structure of the government as that its several constituent parts may, by their mutual relations, be the means of keeping each other in their proper places.. ("Federalist Papers")

..정부를 구성하는 다수의 기관들이 그들의 상호 관계를 고려하고 서로가 서로를 월권하지 않도록 하는 방식으로 정부의 내부구조를 고안하여..(연장주의자 논집)

☐ **hazard** /ˈhæzərd/   v. to offer with the possibility of facing criticism

(= suggest, proffer, propose)

I will hazard a few general observations, which may perhaps place it in a clearer light, and enable us to form a more correct judgment... ("Federalist Papers")

어쩌면 그것을 더욱 명확하게 설명하고 우리로 하여금 더 정확한 판단을 내리게 도와 줄 수 있는 몇 가지 관찰한 바를 내가 비판받을 각오로 제시하겠다. (연방주의자 논집)

☐ **extent** /ɪkˈstent/   n. scope

(= degree, amount, level, range, magnitude)

..which to a certain extent is admitted on all hands to be essential to the preservation of liberty.. ("Federalist Papers")

..자유를 수호하기 위하여 매우 중요하다고 모든 사람들이 어느 정도 인정하는..(연방주의자 논집)

☐ **constitute** /ˈkɑːnstɪtuːt/   v. to compose or form

(= comprise, represent, form)

..it is evident that each department should have a will of its own; and consequently should be so constituted that the members of each should have as little agency as possible in the appointment of the members of the others.. ("Federalist Papers")

모든 정부부서가 자기만의 의지가 있어야 하는 것은 자명하며; 그 결과로 한 부서의 인원이 다른 부서의 인원의 지명에 가능한 한 관여할 권한이 없도록 하며..(연방주의자 논집)

☐ **magistracy** /ðəˈmædʒɪstrəsi/   n. a civil officer

(= magistrate)

Were this principle rigorously adhered to, it would require that all the appointments for the supreme executive, legislative, and judiciary magistracies should be drawn from the same fountain of authority..("Federalist Papers")

만약 이 원칙이 엄격하게 적용이 된다면, 모든 행정, 입법, 사법부의 공무원들이 같은 수준의 지휘권을 가진 사람들로 지명이 되어야 하고..(연방주의자 논집)

☐ **contemplation** /ˌkɑːntəmˈpleɪʃn/   n. deep thought

(= meditation, consideration, deliberation)

Perhaps such a plan of constructing the several departments would be less difficult in practice than it may in contemplation appear. ("Federalist Papers")

어쩌면 (정부의) 다수의 부서를 구성하는 것을 실행에 옮기기가 생각하는 것 보다 덜 어려울 수도 있고.. (연방주의자 논집)

☐ **confer** /kən'fɜːr/   v. to bestow upon as a gift, favor or honor

(= award, bestow, present, grant)

..secondly, because the permanent tenure by which the appointments are held in that department, must soon destroy all sense of dependence on the authority conferring them. ("Federalist Papers")

..두 번째로, 그 부서에 임명된 자들에게 종신 재직권을 부여하면 그 자리가 제공하는 권위에 (본인들이) 의지해야 한다는 생각이 곧 없어질 것이며..(연장주의자 논집)

☐ **nominal** /'nɑːmɪnl/   adj. being such in name only

(= so-called, titular, putative)

Were the executive magistrate, or the judges, not independent of the legislature in this particular, their independence in every other would be merely nominal. ("Federalist Papers")

만일 행정부의 공무원들이나 재판관들이 이 부분에서 입법부로부터 독립적이지 못하다면, 그들의 다른 부분에서의 독립성도 명목적인 것일 수 밖에 없다. (연방주의자 논집)

☐ **commensurate** /kə'menʃərət/   adj. corresponding in amount

(= equal, corresponding, appropriate, matching)

The provision for defense must in this, as in all other cases, be made commensurate to the danger of attack. ("Federalist Papers")

다른 모든 경우와 마찬가지로 이 경우에도 공격받을 수 있다는 위험과 정비례하여 방어수단을 준비해야 한다. (연방주의자 논집)

☐ **auxiliary** /ɔːg'zɪliəri/   adj. used as a reserve in case of need

(= supplementary, secondary, ancillary)

A dependence on the people is, no doubt, the primary control on the government; but experience has taught mankind the necessity of auxiliary precautions. ("Federalist Papers")

정부를 통제하는 제일의 수단은 국민에 의지하는 것이다; 하지만 인간은 경험을 통해 대비책을 준비해야 한다는 것을 안다. (연장주의자 논집)

□ **palpable** /ˈpælpəbl/   adj. readily or plainly seen

(= manifest, plain, corporeal, tangible)

Here, again, the extent of the Union gives it the most palpable advantage. ("Federalist Papers")

여기서, 다시, 연방의 범위가 가장 유형의 강점을 제공한다. (연방주의자 논집)

□ **conflagration** /ˌkɑːnfləˈɡreɪʃn/   n. a huge fire

(= blaze, inferno, fire)

The influence of factious leaders may kindle a flame within their particular States, but will be unable to spread a general conflagration through the other States. ("Federalist Papers")

파벌 지도자들의 영향력이 자신들의 주(州) 안에서는 작은 불꽃을 일으킬 수는 있으나, 다른 주(州)까지 퍼지는 대화재가 발생하지는 않을 것이다. (연방주의자 논집)

□ **sect** /sekt/

n. a group of people forming a distinct unit within a bigger group of people

(= group, clique, faction, camp, offshoot)

A religious sect may degenerate into a political faction in a part of the Confederacy.. ("Federalist Papers")

연합 형태의 정부 하에서 종교적인 파벌은 정치적 파벌로 전락할 수 있다. (연방주의자 논집)

□ **confederacy** /kənˈfedərəsi/

n. a union or combination of peoples, states or etc.

(= alliance, league)

A religious sect may degenerate into a political faction in a part of the Confederacy.. ("Federalist Papers")

연합 형태의 정부 하에서 종교적인 파벌은 정치적 파벌로 전락할 수 있다. (연방주의자 논집)

☐ **address** /əˈdrɛs/   v. to make a speech

(= lecture, sermon)

No man thinks more highly than I do of the patriotism, as well as abilities, of the very worthy gentlemen who have just addressed the house. ("Give me liberty or give me death")

방금 의회에서 연설하신 자격있는 분들의 애국심과 능력을 나보다 더 높게 인정하는 사람은 없을 겁니다. ("자유가 아니면 죽음을 달라" 연설)

☐ **entertain** /ˌɛntərˈteɪn/   v. to consider

(= contemplate, ruminate, cogitate)

I hope it will not be thought disrespectful to those gentlemen if, entertaining as I do opinions of a character very opposite to theirs. ("Give me liberty or give me death")

혹시 그 신사분들이 내가 그들과 전혀 반대의 의견을 피력함을 모욕으로 생각하지 않았으면 좋겠습니다. ("자유가 아니면 죽음을 달라" 연설)

☐ **proportion** /prəˈpɔːrʃn/   n. a relative amount

(= ratio, comparison)

For my own part, I consider it as nothing less than a question of freedom or slavery; and in proportion to the magnitude of the subject ought to be the freedom of the debate. ("Give me liberty or give me death")

제가 보기에는 이것은 단순히 자유나 구속이냐의 문제인 것 같습니다; 그리고 사안이 중요한 만큼에 비례하여 이 문제에 대한 협의도 자유로왔으면 좋겠습니다. ("자유가 아니면 죽음을 달라" 연설)

☐ **magnitude** /ˈmæɡnɪtuːd/   n. great size, scale or importance

(= amplitude, vastness, volume)

For my own part, I consider it as nothing less than a question of freedom or slavery; and in proportion to the magnitude of the subject ought to be the freedom of the debate. ("Give me liberty or give me death")

제가 보기에는 이것은 단순히 자유나 구속이냐의 문제인 것 같습니다; 그리고 사안이 중요한 만큼에 비례하여 이 문제에 대한 협의도 자유로왔으면 좋겠습니다. ("자유가 아니면 죽음을 달라" 연설)

Practice 9.

Fill in the blank with the word that matches the definition provided

01 The school has two _____ (used as a reserve in case of need) generators in case the electricity is cut off.

02 The excitement wa _____ (plainly seen) in the arena as the game was about to begin.

03 Students must take several _____ (needed or necessary) courses, in order to join the engineering department.

04 Her success is the result of no special _____ (natural talents or character). She is the same as everyone else, except that she tries harder than everyone else.

05 The government's _____ (means to accomplish something) to all problems is to raise taxes.

06 They _____ (to plan with ingenuity) a plan that no one has tried before.

07 Leonard sat in _____ (deep thought) for several days before he accepted the post.

08 The university _____ (to bestow on as an honor) an honorary degree on him.

09 The Principal _____ (to make a speech) the student body every Monday morning.

10 Mr. Williams is the _____ (in name only) President. The company is actually run by the Vice President, Ms Finch.

11 I expect to receive a salary _____ (corresponding in amount) to my experience.

12 We didn't realize the _____ (great size) of work that had to be done until we began the project.

13 The Christian Democratic Party began as a/an _____ (a group within a group) within the National Democratic Party.

14 We do not know yet the _____ (scope) of the damage that yesterday's storm caused.

15 Some people think the increase of immigrants _____ (to compose or form) as a threat to the domestic labor market.

16 I know this is a sensitive topic, but may I _____ (to offer with the possibility of facing criticism) a few questions about your recent scandal?

Class 10

☐ **treason** /ˈtriːzn/   n. the act of betraying one's country

(= betrayal, treachery, perfidy)

Should I keep back my opinions at such a time, through fear of giving offense, I should consider myself as guilty of treason towards my country ("Give me liberty or give me death")

만일 내가 남들에게 모욕감을 줄까 두려워서 나의 의견들을 말하지 않는다면 나는 내 국가에 대한 배신을 저지르는 것입니다. ("자유가 아니면 죽음을 달라" 연설)

☐ **indulge** /ɪnˈdʌldʒ/   v. to let one do something that one enjoys

(= spoil, treat, pamper)

Mr. President, it is natural to man to indulge in the illusions of hope. ("Give me liberty or give me death")

위원장님, 사람이 희망이라는 환상에 푹 빠지는 것은 자연스러운 것입니다. ("자유가 아니면 죽음을 달라" 연설)

☐ **apt to**   (idiom.) have a tendency to ~

(= prone to)

We are apt to shut our eyes against a painful truth, and listen to the song of that siren till she transforms us into beasts. ("Give me liberty or give me death")

우리는 불편한 진실에 눈을 감고 사이렌의 노래소리가 우리를 짐승으로 바꿀 때까지 듣고 있는 경향이 있습니다. ("자유가 아니면 죽음을 달라" 연설)

☐ **arduous** /ˈɑːrdʒuəs/   adj. to be very difficult

(= difficult, grueling, onerous)

Is this the part of wise men, engaged in a great and arduous struggle for liberty? ("Give me liberty or give me death")

이것이 자유를 위해 대단하고도 어려운 투쟁을 해야 하는 것이 현명한 자들의 역할입니까? ("자유가 아니면 죽음을 달라" 연설)

☐ **disposed** /dɪˈspəʊzd/　　　　　　adj. to be willing to do something

(= willing, inclined)

Are we disposed to be of the numbers of those who, having eyes, see not, and, having ears, hear not, the things which so nearly concern their temporal salvation? ("Give me liberty or give me death")

우리는 우리의 현실적인 구원과 관련된 것들을 눈이 있어도 보지 못하고 귀가 있어도 듣지 못하는 그런 사람들이 되고자 하는 겁니까? ("자유가 아니면 죽음을 달라" 연설)

☐ **temporal** /ˈtempərəl/　　　　　　adj. related to current life or this world

(= worldly, secular)

Are we disposed to be of the numbers of those who, having eyes, see not, and, having ears, hear not, the things which so nearly concern their temporal salvation? ("Give me liberty or give me death")

우리는 우리의 현실적인 구원과 관련된 것들을 눈이 있어도 보지 못하고 귀가 있어도 듣지 못하는 그런 사람들이 되고자 하는 겁니까? ("자유가 아니면 죽음을 달라" 연설)

☐ **salvation** /sælˈveɪʃn/

n. the act of saving or protecting from harm, risk or loss

(= rescue)

Are we disposed to be of the numbers of those who, having eyes, see not, and, having ears, hear not, the things which so nearly concern their temporal salvation? ("Give me liberty or give me death")

우리는 우리의 현실적인 구원과 관련된 것들을 눈이 있어도 보지 못하고 귀가 있어도 듣지 못하는 그런 사람들이 되고자 하는 겁니까? ("자유가 아니면 죽음을 달라" 연설)

☐ **anguish** /ˈæŋgwɪʃ/　　　　　　n. extreme sadness

(= torment, agony, suffering)

For my part, whatever anguish of spirit it may cost, I am willing to know the whole truth, to know the worst, and to provide for it. ("Give me liberty or give me death")

제 입장에서는 그 어떤 고통이 수반된다 하더라도 저는 진실을 알고자 하고 최악의 상황을 알고 대비하고자 합니다. ("자유가 아니면 죽음을 달라" 연설)

☐ **solace** /ˈsɑːləs/   n. the feeling of comfort

(= comfort, consolation, relief)

I wish to know what there has been in the conduct of the British ministry for the last ten years to justify those hopes with which gentlemen have been pleased to solace themselves and the House. ("Give me liberty or give me death")

지난 십 년간 영국 정부가 한 행동 중에 어떤 부분이 그분들과 의회에 위안을 주었는지 저는 알고 싶습니다. ("자유가 아니면 죽음을 달라" 연설)

☐ **insidious** /ɪnˈsɪdiəs/   adv. to have evil intent

(= sinister, subtle, sneaky)

(compare: invidious = unenviable, unpleasant)

Is it that insidious smile with which our petition has been lately received? ("Give me liberty or give me death")

우리가 보낸 청원을 받으며 그들이 보였던 사악한 미소가 그것인가요? ("자유가 아니면 죽음을 달라" 연설)

☐ **snare** /sner/   n. a trap to catch animals

(= trap)

Trust it not, sir; it will prove a snare to your feet. ("Give me liberty or give me death")

믿지 마십시요; 그것은 여러분의 발을 묶는 족쇄가 될 것입니다. ("자유가 아니면 죽음을 달라" 연설)

☐ **comport** /kəmˈpɔːrt/   v. to be in agreement

(= agree, conform)

Ask yourselves how this gracious reception of our petition comports with those warlike preparations which cover our waters and darken our land. ("Give me liberty or give me death")

우리가 보낸 청원서를 호의적으로 받아준 것과 지금 우리의 바다와 땅 위에서 진행되고 있는 전쟁 준비가 어떻게 서로 일치하는지 스스로에게 물어 보십시요. ("자유가 아니면 죽음을 달라" 연설)

□ **subjugation** /ˌsʌbdʒuˈɡeɪʃn/   n. defeat

(= suppression, conquest)

These are the implements of war and subjugation; the last arguments to which kings resort.
("Give me liberty or give me death")

이것은 전쟁과 침략의 준비입니다; 더는 대화가 통하지 않을 때 군주가 쓰는 최후의 수단이지요.
("자유가 아니면 죽음을 달라" 연설)

□ **martial**ı /ˈmɑːrʃl/   adj. warlike

(= aggressive, belligerent)

I ask gentlemen, sir, what means this martial array, if its purpose be not to force us to
submission? ("Give me liberty or give me death")

신사 여러분께 묻습니다, 이러한 무력적인 과시가 우리를 예속시키기 위한 것이 아니면 무엇인가요?
("자유가 아니면 죽음을 달라" 연설)

□ **array** /əˈreɪ/

n. order or arrangement, as of troops drawn up for battle

(= collection, display, grouping)

I ask gentlemen, sir, what means this martial array, if its purpose be not to force us to
submission? ("Give me liberty or give me death")

신사 여러분께 묻습니다, 이러한 무력적인 과시가 우리를 예속시키기 위한 것이 아니면 무엇인가요?
("자유가 아니면 죽음을 달라" 연설)

□ **rivet** /ˈrɪvɪt/   v. to secure, bind

(= fasten, attach)

They are sent over to bind and rivet upon us those chains which the British ministry have
been so long forging. ("Give me liberty or give me death")

영국 정부가 그토록 오랫동안 주물하던 쇠사슬을 우리에게 채우기 위해 보내지는 것입니다. ("자유가
아니면 죽음을 달라" 연설)

□ **entreaty** /ɪnˈtriːti/   n. a polite and serious request

(= appeal, plea, petition)

Shall we resort to entreaty and humble supplication? ("Give me liberty or give me death")

우리는 최종적으로 간청과 겸손한 애원을 시도해 볼까요? ("자유가 아니면 죽음을 달라" 연설)

☐ **supplication** /ˌsʌplɪˈkeɪʃn/

n. a prayer to God or a respectful request to a person of authority

(= entreaty, plea, appeal)

Shall we resort to entreaty and humble supplication? ("Give me liberty or give me death")

우리는 최종적으로 간청과 겸손한 애원을 시도해 볼까요? ("자유가 아니면 죽음을 달라" 연설)

☐ **beseech** /bɪˈsiːtʃ/　　　　　　　v. to beg, to entreat

(= implore, request)

Let us not, I beseech you, sir, deceive ourselves. ("Give me liberty or give me death")

여러분께 간청 드리온데, 우리 자신을 속이지 맙시다. ("자유가 아니면 죽음을 달라" 연설)

☐ **implore** /ɪmˈplɔːr/　　　　　　v. to beg, to entreat

(= beseech, request)

We have prostrated ourselves before the throne, and have implored its interposition to arrest the tyrannical hands of the ministry and Parliament. ("Give me liberty or give me death")

우리는 왕 아래에 허리를 숙이고 그가 정부와 의회의 폭군과 같은 행동을 중재해달라고 간청하였습니다. ("자유가 아니면 죽음을 달라" 연설)

☐ **interposition** /ɪntərpəzíʃən/

n. the legal intervention between two parties in dispute

(= intervention)

We have prostrated ourselves before the throne, and have implored its interposition to arrest the tyrannical hands of the ministry and Parliament. ("Give me liberty or give me death")

우리는 왕 아래에 허리를 숙이고 그가 정부와 의회의 폭군과 같은 행동을 중재해달라고 간청하였습니다. ("자유가 아니면 죽음을 달라" 연설)

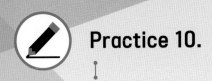

Practice 10.

Fill in the blank with the word that matches the definition provided

01 While his mother is very spiritual, David is more consumed with _____ (worldly) interests.

02 Howard cried in _____ (extreme sadness) when his pet dog died.

03 We are _____ (willing) to continue our struggle until our demands are met.

04 Imperial Japan's _____ (suppression) of Korea lasted for 36 years.

05 It is clear that the enemy had _____ (war-like) intentions.

06 The defendant's mother made a heartfelt _____ (a polite and serious request) to the judge to set her son free.

07 Brian is _____ (have a tendency to) to blaming other people for his faults.

08 After a/an _____ (to be very difficult) hike, we finally reached the summit of the mountain.

09 Our friendship is _____ (secured) on our mutual respect for each other.

10 The café had an impressive _____ (collection, arrangement) of CDs and LPs.

11 Laura _____ (begged) her grandfather to stop drinking, before he loses his health.

12 Children that age only find _____ (the feeling of comfort) in the arms of their mothers.

13 I was not aware of what a/an _____ (having evil intent) side he had.

14 The conclusion does not _____ (be in agreement) with the logic.

15 It is not good to _____ (to let do as one wants) your children too much: some discipline is required.

Class 11

☐ **slighted** /slaɪt/   adj. to be insulted

(= affronted, insulted, miffed)

Our petitions have been slighted. ("Give me liberty or give me death")

우리의 청원서는 무시되었습니다. ("자유가 아니면 죽음을 달라" 연설)

☐ **spurn** /spɜːrn/   v. to reject

(= reject, snub, scorn)

we have been spurned, with contempt, from the foot of the throne! ("Give me liberty or give me death")

우리는 왕의 발 아래에서 내쳐지고 멸시받았습니다. ("자유가 아니면 죽음을 달라" 연설)

☐ **remonstrance** /rɪˈmɑːnstrəns/   n. objections

(= protest, complaint, petition)

..our remonstrances have produced additional violence and insult ("Give me liberty or give me death")

우리의 항의는 추가로 폭력과 모욕을 받았습니다. ("자유가 아니면 죽음을 달라" 연설)

☐ **inviolate** /ɪnˈvaɪələt/   adj. free from violation

(= unbroken, untouched, unadulterated)

If we wish to be free--if we mean to preserve inviolate those inestimable privileges for which we have been so long contending ("Give me liberty or give me death")

우리가 자유롭고 싶으면—우리가 그토록 오랫동안 쟁취하고자 했던 더없이 중요한 권리들을 유지하고 싶다면 ("자유가 아니면 죽음을 달라" 연설)

☐ **formidable** /ˈfɔːrmɪdəbl/   adj. great and impressive

(= impressive, astounding, remarkable)

They tell us, sir, that we are weak; unable to cope with so formidable an adversary. ("Give me liberty or give me death")

그들은, 여러분, 우리가 약하다고 합니다; 저토록 엄청난 적을 당해낼 수 없다고. ("자유가 아니면 죽음을 달라" 연설)

□ **irresolution** /ˌɪˌrezə'luːʃn/   n. the inability to make a decision

(= indecision, indecisiveness)

Shall we gather strength by irresolution and inaction? ("Give me liberty or give me death")

우유부단함과 무대책으로 힘이 길러지나요? ("자유가 아니면 죽음을 달라" 연설)

□ **supine** /'suːpaɪn/   adj. to be lying on one's back

Shall we acquire the means of effectual resistance by lying supinely on our backs and hugging the delusive phantom of hope.. ("Give me liberty or give me death")

우리가 바닥에 등을 대고 누워서 사라져가는 희망의 환상을 끌어안고 있으면 효과적인 저항책이 생기나요? ("자유가 아니면 죽음을 달라" 연설)

□ **extenuate** /ɪksténjuèit/

v. to represent a fault as being less serious than it seems

It is in vain, sir, to extenuate the matter. ("Give me liberty or give me death")

사건의 심각성을 축소하는 것은 소용없습니다. ("자유가 아니면 죽음을 달라" 연설)

□ **conduce** / kəndjúːs /   v. to contribute or lead to a specific result

(= partake, contribute, take part)

..it appears to me proper, especially as it may conduce to a more distinct expression of the public voice, that I should now apprise you of the resolution I have formed.. ("President George Washington's Farewell Address")

지금 나의 결심을 여러분께 밝히는 것이 옳은 일인 것 같습니다. 특히나 그 결과로 더 활발한 대중의 의견 표명을 이끌 것 같기 때문에. (워싱턴 대통령의 퇴임사)

□ **apprise** /ə'praɪz/   v. to give notice

(= inform, explain, impart, acquaint)

..that I should now apprise you of the resolution I have formed.. ("President George Washington's Farewell Address")

..지금 여러분께 제 결정을 알려드려야 할 것 같습니다. (워싱턴 대통령의 퇴임사)

☐ **appertain** /ˌæpərˈteɪn/   v. to be a part of

(= relate, belong, pertain)

..be assured that this resolution has not been taken without a strict regard to all the considerations appertaining to the relation which binds a dutiful citizen to his country.. ("President George Washington's Farewell Address")

나는 내가 이 결정을 내리기 전에 의무감 충만한 한 국민으로서 참고해야 할 모든 사항들에 대해 엄중하게 숙고해보았다는 확신을 드릴 수 있습니다. (워싱턴 대통령의 퇴임사)

☐ **diminution** /ˌdɪmɪˈnuːʃn/   n. reduction

(= decrease, lessening, attenuation, contraction)

..I am influenced by no diminution of zeal for your future interest.. ("President George Washington's Farewell Address")

여러분들의 미래의 이익에 대한 나의 열정이 추호도 줄어들지 않았으며.. (워싱턴 대통령의 퇴임사)

☐ **inclination** /ˌɪnklɪˈneɪʃn/   n. preference

(= disposition, proclivity, preference, penchant)

The acceptance of, and continuance hitherto in, the office to which your suffrages have twice called me have been a uniform sacrifice of inclination to the opinion of duty and to a deference for what appeared to be your desire. ("President George Washington's Farewell Address")

여러분들의 투표로 제가 두 번이나 연임한 이 직책을 수용하고 유지한 것은 제게는 의무감에 일률적으로 한 희생이며 여러분들의 희망에 대한 저의 존경심에서 유발한 것입니다. (워싱턴 대통령의 퇴임사)

☐ **deference** /ˈdefərəns/   n. respect

(= esteem, regard, admiration, reverence)

The acceptance of, and continuance hitherto in, the office to which your suffrages have twice called me have been a uniform sacrifice of inclination to the opinion of duty and to a deference for what appeared to be your desire. ("President George Washington's Farewell Address")

여러분들의 투표로 제가 두 번이나 연임한 이 직책을 수용하고 유지한 것은 제게는 의무감에 일률적으로 한 희생이며 여러분들의 희망에 대한 저의 존경심에서 유발한 것입니다. (워싱턴 대통령의 퇴임사)

☐ **perplexed** /pər'plekst/   adj. full of confusion and complications

(= bewildered, befuddled, disconcerted, confounded)

..but mature reflection on the then perplexed and critical posture of our affairs with foreign nations.. ("President George Washington's Farewell Address")

그러나 그 당시 우리의 혼란스럽고 위태로운 외교상황을 지금에 와서 성숙한 자세로 회상해보면.. (워싱턴 대통령의 퇴임사)

☐ **impel** /ɪm'pel/   v. to urge to action through moral pressure

(= compel, urge, induce, coerce)

..and the unanimous advice of persons entitled to my confidence, impelled me to abandon the idea. ("President George Washington's Farewell Address")

그리고 내가 믿는 사람들의 한결 같은 충고가 나로 하여금 그 생각을 버리게 하였습니다. (워싱턴 대통령의 퇴임사)

☐ **rejoice** /rɪ'dʒɔɪs/   v. to celebrate

(= cheer, exult)

I rejoice that the state of your concerns no longer renders the pursuit of inclination incompatible with the sentiment of duty or propriety... ("President George Washington's Farewell Address")

나는 더 이상 내가 하고 싶은 일과 의무감이나 예의범절상 해야 하는 일이 서로 호환되지 않음이 여러분들의 이해관계와 맞물려 잊지 않음에 크게 기뻐하고.. (워싱턴 대통령의 퇴임사)

☐ **propriety** /prə'praɪəti/

n. conforming to the prevailing standards of behavior and speech

(= politeness, decorum, decency, appropriateness)

I rejoice that the state of your concerns no longer renders the pursuit of inclination incompatible with the sentiment of duty or propriety... ("President George Washington's Farewell Address")

나는 더 이상 내가 하고 싶은 일과 의무감이나 예의범절상 해야하는 일이 서로 호환되지 않음이 여러분들의 이해관계와 맞물려 잊지 않음에 크게 기뻐하고.. (워싱턴 대통령의 퇴임사)

☐ **admonish** /əd'mɑːnɪʃ/   v. to give warning about

(= reprove, caution, reprimand, reproach, chide)

..every day the increasing weight of years admonishes me more and more that the shade of retirement is as necessary to me as it will be welcome.. ("President George Washington's Farewell Address")

..매일매일 느끼는 세월의 무게가 나에게 은퇴의 필요성과 반가움을 지속적으로 경고하는데.. (워싱턴 대통령의 퇴임사)

☐ **steadfast** /'stedfæst/   adj. showing no sign of weakening

(= unwavering, resolute, persistent, dedicated, loyal)

..still more for the steadfast confidence with which (my country) has supported me.. ("President George Washington's Farewell Address")

..더욱이 (내 나라가) 나를 뚝심있는 믿음을 가지고 지지해 준 것이... (워싱턴 대통령의 퇴임사)

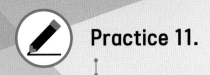

Practice 11.

Fill in the blank with the word that matches the definition provided

01 The lawyer tried to _____ (represent a fault as being less serious than it seems) his client's behavior so she would get a short jail term.

02 Frugality when young _____ (specifically lead to) to prosperity when old.

03 Kenneth has _____ (given notice) his employer that he will resign at the end of the month.

04 He lay on the floor in a/an _____ (lying on one's back) position for hours.

05 Mark always treats his seniors with _____ (respect).

06 Sometimes one must fight to preserve one's _____ (free from violation) rights.

07 Gary fought many boxing matches before, but he never faced an opponent as _____ (great and impressive) as Tom.

08 Craig's _____ (preference) to fine dining has made him most knowledgeable in where to find the best restaurants in the city.

09 Sandy was _____ (insulted) by Harry's comment about her family.

10 Emily _____ (rejected) Jack's displays of affection.

11 Clint is _____ (showing no signs of weakening) in his belief that hard work always pays off.

12   The entire country _____ (celebrated) when their national team reached the semi-finals of the World Cup Games.

13   In some countries it is against _____ (conforming to standards of behavior) for a man and woman to hold hands in public.

14   My Dad never _____ (to give warning about) me about my grades, but whenever I did something he thought to be impolite, he scolded me very sternly.

15   I was _____ (full of confusion) at the strange question, but I tried to answer it as sincerely as possible.

16   The _____ (reduction) of population growth has sparked a serious conversation about accepting more immigrants in the future.

Find the correct word which can replace the bold phrase in the following sentences. Change the word form appropriately to fit the sentence, if necessary

insidious, beseech, impediment, auxiliary, patronize, inflame, frivolous, endowment, prevail, inducement, nominal, discern, integrity, contrive, subservient

01   A good politician must be able to _____ a right policy from a popular policy.

02   The man is too _____ and self-centered to expect him to act in the interest of others.

03   With only two days left to finish his paper, Larry _____ Brian for help.

04   High oil prices have become a serious _____ to the world's economic growth.

05   Harry possesses many special _____ such as intelligence, curiosity, tenacity and endurance that make him a brilliant scholar.

06   The politician's comments blaming immigrants for social unrest _____ many people.

07   John's wife views John's hobby of making plastic models as a _____ waste of time.

08   He was viewed as a man of _____ and unable to commit acts of perfidy.

09   The two hostages _____ a plan to trick their kidnappers and escape.

10 In my grandfather's day, most wives were obedient to their husbands, but now, husbands are usually _____ to their wives.

11 Life sometimes seems unfair but remember that justice always _____.

12 The government has announced _____ policies to encourage couples to have more babies.

13 My dad is only the _____ head of our family: Mom makes all the important decisions.

14 The cabin in the woods is connected to the electricity grid but also has a gasoline generator as an _____ power source.

15 My grandmother has _____ the same convenience store in her neighborhood for over 30 years.

steadfast, address, inviolate, deference, contemplation, entreaty, artifice, covert, rejoice, magnitude, perplexed, palpable, temporal, subjugation, spurn, surveillance

16 Despite the defendant's family's earnest _____ for a lenient ruling, the judged sentenced the defendant to 15 years in prison.

17 Zhu Ge Liang defeated his enemy's 20,000 troops with only 3,000 troops through _____.

18 The police had the suspect under covert _____ for weeks.

19 When the war was finally over, the entire country _____.

20 Even though his first two businesses failed, George was _____ in his determination to succeed.

21 The President will _____ the nation for the first time since his re-election next week.

22 When we heard that James was not hurt in the accident, our relief was _____.

23 In the Kingdom of Bhutan, the King is both the spiritual and _____ leader of the country.

24 The _____ of native Indians by the Americans was not a peaceful process.

25 I realized that Robert's anger was deeper than I thought because he _____ all my gestures to reconcile with him.

26 When I was a child, my father's authority within my family was _____.

27 On Memorial Day, the national flag is raised at half-mast in _____ to the soldiers who sacrificed their lives for this country.

28 After several days of deep _____, Simon decided to quit his job and start his own business.

29 At the time the decision was made, no one realized the _____ of problems this decision would cause.

30 When the man the police thought was the culprit was proved innocent, the police was _____.

Select the pair of words that most nearly expresses the same relationship

31 frivolous: trivial
    A. zeal: energy
    B. animosity: magnanimity
    C. mercantile: temporal
    D. enlightened: old-fashioned

32 prevail: succumb
A. espouse: assimilate
B. cabal: faction
C. assistance: impediment
D. requisite: necessary

33 commensurate: corresponding
A. espouse: assimilate
B. conflagration: inferno
C. ruminate: sect
D. treason: alliance

34 disposed: unwilling
A. secular: temporal
B. solace: worry
C. behave: comport
D. plea: entreaty

35 beseech: implore
A. inviolate: infringed
B. supine: standing
C. diminution: increase
D. esteem: reverence

36 propriety: decorum
A. weak: steadfast
B. reprimand: admonish
C. array: rejection
D. salvation: declaration

37 tangible: palpable
A. diffusive: collective
B. deception: truth
C. upend: invert
D. dominant: subservient

38 agitate: provoke
A. annoy: vex
B. creditor: debtor
C. enlightened: prejudiced
D. helm: faction

39   obnoxious: ill-behaved
     A. oppose: patronize
     B. discern: avoid
     C. capsize: impart
     D. affronted: slighted

40   mischief: damage
     A. contend: perish
     B. domination: eminence
     C. animosity: friendliness
     D. apportionment: medium

Choose the word that isn't a synonym

41   helm – vice – controls

42   acrimony – hostility – conjecture

43   trivial – frivolous – obedient

44   prejudice – predominate – prevail

45   inference – extrapolation – manifestation

46   assimilate – patronize – integrate

47   overturn – capsize – discern

48   factious – divisive – mandatory

49   aptitude – magnitude – faculty

50   conflagration – deliberation – contemplation

51   spurn – secure – rivet

52   unadulterated – unscrupulous – inviolate

53   appropriateness – penchant – inclination

54   belligerent – martial – grueling

55   apt – snare – trap

56   salvation – consolation – rescue

57   comport – implore – behave

58   fervor – ardor – anguish

59   corporeal – tangible – informed

60   partake – protest – remonstrate

61   collection – array – perfidy

62   ruminate – cogitate – scheme

63   expedient – obligatory – requisite

64   diffusive – disseminative – consonant

65   impartial – biased – objective

☐ **annals** /ˈænlz/   n. historical records

(= archives, chronicles, histories, accounts)

...let it be remembered... as an instructive example in our annals... ("President George Washington's Farewell Address")

..기억되기 바랍니다.. 우리의 역사적인 기록 내의 교훈적인 예로.. (워싱턴 대통령의 퇴임사)

☐ **vicissitude** /vɪˈsɪsɪtuːd/   n. variation in life

...amidst appearances sometimes dubious, vicissitudes of fortune often discouraging, ("President George Washington's Farewell Address")

..가끔식 우리 운의 불확실한 우여곡절이 (우리를) 실망스럽게 하더라도.. (워싱턴 대통령의 퇴임사)

☐ **countenance** /ˈkaʊntənəns/   v. to tolerate or endure

(= tolerate, allow, approve, endure)

..in situations in which not unfrequently want of success has countenanced the spirit of criticism.. ("President George Washington's Farewell Address")

..비판의 정신을 성공을 원하는 우호적인 정신으로 인내한 상황.. (워싱턴 대통령의 퇴임사)

☐ **solicitude** /səˈlɪsɪtuːd/   n. excessive attentiveness

(= concern, apprehension, attentiveness, consideration)

But a solicitude for your welfare, which cannot end but with my life... ("President George Washington's Farewell Address")

..내 삶이 끝나기 전에는 끝나지 않을 여러분의 행복에 대한 나의 간절한 걱정이.. (워싱턴 대통령의 퇴임사)

☐ **interwoven** /ˌɪntərˈwiːv/   adj. interconnected

(= intertwined, entwined, knit, meshed)

Interwoven as is the love of liberty with every ligament of your hearts, no recommendation of mine is necessary to fortify or confirm the attachment. ("President George Washington's Farewell Address")

여러분의 심장 속의 모든 연대와 맞물려 있는 자유에 대한 사랑과 같이, 그 연대를 강화하거나 확인하기 위해 나의 권유 따위는 필요하지 않으며.. (워싱턴 대통령의 퇴임사)

☐ **pillar** /ˈpɪlər/

n. an upright structure made of stone, brick or metal that supports a superstructure

(= column, stake, mast)

..for it is a main pillar in the edifice of your real independence.. ("President George Washington's Farewell Address")

여러분의 진정한 자유라는 건축물을 떠 받치는 주 기둥이기 때문입니다. (워싱턴 대통령의 퇴임사)

☐ **edifice** /ˈedɪfɪs/   n. a large building

(= structure, construction)

..for it is a main pillar in the edifice of your real independence.. ("President George Washington's Farewell Address")

여러분의 진정한 자유라는 건축물을 떠 받치는 주 기둥이기 때문입니다. (워싱턴 대통령의 퇴임사)

☐ **artifice** /ˈɑːrtɪfɪs/   n. deception

(= deceit, cunning, trickery, ruse)

..many artifices (will be) employed to weaken in your minds the conviction of this truth.. ("President George Washington's Farewell Address")

이 진실에 대한 여러분의 믿음을 약화시키기 위해 사용되는 여러 가지 책략들.. (워싱턴 대통령의 퇴임사)

☐ **battery** /ˈbætəri/   n. the act of beating or battering

(= attack, bombardment, assault)

..as this is the point in your political fortress against which the batteries of internal and external enemies will be most constantly and actively (though often covertly and insidiously) directed... ("President George Washington's Farewell Address")

..이 지점에서 여러분들의 정치적인 요새를 향해 내외부의 적들이 지속적이고 활동적으로 (하지만 많은 경우에 은밀하고 사악하게) 집중포화를 할 것이며.. (워싱턴 대통령의 퇴임사)

□ **covert** /ˈkəʊvɜːrt/   adj. done unnoticeably

(= clandestine, concealed, furtive, stealthy)

..as this is the point in your political fortress against which the batteries of internal and external enemies will be most constantly and actively (though often covertly and insidiously) directed... ("President George Washington's Farewell Address")

..이 지점에서 여러분들의 정치적인 요새를 향해 내외부의 적들이 지속적이고 활동적으로 (하지만 많은 경우에 은밀하고 사악하게) 집중포화를 할 것이며.. (워싱턴 대통령의 퇴임사)

□ **insidious** /ɪnˈsɪdiəs/   adj. stealthily treacherous

(= sinister, crafty, deceptive, devious)

..as this is the point in your political fortress against which the batteries of internal and external enemies will be most constantly and actively (though often covertly and insidiously) directed... ("President George Washington's Farewell Address")

..이 지점에서 여러분들의 정치적인 요새를 향해 내외부의 적들이 지속적이고 활동적으로 (하지만 많은 경우에 은밀하고 사악하게) 집중포화를 할 것이며.. (워싱턴 대통령의 퇴임사)

□ **palladium** /pəˈleɪdiəm/   n. something believed to ensure protection

(= safeguard)

..accustoming yourselves to think and speak of (your national union) as of the palladium of your political safety and prosperity.. ("President George Washington's Farewell Address")

..(여러분의 국가 연방이) 여러분들의 정치적 안전과 번영을 보호해 주는 수호자로 생각하는 데 익숙해지며.. (워싱턴 대통령의 퇴임사)

□ **indignant** /ɪnˈdɪɡnənt/   adj. expressing strong displeasure

(= irate, vexed, annoyed, piqued)

..and indignantly frowning upon the first dawning of every attempt to alienate any portion of our country from the rest, or to enfeeble the sacred ties which now link together the various parts. ("President George Washington's Farewell Address")

..그리고 우리 나라의 한 부분을 나머지 부분으로부터 이간하려는 시도를 하거나 (우리나라의) 각기 다른 지방들을 서로 연결해 주는 성스러운 매듭을 약화시키고자 하는 시도가 보이는 순간 분함을 느끼고 못마땅해 하며.. (워싱턴 대통령의 퇴임사)

☐ **enfeeble** /ɪn'fiːbl/   v. to cause to become weak

(= weaken, debilitate, enervate, deplete, exhaust)

..and indignantly frowning upon the first dawning of every attempt to alienate any portion of our country from the rest, or to enfeeble the sacred ties which now link together the various parts. ("President George Washington's Farewell Address")

..그리고 우리 나라의 한 부분을 나머지 부분으로부터 이간하려는 시도를 하거나 (우리나라의) 각기 다른 지방들을 서로 연결해 주는 성스러운 매듭을 약화시키고자 하는 시도가 보이는 순간 분함을 느끼고 못마땅해 하며.. (워싱턴 대통령의 퇴임사)

☐ **exalt** /ɪg'zɔːlt/   v. to pay tribute to

(= praise, laud, acclaim, extol, lionize)

The name of American, which belongs to you in your national capacity, must always exalt the just pride of patriotism.. ("President George Washington's Farewell Address")

여러분들의 국적인 미국인이라는 명칭이 항상 애국심을 칭송하게(느끼게) 하고.. (워싱턴 대통령의 퇴임사)

☐ **appellation** /ˌæpə'leɪʃn/   n. an identifying name or title

(= name, designation, title, label)

The name of American.. must always exalt the just pride of patriotism more than any appellation derived from local discriminations. ("President George Washington's Farewell Address")

미국인이라는 명칭이... 다른 어떤 지방의 명칭보다 더 애국심을 칭송하게(느끼게) 만들어야 합니다. (워싱턴 대통령의 퇴임사)

☐ **fraternal** /frə't3ːrnl/   adj. of brothers

(= brotherly, comradely, communal, amicable)

..they tend to render alien to each other those who ought to be bound together by fraternal affection. ("President George Washington's Farewell Address")

..그들은 형제애로 엮여야 되는 사람들의 관계를 서로 소원하게 만드는 경향이 있고.. (워싱턴 대통령의 퇴임사)

☐ **incongruous** /ɪn'kɑːŋgruəs/   adj. out of place

(= odd, inappropriate, absurd, bizarre)

..to make the public administration the mirror of the ill-concerted and incongruous projects of faction.. ("President George Washington's Farewell Address")

국민의 행정부를 파벌의 악한 의도로 고안되고, 자리에 어울리지 않는 과제로 만들기 위해.. (워싱턴 대통령의 퇴임사)

☐ **subvert** /səb'vɜːrt/   v. to overthrow

(= undermine, destabilize, disrupt, topple)

..cunning, ambitious, and unprincipled men will be enabled to subvert the power of the people.. ("President George Washington's Farewell Address")

..교활하고, 야망에 찬 그리고 도덕심 없는 사람들이 국민의 힘을 전복할 수 있게 하고.. (워싱턴 대통령의 퇴임사)

☐ **specious** /'spiːʃəs/   adj. superficially plausible

(= false, misleading, bogus, inaccurate)

Towards the preservation of your government... it is requisite... that you resist with care the spirit of innovation upon (the government's) principles, however specious the pretexts. ("President George Washington's Farewell Address")

여러분의 정부를 유지하기 위해.. 필요한 것은.. 여러분들이 정부의 원칙에 반하는 혁신들을, 아무리 그것들의 전제가 듣기에 좋다 하더라도, 조심스럽게 거부하는 것이.. (워싱턴 대통령의 퇴임사)

Practice 13.

Fill in the blank with the word that matches the definition provided

01 I was touched by his _____ (excessive attentiveness) towards my family.

02 Gold threads were _____ (knit) within the dark blue fabric.

03 The cathedral was held up by 120 _____ (column) 80 feet high.

04 The towering _____ (large building) can be seen from miles away.

05 We are not trying to _____ (overthrow) the government: we only want the government to acknowledge the injustices that are happening.

06 Roger Federer is arguably the greatest tennis player in the _____ (historical records) of the sport's history.

07 It was difficult to believe the _____ (variations in life) my grandmother went through during her life.

08 Mrs. Wilson was _____ (expressing strong displeasure) when she heard that her daughter was made to stand outside in the pouring rain.

09 Winston was charged with _____ (the act of beating), after he put Peter in the hospital in a fist fight.

10 I saw Dwayne steal a/an _____ (done unnoticeably) glance at the wall clock during my presentation.

11 I never imagined William would be capable of such _____ (deception): he seemed like a very honest person.

12 In church, everyone _____ (pays tribute to) God through prayer.

13 Justine gives his younger brother Joshua _____ (brotherly) advice whenever he can.

14 The clothes Richard wore to work today were most _____ (out of place).

15 Years of working in the coal mines have _____ (to make weak) Mr. Gregory to the point of losing his health.

☐ **intimate** /ˈɪntɪmət/   v. to make known indirectly

(= insinuate, hint, imply, infer, allude)

I have already intimated to you the danger of parties in the State. ("President George Washington's Farewell Address")

나는 이미 여러분에게 파벌의 위험성을 알렸습니다. (워싱턴 대통령의 퇴임사)

☐ **foment** /fəʊˈment/   v. to instigate or foster (discord or rebellion)

(= provoke, encourage, germinate, ferment, aggravate)

..foments occasionally riot and insurrection.. ("President George Washington's Farewell Address")

..가끔씩 폭동과 내란을 선동하고.. (워싱턴 대통령의 퇴임사)

☐ **cast** /kæst/   n. outward form

(= appearance)

..and in governments of a monarchical cast, patriotism may look with indulgence, if not with favor, upon the spirit of party.. ("President George Washington's Farewell Address")

전제군주제 하의 정부에서는 애국심을 가진 사람들이 파벌에 대해서는 좋게 생각하지 않더라도 묵인할 수는 있는 것이라 할 수 있지만.. (워싱턴 대통령의 퇴임사)

☐ **indulgence** /ɪnˈdʌldʒəns/   n. tolerant treatment

(= tolerance, lenience, clemency, absolution, forbearance)

..and in governments of a monarchical cast, patriotism may look with indulgence, if not with favor, upon the spirit of party.. ("President George Washington's Farewell Address")

전제군주제 하의 정부에서는 애국심을 가진 사람들이 파벌에 대해서는 좋게 생각하지 않더라도 묵인할 수는 있는 것이라 할 수 있지만.. (워싱턴 대통령의 퇴임사)

☐ **salutary** /'sæljəteri/   adj. promoting some beneficial purpose

(= helpful, useful, beneficial, productive)

From (governments') natural tendency, it is certain there will always be enough of that spirit for every salutary purpose. ("President George Washington's Farewell Address")

정부들의 자연스런 성향으로 볼 때, 모든 유익한 목적(의 달성)을 위한 그런 정신은 항상 충분히 있을 것입니다. (워싱턴 대통령의 퇴임사)

☐ **mitigate** /'mɪtɪgeɪt/   v. to make less severe

(= alleviate, lessen, allay, assuage, abate)

And there being constant danger of excess, the effort ought to be by force of public opinion, to mitigate and assuage it. ("President George Washington's Farewell Address")

그리고 항상 과할 수 있는 위험이 있기 때문에, 그런 노력은 국민의 여론에 의해 강요되어야 그것을 중재하고 진정시킬 수 있을 것입니다. (워싱턴 대통령의 퇴임사)

☐ **assuage** /ə'sweɪdʒ/   v. to make milder or less severe

(= moderate, ease, appease, temper, pacify)

And there being constant danger of excess, the effort ought to be by force of public opinion, to mitigate and assuage it. ("President George Washington's Farewell Address")

그리고 항상 과할 수 있는 위험이 있기 때문에, 그런 노력은 국민의 여론에 의해 강요되어야 그것을 중재하고 진정시킬 수 있을 것입니다. (워싱턴 대통령의 퇴임사)

☐ **vigilance** /'vɪdʒɪləns/   n. watchfulness

(= attentiveness, caution, observance, alertness)

A fire not to be quenched, it demands a uniform vigilance to prevent its bursting into a flame.. ("President George Washington's Farewell Address")

끌 수 없는 불꽃이기 때문에, 항상 그것이 큰 불로 번지지 않게끔 지속적인 경계를 해야 합니다. (워싱턴 대통령의 퇴임사)

☐ **score** /skɔːr/   n. twenty

Four score and seven years ago our fathers brought forth, upon this continent, a new nation.. ("Gettysburg Address")

팔십하고 칠 년 전에 우리의 선조들은 이 땅에 새로운 나라를 건설하였습니다. (링컨의 게티스버그 연설)

☐ **conceive** /kən'siːv/　　　　　v. to imagine or believe something

(= envisage, imagine, visualize)

Now we are engaged in a great civil war, testing whether that nation, or any nation so conceived and so dedicated, can long endure. ("Gettysburg Address")

지금 우리는 과연 그 나라가, 혹은 그런 방법으로 고안되고 축성된 나라가 오래 지속될 수 있는지 시험하는 엄청난 내전 중에 있습니다. (링컨의 게티스버그 연설)

☐ **endure** /ɪn'dʊr/　　　　　v. to continue to exist

(= last, continue)

Now we are engaged in a great civil war, testing whether that nation, or any nation so conceived and so dedicated, can long endure. ("Gettysburg Address")

지금 우리는 과연 그 나라가, 혹은 그런 방법으로 잉태되고 헌신한 나라가 오래 지속될 수 있는지 시험하는 엄청난 내전 중에 있습니다. (링컨의 게티스버그 연설)

☐ **propriety** /prə'praɪəti/

n. quality of being socially or morally acceptable

(= correctness, decency, politeness, decorum)

This we may, in all propriety do. ("Gettysburg Address")

그것은 우리가 마땅하고 옳게 할 일입니다. (링컨의 게티스버그 연설)

☐ **consecrate** /'kɑːnsɪkreɪt/　　　　　v. to declare something as holy

(= sanctify, bless, devote, hallow)

But in a larger sense, we cannot dedicate, we cannot consecrate, we cannot hallow, this ground. ("Gettysburg Address")

보다 넓은 의미에서 우리는 이 땅을 헌정하거나, 축성하거나, 신성하게 할 수는 없습니다. (링컨의 게티스버그 연설)

☐ **hallow** /hælou/　　　　　v. to set apart as being holy

(= consecrate, sanctify)

But in a larger sense, we cannot dedicate, we cannot consecrate, we cannot hallow, this ground. ("Gettysburg Address")

보다 넓은 의미에서 우리는 이 땅을 헌정하거나, 축성하거나, 신성하게 할 수는 없습니다. (링컨의 게티스버그 연설)

☐ **in vain**   adv. without success

(= uselessly, pointlessly)

that we here highly resolve that these dead shall not have died in vain, ("Gettysburg Address")

우리는 이곳에서 죽은 자들이 헛되이 죽은 것이 아님을 다짐합니다. (링컨의 게티스버그 연설)

☐ **emancipation** /ɪˌmænsɪˈpeɪʃn/   n. the act of freeing or state of being free

(= liberation, freedom, deliverance)

The Emancipation Declaration

노예해방선언문

☐ **issue** /ˈɪʃuː/   v. to make known

(= announce, release, publish, deliver)

Whereas on the 22nd day of September, A.D. 1862, a proclamation was issued by the President of the United States ("The Emancipation Declaration")

1862년 9월 22일, 미국의 대통령이 선언문을 공표했다. (노예해방선언문)

☐ **designate** /ˈdezɪɡneɪt/   v. to formally give a description or name

(= assign, call, label, name)

That on the 1st day of January, A.D. 1863, all persons held as slaves within any State or designated part of a State shall be then, thenceforward, and forever free ("The Emancipation Declaration")

서기 1863년 1월 1일과 그 이후로 그 어떤 주(州)나 주의 일부분에서 노예로 잡혀 있는 모든 사람은 영원히 자유의 몸이 된다. (노예해방선언문)

☐ **thenceforward** /ˌðensˈfɔːrθ/   adv. from that point on

(= thence, from then on)

That on the 1st day of January, A.D. 1863, all persons held as slaves within any State or designated part of a State shall be then, thenceforward, and forever free ("The Emancipation Declaration")

서기 1863년 1월 1일과 그 이후로 그 어떤 주(州)나 주(州)의 일부분에서 노예로 잡혀 있는 모든 사람은 영원히 자유의 몸이 된다. (노예해방선언문)

☐ **aforesaid** /əˈfɔːrmenʃənd/   adj. mentioned before

(= aforementioned, above-mentioned, said)

That the executive will on the 1st day of January aforesaid, by proclamation, designate the States and parts of States, if any, in which the people thereof, respectively, shall then be in rebellion against the United States ("The Emancipation Declaration")

행정부가 상기에 명기된 1월 1일 이후부터, 선언문에 의하여, 해당 주나 주의 일부분의 주민들을 미국의 정부를 상대로 반란 중인 것으로 지명한다. (노예해방선언문)

☐ **countervail** /kàuntərvéil/   v. to act against with equal power or force

(= counteract, offset)

..in the absence of strong countervailing testimony.. ("The Emancipation Declaration")

..반대의 경우를 강력히 입증하는 증언이 없을 경우.. (노예해방선언문)

Practice 14.

Fill in the blank with the word that matches the definition provided

01 There are some _____ (promoting some beneficial purpose) lessons to take away from our defeat today.

02 Apologizing will not _____ (make less severe) the seriousness of your mistake.

03 The sight was _____ (to declare something as holy) by the Catholic Pope in 1998.

04 Mr. Tucker will be three _____ (twenty) years of age next week.

05 Ruth sprayed air-freshener everywhere to _____ (to act against in equal power) the awful smell.

06 The most important job of the new President will be to _____ (to appease or pacify) the disappointment that many citizens have of the previous government.

07 The company guards its technical secrets with great _____ (watchfulness).

08 The director _____ (to imagine something) the movie more than a decade before the technology to make such a movie was available.

09 Many Pilgrims immigrated to North America seeking religious _____ the state of being free).

10 As of this year, all buildings over five stories have been _____ (formerly give a description) as "no smoking" zones.

11 Her sons can be rowdy, but Gloria deals with them with _____ (tolerant treatment).

12 The Su Dynasty was founded to _____ (to continue to exist) for 1,000 years, but it only lasted for 60.

13 Mary _____ (make known indirectly) that sometimes Frank's directness makes her uncomfortable.

14 When it happened, the Russian Revolution shook an unsuspecting world to its core, but in reality the mood for a social upheaval had _____ (to instigate or foster) for more than a century within the Russian Empire.

☐ **testimony** /ˈtestɪməʊni/   n. evidence in support of a fact or statement

(= proof, evidence, witness, verification)

..in the absence of strong countervailing testimony, be deemed conclusive evidence that such State and the people thereof are not then in rebellion against the United States. ("The Emancipation Declaration")

..반대의 경우를 강력히 입증하는 증언이 없을 경우, 상기된 주와 그의 주민들이 미국 정부를 상대로 반란 중임을 증명하는 증거로 간주된다. (노예해방선언문)

☐ **deem** /diːm/   v. to hold as an opinion

(= believe, suppose, estimate, reckon)

..in the absence of strong countervailing testimony, be deemed conclusive evidence that such State and the people thereof are not then in rebellion against the United States. ("The Emancipation Declaration")

..반대의 경우를 강력히 입증하는 증언이 없을 경우, 상기된 주와 그의 주민들이 미국 정부를 상대로 반란 중임을 증명하는 증거로 간주된다. (노예해방선언문)

☐ **by virtue of**   idiom. thanks to

(= because of, by reason of)

Now, therefore, I, Abraham Lincoln, President of the United States, by virtue of the power in me vested as Commander-In-Chief of the Army and Navy of the United States.. ("The Emancipation Declaration")

그러므로 나, 미국 대통령 아브라함 링컨은 미국의 육군과 해군의 최고사령관으로서 내게 주어진 권력에 의해.. (노예해방선언문)

☐ **suppress** /səˈpres/   v. to force an activity to stop

(= subdue, quell, dominate, overpower)

..as a fit and necessary war measure for suppressing (the) said rebellion.. ("The Emancipation Declaration")

..상기한 반란을 진압하기 위해 전시에 준하는 필요한 조처로.. (노예해방선언문)

☐ **enjoin** /ɪnˈdʒɔɪn/　　　　　　v. to direct or order to do something

(= command, instruct, bid, direct)

And I hereby enjoin upon the people so declared to be free to abstain from all violence, unless in necessary self-defense.. ("The Emancipation Declaration")

그리고 나는 (자유의 몸으로) 선언된 사람들이 정당방위의 경우를 제외한 그 어떠한 폭력적인 행동도 삼가 할 것을 명령한다. (노예해방선언문)

☐ **abstain** /əbˈsteɪn/　　　　　　v. to hold back voluntarily

(= restrain, withdraw, refrain, desist, curb)

And I hereby enjoin upon the people so declared to be free to abstain from all violence, unless in necessary self-defense.. ("The Emancipation Declaration")

그리고 나는 (자유의 몸으로) 선언된 사람들이 정당방위의 경우를 제외한 그 어떠한 폭력적인 행동도 삼가 할 것을 명령한다. (노예해방선언문)

☐ **faithful** /ˈfeɪθfl/

adj. strict or thorough in the performance of duty

(= true, loyal, trustworthy, staunch)

I recommend to them that, in all case when allowed, they labor faithfully for reasonable wages. ("The Emancipation Declaration")

나는 그들이 허락되는 한 정당한 임금을 받기 위해 성실하게 노동할 것을 권유한다. (노예해방선언문)

☐ **wage** /weɪdʒ/

n. money received in exchange for work or services provided

(= salary, remuneration, pay)

I recommend to them that, in all case when allowed, they labor faithfully for reasonable wages. ("The Emancipation Declaration")

나는 그들이 허락되는 한 정당한 임금을 받기 위해 성실하게 노동할 것을 권유한다. (노예해방선언문)

☐ **suitable** /ˈsuːtəbl/   adj. to be appropriate

(= appropriate, fitting, proper, seemly)

I further declare and make known that such persons of suitable condition will be received into the armed service of the United States.. ("The Emancipation Declaration")

적절한 (정신/건강) 상태의 사람들은 미국의 국군에 받아들여질 것임을 선언한다. (노예해방선언문)

☐ **garrison** /ˈɡærɪsn/   v. to provide with troops

(= man, guard)

..to garrison forts, positions, stations, and other places, and to man vessels of all sorts in said service. ("The Emancipation Declaration")

.. 요새, 위치, 역 그리고 다른 곳에 수비대로 주둔하고, 앞서 명기한 해군에 모든 종류의 군선에 승선할 것을.. (노예해방선언문)

☐ **man** /mæn/   v. provide with manpower

(= staff, work, garrison)

..to garrison forts, positions, stations, and other places, and to man vessels of all sorts in said service. ("The Emancipation Declaration")

.. 요새, 위치, 역 그리고 다른 곳에 수비대로 주둔하고, 앞서 명기한 해군에 모든 종류의 군선에 승선할 것을.. (노예해방선언문)

☐ **warrant** /ˈwɔːrənt/   v. to give reason or sanction for

(= justify, attest, merit, necessitate)

And upon this act, sincerely believed to be an act of justice, warranted by the Constitution upon military necessity.. ("The Emancipation Declaration")

이러한 행동이, 진실로 정의로운 행동으로 간주되고, 헌법에 군사적 필요성이라고 정당화된 행동임을.. (노예해방선언문)

☐ **invoke** /ɪnˈvəuk/   v. to call for with earnest desire

(= appeal to, call upon, beseech, implore)

I invoke the considerate judgment of mankind and the gracious favor of Almighty God. ("The Emancipation Declaration")

나는 인류의 너그러운 판단과 전지전능한 하느님의 가호에 호소한다. (노예해방선언문)

☐ **amicable** /ˈæmɪkəbl/   adj. friendly

(= good-natured, cordial, agreeable, polite)

At the proposal of the Russian Imperial Government...instructions have been transmitted to the minister of the United States at St. Petersburg to arrange by amicable negotiation the respective rights and interests of the two nations on the northwest coast of this continent. ("Monroe Doctrine")

러시아 제국의 요청에 의해⋯이 대륙의 북서 지역에 위치한 두 나라의 권리와 이해관계가 우호적인 대화로 조정될 수 있도록 상트 페테스부르그에 위치한 미국의 대사관에 지시사항이 전달되었다. (먼로 선언문)

☐ **accede** /əkˈsiːd/   v. to agree

(= agree, assent, consent, comply)

A similar proposal has been made by His Imperial Majesty to the Government of Great Britain, which has likewise been acceded to. ("Monroe Doctrine")

대영제국 정부의 국왕폐하에게도 비슷한 요청이 전달되었으며, 마찬가지로 동의하였다. (먼로 선언문)

☐ **manifest** /ˈmænɪfest/   v. to plainly show

(= demonstrate, display, exhibit, establish)

The Government of the United States has been desirous by this friendly proceeding of manifesting the great value which they have invariably attached to the friendship of the Emperor and their solicitude to cultivate the best understanding with his Government. ("Monroe Doctrine")

미국 정부는 이러한 우호적인 진행상황을 통해 황제폐하와의 우정을 유지하고 그의 정부와 최상의 이해관계를 조성하고자 큰 정성을 들여 얻는 큰 가치를 실현하고자 한다. (먼로 선언문)

☐ **solicitude** /səˈlɪsɪtuːd/   n. excessive attentiveness

(= attentiveness, consideration, care)

The Government of the United States has been desirous by this friendly proceeding of manifesting the great value which they have invariably attached to the friendship of the Emperor and their solicitude to cultivate the best understanding with his Government. ("Monroe Doctrine")

미국 정부는 이러한 우호적인 진행상황을 통해 황제폐화와의 우정을 유지하고 그의 정부와 최상의 이해관계를 조성하고자 큰 정성을 들여 얻는 큰 가치를 실현하고자 한다. (먼로 선언문)

☐ **colonization** /ˌkɑːlənəˈzeɪʃn/　　　n. the establishment of a colony

(= occupation, annexation, establishment)

..the American continents, by the free and independent condition which they have assumed and maintain, are henceforth not to be considered as subjects for future colonization by any European powers.. ("Monroe Doctrine")

아메리카 대륙들은, 그들이 받아들이고 유지하는 자유롭고 독립적인 상태에 의거, 앞으로 유럽 열강들의 식민지의 대상이 될 수 없다.. (먼로 선언문)

☐ **moderation** /ˌmɑːdəˈreɪʃn/　　　n. avoidance of extremes

(= restraint, control, temperance, balance)

It was stated at the commencement of the last session that a great effort was then making in Spain and Portugal to improve the condition of the people of those countries, and that it appeared to be conducted with extraordinary moderation. ("Monroe Doctrine")

지난 번 회의 모두에서 발표되기를 스페인과 포르투갈에서 자국국민들의 형편을 개선시키기 위한 대단한 노력이 진행되고 있으며 그것을 보통 이상의 절제하에서 진행하고 있는 듯하다. (먼로 선언문)

☐ **intercourse** /ˈɪntərkɔːrs/

n. dealings or communications between individuals, groups or countries

(= communication, interaction, association)

Of events in that quarter of the globe, with which we have so much intercourse and from which we derive our origin, we have always been anxious and interested spectators. ("Monroe Doctrine")

우리와 많은 교류가 있고 우리의 근원지인 지구의 그 쪽에서 일어나는 일에 대해 우리는 항상 걱정스러워 하고 관심을 보이는 관전자들이었다. (먼로 선언문)

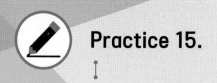

Practice 15.

Fill in the blank with the word that matches the definition provided

01 His manager warned Stewart that his clothes were not _____ (to be appropriate) to wear to the office.

02 In the absence of men, the compound was _____ (to provide with troops) by the women and teenaged boys.

03 If I don't go to work, Richard must _____ (provide manpower) the store alone.

04 We were always _____ (friendly) towards each other but were never really friends.

05 I do not _____ (to agree) to the terms.

06 I have been a/an _____ (loyal) reader of Time Magazine for 10 years.

07 He lives alone and has no _____ (communication with others) with anyone.

08 The sparse decorations of his small apartment is _____ (evidence in support of fact or statement) to the frugal life Mr. Hawk lived.

09 The professor _____ (to believe or reckon) my excuse acceptable.

10 I tried to _____ (to force to stop) my hick-ups during the concert but couldn't.

11 Many European Countries have _____ (to order to do something) advertisers to stop using models that are unhealthily skinny.

12 His philanthropic actions _____ (plainly show) a truly benevolent character.

13 His doctor told Richard that he must drink in _____ (avoidance of excess).

14 I'm trying to lose weight by _____ (to hold back voluntarily) from eating much.

15 I can't imagine what I could have done to _____ (to give reason for) Henry's anger at me.

16 The assailant's mother _____ (to call for with earnest desire) the victim's family to forgive her son.

Class 16

□ **spectator** /'spekteɪtər/   n. someone who watches

(= viewer, watcher, observer)

Of events in that quarter of the globe, with which we have so much intercourse and from which we derive our origin, we have always been anxious and interested spectators. ("Monroe Doctrine")

우리와 많은 교류가 있고 우리의 근원지인 지구의 그 쪽에서 일어나는 일에 대해 우리는 항상 걱정스러워하고 관심을 보이는 관전자들이었다. (먼로 선언문)

□ **comport** /kəm'pɔːrt/   v. to be in agreement

(= agree, correspond)

In the wars of the European powers in matters relating to themselves we have never taken any part, nor does it comport with our policy to do so. ("Monroe Doctrine")

유럽의 강호들이 자국과 관련된 일로 서로 치룬 전쟁에 우리는 한 번도 참여해 본 적이 없으며 참여하는 것이 우리의 정책과 일치하지도 않는다. (먼로 선언문)

□ **menace** /'menəs/   v. to threaten

(= threaten, jeopardize, imperil, intimidate)

It is only when our rights are invaded or seriously menaced that we resent injuries or make preparation for our defense. ("Monroe Doctrine")

우리의 권리들이 침탈되고 위협 당할 때 우리는 받은 상처를 분하게 여기고 우리의 방어를 준비한다. (먼로 선언문)

□ **hemisphere** /'hemɪsfɪr/   n. half of a sphere

With the movements in this hemisphere we are of necessity more immediately connected.. ("Monroe Doctrine")

우리는 우리가 속한 반구 내의 움직임에 필요상 더 직접적으로 연관되어 있다.. (먼로 선언문)

□ **felicity** /fə'lɪsəti/　　　　　　　n. happiness

(= contentment, pleasure, blessedness, bliss)

and to the defense of our own, which has been achieved by the loss of so much blood and treasure, and matured by the wisdom of their most enlightened citizens, and under which we have enjoyed unexampled felicity, this whole nation is devoted. ("Monroe Doctrine")

그리고 많은 피를 쏟고 재산의 피해를 입고 얻은, 가장 개화된 국민들의 현명함에 의해 성숙된, 그리고 그 결과 전에 없는 행복을 누리고 있는 우리 국가의 방어에 온나라가 헌신한다. (먼로 선언문)

□ **candor** /'kændər/　　　　　　　n. frankness

(= openness, honesty, truthfulness, sincerity)

We owe it, therefore, to candor and to the amicable relations existing between the United States and those powers to declare that we should consider any attempt on their part to extend their system to any portion of this hemisphere as dangerous to our peace and safety. ("Monroe Doctrine")

우리는 정직함과 미국과 상기 국가들간에 유지되는 상호 우호적인 관계를 고려하여 그 국가들이 자국의 정부형태를 우리가 속한 반구로 뻗치고자 하는 그 어떤 노력도 미국의 평화와 안전에 위험한 일로 치부하겠다고 선언한다. (먼로 선언문)

□ **amicable** /'æmɪkəbl/　　　　　　　adj. friendly

(= good-natured, harmonious, cordial)

We owe it, therefore, to candor and to the amicable relations existing between the United States and those powers to declare that we should consider any attempt on their part to extend their system to any portion of this hemisphere as dangerous to our peace and safety. ("Monroe Doctrine")

우리는 정직함과 미국과 상기 국가들간에 유지되는 상호 우호적인 관계를 고려하여 그 국가들이 자국의 정부형태를 우리가 속한 반구로 뻗치고자 하는 그 어떤 노력도 미국의 평화와 안전에 위험한 일로 치부하겠다고 선언한다. (먼로 선언문)

□ **interposition** /ɪntərpəzíʃən/　　　　　　　n. intervention

(= interruption, interference, meddling)

But with the Governments who have declared their independence... and whose independence we have acknowledged, we could not view any interposition for the purpose of oppressing them... by any European power in any other light than as the manifestation of an unfriendly disposition toward the United States. ("Monroe Doctrine")

그러나 독립을 선언한 국가들.. 특히 우리가 그 독립을 인정한 국가를 탄압하기 위해 어떤 유럽의 국가가 간섭하는 행위는 미국에 대한 적대행위로 간주할 수 밖에 없다. (먼로 선언문)

☐ **manifestation** /ˌmænɪfeˈsteɪʃn/   n. outward appearance

(= display, expression, indication)

But with the Governments who have declared their independence... and whose independence we have acknowledged, we could not view any interposition for the purpose of oppressing them... by any European power in any other light than as the manifestation of an unfriendly disposition toward the United States. ("Monroe Doctrine")

그러나 독립을 선언한 국가들.. 특히 우리가 그 독립을 인정한 국가를 탄압하기 위해 어떤 유럽의 국가가 간섭하는 행위는 미국에 대한 적대행위로 간주할 수 밖에 없다. (먼로 선언문)

☐ **disposition** /ˌdɪspəˈzɪʃn/   n. prevailing tendency

(= nature, character, temperament)

But with the Governments who have declared their independence... and whose independence we have acknowledged, we could not view any interposition for the purpose of oppressing them... by any European power in any other light than as the manifestation of an unfriendly disposition toward the United States. ("Monroe Doctrine")

그러나 독립을 선언한 국가들.. 특히 우리가 그 독립을 인정한 국가를 탄압하기 위해 어떤 유럽의 국가가 간섭하는 행위는 미국에 대한 적대행위로 간주할 수 밖에 없다. (먼로 선언문)

☐ **adhere** /ədˈhɪr/   v. to stay attached

(= follow, obey, observe)

In the war between those new Governments and Spain we declared our neutrality at the time of their recognition, and to this we have adhered, and shall continue to adhere.. ("Monroe Doctrine")

그러한 신생독립국이 독립을 선언했을 때 우리는 인정했고 그들과 스페인 간의 전쟁에서 우리는 중립을 선언했고, 지금도 그 중립을 유지하며 앞으로도 그럴 것이다. (먼로 선언문)

☐ **adduce** /əˈduːs/   v. to site as evidence

(= offer, present, cite)

Of this important fact no stronger proof can be adduced than that the allied powers should have thought it proper, on any principle satisfactory to themselves, to have interposed by force in the internal concerns of Spain. ("Monroe Doctrine")

이 중요한 사실의 가장 확실한 증거는 연합 국가들이 그들에게만 만족스러운 이유로 스페인의 내정에 간섭하는 것이 옳은 것이라고 생각했다는 것이다. (먼로 선언문) (먼로 선언문)

☐ **de facto** /ˌdeɪˈfæktəʊ/   adj. actual

(= genuine, actual, effective)

Our policy in regard to Europe... nevertheless remains the same, which is, not to interfere in the internal concerns of any of its powers; to consider the government de facto as the legitimate government for us; ("Monroe Doctrine")

우리의 유럽과 관련한 정책은... 그럼에도 불구하고 변동이 없으며, 그것은 유럽의 어떤 국가의 내정에도 관여하지 않겠다는 것이고, 현재 존재하는 정부들을 합법적인 정부로 인정하겠다는 것이다. (먼로 선언문)

☐ **conspicuous** /kənˈspɪkjuəs/   adj. clearly visible

(= noticeable, exposed, prominent, evident)

But in regard to those continents circumstances are eminently and conspicuously different. ("Monroe Doctrine")

그러나 그 대륙들과 관련해서는 상황이 확연하고 확실하게 다르다. (먼로 선언문)

☐ **subdue** /səbˈduː/   v. to subjugate

(= overpower, conquer, vanquish, overwhelm)

If we look to the comparative strength and resources of Spain and those new Governments, and their distance from each other, it must be obvious that she can never subdue them. ("Monroe Doctrine")

스페인과 신생독립국가들 간의 국력의 차이와 그들 간의 물리적인 거리를 생각한다면, 스페인이 그들을 복종시킬 수 없다는 것이 자명해진다. (먼로 선언문)

☐ **impartial** /ɪmˈpɑːrʃl/   adj. to be neutral

(= neutral, unbiased, objective, nonaligned)

A very limited statement of the argument for impartial suffrage, and for including the black man in the body politic, would require more space than can be reasonably asked here.

("Appeal to Congress for Impartial Suffrage by Frederick Douglass")

모든 사람에게 투표권을 제공해야 되는 이유와 투표권자들에 흑인들을 포함해야 되는 이유에 대해서 아주 국한적으로라도 주장하기 위해서는 여기서 제공된 것보다 많은 공간이 필요할 것이다. ("공정한 투표권에 대한 호소문" 프레데릭 더글러스)

☐ **body politic**

n. the state, people regarded as a political body under an organized government

A very limited statement of the argument for impartial suffrage, and for including the black man in the body politic, would require more space than can be reasonably asked here. ("Appeal to Congress for Impartial Suffrage by Frederick Douglass")

모든 사람에게 투표권을 제공해야 되는 이유와 투표권자들에 흑인들을 포함해야 되는 이유에 대해서 아주 국한적으로라도 주장하기 위해서는 여기서 제공된 것보다 많은 공간이 필요할 것이다. ("공정한 투표권에 대한 호소문" 프레데릭 더글러스)

☐ **manhood** /ˈmænhʊd/   n. the state of being a man

(= adulthood, maturity)

It is no less a crime against the manhood of a man, to declare that he shall not share in the making and directing of the government under which he lives, than to say that he shall not acquire property and education. ("Appeal to Congress for Impartial Suffrage by Frederick Douglass")

한 사람에게 그가 살고 있는 국가의 정부의 형성과 지휘에 관여하지 못한다 선언하는 것은 그가 재산을 형성하지 못하거나 교육을 받지 못한다고 말하는 것에 비해 가벼운 범죄가 아니다. ("공정한 투표권에 대한 호소문" 프레데릭 더글러스)

☐ **enfranchisement** /ɪnˈfræntʃaɪzmənt/

n. the state of allowing to vote

(= suffrage, empowerment, voting right)

The fundamental and unanswerable argument in favor of the enfranchisement of the black man is found in the undisputed fact of his manhood. ("Appeal to Congress for Impartial Suffrage by Frederick Douglass")

흑인에게도 투표권이 주어져야 한다는 가장 원칙적이고 이의를 달 수 없는 주장은 그가 인간이라는 데에 있다. ("공정한 투표권에 대한 호소문" 프레데릭 더글러스)

□ **sustain** /sə'steɪn/

v. continue or maintain for a certain period of time

(= maintain, prolong, protract)

He is a man, and by every fact and argument by which any man can sustain his right to vote, the black man can sustain his right equally. ("Appeal to Congress for Impartial Suffrage by Frederick Douglass")

그는 인간이고, 다른 인간이 투표권을 가질 수 있는 권리가 있듯이 흑인에게도 동등하게 그 권리가 주어진다. ("공정한 투표권에 대한 호소문" 프레데릭 더글러스)

Practice 16.

Fill in the blank with the word that matches the definition provided

01 The two men are rivals on the tennis court, but, off-court, they have a/an _____ (friendly) relationship.

02 I am of the _____ (prevailing tendency) to always tell the truth if I can.

03 What I am about to ask you is very important, so I want you to answer with perfect _____ (frankness), OK?

04 At 197cm and 120kg, Jake is always _____ (clearly visible).

05 The police used water cannons and tear gas to _____ (overpower) the violent protestors.

06 Jake remained _____ (neutral), while Jesse and Richard argued.

07 When my mom and my grandmother argue, my dad can only be a/an _____ (a person who watches).

08 When an unknown man _____ (threatened) the children in the playground, one of the parents called the police immediately.

09 Aaron said that the secret to his success was to seek smart people's advice and _____ (stay attached) to it.

10 Although Mr. Higgins is the Chairman, Mr. White is the _____ (actual) head of the company.

11 The recent demonstrations are a/an _____ (outward appearance) of the people's discontent.

12 When his five children and 16 grandchildren all gathered for his birthday party, Mr. Crowley exclaimed: "I there any _____ (happiness) greater than this?"

13 I have always been careful to have my words and actions _____ (be in agreement).

14 With his father dead and mother ill, Henry had to reach _____ (the state of being a man) quickly.

15 I have trouble _____ (maintaining something for a time) my concentration for prolonged periods of time.

☐ **banish** /ˈbænɪʃ/   v. to send away or prevent from entering

(= expel, evict, oust, deport)

The doctrine that some men have no rights that others are bound to respect, is a doctrine which we must banish as we have banished slavery, from which it emanated. ("Appeal to Congress for Impartial Suffrage by Frederick Douglass")

다른 사람에게는 인정되는 권리를 어떤 사람들에게는 인정되지 않는다는 주장은 그러한 주장을 나오게 한 노예제도를 우리가 추방했듯이 추방해야 한다. ("공정한 투표권에 대한 호소문" 프레데릭 더글러스)

☐ **emanate** /ˈeməneɪt/   v. to flow out, issue or proceed

(= radiate, spring, emit)

The doctrine that some men have no rights that others are bound to respect, is a doctrine which we must banish as we have banished slavery, from which it emanated. ("Appeal to Congress for Impartial Suffrage by Frederick Douglass")

다른 사람에게는 인정되는 권리를 어떤 사람들에게는 인정되지 않는다는 주장은 그러한 주장을 나오게 한 노예제도를 우리가 추방했듯이 추방해야 한다. ("공정한 투표권에 대한 호소문" 프레데릭 더글러스)

☐ **annihilation** /əˌnaɪəˈleɪʃn/   n. total destruction

(= obliteration, extermination, eradication)

The result is a war of races, and the annihilation of all proper human relations. ("Appeal to Congress for Impartial Suffrage by Frederick Douglass")

그것의 결과는 인종 간의 전쟁이고, 모든 적절한 인간관계의 말살이다. ("공정한 투표권에 대한 호소문" 프레데릭 더글러스)

☐ **abstract** /ˈæbstrækt/   adj. not practical

(= theoretical, intangible, conceptual, speculative)

But suffrage for the black man, while easily sustained upon abstract principles, demands consideration upon what are recognized as the urgent necessities of the case. ("Appeal to Congress for Impartial Suffrage by Frederick Douglass")

하지만 흑인에게 투표권을 제공하는 일은 추상적 원칙상으로는 쉽게 주장할 수 있으나 그것을 현실화하기 위해서 어떤 급한 조처를 취해야 하는지 생각해보게 만든다. ("공정한 투표권에 대한 호소문" 프레데릭 더글러스)

□ **render** /ˈrendər/   v. to cause to be or become

(= make, turn into)

It is a measure of relief – a shield to break the force of a blow already descending with violence, and render it harmless. ("Appeal to Congress for Impartial Suffrage by Frederick Douglass")

그것은 구호의 조치이다 – 폭력적으로 이미 내려쳐지고 있는 구타의 세력을 막아주고 무력화 하는 방패이다. ("공정한 투표권에 대한 호소문" 프레데릭 더글러스)

□ **strife** /straɪf/   n. strong disagreement or fight

(= conflict, discord, trouble, contention, dissention)

Peace to the country has literally meant war to the loyal men of the South, white and black; and black suffrage is the measure to arrest and put an end to that dreadful strife. ("Appeal to Congress for Impartial Suffrage by Frederick Douglass")

이 나라의 평화는 남부의 충성스러운 백인과 흑인들에게 전쟁을 뜻하였고; 그러한 갈등을 멈추게 하는 조처가 흑인에게 투표권을 제공하는 것이다. ("공정한 투표권에 대한 호소문" 프레데릭 더글러스)

□ **perpetuate** /pərˈpetʃueɪt/   v. to continue forever

(= continue, maintain, preserve, propagate)

(Black men) are too numerous and useful to be colonized, and too enduring and self-perpetuating to disappear by natural causes. ("Appeal to Congress for Impartial Suffrage by Frederick Douglass")

(흑인들은) 식민화 하기엔 숫자가 너무 많고, 자연적인 이유로 없어지기에는 너무 인내심이 강하고 생명력이 강하다. ("공정한 투표권에 대한 호소문" 프레데릭 더글러스)

□ **for weal or woe**   idiom. happiness or sadness

(= whether happy or sad)

Here they are, four millions of them, and, for weal or woe, here they must remain. ("Appeal to Congress for Impartial Suffrage by Frederick Douglass")

좋건 싫건, 그들은, 사백만 명이, 여기에 있고 계속 여기에 머물 것이다. ("공정한 투표권에 대한 호소문" 프레데릭 더글러스)

☐ **parallel** /ˈpærəlel/   adj. extending in the same direction

(= equivalent, corresponding, matching)

Their history is parallel to that of the country.. ("Appeal to Congress for Impartial Suffrage by Frederick Douglass")

그들의 역사와 이 나라의 역사는 평행하다. ("공정한 투표권에 대한 호소문" 프레데릭 더글러스)

☐ **agony** /ˈægəni/   n. extreme physical or mental pain

(= anguish, misery, torture, distress)

..but while the history of the (country) has been cheerful and bright with blessings, (black men's) has been heavy and dark with agonies and curses. ("Appeal to Congress for Impartial Suffrage by Frederick Douglass")

하지만 이 나라의 역사가 유쾌하고 축복이 가득하다면, (흑인들의 역사는) 고통과 저주로 무겁고 어두웠다. ("공정한 투표권에 대한 호소문" 프레데릭 더글러스)

☐ **bondage** /ˈbɑːndɪdʒ/   n. involuntary servitude

(= repression, oppression, servitude, suppression)

..(Black men) have emerged at the end of two hundred and fifty years of bondage, not morose, misanthropic, and revengeful, but cheerful, hopeful, and forgiving. ("Appeal to Congress for Impartial Suffrage by Frederick Douglass")

...(흑인들은) 250년간의 구속을 벗어나 비통하고 염세적이며 복수심에 가득찬 상태가 아니라 흥겹고, 희망적이며 관대하다. ("공정한 투표권에 대한 호소문" 프레데릭 더글러스)

☐ **morose** /məˈrəʊs/   adj. very sad

(= glum, depressed, lugubrious, forlorn)

..(Black men) have emerged at the end of two hundred and fifty years of bondage, not morose, misanthropic, and revengeful, but cheerful, hopeful, and forgiving. ("Appeal to Congress for Impartial Suffrage by Frederick Douglass")

...(흑인들은) 250년간의 구속을 벗어나 비통하고 염세적이며 복수심에 가득찬 상태가 아니라 흥겹고, 희망적이며 관대하다. ("공정한 투표권에 대한 호소문" 프레데릭 더글러스)

☐ **misanthropic** /ˌmɪsənˈθrɑːpɪk/   adj. disliking or mistrusting mankind

(= antisocial, cynical, distrustful)

..(Black men) have emerged at the end of two hundred and fifty years of bondage, not morose, misanthropic, and revengeful, but cheerful, hopeful, and forgiving. ("Appeal to Congress for Impartial Suffrage by Frederick Douglass")

...(흑인들은) 250년간의 구속을 벗어나 비통하고 염세적이며 복수심에 가득찬 상태가 아니라 흥겹고, 희망적이며 관대하다. ("공정한 투표권에 대한 호소문" 프레데릭 더글러스)

☐ **implore** /ɪmˈplɔːr/

v. to ask for something in a forceful, emotional way

(= beseech, beg, plead, entreat)

The spectacle of these dusky millions thus imploring, not demanding, is touching. ("Appeal to Congress for Impartial Suffrage by Frederick Douglass")

이 검게 탄 수백만 명이 강력히 요구하지 않고 간청하는 모습은 매우 감동적이다. ("공정한 투표권에 대한 호소문" 프레데릭 더글러스)

☐ **waive** /weɪv/   v. to give up or forgo

(= forego, surrender, relinquish, abandon, renounce)

Hardships, services, sufferings, and sacrifices are all waived. ("Appeal to Congress for Impartial Suffrage by Frederick Douglass")

고생, 수발, 고통 그리고 희생은 모두 없던 일로 치부한다. ("공정한 투표권에 대한 호소문" 프레데릭 더글러스)

☐ **notwithstanding** /ˌnɑːtwɪθˈstændɪŋ/   adv. in spite of

(= despite, although, albeit)

It is true that, notwithstanding their alleged ignorance, they were wiser than their masters, ("Appeal to Congress for Impartial Suffrage by Frederick Douglass")

그들의 소위 무식함에도 불구하고 그들을 소유했던 주인들보다 현명했다는 것은 사실이다. ("공정한 투표권에 대한 호소문" 프레데릭 더글러스)

☐ **alleged** /əˈledʒd/   adj. asserted without proof

(= claimed, asserted, supposed, assumed, purported)

It is true that, notwithstanding their alleged ignorance, they were wiser than their masters,
("Appeal to Congress for Impartial Suffrage by Frederick Douglass")

그들의 소위 무식함에도 불구하고 그들을 소유했던 주인들보다 현명했다는 것은 사실이다. ("공정한 투표권에 대한 호소문" 프레데릭 더글러스)

☐ **entail** /ɪnˈteɪl/   v. to involve or cause

(= require, bring about, necessitate, demand)

..the Rebels might have succeeded in breaking up the Union, thereby entailing border wars and troubles of unknown duration and incalculable calamity.. ("Appeal to Congress for Impartial Suffrage by Frederick Douglass")

..반군은 연방을 와해하는 데 성공할 수 있었고, 그렇게 되었다면 이 나라에서는 국경마다 전쟁과 소요가 끝 없는 기간동안 피해를 가늠할 수 없는 규모로 일어났을 것이다. ("공정한 투표권에 대한 호소문" 프레데릭 더글러스)

☐ **incalculable** /ɪnˈkælkjələbl/   adj. unable to calculate

(= countless, innumerable, multitudinous, inestimable)

..the Rebels might have succeeded in breaking up the Union, thereby entailing border wars and troubles of unknown duration and incalculable calamity.. ("Appeal to Congress for Impartial Suffrage by Frederick Douglass")

..반군은 연방을 와해하는 데 성공할 수 있었고, 그렇게 되었다면 이 나라에서는 국경마다 전쟁과 소요가 끝 없는 기간동안 피해를 가늠할 수 없는 규모로 일어났을 것이다. ("공정한 투표권에 대한 호소문" 프레데릭 더글러스)

☐ **calamity** /kəˈlæməti/   n. an event that causes much damage

(= disaster, catastrophe, misfortune, mishap)

..the Rebels might have succeeded in breaking up the Union, thereby entailing border wars and troubles of unknown duration and incalculable calamity.. ("Appeal to Congress for Impartial Suffrage by Frederick Douglass")

..반군은 연방을 와해하는 데 성공할 수 있었고, 그렇게 되었다면 이 나라에서는 국경마다 전쟁과 소요가 끝 없는 기간동안 피해를 가늠할 수 없는 규모로 일어났을 것이다. ("공정한 투표권에 대한 호소문" 프레데릭 더글러스)

Practice 17.

Fill in the blank with the word that matches the definition provided

01 An interesting point about New York City is that despite the various pollution and hygiene issues that such a huge metropolis _____ (involves), its tap water is surprisingly clean and drinkable.

02 The bus and subway routes are _____ (extending in the same direction) for miles from this point on.

03 I could tell that Frank was in _____ (extreme pain) by his grimaced face.

04 The movie is about how Moses led his people out of _____ (involuntary servitude).

05 Dr. Cooper has become _____ (disliking other people) and cynical in his old age.

06 The Russian writer Alexander Solzhenitsyn was _____ (sent away) from the Soviet Union in the 1970s.

07 Confidence _____ (flows out) from Sebastian.

08 North Korea knows that to start a war with South Korea means its _____ (total destruction).

09 The storm was a huge _____ (a very damaging event) to the region.

10 There has been constant civil _____ (strong disagreement or fighting) within the country for decades.

11 It is foolish for Reuben to think that he can _____ (continue forever) his dependency on his parents for financial help.

12 I find most classical music written since the early 20th century is too _____ (conceptual and theoretical) for my taste.

13 The sight of the audience looking at him _____ (caused to be) Luke's courage useless.

14 I _____ (to ask in a forceful way) David to share his class notes, but he refused.

15 The landlord promised the tenants that he would _____ (give up or forego) the last month's rent if they agreed to lease the house for two years.

16 The _____ (asserted without proof) suspect had no alibi to prove his innocence.

17 Andrew looked _____ (very sad) at his father's funeral.

Find the correct word which can replace the bold phrase in the following sentences. Change the word form appropriately to fit the sentence, if necessary

hallow, countervail, moderation, insidious, foment, salutary, assuage, warrant, abstain, man, annals, edifice, indignant, specious, enjoin

01 Winston Churchill's exploits as a young officer in Africa have become a legend in the _____ of British military history.

02 The Taj Mahal is one of the most recognized _____ in the world.

03 The spread of the disease has been _____, and now over a million people have contracted it, some health officials say.

04 James' mother was _____ when James was caught stealing from the grocery store.

05 The former Director's excuse for his sudden resignation was quite _____, but people within the company knew that the reason was because he was under suspicion of fraud.

06 The opposition leader used the scandal to _____ anti-government sentiments in the public.

07 His reprimand, although unpleasant, was a _____ reminder to me to never overestimate my importance.

08 No Japanese politician has been able to fully _____ the hostility that Koreans and Chinese feel towards Japan for the crimes it committed during World War 2.

09 This church was _____ by the Pope upon its construction in 1976.

10 During the cold war, the U.S. and Soviet Union each developed more and more destructive weapons to _____ each other's military power.

11 When Mrs. Keller learned of her son's excessive spending, she _____ him to live more frugally.

12 Mr. Anderson's doctor warned him that he must _____ from excessive drinking and smoking or he won't live for another ten years.

13 All the entrances to foreign embassies were _____ by soldiers.

14 Having found evidence that the two students cheated, the Principal felt that the situation _____ the students to be expelled.

15 Drinking too much alcohol is bad for your health, but drinking in _____ is considered to be harmless.

bondage, implore, entail, solicitude, incongruous, strife, banish, abstract, menace, conspicuous, manifestation, spectator, calamity, agony

16 The new stadium can hold over 40,000 _____.

17 Sick of being bullied, Henry decided that he would no longer be _____ by the bigger kids at school.

18 Because Uncle got drunk and made a fool of himself at Aunt Mary's wedding, Grandmother _____ him from all future family gatherings.

19 Having had an unhappy childhood, Gloria finally found domestic _____ when she met and married Jake.

20 Kelly said that she would wear a bright red jacket to be _____ in the crowd.

21 I found his poetry to be too _____: I couldn't understand a single word of it.

22 To ignore injustice is to _____ it.

23 Jason considered his parents to be overly restrictive and could not wait until he entered college, so he could be free from their _____.

24 When Susie informed her boss that she was resigning, he _____ her to stay.

25 A job that pays well usually _____ very hard work.

26 Thanks to the excellent cooperation between the police, the fire department and medical staff at local hospitals, a large _____ was avoided when the hurricane hit the area.

27 When Mr. Brooks heard that his father had passed away, he cried out in _____.

28 My father's _____ of affection to me is usually expressed with money.

29 We were touched by the _____ of our hosts during the time of our stay.

30 That my grandmother still uses a 2G phone seems very _____ in this age of smart phones.

Select the pair of words that most nearly expresses the same relationship

31 brother: fraternal
    A. mother: maternal
    B. children: frivolous
    C. strength: enfeeble
    D. attack: battery

32   moderation: abstain
     A. accede: disagree
     B. garrison: hemisphere
     C. solicitude: care
     D. faithful: perfidy

33   remuneration: wage
     A. suppress: overcome
     B. testimony: intercourse
     C. treachery: candor
     D. obey: adhere

34   emancipation: imprisonment
     A. aforesaid: undisclosed
     B. endure: continue
     C. beneficial: salutary
     D. praise: extol

35   devious: insidious
     A. disconnected: interwoven
     B. trickery: artifice
     C. countenance: disapproval
     D. irate: exalted

36   undermine: subvert
     A. announce: intimate
     B. misleading: specious
     C. mitigate: manifest
     D. clemency: palladium

37   sanctify: consecrate
     A. mean: amicable
     B. assent: intimidate
     C. merit: necessitate
     D. adhere: vanquish

38 suffrage: enfranchisement
    A. protract: sustain
    B. banish: welcome
    C. radiate: annihilate
    D. harmony: strife

39 parallel: equivalent
    A. waive: accept
    B. morose: forlorn
    C. proven: alleged
    D. unbiased: subjective

40 temperament: disposition
    A. felicity: agony
    B. emancipation: colonization
    C. designate: mitigate
    D. invoke: beseech

Choose the word that isn't a synonym

41 helpful – trivial – salutary

42 allude – intimate – partake

43 hazard – foster – foment

44 vicissitude – rescue – salvation

45 edifice – artifice – structure

46 annoyed – indignant – countenance

47 furtive – exhaust – covert

48 inappropriate – insidious – incongruous

49 assuage – mitigate – endure

50 issue – sanctify – hallow

51 vigilance – spectacle – display

52 consonant – compatible – cordial

53 command – patronize – enjoin

54 conceive – conquer – prevail

55 bombardment – assault – subjugation

56 warrant – attach – rivet

57 imagine – envisage – obviate

58 alleged – fallible – imperfect

59 renounce – insinuate – forego

60 manifestation – decorum – propriety

61 announce – issue – offset

62 suppose – deem – exult

63 suitable – unadulterated – inviolate

64 inclination – penchant – solicitude

65 assent – menace – intimidate

☐ **exploit** /ɪkˈsplɔɪt/   n. a striking or noble deed, a heroic act

(= feat, deed, achievement)

Many daring exploits will be told to their credit. ("Appeal to Congress for Impartial Suffrage by Frederick Douglass")

그들은 많은 용맹한 활약을 하였다. ("공정한 투표권에 대한 호소문" 프레데릭 더글러스)

☐ **ford** /fɔːrd/

v. to cross a river or stream usually on foot or by car

(= cross, wade, traverse)

It will tell how they forded and swam rivers.. ("Appeal to Congress for Impartial Suffrage by Frederick Douglass")

그것은 그들이 어떻게 강을 건너고 개울을 헤쳐 나갔는지 말해 줄 것이다. ("공정한 투표권에 대한 호소문" 프레데릭 더글러스)

☐ **brier** /ˈbraɪər/   n. thorny plants

(= thorns, bushes)

..how they toiled in the darkness of night through the tangled marshes of briers and thorns.. ("Appeal to Congress for Impartial Suffrage by Frederick Douglass")

그들이 어떻게 어두운 밤에 뒤엉킨 가시덤불을 헤치고 어렵게 나갔는지.. ("공정한 투표권에 대한 호소문" 프레데릭 더글러스)

☐ **despise** /dɪˈspaɪz/   v. to intensely hate

(= loathe, scorn, spurn, deride)

It will tell how these poor people, whose rights we still despised, behaved to our wounded soldiers, when found cold, hungry, and bleeding on the deserted battle-field.. ("Appeal to Congress for Impartial Suffrage by Frederick Douglass")

그것은 우리가 아직도 권리를 증오하는 이 가련한 사람들이, 전장에서 춥고 배고프고 피 흘리는 우리의 부상 입은 병사들에게 어떻게 행동했는지 말해줄 것이다. ("공정한 투표권에 대한 호소문" 프레데릭 더글러스)

☐ **wretched** /ˈretʃɪd/   adj. very bad or unfortunate

(= pitiful, awful, dejected, abject, miserable)

..how (black men) assisted our escaping prisoners from Andersonville, Belle Isle, Castle Thunder, and elsewhere, sharing with (wounded soldiers) their wretched crusts, ("Appeal to Congress for Impartial Suffrage by Frederick Douglass")

..(흑인들이) 앤더슨빌이나, 벨르아일, 캐슬썬더 혹은 다른 곳에서 도망치는 포로들을 어떻게 돕고, (부상자들과) 보잘 것 없는 빵 껍질도 나눈 사실을.. ("공정한 투표권에 대한 호소문" 프레데릭 더글러스)

☐ **afford** /əˈfɔːrd/   v. to give or provide

(= provide, present, offer)

..and otherwise affording them aid and comfort.. ("Appeal to Congress for Impartial Suffrage by Frederick Douglass")

..다른 방법으로 구호와 안락함을 제공하는.. ("공정한 투표권에 대한 호소문" 프레데릭 더글러스)

☐ **violation** /ˌvaɪəˈleɪʃn/

n. a breach or infringement of a law or regulation

(= breach, disobedience, infringement, abuse, defiance)

..fighting against a foe that denied (black men) the rights of civilized warfare, and for a government which was without the courage to assert those rights and avenge their violation in their behalf.. ("Appeal to Congress for Impartial Suffrage by Frederick Douglass")

신사적인 전쟁을 할 권리를 (흑인들에게) 허락하지 않았던 적에 대항하여 싸우며, 흑인에게 그러한 권리를 부여하여 그들의 권리가 침탈된 것을 앙갚음해 줄 용기도 없는 정부를 위해 싸운.. ("공정한 투표권에 대한 호소문" 프레데릭 더글러스)

☐ **fortification** /ˌfɔːrtɪfiˈkeɪʃn/   n. something that fortifies or protects

(= strengthening, defenses)

..with what gallantry they flung themselves upon Rebel fortifications, meeting death as fearlessly as any other troops in the service. ("Appeal to Congress for Impartial Suffrage

by Frederick Douglass")

그들이 얼마나 용감하게 반군의 요새에 대항하여 몸을 던졌는지, 그 어떤 군사보다도 더 용감하게 죽음을 맞이하며.. ("공정한 투표권에 대한 호소문" 프레데릭 더글러스)

☐ **reliance** /rɪˈlaɪəns/   n. the act of relying on something

(= dependence, confidence, faith)

But upon none of these things is reliance placed. ("Appeal to Congress for Impartial Suffrage by Frederick Douglass")

그러나 이러한 것들 어디에도 의지하지 않는다. ("공정한 투표권에 대한 호소문" 프레데릭 더글러스)

☐ **disposition** /ˌdɪspəˈzɪʃn/   n. the way someone tends to feel or behave

(= nature, temperament, personality)

These facts speak to the better dispositions of the human heart.. ("Appeal to Congress for Impartial Suffrage by Frederick Douglass")

이러한 사실들은 인간의 양심(의 기질)을 개선시킨다. ("공정한 투표권에 대한 호소문" 프레데릭 더글러스)

☐ **gratitude** /ˈɡrætɪtuːd/   n. the state of feeling grateful

(= thankfulness, appreciation)

Something, too, might be said of national gratitude. ("Appeal to Congress for Impartial Suffrage by Frederick Douglass")

국가적 차원의 감사함에 대해서는 할 말이 있다. ("공정한 투표권에 대한 호소문" 프레데릭 더글러스)

☐ **espouse** /ɪˈspaʊz/   v. to adopt or embrace as a cause

(= adopt, advocate, promote, champion)

We asked the (black men) to espouse our cause, to be our friends, to fight for us, and against their masters.. ("Appeal to Congress for Impartial Suffrage by Frederick Douglass")

우리는 흑인들에게 우리의 목표를 공감하고, 우리의 친구가 되어 달라 하고, 그들의 주인에 대항하여 우리를 위해 싸워달라고 요청했다. ("공정한 투표권에 대한 호소문" 프레데릭 더글러스)

□ **vanquish** /ˈvæŋkwɪʃ/　　　　　　v. to defeat completely

(= conquer, crush, annihilate, subjugate)

..helped us to conquer their masters, and thereby directed toward themselves the furious hate of the vanquished.. ("Appeal to Congress for Impartial Suffrage by Frederick Douglass")

우리를 도와 그들의 주인들을 무찌르고, 그로써 전쟁의 패자들의 엄청난 분노가 그들을 향하게 되었고.. ("공정한 투표권에 대한 호소문" 프레데릭 더글러스)

□ **pertinence** /ˈpɜːrtnəns/

n. the state of relating directly to the matter at hand

(= relevance, appropriateness, suitability, aptness)

..the appeal for impartial suffrage addresses itself with great pertinence to the darkest, coldest, and flintiest side of the human heart.. ("Appeal to Congress for Impartial Suffrage by Frederick Douglass")

공정한 투표권에 대한 호소는 인간 양심의 가장 어둡고, 차갑고, 무감정한 면에 아주 관련있게 다가간다. ("공정한 투표권에 대한 호소문" 프레데릭 더글러스)

□ **righteousness** /ˈraɪtʃəsnəs/　　　　n. the quality of being right or just

(= virtue, morality, decency, rectitude)

..the appeal for impartial suffrage would wring righteousness from the unfeeling calculations of human selfishness. ("Appeal to Congress for Impartial Suffrage by Frederick Douglass")

공정한 투표권에 대한 호소는 인간의 이기심에서 유발되는 무감정한 계산으로부터 정의를 뽑아낼 것이다. ("공정한 투표권에 대한 호소문" 프레데릭 더글러스)

□ **wring** /rɪŋ/　　　　　　v. to twist forcibly

(= twist, mangle, squeeze)

...the appeal for impartial suffrage... will wring righteousness from the unfeeling calculations of human selfishness. ("Appeal to Congress for Impartial Suffrage by Frederick Douglass")

공정한 투표권에 대한 호소는 인간의 이기심에서 유발되는 무감정한 계산으로부터 정의를 뽑아낼 것이다. ("공정한 투표권에 대한 호소문" 프레데릭 더글러스)

☐ **indictment** /ɪnˈdaɪtmənt/   n. the state of being on trial

(= charge, prosecution)

I stand before you tonight under indictment for the alleged crime of having voted at the last presidential election.. ("On Women's Right to Vote, Susan B. Anthony")

저는 지난번 대통령 선거에서 투표권을 행사한 범죄를 저질렀다는 혐의로 여러분 앞에 서 있습니다. ("여성의 투표권에 대하여"연설, 수잔 B.안소니)

☐ **deny** /dɪˈnaɪ/   v. to refuse to agree to

(= reject, contradict, repudiate, negate)

I not only committed no crime, but, instead, simply exercised my citizen's rights, guaranteed to me and all United States citizens by the National Constitution, beyond the power of any state to deny. ("On Women's Right to Vote, Susan B. Anthony")

저는 아무런 범죄도 저지르지 않았으며, 그대신 단순히 저와 모든 미국국민들에게 헌법이 보장해 준, 그리고 어떤 주(州)에서도 거부할 힘이 없는 권리를 행사했을 뿐입니다. ("여성의 투표권에 대하여"연설, 수잔 B.안소니)

☐ **downright** /ˈdaʊnraɪt/   adv. thoroughly

(= absolutely, completely; 순전히, 완전히)

..while (women) are downright denied the use of the only means of securing them provided by this democratic-republican government - the ballot. ("On Women's Right to Vote, Susan B. Anthony")

여성들에게는 이 민주주의 공화국 내에서 그들을 보호해 줄 유일한 권리인 투표권을 행사하는 것이 대놓고 거부되고.. ("여성의 투표권에 대하여"연설, 수잔 B.안소니)

☐ **mockery** /ˈmɑːkəri/   n. a subject or occasion of derision

(= ridicule, derision; 조롱)

She was insulted by their mockery. ("On Women's Right to Vote, Susan B. Anthony")

그녀는 그들의 조롱에 모욕감을 느꼈습니다. ("여성의 투표권에 대하여"연설, 수잔 B.안소니)

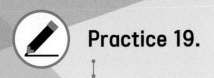

Practice 19.

Fill in the blank with the word that matches the definition provided

01 He performed _____ (heroic acts) that were worthy of mentioning in history books.

02 In the middle ages, this city was renowned for its strong _____. (defenses)

03 Grace showed her _____ (thankfulness) to her parents by doing her best in school.

04 Having been raised in the United States, James found it difficult to _____ (embrace as a cause) the rigid sense of seniority that everyone adheres to in Korea.

05 When the police asked the woman to testify against her son, the accused woman _____ (absolutely) refused to cooperate.

06 The first movie in the "Rocky" series was a masterpiece: by the time the fifth movie was made, it became a/an _____ of cinema. (subject of derision)

07 My three years in boarding school were absolutely _____ (very bad). I am so glad I don't have to go back.

08 He was not a man of genial _____ (temperament, personality): in fact, I think I never saw him smile.

09 Mike was upset that his team mates didn't _____ (to give or provide) him the support he expected from them.

10 Please come to the next meeting on time. I absolutely _____ (intensely hate) wasting time waiting for other people to show up.

11   In the United States, restricting gun ownership is a/an _____ (breach of a regulation) of a constitutional right.

12   Do not try to _____ (cross a river or stream) the river by yourself, the water is much deeper than it looks from the surface.

13   Making the ethical choice whether in all circumstances is the sign of _____. (moral correctness)

14   Henry _____ (twisted forcibly) his wet shirts and hung them to dry.

15   The accused man _____ (refuse to agree to) his involvement with the crime.

16   Life is not a video game: you do not _____ (defeat or conquer) a boss at the end.

17   Personal connections or family ties should have no _____ (relevance) in the hiring process.

Class 20

□ **ballot** /ˈbælət/   n. vote

(= vote, poll; 투표, 투표용지)

And it is a downright mockery to talk to women of their enjoyment of the blessings of liberty while they are denied the use of the only means of securing them provided by this democratic-republican government - the ballot. ("On Women's Right to Vote, Susan B. Anthony")

여성들에게 이 민주주의 공화국 내에서 그들을 보호해 줄 유일한 권리인 투표권을 행사하는 것이 대놓고 거부되고 있는 마당에 그들이 자유의 축복을 누리고 있다고 말하는 것은 웃기는 소리입니다. ("여성의 투표권에 대하여"연설, 수잔 B.안소니)

□ **ex post facto**   n. a retroactive law

For any state to make sex a qualification that must ever result in the disfranchisement of one entire half of the people, is to pass a bill of attainder, or, an ex post facto law, and is therefore a violation of the supreme law of the land. ("On Women's Right to Vote, Susan B. Anthony")

어떤 주에서 투표할 권리를 성별로 정한다고 결정할 경우 주민의 절반의 투표권을 빼앗아 가는 결과를 가지고 올 것이며, 그것은 사법 박탈권을 승인하는 것이며 혹은 소환법을 제정하는 것이고 그것은 이 나라의 상위법의 위반입니다. ("여성의 투표권에 대하여"연설, 수잔 B.안소니)

□ **odious** /ˈəʊdiəs/   adj. deserving or causing hatred

(= hateful, horrible, heinous, gruesome, horrendous)

It is an odious aristocracy.. ("On Women's Right to Vote, Susan B. Anthony")

그것은 사악한 독재주의입니다. ("여성의 투표권에 대하여"연설, 수잔 B.안소니)

□ **oligarchy** /ˈɑːləɡɑːrki/

n. a form of government in which all power is vested in a few persons or in a dominant class

(= totalitarianism, dictatorship, tyranny)

..a hateful oligarchy of sex.. ("On Women's Right to Vote, Susan B. Anthony")

그것은 사악한 독재주의입니다. ("여성의 투표권에 대하여"연설, 수잔 B.안소니)

☐ **ordain** /ɔːr'deɪn/   v. to order or command, to destine

(= order, proclaim, dictate, decree, command)

..this oligarchy of sex, which makes father, brothers, husband, sons, the oligarchs over the mother and sisters, the wife and daughters, of every household - which ordains all men sovereigns, all women subjects.. ("On Women's Right to Vote, Susan B. Anthony")

이러한 성별에 의한 독재는 모든 집안의 아버지, 형제, 남편, 아들을 그들의 어머니, 누이, 부인과 딸을 지배하는 군주로 임명하며, 모든 여성들은 그의 지배를 받는 백성이 되는데.. ("여성의 투표권에 대하여"연설, 수잔 B.안소니)

☐ **sovereign** /'sɑːvrɪn/   n. king or monarch

(= ruler, monarch, potentate)

..this oligarchy of sex, which makes father, brothers, husband, sons, the oligarchs over the mother and sisters, the wife and daughters, of every household - which ordains all men sovereigns, all women subjects.. ("On Women's Right to Vote, Susan B. Anthony")

이러한 성별에 의한 독재는 모든 집안의 아버지, 형제, 남편, 아들을 그들의 어머니, 누이, 부인과 딸을 지배하는 군주로 임명하며, 모든 여성들은 그의 지배를 받는 백성이 되는데.. ("여성의 투표권에 대하여"연설, 수잔 B.안소니)

☐ **subject** /'sʌbdʒɪkt/   n. people under the rule of a monarch

(= subordinate, citizen, people)

..this oligarchy of sex, which makes father, brothers, husband, sons, the oligarchs over the mother and sisters, the wife and daughters, of every household - which ordains all men sovereigns, all women subjects.. ("On Women's Right to Vote, Susan B. Anthony")

이러한 성별에 의한 독재는 모든 집안의 아버지, 형제, 남편, 아들을 그들의 어머니, 누이, 부인과 딸을 지배하는 군주로 임명하며, 모든 여성들은 그의 지배를 받는 백성이 되는데.. ("여성의 투표권에 대하여"연설, 수잔 B.안소니)

☐ **dissension** /dɪ'senʃn/   n. strong disagreement

(= disagreement, opposition, discord, rebellion)

..carries dissension, discord, and rebellion into every home of the nation.. ("On Women's Right to Vote, Susan B. Anthony")

이 나라의 모든 가정에 불화, 불협과 반항을 가지고 옵니다. ("여성의 투표권에 대하여"연설, 수잔 B.안소니)

☐ **hardihood** /hɑ́ːrdihùd/   n. boldness

(= daring, courage, audacity, self-assurance, durability)

Are women persons? And I hardly believe any of our opponents will have the hardihood to say they are not. ("On Women's Right to Vote, Susan B. Anthony")

여성은 인간인가요? 저는 반대하시는 분 중에 아니라고 대답할 수 있는 뻔뻔함을 가진 분은 없을 거라고 생각합니다. ("여성의 투표권에 대하여"연설, 수잔 B.안소니)

☐ **immunity** /ɪ'mjuːnəti/   n. exemption from obligation

(= exemption, exception, liberation)

Being persons, then, women are citizens; and no state has a right to make any law, or to enforce any old law, that shall abridge their privileges or immunities. ("On Women's Right to Vote, Susan B. Anthony")

그렇다면, 여성은 인간이기 때문에 시민이기도 합니다; 그러므로 어떤 주도 여성의 권리나 면제권을 축소할 수 있는 법을 제정하거나 오래된 법을 근거로 강제할 권리는 없습니다. ("여성의 투표권에 대하여"연설, 수잔 B.안소니)

☐ **discrimination** /dɪˌskrɪmɪ'neɪʃn/

n. the act of treating a group of people unfairly from others

(= prejudice, unfairness, bias, favoritism)

Hence, every discrimination against women in the constitutions and laws of the several states is today null and void, ("On Women's Right to Vote, Susan B. Anthony")

그러므로, 몇몇 주가 제정한 주헌법과 일반법 하에서 자행되는 여성의 차별은 오늘부터 무효입니다. ("여성의 투표권에 대하여"연설, 수잔 B.안소니)

☐ **null and void**   idiom. no longer effective

(= valueless, invalid, unacceptable)

Hence, every discrimination against women in the constitutions and laws of the several states is today null and void, ("On Women's Right to Vote, Susan B. Anthony")

그러므로, 몇몇 주가 제정한 주헌법과 일반법 하에서 자행되는 여성의 차별은 오늘부터 무효입니다. ("여성의 투표권에 대하여"연설, 수잔 B.안소니)

☐ **consecration** /ˌkɑːnsɪˈkreɪʃn/   n. ordination to a sacred office

(= sanctification, dedication, blessing)

..this is a day of national consecration. ("Franklyn D. Roosevelt's Inauguration Speech, 1933")

..오늘은 국가헌신의 날입니다. (프랭클린 D.루즈벨트 대통령 취임사 1933)

☐ **induction** /ɪnˈdʌkʃn/   n. formal installation in an office

(= inauguration, installment, entree)

And I am certain that on this day my fellow Americans expect that on my induction into the presidency, I will address them with a candor and a decision which the present situation of our people impels. ("Franklyn D. Roosevelt's Inauguration Speech, 1933")

저는 오늘 저의 취임을 맞아 저의 동료 미국인들이 지금 처한 상황이 요구하는 정직과 결정에 대해 이야기해 줄 것을 기대하고 있다고 확신합니다. (프랭클린 D.루즈벨트 대통령 취임사 1933)

☐ **candor** /ˈkændər/   n. the state of being frank or open

(= frankness, honesty, sincerity)

And I am certain that on this day my fellow Americans expect that on my induction into the presidency, I will address them with a candor and a decision which the present situation of our people impels. ("Franklyn D. Roosevelt's Inauguration Speech, 1933")

저는 오늘 저의 취임을 맞아 저의 동료 미국인들이 지금 처한 상황이 요구하는 정직과 결정에 대해 이야기해 줄 것을 기대하고 있다고 확신합니다. (프랭클린 D.루즈벨트 대통령 취임사 1933)

☐ **impel** /ɪmˈpel/   v. to drive or urge forward

(= push, compel, urge, oblige, induce)

And I am certain that on this day my fellow Americans expect that on my induction into the presidency, I will address them with a candor and a decision which the present situation of our people impels. ("Franklyn D. Roosevelt's Inauguration Speech, 1933")

저는 오늘 저의 취임을 맞아 저의 동료 미국인들이 지금 처한 상황이 요구하는 정직과 결정에 대해 이야기해 줄 것을 기대하고 있다고 확신합니다. (프랭클린 D.루즈벨트 대통령 취임사 1933)

☐ **paralysis** /pə'ræləsɪs/   n. state of helpless inactivity

(= immobility, stoppage)

So, first of all, let me assert my firm belief that the only thing we have to fear is fear itself - nameless, unreasoning, unjustified terror which paralyses needed efforts to convert retreat into advance. ("Franklyn D. Roosevelt's Inauguration Speech, 1933")

우선 확실하게 말하고 싶은 것은 우리가 두려워 할 것은 두려움 밖에 없다는 저의 신념입니다 - 후퇴를 전진으로 전환하는데 필요한 노력을 마비시키는 이름없는, 이유없는, 정당화되지 않은 공포. (프랭클린 D.루즈벨트 대통령 취임사 1933)

☐ **vigor** /'vɪgər/   n. active strength or force

(= energy, drive, potency, vitality, verve)

In every dark hour of our national life, a leadership of frankness and of vigor has met with that understanding and support of the people themselves which is essential to victory. ("Franklyn D. Roosevelt's Inauguration Speech, 1933")

우리의 역사에서 암울한 시간이 도래할 때마다, 승리를 위해 필요한 정직하고 활력있는 지도력이 국민의 이해심과 지지를 받았습니다. (프랭클린 D.루즈벨트 대통령 취임사 1933)

☐ **curtailment** /kɜːr'teɪlmənt/   n. a state of cutting something short

(= abridgement, limitation, curbing)

..government of all kinds is faced by serious curtailment of income.. ("Franklyn D. Roosevelt's Inauguration Speech, 1933")

..모든 형태의 정부들이 심각한 수입의 축소를 경험합니다. (프랭클린 D.루즈벨트 대통령 취임사 1933)

☐ **wither** /'wɪðər/   v. to become very weak, for flowers to wilt

(= shrivel, wilt, fade, weaken, wane)

..the withered leaves of industrial enterprise lie on every side.. ("Franklyn D. Roosevelt's Inauguration Speech, 1933")

산업발달의 시든 낙엽이 모든 길바닥에 떨어졌습니다. (프랭클린 D.루즈벨트 대통령 취임사 1933)

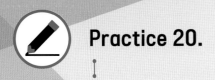

Practice 20.

Fill in the blank with the word that matches the definition provided

01 Mike had the _____ (boldness) to stand against the school bully.

02 This school does not allow any form of _____ (prejudice) – people of all racial, religious and political background are welcome.

03 During the baptismal ceremony, the priest will _____ (sanctify) the infant in front of his parents.

04 The news reported that a record number of people cast their _____ (vote) today at the general elections.

05 My loyalty to Frank _____ (to urge or compel) me to stop him from making a mistake.

06 The stock market was in a state of _____ (state of helpless inactivity) – all trading had stopped.

07 Mr. Moses is 95 year old, but he's still full of _____ (energy and strength)

08 If I don't _____ (cut short) my spending, I will go broke soon.

09 The flowers that were fresh only this morning have begun to _____. (wilt)

10 I spent a/an _____ (deserving hatred) summer working in a duck farm in Australia: I'm never doing that again.

11 I said goodbye to him, but I had the feeling that fate would _____ (order or command) us to meet again.

12 Queen Elizabeth II is the _____ (ruling monarch) of Canada.

13 There was some _____ (strong disagreement) between the members of the group, but they always did good work.

14 The new Governor was _____ (formally install in an office) into office today.

15 My parents say that the secret to their happy marriage is complete _____ (frankness) to each other.

Class 21

☐ **produce** /prə'duːs/   n. crops or products

(= foodstuffs, harvest)

..farmers find no markets for their produce; and the savings of many years in thousands of families are gone. ("Franklyn D. Roosevelt's Inauguration Speech, 1933")

..농부들은 그들의 농산품을 팔 수 있는 시장이 없고; 수천의 가족이 수년간 저축한 돈은 다 사라졌습니다. (프랭클린 D.루즈벨트 대통령 취임사 1933)

☐ **stricken** /'strɪkən/

adj. wounded, afflicted with a disease or affected with grief

(= suffering, troubled, tormented)

We are stricken by no plague of locusts. ("Franklyn D. Roosevelt's Inauguration Speech, 1933")

메뚜기 떼가 창궐하여 큰 피해를 입고 있습니다. (프랭클린 D.루즈벨트 대통령 취임사 1933)

☐ **locust** /'ləʊkəst/   n. grasshopper

We are stricken by no plague of locusts. ("Franklyn D. Roosevelt's Inauguration Speech, 1933")

메뚜기 떼가 창궐하여 큰 피해를 입고 있습니다. (프랭클린 D.루즈벨트 대통령 취임사 1933)

☐ **peril** /'perəl/   n. great danger

(= danger, risk, hazard)

Compared with the perils which our forefathers conquered, because they believed and were not afraid. ("Franklyn D. Roosevelt's Inauguration Speech, 1933")

우리의 선조들이 극복한 위험과 비교하면, 그들은 신념이 있었고 두려워하지 않았기 때문입니다. (프랭클린 D.루즈벨트 대통령 취임사 1933)

☐ **bounty** /'baʊnti/   n. generosity in giving

(= generosity, charity, philanthropy, abundance)

Nature still offers her bounty and human efforts have multiplied it. ("Franklyn D. Roosevelt's Inauguration Speech, 1933")

자연은 아직도 너그러움을 선사하고 인간의 노력은 그 너그러움을 배가합니다. (프랭클린 D.루즈벨트 대통령 취임사 1933)

☐ **incompetence** /ɪn'kɑːmpɪtəns/   n. inability to do required work

(= ineptitude, inability, ineffectiveness)

..this is because the rulers of the exchange of mankind's goods have failed, through their own stubbornness and their own incompetence, have admitted their failure, and have abdicated. ("Franklyn D. Roosevelt's Inauguration Speech, 1933")

..그 이유는 인간의 생산품을 교환하던 시장의 지배자들이, 그들의 고집과 무능함으로 인해 실패하고, 실패를 인정하고 퇴위하였기 때문입니다. (프랭클린 D.루즈벨트 대통령 취임사 1933)

☐ **abdicate** /'æbdɪkeɪt/   v. to give up a throne, position or responsibility

(= renounce, relinquish, resign, abandon)

..this is because the rulers of the exchange of mankind's goods have failed, through their own stubbornness and their own incompetence, have admitted their failure, and have abdicated. ("Franklyn D. Roosevelt's Inauguration Speech, 1933")

..그 이유는 인간의 생산품을 교환하던 시장의 지배자들이, 그들의 고집과 무능함으로 인해 실패하고, 실패를 인정하고 퇴위하였기 때문입니다. (프랭클린 D.루즈벨트 대통령 취임사 1933)

☐ **unscrupulous** /ʌn'skruːpjələs/   adj. to have no moral standards

(= dishonest, unprincipled, immoral, devious)

Practices of the unscrupulous money changers stand indicted in the court of public opinion ("Franklyn D. Roosevelt's Inauguration Speech, 1933")

도덕심이 결여된 현금교환자들의 행위가 여론의 법정에 기소되었습니다. (프랭클린 D.루즈벨트 대통령 취임사 1933)

☐ **indict** /ɪn'daɪt/   v. to officially charge of a crime

(= accuse, charge, prosecute)

Practices of the unscrupulous money changers stand indicted in the court of public opinion ("Franklyn D. Roosevelt's Inauguration Speech, 1933")

도덕심이 결여된 현금교환자들의 행위가 여론의 법정에 기소되었습니다. (프랭클린 D.루즈벨트 대통령 취임사 1933)

☐ **outworn** /ˈaʊtwɔːrn/   adj. not used because it is too old

(= obsolete, antiquated, archaic, outdated)

But their efforts have been cast in the pattern of an outworn tradition. ("Franklyn D. Roosevelt's Inauguration Speech, 1933")

그러나 그들의 노력은 오래되어 낙후된 전통이라고 내쳐졌습니다. (프랭클린 D.루즈벨트 대통령 취임사 1933)

☐ **lure** /lʊr/

n. an object used to trick someone into doing something he should not do

(= entice, tempt, attract, ensnare)

Stripped of the lure of profit by which to induce our people to follow their false leadership, they have resorted to exhortations, pleading tearfully for restored confidence. ("Franklyn D. Roosevelt's Inauguration Speech, 1933")

그들의 헛된 지도력에 우리 국민들이 속아서 따라오게 만들 수 있는 이익의 미끼를 빼앗긴 후 그들은 다시 한 번 믿어달라고 눈물로 호소하고 있습니다. (프랭클린 D.루즈벨트 대통령 취임사 1933)

☐ **exhortation** /ˌegzɔːrˈteɪʃn/   n. a speech to persuade, inspire or encourage

(= appeal, urging, encouragement)

Stripped of the lure of profit by which to induce our people to follow their false leadership, they have resorted to exhortations, pleading tearfully for restored confidence. ("Franklyn D. Roosevelt's Inauguration Speech, 1933")

그들의 헛된 지도력에 우리 국민들이 속아서 따라오게 만들 수 있는 이익의 미끼를 빼앗긴 후 그들은 다시 한 번 믿어달라고 눈물로 호소하고 있습니다. (프랭클린 D.루즈벨트 대통령 취임사 1933)

☐ **possession** /pəˈzeʃn/   n. the state of owning something

(= ownership, custody, proprietorship)

Happiness lies not in the mere possession of money; it lies in the joy of achievement, in the thrill of creative effort. ("Franklyn D. Roosevelt's Inauguration Speech, 1933")

행복은 단순히 돈을 소유하는 것에서 오는 것이 아니고; 행복은 무언가를 달성할 때의 즐거움, 노력을 창조할 때의 희열에서 오는 것입니다. (프랭클린 D.루즈벨트 대통령 취임사 1933)

··

□ **stimulation** /ˌstɪmjuˈleɪʃn/   n. the rousing of action or effort

(= stimulus, incentive, inspiration, prompt)

The joy, the moral stimulation of work no longer must be forgotten in the mad chase of evanescent profits. ("Franklyn D. Roosevelt's Inauguration Speech, 1933")

한 순간에 없어지는 이익만을 쫓다가 노동이 주는 도덕적인 자극과 희열을 잊어버리는 일은 더는 없어야 합니다. (프랭클린 D.루즈벨트 대통령 취임사 1933)

··

□ **evanescent** /ˌevəˈnesnt/   adj. gradually disappearing, quickly passing

(= fleeting, temporary, ephemeral, transient)

The joy, the moral stimulation of work no longer must be forgotten in the mad chase of evanescent profits. ("Franklyn D. Roosevelt's Inauguration Speech, 1933")

한 순간에 없어지는 이익만을 쫓다가 노동이 주는 도덕적인 자극과 희열을 잊어버리는 일은 더는 없어야 합니다. (프랭클린 D.루즈벨트 대통령 취임사 1933)

··

□ **minister** /ˈmɪnɪstər/   v. to attend to one's needs, to take care of

(= attend, care for, aid, comfort)

These dark days, my friends, will be worth all they cost us if they teach us that our true destiny is not to be ministered unto but to minister to ourselves, to our fellow men. ("Franklyn D. Roosevelt's Inauguration Speech, 1933")

우리가 우리의 운명이 어떤 사물을 섬기는 게 아니라 우리 자신들과 우리의 형제들을 섬기는 데 있다는 것을 깨달을 수만 있다면 지금의 어두운 날들은, 여러분, 가치가 있습니다. (프랭클린 D.루즈벨트 대통령 취임사 1933)

··

□ **falsity** /ˈfɔːlsəti/   n. the state of being false or untrue

(= false, fallacy, untruth)

Recognition of that falsity of material wealth as the standard of success goes hand in hand with the abandonment of the false belief that public office and high political position are to be valued only by the standards of pride of place and personal profit... ("Franklyn D. Roosevelt's Inauguration Speech, 1933")

성공의 기준이 금전적인 부유함이라는 믿음의 허위성을 인정하는 것과 공직과 정치적인 직책의 가치는 그 위치에 있음으로 얻는 자존감 및 개인적 이익으로만 가늠한다는 잘못된 믿음과 같이 가야 합니다.. (프랭클린 D.루즈벨트 대통령 취임사 1933)

☐ **conduct** /kənˈdʌkt/   n. behavior, direction of management

(= behavior, management, comportment, mien)

..and there must be an end to a conduct in banking and in business which too often has given to a sacred trust the likeness of callous and selfish wrongdoing.. ("Franklyn D. Roosevelt's Inauguration Speech, 1933")

..그리고 금융과 사업에 있어서 성스러운 신뢰가 마치 무신경하고 이기적인 나쁜 짓인 것처럼 보이게 하는 행위를 그만둬야 합니다. (프랭클린 D.루즈벨트 대통령 취임사 1933)

☐ **callous** /ˈkæləs/   adj. showing no concern

(= heartless, unfeeling, uncaring, unsympathetic)

..and there must be an end to a conduct in banking and in business which too often has given to a sacred trust the likeness of callous and selfish wrongdoing.. ("Franklyn D. Roosevelt's Inauguration Speech, 1933")

..그리고 금융과 사업에 있어서 성스러운 신뢰가 마치 무신경하고 이기적인 나쁜 짓인 것처럼 보이게 하는 행위를 그만둬야 합니다. (프랭클린 D.루즈벨트 대통령 취임사 1933)

☐ **signify** /ˈsɪgnɪfaɪ/   v. to be a sign of

(= mean, indicate)

..we observe today not a victory of party, but a celebration of freedom--symbolizing an end, as well as a beginning--signifying renewal, as well as change. ("Inaugural Address of John F. Kennedy, 1961")

..우리는 오늘 하나의 당의 승리가 아니라, 자유의 축제를 목격합니다—하나의 끝이자 시작을 상징하는—재시작 및 변화를 의미하는. (존 F.케네디 대통령의 취임사 1961)

01 Most people who have achieved money and fame will tell you that both are
_____. (quickly passing)

02 Dr. Roberts, who is in his eighties, says he spends his free time solving high school math
questions because he enjoys the mental _____ (stimulus).

03 The King was in his nineties but still showed no intention of _____ (giving up
one's throne).

04 His blatant disregard for other people's feelings and _____ (showing no concern)
refusal to accept excuses make him the most feared manager within the entire company.

05 Many articles said the government's foreign policy decisions _____ (be a sign of) a
new direction for the current administration.

06 The mayor denied all accusations of his involvement in _____ (having no principles)
behavior.

07 The former diplomat was _____ (officially charged of a crime) for passing state
secrets to foreign intelligence agencies.

08 Jack's mother told him to be late for the family dinner at his own _____. (great danger)

09 Since Mrs. Heller hurt her leg, her daughter Sally moved in with her to _____
(take care of) to her needs.

10 The bicycle I found in my grandfather's shed seemed quite _____ (not used because
old age), but I figured I could fix it.

11 Paul tried to _____ (trick or tempt) the stray cat into his house with a piece of ham.

12 When I visited the Farbers, the whole family was _____ (afflicted with disease) with the flu.

13 The cheating students were suspended for ungentlemanly _____. (behavior)

14 David's mother's _____ (speech to persuade) to David to stop smoking fell on deaf ears.

15 The area is blessed with abundant natural _____. (generosity in giving)

16 The opposition parties accused the government of _____. (incapability)

☐ **renewal** /rɪˈnuːəl/   n. the act of starting something again

(= rebirth, rekindling,)

..we observe today not a victory of party, but a celebration of freedom--symbolizing an end, as well as a beginning--signifying renewal, as well as change. ("Inaugural Address of John F. Kennedy, 1961")

..우리는 오늘 하나의 당의 승리가 아니라, 자유의 축제를 목격합니다—하나의 끝이자 시작을 상징하는—재시작 및 변화를 의미하는. (존 F.케네디 대통령의 취임사 1961)

☐ **solemn** /ˈsɑːləm/   adj. serious and earnest

(= sincere, earnest, grave, firm)

For I have sworn before you and Almighty God the same solemn oath our forebears prescribed nearly a century and three quarters ago. ("Inaugural Address of John F. Kennedy, 1961")

왜냐하면 저는 거의 일세기와 75년 전 우리의 선조들이 규정한 성스러운 맹세를 오늘 여러분과 전능한 신 앞에 하였습니다. (존 F.케네디 대통령의 취임사 1961)

☐ **forebear** /ˈfɔːrber/   n. ancestor or forefather

(= ancestor, predecessor)

For I have sworn before you and Almighty God the same solemn oath our forebears prescribed nearly a century and three quarters ago. ("Inaugural Address of John F. Kennedy, 1961")

왜냐하면 저는 거의 일세기와 75년 전 우리의 선조들이 규정한 성스러운 맹세를 오늘 여러분과 전능한 신 앞에 하였습니다. (존 F.케네디 대통령의 취임사 1961)

☐ **prescribe** /prɪˈskraɪb/

v. lay down a rule or course of action to be followed

(= stipulate, recommend, advise, counsel)

For I have sworn before you and Almighty God the same solemn oath our forebears prescribed nearly a century and three quarters ago. ("Inaugural Address of John F. Kennedy, 1961")

왜냐하면 저는 거의 일세기와 75년 전 우리의 선조들이 규정한 성스러운 맹세를 오늘 여러분과 전능한 신 앞에 하였습니다. (존 F.케네디 대통령의 취임사 1961)

☐ **mortal** /ˈmɔːrtl/   adj. belonging to this world

(= worldly, human, temporal)

For man holds in his mortal hands the power to abolish all forms of human poverty and all forms of human life. ("Inaugural Address of John F. Kennedy, 1961")

왜냐하면 인간은 자기 힘으로 모든 기아를 박멸할 힘이 있고 동시에 인류 전체를 박멸할 힘이 있기 때문입니다. (존 F.케네디 대통령의 취임사 1961)

☐ **heir** /er/

n. someone who has the right to inherit a person's money, property, or title when that person dies

(= successor, inheritor, beneficiary)

We dare not forget today that we are the heirs of that first revolution. ("Inaugural Address of John F. Kennedy, 1961")

오늘 잊어서는 안 되는 것이 우리는 첫 번째 혁명의 후계자들입니다. (존 F.케네디 대통령의 취임사 1961)

☐ **foe** /fəʊ/   n. enemy

(= opponent, rival, antagonist)

Let the word go forth from this time and place, to friend and foe alike, that the torch has been passed to a new generation of Americans.. ("Inaugural Address of John F. Kennedy, 1961")

이시간에 이곳에서 친구와 적에게 동시에 고하노니, 그 횃불은 새로운 세대의 미국인들에게 전달되었습니다. (존 F.케네디 대통령의 취임사 1961)

☐ **tempered** /ˈtempər/

adj. made less intense or violent, especially by the influence of something good or benign

(= moderated, mitigated, lightened, palliated)

..born in this century, tempered by war, disciplined by a hard and bitter peace, proud of our ancient heritage.. ("Inaugural Address of John F. Kennedy, 1961")

..금세기에 태어나고, 전쟁을 거치면서 순해지고, 어렵고 쓸쓸한 평화를 거치면서 훈육되고, 우리의 과거 유산에 자부심을 느끼는.. (존 F.케네디 대통령의 취임사 1961)

□ **heritage** /ˈherɪtɪdʒ/   n. something reserved for descendants

(= inheritance, legacy, custom, tradition)

..born in this century, tempered by war, disciplined by a hard and bitter peace, proud of our ancient heritage.. ("Inaugural Address of John F. Kennedy, 1961")

..금세기에 태어나고, 전쟁을 거치면서 순해지고, 어렵고 쓸쓸한 평화를 거치면서 훈육되고, 우리의 과거 유산에 자부심을 느끼는.. (존 F.케네디 대통령의 취임사 1961)

□ **venture** /ˈventʃər/

n. a project or activity which is new, exciting, and difficult because it involves the risk of failure

(= business enterprise, undertaking, endeavor, mission)

United, there is little we cannot do in a host of cooperative ventures.. ("Inaugural Address of John F. Kennedy, 1961")

우리가 힘을 합쳐 하지 못할 협력적 사업이 없습니다. (존 F.케네디 대통령의 취임사 1961)

□ **asunderr** /əˈsʌndər/   adv. into parts or pieces

(= apart, in pieces, in bits)

Divided, there is little we can do--for we dare not meet a powerful challenge at odds and split asunder. ("Inaugural Address of John F. Kennedy, 1961")

흩어진다면 우리가 할 수 있는 것이 별로 없습니다—왜냐하면 우리는 서로 반감을 느끼고 뿔뿔히 흩어진 상태에서 감히 강력한 도전을 받아들이지 못할 것이기 때문입니다. (존 F.케네디 대통령의 취임사 1961)

□ **struggle** /ˈstrʌgl/

v. to contend with an adversary or opposing force

(= resist, fight, brawl, battle)

To those peoples in the huts and villages across the globe struggling to break the bonds of mass misery, we pledge our best efforts to help them help themselves.. ("Inaugural Address of John F. Kennedy, 1961")

지구상에 흩어져 움막과 촌락에 살면서 대규모 가난의 고리를 끊으려고 투쟁하는 사람들에게는 그들이 그들 스스로를 도울 수 있도록 우리가 도움을 줄 것을 맹세합니다. (존 F.케네디 대통령의 취임사 1961)

☐ **subversion** /səbˈvɜːrʒn/   n. attempt to weaken or destroy

(= rebellion, sedition, insurrection, mutiny)

Let all our neighbors know that we shall join with them to oppose aggression or subversion anywhere in the Americas. ("Inaugural Address of John F. Kennedy, 1961")

우리의 이웃들에게는 아메리카 대륙 어디선가에 만약에 그들이 탄압과 반란에 대항하여 싸운다면 우리가 동참할 것이라는 걸 알립니다. (존 F.케네디 대통령의 취임사 1961)

☐ **outpace** /ˌaʊtˈpeɪs/   v. to surpass or exceed

(= surpass, exceed, beat, outperform)

To that world assembly of sovereign states, the United Nations, our last best hope in an age where the instruments of war have far outpaced the instruments of peace, we renew our pledge of support. ("Inaugural Address of John F. Kennedy, 1961")

전쟁의 도구들이 평화의 도구들보다 훨씬 더 발달한 시대의 마지막 희망인, 독립 국가들의 연합, 유엔에게는 우리의 지지를 다시 한 번 맹세합니다. (존 F.케네디 대통령의 취임사 1961)

☐ **forum** /ˈfɔːrəm/   n. a meeting place for discussion

(= conference, council, roundtable, discussion)

..to prevent it from becoming merely a forum for invective.. ("Inaugural Address of John F. Kennedy, 1961")

..그곳이 단순히 비난의 장이 되지 않게끔 하기 위하여.. (존 F.케네디 대통령의 취임사 1961)

☐ **invective** /ɪnˈvektɪv/

n. vehement or violent denunciation, censure, or reproach

(= diatribe, criticism, tirade, abuse, polemic)

..to prevent it from becoming merely a forum for invective.. ("Inaugural Address of John F. Kennedy, 1961")

..그곳이 단순히 비난의 장이 되지 않게끔 하기 위하여.. (존 F.케네디 대통령의 취임사 1961)

☐ **engulf** /ɪnˈgʌlf/   v. to completely cover

(= overwhelm, surround, immerse, consume, whelm)

..that both sides begin anew the quest for peace, before the dark powers of destruction unleashed by science engulf all humanity in planned or accidental self-destruction. ("Inaugural Address of John F. Kennedy, 1961")

과학이 풀어놓은 어두운 세력이 의도했거나 실수로거나 전 인류를 감싸기 전에, 양측이 평화를 위한 노력을 다시 시작하자는 것.. (존 F.케네디 대통령의 취임사 1961)

☐ **anew** /əˈnuː/   adv. do again

(= again, once more, over, afresh)

So let us begin anew – remembering on both sides that civility is not a sign of weakness. ("Inaugural Address of John F. Kennedy, 1961")

그러니 새롭게 시작합시다—양측 모두 예절을 지키는 것이 약함을 보이는게 아니라는 것을 기억하며. (존 F.케네디 대통령의 취임사 1961)

☐ **civility** /səˈvɪləti/   n. a polite action or polite expression

(= affability, manners, politeness, decorum, courtesy)

So let us begin anew – remembering on both sides that civility is not a sign of weakness. ("Inaugural Address of John F. Kennedy, 1961")

그러니 새롭게 시작합시다—양측 모두 예절을 지키는 것이 약함을 보이는게 아니라는 것을 기억하며. (존 F.케네디 대통령의 취임사 1961)

☐ **endeavor** /ɪnˈdevər/   n. a strenuous effort

(= effort, attempt)

The energy, the faith, the devotion which we bring to this endeavor will light our country and all who serve it. ("Inaugural Address of John F. Kennedy, 1961")

이 노력에 우리가 깃드는 에너지와 헌신이 우리나라와 우리나라를 섬기는 모든 사람에게 광명을 가져다 줄 것입니다. (존 F.케네디 대통령의 취임사 1961)

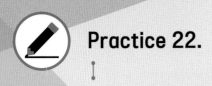

Practice 22.

Fill in the blank with the word that matches the definition provided

01   When one loses one's health, _____ (of this world) matters such as money and
      career do not matter much.

02   I am very happy with the _____ (starting something new) of interest in Korean
      traditional alcoholic drinks.

03   The coach warned the players that he will kick out anyone, who does not abide by the
      rules he _____, (lay down a rule) off the team.

04   Mr. Cuthbert's recent business _____ (a business enterprise) made him over five
      million dollars.

05   Many families were torn _____ (into pieces) during the war.

06   Many refugees immigrated to Canada to start their lives _____. (do again)

07   Mr. Miller trains the waiters at his restaurant to always treat its customers with _____.
      (polite action)

08   Professor Higgins warned the lagging student that she will have to make a great _____
      (a strenuous effort) to catch up with the course.

09   Social media has become an important _____ (place for discussion) for positive
      debate.

10   The two candidates hurled _____ (violent denunciations) at each other during the
      televised debate.

11 If we refuse to learn from the experiences of our _____ (ancestors), we are doomed to repeat their mistakes.

12 When the king dies without naming a/an _____ (successor), a bloody struggle for the throne ensued for over ten years.

13 Since the original movie was too violent to show on television, a/an _____ (made less violent) version was aired.

14 The terrorist organization's objective was the total _____ (weakening or destruction) of Western civilization.

15 The atmosphere at Mr. Harding's funeral was far from sad and _____ (serious and earnest); in fact, it was almost gay and jovial – just like Mr. Harding would have wanted it to be.

16 Korea is a country of rich historical _____. (something reserved for descendants)

17 When Mr. Richards saw so many people gathered for his retirement party, he was _____ (completely covered) by a feeling of gratitude.

Class 23

□ **conscience** /ˈkɑːnʃəns/

n. the inner sense of what is right or wrong in one's conduct or motives, impelling one
   toward right action

adj. conscientious

(= ethics, principles, morality)

*With a good conscience our only sure reward, with history the final judge of our deeds, let
us go forth to lead the land we love.. ("Inaugural Address of John F. Kennedy, 1961")*

가책 없는 양심만을 상으로 받으며, 역사만이 우리의 행동의 마지막 심판임을 기대하며 사랑으로 우리
나라를 이끕시다. (존 F.케네디 대통령의 취임사 1961)

□ **score** /skɔːr/   n. a group of twenty

(= twenty)

*Five score years ago, a great American, in whose symbolic shadow we stand today, signed
the Emancipation Proclamation. ("I have a dream – Dr. Martin Luther King, Jr")*

우리는 지금 한 훌륭한 미국인의 상징적인 그림자에 서 있는데 백년 전에 그분이 노예해방선언문에
서명을 하셨습니다. ("나에게 꿈이 있습니다" 연설 – 마틴 루터 킹 목사)

□ **momentous** /moʊˈmentəs/   adj. of great importance or consequences

(= significant, historic, crucial, decisive)

*This momentous decree came as a great beacon light of hope to millions of black slaves
who had been seared in the flames of withering injustice. ("I have a dream – Dr. Martin
Luther King, Jr")*

이 역사적인 선언문은 기를 죽이는 불평등의 불꽃에 데인 수백만 명의 흑인 노예들에게 희망의 불빛을
보여주었습니다. ("나에게 꿈이 있습니다" 연설 – 마틴 루터 킹 목사)

□ **beacon** /ˈbiːkən/   n. a light or fire that acts as a signal or guide

(= signal, guiding-light, sign)

This momentous decree came as a great beacon light of hope to millions of black slaves who had been seared in the flames of withering injustice. ("I have a dream – Dr. Martin Luther King, Jr")

이 역사적인 선언문은 기를 죽이는 불평등의 불꽃에 데인 수백만 명의 흑인 노예들에게 희망의 불빛을 보여주었습니다. ("나에게 꿈이 있습니다" 연설 – 마틴 루터 킹 목사)

☐ **sear** /sɪr/

v. to burn the surface with a sudden intense heat

(= scorch, burn, singe, solder)

This momentous decree came as a great beacon light of hope to millions of black slaves who had been seared in the flames of withering injustice. ("I have a dream – Dr. Martin Luther King, Jr")

이 역사적인 선언문은 기를 죽이는 불평등의 불꽃에 데인 수백만 명의 흑인 노예들에게 희망의 불빛을 보여주었습니다. ("나에게 꿈이 있습니다" 연설 – 마틴 루터 킹 목사)

☐ **wither** /ˈwɪðər/   v. to become very weak

(= shrivel, wilt, weaken, wane)

This momentous decree came as a great beacon light of hope to millions of black slaves who had been seared in the flames of withering injustice. ("I have a dream – Dr. Martin Luther King, Jr")

이 역사적인 선언문은 기를 죽이는 불평등의 불꽃에 데인 수백만 명의 흑인 노예들에게 희망의 불빛을 보여주었습니다. ("나에게 꿈이 있습니다" 연설 – 마틴 루터 킹 목사)

☐ **captivity** /kæpˈtɪvəti/   n. the state of being imprisoned

(= imprisonment, detention, incarceration, confinement)

It came as a joyous daybreak to end the long night of their captivity. ("I have a dream – Dr. Martin Luther King, Jr")

기나긴 감금의 밤 끝에 찾아 온 환희의 새벽이었습니다. ("나에게 꿈이 있습니다" 연설 – 마틴 루터 킹 목사)

☐ **crippled** /ˈkrɪpld/   adj. anything that is impaired or damaged

(= damaged, lame, retarded)

One hundred years later, the life of the black man is still sadly crippled by the manacles of segregation and the chains of discrimination. ("I have a dream – Dr. Martin Luther King, Jr")

백년이 지난 후, 흑인은 아직도 인종분리정책이라는 수갑과 인종차별이라는 쇠사슬로 인해 불구의 삶을 살고 있습니다. ("나에게 꿈이 있습니다" 연설 – 마틴 루터 킹 목사)

☐ **manacles** /ˈmænəklz/   n. hand-cuffs

(= shackles, fetters, restraints)

One hundred years later, the life of the black man is still sadly crippled by the manacles of segregation and the chains of discrimination. ("I have a dream – Dr. Martin Luther King, Jr")

백년이 지난 후, 흑인의 아직도 인종분리라는 수갑과 인종차별이라는 쇠사슬로 인해 불구의 삶을 살고 있습니다. ("나에게 꿈이 있습니다" 연설 – 마틴 루터 킹 목사)

☐ **segregation** /ˌsegrɪˈgeɪʃn/

n. the state of being separated or isolated from the main body or a group (= separation, isolation, exclusion, apartheid)

One hundred years later, the life of the black man is still sadly crippled by the manacles of segregation and the chains of discrimination. ("I have a dream – Dr. Martin Luther King, Jr")

백년이 지난 후, 흑인의 아직도 인종분리라는 수갑과 인종차별이라는 쇠사슬로 인해 불구의 삶을 살고 있습니다. ("나에게 꿈이 있습니다" 연설 – 마틴 루터 킹 목사)

☐ **prosperity** /prɑːˈsperəti/

n. condition in which a person or community is doing well financially

(= wealth, affluence, opulence, fortune)

One hundred years later, the black man lives on a lonely island of poverty in the midst of a vast ocean of material prosperity. ("I have a dream – Dr. Martin Luther King, Jr")

백년이 지난 후, 흑인은 물질적 풍요의 바다 한 가운데에 떠 있는 가난이라는 섬에 혼자 고립되어 있습니다. ("나에게 꿈이 있습니다" 연설 – 마틴 루터 킹 목사)

☐ **languish** /ˈlæŋgwɪʃ/   v. to remain and suffer

(= suffer, decay, deteriorate, flag)

One hundred years later, the Negro is still languishing in the corners of American society and finds himself an exile in his own land. ("I have a dream – Dr. Martin Luther King, Jr")

백년이 지난 후, 흑인은 아직도 미국 사회의 구석에서 고생하고 있으며 자기의 땅에서 추방된 자로 살고 있는 자신을 발견합니다. ("나에게 꿈이 있습니다" 연설 – 마틴 루터 킹 목사)

☐ **exile** /ˈeksaɪl/

n. someone who is forced to live outside of his home country

(= refugee, émigré, deportee)

One hundred years later, the Negro is still languishing in the corners of American society and finds himself an exile in his own land. ("I have a dream – Dr. Martin Luther King, Jr")

백년이 지난 후, 흑인은 아직도 미국 사회의 구석에서 고생하고 있으며 자기의 땅에서 추방된 자로 살고 있는 자신을 발견합니다. ("나에게 꿈이 있습니다" 연설 – 마틴 루터 킹 목사)

☐ **dramatize** /ˈdræmətaɪz/

v. to express oneself in a dramatic or exaggerated way

(= exaggerate, embellish, overstate)

So we have come here today to dramatize a shameful condition. ("I have a dream – Dr. Martin Luther King, Jr")

그래서 우리는 오늘 수치스러운 상황을 극화시키기 위해 오늘 이 자리에 모였습니다. ("나에게 꿈이 있습니다" 연설 – 마틴 루터 킹 목사)

☐ **cash a check**

idiom. to exchange a check for the same amount in cash

In a sense we have come to our nation's capital to cash a check. ("I have a dream – Dr. Martin Luther King, Jr")

어떤 의미에서 우리는 수표를 현금화 하러 우리나라의 수도에 왔습니다. ("나에게 꿈이 있습니다" 연설 – 마틴 루터 킹 목사)

☐ **promissory note** /ˈprɑːmɪsɔːri nəʊt/

n. a financial instrument that promises to pay a certain amount to the note holder

When the architects of our republic wrote the magnificent words of the Constitution and the Declaration of Independence, they were signing a promissory note to which every American was to fall heir. ("I have a dream – Dr. Martin Luther King, Jr")

이 나라의 설계자들이 이 나라의 위대한 헌법과 노예해방선언문을 집필할 때, 그들은 모든 미국인들이 수혜자가 될 하나의 약속어음에 서명을 한 것입니다. ("나에게 꿈이 있습니다" 연설 – 마틴 루터 킹 목사)

☐ **default** /dɪˈfɔːlt/　　　　　　　　v. to fail to meet a financial obligation

(= nonpayment, nonattendance)

It is obvious today that America has defaulted on this promissory note insofar as her citizens of color are concerned. ("I have a dream – Dr. Martin Luther King, Jr")

오늘 자명한 것은 적어도 이 나라의 유색인종과 관련해서는 미국이 그 약속어음을 지급불능 처리한 것입니다. ("나에게 꿈이 있습니다" 연설 – 마틴 루터 킹 목사)

☐ **insofar as** /ˌɪnsəˈfɑːr əz/　　　　idiom. as long as

It is obvious today that America has defaulted on this promissory note insofar as her citizens of color are concerned. ("I have a dream – Dr. Martin Luther King, Jr")

오늘 자명한 것은 적어도 이 나라의 유색인종과 관련해서는 미국이 그 약속어음을 지급불능 처리한 것입니다. ("나에게 꿈이 있습니다" 연설 – 마틴 루터 킹 목사)

☐ **hallowed** /ˈhæləʊd/

adj. respected and admired because something is old or important

(= sacred, holy)

We have also come to this hallowed spot to remind America of the fierce urgency of now. ("I have a dream – Dr. Martin Luther King, Jr")

우리는 미국에게 지금 상황의 급박성을 상기시키려 이 성스러운 자리에 왔습니다. ("나에게 꿈이 있습니다" 연설 – 마틴 루터 킹 목사)

☐ **tranquilizing**　　　　　　adj. making or becoming calm and quiet

(= calming, soothing, sedative, soporific)

This is no time to engage in the luxury of cooling off or to take the tranquilizing drug of gradualism. ("I have a dream – Dr. Martin Luther King, Jr")

지금 한가하게 머리를 식히자느니 점진주의라는 마취약을 복용하자느니 할 여유가 없습니다. ("나에게 꿈이 있습니다" 연설 – 마틴 루터 킹 목사)

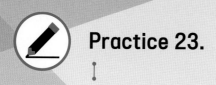

Practice 23.

Fill in the blank with the word that matches the definition provided

01 Eating all my little brother's Halloween candy does not trouble my _____. (principals)

02 The school still enforces gender _____ (separation): boys and girls are not taught in the same classroom.

03 Sociologists say that, despite the many conflicts we see today, the world is experiencing an unprecedented period of peace and _____ (affluence).

04 Many wild animals cannot survive in _____. (the state of being imprisoned)

05 They navigated our boat towards the shining _____. (a light signal)

06 There was about a/an _____ (group of twenty) of people waiting in line.

07 At 38, Ulysses Grant made the _____ (of great importance) decision to rejoin the Army.

08 If the management of the company cannot raise U$2 million by the end of the month, the company will _____. (fail to meet financial obligations)

09 This land is considered _____ (sacred) by the natives.

10 Aleksandr Solzhenitsyn was a/an _____ (someone who is forced to live outside his country) from the Soviet Union from 1974 until his return to Russia in 1994.

11 Mr. Keller always _____ (express in an exaggerated way) when telling the story of how he stopped a burglar in a mall parking lot.

12 Half a year after the flood, many refugees still _____ (remain and suffer) in makeshift shelters waiting for their homes to be restored.

13 To me, fishing has a/an _____ (calming) effect: it puts me at peace.

14 Dr. Hawking's body is _____ (impaired or damaged) by disease, but his mental faculties are sharper than those of most other people.

15 I _____ (burned the surface) my hand on the stove.

16 He was such a robust man, but like everyone he has _____ (become weak) with old age.

Find the correct word which can replace the bold phrase in the following sentences. Change the word form appropriately to fit the sentence, if necessary

> **gratitude, hardihood, exploit, despise, violation, odious, mockery, impel, vigor, wither, produce, ordain, discrimination, bounty, incompetent**

01 William's description of his _____ in the army were too fantastic to be true.

02 When Gloria was young, she _____ always being the tallest girl in her class, but now that she is an adult, she doesn't mind being a tall woman.

03 The Philippines and the Vatican are the only remaining countries where divorce is a _____ of law.

04 The students showed their _____ towards their substitute teacher by throwing a farewell party for him on his last day.

05 That Michael married a woman half his age was a subject of some _____: his friends jokingly called him a "kidnapper".

06 Many Westerners who visit Korea think that eating live octopus is quite _____.

07 During World War Two, the British Prime Minister, Winston Churchill believed that fate had _____ him to be the savior of Great Britain.

08 The politician had the _____ to deny his involvement in the scandal even when the media had provided proof.

09 It is hard to imagine now, but racial _____ was prevalent in the United States' public school system as recently as the 1960s.

10 The judge said that although there was some evidence that suggested the defendant's innocence, he has reasons that _____ him to rule the defendant to be guilty.

11 Even at 85, Mr. Massey has not lost his _____: he still swims 2km a day.

12 My wife doesn't like to receive flowers because she gets depressed when they _____.

13 During the summer and autumn, we buy our groceries at the open farmers' market because the _____ sold there is much fresher.

14 The clinic is operated by the _____ of public donations and philanthropic support.

15 The reason that public officials cannot launch long term plans is that they are deemed _____ if they don't show visible improvements within a year.

venture, beacon, evanescent, conduct, callous, tempered, prescribe, civility, conscience, solemn, outpace, engulf, outworn, lure, possession

16 Apparently the idea of working for a large conglomerate is _____: more and more college graduates choose to work independently.

17 The prospect of money can _____ young people into dabbing in illegal activities.

18 The police had tracked down the man that stole the paintings, but unfortunately, they were no longer in his _____.

19 The brief and _____ period of economic growth has passed, and the world has plunged into a recession once again.

20   The students who were caught cheating were accused of ungentlemanly _____ and set under detention.

21   Her husband's _____ disregard for her feelings made Jane very angry.

22   News caster's voice was _____ when he announced that many people were killed and hurt in a terrible explosion.

23   Company regulations _____ that all employees must carry identification cards at all times.

24   The right wing newspaper's editorial was a _____ version of that of the left wing's, but it still criticized the government for its incompetence.

25   The two former rival companies have decided to cooperate and set up a joint _____.

26   The U.S's space program, although launched after the Soviets launched their first satellite, soon _____ the Soviet Union's program.

27   Whenever the actor makes a public appearance, he is _____ by fans, photographers, and paparazzi.

28   Jane's parents greeted Jane's boyfriend with _____ but not with warmth.

29   Henry could see the answers on his friend's test sheet clearly, but it went against his _____ to copy them.

30   Far on the horizon, the sailors saw the lighthouse _____ that would guide their ship to dock.

Select the pair of words that most nearly expresses the same relationship

31 lame: crippled
    A. prosperity: poverty
    B. languish: perpetuate
    C. tranquilizing: soothing
    D. combination: segregation

32 diatribe: praise
    A. tempered; exaggerated
    B. rival: foe
    C. descendant: heir
    D. wretched: evanescent

33 ford: traverse
    A. enumeration: edifice
    B. vanquish: conquer
    C. fortification: propensity
    D. abstinence: pertinence

34 repudiate: deny
    A. induction: intimate
    B. derision: mockery
    C. indulgence: convulsion
    D. charter: pillar

35 candor: artifice
    A. amicable: antagonistic
    B. disclose: impart
    C. impartial: neutral
    D. accept: expose

36 misanthropic: social
    A. disaster: calamity
    B. rejoice: cheer
    C. appropriate: incongruous
    D. unwavering: steadfast

37 appertain: relate
   A. stricken: praised
   B. extenuate: indict
   C. impediment: incompetence
   D. chronicles: annals

38 faculty: talent
   A. specious: callous
   B. extol: laud
   C. useful: frivolous
   D. designate: wilt

39 conjecture: speculation
   A. evanescent: subservient
   B. hint: insinuate
   C. conquer: supine
   D. countervail: topple

40 perpetuate: endure
   A. vicissitude: falsity
   B. auxiliary: requisite
   C. moderate: exhort
   D. confused: perplexed

Choose the word that isn't a synonym

41 heritage – enterprise – legacy

42 insurrection – subversion – forum

43 helm – criticism – invective

44 momentum – conscience – morality

45 singe – scorch – wither

46 lame - specious – crippled

47 shackles – fetters – annals

48 decorum – incarceration – civility

49 languish – embellish – deteriorate

50 sedative – tranquilizing – overwhelming

51 refugee – exile – deed

52 fortune – non-payment – default

53 indictment – attentiveness – solicitude

54 squeeze – adopt – wring

55 hardihood – monarch – sovereign

56 sanctify – curtail – consecrate

57 stricken – afflicted – irate

58 devious – obsolete – unscrupulous

59 renewal – conduct – behavior

60 endeavor – enemy – foe

Class 25

□ **desolate** /ˈdesələt/   adj. empty of people and lacking of comfort

(= forlorn, deserted, bleak, barren)

Now is the time to rise from the dark and desolate valley of segregation to the sunlit path of racial justice. ("I have a dream – Dr. Martin Luther King, Jr")

이제는 어둡고 황량한 인종분리라는 골짜기에서 나와 인종 정의의 밝은 길로 나아가야 할 때입니다. ("나에게 꿈이 있습니다" 연설 – 마틴 루터 킹 목사)

□ **sweltering** /ˈsweltərɪŋ/   adj. to extremely hot and uncomfortable

(= boiling, scorching, torrid, blistering)

This sweltering summer of the Negro's legitimate discontent will not pass until there is an invigorating autumn of freedom and equality. ("I have a dream – Dr. Martin Luther King, Jr")

흑인의 정당화된 불만의 뜨거운 여름은 활기가 돌게 해주는 자유와 평등의 가을이 오기 전에는 끝나지 않을 것입니다. ("나에게 꿈이 있습니다" 연설 – 마틴 루터 킹 목사)

□ **invigorate** /ɪnˈvɪɡəreɪt/   v. to fill with life and energy

(= energize, refresh, revitalize, enliven, galvanize)

This sweltering summer of the Negro's legitimate discontent will not pass until there is an invigorating autumn of freedom and equality. ("I have a dream – Dr. Martin Luther King, Jr")

흑인의 정당화된 불만의 뜨거운 여름은 활기가 돌게 해주는 자유와 평등의 가을이 오기 전에는 끝나지 않을 것입니다. ("나에게 꿈이 있습니다" 연설 – 마틴 루터 킹 목사)

□ **degenerate** /dɪˈdʒenəreɪt/   v. to worsen or weaken

(= deteriorate, disintegrate, worsen, collapse)

We must not allow our creative protest to degenerate into physical violence. ("I have a dream – Dr. Martin Luther King, Jr")

우리는 우리의 창의적인 항의가 육체적 폭력으로 전락하지 않도록 해야 합니다. ("나에게 꿈이 있습니다" 연설 – 마틴 루터 킹 목사)

□ **militancy** /ˈmɪlɪtənsi/   n. aggressiveness

(= combativeness, hostility, violence, belligerence)

The marvelous new militancy which has engulfed the black community must not lead us to a distrust of all white people..("I have a dream – Dr. Martin Luther King, Jr")

흑인 사회에 새롭게 생긴 대단한 투지가 모든 백인들에 대한 불신으로 이어져서는 안 됩니다. ("나에게 꿈이 있습니다" 연설 – 마틴 루터 킹 목사)

□ **inextricable** /ˌɪnɪkˈstrɪkəbl/   adj. unable to consider separately

(= involved, tangled, inseparable, indivisible)

They have come to realize that their freedom is inextricably bound to our freedom..("I have a dream – Dr. Martin Luther King, Jr")

그들은 우리의 자유와 그들의 자유가 불가분의 관계라는 것을 이해하게 되었습니다. ("나에게 꿈이 있습니다" 연설 – 마틴 루터 킹 목사)

□ **devotee** /ˌdevəˈtiː/   n. someone who is devoted

(= enthusiast, supporter, aficionado)

There are those who are asking the devotees of civil rights, "When will you be satisfied?" ..("I have a dream – Dr. Martin Luther King, Jr")

시민의 권리를 추종하는 사람에게 "당신은 언제 만족할 겁니까?"라고 묻는 사람들이 있습니다. ("나에게 꿈이 있습니다" 연설 – 마틴 루터 킹 목사)

□ **selfhood** /ˈselfhʊd/   n. the state having an identity

(= identity)

We can never be satisfied as long as our children are stripped of their selfhood and robbed of their dignity by signs stating "For Whites Only". ("I have a dream – Dr. Martin Luther King, Jr")

우리는 우리의 아이들의 자존감을 벗기고 그들의 존엄성을 빼앗는 "백인 전용"이라는 표지판이 계속 존재하는 한 만족하지 않을 것입니다. ("나에게 꿈이 있습니다" 연설 – 마틴 루터 킹 목사)

☐ **trials and tribulations**   idiom. difficulties and troubles

I am not unmindful that some of you have come here out of great trials and tribulations. ("I have a dream – Dr. Martin Luther King, Jr")

저는 여러분 중에 많은 시련과 우여곡절을 겪은 끝에 오늘 여기에 오신 분들이 있다는 걸 압니다. ("나에게 꿈이 있습니다" 연설 – 마틴 루터 킹 목사)

☐ **quest** /kwest/   n. a long and difficult search for something

(= expedition, pursuit)

Some of you have come from areas where your quest for freedom left you battered by the storms of persecution and staggered by the winds of police brutality. ("I have a dream – Dr. Martin Luther King, Jr")

여러분들 중에 어떤 분들은 자유를 향한 탐구가 탄압의 폭풍우를 맞고 경찰 폭력의 강풍에 휘청거리게 만드는 지역에서 오셨습니다. ("나에게 꿈이 있습니다" 연설 – 마틴 루터 킹 목사)

☐ **brutality** /bruːˈtæləti/   n. the quality of being extremely cruel

(= cruelty, violence, ruthlessness, harshness)

Some of you have come from areas where your quest for freedom left you battered by the storms of persecution and staggered by the winds of police brutality. ("I have a dream – Dr. Martin Luther King, Jr")

여러분들 중에 어떤 분들은 자유를 향한 탐구가 탄압의 폭풍우를 맞고 경찰 폭력의 강풍에 휘청거리게 만드는 지역에서 오셨습니다. ("나에게 꿈이 있습니다" 연설 – 마틴 루터 킹 목사)

☐ **redemptive** /rɪˈdemptɪv/   adj. serving to redeem

(= liberating, redeeming, rescuing)

You have been the veterans of creative suffering. Continue to work with the faith that unearned suffering is redemptive. ("I have a dream – Dr. Martin Luther King, Jr")

여러분들은 창조적인 수난의 베테랑이 되셨습니다. 계속해서 정당화되지 않는 수난은 구원의 수난이라는 신념을 가지고 계속 정진하시기 바랍니다. ("나에게 꿈이 있습니다" 연설 – 마틴 루터 킹 목사)

☐ **nullification** /nʌˌləfɪkéiʃən/   n. the act or instance of nullifying

(= invalidation, annulment, abolishment)

I have a dream that one day, down in Alabama, with its vicious racists, with its governor having his lips dripping with the words of interposition and nullification.. ("I have a dream – Dr. Martin Luther King, Jr")

저의 꿈은 언젠가, 잔혹한 인종차별주의자들이 모여있고, 주지사의 입에서 주권(州權) 우위설과 연방법령 실시거부와 같은 말이 나오는, 앨라배마에서.. ("나에게 꿈이 있습니다" 연설 – 마틴 루터 킹 목사)

☐ **hew** /hjuː/

v. to cut a big piece of wood or rock to make a smaller one

(= cut, carve, shape)

With this faith we will be able to hew out of the mountain of despair a stone of hope. ("I have a dream – Dr. Martin Luther King, Jr")

우리의 신념으로 절망의 산에서 작은 희망의 돌을 캐어 낼 것입니다. ("나에게 꿈이 있습니다" 연설 – 마틴 루터 킹 목사)

☐ **jangle** /ˈdʒæŋgl/   v. to make a ringing noise

(= ring, jingle, clang)

With this faith we will be able to transform the jangling discords of our nation into a beautiful symphony of brotherhood. ("I have a dream – Dr. Martin Luther King, Jr")

이 신념으로 우리는 이 나라의 짤랑거리는 불협화음을 형제애의 아름다운 교향곡으로 바꿀 것입니다. ("나에게 꿈이 있습니다" 연설 – 마틴 루터 킹 목사)

☐ **discord** /ˈdɪskɔːrd/   n. lack of harmony

(= disagreement, dissonance, disharmony, cacophony)

With this faith we will be able to transform the jangling discords of our nation into a beautiful symphony of brotherhood. ("I have a dream – Dr. Martin Luther King, Jr")

이 신념으로 우리는 이 나라의 짤랑거리는 불협화음을 형제애의 아름다운 교향곡으로 바꿀 것입니다. ("나에게 꿈이 있습니다" 연설 – 마틴 루터 킹 목사)

☐ **hamlet** /ˈhæmlət/   n. a very small village

(= village, small town)

And when this happens, when we allow freedom to ring, when we let it ring from every village and every hamlet, ("I have a dream – Dr. Martin Luther King, Jr")

그리고 이것이 현실이 되었을 때, 우리가 자유가 울리게 할 때, 우리가 모든 마을과 촌락에서 자유가 울리게 할 때.. ("나에게 꿈이 있습니다" 연설 - 마틴 루터 킹 목사)

☐ **cabinet** /ˈkæbɪnət/

n. an advisory body to the President, consisting of the heads of the 13 executive departments of the Federal Government

(= council, advisory board)

"Some of your Cabinet members don't seem loyal..." ("Jimmy Carter's Crisis of Confidence Speech, 1979")

당신의 내각 구성원 중 일부가 충성심이 없어 보입니다. (지미 카터 대통령의 "신뢰의 위기" 연설 1979)

☐ **inflation** /ɪnˈfleɪʃn/   n. the rising of prices of general goods

(= increase, rise)

When we import oil we are also importing inflation plus unemployment.. ("Jimmy Carter's Crisis of Confidence Speech, 1979")

우리가 원유를 수입 할 때, 물가상승과 실업도 수입합니다. (지미 카터 대통령의 "신뢰의 위기" 연설 1979)

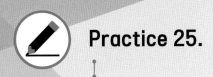

Practice 25.

Fill in the blank with the word that matches the definition provided

01 My _____ (a long and difficult search) for knowledge will never stop.

02 Many of the dogs in the shelter experienced _____ (extreme cruelty) and so are weary of trusting people.

03 The _____ (combativeness) of the protestors shocked everyone.

04 Only three decades ago, this thriving town was only a small _____. (small village)

05 I _____ (make a ringing noise) the doorbell several times before someone came to answer.

06 Like all families, we have our mix of harmony and _____. (lack of harmony)

07 The meeting soon _____ (to worsen) into a yelling match.

08 Our house looked so _____ (empty of people and lacking comfort) after all the furniture had been moved out.

09 Singapore sits right on the equator, so the weather is _____ (extremely hot) all year round.

10 At the end of the movie, the antagonist saves the life of the hero and dies in a/an _____ (serving to redeem) sacrifice of his own life.

11 It is almost impossible for a young family to find housing downtown because of _____. (rising prices)

12 Few people know that Chris, who is a professional wrestler, is a/an _____ (someone who is devoted) of romantic novels in his spare time.

13 The store owner came to the conclusion that customer service and revenue increase have a/an _____ (unable to consider separately) link.

14 Many people gathered in front of the court to demand of the _____ (annulment) of the recent ruling.

15 A tall glass of ice-tea always _____ (to fill with energy) me after my work out.

☐ **vivid** /ˈvɪvɪd/   adj. strong and clear

(= graphic, striking, lively, lucid, clear)

And this is one of the most vivid statements: "Our neck is stretched over the fence and OPEC has a knife." ("Jimmy Carter's Crisis of Confidence Speech, 1979")

그리고 이것이 가장 생생한 발언 중 하나입니다: "우리의 목이 담장에 걸쳐 늘어져 있고 세계 석유 수출국 기구가 칼을 들고 있다." (지미 카터 대통령의 "신뢰의 위기" 연설 1979)

☐ **cartel** /kɑːrˈtel/

n. an international syndicate formed to regulate prices or output of some field of business

(= union, league, association)

There will be other cartels and other shortages. ("Jimmy Carter's Crisis of Confidence Speech, 1979")

다른 카르텔과 다른 부족이 발생할 겁니다. (지미 카터 대통령의 "신뢰의 위기" 연설 1979)

☐ **campaign** /kæmˈpeɪn/

n. a competition by rival political candidates for political office

That's why I've worked hard to put my campaign promises into law - and I have to admit, with just mixed success. ("Jimmy Carter's Crisis of Confidence Speech, 1979")

그런 이유로 저는 저의 공약을 법으로 제정하기 위해 많은 노력을 하였습니다만 – 솔직히 성공률은 반반입니다. (지미 카터 대통령의 "신뢰의 위기" 연설 1979)

☐ **erosion** /ɪˈrəʊʒn/   n. destruction by slow disintegration

(= corrosion, loss, wearing away)

The erosion of our confidence in the future is threatening to destroy the social and the political fabric of America. ("Jimmy Carter's Crisis of Confidence Speech, 1979")

우리의 신뢰의 부식은 미국의 미래 사회적 정치적 구조를 파괴할 위협을 하고 있습니다. (지미 카터 대통령의 "신뢰의 위기" 연설 1979)

☐ **self-indulgence** /self-ın'dʌldʒəns/   n. tendency to indulge one's desires

(= decadence, indulgence, hedonism, self-centeredness)

..too many of us now tend to worship self-indulgence and consumption. ("Jimmy Carter's Crisis of Confidence Speech, 1979")

..우리 중의 너무 많은 숫자가 방종과 소비를 숭배하고 있습니다. (지미 카터 대통령의 "신뢰의 위기" 연설 1979)

☐ **reassurance** /ˌriːə'ʃʊrəns/   n. a feeling of comfort

(= assurance, encouragement, hope, comfort)

This is not a message of happiness or reassurance, but it is the truth and it is a warning. ("Jimmy Carter's Crisis of Confidence Speech, 1979")

이것은 행복이나 안심을 위해 드리는 말이 아니라 현실이고 경고입니다. (지미 카터 대통령의 "신뢰의 위기" 연설 1979)

☐ **mainstream** /'meɪnstriːm/   n. the principal trend of society

(= convention)

..our people have turned to the Federal Government and found it isolated from the mainstream of our Nation's life.. ("Jimmy Carter's Crisis of Confidence Speech, 1979")

..국민들은 연방정부에 의지하려 하였으나 이 정부가 우리 나라의 주류의 삶으로부터 동떨어져 있다는 걸 알았습니다. (지미 카터 대통령의 "신뢰의 위기" 연설 1979)

☐ **evasiveness** /ɪ'veɪsɪvnəs/   n. the tendency to avoid an issue

(= ambiguousness, elusiveness, equivocation, indirectness)

The people are looking for honest answers, not easy answers; clear leadership, not false claims and evasiveness and politics as usual. ("Jimmy Carter's Crisis of Confidence Speech, 1979")

국민들은 쉬운 해답이 아닌 솔직한 해답을 원하고 있고, 일상이 되어버린 거짓 주장과 본질을 피하는 말 그리고 정치적 술수가 아닌 투명한 지도력을 원합니다.

☐ **paralysis** /pə'ræləsɪs/   n. a state of helpless inactivity

(= inactivity, stoppage, immobility)

Often you see paralysis and stagnation and drift. ("Jimmy Carter's Crisis of Confidence Speech, 1979")

마비와 침체 그리고 표류를 자주 목격합니다. (지미 카터 대통령의 "신뢰의 위기" 연설 1979)

☐ **stagnation** /stæg'neɪʃn/   n. the state of being sluggish and dull

(= inaction, torpor, sluggishness)

Often you see paralysis and stagnation and drift. ("Jimmy Carter's Crisis of Confidence Speech, 1979")

마비와 침체 그리고 표류를 자주 목격합니다. (지미 카터 대통령의 "신뢰의 위기" 연설 1979)

☐ **fragmentation** /ˌfrægmen'teɪʃn/   n. the state of dividing into many pieces

(= disintegration, breakup, crumbling, shattering)

One is a path I've warned about tonight, the path that leads to fragmentation and self-interest. ("Jimmy Carter's Crisis of Confidence Speech, 1979")

한 개는 제가 오늘 저녁에 경고 드린 길입니다. 분열과 이기주의로 이끄는 길. (지미 카터 대통령의 "신뢰의 위기" 연설 1979)

☐ **route** /ruːt/   n. a passage way

(= course, road, path)

It is a certain route to failure. ("Jimmy Carter's Crisis of Confidence Speech, 1979")

무조건 실패로 가는 길입니다. (지미 카터 대통령의 "신뢰의 위기" 연설 1979)

☐ **quota** /'kwəʊtə/   n. a prescribed share

(= share, allocation, portion, ration)

These quotas will ensure a reduction in imports even below the ambitious levels we set at the recent Tokyo summit. ("Jimmy Carter's Crisis of Confidence Speech, 1979")

이 할당량은 우리가 최근 도쿄회의에서 선정한 의욕적인 수준보다도 낮게 수입량을 축소해 줄 것입니다. (지미 카터 대통령의 "신뢰의 위기" 연설 1979)

☐ **denomination** /dɪˌnɑːmɪ'neɪʃn/
n. the face value of money or financial instruments

(= face value)

The corporation I will issue up to $5 billion in energy bonds, and I especially want them to be in small denominations so that average Americans can invest directly in America's energy security. ("Jimmy Carter's Crisis of Confidence Speech, 1979")

저는 50억 불에 해당하는 에너지 채권을 발행하여 그 수입으로 기업을 설립하고자 합니다. 그리고 그 채권은 특히 소액 액면가로 발행이 되어 보통의 미국인이 우리의 에너지 안보에 직접 투자를 할 수 있게 하고 싶습니다. (지미 카터 대통령의 "신뢰의 위기" 연설 1979)

☐ **legislation** /ˌledʒɪsˈleɪʃn/　　　n. the act of enacting laws

(= lawmaking, legislature, law)

I will soon submit legislation to Congress calling for the creation of this Nation's first solar bank. ("Jimmy Carter's Crisis of Confidence Speech, 1979")

저는 곧 상원에 새로운 법안을 상정하여 그들이 우리나라 최초의 태양열 은행을 설립토록 요청할 것입니다. (지미 카터 대통령의 "신뢰의 위기" 연설 1979)

☐ **windfall** /ˈwɪndfɔːl/　　　n. an unexpected gain

(= bonus, premium, extra)

These efforts will cost money, a lot of money, and that is why Congress must enact the windfall profits tax without delay. ("Jimmy Carter's Crisis of Confidence Speech, 1979")

이러한 노력을 현실화 하는 데는 아주 많은 돈이 필요하며, 그렇기 때문에 상원에서는 지체 없이 우발소득세를 입법화 해야 합니다. (지미 카터 대통령의 "신뢰의 위기" 연설 1979)

☐ **mandate** /ˈmændeɪt/　　　v. to give an order

(= decree, dictate, assign, require)

I'm asking Congress to mandate, to require as a matter of law, that our Nation's utility companies cut their massive use of oil by 50 percent within the next decade. ("Jimmy Carter's Crisis of Confidence Speech, 1979")

저는 상원에 요청하여 우리나라의 공공사업 회사들이 앞으로 10년 내에 원유 사용량을 50% 줄이도록 법으로 정하게 할 겁니다. (지미 카터 대통령의 "신뢰의 위기" 연설 1979)

☐ **utility** /juːˈtɪləti/　　　n. a public service

(= public service)

I'm asking Congress to mandate, to require as a matter of law, that our Nation's utility companies cut their massive use of oil by 50 percent within the next decade, ("Jimmy Carter's Crisis of Confidence Speech, 1979")

저는 상원에 요청하여 우리나라의 공공사업 회사들이 앞으로 10년 내에 원유 사용량을 50% 줄이도록 법으로 정하게 할 겁니다. (지미 카터 대통령의 "신뢰의 위기" 연설 1979)

□ **refinery** /rɪ'faɪnəri/

n. a factory for the refining of crude oil into gasoline and other petrochemical products

(= processing plant)

But when this Nation critically needs a refinery or a pipeline, we will build it. ("Jimmy Carter's Crisis of Confidence Speech, 1979")

그러나 우리나라가 정유소나 파이프라인이 급하게 필요한 경우에는 짓겠습니다. (지미 카터 대통령의 "신뢰의 위기" 연설 1979)

□ **ration** /'ræʃn/   v. to restrict the consumption of

(= limit, control, restrict, apportion, allot)

I ask Congress to give me authority for mandatory conservation and for standby gasoline rationing. ("Jimmy Carter's Crisis of Confidence Speech, 1979")

저는 상원에게 제게 휘발유의 의무적인 절약 및 유사시에 휘발유 배급제도를 명령할 수 있는 권한을 달라고 요청하겠습니다. (지미 카터 대통령의 "신뢰의 위기" 연설 1979)

Practice 26.

Fill in the blank with the word that matches the definition provided

01 Living on a tight budget, my only _____ (decadence) is to dine at a four-star restaurant once a month.

02 Traffic is too congested: we must take an alternative _____ (passage way).

03 The company _____ (gave an order) Arthur's firm to undertake the huge production project.

04 Since I'm on a diet, I have to _____ (restrict consumption) my food so I don't exceed 2,000 calories a day.

05 I lost my interest in the band when it stopped being "indie" and became _____. (the principal trend of society)

06 I am sick of your _____ (tendency to avoid an issue): can't you give me a straight answer?

07 I cannot leave work until I achieve my production _____ (prescribed share)

08 Can you break this hundred dollar bill into bills of smaller _____? (face value)

09 I made a/an _____ (unexpected gain), when I received a tax refund from the government.

10 Martin's winking at me and saying "trust me" gave me no _____. (feeling of comfort)

11 The witness gave a very _____ (strong and clear) account of the accident.

12 With a month till the election, each candidate's _____ (competition for public office) was in full swing.

13 The government's mismanagement of the crisis caused much _____ (slow disintegration) in the public's confidence.

14 At 64, he suffered a stroke and now half his body in afflicted with _____. (a state of inactivity)

15 The economic _____ (the state of being sluggish and dull) has continued for over a decade.

16 The labor union is fraught with _____. (the state of being divided into many pieces)

☐ **rekindle** /ˌriːˈkɪndl/   v. to cause to arouse again

(= renew, regenerate, revitalize, refresh)

It can rekindle our sense of unity, our confidence in the future, and give our Nation and all of us individually a new sense of purpose. ("Jimmy Carter's Crisis of Confidence Speech, 1979")

저는 우리의 일체감과 미래에 대한 확신을 다시 지필 수 있고, 우리 국가와 국민 모두에게 새로운 목표의식을 드릴 수 있습니다. (지미 카터 대통령의 "신뢰의 위기" 연설 1979)

☐ **agenda** /əˈdʒendə/   n. matters to be discussed

(= plan, outline, memo)

You can help me to develop a national agenda for the 1980s. ("Jimmy Carter's Crisis of Confidence Speech, 1979")

여러분들은 제가 1980년대를 위한 국가의 의제를 개발하는 것을 도와주실 수 있습니다. (지미 카터 대통령의 "신뢰의 위기" 연설 1979)

☐ **treasury** /ˈtreʒəri/   n. funds of the government

(= coffers, reserves, government funds)

We can spend until we empty our treasuries, and we may summon all the wonders of science. ("Jimmy Carter's Crisis of Confidence Speech, 1979")

우리는 국고가 바닥이 날 때까지 지불을 할 수 있고, 과학이 제공하는 모든 경이로움을 소환할 수 있습니다. (지미 카터 대통령의 "신뢰의 위기" 연설 1979)

☐ **for the sake of**   idiom. for the benefit of

(= for the good of)

With God's help and for the sake of our Nation, it is time for us to join hands in America. ("Jimmy Carter's Crisis of Confidence Speech, 1979")

하느님의 가호와 우리 나라를 위해, 이제는 모든 미국인들이 손을 잡을 때입니다.

☐ **impose** /ɪmˈpəʊz/

v. to use authority to force something upon someone

(= inflict, oblige, compel, force)

But there remain armed guards and checkpoints all the same—still a restriction on the right to travel, still an instrument to impose upon ordinary men and women the will of a totalitarian state. ("Ronald Reagan's Berlin Wall Speech, 1987")

그러나 여전히 무장 경비병과 검문소들이 있습니다 – 아직도 보통의 남녀에게 전체국가의 의지를 강요하는 수단인 여행의 통제가 이뤄집니다. (레이건 대통령의 베를린 장벽 연설, 1987)

☐ **gash** /gæʃ/ n. a long deep cut

(= slash, tear, laceration, incision)

..those barriers cut across Germany in a gash of barbed wire, concrete, dog runs, and guard towers.. ("Ronald Reagan's Berlin Wall Speech, 1987")

..그러한 장애물들, 가시철사, 콘크리트, 경비견의 순찰 그리고 경비 타워들로 이뤄진 크고 깊은 상처가 독일을 가로질러 있습니다. (레이건 대통령의 베를린 장벽 연설, 1987)

☐ **lament** /ləˈment/ v. to express deep sorrow

(= mourn, grieve, weep, bewail, bemoan)

Yet I do not come here to lament. ("Ronald Reagan's Berlin Wall Speech, 1987")

그러나 저는 비통해 하려 이 자리에 온 건 아닙니다. (레이건 대통령의 베를린 장벽 연설, 1987)

☐ **commemorate** /kəˈmeməreɪt/ v. to celebrate

(= honor, memorialize, venerate)

I saw a display commemorating this 40th anniversary of the Marshall Plan. ("Ronald Reagan's Berlin Wall Speech, 1987")

저는 마샬계획의 40주년 행사를 기념하는 설치물을 보았습니다. (레이건 대통령의 베를린 장벽 연설, 1987)

☐ **utter** /ˈʌtər/ adj. absolute

(= complete, sheer, downright, absolute)

From devastation, from utter ruin, you Berliners have, in freedom, rebuilt a city that once again ranks as one of the greatest on earth. ("Ronald Reagan's Berlin Wall Speech, 1987")

여러분 베를린인들은 파괴와 완전한 폐허로부터 다시 지구상에서 가장 훌륭한 도시중 하나로 칭송 받는 도시를 재건하였습니다. (레이건 대통령의 베를린 장벽 연설, 1987)

☐ **token** /'təʊkən/   adj. perfunctory

(= empty, nominal, symbolic)

Or are they token gestures, intended to raise false hopes in the West...("Ronald Reagan's Berlin Wall Speech, 1987")

아니면 그것들은 그저 형식적인 행동인가요. 서방세계의 헛된 희망을 부추기고자 하는.. (레이건 대통령의 베를린 장벽 연설, 1987)

☐ **deterrence** /dɪ'tɜːrəns/

n. the act of discouraging an enemy from attacking by the capacity or threat of retaliating

(= dissuasion, pre-emption, prevention, restriction)

..research to base deterrence not on the threat of offensive retaliation, but on defenses that truly defend.. ("Ronald Reagan's Berlin Wall Speech, 1987")

..(전쟁)억지력을 공격적 보복행위가 아닌, 오로지 방어만을 위한 억지력을 개발하기 위한 연구.. (레이건 대통령의 베를린 장벽 연설, 1987)

☐ **aviation** /ˌeɪvi'eɪʃn/   n. air travel or air transport

(= flight, flying)

We look to the day when West Berlin can become one of the chief aviation hubs in all central Europe. ("Ronald Reagan's Berlin Wall Speech, 1987")

우리는 베를린이 중앙유럽에서의 핵심 항공 중심지 중 하나가 되는 날을 기대합니다. (레이건 대통령의 베를린 장벽 연설, 1987)

☐ **hub** /hʌb/   n. center

(= middle, core, heart, pivot)

We look to the day when West Berlin can become one of the chief aviation hubs in all central Europe. ("Ronald Reagan's Berlin Wall Speech, 1987")

우리는 베를린이 중앙유럽에서의 핵심 항공 중심지 중 하나가 되는 날을 기대합니다. (레이건 대통령의 베를린 장벽 연설, 1987)

□ **implicit** /ɪmˈplɪsɪt/   adj. not explicit

(= embedded, implied, contained, tacit)

Today the city thrives in spite of the challenges implicit in the very presence of this wall. ("Ronald Reagan's Berlin Wall Speech, 1987")

오늘날 이 장벽이 존재함으로 암시되는 여러 가지 도전에도 불구하고 이 도시는 번창하고 있습니다. (레이건 대통령의 베를린 장벽 연설, 1987)

□ **fortitude** /ˈfɔːrtɪtuːd/   n. mental and emotional strength

(= strength, courage, resilience, grit)

Certainly there's a great deal to be said for your fortitude, for your defiant courage. ("Ronald Reagan's Berlin Wall Speech, 1987")

여러분들의 강인함과 불굴의 용기에 대해 하고 싶은 말이 많습니다. (레이건 대통령의 베를린 장벽 연설, 1987)

□ **disabuse** /ˌdɪsəˈbjuːz/   v. to free from deception or error

(= disillusion, enlighten, deprive)

No one could live long in Berlin without being completely disabused of illusions. ("Ronald Reagan's Berlin Wall Speech, 1987")

베를린에 오래 살면서 환상에서 깨어나지 않는 사람은 없습니다. (레이건 대통령의 베를린 장벽 연설, 1987)

□ **affront** /əˈfrʌnt/   n. insult

(= slur, slight, offense, disrespect, injury)

The totalitarian world finds even symbols of love and of worship an affront. ("Ronald Reagan's Berlin Wall Speech, 1987")

전체주의 세계는 사랑과 예배의 상징들도 모욕이라고 생각합니다. (레이건 대통령의 베를린 장벽 연설, 1987)

□ **secular** /ˈsekjələr/   adj. non-religious

(= worldly, non-religious, material, lay)

Years ago, before the East Germans began rebuilding their churches, they erected a secular structure: the television tower at Alexander Platz. ("Ronald Reagan's Berlin Wall Speech, 1987")

수년 전, 동독 사람들이 그들의 교회를 재건축하기 전에 속세의 건물을 지었습니다: 알렉산더 플라츠에 있는 텔레비전 송출 타워입니다. (레이건 대통령의 베를린 장벽 연설, 1987)

☐ **exhaustion** /ɪgˈzɔːstʃən/　　　　n. extreme tiredness

(= fatigue, overtiredness, enervation)

We have seen the state of our Union in the endurance of rescuers working past exhaustion. ("George W. Bush's Post 9-11 Speech, 2001")

우리는 탈진의 상태를 넘어서까지 일하는 구조자들의 지구력을 보며 우리의 연방의 현실을 보았습니다. (조지 W.부시 대통령의 911 테러 후 연설)

☐ **unfurl** /ˌʌnˈfɜːrl/　　　　v. to unfold

(= unfold, expand, open up, spread out)

We've seen the unfurling of flags, ("George W. Bush's Post 9-11 Speech, 2001")

우리는 국기가 펼쳐지는 것을 보았습니다. (조지 W.부시 대통령의 911 테러 후 연설)

Practice 27.

Fill in the blank with the word that matches the definition provided

01   I _____ (express sorrow) when my best friend moved to another country.

02   Americans _____ (celebrate) independence on the 4th of July.

03   The Ministry of Transportation announced that it would strictly _____ (use authority to force) traffic regulations from January 1st.

04   I made a criticism, but he took it as a/an _____. (insult)

05   Just because Michael is a priest, it doesn't mean that he doesn't have _____ (worldly) needs.

06   I watched a little known movie about Mozart, which _____ (caused to arouse again) my love of classical music.

07   His behavior can be described only as _____ (absolute) foolishness.

08   When he stood up after falling off his bicycle, Greg noticed a long _____ (long deep cut) running down his leg, bleeding profusely.

09   My work is so tiring that every night I collapse on my bed in _____ (extreme tiredness)

10   Henry noticed a hint of _____ (implied) criticism in Helen's comment.

11   Our opponents may be more experienced, but we have more _____. (mental strength)

12 He made a/an _____ (perfunctory) gesture of reconciliation, but I knew he wasn't sincere.

13 The company is branching out into the field of _____ (air travel).

14 Seoul, Shanghai and Tokyo are all competing to be the aviation _____ (center) of Asia.

15 As there are many points to discuss on the _____ (matters to be discussed), let us begin our meeting.

Class 28

☐ **resolution** /ˌrezəˈluːʃn/   n. firmness of purpose

(= resolve, determination, doggedness, tenacity)

Our grief has turned to anger and anger to resolution. ("George W. Bush's Post 9-11 Speech, 2001")

우리의 슬픔은 분노가 되고, 분노는 결단력이 되었습니다. (조지 W.부시 대통령의 911 테러 후 연설)

☐ **cleric** /ˈklerɪk/   n. a member of clergy

(= priest, minister, ecclesiastic)

The terrorists practice is a fringe form of Islamic extremism that has been rejected by Muslim scholars and the vast majority of Muslim clerics.. ("George W. Bush's Post 9-11 Speech, 2001")

테러리스트 행위는 이슬람 극단주의의 한 비주류 움직임이며 무슬림 학자들과 다수의 이슬람 종교인들이 거부합니다. (조지 W.부시 대통령의 911 테러 후 연설)

☐ **fringe** /frɪndʒ/   adj. of the outer edge

(= peripheral, outlying, marginal, radical)

The terrorists practice a fringe form of Islamic extremism that has been rejected by Muslim scholars and the vast majority of Muslim clerics.. ("George W. Bush's Post 9-11 Speech, 2001")

테러리스트 행위는 이슬람 극단주의의 한 비주류 움직임이며 무슬림 학자들과 다수의 이슬람 종교인들이 거부합니다. (조지 W.부시 대통령의 911 테러 후 연설)

☐ **pervert** /pərˈvɜːrt/   v. to turn away from the right course

(= distort, misrepresent, deprave, spoil, corrupt)

..a fringe movement that perverts the peaceful teachings of Islam. ("George W. Bush's Post 9-11 Speech, 2001")

..평화로운 이슬람의 가르침을 왜곡하는 비주류 움직임.. (조지 W.부시 대통령의 911 테러 후 연설)

☐ **abet** /ə'bet/   v. to assist or encourage

(= support, urge, connive, incite)

By aiding and abetting murder, the Taliban regime is committing murder. ("George W. Bush's Post 9-11 Speech, 2001")

살인을 돕고 사주함으로써 탈레반 정권은 살인을 저지르고 있습니다. (조지 W.부시 대통령의 911 테러 후 연설)

☐ **blaspheme** /blæs'fiːm/   v. to insult religion

(= curse, swear, cuss)

..those who commit evil in the name of Allah blaspheme the name of Allah. ("George W. Bush's Post 9-11 Speech, 2001")

..알라신의 이름으로 악을 자행하는 자는 알라신의 이름을 모독하는 자입니다. (조지 W.부시 대통령의 911 테러 후 연설)

☐ **atrocity** /ə'trɑːsəti/   n. behavior or action that is wicked or ruthless

(= violence, viciousness, cruelty, barbarism)

With every atrocity, they hope that America grows fearful, retreating from the world and forsaking our friends. ("George W. Bush's Post 9-11 Speech, 2001")

그들은 악행을 저지르면 미국이 겁에 질리고 세상과 멀어지며 우리의 친구들을 멀리할 것이라고 기대합니다. (조지 W.부시 대통령의 911 테러 후 연설)

☐ **pretense** /'priːtens/   n. a false show of something

(= fabrication, hoax, deception, subterfuge, deceit)

We're not deceived by their pretenses to piety. ("George W. Bush's Post 9-11 Speech, 2001")

우리는 그들의 가식적 독실함에 속지 않습니다. (조지 W.부시 대통령의 911 테러 후 연설)

☐ **piety** /'paɪəti/   n. religious reverence

(= piousness, devoutness, devotion)

We're not deceived by their pretenses to piety. ("George W. Bush's Post 9-11 Speech, 2001")

우리는 그들의 가식적 독실함에 속지 않습니다. (조지 W.부시 대통령의 911 테러 후 연설)

□ **safeguard** /'seɪfgɑːrd/   v. to protect

(= defend, preserve, uphold)

He will lead, oversee and coordinate a comprehensive national strategy to safeguard our country against terrorism and respond to any attacks that may come. ("George W. Bush's Post 9-11 Speech, 2001")

그는 우리나라를 테러 행위로부터 보호하고 향후 받을 수 있는 그 어떤 공격에도 대응하기 위해 조성되는 통합적인 국가 전략을 이끌 것입니다. (조지 W.부시 대통령의 911 테러 후 연설)

□ **rally** /'ræli/   v. to draw or call together for a common action

(= unite, assemble, gather, collect)

The civilized world is rallying to America's side. ("George W. Bush's Post 9-11 Speech, 2001")

문명세계가 미국의 곁으로 집결합니다. (조지 W.부시 대통령의 911 테러 후 연설)

□ **bestow** /bɪ'stəʊ/   v. to present as a gift

(= give, confer, bequeath, grant)

I stand here today humbled by the task before us, grateful for the trust you have bestowed, mindful of the sacrifices borne by our ancestors. ("Barack Obama's Inauguration Speech, 2009")

저는 오늘 이 자리에서 우리 앞에 놓여진 과제에 겸손하며, 여러분들이 주신 믿음에 감사하며, 우리의 선조들이 겪은 희생을 기억합니다. (조지 W.부시 대통령의 911 테러 후 연설)

□ **amidst** /əmídst/   preposition. in the middle of

(= among, within, amid, during)

Yet, every so often the oath is taken amidst gathering clouds and raging storms. ("Barack Obama's Inauguration Speech, 2009")

그럼에도 불구하고 가끔씩 다가오는 먹구름과 내리치는 폭풍우의 와중에 맹세를 해야 합니다. (버락 오바마 대통령의 취임사 2009)

□ **forbearer**   n. ancestor

(= ancestor, forefather)

...because "We the People" have remained faithful to the ideals of our forbearers, and true to our founding documents. ("Barack Obama's Inauguration Speech, 2009")

..왜냐 하면, "우리 국민들은" 우리의 선조들의 이상에 충실하고, 우리의 건국 문서에 충직하였기 때문입니다. (버락 오바마 대통령의 취임사 2009)

☐ **petty** /ˈpeti/   adj. of little or no importance

(= trivial, inconsequential, insignificant, trifling, paltry)

On this day, we come to proclaim an end to the petty grievances and false promises, ("Barack Obama's Inauguration Speech, 2009")

오늘, 우리는 째째한 불만사항과 거짓 약속의 종말을 선언합니다. (버락 오바마 대통령의 취임사 2009)

☐ **recrimination** /rɪˌkrɪmɪˈneɪʃn/

n. the act of bringing countercharge against an accuser

(= accusation, countercharge, counter-allegation, retort, retaliation)

..the recriminations and worn-out dogmas, that for far too long have strangled our politics. ("Barack Obama's Inauguration Speech, 2009")

..우리의 정치를 너무 오랫동안 옥죄었던 비난과 낡아빠진 독단들.. (버락 오바마 대통령의 취임사 2009)

☐ **faint-hearted** /ˌfeɪnt ˈhɑːrtɪd/

adj. lacking courage, n. someone who lacks courage

(= fearful, timorous, apprehensive, tentative)

It has not been the path for the faint-hearted.. ("Barack Obama's Inauguration Speech, 2009")

그것은 심약한 사람들을 위한 길이 아니었습니다. (버락 오바마 대통령의 취임사 2009)

☐ **lash** /læʃ/   n. stroke

(= hit, blow, belt)

..endured the lash of the whip and plowed the hard earth. ("Barack Obama's Inauguration Speech, 2009")

채찍질을 견디고 땅을 갈아엎었으며.. (버락 오바마 대통령의 취임사 2009)

☐ **whip** /wɪp/   n. an instrument for striking

(= lash, rod, belt)

..endured the lash of the whip and plowed the hard earth. ("Barack Obama's Inauguration Speech, 2009")

채찍질을 견디고 땅을 갈아엎었으며.. (버락 오바마 대통령의 취임사 2009)

☐ **temper** /ˈtempər/   v. to soften or tone down

(= mitigate, alleviate, soften, assuage, palliate)

..our security emanates from the justness of our cause, the force of our example, the tempering qualities of humility and restraint. ("Barack Obama's Inauguration Speech, 2009")

우리의 안전은 우리의 대의의 정당성, 우리의 본보기의 힘, 그리고 겸손과 절제의 순화해주는 힘으로부터 나옵니다. (버락 오바마 대통령의 취임사 2009)

Practice 28.

Fill in the blank with the word that matches the definition provided

01 It is good to know that there are still people who _____ (protect) the traditional customs of our country.

02 On the day David arrived home from the hospital, all his friends _____ (called together for a common action) in front of his house to show their support.

03 There was _____ (firmness of purpose) in her eyes, when Mandy vowed that she would do better next semester.

04 Catholic, Christian and Muslim _____ (members of clergy) joined forces to condemn violence and promote peace and harmony.

05 My father has never given me money, but he did _____ (present as a gift) upon me the wisdom to live a fulfilling life.

06 The media's criticism of the government does not seem to _____ (tone down).

07 I am not so _____ (lacking courage) as to blame my mistakes on other people.

08 When rock and roll was first introduced, many people discarded it as a/an _____ (of the outer age) style of music that would not last.

09 We've had _____ (of little importance) bickerings from time to time, but we've been friends for over ten years.

10 The debate turned into a forum for mutual _____ (the act of bringing countercharges to an accuser)

11   There are no holy wars or good wars: all wars are _____. (wicked or evil activities)

12   When he was young his dream was to be a musician, but life's ups and down _____ (turn away from the right course) him to a career in crime.

13   The poor man fainted after receiving one _____ (stroke) from the policemen's baton.

14   Macbeth was _____ (assisted or encouraged) to murder by his wife.

15   Being an atheist does not give one the right to _____ (to insult religion) religions.

16   His _____ (a false show) fools no one.

☐ **specter** /ˈspektər/   n. some object or source of terror

(= threat, menace, shadow, possibility)

With old friends and former foes, we will work tirelessly to lessen the nuclear threat, and roll back the specter of a warming planet. ("Barack Obama's Inauguration Speech, 2009")

우리는 오래된 친구와 과거의 적과 함께 핵 위협을 줄이고자 쉼 없이 일을 할 것이며 지구온난화의 위협을 줄일 것입니다. (버락 오바마 대통령의 취임사 2009)

☐ **outlast** /ˌaʊtˈlæst/   v. to endure longer than

(= outlive, survive, endure)

..you cannot outlast us, and we will defeat you. ("Barack Obama's Inauguration Speech, 2009")

..당신들은 우리보다 오래 존재할 수 없습니다, 우리가 당신들을 멸할 것입니다. (버락 오바마 대통령의 취임사 2009)

☐ **patchwork** /ˈpætʃwɜːrk/

n. something made up from an incongruous variety of pieces

(= hodge-podge, mixture, collage, assortment)

For we know that our patchwork heritage is a strength, not a weakness.. ("Barack Obama's Inauguration Speech, 2009")

왜냐하면 우리는 우리의 서로 다른 문화가 합쳐져 생긴 유산이 취약점이 아니라 장점인 것을 알고 있기 때문입니다. (버락 오바마 대통령의 취임사 2009)

☐ **usher** /ˈʌʃər/   v. to show someone where to go

(= escort, accompany, shepherd, guide)

America must play its role in ushering in a new era of peace. ("Barack Obama's Inauguration Speech, 2009")

미국은 새로운 평화의 시대가 도래하는 데 안내원의 역할을 해야 합니다. (버락 오바마 대통령의 취임사 2009)

☐ **clench** /klentʃ/   v. to curl your fingers into a tight fist

(= tighten, clasp, clamp)

..but that we will extend a hand if you are willing to unclench your fist. ("Barack Obama's Inauguration Speech, 2009")

..당신들이 꽉 움켜진 주먹을 펼 의향이 있다면 우리는 당신을 향해 손을 내뻗을 것입니다.

☐ **embody** /ɪmˈbɑːdi/   v. to be a symbol or expression of an idea

(= exemplify, symbolize, represent, personify)

We honor them not only because they are guardians of our liberty, but because they embody the spirit of service.. ("Barack Obama's Inauguration Speech, 2009")

우리는 그들이 우리의 자유의 수호인일 뿐 아니라 그들이 헌신의 상징이기 때문에 그들에게 존경을 표합니다. (버락 오바마 대통령의 취임사 2009)

☐ **levee** /ˈlevi/   n. an embankment along a river

(= embankment, bank, wall)

It is the kindness to take in a stranger when the levees break.. ("Barack Obama's Inauguration Speech, 2009")

강둑이 터져 홍수가 날 때 일면식 없는 사람을 자기 집으로 들이는 것 같은 친절입니다. (버락 오바마 대통령의 취임사 2009)

☐ **storm** /stɔːrm/   v. to enter or leave a place quickly and noisily

(= stamp, stalk, march)

It is the firefighter's courage to storm a stairway filled with smoke.. ("Barack Obama's Inauguration Speech, 2009")

연기로 가득찬 층계를 뛰어올라가는 소방관의 용기입니다. (버락 오바마 대통령의 취임사 2009)

☐ **virtue** /ˈvɜːrtʃuː/   n. thinking and doing what is right

(= goodness, integrity, honesty, morality)

With hope and virtue, let us brave once more the icy currents, and endure what storms may come. ("Barack Obama's Inauguration Speech, 2009")

희망과 선행을 가지고 우리가 얼음이 떠가는 물줄기를 헤치고 나갈 수 있게, 그 어떤 폭풍우가 쳐도 견딜 수 있게 허락해 주십시오. (버락 오바마 대통령의 취임사 2009)

☐ **brave** /breɪv/

v. to deliberately expose oneself to difficulty or danger

(= face, endure, suffer, confront)

With hope and virtue, let us brave once more the icy currents, and endure what storms may come. ("Barack Obama's Inauguration Speech, 2009")

희망과 선행을 가지고 우리가 얼음이 떠가는 물줄기를 헤치고 나갈 수 있게, 그 어떤 폭풍우가 쳐도 견딜 수 있게 허락해 주십시오. (버락 오바마 대통령의 취임사 2009)

☐ **falter** /ˈfɔːltər/   v. to lose power or strength in an uneven way

(= waver, weaken, abate, stagger, stumble)

..that we did not turn back nor did we falter.. ("Barack Obama's Inauguration Speech, 2009")

..우리가 등돌리지도 휘청거리지도 않았습니다. (버락 오바마 대통령의 취임사 2009)

☐ **allegiance** /əˈliːdʒəns/   n. support and loyalty

(= loyalty, commitment, adherence, fidelity)

What makes us exceptional -- what makes us American -- is our allegiance to an idea articulated in a declaration made more than two centuries ago: ("Barack Obama's Inauguration Speech, 2013")

우리를 특별하게 만드는 것 – 우리를 미국인으로 만드는 것 – 은 우리가 무려 2세기 전의 선언문에 설명된 이상에 충성한다는 것입니다. (버락 오바마 대통령의 취임사 2009)

☐ **outworn** /ˈaʊtwɔːrn/   adj. worn out

(= decrepit, obsolete, antiquated, archaic)

We understand that outworn programs are inadequate to the needs of our time. ("Barack Obama's Inauguration Speech, 2013")

우리는 오래된 프로그램들이 이 시대의 요구에 불충분하다는 것을 압니다. (버락 오바마 대통령의 취임사 2009)

☐ **revamp** /ˌriːˈvæmp/   v. to make changes of improvement

(= refurbish, restore, overhaul, make over)

So we must harness new ideas and technology to remake our government, revamp our tax code, reform our schools, ("Barack Obama's Inauguration Speech, 2013")

우리는 우리의 정부를 재건하고, 세법을 개선하고, 학교를 개혁하기 위해 새로운 아이디어를 활용해야 합니다. (버락 오바마 대통령의 취임사 2009)

......

□ **creed** /kriːd/   n. set of beliefs or principles

(= faith, dogma, credo, principle, belief)

That is what will give real meaning to our creed. ("Barack Obama's Inauguration Speech, 2013")

그것은 우리의 신조에 참 의미를 부여할 것입니다. (버락 오바마 대통령의 취임사 2009)

......

□ **vigilant** /ˈvɪdʒɪlənt/

adj. to give careful attention to noticing any danger or trouble

(= watchful, attentive, cautious, observant)

The knowledge of their sacrifice will keep us forever vigilant against those who would do us harm. ("Barack Obama's Inauguration Speech, 2013")

그들이 우리를 위해 한 희생의 기억이 우리에게 해를 가하고자 하는 사람들에 대한 경계심을 항상 가지게 해줄 것입니다. (버락 오바마 대통령의 취임사 2009)

......

□ **unsung** /ˌʌnˈsʌŋ/

adj. to not be praised or acknowledged, especially when deserving to be praised or acknowledged

(= unrecognized, nameless, unacknowledged, unrewarded)

.. just as it guided all those men and women, sung and unsung, who left footprints along this great land.. ("Barack Obama's Inauguration Speech, 2013")

.. 추앙을 받건 잊혀졌건 이 위대한 땅에 발자국을 남긴 많은 남녀들을 안내하였듯이.. (버락 오바마 대통령의 취임사 2009)

......

□ **absolutism** /ˈæbsəluːtɪzəm/

n. a political system in which one ruler or leader has complete authority or power over a country

(= totalitarianism, despotism, dictatorship, autocracy)

We cannot mistake absolutism for principle…("Barack Obama's Inauguration Speech, 2013")

우리는 절대주의를 원칙으로 오해하면 안 됩니다. (버락 오바마 대통령의 취임사 2009)

☐ **succumb** /sə'kʌm/   v. to give in

(= yield, surrender, capitulate, accede)

..we have never relinquished our skepticism of central authority, nor have we succumbed to the fiction that all society's ills can be cured through government alone. ("Barack Obama's Inauguration Speech, 2013")

..우리는 중앙집권적인 권력에 대한 비관적인 생각을 포기한 적도 없고, 모든 사회악을 정부 혼자서 해결해줄 수 있다는 허구에 빠진 적도 없습니다. (버락 오바마 대통령의 취임사 2009)

☐ **relinquish** /rɪ'lɪŋkwɪʃ/   v. to give up voluntarily

(= surrender, abandon, resign, renounce)

..we have never relinquished our skepticism of central authority, nor have we succumbed to the fiction that all society's ills can be cured through government alone. ("Barack Obama's Inauguration Speech, 2013")

..우리는 중앙집권적인 권력에 대한 비관적인 생각을 포기한 적도 없고, 모든 사회악을 정부 혼자서 해결해줄 수 있다는 허구에 빠진 적도 없습니다. (버락 오바마 대통령의 취임사 2009)

Practice 29.

Fill in the blank with the word that matches the definition provided

01 These boots are too _____ (worn out) for hiking.

02 The new mayor promised to _____ (to make improvements) the decrepit public transportation system of the city.

03 His speech _____ (symbolized) the spirit of perseverance.

04 I was enjoying a quiet morning in the café, when a bunch of boisterous teenagers _____ (entered noisily) in.

05 The professor called my paper a/an _____ (made up of pieces) of incongruent ramblings.

06 The maître d' _____ (showed where to go) us to our table, where our friends were waiting.

07 He _____ (made a fist) his fists in anger.

08 Andy's face was as white as if he had seen a/an _____ (some object of terror)

09 Bill always complains of being ill, but he is actually very healthy and will probably _____ (endure longer than) all the rest of us.

10 Nowadays, most people will change jobs at the drop of the hat when offered more money – no one has _____ (loyalty) to one's employers anymore.

11 A true person of _____ (integrity) is one that does as if someone is looking when no one is looking.

12 Some say that, in modern times, we need to be paranoid and _____ (extremely watchful of any danger) to survive.

13 We do the unappreciated, _____ (unrecognized) work that no one else wants to do.

14 Calm down. Do not _____ (give in) to anger and do something rash.

15 The founder of the company _____ (gave up voluntarily) his authority when he turned 65.

16 Many police officers and volunteers _____ (deliberately expose oneself to danger) through the forest to find the missing boy.

17 The wind was so strong I _____ (stumbled) while walking to my car.

Find the correct word which can replace the bold phrase in the following sentences. Change the word form appropriately to fit the sentence, if necessary

reassurance, rekindle, mainstream, ration, degenerate, despised, hamlet, vivid, fragmentation, windfall, mandate, inextricable, quest, discord, sweltering

01 The heat outside was so _____ that I was sweating profusely by the time I walked around the block.

02 The famous pianist Frank Dillard says that when he was a boy, he _____ going to piano classes while his friends were in the park playing baseball.

03 What was supposed to be a civilized discussion quickly _____ into a yelling match between the two opposing groups.

04 Most people nowadays agree that global warming is _____ to carbon emissions.

05 Most of modern South American countries speak Spanish because Spain was the first country to send explorers to the continent in its _____ for gold.

06 In running a democracy, some _____ is considered healthy because it means that no one is afraid to speak out his own opinion.

07 George seems like an urban gentleman, but he actually grew up in a small _____ in the country.

08 We were terrified when grandmother told us _____ stories of how she escaped from North Korea right before the war.

09 Dad told me to trust him to make me a good baseball player, but, frankly, he didn't give me much _____.

10 Not many people know that hip-hop music had been around for more than a decade before it entered the _____ in the late 1980s.

11 During the 1970s, there was much _____ in the U.S. due to the divided public opinion about the country's involvement in the Vietnam War.

12 Dad received a sudden _____ of U$2,000 in the form of a tax refund.

13 The new tax law _____ that high income earners must pay more in income tax.

14 With very little water left, we had to _____ what was left for drinking and cooking and stop usage for washing.

15 Finding my old comic books in my parents' attic has _____ my love for super-hero comics.

---

token, hub, affront, resolution, impose, commemorate, fringe, safeguard, bestow, temper, usher, abet, atrocity, pretense, brave

16 Many women argue that modern system still _____ unfair demands on women.

17 The Post Service decided to issue a new postal stamp to _____ the 70th anniversary of the ending of WWII.

18 The government promised to take measures to reduce the unemployment rate but, so far, has only made _____ gestures.

19 The international airports in Inchon, Shanghai and Osaka are in competition to become the transportation _____ of Asia.

20 Many immigrants took the politician's claim that illegal immigrants are causing many problems in the country as an _____.

21 Everyone could see that Sarah's _____ to win the competition was firm.

22 In the last election, the three main parties won over 94% of all votes while the four _____ parties only won 6%.

23 Macbeth's wife _____ Macbeth in the murder of the Scottish King.

24 The Nuremburg trials disclosed many of the horrible _____ the Nazis committed during WWII.

25 When Carry introduced her boyfriend to her mother, she asked all kinds of embarrassing questions, under the _____ of being interested in him.

26 We must take measures to _____ the environment now, so that future generations may enjoy an uncontaminated environment.

27 Many socio-economists believe that the reason for higher savings rates of Asians compared to those of Americans or Europeans is that Asians feel more social pressure to _____ a large portion of their wealth to their children before they die.

28 Try as she did, Helen found it hard to _____ her anger at the man who robbed her store, when she saw him in the defense stand in the court room.

29 Having identified himself to the receptionist, Greg was quickly _____ into a conference room where interviews were to be carried out.

30 Realizing that his daughter was still stuck in the burning hut, Karl _____ the flames to save her.

Select the pair of words that most nearly expresses the same relationship

31   renounce: relinquish
      A. unsung: lionized
      B. revamp: continue
      C. allegiance: loyalty
      D. falter: energize

32   obsolete: outworn
      A. creed: vigilance
      B. succumb, surrender
      C. virtue: betrayal
      D. embody: overwhelm

33   clench: tighten
      A. usher: evict
      B. whip: extol
      C. petty: lame
      D. specter: threat

34   rally: disperse
      A. timorous: courageous
      B. unanimous: undivided
      C. abolish: entertain
      D. artifice: indulgence

35   windfall: bonus
      A. lash: storm
      B. pious: blasphemous
      C. patchwork: assortment
      D. pervert: preserve

36   hub: fringe
      A. token: sincere
      B. mourn: lament
      C. dissuasion: aviation
      D. exhausted: enervated

37 fortitude: resilience
    A. denomination: disintegration
    B. ration: infringe
    C. erosion: convention
    D. slight: offense

38 jangle: ring
    A. cartel: inflation
    B. nullification: annulment
    C. brutality: magnanimity
    D. foe: devotee

39 interwoven: inextricable
    A. barren: desolate
    B. redemptive: amicable
    C. nominal: commensurate
    D. invert: discern

40 immobility: paralysis
    A. impediment: route
    B. evasive: hallowed
    C. dramatize: embellish
    D. rudeness: civility

Choose the word that isn't a synonym

41 mandate – languish – deteriorate

42 default – oblige – impose

43 hallowed – sacred – asunder

44 torrid – infringed – sweltering

45 barren – refresh – invigorate

46 cruelty – entreaty – brutality

47 discord – dissonance – diffusive

48 hamlet – cabinet – village

49   association – folly – cartel

50   patronize – abandon – relinquish

51   autocracy – enfranchisement – absolutism

52   creed – dogma – constituent

53   intrigue – embankment – levee

54   unfurl – bestow – confer

55   secular – temporal – pious

56   evasive – redemptive – elusive

57   agenda – plan – strife

58   resilience – fortitude – affront

59   insidious – implicit – implied

60   deception – pretense – manifestation

Class 31

□ **lofty** /ˈlɔːfti/   adj. very tall or high

(= high)

One can see the lofty tower of the church from far away.

멀리서 그 높은 탑을 볼 수 있다.

             adj. showing a proud or superior attitude

(= arrogant, condescending)

He spoke in a lofty manner that left many feeling insulted.

그가 거만한 말투를 써서 많은 사람들이 모욕감을 느꼈다.

□ **distinct** /dɪˈstɪŋkt/   adj. not the same

(= different, separate)

Potatoes come in many distinct varieties.

감자는 종류가 다양하다.

             adj. unmistakable

(= definite)

Cilantro is a herb with a distinct taste.

고수는 특이한 향이 나는 허브이다.

□ **graze** /greɪz/   v. to feed on growing grass

Sheep graze in the fields all day.

양들이 온종일 들에서 풀을 뜯고 있다.

             v. to touch lightly in passing

He tried to punch me, but his fist only grazed my arm.

그는 나에게 주먹을 날렸지만, 내 팔에 스치기만 하였다.

□ **posture** /ˈpɑːstʃər/   n. the way one holds one's body

(= pose, position)

Good posture helps young children to grow taller.

좋은 자세를 취하는 것이 아이들이 키가 크게 자라는 데 도움을 준다.

       v. to assume a particular position

Raymond postured as if he were a martial arts specialist.

레이먼드는 그가 마치 무술고수인 것처럼 폼을 잡았다.

□ **motion** /ˈmoʊʃn/   v. to signal

(= signal)

I motioned to him to be quiet.

나는 그에게 조용히 하라고 손짓을 했다.

n. a suggestion on which members at a meeting must vote

I will cast a vote against the motion.

나는 그 안건에 반대표를 던졌다.

□ **shed** /ʃed/   v. to lose or give up

(= lose)

Deciduous trees shed their leaves in the autumn.

낙엽수림은 가을이 되면 잎이 떨어진다.

       v. to cause to flow

(= run)

I shed copious tears while watching the sad movie.

나는 슬픈 영화를 보면서 눈물을 한 바가지로 흘렸다.

□ **punctuate** /ˈpʌŋktʃueɪt/

v. to add marks to writing to make the meaning clear

n. punctuation

Try to punctuate your sentences more clearly.

문장을 쓸 때 구둣점을 더 확실하게 찍도록 해 봐.

v. to interrupt from time to time

His speech was punctuated by applause from the audience.

그가 연설하는 동안 가끔씩 청중들이 박수를 보냈다.

☐ **inept** /ɪˈnept/   adj. lacking in skill or ability

(= unskillful, bungling)

He is skilled at doing research but inept at presenting the results of that research.

그는 연구실력은 출중하지만 연구결과를 발표하는 데는 서투르다.

adj. not suitable for the occasion

(= inappropriate)

He made an inept joke.

그는 적절치 못한 농담을 했다.

☐ **brisk** /brɪsk/   adj. quick and active

(= quick, energetic)

I take a brisk walk during my lunch break every day.

나는 점심시간마다 짧고 빠른 산책을 한다.

adj. stimulating, refreshing

A brisk wind blew in from the sea.

상쾌한 바닷바람이 불었다.

☐ **appropriate** /əˈprəʊpriət/   adj. suitable or right for the purpose

(= suitable)

Always wear appropriate clothing when going to an interview.

면접을 하러 갈 때는 항상 적절한 옷차림을 하도록 해.

v. to set aside for a particular purpose

The company appropriates a certain percentage of profits for charity.

그 회사는 이익금 중 일부를 기부한다.

☐ **compose** /kəmˈpəʊz/   v. to create or write a poem or music

(= write, create)

n. composition

Mozart composed his first symphony when he was seven.

모짜르트는 일곱 살 때 첫 교향곡을 작곡하였다.

v. to quiet or calm

(= soothe, pacify)

n. composure

Please compose yourself. It's nothing to get excited about.

진정하세요. 흥분할 일 아닙니다.

□ **trace** /treɪs/   n. a very small amount

(= sign, speck)

There was a trace of blood at the crime scene.

범죄현장에 아주 미량의 혈흔이 있었다.

n. a mark or sign left behind

The airplane vanished from the radar without a trace.

비행기가 레이더에서 흔적도 없이 사라졌다.

□ **trace** /treɪs/   v. to follow the trail of

(= locate, pursue, track)

All the evidence trace to this house.

모든 증거가 그의 집을 가리켰다.

v. to copy through thin paper

I traced the picture to my notebook.

나는 공책에 그 그림을 베껴 그렸다.

□ **loom** /luːm/   n. a machine or device for weaving cloth

In the past a family's loom was handed down from mother to daughter.

과거에는 배틀을 어머니가 딸에게 대물림해주었다.

v. to appear suddenly

A bear loomed out of the trees, frightening the campers.

숲 속에서 곰이 갑자기 등장해 캠핑족들이 다들 놀랐다.

v. to get frighteningly close

While Terry was wasting time, final exams loomed.

테리가 시간을 낭비하는 동안 기말시험은 부쩍 앞으로 다가왔다.

☐ **lull** /lʌl/   n. a temporary calm or quiet period

(= break, hiatus, calm)

Dad is usually very busy with his business, but he enjoys a lull during the summer.

아버지는 항상 사업으로 바쁘시지만 여름에는 한시적으로 한가한 시간을 보내신다.

                                                                    v. to cause to relax

(= relax, soothe)

His mother's voice lulled to boy to sleep.

엄마의 나긋나긋한 목소리가 아이를 잠들게 하였다.

Practice 31.

01 I used my dad's old diary to _____ (follow the trail of) the journey he took when he was my age.

02 I was so distraught at the news that I found it difficult to _____ (calm) myself.

03 After I _____ (set aside) money for my bills, food and a small savings account, I have almost nothing left for leisure.

04 If Mozart were alive today, he would most likely _____ (write music) on a computer.

05 I thought the clothes he was wearing was _____ (not suitable for the occasion) for a job interview.

06 _____ (small amounts) of iridium, a very rare substance, found under the ground proved that this was the site where a meteor struck the Earth over a billion years ago.

07 Johnnie attempted to kick the ball in mid-air, but his foot only _____ (touch lightly in passing) the ball.

08 Over 70 percent of the delegates cast votes against the _____ (a suggestion to be voted on).

09 She tried to remain calm, but there was a/an _____ (unmistakable) edginess in her voice.

10 Dr. Roberts _____ (interrupt from time to time) his speech with several jokes and humorous anecdotes.

11 Every spring, my cats and dogs _____ (lose) so much hair that I constantly have to vacuum my apartment.

12 After several _____ (quick and active) morning meetings, the rest of my day was quite leisurely.

13 There has been a _____ (temporary quiet period) in traffic violations since the police announced that they will enforce traffic laws very strictly in the future.

14 While the many people were engulfed in euphoria, some warned that a crisis _____ (is very close).

☐ **charge** /tʃɑːrdʒ/   n. a duty or responsibility

(= care, trust)

Mr. Douglas is the Chairman, so he doesn't have charge of the day to day operations of the company.

더글러스 씨는 회장이기 때문에 회사의 세세한 업무는 책임지지 않는다.

She was introduced to the nature of the charge that was thrust upon her.

그녀는 책임져야 할 업무에 대해 지침을 받았다.

☐ **subject** /ˈsʌbdʒɪkt/

n. a person who is under the rule of a sovereign

(= citizen, subordinate)

He was a ruthless king, and his subjects secretly despised him.

그는 잔혹한 군주였고, 백성들은 은밀하게 그를 경멸하였다.

☐ **form** /fɔːrm/   n. a customary order of doing something

(= formality, custom)

He followed form and asked his mother to speak to a match-maker to arrange his marriage with the girl.

그는 관습대로 어머니에게 중매인에게 말하여 그와 여자의 결혼을 주선해 달라고 요청했다.

☐ **qualify** /ˈkwɑːlɪfaɪ/   v. to modify or limit in some way.

(= restrict, moderate, temper, modify)

Let me qualify my statement. I didn't mean that my job is useless. It's just that I wish for more challenging work.

제가 한 말에 제한을 걸겠습니다. 제 일이 쓸모없다는 말이 아니라 좀 더 진취적인 일을 하고 싶다는 말이었습니다.

□ **industry** /ˈɪndəstri/   n. energetic, devoted attitude at work

(= diligence, passion)

The young man had the industry expected of an ambitious and outgoing new employee.

그 젊은이는 야망 있고 외향적인 신입사원에게 기대되는 근면성이 있었다.

□ **constitution** /ˌkɑːnstɪˈtuːʃn/   n. physical character of the body

(= health, disposition)

He was a bright fellow but of a weak constitution, which prevented him from participating in the various activities that are reserved for people his age.

그는 머리는 영리하였으나 신체적으로 약했다. 그래서 그 나잇 또래의 아이들이 참여하는 여러 가지 활동에 참여할 수 없었다.

□ **husbandry** /ˈhʌzbəndri/   n. farming

(= farming, agriculture, crop growing)

His family has been in animal husbandry for four generations.

그의 집안은 4대째 목축업을 하고 있다.

     n. careful and thrifty management

(= thriftiness, frugality, conservation)

During times of drought, the local people must exercise strict husbandry of their food reserves to prevent starvation.

가뭄 기간에 현지 사람들은 그들의 식량을 엄격히 절약해야 기아를 방지할 수 있다.

□ **faculty** /ˈfæklti/   n. the ability for a particular kind of action

(= ability, facility, capability, capacity)

Although my great grandfather is 96, he still retains all his mental and physical faculties perfectly.

우리 할아버지는 96세이지만 아직도 정신적, 육체적 능력을 완벽히 보유하신다.

□ **sublime** /səˈblaɪm/   adj. impressing the mind

(= awesome, inspiring, superb)

The Kingdome of Bhutan is famous for its sublime beauty.
부탄 왕국은 경이로운 아름다움으로 유명하다.

☐ **subliminal** /ˌsʌbˈlɪmɪnl/   adj. affecting without awareness

(= subconscious, unconscious, unintentional, hidden)

Scientists have discovered that, in a conversation, we understand only 25% from the spoken words and the remaining 75% from subliminal body language.
과학자들에 의하면 우리는 대화의 내용을 언어로 25%, 그리고 무의식적인 몸동작으로 75% 이해한다.

☐ **sublimate** /ˈsʌblɪmeɪt/

v. to direct negative energy to a more socially acceptable activity

(= channel, redirect, reroute)

He was a juvenile delinquent, but as he matured, he learned to sublimate his anti-social tendencies to fighting crime in the police force.
그는 어려서 청소년 범죄자였지만 나이가 들고는 그의 반사회적인 성향을 경찰에서 범죄와 싸우는 것으로 해소하였다.

☐ **temperament** /ˈtemprəmənt/

n. the mental, physical and emotional traits of a person

(= nature, character, disposition)

He was a leader by temperament.
그에게는 리더 기질이 있다.

☐ **culture** /ˈkʌltʃər/

n. a cultivation of microorganisms such as bacteria

Greek yogurt is made from special cultures extracted from milk.
그리스 요거트는 우유에서 추출하는 특별한 균으로 만들어진다.

v. to grow microorganisms such as bacteria

Alexander Hamilton was the first person to culture bacteria extracted from bread mold and discover penicillin.
알렉산더 플레밍은 최초로 빵 곰팡이에서 추출한 균을 배양하여 페니실린을 발견한 사람이다.

☐ **strain** /streɪn/   n. a variety of micro organisms

(= type, variety)

In 1982, scientists discovered a strain of virus in a patient that was up till then known only to afflict wild monkeys.

1982년에 과학자들은 그때까지 야생 원숭이에게만 존재한다고 알려진 바이러스를 환자에게서 발견했다.

n. a body of decedents from the same ancestor

(= breed, species, kind)

Darwin discovered that all the finches on the Galapagos Islands were of the same strain despite having differently shaped beaks.

다윈은 갈라파고스의 모든 핀치가 부리 모양은 다 다르지만 같은 종의 새라는 걸 발견했다.

v. to pour liquid through a filter to hold back the denser solid matter

(= filter, sieve)

After boiling the potatoes until they are tender, strain the water and let them cool.

푹 익을 때까지 감자를 삶고 나서 물을 부어내고 식히세요.

☐ **game** /geɪm/
adj. of an animal or bird hunted chiefly for sport

Aside from being famous as one of the most successful Presidents in U.S. history, Theodore Roosevelt was also an accomplished hunter, who hunted big game animals like lions and elephants in Africa.

테오도어 루스벨트는 미국 역사상 가장 유명한 대통령 중의 하나였을 뿐만 아니라 아프리카에서 사자나 코끼리 같은 큰 동물을 사냥하는 매우 숙달된 사냥꾼이기도 하였다.

☐ **game** /geɪm/
adj. willing to do something that is usually dangerous or risky

(= willing, ready, inclined)

Although I was scared, I was game to try skydiving.

n. authorization

(= authorization, permission, approval)

The Free Trade Agreement requires the sanction of congress.

나는 겁은 났지만 스카이다이빙을 시도할 의향이 있었다.

□ **sanction(s)** /ˈsæŋkʃn/   n. authorization

(=authorization, permission, approval)

The Free Trade Agreement requires the sanction of congress.

자유무역협정이 체결되기 위해서는 상원의 비준이 필요하다.

                         n. restrictions

(= restrictions, penalty, ban)

During the era of Apartheid, economic sanctions were imposed on South Africa.

인종차별 정책 중에 남아프리카 공화국에 경제 제재가 가해졌다.

□ **institution** /ˌɪnstɪˈtuːʃn/   n. an established custom

(= tradition, convention, ritual, custom)

People of the older generation say that Westernization has ruined many traditional institutions.

나이든 세대의 사람들은 서방화가 많은 전통 관습을 망쳐 놓았다고 말한다.

                         n. a famous person

(= celebrity)

After serving in the Constitutional Court for over 40 years, Justice Higgins is an institution within the American judiciary system.

헌법재판소에서 40년간 재직한 히긴스 판사는 미국의 사법부 내에서 유명인사이다.

□ **institutionalize**
v. to place in an institution (usually such as a hospital, rehab center or old people's home)

Gary's addiction to alcohol was so severe that his family had him institutionalized.

게리의 알코올 중독이 너무 심해 그의 가족은 그를 재활병원에 입원시켰다.

□ **municipal** /mjuːˈnɪsɪpl/
adj. pertaining to the internal affairs of a state or country

(= internal)

In the decades leading up to the Civil War, the U.S. regarded slavery as a municipal issue and didn't take kindly to criticisms from Europe.

남북전쟁이 일어나기 이전 수십 년 동안 미국에서는 노예제도를 국내의 문제로 간주하여 유럽에서 들려오는 비판의 목소리를 달가워하지 않았다.

☐ **fowl** /faʊl/

n. a bird (especially one that is domesticated for consumption as food for humans)

(= bird, chicken)

The bird flu spread like wildfire, killing thousands of fowl.

조류독감이 들불처럼 번지며 수천 마리의 닭과 가금을 죽였다.

☐ **inclination** /ˌɪnklɪ'neɪʃn/   n. a tendency towards a certain condition

(= disposition, penchant, fondness)

At social gatherings, my inclination is to sit quietly in the corner: I am an introvert.

모임 장소에 가면 나는 주로 구석에 가만히 앉아 있는 경향이 있다: 나는 내성적이다.

☐ **inclination**   n. a slope

(= slope, slant, gradient)

The light house was on top of a hill with a steep inclination.

등대는 가파른 언덕 꼭대기에 있었다.

☐ **to put on an air**   idiom. to pretend to be good or superior

(= to act superior, to be arrogant)

Despite being an extremely rich and important person, Mark does not put on airs.

매우 돈이 많고 중요한 사람임에도 불구하고 마크는 거드름을 피우지 않는다.

01 Mr. Druid was wrong to initiate the marketing plan without receiving _____ (authorization) from the company management.

02 The _____ (slope) of the hill was so steep that it was impossible to walk up.

03 James is not a vegetarian, but he abstains from eating red meat: I'll fix him a/an _____(bird) dish.

04 With his wife dead and his daughter working full time, Mr. Williams had to be _____ (sent to an old people's home)

05 His boss told George to show more _____ (energetic attitude towards work) at his job.

06 They misunderstood my meaning because I wasn't allowed to _____ (modify) my statement.

07 I can't explain why these ceremonies are done this way: I only follow the _____ (custom) I learned from my elders when I was young.

08 I dared my friends to come bungee jumping with me, but no one was _____ (illing)

09 Boil the vegetables for half an hour and _____ (filter) the liquid, to use later.

10 The vet took a cotton-swab, wiped the inside of my dog's mouth and _____ grew bacteria) the germs to see if the dog was infected by any kind of virus.

11 When a teenager, William would get very depressed, but he soon learned to _____ (channel or reroute) this negative energy into writing, and that's how he became an author.

12 Mr. King, the most popular teacher in school, has taught French at this school for over 25 years. He is something of a/an _____ (celebrity) among the students and graduates.

13 From a very young age, Dr. Hawking had the _____ (ability) to understand very complex issues.

14 With the harvest being bad, the villagers will have to exercise extreme _____ (conservation) to survive the winter.

15 When 21, William married a bubbly 17 year old girl with a healthy _____ (physical character), and during their 65 year marriage, they sired 6 children, 21 grandchildren and 54 great grandchildren.

16 Sandra found most of the art works collected in the museum to be _____ (very impressive).

obtuse vs obdurate vs obfuscate

obtuse /əb'tu:s/   adj. lacking wit

(= dull-witted, simpleminded, stupid, thick)

His obtuse questions vexed everyone.

그의 아둔한 질문들이 모두를 짜증나게 했다.

obdurate /'ɑ:bdərət/   adj. being stubborn

(= obstinate, inflexible, pigheaded, unbending)

We don't understand the reason for his obdurate refusal to our proposal.

그가 우리 제안을 저렇게 고집스럽게 거부하는 이유를 모르겠다.

obfuscate /'ɑ:bfəskeɪt/   v. to obscure (the truth)

(= obscure, complicate, confuse)

Sometimes having too much information will only just obfuscate the situation more.

어떨 때는 정보가 너무 많은 것이 상황을 더 혼란스럽게만 할 수 있다.

ethereal vs ephemeral

ethereal /ɪ'θɪriəl/   adj. extremely delicate and refined

(= fragile, frail, delicate)

She had an ethereal beauty.

그녀는 천상의 아름다움을 가졌다.

ephemeral /ɪ'femərəl/   adj. passing quickly

(= fleeting, brief, transitory, evanescent)

Life is ephemeral.

삶은 덧없다.

tantalize vs titillate vs palpitate

tantalize /ˈtæntəlaɪz/   v. to tease by arousing expectation
(= entice, provoke, frustrate)

Jim tantalized me by giving me one raisin at a time when he knew I was hungry.
짐은 내가 배고픈 걸 알면서도 건포도를 하나씩 주며 감질나게 했다.

titillate /ˈtɪtɪleɪt/   v. to excite
(= rouse, tempt, excite)

Television networks have jacked up the level of violence and adult content in programs to titillate their viewers.
텔레비전 방송국들은 폭력물 및 성인 컨텐츠를 늘려 시청자들을 매료시키려 한다.

palpitate /ˈpælpɪteɪt/   v. to beat with unusual rapidity
(= beat, throb, pulse, pulsate, pound)

Henry felt his heart palpitating harder when he saw Janet walking towards him.
헨리는 자넷이 그를 향해 걸어오는 것을 보자 가슴이 뛰기 시작했다.

odious vs onerous vs ominous

odious /ˈəʊdiəs/   adj. deserving or causing hatred
(= hateful, abhorrent, loathsome, detestable)

Many Westerners consider eating live octopus odious, but in Korea, live octopus is a delicacy many people enjoy.
많은 서양인들은 생낙지를 먹는 것을 끔찍하게 생각하지만, 한국에서는 많은 사람들이 생낙지를 별미로 즐겨 먹는다.

onerous /ˈəʊnərəs/   adj. causing hardship
(= burdensome, arduous, difficult)

With Janet's mother travelling out of town, Janet has the onerous task of taking care of her three rambunctious younger brothers for two days.

자넷의 어머니가 도시 밖으로 여행하는 동안, 자넷은 세 명의 날뛰는 남동생들을 이틀 간 돌보아야 하는 힘겨운 일을 맡았다.

ominous /ˈɑːmɪnəs/　　　　　　　　adj. foreboding evil

(= threatening, warning, menacing)

An ominous silence engulfed the room.

불길한 침묵이 방을 에워쌌다.

☐ **meander vs wander**

meander /miˈændər/　　　　　　　v. to wander aimlessly

(= wander, ramble, roam)

We meandered the streets for hours deep in conversation.

우리는 몇 시간 동안 깊은 대화를 하며 길을 싸돌아다녔다.

wander /ˈwɑːndər/　　　　　　　　v. to go without aim or purpose

(= ramble, roam, meander)

Stay here. Do not wander off.

여기 있어. 아무데도 가지 마.

☐ **ingenuous vs ingenious**

ingenuous /ɪnˈdʒenjuəs/　　　　　adj. to be very trusting

(= trusting, innocent, gullible, naïve)

If you believe that you can score high in the SAT just by watching this lecture once, you are ingenuous.

당신이 이 강의를 한 번 들었다고 SAT에서 고득점을 받을 거라고 생각한다면 매우 순진한 겁니다.

ingenious /ɪnˈdʒiːniəs/　　　　　　adj. to be very clever

(= clever, resourceful, imaginative, creative)

We launched an ingenious plan to strike revenge on our enemies.

우리는 적군에게 복수를 가할 기발한 계획을 짰다.

□ melee vs milieu

melee /ˈmeɪleɪ/   n. a noisy confusing fight

(= fight, brawl, ruckus, skirmish)

The argument soon developed into a full melee that continued until the police arrived.

단순한 의견 충돌이 곧 시끌벅적한 싸움으로 번져 경찰이 올 때까지 계속되었다.

milieu /mɪlˈjuː/   n. social and cultural surroundings

(= environment, background, ambiance, setting)

At the time, the social milieu of her country prevented her from marrying a man from a poor family

그 당시 그녀가 살았던 나라의 사회 분위기상 그녀가 가난한 집의 남자와 결혼하는 것은 불가능하였다.

□ affect vs effect

affect /əˈfekt/   v. to impress the mind or move the feelings of

(= influence)

n. affect

This book affected my life in many ways.

이 책은 내 인생에 큰 영향을 끼쳤다.

affect /əˈfekt/   v. to give the appearance of

(= pretend, feign)

affected /ɪˈfekt/   adj.

While affecting indifference, he pried information from her without her noticing.

그는 무관심한 척하면서도 그녀 모르게 정보를 빼내려하였다.

effect   n. a result or consequence

(= result, consequence, outcome, conclusion)

v. effect

This cough syrup has a strange effect on me. I feel drowsy.

기침 시럽을 먹었더니 이상한 부작용이 생긴다. 졸리다.

□ founder vs found

founder /ˈfaʊndər/   v. to stumble or breakdown
(= stumble, wallow, fail)

The company that Greg's mother had founded 20 years ago foundered under his leadership.
그레그의 어머니가 20년 전에 창업한 회사가 그의 지도 아래 휘청거렸다.

found /faʊnd/   v. to set up
(= create, establish)

The company that Greg's mother had founded 20 years ago foundered under his leadership.
그레그의 어머니가 20년 전에 창업한 회사가 그의 지도 아래 휘청거렸다.

□ epidemic vs pandemic

epidemic /ˌepɪˈdemɪk/   n. a temporary prevalence of a disease
(= outbreak, plague, scourge)

A flu epidemic is spreading in the area.
독감 전염병이 그 지역에 돌고 있다.

pandemic /pænˈdemɪk/   n. an epidemic over a large area
(= contagion, plague)

The avian flu pandemic spread throughout many countries in Asia.
조류독감 대유행병이 아시아의 여러 국가에 퍼졌다.

Practice 33.

Fill in the blank with the word that matches the definition provided

01 Before I knew it, I was in the middle of a/an _____ (noisy fight) and got a bloody nose.

02 It's already mid-March, but this _____ (obstinate) cold spell won't go.

03 To become a husband and father is quite a/an _____ (difficult) but honorable job.

04 The picture on the cover of the book has nothing to do with the story: it is only there to _____ (excite) you into buying the book.

05 Right before walking on stage, Gemma felt her heart _____ (beat) so hard that she feared it would burst out of her chest.

06 Jake was quite uncomfortable within this new _____ (social surrounding) that his new found fame ushered him into.

07 The con-man prays on the innocent young people or the _____ (overly trusting) old timers.

08 I hinted at Jamie many times, but he was too _____ (dull witted) to get my point.

09 In the current economic depression, many multinational corporations are _____ (stumbling).

10 A particularly viral flu _____ (a temporary prevalence of a disease) is spreading through the city this winter.

11 While Nancy was on the phone, her dad fussed in the kitchen, _____ (giving the appearance) indifference, but secretly he was trying to listen to the conversation.

12   His career as a singer was _____ (passing quickly), and soon he found himself searching for a job as a computer programmer again.

13   Don't listen to politicians: they only _____ (obscure) the main issues.

14   Helen found her Alzheimer stricken grandfather _____ (going without aim) in the streets.

15   I find these medieval portraits to be disconcerting and _____ (deserving hatred). It feels like the eyes follow you when you move.

Class 34

□ **catastrophe vs. cataclysm vs. maelstrom**

catastrophe /kəˈtæstrəfi/   n. a disastrous event

(= disaster, calamity, devastation)

         adj. catastrophic

The hurricane was a catastrophe, killing two people and displacing more than 500 people.

허리케인은 참사였다. 두 명의 목숨을 앗아가고 500명이 집을 잃었다.

cataclysm /ˈkætəklɪzəm/   n. an event that causes great change or harm

(= catastrophe, disaster, upheaval, debacle)

         adj. cataclysmic

Lay people cannot understand how, with so many so-called economists and financial analysts existing in the world, no one saw the financial cataclysm of 2008 coming.

비전문가들 입장에서 이해가 안 되는 것이 어떻게 전 세계에 그렇게 많은 소위 경제학자들 및 금융분석가들이 존재하는 데 2008년 금융위기라는 재앙이 다가오고 있다는 것을 아무도 예견하지 못했다는 것이다.

maelstrom /ˈmeɪlstrəm/   n. turbulent confusion

(= tumult, turbulence, flurry, scramble)

Even though the war was over, it took years for the social and political maelstrom to die down and return life to normal.

전쟁은 끝났지만 전쟁이 만든 사회적 정치적 대혼란이 누그러지고 삶이 정상적으로 돌아오는데까지 몇 년 걸렸다.

□ **contrition vs. attrition**

contrition /kənˈtrɪʃn/   n. sincere penitence or remorse

(= remorse, repentance, sorrow, apology)

The convicted man shed tears of contrition at his trial.

구속된 남자가 참회의 눈물을 흘렸다.

attrition /əˈtrɪʃn/

n. the process of steadily reducing the strength of an enemy

(= erosion, wearing away)

The Gulf War was a war of attrition

걸프전은 소모전이었다.

□ **macerate vs. lacerate**

macerate /ˈmæsəreɪt/   v. to soften by steeping in liquid

(= soak, saturate)

You need to macerate these mushrooms before cooking them with the other vegetables.

다른 채소와 요리하기 전에 이 버섯들을 물에 불려야 합니다.

macerate /ˈmæsəreɪt/   v. to grow thin

(= starve, slim, waste away)

Everyone macerated during the war because there was a shortage of food supplies.

전쟁 중에 식량이 모자라 모든 사람들이 심하게 말라갔다.

lacerate /ˈlæsəreɪt/   v. to tear roughly

(= slash, tear, cut)

The thorn bushes lacerated his arms and hands as he tried to wade through them.

그가 가시덤불을 헤치고 나가는 동안 그의 팔이 심하게 긁혀 상처가 났다.

□ **compliment vs. complement**

complimentt /ˈkɑːmplɪmənt/   v. to give praise

(= praise, congratulate, approve)

n. compliment

Let me compliment you on your great work.

대단한 작업을 한 당신에게 칭찬을 보냅니다.

complement /ˈkɑːmplɪment/   v. to supplement

(= accompany, balance, complete, add)

                                       n. complement

He complemented my report by providing excellent charts and graphs.

그는 나의 보고서에 훌륭한 챠트와 그래프를 삽입하여 보충했다.

□ verdant vs. arboreal

verdant /ˈvɜːrdnt/   adj. green with vegetation

(= lush, green)

The field turned verdant after the rain shower.

소나기가 온 후 들판이 온통 초록색이 되었다.

arboreal /ɑːrˈbɔːriəl/   adj. adapted for living or moving in trees

This Papua New Guinean tribe lives an arboreal lifestyles away from the predators that roam the ground.

이 파푸아뉴기니 부락은 땅에 돌아다니는 맹수들을 피해 나무 위에서 생활한다.

□ bucolic vs. pastoral

bucolic /bjuːˈkɑːlɪk/   adj. of the countryside or country lifestyle

(= pastoral, idyllic, rustic, rural)

Clark Kent was adopted by an old couple from a small bucolic village in Kansas.

클라크 켄트는 캔사스의 작은 시골 마을에 사는 노부부에게 입양이 되었다.

pastoral /ˈpæstərəl/

adj. pertaining to the country or country life style

(= rustic, rural, countryside)

After three years in the country, I have grown quite accustomed to the pastoral lifestyle.

시골에 3년 정도 살다보니 전원생활에 꽤나 익숙해졌다.

□ **philanthropic vs. altruistic**

philanthropic /ˌfɪlən'θrɑːpɪk/
adj. showing concern for humanity by doing charitable deeds

(= charitable, benevolent, humanitarian, generous)

n. philanthropy

n. philanthropist

He is involved in many philanthropic activities.
그는 많은 자선사업에 관여한다.

altruistic /ˌæltru'ɪstɪk/
adj. devoted to the welfare of others
(= unselfish, humane, selfless)

n. altruism

n. altruist

Mother Teresa lived a truly altruistic life.
테레사 수녀는 매우 이타적인 삶을 살았다.

□ **instill vs. install**

instill /ɪn'stɪl/
v. to infuse slowly into the mind or feelings
(= impart, inculcate, implant, infuse)

Whenever Dad was home, he instilled a sense of fear in my brothers and me.
아버지가 집에 계실 때 나와 내 형제들에게 공포심을 심어주신다.

install /ɪn'stɔːl/
v. to connect or service or use
(= connect, mount, position)

I installed a game console on the TV in my room.
나는 내 방의 텔레비전에 게임 콘솔기를 설치했다.

□ **imminent vs. eminent**

imminent /'ɪmɪnənt/
adj. about to happen
(= looming, impending, pending)

Look at the clouds! A rain shower is imminent.

저 구름 좀 봐! 곧 소나기가 들이닥칠 것 같아.

eminent /ˈemɪnənt/   adj. well-known and respected

(= renowned, distinguished, prominent, reputed)

I will take a class in economics from a renowned professor next semester.

나는 다음 학기에 매우 저명한 교수님의 경제학 강의를 수강할 것이다.

☐ **illusion vs. allusion**

illusion /ɪˈluːʒn/

n. something that deceives by giving the false impression of reality

(= delusion, deception, fantasy, dream)

adj. illusionary

He was under that illusion that he will score high in the upcoming SAT.

그는 그가 곧 치를 SAT 시험에 고득점을 받을 거라는 환상에 빠져있다.

allusion /əˈluːʒn/   n. a passing or casual reference

(= reference, mention, insinuation)

v. to allude

During the debate, one candidate made several indirect allusions to the other's history of conviction.

토론 중에 한 후보가 상대편 후보의 전과기록에 대해 몇 차례 간접적으로 언급을 했다.

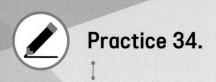

Practice 34.

Fill in the blank with the word that matches the definition provided

01 In a show of _____ (sincere remorse), Jackson brought a huge cake with the words "Please, forgive me," written on it.

02 When I threw bread crumbs in the pond, instantly the water became a/an _____ (turbulent confusion), as huge koi lunged for the food.

03 Jim was _____ (grow thin) beyond recognition from overwork and stress.

04 Just before the game began, Coach Roberts tried to _____ (infuse into the mind) a sense of determination and fighting spirit in his team.

05 It is a mistake to think that businesses involve themselves in charities only from purely _____ (devoted to the welfare of others) motives.

06 The area is now engulfed by real-estate development. Gone are the _____ (of the country-side) pastures and farms that the area was once famous for.

07 Much of the region's _____ (green with vegetation) countryside has been destroyed in the hurricane.

08 The restaurant's excellent menu is _____ (supplemented) by a superb wine list.

09 The idea that you will be out of your parents' influence once you move out of their house is a/an _____ (deception).

10 She was made uncomfortable by his veiled _____ (casual reference) to her previous SAT score.

11 I like to _____ (soak in liquid) cherries in brandy. They taste great as toppings for ice cream sundaes.

12 Last night, when I tried to bathe my cat, she _____ (tore roughly) my arms.

13 Man evolved from ancestors that were most likely _____ (living in trees).

Ⅰ

Fill the blank with a word from the box

> **founder, altruistic, vacillate, gesticulate, institution, eminent, strain, formidable, charge, industry, onerous, contrition, complement, obdurate, ingenuous**

01 Although Allan joined the Royale Army to fight the Nazis, his _____ was to shine General Klift's shoes and iron his uniform, and so he never fired a single shot during the entire war.

02 Every one of them is an outstanding baseball player, and, together, they make a/an _____ team.

03 Cortney _____ between vacationing in Montana horseback riding or in Vermont skiing.

04 Milton Hershey was a man of exceptional _____, opening his first store at 18 and ultimately founding the largest confectionary company in the United States when he was 26.

05 The bartender shook all the ingredients with ice in a cocktail shaker and _____ the liquid in a tall thin glass.

06 Our basketball team's coach's and assistant coach's different styles _____ each other very well.

07 His motive for helping others is truly _____: he genuinely is concerned for the welfare of everyone.

08 Charles' father is none other than the _____ biologist, Dr. Markus Gibson.

09 Jack has been trying to get his father to quit smoking for years, but it's not been easy to persuade the _____ old man.

10 It is _____ to think that politicians are not motivated by money and power.

11 The general consensus was that regional packs such as NATO would _____ after the end of the cold war, but this has been proven wrong.

12 My first responsibility as Manager was the _____ job of informing several employees that they are being let go due to the recession.

13 Any man who does not feel a sense of _____ at the twilight of his life is a fool.

14 The old-man selling balloons in the park is a kind of a/an _____ in this area. He's been selling them at the same spot for 40 years.

15 Being too far to be heard from across the street, Michael _____ to George to phone him.

odious, sanction, tantalize, sublimate, found, cataclysm, epidemic, charge, macerate, pastoral, inclination, melee, meander, obtuse, arboreal

16 After leaving the cut-throat world of business, Mark Wood retreated to a quiet ranch in Idaho to live in a quiet and _____ surrounding.

17 Sloths are truly _____ animals: they almost never come down from the tree that they live in.

18 Make sure to _____ all your dry vegetables before you begin cooking this dish.

19 The city of New Orleans has never really recovered from the _____ of hurricane Katrina that hit in 2005.

20 Cell-phone addition is a new _____; there are millions of people afflicted by it.

248

21 The oldest company still in business is Congo Gumi Construction of Japan, which was _____ in 578 AD.

22 There was a scuffle, and I lost my hat and scarf in the _____.

23 Having finished their work, Mr. Grouse and his friends _____ the streets until they found a suitable pub for a drink and supper.

24 I find it _____ that I have to wake up tomorrow morning at 5 to go to the airport to pick up my boss.

25 The ultimate _____ the government can impose on a corporation is to undergo a tax investigation.

26 Don't _____ me with your circumlocution. Just tell me straight what the problem is.

27 Einstein was brilliant in science, but when it came to everyday living, he was quite _____.

28 Dr. Jones, a leading archeologist, didn't mind that neither of his children had the slightest _____ to follow his footsteps into archeology.

29 Afterschool sports programs are an excellent forum for underprivileged students to _____ their rebellious tendencies into sporting activities.

30 While Dick's father was away, he left Dick's younger brothers and sister under Dick's _____.

Choose the right word

31 Some of my boss' questions seemed obtuse/obdurate/ominous at first, but I soon realized they were actually quite insightful.

32 When Jed heard the lacerating/titillating/palpitating offer the company made to him, he found it difficult to refuse.

33 Many people lost touch with their families during the meandering/milieu/maelstrom of the Korean War and lived for decades without knowing their fates.

34 The convicted criminal showed no attrition/contrition/émigré while the judge sentenced him to 20 years in prison.

35 The actor Christian Bale lacerated/lactated/macerated himself from 80kg to 62kg to play a man suffering from insomnia in the movie "the Machinist".

36 Although Mr. Harris was in his seventies, he never made any intimation/intimacy/emancipation of planning to retire.

37 The college has decided to dispose of its archaic/complemented/bucolic and cryptic scoring system and replace it with a new one.

Class 36

formative vs. formidable

formative /ˈfɔːrmətɪv/   adj. relating to development or growth

(= determinative, influential, seminal, shaping)

He was born in Busan but spent his formative years in Los Angeles.

그는 부산에서 태어났지만 가치관이 형성되는 기간은 로스엔젤레스에서 보냈다.

formidable /ˈfɔːrmɪdəbl/   adj. of great strength

(= daunting, impressive, arduous, intimidating)

We are up against a formidable team in our next football game.

우리는 다음 경기에서 매우 강력한 팀을 상대한다.

regiment vs regimen

regiment /ˈredʒɪmənt/   n. a military unit of ground forces
He volunteered to join the air-borne regiment.

그는 공수부대에 자원을 했다.

regimen /ˈredʒɪmən/
n. a regulated course, such as a diet, exercise or manner of living, intended to preserve
    or restore health

(= routine, regime, program)

The doctor started her on a regimen of medication and exercise to manage her high blood pressure.

의사는 그녀의 고혈압 치료를 위해 약과 운동을 병행하는 식이요법을 시작하도록 하였다.

□ oscillate vs. vacillate

oscillate /ˈɑːsɪleɪt/   v. to swing or move to and from

(= waver, fluctuate, swing, equivocate)

The needle on the dial was oscillating madly.

다이얼의 바늘이 심하게 흔들렸다.

vacillate /ˈvæsəleɪt/   v. to sway unsteadily

(= sway, waver, fluctuate)

As always, he will vacillate until the last moment before he makes up his mind.

항상 그렇듯이 그는 마지막 결단을 내릴 때까지 마음을 먹지 못하고 갈팡질팡하였다.

□ auspicious vs. suspicious

auspicious /ɔːˈspɪʃəs/   adj. favored by fortune

(= propitious, opportune, favorable)

Rain or snow on a wedding day is seen as an auspicious sign that the married couple will live happily.

결혼하는 날에 비나 눈이 내리는 것은 부부가 행복해질 것이라는 상서로운 징조로 간주된다.

suspicious /səˈspɪʃəs/   adj. causing distrust

(= dubious, untrustworthy, questionable)

A suspicious man was lurking at the entrance of the bank for hours.

은행 입구에서 퇴근 시간 이후에 수상한 남자가 얼쩡거렸다.

□ gestate vs. gesticulate

gestate /ˈdʒesteɪt/

v. to carry in the womb during a period of pregnancy

Did you know that an elephant gestates for over 20 months?

너는 코끼리의 잉태기간이 20개월이라는 걸 알고 있었니?

gestate /ˈdʒesteɪt/   v. to think of and develop slowly in the mind

He gestated the idea for his business for over ten years before he finally decided to realize it.

그는 마침내 사업을 시작하기 전에 사업에 관한 아이디어를 십 년간 머릿속에서 천천히 개발하였다.

gesticulate /dʒeˈstɪkjuleɪt/

v. express with body motions such as waving the arms

(= gesture, signal, motion, sign)

Not speaking a word of Italian, Brian tried to gesticulate his innocence to the Italian policeman who caught him running a red traffic light.

이태리어를 한 마디도 모르는 브라이언은 자기가 빨간 신호등을 그냥 지나치는 걸 적발한 이태리의 경찰관에게 왜 자기가 무죄인지 손짓발짓으로 설명하려 하였다.

☐ plethora vs. myriad

plethora /ˈpleθərə/   n. an overabundance

(= excess, surfeit, glut, surplus)

⇔ paucity

There is no way I can answer the plethora of emails I receive every day.

내가 하루에 받는 무수히 많은 이메일을 다 회신하기란 불가능하다.

myriad /ˈmɪriəd/   n. a great number of things

(= countless, innumerable, multitude)

Jack found that he had a myriad of things to do when he returned from his weeklong vacation.

잭은 일주일간의 휴가에서 돌아온 후 해야 할 일이 무수히 많은 것을 발견했다.

☐ gregarious vs. garrulous

gregarious /grɪˈgeriəs/   adj. fond of the company of others

(= outgoing, sociable, extroverted, convivial)

He has an outgoing and gregarious character.

그는 외향적이고 남들과 잘 어울리는 성격이다.

garrulous /ˈgærələs/   adj. excessively talkative

(= talkative, chatty, effusive, loquacious)

Mrs. Shim is so garrulous that I stopped to say hello to her and ended up listening to her complain about her husband for over half an hour.

심 여사님은 얼마나 수다스러운지 내가 잠깐 인사하려고 멈췄다가 그녀가 남편 흉보는 이야기를 삼십 분간 들었다.

□ intimation vs. intimacy

intimation /ˌɪntɪˈmeɪʃn/   n. making known indirectly

(= hint, suggestion, indication)

v. intimate

The band's decision to break up was very surprising since there was no intimation of any disharmony amongst the members.

그 밴드가 해체했다는 소식은 매우 놀라웠다. 왜냐하면 멤버 간에 어떤 불화가 있었다는 소식이 간접적으로라도 새어 나오지 않았기 때문에.

intimacy /ˈɪntɪməsi/   n. a close relationship

(= familiarity, closeness, tenderness)

adj. intimate

Howard never felt any intimacy between his father and him.

하워드는 그와 아버지 간에 그 어떤 친근함도 느끼지 못했다.

□ archaic vs. arcane

archaic /ɑːrˈkeɪɪk/   adj. very old

(= ancient, outdated, prehistoric)

The band used an archaic piano in their recording to get the 1920s type of feel in their song.

그 밴드는 1920년대 분위기의 곡을 녹음하기 위해 아주 오래된 피아노를 사용하였다.

arcane /ɑːrˈkeɪn/   adj. mysterious

(= mysterious, secret, esoteric, obscure)

Many people find it difficult to understand the rather arcane method of scoring the SAT test.

많은 사람들이 꽤나 불가사의한 SAT 시험 채점 방식을 이해하기 어려워한다.

□ emaciate vs. emancipate

emaciate /iméiʃièit/   v. to become abnormally thin
(= thin)

His disease emaciated him beyond recognition.

그는 병에 걸려 알아보기 어려울 정도로 야위었다.

emancipate /ɪˈmænsɪpeɪt/   v. to set free
(= free, liberate, release)

It is ironic that slavery was rampant in some African areas well into the 20th century when slaves were emaciated in 1864 in the United States.

노예제도가 미국에서는 1864년에 폐지되었는데 아프리카의 몇몇 지역에서는 20세기 중반까지 성행했다는 것은 아이러니한 일이다.

□ ravenous vs famished vs voracious

ravenous /ˈrævənəs/   adj. very hungry
(= greedy, voracious, starving)

With three ravenous teenagers to feed, Martha spends a lot of money on groceries.

세 명의 먹성 좋은 십대 아이들을 키우는 마사는 식료품 구매에 많은 돈을 쓴다.

famished /ˈfæmɪʃt/   adj. starving
(= hungry, rapacious, underfed)

By the time I come home from classes, I'm usually famished.

수업이 끝나고 집에 돌아올 때 쯤이면 나는 굶어죽기 일보직전이다.

voracious /vəˈreɪʃəs/   adj. craving for food
(= insatiable, avid, greedy)

After skiing for five hours, we all developed voracious appetites.

다섯 시간 스키를 탄 후 우리는 엄청나게 배가 고팠다.

Practice 36.

Fill in the blank with the word that matches the definition provided

01 It is known that some sharks _____ (be pregnant) for over three years.

02 Mr. and Mrs. Wilson spent their _____ (relating to growth) years in very different surroundings.

03 After a long illness, he looked frail and _____ (very thin).

04 At Helen's wedding, her grandmother was sad that her husband didn't live long enough to witness this _____ (favored by fortune) event.

05 Being a parent, Martha _____ (swing back and forth) between worry and happiness on a daily basis.

06 It was clear I needed to hire a lawyer who understood all the _____ (mysterious) details of the agreement.

07 The software they were using was _____ (old and useless) and needed to be updated.

08 Through the window, I could see Nancy waving her arms and _____ (express in bodily motions) madly, but I couldn't understand what she meant.

09 By the time we returned from our hike, I was _____ (very hungry).

10 When raising children, you will face a/an _____ (great number) of problems.

11 The doctor has prescribed a/an _____ (routine) for you, so you take care to strictly follow it.

12 I was surprised that Harold was admitted to a hospital. There was no _____ (making known indirectly) of him being ill when I saw him last week.

13 At first, Gloria seemed timid and shy, but once I got to know her better, she became quite _____ (talkative).

14 I immediately became friends with Helen's husband, Mike. He seemed like a very easygoing, _____ (fond of the company of others) guy.

☐ **veracious vs. voracious**

veracious /vəréiʃəs/   adj. habitually truthful

(= honest, ethical, truthful)

Every politician sounds veracious during election time.

모든 정치인들은 선거철이 되면 매우 솔직한 사람처럼 행동한다.

voracious /və'reɪʃəs/   adj. craving for food

(= insatiable, avid, greedy)

After skiing for five hours, we all developed voracious appetites.

다섯 시간 스키를 탄 후 우리는 엄청나게 배가 고팠다.

☐ **posterity vs. prosperity**

posterity /pɑː'sterəti/   n. succeeding generations collectively

(= descendants, successors, progeny, lineages)

Posterity may remember him differently from the way he is portrayed by his supporters.

그가 후세에게 받는 평가는 현재 그가 그의 지지자에게 받는 평가와 다를지도 모른다.

prosperity /prɑː'sperəti/   n. a successful condition

(= wealth, affluence, richness)

He achieved much prosperity and happiness later in his life.

그는 삶의 후반에 많은 부유함과 행복을 이뤘다.

☐ **canine vs. feline vs. bovine vs. lupine**

canine /'keɪnaɪn/   adj. of dogs
                               n. canine tooth

Every morning you can see Mr. Dickens walking with his canine buddy along the dock.
매일 아침 디킨스씨가 부둣가에서 그의 댕댕이 친구와 함께 산책하는 걸 볼 수 있다.

feline /ˈfiːlaɪn/   adj. of cats
Lions are the only feline species that are social animals.
사자는 고양이과 동물 중 유일하게 사회적인 동물이다.

bovine /ˈbəʊvaɪn/   adj. of cows
(= dimwitted, dumb)

Foot-and-mouth disease is not strictly a bovine disease; it harms pigs as well as cattle.
수족구는 엄격히 말하면 소만 걸리는 병이 아니다; 소 뿐만 아니라 돼지도 감염이 된다.

lupine /ˈluːpaɪn/   adj. of wolves
There are many stories about lupine man-beasts, otherwise known as "werewolves", in western folklore.
서양 미신에 늑대인간이라고 알려진 사람 늑대 괴수에 대한 이야기가 많다.

··

□ **perdition vs. purgatory vs. providence**

perdition /pɜːrˈdɪʃn/
n. the final punishment waiting for wicked people

(= hell, damnation, purgatory)

I tried to warn him that he was on the path to perdition.
그것은 지옥으로 가는 길이라고 그에게 경고했다.

purgatory /ˈpɜːrɡətɔːri/   n. a place of suffering or torment
(= anguish, hell, suffering)

I can't quit now. I've been through purgatory to get to this point.
지금 그만 둘 수는 없어. 여기까지 오느라고 지옥의 문턱까지 갔다 왔는데.

providence /ˈprɑːvɪdəns/   n. God
(= God, the Lord, the Maker, the man upstairs)

에드몬드는 하느님이 그를 하인으로 부려 그에게 해를 입힌 자들에게 복수를 하는 운명을 주신 걸로 생각했다.

provident
adj. prudent, frugal, wise

Edmond regarded himself as a minion of Providence destined to punish those who wronged him.

나는 수입의 1/3은 항상 저금하라는 우리 아버지의 현명한 충고를 듣는다.

providence /'prɑːvɪdəns/
n. good luck

(= fate, fortune, outside influence)

It can only be regarded as an act of Providence that we got this far!

우리가 여기까지 온 것도 천운이라고 밖에 말할 수 없어!

□ persecute vs. prosecute

persecute /'pɜːrsɪkjuːt/
v. to oppress or bully (usually for racial, political or religious reasons)

(= torment, oppress, harass, intimidate)

Koreans were persecuted by the Japanese during the years of Japanese Occupation.

일제 식민시대 동안 한국인들은 일본인들에게 박해를 받았다.

prosecute /'prɑːsɪkjuːt/
v. to bring legal action against an offense

(= indict, accuse, put on trial)

The warning sign said that violators will be prosecuted.

경고문에 규칙을 어기는 자들은 기소된다고 쓰여 있었다.

□ boon vs. bane

boon /buːn/
n. something to be thankful for

(= benefit, advantage, bonus, gain)

The development of the internet is perhaps the greatest boon to our society in the past 20 years.

지난 20년 동안 우리 사회의 가장 유익한 발전은 인터넷의 발명일 것이다.

bane /beɪn/
n. something that ruins or spoils

(= nuisance, misery, pest, curse)

There was no bane in my life until we adopted that dog.

저 개를 입양하기 전까지 내 인생에 나쁜 일이라고는 없었어.

□ émigré vs. protégé

émigré /ˈemɪgreɪ/
n. a person who is forced to leave his country for political reasons

(= emigrant, exile, expatriate, deportee)

Andrei Sakharov was an émigré from the former Soviet Union.
안드레이 사하로프는 소련에서 추방된 사람이었다.

protégé /ˈprəʊtəʒeɪ/
n. a person under the patronage or care of someone interested in his career

(= successor, charge, apprentice, understudy)

Jack Welch picked three protégés to train in the hope that one of them will be his successor.
잭 웰치는 그 중 한 명이 그의 후계자가 될 것을 기대하며 후견인 세 명을 지명하여 훈련시켰다.

□ avaricious vs. rapacious

avaricious /ˌævəˈrɪʃəs/   adj. extremely greedy
(= greedy, avid, covetous)

He was an avaricious man – always wanting more.
그는 탐욕스러운 사람이었다 – 그는 만족을 모른다.

rapacious /rəˈpeɪʃəs/   adj. extremely greedy
(= predatory, extortionate, voracious)

He is nothing but a rapacious sinner
그는 탐욕스러운 죄인일 뿐이다.

□ conflagration vs. deluge

conflagration /ˌkɑːnfləˈgreɪʃn/   n. a huge and destructive fire
(= inferno, blaze)

San Francisco was almost entirely burned off the map in a conflagration in 1906.

1906년의 대화재로 샌프란시스코는 거의 지도상에서 없어질 뻔 했다.

deluge /ˈdeljuːdʒ/   n. a huge flood
(= flood, inundation)

v. deluge

After the hurricane Katrina totally destroyed New Orleans, the inhabitants were then caught in a deluge.

뉴올리언즈가 허리케인 카타리나에 의해 완전히 파괴된 후, 주민들은 또 홍수를 겪었다.

□ insipid vs. intrepid

insipid /ɪnˈsɪpɪd/
adj. without sufficient taste to be pleasing, as in food and drink

(= dull, bland, tasteless, flavorless)

The soup was insipid and the main dish, too salty.

스프는 간이 싱거웠고, 주요리는 너무 짰다.

intrepid /ɪnˈtrepɪd/   adj. having no fear
(= fearless, bold, valiant)

He made the intrepid attempt at taking the SAT exam without studying at all!

그는 공부를 하나도 하지 않고 SAT를 치르는 간 큰 시도를 하였다!!

□ devious vs. dubious

devious /ˈdiːviəs/   adj. not straightforward
(= deceitful, scheming, underhanded, conniving)

Many people claim that he made money through devious means

많은 사람들이 그가 옳지 못한 방법으로 돈을 벌었다고 주장한다.

dubious /ˈduːbiəs/   adj. marked by doubt
(= doubtful, uncertain, ambiguous)

Many people think that his claims are dubious.

많은 사람들이 그의 주장이 근거가 없다고 생각한다.

□ insidious vs. invidious

insidious /ɪnˈsɪdiəs/　　　　　adj. slowly spreading evil

(= sinister, treacherous, deceptive, sneaky)

Many adults think that playing video games for too long causes insidious harm to young people.

많은 어른들은 너무 오랫동안 비디오 게임을 하는 것은 젊은이들에게 은밀하게 퍼지는 해악을 입힌다고 생각한다.

invidious /ɪnˈvɪdiəs/　　　　　adj. arousing resentment

(= unenviable, unpleasant, discriminatory, odious)

I was in the invidious position of being stuck between my ex-girlfriend and current girlfriend arguing.

나는 나의 전 여친과 현 여친이 다투는 가운데 끼는 불쾌한 위치에 있었다.

01 Not many people know that Ludwig von Beethoven was Joseph Hayden's _____ (person under patronage).

02 Our dog causes so much trouble that it has become the _____ (something that ruins) of our lives.

03 The politician was _____ (put on trial) for taking bribes from corporate supporters.

04 Alex made the rather _____ (doubtful) claim that his family are descendants of aristocrats in Imperial Russia.

05 I thought the soup was too bland and tasted _____ (bland) to me.

06 During World War II, _____ (brave) men as young as 19 volunteered to join the army.

07 I am not lonely. Everywhere I go, I take my _____ (of dog) friend, Jack, with me.

08 Just as the music of Bach, Mozart and Beethoven will be cherished by _____ (future generations), so will the music of the Beatles.

09 The truth can sometimes hurt, but one must always be _____ (telling the truth).

10 Professor Schroedinger was one of the scientist _____ (exile) that fled Europe when WWII began.

11 When I finished my presentation, I was faced with a/an _____ (flood) of questions.

12 The book seems harmless, but many people think it has a/an _____ (slowly spreading evil) effect on the minds of young people.

13 I had the _____ (arousing resentment) task of telling James that the company was letting him go.

14 Only the shrewdest and most _____ (deceitful) politician can survive in this political jungle for over three decades.

15 The earthquake lasted only 15 seconds, but it triggered a/an _____ (huge fire) that destroyed most of the city.

Class 38

□ **deference vs. reverence**

deference /ˈdefərəns/   n. respectful regards

(= respect, esteem, regard, admiration)

    adj. deferential

The flag is flown at half-mast on Memorial Day in deference to those who sacrificed their lives for their country.

현충일에는 나라를 위해 목숨을 바친 사람들을 기리기 위해 조기가 계양된다.

reverence /ˈrevərəns/   n. feeling or attitude of deep respect

(= veneration, admiration, awe)

    adj. reverential
    v. to revere

The letter from his son showed deep reverence and love for his father.

그의 아들로부터 받은 편지에는 아버지에 대한 깊은 존경심이 보인다.

□ **tepid vs turbid vs turgid vs torrid**

tepid /ˈtepɪd/   adj. that state of being neither cold or hot

(= lukewarm, half-hearted)

Some say that it is better to drink tepid water than it is to drink cold water to quench thirst.

어떤 사람들은 갈증을 해소하기 위해서는 찬물보다는 미지근한 물을 마시는 게 더 도움이 된다고 한다.

turbid /ˈtɜːrbɪd/   adj. muddy and unclear

(= muddy, cloudy, opaque)

Makoli is a turbid, milky alcoholic beverage of Korea made from rice.

막걸리는 쌀로 만든 한국의 탁하고 우유 같은 술이다.

turgid /ˈtɜːrdʒɪd/   adj. boring and difficult to understand

(= boring, pompous, stuffy)

His turgid lecture was boring and exhausting.

그의 복잡하고 따분한 강의는 듣기가 지루하고 피곤하다.

torrid /ˈtɔːrɪd/   adj. extremely hot or passionate

(= hot, sweltering, scorching, boiling)

It was impossible to think straight in the torrid weather.

날씨가 너무 더워서 똑바로 생각을 할 수가 없었다.

□ **forage vs. rummage**

forage /ˈfɔːrɪdʒ/   v. to wander about seeking something

(= search, seek, scavenge, rummage)

We spent the afternoon foraging through the forest for wild mushrooms.

우리는 낮에 숲 속에서 야생 버섯을 찾으러 돌아다녔다.

rummage /ˈrʌmɪdʒ/   v. to search actively for

(= search, delve, hunt)

John rummaged around in his backpack looking for his bus pass.

존은 버스 카드를 찾으려고 가방 안을 뒤적거렸다.

□ **philistine vs. philanthropist**

philistine /ˈfɪlɪstiːn/   n. a person lacking in culture

(= barbarian, boor)

Many of the older generation think that the younger generation are mostly comprised of philistines.

나이든 세대 사람들 중에 많은 사람이 젊은 세대 사람들은 거의 다 속물이라고 생각한다.

philanthropist /fɪˈlænθrəpɪst/   n. a person who practices philanthropy

(= altruist, humanitarian)

The young miser becomes the old philanthropist.

젊은 구두쇠가 늙은 자선사업가가 된다.

□ **quiescent vs. acquiescent**

quiescent /kwi'esnt/   adj. being at rest

(= calm, inactive, dormant, gentle)

After the raging storm, the sky grew quiescent and bright.

휘몰아치던 폭풍우 후에 하늘이 조용해지고 밝아졌다.

acquiescent /ˌækwi'esnt/   adj. quietly agreeing

(= yielding, accepting, submissive, consenting)

After stubbornly rejecting the offer for days, George suddenly was acquiescent after talking to his lawyer.

며칠간 고집스럽게 거부하던 죠지는 변호사와 대화한 후에 갑자기 순응적이 되었다.

□ **sallow vs. sanguine vs. pallid**

sallow /'sæləʊ/   adj. of a sickly yellowing color

(= yellow, sickly)

I could tell he was very ill by his sallow complexion.

그의 안색이 누런 걸로 보아 그가 많이 아프다는 걸 알 수 있었다.

sanguine /'sæŋgwɪn/   adj. of a reddish complexion

(= red, ruddy, rosy-cheeked)

His sanguine face beamed of good health.

그의 생기있는 얼굴이 그가 매우 건강하다는 걸 알려줬다.

sanguine   adj. positive

(= confident, optimistic, hopeful)

He had a sanguine view of his future.

그는 그의 미래에 대한 매우 낙관적인 전망을 한다.

pallid /'pælɪd/   adj. pale

(= white, ashen, sallow)

His usually white complexion was even more pallid today.

평소에도 하얀 그의 안색이 오늘따라 유난히 창백해 보였다.

268

□ benefactor vs. beneficiary

benefactor /ˈbenɪfæktər/   n. a person who proffers benefits to others
(= sponsor, patron, supporter)

The children's hospital received a huge donation from an anonymous benefactor.
어린이 병원이 무명의 후견인으로부터 큰 액수의 기부금을 받았다.

beneficiary /ˌbenɪˈfɪʃieri/   n. a person who receives a benefit from others
(= recipient, receiver)

His business was the beneficiary of the turbulent times just after the war, when there were many opportunities for people who were industrious to take advantage of them.
그의 사업은 근면한 사람들이 이용할 수 있는 기회들이 많았던 전쟁 후의 혼란기의 혜택을 받았다.

□ exacerbate vs exasperate

exacerbate /ɪgˈzæsərbeɪt/   v. to make worse
(= worsen, aggravate, impair)

Henry realized that his efforts to cheer her up were only exacerbating her anger.
헨리는 그녀가 기운을 내게 하기 위해 하는 그의 행동들이 그녀의 화만 더 돋운다는 걸 깨달았다.

exasperate /ɪgˈzæspəreɪt/   v. to infuriate
(= infuriate, madden, frustrate, irritate)

Henry's jokes only exasperated her more.
헨리의 농담들이 그녀를 더 화나게만 했다.

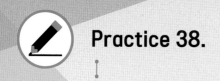

Practice 38.

Fill in the blank with the word that matches the definition provided

01 These fluorescent lamps make everyone look so _____ (having a white complexion).

02 Many economists are quite _____ (positive) about the economic prospects of the U.S. in the next few years.

03 Henry's laziness _____ (made angry) his mother often.

04 The well water was so _____ (unclear) that I decided not to drink it.

05 June was usually _____ (quietly agreeing) to her mother's wishes, but this time, she readily disobeyed.

06 Nowadays, children are not taught to treat their parents with _____ (respect).

07 Queen Elizabeth I was known to eat sweets constantly, thinking that it would give her sweet smelling breath, but little did she know that it only _____ (made worse) her bad breath.

08 When Henry was 22, he became the sole _____ (receiver of a benefit) of his late grandfather's estate, which was valued at more than USD50 million.

09 Mrs. Goldberg _____ (searched actively) all day through the cellar looking for her old photo albums.

10 Sitting in an air-conditioned office all day, Mr. Drummond had no idea how _____ (extremely hot) the weather was.

11   Grandmother looked _____ (having a yellow complexion) and weak in her hospital bed.

12   In my profession, autumns to springs are quite hectic, but summers are _____ (being at rest).

13   At the motel, I only got _____ (not warm or cold) water, no matter which direction I turned the faucet.

Class 39

□ indigent vs. indignant

indigent /'ɪndɪdʒənt/   adj. poor
(= poor, needy, impoverished, destitute)

n. indigence

He comes from an indigent family.
그는 가난한 집안 출신이다.

indignant /ɪn'dɪgnənt/
adj. feeling displeasure at something unjust or insulting

(= irate, vexed, outraged, incensed)

He was indignant at the unfair way he was treated.
그는 불공평한 대우를 받은 것에 대해 분했다.

□ brisk vs. brusque

brisk /brɪsk/   adj. quick and active
(= lively, quick, rapid)

He walked at such a brisk pace that his companions had to run to catch up with him.
그는 너무 잰걸음으로 걸어 같이 가는 사람들이 달려야 따라잡을 수 있었다.

brisk /brɪsk/   adj. cold and refreshing
(= cool, invigorating, refreshing)

A brisk wind blew across the lake.
호수 너머로 상쾌한 바람이 불어왔다.

brisk /brɪsk/   adj. abrupt and business like
(= abrupt, curt, brusque, hurried)

She was surprised by his brisk tone of voice.

그의 사무적이고 딱딱한 말투에 그녀는 놀랐다.

brusque /brʌsk/   adj. abrupt and business like

(= abrupt, curt, offhand, gruff)

The fact that the doctor explained to him that he had cancer in such a brusque manner amplified Kevin's shock even more.

그가 암에 걸렸다는 사실을 알리면서 의사가 쓴 너무나 딱딱하고 사무적인 말투가 케빈의 충격을 가중시켰다.

☐ **inapt vs. inept**

inapt /inǽpt/   adj. unsuitable

(= inappropriate, unfit, tactless, irrelevant)

Janet's mother commented that Janet's clothes were inapt for a teenager to wear.

자넷의 어머니는 자넷이 입은 옷이 청소년이 입기에 부적절한 것이라고 말했다.

inept /ɪˈnept/   adj. not capable of

(= incompetent, inexpert, clumsy, maladroit)

I am the wrong person to ask for help in making a cabinet as I am inept in carpentry.

나는 목공을 전혀 모르는 사람이라 내게 캐비닛을 만드는 것을 도와달라고 부탁하지 않는 것이 좋다.

☐ **envoy vs. convoy**

envoy /ˈenvɔɪ/   n. a diplomatic agent

(= emissary, diplomat, representative)

He was sent as a Presidential envoy.

그는 대통령의 특사로 파견되었다.

convoy /ˈkɑːnvɔɪ/   n. the protection provided by an esc

(= protection)

The foreign envoy was surrounded by a convoy of police cars.

외국의 특사가 경찰차의 호위를 받았다.

□ **entropy vs. atrophy**

entropy /ˈentrəpi/   n. a measure of randomness

(= chaos)

In the stock market, entropy rules.

주식 시장에서는 무질서가 지배한다.

atrophy /ˈætrəfi/

n. the wasting away of the entire body or a part of it

(= degeneration, deterioration, weakening)

      v. atrophy

Once a person loses the use of his legs, they will eventually atrophy.

사람이 다리의 사용 능력을 잃으면 그 다리는 점점 퇴화한다.

□ **timber vs. timbre**

timber /ˈtɪmbər/   n. wood usable to structural uses

(= wood, lumber)

Natives traditionally built their houses with mud bricks as there were no trees to fell and use as timber.

근처에 목재로 사용하기 위해 벨 나무가 없어서 원주민들은 진흙 벽돌로 집을 지었다.

timbre /ˈtæmbər/   n. quality of sound

(= resonance, tone, pitch)

His voice had a distinct timbre that made him recognizable as soon as he began to speak.

그의 목소리는 독특한 억양이 있어 그가 말하기 시작하면 금방 그의 목소리라는 걸 알 수 있다.

□ **capricious vs. capacious**

capricious /kəˈprɪʃəs/   adj. subject to unpredictable change

(= impulsive, fickle, erratic, unpredictable)

He was so capricious that he would change his mind twenty times before making a final decision.

그는 얼마나 변덕이 심한지 결심을 하기 전에 스무 번도 더 생각을 바꾼다.

capacious /kə'peɪʃəs/   adj. full of space

(= roomy, spacious, ample, extensive)

Houses in the countryside are usually more capacious than those in the city.

시골의 집들이 대개 도시의 집들보다 공간이 넓다.

□ **urban vs. urbane**

urban /'ɜːrbən/   adj. relating to the city

(= city, town, metropolitan)

I can understand how some people say they would like to live in the country someday, but I would much rather live in an urban environment.

나는 왜 어떤 사람들이 언젠가 전원에서 살고 싶다고 말하는지 이해는 가지만, 나는 도심에서 차라리 더 살고 싶다.

urbane /ɜːr'beɪn/   adj. reflecting elegance and sophistication

(= polished, courteous, refined, stylish)

Whenever I look in the mirror, I see an urbane gentleman staring back at me.

내가 거울을 들여다 보면, 아주 세련된 신사가 나를 보고 있다.

□ **empathy vs antipathy**

empathy /'empəθi/

n. the ability to share and understand another persons' feelings as if they are your own

(= sympathy, understanding, compassion, identification)

I felt empathy for my younger brother who began to study for his SAT.

나는 SAT 공부를 시작한 나의 동생에게 동정을 느낀다.

antipathy /æn'tɪpəθi/   n. a natural aversion

(= opposition, aversion, hostility, hatred)

Although the two men seemingly argue all the time, there is no real antipathy between them.

그 두 사람은 항상 싸우는 것 같지만 그들 간에 진짜 적대감은 없다.

□ efficient vs. efficacious

efficient /ɪˈfɪʃnt/   adj. performing in the best possible manner

(= competent, effective, capable)

He is an efficient employee.

그는 매우 효율적인 직원이다.

efficacious /ˌefɪˈkeɪʃəs/   adj. capable of having the desired result

(= effective, efficient, useful)

The medicine proved efficacious in relieving my headache.

그 약이 내 두통을 치료하는 데 효과적이었다.

□ benevolent vs. malevolent

benevolent /bəˈnevələnt/   adj. extremely kind and generous

(= kind, caring, compassionate, munificent)

                 n. benevolence

The benevolent child shared his lunch with his friend

관대한 아이가 그의 점심을 친구와 나눠 먹었다.

malevolent /məˈlevələnt/   adj. evil and wicked

(= malicious, spiteful, vindictive)

                 malevolence

Some people think my boss is malevolent, but he only wants everyone to do his best in his job.

어떤 사람들은 나의 보스가 사악하다고 생각하지만, 그는 단지 모든 사람들이 자기 일을 최고로 잘하기를 원할 뿐이다.

□ magnanimity vs. clemency

magnanimity /ˌmæɡnəˈnɪməti/   n. generosity of spirit

(= generosity, benevolence, altruism, fairness)

                 adj. magnanimous

The man had the magnanimity to forgive the person who insulted him publicly.

그는 공개적으로 그를 모욕한 사람을 용서할 만큼의 관대함이 있다.

clemency /ˈklemənsi/   n. kindness of heart

(= mercy, leniency, forgiveness)

The judge showed no clemency when sentencing the convicted murderer.

판사는 기소된 살인자에게 형을 선고할 때 전혀 관용을 베풀지 않았다.

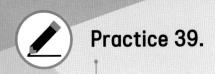

Practice 39.

Fill in the blank with the word that matches the definition provided

01 Our hotel room was quite _____ (full of space) with enough space for all four of us.

02 The singer possesses a voice with arguably the most distinctive _____ (quality of sound) in the music industry.

03 One's language speaking ability is the same as any other physical ability in that it will _____ (deterioration) if not used.

04 As we drove closer to the border, we saw many _____ (protection provided by vehicles) of army vehicles.

05 Do not ask Jacob to make a toast; he is a man _____ (incapable) of humor.

06 It is irrational to ask for _____ (leniency) when you have committed the same offense three times.

07 Jennifer has a/an _____ (extremely kind) soul; she wouldn't hurt a fly.

08 The nasal spray I used was very _____ (effective) in relieving my nasal congestion.

09 After having her purse stolen and suffering from motion sickness in a Manhattan taxi, Nelly has developed a/an _____ (natural aversion) to New York.

10 Traffic congestions, noise pollution and bad air quality are normal parts of everyday _____ (of the city) life.

11 As Robert reached 30, he lost most of his boyish looks and took on a more _____ charm.

12 Kurt is so _____ (subject to frequent change) that he changed the restaurant reservations three times before the date of the event.

13 On his first day in medical school, Dr. Roberts was taught that the most important virtue a doctor must possess is _____ (compassion).

14 His action could only be described as _____ (having evil intent): why would anyone choose to steal money from a charity fund?

Fill the blank with a word from the box

> **sallow, exacerbate, indigent, gregarious, posterity, canine, brisk, dubious, boon, insipid, forage, acquiescent, convoy, capricious, magnanimity**

01 After spending three months in Milan drinking strong Italian coffee, the coffee in L.A. tasted a bit _____.

02 Jake _____ through his backpack looking for his bus pass.

03 Although Neil is Gary's brother, Gary doesn't expect Neil to be _____ with his recent life decision.

04 I could tell from his _____ face that he had been more ill than he led me to believe over the phone.

05 The jury was expected to show no _____ to the convicted murderer when deciding his sentence.

06 After an exceptionally hot and muggy summer, I welcome these _____ autumn days.

07 The _____ account of the witnesses were proven correct after the police investigation.

08 Many of the drugs prescribed for the disease ultimately resulted in _____ the symptoms.

09 The twins are exact opposites: Johnny is _____ and outgoing, while Hank is introverted and shy.

10 Mozart and Beethoven's music will be enjoyed for _____.

11 Some people say that dogs can understand their masters' emotions, but scientists say that the _____ brain is wired totally differently from that of humans, so such empathy is impossible.

12 The internet has proven a/an _____ for students who no longer have to spend long hours in libraries researching.

13 Samuel is from a/an _____ family. That is why he watches every penny he uses.

14 Soon after the police stopped all the cars on the freeway, a/an _____ of black vehicles rushed by.

15 The weather at this time of the year can be quite _____. One day, it will be bright and warm; on the next day, it will be cold and windy.

empathy, urbane, gestate, inapt, bane, feline, famished, avaricious, myriad, clemency, brusque, envoy, reverence, dubious, philistine

16 The family of the accused man pleaded for _____ to the judge.

17 Kim's brilliance as a novelist comes with her _____ with what readers want.

18 The rambunctious boy has turned into a charming, _____ gentleman.

19 The two governments agreed to exchange _____ to begin the peace process.

20 Bill is not good at social events: he can't seem to control his impulse to make _____ comments.

21 He was pale, of _____ manners, somewhat given to affectation, but of immaculate dress and generous to his enemies.

22   I know a bit about music and art, but in reality, I'm only a/an _____.

23   When I saw my dad at his job as fire marshal of our town, I found a new _____ for him.

24   The first few business ideas of Glenn's were quite _____, but later he hit the jackpot with his on-line sporting goods mall.

25   There are too many _____ people in the world today: we should all think of others' welfare more.

26   Mrs. Kent's oldest three sons are all very successful, but her fourth son is the _____ in her life.

27   She remained silent, with a/an _____ smile spreading on her face.

28   I've been on a diet for a week now, so I am constantly _____.

29   We looked up at the sky and saw a/an _____ of stars.

30   Larry was stumped for days, when a solution slowly began to _____ in his mind.

Choose the correct word

31   The **verdant/bucolic/bovine** vines hid the entrance of the cottage from the street.

32   Henry's joking **delusion/illusion/allusion** that a woman's place is in the kitchen upset Grace.

33   The investigative reporters could not disclose his findings yet because there was only **formative/fragmentary/formidable** evidence to incriminate the senator in the scandal.

34   The investigator regarded the suspect's alibi to be auspicious/propitious/dubious.

35   Miles advised Lance that there were a paucity/plethora/bane of reasons for Lance to begin or not begin his own business, so the important thing is for Lance to follow his gut feeling.

36   It is ironic how, after the early Christians endured prosecution/persecution/perspiration for centuries, in later history it was the Christians who harassed people of other faiths.

37   Nicholas was the fifth son of a Russian protégé/émigré/apprentice who moved to Chicago from Russia in search of religious freedom in the 1920s.

38   My first responsibility as manager was the insidious/insipid/invidious job of telling several employees that they were being laid off as a consequence of the recession.

39   Analysts' forecasts that the demand for smart devices would grow tepid/turgid/turbid this year have been proved wrong.

40   The young philistine/philanthropist/connoisseur inherited his concern for the welfare of others from his father.

41   Frank was indignant/indigent/emaciated when the professor praised only Jake for his work though the project was submitted under the names of both of them.

42   The terrorist attack was criticized as a great act of malevolence/magnanimity/clemency.

Ted Chung
유학/SAT/ACT 필수 Vocabulary

| The Bodacious Book of |

Voluminous Vocabulary

Series 1-Core

(from Founding Documents and
Great American Conversations)

-Answers -

Class 01 Answers

01 unanimous   adj. 만장일치의
위원회 위원들이 만장일치로 그랜트 씨를 새로운 의장으로 선출하였다.

02 tyranny   n. 압제, 폭압
지역 주민들은 부패한 경찰들의 폭압으로부터 아무런 보호를 받지 못했다.

03 assume   v. 책임을 맡다
법원이 아이의 복지를 책임지기로 하였다.

04 station   n. 지위, 위상
그는 왕의 사촌으로서 왕의 부재에 내정에 관여해야 하는 지위이다.

05 impelled   v. ~ 해야만 하게 하다
증거는 용의자가 유죄임을 증명했지만, 형사는 사건을 추가적으로 조사해야 할 것만 같은 느낌을 받았다.

06 inalienable   adj. 양도/이양할 수 없는
두 국가는 섬은 각자의 영토이고, 양도할 수 없는 일부라고 선언했다.

07 declaration   n. 선언, 공표
일본 총리는 일본의 영토를 지나는 미사일을 발사하는 것은 전쟁 선언과 다름없다고 하며 북한을 비난했다.

08 candid   adj. 솔직한
법원에서 증언을 할 때 솔직해야 한다.

09 altered   v. 바꾸다, 수정하다
회사의 조직 구조는 20년 동안 바뀌지 않았다.

10 prudence
n. 신중, 조심, 사려 분별
요즘과 같이 미래를 예측할 수 없는 시기에 신중함을 유지하는 것이 최선의 해결책이다.

11 institute
v. 도입하다, 시작하다
경찰서장은 사건 조사를 맡을 임시 조직을 도입할 것이라고 공지했다.

12 usurpation
n. 불법 권리 침해, 침략
최근 개인정보 관련 심사를 확장하겠다는 정부의 결정을 많은 사람들이 불법 권리 침해의 일종으로 간주하며 반대한다.

13 constrain   v. 강요하다
유태인 어머니들은 자녀에게 결혼을 강요하는 사람들로 유명하다.

14 ephemeral
adj. 수명이 짧은, 순식간의
아버지께서 젊음은 순식간에 지나가니, 즐기라고 말씀하셨다.

15 disposed
adj. ~ 할 마음이 있는, 경향이 있는
자넷은 케빈과 남매 사이이기에 케빈의 모든 말에 동의하는 경향이 있었다.

01 formidable
adj.어마어마한, 공포심을 유발하는
나는 공포심을 유발하는 상대와 맞서야 했지
만, 연습 때만큼 실력발휘를 하면 그를 이길
수 있다고 믿었다.

02 tenure   n. 재임 기간, 재임
몇몇 사람들은 단일 5년의 재임 기간이 교육
감으로서 의미 있는 정책을 도입하기에는 짧
다고 말한다.

03 suspend
v. 일시적으로 중단하다, 연기하다, 보류하다
가게는 해당 제품 판매를 추가 공지가 있을 때
까지 일시적으로 중단하겠다고 알렸다.

04 pressing   adj. 긴급한
운영자는 근로자들에게 긴급한 문제가 없으면
가도 된다고 말했다.

05 annihilation   n. 전멸
오펜하이머 박사는 선진국들 간에 계속적으로
파괴적인 무기 개발경쟁이 지속된다면 인간의
전멸로 이어질 수 있다고 경고했다.

06 compliance   n. 준수, 협조
한국지사가 있는 외국계 기업은 한국의 법을
완전히 준수할 것을 반드시 보장해야 한다.

07 depository   n. 보관소
레오나르도 다 빈치의 유명한 벽화 "최후의 만
찬"이 위치한 교회는 제2차 세계대전 중 탄약
보관소로 사용됐었다.

08 inestimable
adj. 헤아릴 수 없는, 계산할 수 없는
뉴스에서 허리케인이 지나간 경로에 헤아릴
수 없는 피해를 줬다고 보도했다.

09 obstructed   v. 막다, 차단하다
해돋이의 경치는 지평선 너머에 두꺼운 구름
으로부터 차단되었다.

10 wholesome   adj. 건강에 좋은
학교 식당에서 파는 음식은 고급스럽지 않더
라도, 건강에 좋다.

11 dissolution
n. (사업상 관계의) 해소, 해체
이 나라에서는 한 기업의 해체는 설립보다 오
래 걸린다.

12 appropriation
n. 특정 목적을 위한 돈의 책정액
시 정부는 모든 지하철 역의 에스컬레이터
설치를 위해 천만 달러가 넘는 책정액을 확
정했다.

13 convulsion   n. 격동, 혼란
스캔들은 국가 전체에 혼란을 불러일으켰다.

14 at large
idiom. 대체적으로, 전반적으로
많은 정치인들은 일반 여론을 이해하지 못한다.

15 relinquish   v. 포기하다
대통령이 범죄를 지었다는 것이 증명되었을
때, 그는 모든 권위를 즉시 부통령에게 포기할
것을 강요 받았다.

01 acquiesce
v. 묵인하다, 복종하다, 동의하다
나는 결론에 동의하지 않았다: 동의하기에 너무 쩨쩨한 일이었기 때문에.

02 swarm
n. (한 방향으로 이동하는 곤충의) 떼
우리는 벌집 주위에 벌 떼가 있었기 때문에 벌집 근처로 가지 못했다.

03 appealed
v. 마음을 끌다, 동조를 요청하다
많은 사회 지도자들은 대중에게 침착하라고 마음을 끌었다.

04 abolished
v. 폐지하다
많은 사람들은 사형제도가 미국의 여러 주에서 폐지되지 않았다는 사실을 이상하게 여긴다.

05 constrain
v. 강요하다, ~ 하게 만들다
증인이 경찰에게 말을 하지 않자, 경찰들은 그를 체포하겠다고 위협하며 말을 하게 하려고 했다.

06 rectitude
n. 도덕적 청렴
그는 도덕적 청렴이 몸에 밴 사람의 한 예시다.

07 divine
adj. 신의, 신성한
솔로몬은 하느님께 기도하며 신의 도움을 요청했다.

08 brethren
n. 형제(같은 사람)
내전에서 우리는 형제와 같은 사람들과 싸워야 했다.

09 abdicated
v. 왕위에서 물러나다, 퇴위하다, 권력을 포기하다
영국의 애드워드 3세는 낭만의 왕으로 알려져 있다: 그는 사랑하는 미국 출신의 한 번 결혼한 경험이 있는 여성과 결혼하기 위해 왕위에서 물러났다.

10 plunder
v. 약탈하다, 강탈하다
중세 전쟁 때, 성이 정복된 후, 전쟁에서 승리한 군대는 3일 동안 성이 위치한 도시 내부에서 약탈할 권한을 얻었다.

11 ravaged
v. 파괴하다, 피폐하게 만들다
몇몇 상점들은 밤새 도둑들에 의해 파괴되었다.

12 perfidy
n. 배신
놀랍게도, 의심 가득한 본성을 가진 스탈린은 히틀러가 둘의 1941년 비밀의 불가침 조약 이후 배신을 할 것이라고 예상하지 못했다.

13 insurrection
n. 반란 사태
시위자들은 반란을 일으키려고 한다는 의혹을 받았다.

14 unwarrantable
adj. 정당하지 않은
비합리적인 손님은 계속 정당하지 않은 요청을 했다.

01 concur   v. 동의하다
나는 외국인 이민자들이 국내 실업 문제를 일으키는 주범이라는 의견에 동의하지 않는다.

02 ratified   v. 비준하다
조약은 UN의 모든 소속 국가들에 의해 비준되었다.

03 prohibited   v. 금하다
이 공원에서는 5월에서 9월까지 동물을 사냥하는 것이 금지되어 있다.

04 abridge   v. 줄이다, 요약하다
교수는 Francis에게 보고서가 너무 길어서 줄이라고 했다.

05 indictment   n. 고발, 기소
거짓말을 한 정치인은 위증죄로 기소될 것으로 보인다.

06 impartial   adj. 공정한
그의 판단이 공정했다는 점이 의심스럽다.

07 enumeration   n. 목록, 일람표
토론의 끝에, 각 후보자는 본인의 장단점들을 솔직하게 나열해야 한다.

08 tranquility   n. 평온함
스탠리 공원은 밴쿠버의 북적이는 시내에서 불과 몇 분 떨어진 곳에 위치하고 있고, 사람들이 자연의 평온함을 만끽할 수 있는 공간이다.

09 welfare
n. 행복, (개인, 단체의) 안녕
사람들은 투표가 필요한 순간에만 유권자에게 잘하고, 일 자체가 유권자들의 행복을 위해 노력해야 한다는 것을 잊는 정치인들에게 지쳤다.

10 posterity   n. 후세, 후대
아우슈비츠 강제 수용소가 위치했던 곳에는 현재 아우슈비츠–비르케나우 국립박물관이 있고, 후세에게 제2차 세계대전 동안 발생한 끔찍한 전쟁범죄를 상기시키기 위해 설립되었다.

11 propensity   n. 경향
대부분의 벌은 노란색에 끌리는 경향이 있다.

12 vices   n. 악덕 행위
음주와 흡연은 대중의 가장 흔한 악덕 행위들이다.

13 vested
v. (권리 등의) 소유가 확정된, 기득의
대부분의 민주주의 국가들에서 최상위의 법적 판단을 내릴 수 있는 권리는 대법원이 소유하고 있다.

14 apportion   v. 나누다, 배분하다
다섯 명이서 샌드위치 네 개를 나눠 먹어야 하는 상황이어서 모두 내가 샌드위치를 정확하게 배분하는 것에 대해 불안해 했다.

15 beneficent
adj. 의 득을 보다, 혜택을 입다
Thatcher 씨는 어렸을 때, 집안이 가난해서 저소득층을 위한 복지 정책의 혜택을 받아야 했다.

16 infringed   v. 위반하다, 침해하다
기사는 후보자의 개인적인 재정 상황에 대한 질문을 하며 그의 사생활 침해를 했다.

17 quartered   v. 숙사를 얻은
난민들은 당분간 임시 변통 오두막에서 숙사를 얻게 되었다.

Class 05

01 obviate
v. (문제나 필요성을) 제거하다, 배제하다, 방지하다
대통령이 특정 후보자에 대한 지지를 표출했다고 해당 후보자의 자격을 검증해야 할 필요성이 배제되지 않는다.

02 mischief   n. 나쁜 짓, 장난, 피해
고등학교 졸업한 지 15년이 됐는데도 Beecham 선생님은 여전히 나를 화학 시간에 장난치던 학생으로 기억하고 계신다.

03 adverse
adj. 부정적인, 불리한, 반대하는
나는 공정하지 않은 방식으로 목표를 달성하는 것에 반대한다.

04 subsist
v. 근근이 살아가다, 유지되다
이 지역에 사는 몇몇 주민들은 하루 한 끼로 근근이 생활할 정도로 가난하다.

05 reciprocal   adj. 상호간의, 동등한
그는 내 생일날 좋은 선물을 보내줬기 때문에, 나도 동등한 제스처를 해줘야만 할 것 같다.

06 folly   n. 어리석음
아버지는 내가 안정적인 직장을 포기하고 창업을 했을 때 어리석은 행동이라고 하셨다.

07 perished   v. 죽다
많은 사람들이 지난 주말 해안을 강타한 거대한 허리케인으로 인해 사망했다.

08 adversaries   n. 적
두 남성은 몇 년 동안 다투고 싸웠지만, 사실 서로 적은 아니다.

09 latent
adj. 보이지 않으나 실존하는, 잠복해 있는
미국에서 인종차별은 완전히 사라진 적이 없다; 여전히 잠복해 있다.

10 specious   adj. 그럴듯한
교수는 Geoff의 그럴듯한 변명을 꿰뚫어 보았다.

11 unwarrantable
adj. 용서할 수 없는, 변호할 수 없는
많은 사람들은 정부가 몇 년 동안 실업 문제를 해결하려고 했으나 진전을 이루지 못한 점을 용서할 수 없다고 한다.

12 contend   v. 주장하다, 다투다
너의 설명이 논리적이지 않다고 주장해야만 할 것 같아.

13 faculties   n. 선천적인 능력
내 증조할아버지는 94세지만, 선천적인 신체적, 정신적 능력들은 여전하시다.

14 overbearing
adj. 고압적인, 권위적인
데이빗이 너보다 직급이 낮다고 해서 그에게 고압적으로 대할 수 있다고 생각하지 마.

15 actuated
v. 행동을 하게 하다, 작동시키다
그들의 협동은 Harry를 이기고 싶은 공통적인 바람에 의해 작동되었다.

01 perfidy   n. 배신
장군은 정직한 사람으로 알려져 있던 분이라 그가 배신을 저지를 것이라고 아무도 생각하지 못했다.

02 conjure   v. 간청하다
국가적인 비상사태를 맞아 대통령이 국민들에게 강인하고 용기를 잃지 않기를 간청하였다.

03 unanimous   adj. 만장일치의
이사회는 제안을 만장일치로 거절했다.

04 station   n. 지위, 위상
공작과 공작부인은 딸이 평민과 결혼하고 싶은 소원을 그들의 지위가 유지되는 이상 허용하지 못한다고 하며 반대했다.

05 unalienable   adj. 양도/이양할 수 없는
여성의 투표권은 이양할 수 없는 것처럼 여겨지지만, 이 권리가 헌법에 의해 보장된 지 100년이 채 되지 않았다.

06 abolished   v. 폐지하다
사형제도는 많은 나라에서 폐지되었지만, 미국의 31개의 주에서는 아직 합법적이다.

07 disposed   adj. ~할 마음이 있는, 경향이 있는
Blaire 의사선생님은 개인 병원을 50년 이상 운영해왔지만, 아직 은퇴할 마음이 없다.

08 assent   n. 승인서, 동의
탐험에 참여하고 싶으면, 법적 보호자가 서명을 한 동의서를 제출해야 한다.

09 pressing   adj. 긴급한
우리는 회의 시간을 사소한 사항을 논의하며 낭비한 바람에 긴급한 문제들을 해결할 시간이 없었다.

10 abdicate   v. 왕위에서 물러나다, 퇴위하다, 권력을 포기하다
애드워드 8세는 이혼을 한 미국인 여성과 결혼하기 위해 자발적으로 왕위에서 물러났다.

11 latent   adj. 보이지 않으나 실존하는, 잠복해 있는
어른이 되면 우리는 많은 어린이 동화에 인간의 행동에 대한 신랄한 풍자가 잠복해있음을 발견하게 된다.

12 prohibited   v. 금하다
나는 독실한 불교도로서 술을 먹거나 고기를 먹는 행위가 금지된다.

13 subsisted   v. 근근이 살아가다, 유지되다
사업가와 정치인의 친밀한 관계는 항상 근근이 유지되어 왔다.

14 faculties   n. 선천적인 능력
90대 남성이지만 Davis 씨의 능력들이 놀랍게도 온전하다; 그는 생계를 유지하기 위해 택시 운전사로 일을 한다.

15 formidable   adj. 어마어마한, 공포심을 유발하는
첫 대결에서 로버트는 제임스에게 상대가 되지 않았다. 3년 후, 로버트는 어마어마한 라이벌로 성장하여, 제임스가 각오하고 대결에 임해야 하는 상황이다.

16 acquiesce   v. 묵인하다, 복종하다, 동의하다
범인이 저지른 불법 행위의 범위를 보면, 그의 상사들은 아마 그런 행동을 지시하지는 않았을 테지만, 적어도 동의는 했을 것으로 추정할 수 있다.

17 posterity   n. 후세, 후대
많은 사람들은 기후 변화 문제가 지금 해결되지 않으면 그의 대가로 후세가 굉장히 고생할 것으로 생각한다.

18 apportioned   v. 나누다, 배분하다
Harrison 씨가 죽었을 때, 그의 자산은 자녀에게 나누어지지 않고, 자선단체에 기부되었다.

19 infringe v. 위반하다, 침해하다
야생 동물에게 공격을 당하는 사건의 증가 원인은 인간이 그들의 자연 서식지를 계속해서 침해하기 때문이다.

20 propensity n. 경향, 성향
케빈의 사탕을 좋아하는 성향은 그가 쇼콜라티에가 되게 한 핵심적인 동기이다.

21 perished v. 죽다
많은 정치범들은 스탈린의 테러 정권 아래 1920년대와 1940년대 사이 시베리아 교정 노동 수용소에서 죽었다.

22 obviated v. (문제나 필요성을) 제거하다, 배제하다, 방지하다
이메일은 기업들이 팩시밀리 머신 또는 텔렉스 머신 등 전통적인 커뮤니케이션 장비를 구비할 필요성을 제거했다.

23 adverse adj. 부정적인, 불리한, 반대하는
북아메리카 최초의 서구 정착민들은 부정적인 환경을 견뎌야 했다: 질병, 거친 날씨와 적대적인 원주민들은 그의 일부일 뿐이다.

24 folly n. 어리석음
Henrietta가 사위에게 기독교 신자가 될 것을 설득하려고 했을 때, 그녀의 남편은 종교를 타인에게 강제로 요구하는 행위의 어리석음을 상기시켰다.

25 magnanimity n. 아량, 관대함, 담대함
당신이 공개선상에서 망신시킨 사람에게 관대함을 기대하는 것은 말이 되지 않는다.

26 annihilation n. 전멸
오늘날 핵전쟁이 일어나면, 인류의 전멸을 뜻할 것이다.

27 tenure n. 재임 기간, 재임
한국의 대통령은 5년 단임제로 재임한다.

28 abolished v. 폐지하다
아이러니하게도, 노예제도는 미국에서 폐지된 이후에도 몇몇 아프리카 국가들에서 존재했다.

29 ravaged v. 파괴하다, 피폐하게 만들다
두 개의 태풍은 여러 명의 사망, 수천 명의 상해, 그리고 수백만 달러의 손해를 일으키는 등 나라에 큰 큰 피해를 입혔다.

30 tranquility n. 평온함
그의 아내가 세 자녀를 데리고 시댁에 머칠간 갔을 때, 데이브는 드물게 몇 년만에 혼자 있는 평온함을 즐겼다.

31 적: 아군 (반의어)
A. 중립적인: 편파적인
B. 복지: 안전
C. 신: 신
D. 형제: 동지

32 초토화시키다: 재건하다 (반의어)
A. 경련: 발작
B. 피로: 피로하게 만들다
C. 방해하다: 방해물을 제거하다
D. 연기/유보하다: 보류하다

33 건강에 좋은: 건강한 (동의어)
A. 견딜 수 있는: 견딜 수 없는
B. 솔직한: 솔직한
C. 수명이 짧은: 영원한
D. 신중함: 부주의한

34 도입하다: 설립하다 (동의어)
A. 변경하다: 멈추다
B. 신중함: 오만함
C. 횡포한: 관대함
D. ~하게 만들다: 해내다, 몰다

35 포기하다: 유지하다 (반대어)
A. 준수: 불복종, 반항
B. 반란 사태: 용병
C. 떼: 무리
D. 약탈하다: 약탈하다

36 배신: 충성 (반대어)
A. 혈족: 친족, 연대감
B. 반대하다: 묵인하다
C. 평온함: 고요함
D. 자녀: 후세

37 자선의: 악의적인 (반대어)
A. 동의하다: 동의하다
B. 금하다: 금하다
C. 축소시키다: 압축하다
D. 탐탁찮아 하다: 비준하다

38 숙소: 집 (동의어)
A. 부분적인: 중립적인
B. 파벌: 집단
C. 범죄: 목록
D. 그럴듯한: 정확한

39 절대 확실한: 완벽한 (동의어)
A. 상호간의: 어울리는
B. 구성하다: 신나게 하다
C. 소유주: 직원
D. 잠재적인: 근본적인

40 전하다: 주지 않다 (반대어)
A. 백치: 어리석음
B. 기소: 기소, 혐의
C. 친절한: 고압적인
D. 위반하다: 간섭하는

41 (반박의 여지가 없는 – 덧없는 – 허무하게 지나가는

42 (~할 마음이 있는 – ~ 할 경향이 있는 – 솔직한

43 적응 – 동의 – 동의

44 배반 – 정직 – 정확함

45 사악함 – 범죄 – 연합

46 부정확한 – 젠체하는 – 잘못된

47 전하다 – 전달하다 – 작동시키다

48 상호간의 – 잠재적인 – 표면 밑에 있는

49 용해시키다 – 의존하다 – 흩어지다

50 보관소 – 거처 – 재고품

51 도용 – 종료 – 해산, 소멸

52 뒤지다 – 애원하다 – 청원하다

53 선언하다 – 임명하다 – 간청하다

54 수여하다 – 포기하다 – 수여하다

55 압축하다 – 압축하다 – 넘다

56 목표 – 기소 – 기소

57 맡기다 – 찬성하다 – 비준하다

58 지속되는 기간 – 재임 기간 – 법관

59 증서 – 훔치다 – 헌장

60 강요하다 – 압박하다 – 포기하다

61 반란 – 자비심 – 반란

62 지위, 계급 – 선언 – 지위, 위상

63 수여하다 – 기부하다 – 추정하다

64 변경하다 – 강요하다 – 개정하다

65 재량 – 압박 – 압제, 폭압

01 animosity n. 반감, 적대감
두 남성은 항상 싸우지만, 서로에 대해 반감을 갖고 있진 않다.

02 integrity n. 진실성, 온전함
그녀는 부유하거나 교육을 잘 받은 사람이 아니지만, 행동에서 온전함이 드러난다.

03 apportionment n. 배분, 할당
관계자들은 판매 계약 원본에 토지 배분 관련 사항이 자세하게 명시되지 않아 몇 년간 분쟁을 벌였다.

04 inference n. 추론(한 것)
경찰은 범죄 현장에서 일어난 일에 대한 논리적인 추론이 가능하도록 충분한 증거 확보를 했다고 발표했다.

05 frivolously adj. 경박하게, 장난삼아
마이클의 어머니는 그에게 묻는 질문에 계속 경박하게 대답하면 크게 혼낼 것이라고 경고했다.

06 zeal n. 열의
그는 재능이 있지만, 굉장한 음악가가 되기 위한 열의가 부족하다.

07 speculation n. 추측, 어림짐작
개리가 범죄를 저질렀다는 증거는 없다: 모든 소문과 비난은 추측에 의한 것이다.

08 preeminence n. 탁월함
화가는 자신의 탁월함을 약간의 재능, 좋은 교육과 많은 연습의 결과로 봤다.

09 inflame v. 흥분/격분시키다, 화나게 하다
난 그녀를 화나게 할 의도는 없었는데, 왠지 모르게 내 질문에 화를 냈다.

10 enlightened adj. 깨우친, 계몽된, 교화된
대부분의 사람들은 그런 미신을 믿기에는 너무 교화됐다.

11 subservient adj. 누구한테나 순종하는, 굴종하는
40년 동안 집사였기 때문인지, Ustinov씨는 그의 순종적인 성격을 바꿀 수 없는 것 같았다.

12 helm n. 지도적 지위, (배의) 키
이 회사는 마치 아무도 키를 조정하지 않는 배와 같다.

13 prevail v. 승리하다
전쟁 초기에 양쪽 모두 각자 승리할 확신이 있었다.

14 mercantile adj. 상업(무역)의
르네상스 시대 때, 베니스는 지중해 지역에서 가장 큰 무역 항구였다.

15 biases v. 편견을 갖게 하다
헨리는 지난번 셰퍼드에게 물린 기억 때문에 모든 개에 대한 편견이 있다.

01 patronized   v. 후원하다, 애용하다
길모퉁이에 있는 빵집은 60년 동안 영업했고, 우리 할머니는 할아버지와 결혼한 55년 전부터 그 빵집을 애용했다.

02 inducement   n. 유인책, 장려책
정부는 젊은 부부를 대상으로 실질적으로 출산율을 높일 수 있는 장려책을 따로 마련하지 않았다.

03 obnoxious
adj. 아주 불쾌한, 몹시 기분 나쁜
제이크는 모임에서 남들에게 몹시 기분 나쁜 태도를 보인 후, 다시는 초대받지 않았다.

04 intrigue   n. 모의, 음모
그로버 선생님이 해고된 이유는 그와 관련된 음모 때문인 것이 명백했다.

05 assimilated   v. 동화되다
미국으로 이민을 간 지 40년이 지났지만 김씨는 아직 미국 사회에 완전히 동화되지 않았다.

06 medium   n. 매체, 수단
10년이 채 지나지 않았지만, 스마트폰은 세계적으로 가장 많이 쓰이는 통신 수단이 되었다.

07 spectacle   n. 구경거리
난 록펠러 센터의 크리스마스트리 점등식을 본 적이 없었다: 정말 굉장한 구경거리였다.

08 discern
v. 구분하다, 알아차리다
도버 아저씨는 훈련된 눈 덕에 진짜와 위조 지폐를 구분할 수 있다.

09 consonant
adj. 동의하는, 일치하는
아버지의 행동은 언제나 그의 가치관과 일치했다.

10 efficacy   n. 효험, 효능
난 대체 의약품에 대한 신뢰가 없다: 관련 효능에 대한 과학적 근거가 없기 때문이다.

11 constituents   n. 유권자
선두를 달리고 있던 후보자는 유권자들로부터 30% 미만의 표를 받은 것으로 드러났다.

12 diffusive   adj. 널리 퍼진, 분산된
선행에 대한 미담은 널리 퍼진다: 그런 이야기들은 아주 빨리 퍼진다.

13 rendered
v. (어떤 상태가 되게) 만들다, 하다
많은 사람들은 충격적인 허리케인에 의해 집을 잃은 상태가 되었다.

14 impediment   n. 장애물
여전히 진행되고 있는 정치적 갈등은 나라의 경제성장에 큰 장애물이다.

15 inverted   v. 역의, 반대의
스턴트 파일럿은 비행기가 땅에서 10미터 채 뜨지 않은 상태에서 비행기를 반대로 뒤집었다.

16 factious
adj. 파벌적인, 당파심이 강한
파벌적인 분위기는 일반적으로 국가간 경쟁 의식이 자극될 때 수면에 오른다.

Class 09 — Answers

01 auxiliary   adj. 보조의, 예비의
학교에서 정전을 대비해 두 개의 보조 발전기를 마련했다.

02 palpable
adj. 감지할 수 있는, 명백한, 분명한
경기가 시작하려고 하자 경기장 내부에서 기대감을 확실히 느낄 수 있었다.

03 requisite   adj. 필요한
학생들이 공학대학에 소속되려면 몇 가지 필수 강의를 수강해야 한다.

04 endowments   n. (타고난) 재질, 재능
그녀의 성공 비결은 타고난 재능이 아니다. 남들과 똑같지만, 남들보다 몇 배로 노력해서 성공할 수 있었다.

05 expedient   n. 처방, 방책
정부가 모든 문제에 제시하는 방책은 세금 인상이다.

06 contrived   v. 고안하다
그들은 아무도 시도하지 않은 계획을 고안했다.

07 contemplation   n. 숙고, 사색
레너드는 그 직책을 맡기 전에 며칠동안 숙고를 했다.

08 conferred
v. (상, 명예, 학위, 자격 등을) 수여하다
대학교는 그에게 명예 학위를 수여했다.

09 addressed   v. 연설하다
교장선생님은 매주 월요일 아침 전교생들 앞에서 연설을 하셨다.

10 nominal
adj. 명목상의, 이름뿐인
윌리엄스 씨는 명목상 사장이다. 회사는 사실 부사장인 핀치 씨의 지휘 아래 운영된다.

11 commensurate
adj. 어울리는, 상응하는
내 경력에 상응하는 월급을 받기를 기대한다.

12 magnitude   n. 규모
우리는 업무의 규모가 이렇게 큰지 프로젝트를 시작하고 나서야 알았다.

13 sect   n. 종파
기독교 민주당은 전국 민주당의 종파로 시작되었다.

14 extent   n. 정도, 크기
우리는 어제의 폭풍우가 일으킨 피해의 규모 크기를 아직 모른다.

15 constitutes
v. ~을 구성하다, ~이 되다
몇몇 사람들은 이민자의 증가는 국내 노동 시장에 위협 요인이 될 것으로 생각한다.

16 hazard
v. 비난 받을 셈치고 제안/질문하다
민감한 주제인 것은 알지만, 혹시 욕먹을 셈치고 최근 스캔들에 대한 몇 가지 질문을 드려도 될까요?

01 temporal   adj. 현세적인, 속세의
데이비드의 어머니는 굉장히 영적이지만, 그는
속세적인 요소들에 관심이 더 많다.

02 anguish   n. 괴로움, 비통
하워드는 애완견이 무지개 다리를 건넜을 때
괴로움에 눈물을 흘렸다.

03 disposed
adj. 마음이 있는, ~을 생각하는
우리는 요구사항이 받아들여질 때까지 싸울
의향이 있다.

04 subjugation   n. 정복, 점령, 예속
대한민국이 일제에게 점령당한 시기는 36년
동안 지속되었다.

05 martial   adj. 싸움의, 전쟁의
적이 싸울 의도가 있던 사실은 명백하다.

06 entreaty   n. 간청, 애원
피고인의 어머니는 판사에게 진심 어린 간청
을 드리며 아들의 무죄를 빌었다.

07 apt
idiom. 하는 경향이 있는
브라이언은 본인의 잘못을 타인에게 덮어 씌
우려는 경향이 있다.

08 arduous   adj. 몹시 힘든, 고된
몹시 힘든 등산길을 걸은 후, 드디어 산꼭대기
에 도착했다.

09 riveted   v. 고정시키다
우리 우정은 서로에 대한 존중에 의해 고정되
어 있다.

10 array   n. 집합체, 배열
카페는 인상적인 CD, LP 배열을 선보였다.

11 beseeched   v. 간청하다, 애원하다
로라는 할아버지에게 건강을 헤치기 전에 술
을 끊으시라고 간청했다.

12 solace   n. 위안, 위로
아이들은 그 나이에 어머니의 품속에 있을 때
만 위안을 받는다.

13 insidious   adv. 교활한
나는 그가 이렇게나 교활한 면이 있는 줄 몰랐다.

14 comport   v. 일치하다, 동의하다
결론은 논리와 일치하지 않는다.

15 indulge

v. 마음껏 하다, ~가 제멋대로 하게 하다
아이에게 항상 마음껏 행동하게 하는 것은 좋
지 않다: 약간의 훈육도 필요하다.

01 extenuate   v. 변명하다, 경감하다
변호사는 피고인의 형량을 낮추기 위해 그녀의 죄를 경감하려 하였다.

02 conduces
v. 이끌다, 공헌하다, 이바지하다
젊을 때의 검소함은 노후의 부유에 이바지할 것이다.

03 apprised   v. 알리다, 존중하다
케네스는 그의 상사에게 월말에 퇴사할 예정이라고 알렸다.

04 supine   adj. 반듯이 누운
그는 바닥에서 몇 시간 동안 반듯이 누운 자세로 있었다.

05 deference   n. 존중
마크는 항상 선배들을 존중하는 자세로 대한다.

06 inviolate
adj. 존중되어 온, 존중되어야 할, 어길 수 없는
가끔 사람은 본인의 존중되어야 할 권리를 위해 싸워야 한다.

07 formidable   adj. 어마어마한
개리는 많은 복싱 경기에 참여해봤지만, 톰 같은 어마어마한 상대와 대결해본 적은 없다.

08 inclination   n. 의향, ~하는 경향
크레이그의 미식을 탐닉하는 경향 때문에 시내에서 가장 좋은 식당이 어딘지 가장 잘 아는 사람으로 여겨졌다.

09 slighted   adj. 모욕, 무시당한
샌디는 해리가 그녀의 가족에 대해 한 말에 모욕감을 느꼈다.

10 spurned   v. 일축하다, 거절하다
에밀리는 책의 애정 표현들을 일축했다.

11 steadfast   adj. 견고함, 변함없는
클린트는 노력을 하면 반드시 좋은 결과가 있을 것이라는 굳은 믿음을 가지고 있다.

12 rejoiced   v. 크게 기뻐하다
온 국가는 월드컵 대표팀이 준결승 진출을 했을 때 크게 기뻐했다.

13 propriety   n. 예절, 예의범절
어떤 나라에서는 남녀가 공개적 장소에서 손을 잡는 행위는 예의범절에 어긋난다.

14 admonished   v. 꾸짖다, 충고하다
아버지는 나를 성적에 대해 꾸짖은 적은 없지만, 내가 한 행동이 예의 없다고 생각하실 때는 크게 혼내셨다.

15 perplexed   adj. 당혹스러운
이상한 질문에 당혹스러웠지만, 최대한 진정성 있게 답변하려고 노력했다.

16 diminution   n. 축소, 감소
인구 증가율의 감소가 미래에 이민자를 더 많이 유입시켜야 한다는 진지한 논의를 시작하게 했다.

Class 12 Answers

01 discern
v. 구분하다, 알아차리다
실력 있는 정치인은 인기 있는 정책과 '올바른' 정책을 구분할 줄 알아야 한다.

02 insidious   adj. 사악한
그 남자는 남을 배려하는 행동을 하기에는 너무 사악하고 자기중심적이다.

03 beseeched   v. 간청하다, 애원하다
보고서 마감일까지 이틀 남은 상태에서 래리는 브라이언에게 도와달라고 간청했다.

04 impediment   n. 장애물
높은 유가는 세계의 경제성장에 큰 장애물로 작용하고 있다.

05 endowments   n. (타고난) 재질, 재능
해리는 지능, 호기심, 끈기와 인내 등 훌륭한 학자에게 요구되는 많은 재능을 가지고 있다.

06 inflamed
v. 흥분/격분시키다, 화나게 하다
정치인이 사회 불안을 이민자에게 탓하자 많은 사람을 격분시켰다.

07 frivolous
adj. 경박하게, 장난삼아
존의 아내는 존의 플라스틱 모델을 만드는 취미를 경박한 시간 낭비라고 생각했다.

08 integrity   n. 진실성, 온전함
그는 온전하고, 배신을 하지 못하는 남자로 여겨졌다.

09 contrived   v. 고안하다
두 인질은 납치범을 속이고 도망가는 계획을 억지로 세웠다.

10 subservient   adj. 비굴한, 굴종하는
우리 할아버지가 젊으셨을 때는, 아내들은 대부분 남편에게 순종했는데, 요즘은 남편들이 아내에게 굴종하는 입장이다.

11 prevails   v. 승리하다
가끔 인생은 불공평한 것처럼 보일 수 있지만, 정의는 항상 승리한다는 점을 기억해라.

12 inducement   n. 유인책, 장려책
정부는 출산율을 높이기 위한 유인책을 발표했다.

13 nominal
adj. 명목상의, 이름뿐인
우리 아버지는 명목상 가장이시다; 중요한 결정은 사실 어머니께서 하신다.

14 auxiliary   adj. 보조의, 예비의
숲 속의 오두막집은 전력망과 연결되어 있고, 보조의 전력원으로 휘발유 발전기도 마련되어 있다.

15 patronized   v. 후원하다, 애용하다
우리 할머니는 동네 편의점을 30년 동안 애용하셨다.

16 entreaty   n. 간청, 애원
피고인에게 관대한 형량을 위한 가족의 진심 어린 애원을 듣고서도 판사는 피고인에게 징역 15년을 선고했다.

17 artifice   n. 책략, 계략
제갈량은 책략을 통해 오직 3천 명의 군대로 2만 명의 적군을 물리쳤다.

18 surveillance   n. 감시, 원격감시
경찰은 용의자를 몇 주 동안 비밀리에 감시했다.

19 rejoiced   v. 크게 기뻐하다
전쟁이 드디어 끝났을 때, 국민들은 크게 기뻐했다.

20 steadfast   adj. 견고함, 변함없는
처음 시도한 두 번의 사업은 실패했지만, 조지의 성공에 대한 투지는 견고했다.

21 address   v. 연설하다
대통령은 다음 주 재선 이후 처음으로 국민들 앞에서 연설을 할 예정이다.

22 palpable
adj. 감지할 수 있는, 명백한, 분명한, 완전히
제임스가 사고에서 다치지 않았다는 소식을
들었을 때, 우리는 완전히 안심했다.

23 temporal　　　　adj. 현세적인, 속세의
부탄의 왕국에서 왕은 나라의 영적, 현세적 지
도자다.

24 subjugation　　　n. 정복, 점령, 예속
인디언 원주민들이 미국인들에게 점령당하는
과정은 평화롭지 못했다.

25 spurned　　　　　v. 일축하다, 거절하다
나는 로버트가 예상보다 화났다는 사실을 그
와 화해하려는 나의 노력들을 모두 거절했을
때 깨달았다.

26 inviolate
adj. 존중되어 온, 존중되어야 할, 어길 수 없는
어렸을 때, 우리 가족 내에서 아버지의 권위는
무조건 존중되어야 했다.

27 deference　　　　　　　n. 존중
현충일에는 국기를 조기로 게양하여 나라를
위해 목숨을 희생한 병사들에 대한 존중 및 조
의를 표한다.

28 contemplation　　　n. 명상, 사색
며칠 동안 깊은 사색을 한 후, 사이먼은 직업
을 그만두고 창업을 하기로 결심했다.

29 magnitude　　　　　　n. 규모
결정이 내려졌을 때, 아무도 그 결정이 가져올
문제들의 규모를 상상하지 못했다.

30 perplexed　　　　　adj. 당혹스러운
경찰이 용의자로 생각했던 남성이 무죄로 입
증되었을 때, 경찰은 당혹스러웠다.

31 경박한, 하찮은: 사소한, 하찮은 (동의어)
　　A. 열의: 활기, 기운
　　B. 반감, 적대감: 아량, 관대함
　　C. 상업의: 속세의
A.　D. 깨우친, 계몽된: 구식의

32 승리하다: 굴복하다 (반대어)
　　A. 옹호하다: 동화되다
　　B. 도당: 파벌
　　C. 보조: 장애물
　　D. 필요한: 필요한

33 어울리는, 상응하는: 해당하는 (동의어)
　　A. 옹호하다: 동화되다
　　B. 큰 불, 대화재: 불
　　C. 심사숙고하다: 종파
　　D. 반역죄: 동맹

34 ~ 할 마음이 있는, 경향이 있는: 꺼리는, 싫어
하는 (반대어)
　　A. 세속적인: 현세적인, 속세의
　　B. 위안, 위로: 걱정
　　C. 처신하다, (예의 바르게) 행동하다: 처신하
　　　다, 행동하다
　　D. 애원, 간청: 애원, 간청

35 간청하다, 애원하다: 애원하다 (동의어)
　　A. 존중되어 온, 존중되어야 할: 위반하다, 침
　　　해하다
　　B. 반듯이 누운: 서 있는
　　C. 축소, 감소: 증가
　　D. 존경: 숭배

36 예절, 예의범절: 점잖음, 예의 (동의어)
　　A. 약하다: 견고함, 변함없는
　　B. 질책하다: 꾸짖다, 충고하다
　　C. 집합체, 배열: 거절, 폐기
　　D. 구원, 구조: 선언문, 선언

37 실재하는, 만질 수 있는: 감지할 수 있는, 분명
한 (동의어)
　　A. 널리 퍼진, 분산된: 집단의, 단체의
　　B. 속임, 기만: 진실
　　C. 거꾸로 하다: 뒤집다
　　D. 우세한, 지배적인: 비굴한, 굴종하는

38 휘젓다, 뒤흔들다: 도발하다, 화나게 하다 (동
의어)
　　A. 짜증나게 하다: 성가시게 하다
　　B. 채권자: 채무자
　　C. 깨어있는, 계몽된: 편견을 가진
　　D. 지도적 지위: 파벌

39 아주 불쾌한, 몹시 기분 나쁜: 버릇없는 (동의어)
A. 반대하다: 가르치려 들다, 깔보듯 대하다
B. 구분하다, 알아차리다: 피하다
C. 뒤집히다: 전하다, 주다
D. 모욕, 상처: 모욕

40 나쁜 짓, 장난, 피해: 손상, 피해 (동의어)
A. 주장하다, 다투다: 죽다
B. 지배, 우세: 명성, 고지
C. 반감, 적대감: 친절함
D. 배분, 할당: 매체

41 (배의) 키 – 악덕 행위 – 조종 장치

42 악다구니, 악감정 – 적의, 적대감 – 추측

43 사소한, 하찮은 – 경박하게, 하찮은 – 말을 잘 듣는, 순종적인

44 편견 – 지배적인 – 승리하다

45 추론 – 추정 – 징후, 나타남

46 동화되다 – 깔보듯 대하다 – 통합시키다

47 뒤집히다 – 뒤집히다 – 구분하다, 알아차리다

48 당파적인 – 분열을 초래하는 – 필수적인

49 소질 – 규모 – 능력

50 큰불 – 숙고, 숙의 – 사색, 명상

51 일축하다, 거절하다 – 보안 등 확보하다 – 고정시키다

52 완전한, 순수한 – 부도덕한, 무원칙한 – 어길 수 없는, 존중되어야 할

53 타당성 – 애호 – 성향, 의향

54 적대적인 – 싸움의, 전쟁의 – 엄한, 녹초로 만드는

55 하는 경향이 있는 – 덫 – 덫

56 구원, 구조 – 위안 – 구조하다

57 처신하다 – 애원하다 – 처신하다

58 열렬, 열정 – 열정, 열심 – 괴로움, 비통

59 형체를 가진, 물질적인 – 만질 수 있는 – 잘 아는

60 먹다, 참가하다 – 항의, 시위 – 항의하다

61 수집품, 무리 – 집합체, 배열 – 배신

62 심사숙고하다 – 숙고하다 – 계획, 제도

63 방편, 처방 – 의무적인 – 필요한

64 널리 퍼진, 분산된 – 퍼뜨린, 전파한 – 동의하는, 일치하는

65 공정한 – 편향된 – 객관적인

01 solicitude   n. 배려
우리 가족에 대한 그의 배려에 감동받았다.

02 interwoven   adj. 짜여진
남색 천에 금색 실이 사이사이에 짜여졌다.

03 pillars   n. 기둥
성당은 높이가 24미터인 기둥 120개에 의해
받쳐져 있다.

04 edifice   n. 건물, 조직
저 우뚝 솟은 건물은 멀리서도 잘만 보인다.

05 subvert
v. 전복시키다, 뒤엎으려 하다
우리는 정부를 뒤엎으려고 할 마음은 없다; 단
지 정부가 현재 발생하고 있는 부당함을 파악
하고 있기를 바랄 뿐이다.

06 annals   n. 연대기, 연보
로저 페더러는 아마 테니스 역사 연보에서 가
장 훌륭한 선수로 기록되어 있다고 해도 과언
이 아니다.

07 vicissitudes   n. 우여곡절
우리 할머니가 사는 동안 겪은 우여곡절을 믿
기 어려웠다.

08 indignant
adj. 분개한, 분해하는
윌슨 여사는 딸이 폭우 상태에서도 밖에 서 있
어야 했다는 사실을 듣고 분개하셨다.

09 battery   n. 폭행
윈스턴은 주먹다짐으로 피터를 입원하게 한
후 폭행죄를 선고받았다.

10 covert   adj. 비밀의, 은밀한
드웨인이 내가 발표하는 동안 은밀하게 시계
를 쳐다본 것을 봤다.

11 artifice   n. 책략, 계략
윌리엄이 이렇게 책략적으로 행동할 줄은 상
상도 못했다: 굉장히 진실된 사람으로 보였기
때문이다.

12 exalts
v. 승격시키다, 칭찬하다
교회에서 모든 신자들은 기도를 통해 하나님
을 승격시킨다.

13 fraternal   adj. 공제의, 형제간의
저스틴은 남동생 조슈아에게 형제간 조언을
할 수 있을 때마다 한다.

14 incongruous   adj. 어울리지 않는
리처드가 오늘 회사에 입고 온 옷은 업무 분위
기와 전혀 어울리지 않았다.

15 enfeebled
v. 약화시키다, 쇠약하게 하다
그레고리 씨는 수년간 탄광에서 일하며 건강
을 잃을 정도로 쇠약해졌다.

Class 14 Answers

01 salutary
adj. 유익한, 효과가 좋은
오늘의 패배로 유익한 배움을 얻을 수 있다.

02 mitigate   v. 완화시키다, 줄이다
사과한다고 해서 너의 실수의 심각성이 줄어들진 않을 거야.

03 consecrated   v. 축성되다
이 터는 천주교 교황에 의해1998년에 축성되었다.

04 score   n. 20
터커 씨는 다음 주에 60세가 될 예정이다.

05 countervail
v. 무효로 만들다, 대항하다, 상쇄하다
루스는 지독한 냄새를 상쇄시키기 위해 공기 방향제를 온데 간데 뿌렸다.

06 assuage
v. 누그러뜨리다, 진정시키다
신임 대통령의 가장 중요한 업무는 이전 정부가 국민을 실망시킨 부분을 누그러뜨리는 것이다.

07 vigilance   n. 경계, 조심
회사는 기술적 비밀을 조심스럽게 지킨다.

08 conceived   v. 형성하다, 계획하다
감독은 해당 영화를 제작하기 위해 필요한 기술이 개발되기 10년 전에 시놉시스를 계획했다.

09 emancipation   n. 해방
많은 청교도인들은 해방을 위해 북미로 이민을 갔다.

10 designated   v. 지정하다, 지명하다
올해 기준으로, 5층 이상의 모든 건물은 '금연' 구역으로 지정되었다.

11 indulgence
n. 사치, 하고 싶은 대로 함, 관대함
그녀의 아들들은 매우 소란스럽지만, 글로리아는 그들이 하고 싶은 대로 하게 한다.

12 endure
v. 오래가다, 견디다, 지속되다
수나라는 1000년 동안 지속될 기대에 건국되었으나, 60년밖에 지속되지 못했다.

13 intimated   v. 넌지시 알리다
마리는 프랭크의 솔직함이 간혹 그녀를 불편하게 한다고 넌지시 알렸다.

14 fomented   v. 조성하다
러시아 혁명이 발생했을 때 전혀 예상하지 못한 전 세계를 혼란스럽게 했으나, 사실 사회적 격변의 분위기는 러시아 제국 내에서 한 세기 전부터 조성되었다.

01 suitable   adj. 적합한, 적절한
부장님은 스튜어트에게 옷차림이 회사로 입고
오기에는 적절하지 않다고 경고했다.

02 garrisoned   v. 배치하다, 수비대를 배치하다
남자가 부족했기 때문에 해당 지역에는 여성
과 남자 청소년들이 방위대로 배치되었다.

03 man   v. ~에 인원을 배치하다, 지키다
내가 일하러 가지 않으면, 리처트가 혼자 가게
를 지켜야 한다.

04 amicable   adj. 우호적인, 원만한
우리는 서로에게 항상 우호적이었지만 진정한
친구는 아니다.

05 accede   v. 응하다, 동의하다
조건에 동의하지 않는다.

06 faithful   adj. 충실한
나는 타임 잡지를 10년동안 충실하게 읽었다.

07 intercourse   n. 교류
그는 혼자 살고, 그 누구와도 교류를 하지 않
는다.

08 testimony   n. 증거, 증언
호크 씨의 작은 아파트에 있는 소박한 장식들
은 그의 절약하는 생활 습관을 입증하는 증거다.

09 deemed   v. 여기다
교수님은 내 변명을 받아들일 수 있는 사유로
여기셨다.

10 suppress   v. 진압하다, 금하다, 억제하다
난 콘서트 도중에 나오는 딸국질을 억제하려
고 노력했지만 결국 실패했다.

11 enjoined   v. 명하다
다수의 유럽 국가들이 광고주들에게 건강하지
않을 정도로 마른 모델의 고용 금지를 명했다.

12 manifest   v. 나타내다, 나타나다
그의 인자한 행동들은 진심으로 자애로운 성
격을 그대로 나타낸다.

13 moderation   n. 절제, 적당함
의사는 리처드에게 음주는 적당히만 해야 한
다고 말했다.

14 abstaining   v. 삼가다, 끊다
나는 과식을 삼가면서 살을 빼려고 노력하고
있다.

15 warrant   v. 정당하게 만들다, 이유를 주다
헨리가 나한테 화를 내는 것을 정당하게 한 나
의 행동이 무엇이었는지 전혀 모르겠다.

16 invoked   v. 들먹이다, 부르다, 빌다
가해자의 어머니는 피해자의 가족을 불러 자
기 아들의 용서를 빌었다.

Class 16 ●———— 📖 ————● Answers

01 amicable   adj. 우호적인, 원만한
두 남자는 테니스 코트 위에서는 라이벌이지만, 경기장에서 벗어났을 때는 우호적인 관계를 유지한다.

02 disposition   n. 기질, 성향
나는 최대한 항상 진실을 말하려는 성향이 있다.

03 candor   n. 순수성, 솔직함
곧 너에게 할 질문이 많이 중요해서, 완전 솔직하게 대답해줬으면 좋겠어, 알았지?

04 conspicuous
adj. 눈에 잘 띄는, 튀는, 뚜렷한
키 197cm에 몸무게가 120kg 되는 제이크는 어디서든 눈에 잘 띈다.

05 subdue
v. 진압하다, 가라앉히다
경찰은 물대포와 최루 가스로 폭력적인 시위자들을 진압하려고 했다.

06 impartial   adj. 공정한, 중립적인
제시와 리처드가 다투는 중 제이크는 중립적인 태도를 유지했다.

07 spectator
n. 관중, 관객, 보고 있는 자
엄마와 할머니가 말싸움을 할 때, 아빠는 관전자일 수밖에 없다.

08 menaced   v. 위협하다
의문의 남성이 놀이터에 있는 아이들을 위협하자, 부모들 중 한 명이 바로 경찰에게 신고했다.

09 adhere
v. 들러붙다, 부착되다, 준수하다
아론은 똑똑한 사람들의 조언을 구하고, 그 조언을 받아들이는 것이 그의 성공의 비밀이라고 했다.

10 de facto
adj. 사실상의, 실질적인
히긴스 씨가 회장이지만, 화이트씨가 회사의 실질적인 결정권자이다.

11 manifestation   n. 징후, 나타남
최근 시위들은 국민들의 불만의 징후다.

12 felicity
n. 더할 나위 없는 행복
크롤리 씨의 다섯 자녀와 열 여섯 손녀, 손주가 그의 생일을 위해 모였을 때 "이보다 더한 행복이 있을까?"라고 외치셨다.

13 comport   v. 일치하다, 동의하다
나의 행동과 말이 일치하도록 항상 노력해왔다.

14 manhood   n. 성인, 남성성
헨리의 아버지는 돌아가셨고 어머니는 병으로 누워계셔서 그는 빠르게 성인으로 성장했어야 했다.

15 sustaining   n. 유지하는, 지탱하는
나는 오랫동안 집중력을 유지하는 데에 어려움을 겪는다.

01 entails   v. 수반하다

뉴욕의 재미있는 점 중 하나가 큰 도시인 만큼 수반하는 다양한 오염, 청결 관련 문제가 많음에도 불구하고, 수돗물이 마실 수 있을 정도로 깨끗하다는 것이다.

02 parallel   adj. 평행한, 유사한

버스와 지하철 노선은 이 지점에서 몇 킬로미터동안 평행하게 이어진다.

03 agony   n. 극도의 고통

프랭크가 얼굴을 찡그리는 모습을 보며 극도의 고통에 시달리고 있다는 것을 알 수 있었다.

04 bondage   n. 구속, 신체 결박

이 영화는 모세가 그의 사람들을 구속에서부터 벗어나게 한 이야기다.

05 misanthropic

adj. 사람을 싫어하는, 인간을 혐오하는

쿠퍼 박사는 늙으면서 사람을 싫어하고 냉소적으로 변했다.

06 banished   v. 추방하다, 쫓겨나다

러시아 출신 작가 알렉산드르 솔제니친은 소련에서 1970년도에 추방됐다.

07 emanates

v. ~에서 나오다, 발하다

세바스찬한테 자신감이 뿜어 나온다.

08 annihilation   n. 전멸

북한은 남한과의 전쟁이 북한의 전멸을 뜻한다는 것을 알 것이다.

09 calamity   n. 재앙, 재난

폭풍우는 지역의 큰 재앙을 불러왔다.

10 strife   n. 갈등, 불화

국가 내에서 몇십 년간 내란 관련 갈등이 지속되어 왔다.

11 perpetuate

v. 영구화하다, 영속시키다, 계속하다

루벤이 계속 부모님에게 경제적 지원을 받을 생각을 하는 건 어리석다.

12 abstract

adj. 추상적인, 관념적인

20세기 초부터 쓰인 대부분의 클래식 음악은 내 기준으로 지나치게 추상적이다.

13 rendered

v. (어떤 상태가 되게) 만들다, 하다

관객이 루크를 바라보았을 때 그의 용기를 무용지물로 만들었다.

14 implored   v. 애원하다

나는 데이빗에게 수업 필기를 공유해달라고 애원했으나, 끝내 거절당했다.

15 waive   v. 포기하다, 면하다

주인은 세입자들에게 2년 동안 임대하기로 하면 마지막 달의 월세를 면해주겠다고 약속했다.

16 alleged

adj. (근거 없이) 혐의를 제기하다

혐의자는 그의 무죄를 증명할 알리바이가 없었다.

17 morose   adj. 시무룩한, 침울한

앤드류는 그의 아버지의 장례식에서 매우 침울해 보였다.

01 annals   n. 연대기, 연보
윈스턴 처칠이 아프리카에서 젊은 장교로서 이룬 업적들은 영국 군대 연보의 전설로 기억됐다.

02 edifices   n. 건축물, 조직
타지마할은 세계적으로 인정받는 건축물 중 하나다.

03 insidious
adv. 교활한, 은밀히 퍼지는
질병은 은밀히 퍼졌고, 현재 보건 전문가들에 따르면 백만 명 넘게 확진됐다.

04 indignant   adj. 분개한, 분해하는
제임스의 어머니는 그가 식품점에서 무언가를 훔치는 모습을 봤을 때 분개하셨다.

05 specious   adj. 그럴듯한
전 감독이 본인의 갑작스러운 은퇴에 대해 말한 사유가 그럴듯했지만, 내부 직원들은 그가 사기죄로 의심받고 있어서 은퇴한 사실을 알고 있었다.

06 foment   v. 조성하다
야당의 지도자는 스캔들을 이용해 대중의 반국가적 분위기를 조성하고자 했다.

07 salutary
adj. 유익한, 효과가 좋은
그의 질책은 마냥 기분 좋진 않았지만, 나의 가치를 절대 과대평가하지 말라는 유익한 교훈을 남겼다.

08 assuage
v. 누그러뜨리다, 진정시키다
그 어떤 일본 정치인도 한국인과 중국인이 일본이 제2차 세계대전 때 저질렀던 범죄에 대해 느끼는 적대감을 진정시키지 못했다.

09 hallowed
v. 소중한, 신성시되는, 신성한
본 교회는 완공된 1976년 교황에 의해 신성시되었다.

10 countervail
v. 무효로 만들다, 대항하다, 상쇄하다
내전 기간 동안, 미국과 소련은 각자 더더욱 파괴적인 무기를 개발하여 서로의 군사력에 대항했다.

11 enjoined   v. 명하다
켈러 여사가 아들의 과소비 습관에 대해 알게 되었을 때 더욱 검소하게 살라고 명했다.

12 abstain   v. 삼가다, 끊다
앤더슨 씨의 의사가 지나친 음주와 흡연을 끊지 않으면 10년 이상 못 산다고 경고했다.

13 manned
v. ~에 인원을 배치하다, 지키다
해외 대사관의 모든 입구는 군인이 지켰다.

14 warranted
v. 정당하게 만들다, 이유를 주다
두 학생이 부정행위를 했다는 증거를 찾았을 때, 교장선생님은 상황을 고려해서 학생들의 퇴학이 정당하다고 느꼈다.

15 moderation   n. 절제, 적당함
지나친 음주는 건강을 해치지만, 적당한 음주는 무해하다고 여겨진다.

16 spectators
n. 관중, 관객, 보고 있는 자
새로운 스타디움은 4만 명이 넘는 관객을 수용할 수 있다.

17 menaced   v. 위협하다
왕따당하는 것에 지친 헨리는 더 이상 학교에서 그보다 큰 학생들에게 위협당하지 않기를 다짐했다.

18 banished   v. 추방하다, 쫓겨나다
삼촌이 마리 이모의 결혼식에서 취하고 엉뚱하게 행동해서, 할머니는 앞으로 모든 가족 모임에서 그가 못 오도록 추방시켰다.

19 felicity
n. 더할 나위 없는 행복
글로리아는 어린 시절 불행했지만, 제이크와 만나고 결혼하면서 더할 나위 없는 가정의 행복을 찾았다.

20 conspicuous
adj. 눈에 잘 띄는, 튀는, 뚜렷한
켈리는 무리에서 눈에 잘 띄도록 밝은 빨간색 자켓을 입겠다고 했다.

21 abstract
adj. 추상적인, 관념적인
나는 그의 시가 너무 추상적이라고 생각했다: 단 한 단어도 이해할 수 없었다.

22 perpetuate
v. 영구화하다, 영속시키다, 계속하다
불평등을 무시하는 건 불평등을 영속시키는 것과 똑같다.

23 bondage
n. 구속, 신체 결박
제이슨은 부모님이 과하게 보수적이라고 생각했고, 대학에 입학하여 구속에서 벗어나는 날만 기다렸다.

24 implored
v. 애원하다
수지가 사장님에게 퇴사한다는 말씀을 드렸을 때, 그는 회사를 계속 다니라고 애원했다.

25 entails
v. 수반하다
연봉이 높은 직업은 굉장히 어려운 업무를 수반하는 경우가 많다.

26 calamity
n. 재앙, 재난
경찰, 소방대원과 의료진 사이 훌륭한 협동 덕에 지역에 허리케인이 몰아쳤을 때 큰 재앙을 피할 수 있었다.

27 agony
n. 극도의 고통, 비애
브룩스 씨는 아버지가 돌아가셨다는 소식을 듣고 극도의 비애로 울음을 터트렸다.

28 manifestation
n. 징후, 나타남
아버지의 나에 대한 애정은 주로 돈을 통해 나타난다.

29 solicitude
n. 배려
우리가 머무는 동안 주인들의 배려에 감동을 받았다.

30 incongruous
adj. 어울리지 않는
할머니가 아직 2G 폰을 쓰는 것은 오늘날 같은 스마트폰 시대에 어울리지 않는다.

31 형제: 형제간의 (동의어)
A. 어머니: 모성의
B. 어린이: 장난삼아, 경박하게
C. 힘: 약화시키다
D. 공격하다: 폭행

32 절제, 적당한: 삼가다, 끊다 (동의어)
A. 응하다, 오르다: 동의하지 않다
B. 수비대, 배치하다: 반구, 반구체
C. 배려: 보살핌, 관심을 가지다
D. 충실한: 배신

33 보수: 임금 (동의어)
A. 진압하다, 금하다: 극복하다
B. 증거, 증언: 교류
C. 배반: 순수성
D. 따르다, 순종하다: 들러붙다, 부착되다

34 해방: 투옥, 구금 (반대어)
A. 해방: 비밀에 붙여진
B. 오래가다, 견디다: 계속하다
C. 유익한, 이로운: 유익한, 효과가 좋은
D. 칭찬, 찬사: 극찬하다

35 정직하지 못한: 교활한 (동의어)
A. 동떨어진, 연결이 잘 안되는: 짜여진
B. 사기: 책략
C. 지지하다: 반감
D. 성난: 높은, 너무나 기쁜

36 약화시키다: 전복시키다 (동의어)
A. 발표하다: 친한, 사적인
B. 오해의 소지가 있는: 허울만 그럴듯한
C. 완화시키다: 나타나다
D. 관용, 관대한 처분: 보호, 수호

37 신성하게 하다: 축성하다 (동의어)
A. 성질이 나쁜: 친절한
B. 찬성: 겁을 주다

C. 가치, 훌륭함, 받을 만하다: ~을 필요하게
만들다
D. 들러붙다: 완파하다
38 투표권: 참정권 부여 (동의어)
A. 연장하다, 길게 하다: 지속하게 하다
B. 추방하다: 환영하다
C. 내뿜다: 전멸시키다
D. 조화: 갈등
39 평행한: 동등한 (동의어)
A. 포기하다: 받아들이다
B. 시무룩한: 쓸쓸해 보이는
C. 입증된: (근거 없이) 주장된
D. 선입견 없는: 주관적인
40 기질: 기질 (동의어)
A. 더할 나위 없는 행복: 극도의 고통
B. 해방: 식민지화
C. 지정하다: 완화시키다
D. 부르다, 빌다: 간청하다, 애원하다
41 도움 되는 – 사소한 – 유익한
42 암시하다 – 넌지시 알리다 – 먹다, 참가하다
43 위험 – 조성하다 – 조성하다
44 우여곡절 – 구조 – 구원, 구조
45 건축물, 조직 – 책략 – 구조물, 건축물
46 짜증이 난 – 분개한 – 얼굴, 지지하다
47 은밀한 – 기진맥진하게 만들다 – 은밀한
48 부적절한 – 교활한 – 어울리지 않는
49 누그러뜨리다 – 완화시키다 – 견디다, 참다
50 주제 – 신성하게 하다 – 신성하게 하다
51. 조심 – 구경거리, 광경 – 진열, 전시하다
52 동의하는, 일치하는 – 양립될 수 있는, 호환이
되는 – 다정한
53 명령, 명령어 – 깔보듯 대하다 – 명하다
54 상상하다 – 이기다 – 승리
55 포격, 폭격 – 폭행, 공격 – 정복
56 영장, 보증서 – 붙이다, 고정시키다 – 고정하다
57 상상하다 – 예상하다 – 제거하다
58 주장된 – 실수할 수 있는 – 결함이 있는
59 포기하다 – 암시하다 – 포기하다, 앞서다
60 징후, 나타남 – 점잖음, 예의 – 예의범절

61 발표하다 – 발표하다 – 상쇄하다
62 가정하다 – 여기다 – 기뻐서 어쩔 줄 모르다
63 적절한 – 순수한, 완전한 – 침범되지 않은,
어길 수 없는
64 성향 – 애호 – 배려
65 찬성, 승인 – 위협하다 – 겁을 주다

01 exploits   n. 훈공
그는 역사책에 나올만한 훈공을 세웠다.

02 fortifications   n. 방어 시설
중세시대에 이 도시는 강력한 방어 시설을 가진 곳으로 유명했다.

03 gratitude   n. 고마움
그레이스는 학교에서 최선을 다하며 부모님께 감사함을 표현했다.

04 espouse   v. 옹호하다
미국에서 자라서 그런지, 제임스는 한국에서 모두가 따르는 굳건한 수직적 사회구조를 옹호하는 데에 어려움을 겪었다.

05 downright   adv. 완전히
경찰이 여성에게 아들을 상대로 증언해달라고 요청하자, 그녀는 협조를 완전히 거절했다.

06 mockery
n. 조롱, 흉내에 불과한 것
"Rocky" 시리즈의 첫 영화는 명작이었다: 다섯 번째 영화가 제작될 때쯤에는 영화계의 흉내에 불과한 것이 되었다.

07 wretched
adj. 형편없는, 끔찍한, 비참한
기숙학교에서 보낸 3년은 엄청나게 끔찍했다. 안 돌아가도 돼서 너무 기쁘다.

08 disposition   n. 기질, 성향
그는 친절한 기질을 보이는 사람은 아니었다: 실제로 그가 웃는 모습을 본 적이 없는 것 같다.

09 afford   v. 제공하다
마이크는 팀원들이 그가 원했던 지지를 제공하지 않아서 서운했다.

10 despise
v. 경멸하다, 굉장히 싫어하다
제발 다음 회의에는 늦지 말아주세요. 전 다른 사람들 기다리면서 시간 낭비하는 것을 굉장히 싫어합니다.

11 violation   n. 위반, 위배
미국에서 총기 소유를 제한하는 것은 헌법상의 권리에 위배되는 것과 같다.

12 ford   v. (강 등을) 건너다
너 혼자서 강을 건널 생각을 하지 마; 물이 보기보다 훨씬 깊거든.

13 righteousness   n. 정의, 정당
모든 상황에서 윤리적으로 옳은 결정을 하는 것은 정당하다.

14 wrung   v. 짜다, 비틀다
헨리는 젖은 셔츠를 비틀어 짜고 말리려고 널었다.

15 denied   v. 거부하다, 부인하다
용의자는 범죄와의 연관성을 전면 부인했다.

16 vanquish
v. 완파하다, 정복하다, 물리치다
인생은 게임이 아니다: 마지막에 보스를 물리치며 끝내는 것이 아니다.

17 pertinence   n. 적절성, 연관성
인맥이나 가족 관계 등은 채용 과정에 연관이 없어야 한다.

01 hardihood   n. 배짱, 용기
마이크는 교내 불량배에게 맞설 용기를 냈다.

02 discrimination   n. 차별, 안목, 차이
이 학교는 그 어떤 형태의 차별을 허용하지 않는다 – 인종, 종교, 정치적 성향 상관 없이 모든 사람을 환영한다.

03 consecrate   n. 축성하다
세례식에서 신부님은 부모님 앞에서 아기를 축성할 것이다.

04 ballot   n. 투표, 투표용지
뉴스는 오늘 일반 선거에서 역대급 인원의 국민이 투표를 했다고 발표했다.

05 impelled   v. 해야만 하게 하다
프랑크에 대한 나의 충성심 때문에 그가 실수하고 있다고 설득해야만 했다.

06 paralysis   n. 마비
주식 시장은 마비 상태였다 – 모든 거래가 멈췄다.

07 vigor   n. 힘, 활력
모세 씨는 95세지만 여전히 힘이 넘친다.

08 curtail   n. 축소시키다, 줄이다
나는 소비를 줄이지 않으면 곧 파산할 것이다.

09 wither   v. 시들다, 말라 죽다
오늘 아침에만 해도 멀쩡하게 활짝 펴 있던 꽃들이 벌써 시들기 시직했다.

10 odious
adj. 끔찍한, 혐오스러운
난 한 끔찍한 여름방학 동안 호주에서 한 오리농장에서 일했다: 절대 다시 안할 것이다.

11 ordain
v. 임명하다, 명하다, 정하다
그에게 작별인사를 했지만, 운명이 우리를 다시 만나게 정해줬다는 생각이 들었다.

12 sovereign   n. 군주, 국왕
엘리자벳 2세 여왕은 캐나다의 군주다.

13 dissension   n. 불화
모임 내 멤버들 사이에서 항상 약간의 불화가 있었지만, 그들은 항상 일을 잘했다.

14 inducted   n. 취임되다, 인도하다
오늘 새로운 지도자가 취임되었다.

15 candor   n. 솔직
우리 부모님은 그들이 행복한 결혼 생활을 유지하는 비밀이 서로간에 완전하게 솔직한 것이라고 한다.

01 evanescent   adj. 빠르게 사라지는
돈과 명예를 가진 사람들은 대부분 둘 다 빠르게 사라진다고 알려줄 것이다.

02 stimulation   n. 자극
80대인 로버츠 박사는 고등학교 수준 수학 문제가 주는 뇌의 자극이 좋아서 여가시간에 푼다고 하셨다.

03 abdicated   v. 왕위에서 물러나다.
왕은 이미 90대였으나 왕위를 내어 놓을 의지가 전혀 없었다.

04 callous   adj. 냉담한
그의 타인의 감정에 대한 무관심과 변명을 받아들이지 않는 냉담한 자세는 그를 회사 내에서 가장 무서운 사람으로 여겨지게 했다.

05 signify   v. 의미하다, 뜻하다
여러 기사에서 정부의 외교정책 결정들이 현 정권의 새로운 방향성을 뜻한다고 했다.

06 unscrupulous   adj. 부도덕한, 무원칙한
시장은 본인이 부도덕한 행동에 참여하고 있다는 비난을 모두 거부했다.

07 indicted   v. 기소하다
전 외교관은 국가 기밀을 외국 정보 기관에게 넘긴 혐의로 기소됐다.

08 peril   n. 굉장한 위험
책의 어머니는 가족 식사에 늦을 거면 굉장한 위험을 각오하라고 하셨다.

09 minister   v. 일조하다
헬러 부인이 다리를 다친 후 그녀의 딸 샐리는 그녀의 요구에 일조하기 위해 같이 살았다.

10 outworn   adj. 낡은
할아버지의 헛간에서 찾은 자전거는 꽤 낡아 보였지만, 내가 고칠 수 있을 것 같았다.

11 lure   n. 유혹, 매력
폴은 햄 한 조각으로 길고양이를 집으로 유혹하려고 했다.

12 stricken   adj. 시달리는
파버 가족을 방문했을 때, 온 가족이 독감으로 시달리는 중이었다.

13 conduct   n. 행동
부정 행위를 한 학생들은 신사답지 못한 행동으로 정학당했다.

14 exhortation   n. 간곡한 권고, 설득하는 연설
데이빗은 담배를 끊으라는 어머니의 간곡한 권고를 한 귀로 듣고 한 귀로 흘렸다.

15 bounty   n. 너그러움, 풍요로움, 포상금
이 지역은 자연의 풍요로움을 축복받은 곳이다.

16 incompetence   n. 무능
상대 당들은 정부를 무능하다고 비난했다.

01 mortal adj. 속세의, 이 세계에 해당되는, 필멸의
한 사람의 건강이 악화될 때, 돈과 직업 같은 속세의 요소들은 딱히 중요하게 여겨지지 않는다.

02 renewal n. 재개, 부활, 갱신
한국 전통주에 대한 관심이 부활하여 매우 기쁘다.

03 prescribes v. 규정하다
코치는 선수들에게 그가 규정한 규칙을 따르지 않는 사람은 퇴출시키겠다고 경고했다.

04 venture n. 벤처, 모험, 사업
커스벗 씨의 최근 사업은 5백만 달러가 넘는 수익을 창출했다.

05 asunder adv. 산산이, 뿔뿔이
많은 가족들은 전쟁 동안 뿔뿔이 흩어졌다.

06 anew adv. 다시, 새로
많은 난민들은 인생을 새로 시작하기 위해 캐나다로 이민을 갔다.

07 civility n. 공손함, 정중함
밀러 씨는 그의 식당에서 일하는 직원들에게 항상 손님들을 공손함을 가지고 대하라고 훈련시킨다.

08 endeavor n. 노력, 시도
히긴스 교수는 강의 진도에 뒤처지는 학생에게 만회하려면 많은 노력이 필요할 것이라고 주의를 주었다.

06 forum n. 토론장, 포럼
소셜 미디어는 긍정적인 토론을 위한 중요한 장이 되었다.

10 invectives n. 욕설
두 후보자들은 생중계되는 토론 중 서로에게 욕설을 날렸다.

11 forebears n. 선조, 조상
우리가 조상들의 경험으로부터 배우기를 거부한다면, 실수를 반복할 수밖에 없는 운명에 처할 것이다.

12 heir n. 상속인, 계승자, 후계자
왕이 후계자를 지목하지 않은 상태에서 죽자, 왕위를 위한 피 튀기는 싸움이 10년 이상 지속됐다.

13 tempered adj. 완화된, 조절된
원작이 텔레비전 방송으로 송출하기 너무 폭력적이었기에 다소 완화된 버전이 방영됐다.

14 subversion n. 파괴, 멸망
테러범 조직의 목적은 서구 문명의 완전한 멸망이었다.

15 solemn adj. 근엄한, 엄숙한
하딩 씨의 장례식 분위기는 슬프고 근엄하기보다는 사실 그가 원했을 것처럼 기쁘고 쾌활했다.

16 heritage n. 유산
한국은 역사적 유산이 풍부한 나라다.

17 engulfed v. 완전히 에워싸다
리처드 씨는 본인의 은퇴 파티를 찾은 그 많은 손님을 봤을 때, 감사함으로 완전히 에워싼 듯한 느낌이 들었다.

Class 23 📖 Answers

01 conscience   n. 양심, 가책
나는 내 남동생이 받은 할로윈 사탕을 다 먹은 사실에 양심의 가책을 느끼지 않는다.

02 segregation   n. 분리, 구분
학교는 여전히 교내에서 남녀 구분을 강조한다: 남자와 여자는 같은 교실에서 배우지 않는다.

03 prosperity   n. 번창, 번영
사회학자들은 우리가 느끼기에 많은 문제들이 있음에도 불구하고, 지구는 전례없는 평화와 번창의 시기를 겪고 있다고 주장한다.

04 captivity   n. 감금, 억류
많은 야생 동물은 감금 상태에서 살아남을 수 없다.

05 beacon   n. 신호등
그들은 우리 배를 빛이 나는 신호 방향으로 인도했다.

06 score   n. 20
한 20명 정도가 이미 줄에서 대기하고 있었다.

07 momentous   adj. 중대한
38살에 율리시스 그랜트는 군대에 재입대하겠다는 중대한 결정을 내렸다.

08 default   v. 이행하지 않다, 체납하다
회사 경영진이 월말까지 2백만 달러의 수익을 창출하지 못하면 회사의 채무가 이행되지 않을 것이다.

09 hallowed   adj. 신성한
이 토지는 토착민들에게 신성하게 여겨진다.

10 exile   n. 추방된 사람
알렉산드르 솔제니친은 1974년도부터 러시아로 귀화한 1994년까지 소련에서 추방된 사람이었다.

11 dramatizes   v. 극적으로 보이게 하다, 과장하다
켈러 씨는 백화점 주차장에서 강도를 잡았다는 이야기를 할 때마다 과장해서 얘기한다.

12 languish   v. 머물다, 시들해지다
홍수 후 반년이 지났는데도 많은 난민들은 임시 대피소에서 머물며 집이 복원되기를 기다리고 있다.

13 tranquilizing   adj. 안정적
나한테 낚시는 안정적인 효과가 있다; 나를 안심시킨다.

14 crippled   adj. 불구의, 몸을 다친
호킹 박사의 몸은 질병으로 불구의 상태지만, 지적 능력은 대부분의 사람들보다 훨씬 뛰어나다.

15 seared   v. 표면을 데이게 하다
난로에 손을 데었다.

16 withered   v. 약해지다
그는 강한 남자였지만, 모든 사람과 똑같이 나이가 들면서 약해졌다.

314

Class 24 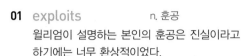 Answers

01 exploits   n. 훈공
윌리엄이 설명하는 본인의 훈공은 진실이라고 하기에는 너무 환상적이었다.

02 despised
v. 경멸하다, 굉장히 싫어하다
글로리아가 어렸을 때는 반에서 키가 제일 큰 학생이라는 사실이 굉장히 싫었지만, 성인이 된 지금 개의치 않는다.

03 violation   n. 위반, 위배
필리핀과 바티칸은 이혼이 위법행위인 유일한 나라들이다.

04 gratitude   n. 고마움
학생들은 보조 교사에 대한 감사함을 수업 마지막 날에 이별 파티를 열면서 표현했다.

05 mockery
n. 조롱, 흉내에 불과한 것
마이클이 본인 나이의 절반인 여자와 결혼했다는 사실은 조롱거리였다: 친구들은 그를 유괴범이라고 장난삼아 부른다.

06 odious
adj. 끔찍한, 혐오스러운
많은 서구 사람들은 한국 사람이 산낙지를 먹는 것을 끔찍하다고 한다.

07 ordained
v. 임명하다, 명하다, 정하다
제2차 세계대전 동안, 영국 총리 윈스턴 처칠은 운명이 그를 영국의 위대한 구세주로 명했다고 믿었다.

08 hardihood   n. 배짱, 용기
그 정치인은 대중매체에서 증거를 제시했을 때도 본인이 스캔들에 연루되어 있지 않다고 주장할 배짱이 있었다.

09 discrimination   n. 차별, 안목, 차이
지금은 상상하기 어렵지만, 인종차별은 미국 공립 학교 체계에서 1960년대까지 흔했다.

10 impel   v. 해야만 하게 하다
판사는 피고인의 무죄를 입증할 증거가 조금 있지만, 피고인에게 유죄를 선고해야만 하는 이유들이 있었다고 말했다.

11 vigor   n. 힘, 활력
85세임에도 불구하고 메시 씨는 활력을 잃지 않았다: 그는 아직도 하루에 2킬로미터를 수영한다.

12 wither   v. 시들다, 말라 죽다
아내는 꽃이 시들 때 우울해져서 꽃을 선물로 받는 것을 싫어한다.

13 produce   n. 생산물, 농작물
여름과 가을 동안 우리는 농작물이 훨씬 신선한 파머스 마켓에서 장을 본다.

14 bounty   n. 너그러움, 포상금
진료소는 너그러운 기부금과 박애주의적 지지에 의해 운영되고 있다.

15 incompetent   adj. 무능한
공무원들이 장기적인 계획을 실행할 수 없는 이유는 1년 이내에 눈에 띄는 발전을 보이지 않으면 무능하다는 평가를 받기 때문이다.

16 outworn   adj. 낡은, 진부한
대기업에서 일을 하고 생각은 진부하다고 여겨지고 있다: 더 많은 대학 졸업생들은 독립적으로 일을 하기를 택하고 있다.

17 lure   n. 유혹, 매력
많은 돈을 만질 수 있는 생각은 젊은이들이 불법 행위를 저지를 유혹을 느끼게 한다.

18 possession   n. 소유물, 보유
경찰은 예술 작품을 훔친 사람을 추적하는 데에 성공했지만, 그 사람은 아쉽게도 작품 자체를 더 이상 보유하고 있지 않았다.

19 evanescent   adj. 빠르게 사라지는
짧고 빠르게 사라지는 경제성장 시기는 지났고, 세계는 다시 불경기에 들어섰다.

20 conduct   n. 행동

부정 행위를 한 학생들은 신사답지 못한 행동으로 정학당했다.

21 callous   adj. 냉담한

제인은 남편이 그녀의 감정에 냉담하게 대해서 화가 났다.

22 solemn   adj. 근엄한, 엄숙한

아나운서가 끔찍한 폭발 사고로 많은 사람들이 사망하고 다쳤다고 엄숙한 목소리로 말했다.

23 prescribe   v. 규정하다

회사에서 모든 직원이 항상 ID카드를 소지하고 있어야 한다고 규정한다.

24 tempered   adj. 완화된, 조절된

우익 언론사의 사설은 좌익의 사설보다 수위가 조절된 버전이지만, 여전히 정부의 무능을 비판했다.

25 venture   n. 벤처, 모험, 사업

두 경쟁사들은 협동하여 공동 벤처 사업을 시작하기로 했다.

26 outpaced   v. 앞지르다, 앞서다

미국의 우주 프로그램은 소련이 첫 위성을 발사한 뒤에 처음 도입됐지만, 빠르게 소련의 프로그램을 앞질렀다.

27 engulfed   v. 완전히 에워싸다

그 배우가 공식 선상에 등장할 때마다 팬, 사진가와 파파라치에 완전히 에워싸여 있다.

28 civility   n. 공손함, 정중함

제인의 부모님은 제인의 남자친구를 정중하게, 그러나 따뜻하지 않게 반겼다.

29 conscience   n. 양심, 가책

헨리는 친구의 시험지에 있는 답안을 또렷하게 볼 수 있었지만 베껴쓰기에는 양심에 어긋났다.

30 beacon   n. 신호등

선원들은 수평선 저 멀리에 배를 부두까지 이끌 등대의 신호등을 봤다.

31 절름발이의: 절름발이의 (동의어)
A. 번영: 가난
B. 약화되다: 영구화하다
C. 진정시키는: 진정하는
D. 조합: 분리

32 비판: 칭찬 (반대어)
A. 조절된: 과장된
B. 경쟁자: 적
C. 자손, 후계자: 계승자, 후계자
D. 끔찍한: 덧없는, 쉬이 사라지는

33 걸어서 건너다: 횡단하다 (동의어)
A. 목록: 건물, 조직
B. 완파하다: 정복하다
C. 방어 시설, 강화: 경향
D. 자제, 금욕: 적절성

34 거부하다: 거부하다 (동의어)
A. 인도, 귀납: 친한, 사적인
B. 조롱: 조롱
C. 사치, 하고 싶은 대로 함: 경련
D. 현장, 선언문: 기둥

35 솔직: 책략 (반대어)
A. 원만한: 적대적인
B. 밝히다: 전하다
C. 공정한: 중립의
D. 받아들이다: 드러내다

36 인간혐오적인: 사회적인 (반대어)
A. 재앙: 재앙
B. 크게 기뻐하다: 환호
C. 적절한: 어울리지 않는
D. 변함없는: 변함없는

37 속하다: 관련시키다 (동의어)
A. 시달리는: 칭찬
B. 경감하다: 기소하다
C. 장애: 무능
D. 연대기: 연대기

38 능력: 재능 (동의어)
A. 그럴듯한: 냉담한
B. 극찬하다: 칭찬하다
C. 유용한: 경솔한
D. 지정하다: 시들다

39 추측: 추측 (동의어)
　　A. 쉬이 사라지는: 굴종하는
　　B. 암시: 암시하는
　　C. 정복하다: 반듯이 누운
　　D. 상쇄하다: 넘어뜨리다

40 영구화하다: 오래가다 (동의어)
　　A. 우여곡절: 허위
　　B. 보조의: 필요한
　　C. 보통의: 촉구하다
　　D. 혼란시키다: 당혹하게 하다

41 유산 – 기업 – 유산

42 반란 사태 – 전복, 파괴 – 토론장

43 (배의) 키 – 비난 – 욕설

44 탄력 – 양심 – 도덕

45 태우다 – 그슬다 – 시들다

46 절름발이의 – 그럴 듯한 – 무능력한

47 구속하다 – 구속하다 – 연대기

48 점잖음 – 투옥, 감금 – 공손함

49 약화되다 – 장식하다 – 악화되다

50 진정제 – 안정되는 – 압도적인

51 난민 – 추방자 – 행위

52 운 – 미지급 – 체납

53 기소 – 조심성 – 배려

54 짜다 – 입양하다 – 짜다

55 배짱 – 군주 – 군주

56 축성하다 – 축소시키다 – 축성하다

57 시달리는 – 괴로워하는 – 성난

58 정직하지 못한 – 한물간 – 부도덕한

59 재개 – 행동 – 행동

60 노력, 시도 – 적 – 적

01 quest   n. 탐구
지식을 위한 탐구는 절대 멈추지 않을 것이다.

02 brutality   n. 잔인함
보호소에 있는 많은 개들은 잔인함을 경험했기 때문에 사람을 믿기 어려워한다.

03 militancy   n. 투쟁성
시위자들의 투쟁성은 모두에게 충격이었다.

04 hamlet   n. 아주 작은 마을
30년 전까지만 해도 이 풍요로운 곳은 하나의 작은 마을이었다.

05 jangled   v. 쨍그렁거리다
누가 대답하기 전까지 초인종을 몇 번이나 울렸다.

06 discord   n. 불협화음, 불화
모든 가족과 똑같이, 우리 가족도 조화와 불화를 다 겪는다.

07 degenerated   v. 악화되다
회의는 빠르게 누가 더 고함을 크게 지르는가를 겨루는 장소로 악화되었다.

08 desolate   adj. 적막한, 외로운
우리 집에 있던 가구가 다 옮겨졌을 때 내부가 너무 적막해 보였다.

09 sweltering   adj. 무더운
싱가포르는 적도 위에 있어서 1년 내내 무덥다.

10 redemptive   adj. 구원하는
영화 끝자락에 적대자는 주인공의 목숨을 구하고 본인의 목숨을 구원하는 희생으로 죽는다.

11 inflation   n. 인플레이션, 물가상승률
젊은 가정이 시내에서 집을 찾는 것은 물가상승률 때문에 거의 불가능하다.

12 devotee   n. 추종자, 열성적인 애호가
프로 레슬링 선수 크리스가 여가 시간에 로맨스 소설을 읽는다는 사실을 아는 사람은 몇 명 되지 않는다.

13 inextricable   adj. 불가분한
가게 주인은 고객 응대 태도와 수익 증가가 불가분한 연관성을 띤다는 결론을 내렸다.

14 nullification   n. 무효
많은 사람들은 최근 판결의 무효를 요구하기 위해 법정 앞에 모였다.

15 invigorates   v. 활기를 북돋우다
헬스 이후 한 잔의 아이스티는 항상 내 활기를 북돋우게 한다.

Class 26

Answers

01 self-indulgence   n. 방종
나는 빠듯한 예산으로 생활하면서 한 달에 딱 한 번 4성 식당에서 저녁 먹는 걸로 방종한다.

02 route   n. 노선
교통상황이 너무 혼잡하다: 별도의 노선으로 가야 할 것 같다.

03 mandated   v. 명령하다
회사는 아서의 기업에게 거대한 제작 프로젝트를 착수하라고 명령했다.

04 ration   v. 제한하다
다이어트하고 있어서 하루 2000 칼로리 넘게 섭취하지 않도록 섭취를 제한해야 한다.

05 mainstream   n. 주류
나는 그 밴드가 인디가 아닌 트렌드를 따르는 대중적 밴드로 전향을 하자 관심을 잃었다.

06 evasiveness   n. 회피적임
너의 회피적인 태도에 이젠 지쳤어: 그냥 정직하게 답변해주면 안돼?

07 quota   n. 한도, 몫, 할당량
오늘의 생산 몫을 도달할 때까지는 퇴근을 못한다.

08 denominations   n. 액면가
이 100달러 지폐를 액면가가 적은 지폐 몇 장으로 교환해줄 수 있어?

09 windfall   n. 뜻밖의 횡재, 이득
정부로부터 세금 환불을 받았을 때 뜻밖의 이득을 얻었다.

10 reassurance   n. 안심
마틴이 나한테 윙크하면서 믿으라는 말을 해도 전혀 안심되지 않았다.

11 vivid   adj. 생생한, 선명한
증인은 사고 당시 있었던 일을 생생하게 설명했다.

12 campaign   n. 선거운동 캠페인
선거까지 한 달 남은 시점에, 각 후보자의 선거운동 캠페인은 풀가동 상태였다.

13 erosion   n. 침식, 부식
정부가 위기를 잘못 대처하면서 대중의 신뢰의 침식을 일으켰다.

14 paralysis   n. 마비
64세에 뇌졸중을 판정받은 그는 이제 반신마비 상태다.

15 stagnation   n. 침체, 부진, 불경기
경제 불경기는 10년 넘게 지속되었다.

16 fragmentation   n. 분열, 조각냄
노동조합은 분열되었다.

Class 27 Answers

01 lamented   v. 애통하다
내 단짝 친구가 다른 나라로 이사를 갔을 때
많이 애통했다.

02 commemorate   v. 기념하다
미국인들은 7월 4일에 미국의 독립을 기념한다.

03 impose   v. 강요하다
교통부는 1월 1일부터 교통 법규를 강요할 것
으로 발표했다.

04 affront   n. 모욕
나는 단지 지적을 했을 뿐인데, 그는 모욕으로
받아들였다.

05 secular   adj. 세속적인
마이클이 목사라고 해서 세속적인 욕구가 없
는 것은 아니다.

06 rekindled   v. 다시 불러일으키다
모짜르트에 대한 별로 알려지지 않은 영화를
본 뒤 클래식 음악에 대한 애정이 되살아났다.

07 utter   adj. 완전, 아주
그의 행동은 완전 어리석었다고 할 수밖에 없다.

08 gash   n. 깊은 상처
그렉은 자전거에서 떨어져 넘어진 뒤 피가 많
이 흐르는 다리에서 깊은 상처를 발견했다.

09 exhaustion   n. 탈진, 기진맥진
매일 밤 탈진 상태로 침대에 쓰러질 정도로 업
무가 힘들다.

10 implicit   adj. 암시된, 내포된
헨리는 헬렌의 말에 내포된 약간의 비판을 포
착했다.

11 fortitude   n. 불굴의 용기
우리의 적은 경험이 더 있을지 몰라도, 우리에
게는 불굴의 용기가 있어.

12 token   adj. 형식적인
그는 형식적으로 화해하려는 행동을 했지만,
나는 진심이 아니라는 것을 알았다.

13 aviation   n. 항공, 비행
기업은 항공업에 진출하고 있다.

14 hub   n. 중심지
서울, 상해와 도쿄는 모두 아시아의 중심지가
될 수 있도록 경쟁하고 있다.

15 agenda   n. 의제, 안건 목록
많은 의제를 논의해야 하니, 회의를 시작합
시다.

01 safeguard   v. 보호하다
아직 우리나라의 전통 관습들을 보호하는 사람들이 있다는 사실로 위안이 된다.

02 rallied
v. 결집하다, 집합하다, 모이다
데이빗이 퇴원해서 집에 오는 날, 친구들이 집 앞에 모여서 그를 응원하는 모습을 보였다.

03 resolution   n. 결단력
맨디가 다음 학기에 더 나은 모습을 보이겠다고 말했을 때 눈에서 결단력이 드러났다.

04 clerics
n. 성직자, 종교 지도자
천주교, 기독교와 무슬림교 성직자들은 협동하여 폭력을 규탄하고 평화와 조화를 촉진하기 위해 노력했다.

05 bestow   v. 수여하다
아버지는 내게 돈을 준 적은 없지만 나에게 만족스러운 삶을 살기 위한 지혜를 수여하셨다.

06 temper   v. 누그러뜨리다
미디어의 정부에 대한 비판은 누그러뜨리지 않았다.

07 faint-hearted
adj. 용기없는, 비겁한
나는 내 실수를 남에게 넘길 정도로 비겁하지 않다.

08 fringe   adj. 외곽의, 바깥
로큰롤이 처음 소개되었을 때, 많은 사람들은 오래 가지 않을 비주류 음악 장르로 여겼다.

09 petty   adj. 사소한
우리 사이에 가끔 사소한 말다툼은 있었지만, 10년 넘게 알고 지낸 친구 사이다.

10 recriminations   n. 비난
토론은 비난의 장으로 바뀌었다.

11 atrocities   n. 잔학한 행위
신성한 전쟁, 좋은 전쟁은 없다: 모든 전쟁은 잔학한 행위다.

12 perverted   v. 비뚤어지게 하다
그의 어릴 적 꿈은 음악가였지만, 크면서 겪은 우여곡절로 비뚤어져 범죄인으로 변했다.

13 lash   n. 채찍질, 강타
가엾은 남성은 경찰봉에 한 번 강타당하자 정신을 잃었다.

14 abetted   v. 사주하다
맥베스는 아내로부터 살인을 사주 받았다.

15 blaspheme
v. 신성 모독적인 발언을 하다
무교라고 해서 종교에 대한 신성 모독적인 발언을 할 권리는 없다.

16 pretense   n. 가식, 가면
그의 가식적인 모습은 그 누구도 속이지 못한다.

01 outworn   adj. 낡은
이 부츠를 신고 등산을 하기에는 너무 낡았다.

02 revamp   v. 개조하다, 개편하다
새로운 시장은 시내의 노쇠한 공공 대중교통 시스템을 개편하기로 약속했다.

03 embodied
v. 포함하다, 담다, 내포하다
그의 연설에 인내의 정신을 포함했다.

04 stormed
v. 쇄도하다, 시끄럽게/빠르게 들어오다/나가다
카페에서 조용한 아침을 즐기고 있던 와중에 왁자지껄한 청소년 무리가 갑자기 시끄럽게 들어왔다.

05 patchwork
n. 여러 조각들로 이뤄진 것
교수님께서 내 보고서가 마구잡이로 구성된 조각들로 이뤄진 것이라고 평가하셨다.

06 ushered   v. 안내하다
웨이터 주임은 우리를 친구들이 기다리고 있는 테이블로 안내했다.

07 clenched   v. 꽉 쥐다
그는 분노에 주먹을 꽉 쥐었다.

08 specter
n. 무서운 것, 망령, 귀신
앤디의 얼굴은 귀신을 본 듯 창백했다.

09 outlast   v. 보다 더 오래가다
빌은 항상 아프다고 징징거리지만, 사실 굉장히 건강하고, 아마 우리보다 오래 살 것이다.

10 allegiance   n. 충성
요즘에 대부분의 사람들은 돈이 더 주겠다는 직업을 가질 수 있다고 하면 바로 이직한다 – 더 이상 고용주들에 대한 충성을 가진 자들이 없다.

11 virtue   n. 진실성
정말 진실성을 가진 사람은 아무도 보고 있지 않을 때에도 누군가가 보고 있는 것처럼 행동하는 사람이다.

12 vigilant
adj. 바짝 경계하는, 조금도 방심하지 않는
어떤 사람들은 현대시대에는 피해망상적으로 모든 것을 바짝 경계해야 살아남을 수 있다고 주장한다.

13 unsung   adj. 찬양받지 못한
우리는 아무도 감사하지 않고 인정해주지도 않으며 그 누구도 하기 싫은 일을 한다.

14 succumb   v. 굴복하다
진정해. 화에 굴복해서 성급한 행동을 하지 마.

15 relinquished   v. 포기하다
기업의 창립자는 65세가 되면서 기업을 이끌기 위한 모든 권한을 포기했다.

16 braved   v. 위험을 대면하다
많은 경찰관과 봉사자들은 실종된 남자아이를 찾기 위해 숲 속에서 위험을 대면했다.

17 faltered
v. 흔들리다, 비틀거리다
차로 걸어가면서 비틀거릴 정도로 바람이 세게 불었다.

01 sweltering   adj. 무더운, 많이 더운
바깥의 날씨가 너무 더워 동네 한 바퀴만 돌았는 데도 땀이 많이 났다.

02 despised   v. 경멸하다
유명 피아니스트인 프랭크 딜러는 그가 소년이었을 때 친구들이 공원에서 야구를 하는 동안 자기는 피아노 연습을 하러 가야 하는 것을 경멸했다고 한다.

03 degenerated   v. 악화되다
교양 있는 회의가 계획되었지만 빠르게 두 경쟁 그룹이 서로에게 소리지르는 다툼으로 악화되었다.

04 inextricable   adj. 불가분한
대부분의 사람들은 지구온난화가 탄소 배출과 불가분하다는 데 동의한다.

05 quest   n. 탐구
스페인이 금을 탐구하는 과정에서 남아메리카로 발을 뻗은 첫 주자였기 때문에 대부분의 남아메리카 국가들에서 스페인어를 구사할 줄 안다.

06 discord   n. 불협화음, 불화
민주주의에서 어느 정도의 불화는 자기 의견을 표현하는 데에 두려움을 느끼지 않는다는 표시로, 건강하다고 여겨진다.

07 hamlet   n. 아주 작은 마을
조지는 도시 남자처럼 보이지만, 사실 시골의 아주 작은 마을에서 자랐다.

08 vivid   adj. 생생한, 선명한
할머니가 전쟁 동안 북한에서 탈출한 생생한 이야기를 하셨을 때 우리는 겁먹었다.

09 reassurance   n. 안심
아빠는 내가 좋은 야구 선수가 되도록 성장시켜주겠다고 믿으라고 하셨는데, 솔직히 크게 안심되지는 않았다.

10 mainstream   n. 주류
힙합이 1980년대 후반에 주류 음악이 되기 이전에도 10년 이상 존재해왔다는 사실을 아는 사람은 몇 없다.

11 fragmentation   n. 분열, 조각냄
1970년대에 미국이 베트남 전쟁에 기여한 정도에 대한 여론의 분열이 있었다.

12 windfall   n. 뜻밖의 횡재, 이득
아버지는 세금 환불로 갑자기 2천 달러가 넘는 횡재를 얻었다.

13 mandates   v. 명령하다
새로운 세법은 고소득층이 소득세를 더 내야 한다고 명령한다.

14 ration   v. 제한하다
물이 얼마 남지 않아 마시고 요리하는 것에만 쓰고 씻는 용도로는 안 쓰도록 제한해야 했다.

15 rekindled   v. 다시 불러일으키다
부모님의 다락방에서 옛날에 읽었던 만화책을 찾으면서 히어로 만화에 대한 애정을 다시 불러일으켰다.

16 imposes   v. 강요하다
많은 여성들은 현대 제도가 여전히 여성에게 불공정한 요구를 강요한다고 주장한다.

17 commemorate   v. 기념하다
우체국은 제2차 세계대전의 종료의 70주년을 기념하기 위해 새로운 우표를 제작하고 발매하기로 했다.

18 token   adj. 형식적인
정부는 실업률을 낮추기 위한 조치를 취하겠다고 약속했지만, 여태까지 형식적인 행동만 취했다.

19 hub   n. 중심지
인천, 상해와 오사카의 국제공항들은 아시아의 교통 중심지가 될 수 있도록 경쟁하고 있다.

20 affront — n. 모욕
많은 이민자들은 정치인이 불법 이민자들이 나라의 여러 문제를 발생시킨다는 주장을 모욕으로 받아들였다.

21 resolution — n. 결단력
모든 사람들이 사라의 승리를 위한 결단력을 느낄 수 있었다.

22 fringe — adj. 외곽의, 바깥
지난 선거에서 세 개의 주요 당이 총 투표의 94%를 차지했고, 네 개의 잔여 당들이 남은 6%를 차지했다.

23 abetted — v. 사주하다
맥베스는 아내로부터 스코틀랜드 왕의 살인을 사주 받았다.

24 atrocities — n. 잔학한 행위
뉘렌베르그 재판은 나치가 제2차 세계대전 동안 저지른 많은 잔학한 행위를 밝혔다.

25 pretense — n. 가식, 가면
캐리가 남자친구를 어머니에게 소개하자, 어머니는 그에게 관심을 가지는 척하며 난처한 질문을 계속 하였다.

26 safeguard — v. 보호하다
후세가 오염되지 않는 환경을 즐길 수 있기 위해 당장 환경을 보호하는 수단을 도입해야 한다.

27 bestow — v. 수여하다
많은 사회경제학자들은 아시아인의 저축률이 미국인이나 유럽인에 비해 높은 이유가 아시아인들은 상대적으로 죽기 전에 재산의 큰 일부를 자녀에게 물려줘야 한다는 사회적 압박감을 느끼기 때문이라고 믿는다.

28 temper — v. 누그러뜨리다
많이 노력했지만, 헬렌은 법정에서 그녀의 가게를 턴 남성을 피고인석에서 봤을 때 화를 누그러뜨리기 어려워했다.

29 ushered — v. 안내하다
접수 담당자에게 신원을 밝힌 뒤, 그렉은 인터뷰가 진행될 회의실로 빠르게 안내되었다.

30 braved — v. 위험을 대면하다
딸이 아직 불에 타는 오두막 안에 있는 사실을 깨달은 후, 칼은 위험을 대면해서 딸을 구하러 갔다.

31 포기하다: 포기하다 (동의어)
A. 찬양 받지 못한: 명사 취급하다
B. 개조하다: 계속하다
C. 충성: 충성
D. 불안정해지다: 활기를 북돋우다

32 한물간: 낡은 (동의어)
A. 신념: 경계
B. 굴복하다: 항복하다
C. 선행: 배신
D. 상징하다: 휩싸다

33 꽉 쥐다: 조여지다 (동의어)
A. 안내하다: 쫓아내다
B. 채찍: 극찬하다
C. 사소한: 절름발이의
D. 무서운 것: 위협적 존재

34 집회: 흩어지다 (반대어)
A. 겁이 많은: 용감한
B. 만장일치의: 분리되지 않은
C. 폐지하다: 접대하다
D. 책략: 하고 싶은 대로 함

35 뜻밖의 횡재: 보너스 (동의어)
A. 후려치다: 쇄도하다
B. 경건한: 불경스러운
C. 여러 조각들로 이뤄진 것: 모음
D. 비뚤어지게 하다: 보존하다

36 중심지: 외곽의 (반대어)
A. 형식적인: 진정한
B. 애도하다: 애통하다
C. 단념: 항공
D. 기진맥진한: 무기력한

37 불굴의 용기: 탄력 (동의어)
A. 액면가: 분해
B. 제한하다: 위반하다
C. 부식, 침식: 관습, 관례
D. 모욕: 모욕, 공격

38 쨍그렁거리다: 울리다 (동의어)
    A. 기업 연합: 물가상승률
    B. 무효: 무효 선언
    C. 잔인성: 관대함
    D. 적: 헌신적인 추종자

39 서로 뒤엉킨, 뗄 수 없는: 불가분한 (동의어)
    A. 황량한: 황량한
    B. 구원하는: 우호적인
    C. 이름뿐인: 상응하는
    D. 뒤집다: 알아차리다

40 부동성: 마비 (동의어)
    A. 장애: 노선
    B. 얼버무리는: 신성한
    C. 극적으로 보이게 하다: 꾸미다
    D. 무례함: 공손함

41 권한 – 악화되다 – 악화되다

42 체납하다 – 의무적으로 하게 하다 – 강요하다

43 신성한 – 신성시되는 – 산산이

44 열렬한, 아주 뜨거운 – 위반하다 – 무더운

45 황량한 – 생기를 되찾게 하다 – 활기를 북돋우다

46 잔인함 – 간청 – 잔인성

47 불화 – 불화 – 잘 퍼지는

48 아주 작은 마을 – 보관장 – 마을

49 협회 – 어리석은 행동 – 기업 연합

50 깔보듯 대하다 – 버리다 – 포기하다

51 독재, 전제주의 – 해방 – 절대주의

52 신념 – 신조 – 주민

53 음모를 꾸미다 – 둑, 제방 – 부두, 제방

54 펼쳐지다 – 수여하다 – 수여하다

55 세속적인 – 현세적인 – 경건한

56 얼버무리는 – 구원하는 – 피하는, 찾기 힘든

57 의제 – 계획 – 갈등

58 포기하지 않는 힘, 회복력 – 불굴의 용기 – 모욕

59 교활함 – 내포된, 암시된 – 함축된

60 속임 – 가식, 가면 – 징후, 나타남

01 trace   v. 추적하다
나는 아버지의 예전 일기로 그가 내 나이였을
때 겪었던 일을 추적했다.

02 compose   v. 가라앉히다
뉴스에 너무 큰 충격을 받아서 흥분을 가라앉
히기 어려웠다.

03 appropriate   v. 책정하다
각종 관리비, 식비, 그리고 작은 저축용 비용을
책정하면 여가를 위해 남는 돈이 거의 없다.

04 compose   v. 작곡하다
모차르트가 오늘 살아있었다면 아마 컴퓨터로
작곡을 했을 것이다.

05 inept   adj. 적합지 않은
그가 입은 옷이 기업 면접에 적합하지 않아 보
였다.

06 traces   n. 흔적
지하에서 발견된 이리듐이라는 굉장히 희귀한
물질의 흔적이 이 지역에 적어도 10억 년 전
지구에 운석이 떨어졌다는 주장을 증명하였다.

07 grazed   v. 살짝 스치다
쟈니는 공이 공중에 있을 때 차려고 했지만,
발이 공을 살짝 스치기만 했다.

08 motion   n. 안건, 의견
대의원들 중 70% 이상이 해당 안건을 반대했다.

09 distinct   adj. 분명한, 확실한
그녀는 침착하려고 했지만, 목소리에서 확실한
날카로움이 들렸다.

10 punctuated   v. 간간이 끼어들다
로버츠 박사는 연설 중에 간간이 농담과 흥미
로운 이야기를 섞었다.

11 shed   v. 털을 갈다, 잃다
봄마다 내 고양이들과 강아지들은 털이 너무
빠져서 수시로 아파트 바닥을 청소기로 밀어
야 한다.

12 brisk   adj. 빠르고 활발한, 활기찬
몇 개의 활기찬 아침 회의 이후, 여유로운 하
루를 보냈다.

13 lull   n. 잠잠한 시기
경찰이 앞으로 교통 관련 법률을 보다 강화시
킨다고 발표하자 대중교통 규칙 위반사항이
잠잠한 시기가 이어졌다.

14 loomed   v. 다가오다, 어렴풋이 나타나다
많은 사람들이 희열에 젖어있을 때 몇 명은 위
기가 다가오고 있다고 경고했다.

01 sanctions   n. 허가
드루이드 씨가 기업 경영진들한테 허가를 받지 않은 상태에 마케팅 전략을 실행한 것은 잘못이었다.

02 inclination   n. 경사
언덕의 경사가 너무 심해서 걸어 올라가는 것조차 불가능했다.

03 fowl
n. 식용새 (닭, 오리, 거위 등)
제임스는 채식주의자는 아니지만 빨간 고기를 최대한 안 먹으려고 하니까 닭 요리를 해줘야겠다.

04 institutionalized
v. 보호 시설로 보내다
윌리엄스 씨의 아내는 사망했고 딸은 정직원으로 근무하고 있었기 때문에 그는 보호 시설로 보내져야 했다.

05 industry   n. 일에 대한 근면성
조지의 상사는 그에게 일에 대한 근면성을 좀 더 보였으면 좋겠다고 전달했다.

06 qualify   v. 수정하다
나는 발언을 수정할 기회가 없었기에 그들은 내 의도를 잘못 해석할 수밖에 없었다.

07 form   n. 방식
이런 의식이 왜 이렇게 진행되는지는 설명하기 어렵다: 난 그저 어렸을 때 어르신들께서 배운 방식을 따를 뿐이다.

08 game
adj. 에 반대하지 않는, 할 의향이 있는
친구들한테 나랑 같이 번지 점프하자고 했는데, 아무도 할 의향이 없었다.

09 strain   v. 필터, 거르다
30분 동안 야채를 끓이고, 국물은 나중에 사용할 수 있도록 따로 걸러 보관하라.

10 cultured   v. 배양하다
수의사는 면봉으로 우리 강아지의 입안을 닦아 세균을 배양한 후 특정 바이러스에 감염되었는지 확인했다.

11 sublimate   v. (방향 등을) 돌리다
청소년이었을 때 윌리엄은 가끔 깊은 우울을 느끼곤 했지만, 빠르게 그 에너지를 글 쓰는 것으로 돌려 작가가 되었다.

12 institution
n. 연예인, 인기 있는 사람
교내에서 가장 인기 있는 교사인 킹 씨는 이 학교에서 25년 넘게 불어를 가르치셨다. 그는 학생들과 동문들 사이 연예인 급으로 유명하다.

13 faculty   n. 능력
호킹 박사는 아주 어린 시절부터 굉장히 복잡한 문제를 이해하는 능력을 가졌다.

14 husbandry   n. 절약
이번 계절에는 수확이 안 좋아서 마을 주민들은 겨울에 살아남기 위해 많은 절약을 해야 할 것이다.

15 constitution   n. 기질, 체질, 체격
21살 때 윌리엄은 명랑하고 건강한 체격을 가진 17살 여자와 결혼했고, 결혼후 65년 동안 6명의 자녀, 21명의 손자와 54명의 증손자를 보았다.

16 sublime   adj. 위대한, 대단한
산드라는 박물관에 있는 대부분의 작품을 대단하게 여겼다.

01 melee   n. 아수라장
무슨 일이 벌어지고 있는지 파악도 못 한 사이에 나는 아수라장 한 가운데에서 맞아 코피가 터졌다.

02 obdurate   adj. 고집 센
이미 3월 중순이지만, 고집 센 추위는 끝날 기미가 안 보인다.

03 onerous   adj. 아주 힘든
남편과 아버지가 되는 것은 아주 힘들지만 영광스러운 일이다.

04 titillate   v. 자극하다
책의 표지는 내용과 아무런 상관이 없다: 단지 책을 구매하도록 자극할 뿐이다.

05 palpitate   v. 두근거리다
무대로 올라가기 직전, 젬마는 두근거리는 심장이 가슴 안에서 터질 것만 같았다.

06 milieu   n. 환경
제이크는 이 유명세가 가져온 새로운 환경이 낯설었다.

07 ingenuous   adj. 순진한, 사람을 잘 믿는
사기꾼은 천진난만한 어린 자들이나 사람을 잘 믿는 노인을 주로 목표로 한다.

08 obtuse   adj. 둔한, 둔감한
제이미한테 몇 번이나 눈치를 줬지만, 그는 이해하기에 너무 둔했다.

09 foundering   v. 실패하다, 침몰하다
지금 같은 경제 불경기에 많은 다국적 기업은 침몰하고 있다.

10 epidemic   n. 유행병
특히 전염성이 강한 유행병이 이번 겨울에 도시 내에 확산되고 있다.

11 affecting   v. ~으로 보이는, 영향을 미치는
낸시가 통화 중이었을 때, 그녀의 아버지가 부엌에서 호들갑을 떨며 무관심한 것처럼 보였지만 사실 통화 내용을 조금이라도 듣고 싶어서 얼쩡거렸다.

12 ephemeral   adj. 수명이 짧은, 단명하는
그의 가수로서의 직업은 수명이 짧았고, 빠르게 다시 프로그래머로서 채용 공고를 찾는 본인의 모습을 발견했다.

13 obfuscate   v. 애매하게 만들다
정치인들의 말을 듣지 마: 제일 중요한 이슈를 애매하게 만들기만 한다.

14 wandering   v. 방랑하는
헬렌은 그녀의 알츠하이머 환자 할아버지가 길거리에서 방랑하는 모습을 목격했다.

15 odious   adj. 끔찍한
나는 이런 중세시대의 초상화들이 불편하고 끔찍하다. 움직일 때 작품 속의 눈이 마치 나를 따라다니는 것 같다.

01 contrition n. 뉘우침
뉘우침을 표현하기 위해 잭슨은 '제발 날 용서해줘'라고 써진 거대한 케이크를 들고 왔다.

02 maelstrom
n. 대혼란, 엄청난 소용돌이
빵가루를 연못에 던지자, 거대한 비단잉어들이 먹이를 먹으려고 하자 물은 엄청난 소용돌이로 요동쳤다.

03 macerated v. 마르다
짐은 과로와 스트레스로 알아보지 못할 정도로 말랐다.

04 instill
v. (서서히) 주입시키다
게임이 시작되기 전에 로버트 코치는 선수들에게 투지와 화이팅 정신을 주입시키고자 노력했다.

05 altruistic adj. 이타적인
기업들이 순수하게 이타적인 목적으로 자선단체 활동을 한다고 생각한다면 잘못된 생각이다.

06 bucolic adj. 목가적인
이 지역은 이제 부동산 개발로 둘러쌓였다. 한때 목가적인 초원과 농장으로 유명했던 지역은 이제 역사로 남을 예정이다.

07 verdant adj. 파릇파릇한
이 지역의 파릇파릇한 시골의 큰 부분이 허리케인으로 파괴되었다.

08 complemented v. 보완하다
식당의 훌륭한 메뉴는 최고의 와인 리스트로 보완되었다.

09 illusion n. 오해, 환상, 환각
독립한 뒤에 부모님의 손에서 벗어날 것이라는 생각은 오해다.

10 allusion n. 언급, 암시, 인유
그가 그녀의 전 SAT 점수를 언급하자 그녀는 불쾌감을 느꼈다.

11 macerate
v. 불리다, 절이다, 적시다
나는 브랜디에 체리를 절이는 것을 좋아한다. 그렇게 불린 체리는 선데이 아이스크림의 꼭대기를 장식하기 좋다.

12 lacerated
v. 찢다, 난도질을 하다, 혹독하게 비판하다
어젯밤, 고양이를 목욕시키려고 했을 때, 고양이는 내 팔을 사정없이 할퀴었다.

13 arboreal adj. 나무 위에서 사는
인간은 아마 나무 위에서 사는 조상들로부터 진화했을 것이다.

01 charge   n. 역할
앨런은 나치와 맞서 싸우기 위해 영국 군대에 입대했지만, 맡은 역할은 클리프트 장군의 신발을 닦고 유니폼을 다리는 것이라 전쟁 내내 총을 한 번도 쏘지 않았다.

02 formidable
adj. 어마어마한, 공포심을 유발하는
그들은 모두 각자 훌륭한 야구 선수고, 함께 있을 때 어마어마한 팀을 이룬다.

03 vacillated
v. 갈팡질팡하다, 흔들리다, 마음이 흔들리다.
코트니는 휴가 기간 중 몬타나에서 승마를 할지, 버몬트에서 스키를 탈지 마음을 정하지 못하고 흔들렸다.

04 industry   n. 일에 대한 근면성
밀톤 허쉬는 일에 대한 근면성이 뛰어난 사람이었다 – 18살에 첫 가게를 열었고 26살에 미국에서 가장 큰 제과회사를 창립했다.

05 strained
v. 거르다, 필터로 거르다
바텐더는 칵테일 쉐이커에 모든 재료와 얼음을 넣어 흔들었고 액체를 높고 얇은 유리잔에 걸러 담았다.

06 complement   v. 보완하다
우리 농구팀 코치들의 서로 다른 지도 스타일은 잘 보완된다.

07 altruistic   adj. 이타적인
그의 타인을 돕기 위한 동기는 정말 이타적이다: 그는 모두의 행복을 위해 진심으로 걱정했다.

08 eminent   adj. 저명한, 탁월한
찰스의 아버지는 이름만 들어도 아는 저명한 생물학자 마커스 깁슨 박사다.

09 obdurate   adj. 고집 센
잭은 몇 년 동안 아버지가 담배를 끊기를 바랐지만, 고집 센 아버지를 설득하기 어렵다.

10 ingenuous
adj. 순진한, 사람을 잘 믿는
정치인에게 돈과 권력이 동기가 되지 않을 것이라는 생각은 순진한 것이다.

11 founder   v. 실패하다, 침몰하다
대부분의 여론은 NATO와 같은 다국적 기구들이 냉전 이후 침몰할 것이라고 생각했지만, 이는 틀렸다고 증명됐다.

12 onerous   adj. 아주 힘든
관리자로서의 첫 업무는 몇몇 직원들에게 그들이 불경기 때문에 구조조정 대상임을 통보하는 아주 힘든 일이었다.

13 contrition   n. 뉘우침
인생의 황혼기에 일종의 뉘우침을 느끼지 않으면 멍청이다.

14 institution
n. 연예인, 인기 있는 사람
공원에서 풍선 파는 아저씨는 이 지역의 연예인이다. 그는 40년 동안 같은 위치에서 풍선을 팔았다.

15 gesticulated   v. 몸짓으로 가리키다
길 건너편에 있어서 안 들렸기 때문에 마이클은 몸짓으로 조지에게 전화하라고 가리켰다.

16 pastoral   adj. 목가적인
극악무도한 업계를 떠나고 마크 우드는 아이다호에 있는 조용한 목장으로 가서 한가하고 목가적인 환경에서 살았다.

17 arboreal   adj. 나무 위에서 사는
나무늘보는 진정 나무 위에서 사는 동물이다: 한 번 살기 시작한 나무 위에서 절대 안 내려온다.

18 macerate   v. 마르다
요리 시작하기 전에 야채를 제대로 말려라.

19 cataclysm   n. 대재앙, 대변동
뉴올리언스는 2005년에 겪은 허리케인 카트리나로 인한 대재앙에서 완전히 회복하지는 않았다.

20 epidemic   n. 유행병
핸드폰 중독은 새로운 유행병이다: 수백만 명이 그로 고통받고 있다.

21 founded   v. 창립하다, 창설하다
역대 가장 오래된 기업은 567년에 창립된 일본의 곤고구미라는 건설 기업이다.

22 melee   n. 아수라장
실랑이가 있었고, 나는 그 아수라장 속에서 모자와 스카프를 잃었다.

23 meandered   v. 거닐다
업무를 끝낸 그라우스 씨와 그의 친구들은 길을 거닐며 저녁먹을 주점을 찾았다.

24 odious
adj. 끔찍한, 혐오스러운
내일 새벽 다섯 시에 일어나 상사를 픽업하러 공항까지 가야 한다는 것은 끔찍한 일이다.

25 sanction   n. 제재
정부가 기업을 대상으로 할 수 있는 가장 효과적인 제재는 세무 사찰이다.

26 tantalize   v. 감질나게 하다
에둘러 말하면서 감질나게 하지 마라. 그냥 문제가 뭔지 똑바로 말해줘.

27 obtuse   adj. 둔한, 둔감한
아인슈타인은 과학 분야에 뛰어났지만, 일상생활 측면에서는 꽤나 둔감했다.

28 inclination   n. 의향, ~하는 경향
훌륭한 고고학자 존스 박사는 자녀들이 고고학을 공부할 의향이 전혀 없다는 점이 신경 쓰이지 않았다.

29 sublimate   v. (방향 등을) 돌리다
방과 후 스포츠 프로그램은 불우한 학생들의 반항적인 경향을 스포츠로 방향을 돌리는 훌륭한 장이다.

30 charge   n. 지휘, 맡은
딕의 아버지가 떠날 때 딕에게 남동생들과 여동생을 돌보라고 맡겼다.

31 <u>둔감한</u> / 고집 센 / 불길한

32 찢다 / <u>자극하다</u> / 두근거리다

33 거닐다 / 환경 / <u>대혼란</u>

34 소모 / <u>뉘우침</u> / 망명자

35 찢다 / 젖을 분비하다 / <u>불리다</u>

36 <u>넌지시 알림</u> / 친밀함 / 해방

37 <u>낡은</u> / 보완된 / 전원의

Class 36  Answers

01 gestate   v. 잉태하고 있다
특정 상어는 3년 이상 잉태를 한다고 알려졌다.

02 formative
adj. 형성과 관련된, 성장과 관련된
윌슨 부부는 각자 굉장히 다른 환경에서 자랐다.

03 emaciated   v. 수척하다
긴 투병 이후, 그는 약하고 수척해 보였다.

04 auspicious
adj. 상서로운, 전조가 좋은
헬렌의 결혼식에서 그녀의 할머니는 헬렌의
할아버지가 이렇게 상서로운 행사를 보지 못
하고 돌아가셔서 슬퍼하셨다.

05 oscillates   v. 왔다 갔다 하다
부모로서 마사는 매일매일 걱정과 행복 사이
를 왔다 갔다 한다.

06 arcane
adj. 불가사의한, 신비로운
계약서의 모든 불가사의할 정도로 복잡한 세
부 사항을 이해하는 변호사를 고용해야 함이
명백했다.

07 archaic   adj. 낡은, 폐물이 된
그들이 사용하고 있던 소프트웨어는 낡아서
업데이트가 필요했다.

08 gesticulating
v. 몸짓으로 가리키다
창문 넘어 낸시가 팔 벌려 인사하며 몸짓으로
이래저래 가리키는 것을 봤는데, 무슨 말을 하
려고 했는지 이해를 못했다.

09 famished
adj. 굶다, 배가 고파 죽을 지경인
등산 후 돌아왔을 때 배가 고파 죽을 지경이었다.

10 myriad   n. 무수히 많음
자녀를 키울 때 무수히 많은 문제를 겪을 것이다.

11 regimen   n. 식이 요법
의사는 네게 식이 요법을 처방해 주셨으니 엄
격하게 따라야 될 거야.

12 intimation   n. 넌지시 알림, 암시
나는 해럴드가 병원에 입원해서 놀랐다. 지난주
에 봤을 때만 해도 아프다는 암시가 없었는데.

13 garrulous   adj. 말이 많은
처음에 글로리아는 소심하고 수줍음을 많이
타는 것처럼 보였는데 알면 알게 될수록 말이
많아졌다.

14 gregarious
adj. 남과 어울리기 좋아하는, 사교적인
나는 헬렌의 남편 마이크를 만나자마자 친해졌
다. 그는 태평하고 사교적인 사람처럼 보였다.

Class 37

01 protégé n. 제자, 후배
베토벤이 하이든의 제자였다는 사실을 아는
사람은 많지 않다.

02 bane n. 골칫거리
우리 강아지는 너무 많은 문제를 일으켜 우리
가족의 골칫거리가 되었다.

03 prosecuted v. 기소하다
정치인은 기업 후견인들로부터 뇌물을 받은
혐의로 기소되었다.

04 dubious adj. 의심하는
알렉스는 본인 가족이 제정 러시아의 귀족의
후손이라는 의심스러운 주장을 했다.

05 insipid
adj. 맛이 없는 (무미한 맛)
수프가 너무 밍밍하고 맛이 안 나는 것 같았다.

06 intrepid n. 용감무쌍한
제2차 세계대전 중 19살 밖에 되지 않는 용감
무쌍한 남자들이 입대를 했다.

07 canine adj. 개의
나는 외롭지 않다. 가는 곳마다 개인 내 친구
잭과 함께 한다.

08 posterity n. 후세
바흐의 음악과 똑같이, 모차르트와 베토벤의
음악, 비틀즈의 음악도 후세에게 간직될 것이다.

09 veracious adj. 진실을 말하는
진실은 상처가 될 수 있지만, 사람은 항상 진
실을 말해야 한다.

10 émigrés n. 망명자
슈뢰딩거 박사는 제2차 세계대전이 시작될 때
유럽을 떠난 망명 과학자들 중 한 명이다.

11 deluge n. 폭우
발표를 마친 후, 폭우 같은 질문 세례를 받았다.

12 insidious
adj. 느리게 퍼지는 교활함/사악함
그 책은 무해한 것처럼 보이지만, 많은 사람들
은 그 책이 젊은이들에게 천천히 악영향을 미
친다고 생각한다.

13 invidious
adj. 불쾌한, 남의 심기를 건드릴
나는 제임스에게 회사가 그를 해고한다고 전
달해야 하는 불쾌한 일을 맡았다.

14 devious adj. 정직하지 못한
가장 똑똑하고 정직하지 못한 정치인만 이 정
치적 정글에서 30년 이상 버틸 수 있다.

15 conflagration n. 큰불
지진은 불과 15초 지속됐지만 도시의 대부분
을 파괴한 큰불을 야기했다.

01 pallid   adj. 창백한
저 형광등은 모든 사람을 창백하게 보이게 한다.

02 sanguine   adj. 낙관적인
많은 경제학자들은 앞으로 몇 년 동안의 미국
경제에 대한 전망을 낙관적으로 본다.

03 exasperated   v. 몹시 화나게 하다
헨리의 게으름은 그의 어머니를 자주 몹시 화
나게 했다.

04 turbid   adj. 탁한, 흐린
우물 안의 물이 탁해서 안 마시기로 했다.

05 acquiescent
adj. 잠자코 동의하는, 묵인하는
준은 어머니의 요구에 주로 동의했지만, 이번
에는 노골적으로 복종하지 않았다.

06 deference   n. 존중
요즘, 아이들은 부모님을 존중해야 된다고 가
르치지 않는다.

07 exacerbated   v. 악화시키다
엘리자베스 1세 여왕은 항상 단 것을 먹는 사
람으로 유명했는데, 그녀는 단 것을 계속 먹으
면 입에서 향긋한 냄새가 날 것이라고 생각했
지만, 막상 그런 행동이 구취를 악화시키기만
한다는 사실은 몰랐다.

08 beneficiary   n. 수혜자
헨리는 22살 때 돌아가신 할아버지의 5천만
달러가 넘는 재산을 받은 수혜자가 되었다.

09 rummaged   v. 뒤지다
골드벅 부인은 하루 종일 옛날 사진첩을 찾으
러 지하 창고를 뒤졌다.

10 torrid   adj. 몹시 더운
드러먼드 씨는 에어컨이 틀어져 있는 사무실
에서 하루 종일 앉아 있다 보니 바깥 날씨가
얼마나 더운지 몰랐다.

11 sallow
adj. 얼굴빛이 약간 누런, 혈색이 안 좋은, 병색이
      완연한.
병실 침대에 누워 있던 할머니는 얼굴빛이 누
렇고 약해 보이셨다.

12 quiescent   adj. 잠잠한
내가 하는 일은 가을에서 봄까지 꽤 바쁘고,
여름에 잠잠하다.

13 tepid   adj. 미지근한
모텔에서 수도꼭지를 어느 방향으로 돌려도
미지근한 물만 나왔다.

Class 39

01 capacious   adj. 널찍한
우리 호텔 방은 꽤 널찍해 네 명 모두 편하게 머물 수 있었다.

02 timbre   n. 음색
그 가수는 음악 업계에서 아마 가장 뚜렷한 음색을 가졌다.

03 atrophy   n. 위축
한 사람의 언어 능력은 다른 신체 능력과 똑같이 사용하지 않으면 위축될 것이다.

04 convoys   n. 호송대
운전하며 국경에 더욱 가까워지자, 군용차 호송대가 많이 보였다.

05 inept   adj. 서투른, 솜씨 없는
제이콥에게 건배 인사를 시키지 마; 그는 유머를 포함한 얘기에 서투른 사람이야.

06 clemency   n. 관용, 관대한 처분
같은 범죄를 세 번이나 저질렀는데 관대한 처분을 요청하는 건 비이성적이다.

07 benevolent   adj. 자애로운
제니퍼는 엄청 자애로운 영혼을 가진 사람이다; 파리도 못 죽인다.

08 efficacious   adj. 효과적인
코분무기는 코막힘을 덜어주는 데에 굉장히 효과적이었다.

09 antipathy   n. 반감
넬리는 지갑을 도난당하고 맨해튼 택시 안에서 멀미를 한 후 뉴욕에 대한 반감이 생겼다.

10 urban   adj. 도시의
교통 혼잡, 소음 공해와 심한 미세먼지는 일반 도시 생활의 정상적인 일부다.

11 urbane   adj. 세련된, 점잖은
로버트가 30세가 되는 과정에서 아이 같은 외모를 잃고 더욱 점잖은 매력의 사람으로 성장했다.

12 capricious   adj. 변덕스러운
커트가 얼마나 변덕스러운지 설명하자면 행사 당일 이전 식당 예약을 세 번이나 변경했다.

13 empathy   n. 공감
의대 입학한 후 첫 날 로버츠 박사는 의사가 가져야 할 가장 중요한 덕목은 동정심이라고 배웠다.

14 malevolent   adj. 악의 있는
그의 행동은 악의적이라고밖에 설명할 수가 없다: 누가 자선기금에서 돈을 훔칠 생각을 할까?

01 insipid
adj. 맛이 없는 (무미한 맛)
밀라노에서 세 달 동안 지내면서 진한 이탈리아 커피에 익숙해져서인지 로스앤젤레스의 커피는 맛이 좀 싱겁게 느껴졌다.

02 foraged
v. ~을 뒤적거리다, ~을 찾다
제이크는 버스 카드를 찾으려고 가방을 뒤적거렸다.

03 acquiescent
adj. 잠자코 동의하는, 묵인하는
닐이 개리와 형제지간이지만, 개리는 닐이 그의 최근 결정에 묵인하기를 바라지 않는다.

04 sallow
adj. 얼굴빛이 약간 누런, 병색이 완연한
그의 누런 얼굴을 보니 그가 통화하면서 그가 설명했던 거보다 사실은 훨씬 더 아프다는 것을 알 수 있었다.

05 magnanimity
n. 아량, 관대함, 담대함
배심원단은 용의자의 형량을 정할 때 관대함을 보이지 않아야 한다.

06 brisk
adj. 빠르고 활발한, 활기찬
역대급으로 덥고 후덥지근한 여름을 보내니 활기찬 가을날이 매우 기대된다.

07 dubious
adj. 의심하는
증인의 의심스러운 증언은 경찰 수사 이후 사실로 증명되었다.

08 exacerbating
v. 악화시키다
질병을 위해 처방된 대부분의 약물은 결과적으로 증상을 더욱 악화시켰다.

09 gregarious
adj. 남과 어울리기 좋아하는, 사교적인
쌍둥이는 서로 반대 성향이다: 쟈니는 사교적이고 외향적인 반면 행크는 내향적이고 수줍음을 많이 탄다.

10 posterity
n. 후세
모차르트와 베토벤의 음악은 후세까지 즐길 것이다.

11 canine
adj. 개의
몇몇 사람들은 개가 주인의 감정을 이해할 수 있다고 하지만, 과학자들은 개의 뇌가 인간의 뇌와 완전히 다른 구조를 가지기 때문에 공감이 불가능하다고 한다.

12 boon
n. 호의, 요긴한 것
인터넷은 도서관에서 긴 시간 동안 연구를 해야 하는 사람들에게 요긴한 것으로 증명되었다.

13 indigent
adj. 궁핍한
사무엘은 궁핍한 가정에서 왔다. 그래서 소비하는 모든 동전까지 신경 쓴다.

14 convoy
n. 호송대
경찰이 고속도로에 있는 모든 차를 멈춰 세운 후 얼마 안 지나서 검은 차량 호송대가 빠르게 지나갔다.

15 capricious
adj. 변덕스러운
이 시기의 날씨는 꽤나 변덕스럽다. 어느 날 밝고 따뜻하고 다음 날 차갑고 바람을 부는 경우가 있다.

16 clemency
n. 관용, 관대한 처분
용의자의 가족은 판사에게 관대한 처분을 해달라고 빌었다.

17 empathy
n. 공감
킴의 소설가로서의 대단함은 독자들이 원하는 바와 공감을 하면서 우러난다.

18 urbane
adj. 세련된, 점잖은
그 난폭했던 아이가 매력적이고 점잖은 어른으로 성장했다.

19 envoys
n. 특사, 결구
두 정부는 평화 협정을 위해 특사를 교환하기로 결정했다.

20 inapt   adj. 적절하지 않은

빌은 사교적 모임에 참여할 때 행동을 제대로 하지 못한다: 적절하지 않은 말을 하는 습관을 통제할 줄 모르는 것 같다.

21 brusque   adj. 무뚝뚝한

그는 창백했고, 무뚝뚝했고, 약간 가장을 하기도 하였으나, 티 하나 없이 깔끔했고 적들에게도 친절했다.

22 philistine   n. 교양 없는 사람, 속물

나는 음악과 예술에 대해 조금 알지만, 사실 속물일 뿐이다.

23 reverence   n. 존경심, 숭배

우리 마을의 소방대장인 아버지가 일을 하는 모습을 봤을 때 그에 대한 새로운 존경심을 느꼈다.

24 dubious   adj. 의심하는

글렌의 첫 사업 구상들은 좀 수상하였지만, 추후에 온라인 스포츠용품 쇼핑몰로 대박을 터트렸다.

25 avaricious   adj. 탐욕스러운, 욕심 많은

요즘 세상에는 욕심 많은 사람이 너무 많다: 우리는 모두 다른 사람의 복지도 조금 더 생각해야 된다.

26 bane   n. 골칫거리

켄트 부인의 첫째, 둘째, 셋째 아들은 크게 성공했지만, 넷째 아들이 그녀의 인생의 골칫거리다.

27 feline   adj. 교양이 같은

그녀는 조용히 있었고, 얼굴에 고양이 같은 웃음을 지었다.

28 famished   adj. 굶다, 배가 고파 죽을 지경인

나는 이제 일주일 동안 다이어트를 해서 그런지 항상 배가 고파 죽을 지경이다.

29 myriad   n. 무수히 많음

우리는 하늘을 올려다보며 무수히 많은 별을 봤다.

30 gestate   v. 잉태하고 있다, 생기다

래리는 며칠 동안 답 없이 고민하고 있었는데 드디어 머릿속에 아이디어가 생기기 시작했다.

31 파릇파릇한 / 전원의 / 소의

32 망상 / 환상 / 암시

33 형성에 중요한 / 단편적인, 부분적인 / 어마어마한

34 상서로운 / 좋은 / 의심하는

35 소량, 부족 / 과다 / 골칫거리

36 기소 / 학대, 박해 / 땀

37 후배 / 망명자 / 견습생

38 교활한 / 맛이 없는 / 남의 심기를 건드릴

39 미지근한 / 복잡하고 따분한 / 탁한, 흐린

40 교양 없는 사람 / 자선가 / 감정가

41 분개한 / 궁핍한 / 쇠약한

42 악의, 나쁜 마음 / 아량, 관대함 / 관용, 관대한 처분

Ted Chung
유학/SAT/ACT 필수 Vocabulary

| The Bodacious Book of |

Voluminous Vocabulary

Series 2-Real

(From Past SAT/ACT Tests)

□ **receptive** /rɪˈseptɪv/   adj. open to reception

(= open, amenable, friendly)

                                   n. reception

The commanding officer was always receptive to the opinions of his subordinates.

총사령관은 그의 부하들의 의견을 항상 경청하였다.

□ **lacquer** /ˈlækər/   n. a type of varnish

(= polish, gloss, varnish)

                                   v. lacquer

The furniture looked old with the lacquer torn off in places.

그 가구는 칠도 여기저기 벗겨지고 매우 낡아 보였다.

□ **endearing** /ɪnˈdɪrɪŋ/   adj. evoking affection

(= appealing, attractive, charming)

                                   v. endear

                                   n. endearment

He was an endearing boy, liked by everyone.

그는 모든 사람들에게 이쁨을 받는 아이였다.

□ **candidacy** /ˈkændɪdəsi/   n. application for a position, role or job

(= application, standing)

그가 대통령 선거에 출마하겠다고 밝혔을 때 많은 사람들이 놀랐다.

□ **candidate**   n. a person applying for a position, role or job

Many were surprised when he announced his candidacy for president.

☐ **engender** /ɪnˈdʒendər/   v. to produce or give rise to

(= produce, provoke, prompt)

His remarks engendered much debate.

그의 발언이 많은 논란을 낳았다.

☐ **ambivalent** /æmˈbɪvələnt/   adj. to have mixed feelings about

(= undecided, uncertain, indecisive)

                                      n. ambivalence

Robert was ambivalent about moving abroad: he was excited about living in a foreign country but also sad to leave his family and friends.

로버트는 외국으로 이사가는 것에 대해 감정이 복잡했다: 외국에 사는 것은 기뻤지만 가족과 친구들을 놔두고 가려니까 슬프기도 했다.

☐ **relish** /ˈrelɪʃ/   v. to enjoy

(= enjoy, savor, appreciate)

                                      n. relish

Henry relished his Sunday tennis games.

헨리는 일요일마다 테니스 치는 것을 매우 즐겼다.

☐ **construe** /kənˈstruː/   v. to deduce by inference or interpretation

(= interpret, take, understand)

Do not construe my silence as agreement.

나의 침묵을 동의라고 해석하지 마십시오.

☐ **calibrate** /ˈkælɪbreɪt/   v. to determine the range or accuracy of

(= adjust, regulate, rectify)

                                      n. calibration

The measuring equipment is very delicate and must be calibrated often.

계측기기들은 매우 민감하며 자주 눈금을 맞춰야 한다.

□ **substantiate** /səbˈstænʃieɪt/   v. to establish by proof or evidence

(= prove, validate, authenticate)

It is an interesting theory that, unfortunately, hasn't been substantiated yet.

그것은 흥미로운 이론이지만 아쉽게도 아직 검증되지는 않았습니다.

□ **scrawl** /skrɔːl/   v. to write awkwardly or illegibly

(= scribble, doodle, jot)

n. scrawl

He quickly scrawled a note and gave it to me.

그는 종이에 급히 뭔가를 끄적여서는 나에게 주었다.

□ **pageant** /ˈpædʒənt/   n. a show or exhibition

(= parade, procession, display)

Norman's mother was the runner up in the Miss America beauty pageant of 1989.

노먼의 어머니는 1989년 미스 아메리카 미인대회에서 2등을 차지하셨다.

□ **traipse** /treɪps/   v. to walk aimlessly

(= trudge, wander, roam)

Gary slowly traipsed home after losing the tennis match.

게리는 테니스 경기에 지고서는 집으로 터벅터벅 걸어갔다.

□ **agitate** /ˈædʒɪteɪt/   v. to disturb or excite emotionally

(= stir, disturb, disquiet)

Jerry's sudden illness agitated his entire family.

제리가 갑자기 병이 나서 모든 가족들이 불안해 했다.

□ **bazaar** /bəˈzɑːr/   n. a middle eastern market place

(= market, open market)

Damascus has one of the biggest bazaars in the world.

다마스커스에는 전 세계에서 가장 큰 바자 시장이 있다.

☐ **candor** /ˈkændər/   n. frankness

(= openness, sincerity, honesty)

                                                          adj. candid

In a rare moment of candor, Eric confessed that he regretted many of his past actions.

어쩌다가 솔직한 이야기를 할 때, 에릭은 자기가 과거에 한 많은 결정을 후회한다고 고백하였다.

☐ **conducive** /kənˈduːsɪv/   adj. contributing to

(= favorable, helpful, encouraging)

Some say globalization is not always conducive to domestic economic growth.

어떤 이들은 세계화가 국내 경제 성장을 항상 도와주는 것은 아니라고 한다.

☐ **procession** /prəˈseʃn/   n. the act of moving along

(= march, parade, line)

There was a long procession of military vehicles leading up to the border.

국경으로 향하는 군용 자동차들의 긴 행렬이 이어졌다.

☐ **pervasive** /pərˈveɪsɪv/   adj. spread throughout

(= enveloping, invasive, persistent)

                                                          v. pervade

As I entered the house, there was a pervasive smell of cooking garlic.

내가 집에 들어서자 온 집안에 마늘 요리하는 냄새가 가득했다.

☐ **flurry** /ˈflɜːri/   n. sudden excitement or confusion

(= disquiet, agitation, flustering)

                                                          v. flurry

There was a flurry of activity in the normally quiet library.

보통 때 조용한 도서관이 갑자기 왁자지껄 해졌다.

Practice 1.

Fill in the blank with the word that matches the definition provided

01 Many students smirked because they felt the school talent competition was only a/an _____ (an exhibition) to display the numerous but mediocre talents of Mary Anderson, the PTA chairwoman's daughter.

02 Dad and my brother Arnie arguing _____ (disturbed emotionally) mom.

03 The Russian president warned that a joint military exercise in the North Sea between the U.K., France, and Germany will be _____ (deduced by inference) as hostility towards the Russian Federation.

04 I _____ (enjoyed very much) the fact that Daniel got in trouble for a misdeed that I committed.

05 William was _____ (to have mixed feelings about) about following his father's footsteps as a doctor: he was happy to carry on a family tradition, but he was also weary that he will always be compared to his father.

06 The government announcement _____ (gave rise to) much public debate.

07 I found nothing about him _____ (evoking affection).

08 Few students in the class could decipher what the professor _____ (wrote awkwardly) on the chalkboard.

09 The police found no evidence to _____ (establish by proof) the suspect's claim.

10 The appearance of a stray cat caused a brief _____ (sudden excitement) in the children's playground.

11 The sound of African drums is _____ (spread throughout) in the artist's music.

12 I had the rare opportunity to watch the _____ (act of moving along) of the royal family while I was visiting London.

13 Prof. Healy's approach to lecturing is try to entertain and edify at the same time; he thinks that an amused student is much more _____ (favorable) to learning.

14 I am convinced that he answered my questions with complete _____ (frankness).

15 You should try to be more _____ (open) to constructive criticism.

☐ **bounty** /ˈbaʊnti/　　　　n. generous gift

(= abundance, plenty, gift)

adj. bountiful

After harvesting, the farmers give thanks to nature's bounty.

수확한 후 농부들은 자연의 너그러움에 감사했다.

☐ **despoil** /dɪˈspɔɪl/　　　　v. to spoil something

(= spoil, defile, wreck)

Uncle Harry's drunken behavior despoiled the jovial mood of the occasion.

즐거운 모임의 분위기를 해리 삼촌이 술을 마시고 주정을 부려 망쳐 놓았다.

☐ **stewardship** /ˈstuːərdʃɪp/

n. the responsibility of looking after something such as property, financial affairs and etc.

(= management, responsibility)

After Gary's father died, the stewardship of the family estate was passed onto Gary's older brother.

게리의 아버지가 돌아가신 후 게리네 가족의 재산 관리권이 게리의 형에게 넘어갔다.

☐ **broach** /broʊtʃ/　　　　v. to initiate a topic for discussion

(= mention, raise, bring up)

Financial matters are a difficult topic to broach – even to your parents.

돈과 관련된 이야기는 꺼내기가 어렵다 – 부모에게게도.

☐ **satiate** /ˈseɪʃieɪt/　　　　v. to satisfy to the full

(= satisfy, quench, gratify)

Perry could satiate his thirst only after drinking two bottles of water.

페리는 물을 두 병이나 마신 후에 갈증을 해소할 수 있었다.

□ **thaw** /θɔː/   v. to melt

(= melt, defrost)

It is best to let frozen meat thaw naturally, rather than defrosting it in a microwave oven.

냉동고기는 자연적으로 녹게 놔두는 것이 전자레인지에서 녹이는 것보다 좋다.

□ **prone to**   idiom. likely to

(= disposed to, inclined to)

Henry was prone to losing items like his keys, pens or phone.

헨리는 열쇠, 펜, 전화 등을 쉽게 잃어버리는 경향이 있다.

□ **prone** /prəʊn/   adj. horizontal

(= lying, flat, level)

Henry was surprised to find his grandfather lying prone on the floor.

헨리는 할아버지가 바닥에 수평으로 반듯이 누워 있는 걸 발견하고 놀랬다.

□ **opine** /əʊˈpaɪn/   v. to express an opinion

(= preach, harangue, speak out)

Too many people opine on issues that they are not qualified to.

너무나 많은 사람들이 자신이 잘 알지도 못하는 것들에 대해 의견을 말한다.

□ **baffle** /ˈbæfl/   v. to confuse

(= confuse, puzzle, stump)

Mars' movement along the night sky baffled ancient astronomers, as it's path was inexplicable from a geocentric viewpoint.

고대 천문학자들은 밤하늘에 보이는 화성의 움직임을 전혀 이해하지 못했다, 왜냐하면, 천동설의 관점에서 설명이 불가능했기 때문이다.

□ **irksome** /ˈɜːrksəm/   adj. causing irritation

(= tiresome, annoying, irritating)

                           v. irk

It's Saturday evening, and I have the irksome responsibility of tending to my sick brother while my friends are at a party.

지금은 토요일 저녁인데 나는 내 친구들이 파티에 가 있는 동안 아픈 동생을 간호해야 하는 짜증나는 책임을 맡았다.

□ **nuisance** /ˈnuːsns/   n. something that bothers or causes irritation

(= irritation, annoyance, pest)

When I was young, my older sister refused to take me anywhere saying I was a nuisance.

내가 어릴 때, 우리 누나는 귀찮게 군다며 나를 어디에도 데려가려 하지 않았다.

□ **intimate** /ˈɪntɪmət/   v. to hint at

(= suggest, hint, imply)

                           n. intimation

Roger intimated his plan to retire only to his closest friends.

로저는 그의 가장 가까운 친구들에게만 그의 은퇴계획에 대해 귀띔해주었다.

□ **tumult** /ˈtuːmʌlt/   n. a violent and noisy disturbance

(= uproar, commotion, clamor)

                           adj. tumultuous

The visit from the famous athlete caused a tumult at our school.

유명한 운동선수가 방문하여 학교에 한차례 소동이 일어났다.

□ **fetish** /ˈfetɪʃ/   n. a blind obsession to something

(= obsession, fixation, passion)

David has developed a fetish for money.

데이빗에게 돈에 대한 집착이 생겼다.

☐ **perseverance** /ˌpɜːrsəˈvɪrəns/   n. steady persistence in spite of obstacles

(= persistence, determination, grit)

v. persevere

Anette's team was losing 2:0 but showed great perseverance and ultimately won the game.

아넷의 팀은 2:0으로 지고 있었으나 엄청난 투지를 발휘하여 결국 게임을 이겼다.

☐ **antipathy** /ænˈtɪpəθi/   n. ill will

(= opposition, aversion, hostility)

The two men constantly bickered, but there was never any real antipathy between them.

그 두 사람은 끝없이 다투었지만, 그들 사이에 진정한 악의는 없었다.

☐ **trifling** /ˈtraɪflɪŋ/   adj. unimportant

(= trivial, petty, negligible)

Global warming is no trifling matter.

지구온난화는 가벼이 여길 문제가 아니다.

☐ **prowl** /praʊl/   v. to move about stealthily hunting for prey

(= stalk, lurk, skulk)

When you see a cat prowl, you can see it still has instincts of a wild animal.

고양이가 살금살금 걸어가는 것을 보면 아직도 야생의 본능이 남아있다는 걸 알 수 있다.

☐ **malignity** /məlígnəti/   n. intense ill will

(= malevolence, wickedness, meanness)

v. malign

Gloria's malignity towards me was so intense that I avoided her.

글로리아의 나에 대한 악감정이 너무나 심해 나는 그녀를 피해 다녔다.

Practice 2.

Fill in the blank with the word that matches the definition provided

01 I'd never felt true _____ (extreme ill will) until I realized James had betrayed me.

02 The appearance of a stray cat caused a brief _____ (noisy disturbance) in the kindergarten playground.

03 By nodding and smiling, the professor _____ (hinted) to Harriet that she was on the right track to solving the problem.

04 Jim considers cleaning the house as a/an _____ (annoyance); I consider it as therapeutic.

05 I can't believe that it is late March, but we're still waiting for the frost to _____. (melt)

06 Mick enjoyed his last biology class where he _____ (satisfied to the full) his morbid fascination by dissecting a frog.

07 When you meet Alice, be careful not to _____ (mention a subject) the topic of her son's accident.

08 We could tell that the obnoxious student's _____ (irritating) questions were beginning to annoy the professor.

09 The ending of the book totally _____ (confused) me; I did not think the story would end that way.

10 Do not go outside the camp boundaries: there are wild animals _____ (move about quietly hunting) in the area.

11 I'm very busy so don't bother me with anything _____. (unimportant)

12 Ever since Henrietta moved to Korea, she has developed a/an _____ (a blind obsession) for spicy food.

13 I noticed that Auntie Babs wanted to _____ (give one's opinion) on the subject on hand.

14 When making a table, be sure that the top board is totally _____. (horizontal)

15 My chance to go to Paris was _____ (spoil something) by the freezing temperature that hit the city.

Class 03

□ **sentinel** /ˈsentɪnl/   n. a guard

(= sentry, watchman, patrol)

He was held in house-arrest with sentinels guarding him around the clock.

그는 24시간 보초의 감시를 받으며 가택연금을 당했다.

□ **slumber** /ˈslʌmbər/   n. sleep or rest

(= rest, sleep, snooze)

After working for hours stacking boxes in the cellar, I fell into a deep slumber.

나는 수시간 동안 창고에서 상자 쌓는 일을 하고 나서 깊은 잠에 빠졌다.

□ **pittance** /ˈpɪtns/   n. small change

(= coppers, pennies, tuppence)

In some underdeveloped countries, many people still labor like slaves for pittance.

어떤 저개발 국가에서는 아직도 많은 사람들이 푼 돈을 받기 위해 노역을 한다.

□ **inexorable** /ɪnˈeksərəbl/   adj. unstoppable

(= inevitable, inevitable, relentless)

An inexorable wave of euphoria swept the nation.

멈출 수 없는 희열이 온 국가를 에워쌌다.

□ **monotonous** /məˈnɑːtənəs/   adj. without variation

(= dull, boring, unvaried)

                                      n. monotone

In my new job, the money is good, but the work is monotonous.

나의 새 직장은, 수입은 좋으나 일 자체는 따분하다.

☐ **malicious** /məˈlɪʃəs/   adj. to be hateful
   (= hateful, malevolent, cruel)

                                  n. malice

My mother has never had a malicious thought in her life.

우리 어머니는 평생 악의를 가진 생각을 한 번도 해 본 적이 없으시다.

☐ **dismay** /dɪsˈmeɪ/   n. sudden disillusionment
   (= disappointment, shock, alarm)

                                  v. dismay

My mother could not hide her dismay at the news of my brother's arrest.

우리 형이 체포되었다는 소식을 듣고 우리 어머니는 놀라움을 숨길 수가 없었다.

☐ **indignation** /ˌɪndɪgˈneɪʃn/   n. righteous anger
   (= anger, resentment, outrage)

                                  adj. indignant

The government's decision to raise taxes was met with indignation by the people.

세금을 올리겠다는 정부의 결정이 많은 사람들을 분개하게 하였다.

☐ **treacherous** /ˈtretʃərəs/   adj. betraying trust
   (= unfaithful, disloyal, deceitful)

                                  n. treachery

The man who was accused of a treacherous crime was proven to be innocent.

흉악한 범죄를 저질렀다는 혐의를 받은 사람이 무죄로 판명되었다.

☐ **critique** /krɪˈtiːk/   n. critical analysis
   (= analysis, assessment, evaluation)

The editorial's negative critique of the new progressive movement was welcomed by many of the conservative middle class.

새로운 진보의 움직임을 부정적으로 평가하는 사설이 많은 중도 보수 서민들로부터 환영을 받았다.

☐ **brawl** /brɔːl/   n. a noisy fight

(= scuffle, fight, clash)

                       v. brawl

The argument soon turned into a brawl.

논쟁이 곧이어 주먹질로 발전했다.

☐ **welter** /'weltər/   n. a confused mass

(= flurry, jumble, confusion)

It is amazing how Professor Higgins can find what he's looking for in the welter of books and papers stacked in his office.

히긴스 교수님이 그의 사무실에 수두룩하게 쌓인 책과 문서에서 뭔가를 찾아낼 수 있다는 것이 신기하다.

☐ **cognitive** /'kɑːgnətɪv/

adj. related to the process of perception or memory

(= mental, intellectual, cerebral)

                       n. cognition

Alzheimer's disease damages one's cognitive abilities.

알츠하이머 병은 사람의 인식력에 피해를 입힌다.

☐ **underpin** /ˌʌndər'pɪn/   v. to reinforce

(= support, buttress, fortify)

The later studies underpinned many of the theories of Albert Einstein.

추후에 나온 많은 연구결과들이 아인슈타인의 이론을 보강하였다.

☐ **reverberate** /rɪ'vɜːrbəreɪt/   v. to echo

(= resound, ring, resonate)

I realized how upset dad was when I could hear his angry voice reverberating within the entire house.

온 집안이 들썩거리게 소리지르는 아버지의 격양된 목소리를 듣고는 그가 얼마나 화가 났는지를 알 수 있었다.

☐ **revamp** /ˌriːˈvæmp/   v. to renovate

(= refurbish, restore, overhaul)

n. revamp

Helen and Eric are staying with us for a few weeks while they revamp their house.

헬렌과 에릭은 그들의 집을 수리하는 동안 우리 집에 며칠 묵을 것이다.

☐ **conjugate** /ˈkɑːndʒəgeɪt/   v. to inflect a verb

n. conjugation

When Koreans first learn to speak English, they often forget to conjugate verbs.

한국인들이 영어를 처음 배울 때 동사의 변화를 자주 잊는다.

☐ **ornate** /ɔːrˈneɪt/   adj. decorative

(= elaborate, decorative, sumptuous)

There was the most ornate Christmas tree I've ever seen standing in the lobby.

내가 본 것 중 가장 장식이 많은 크리스마스 트리가 로비에 서 있었다.

☐ **allude** /əˈluːd/   v. to refer to indirectly

(= refer, mention, indicate)

n. allusion

Norman doesn't like it when other people allude to his family's history.

노먼은 다른 사람들이 그의 가족에 대해 언급하는 것을 싫어한다.

☐ **aggrandize** /əgrǽndaiz /   v. to make greater in power or wealth

(= expand, grow, boost)

n. aggrandizement

Mike's plan was to aggrandize himself by befriending as many rich and influential people as possible.

마이크의 계획은 최대한 많은 부자와 유명인과 사겨서 자기 자신의 위상을 올리려는 것이다.

Practice 3.

Fill in the blank with the word that matches the definition provided

01 She was only 150cm tall and skinny as a twig, but her voice _____ (echoed) throughout the concert hall.

02 The defendant claimed that the plaintiff's accusations are not _____ (supported) by facts.

03 Teaching a child to read at about the age of five has proven to be beneficial to the child's _____ (intellectual) development.

04 Kyle's brain is a/an _____ (an untidy mass) of information both useful and useless.

05 It didn't take long for the argument to escalate into a/an _____ (noisy fight).

06 It was Mark's father who _____ (make greater in wealth) the family business by being one of the first people to utilize internet marketing.

07 When you meet Nathan, do not _____ (refer indirectly) to his height: he's very sensitive about that.

08 The news of the financial crisis put many people in _____ (sudden disillusionment)

09 The politician criticized the newspaper for spreading _____ (with evil intent) lies about him.

10 The popularity of K-Pop seems _____. (unable to stop)

11 At two o'clock in the morning, the baby's fever finally broke and it fell into a deep _____ (sleep).

12 There were _____ (decorative) decorations all over her room.

13 We acquired an old movie studio and _____ (renovated) it into an indoor theme park.

14 No one expected James to be such a _____ (betraying trust) character: he betrayed the trust of everyone who confided in him.

15 The sudden rise of public transportation fares met with much _____ (righteous anger) from citizens.

Class 04

☐ **persecution** /ˌpɜːrsɪˈkjuːʃn/

n. the act of harassing or oppressing based on one's religion, gender, race or political belief.

(= harassment, oppression, maltreatment)

v. persecute

In the late 19th century, many Europeans emigrated to the U.S. to escape persecution.

19세기 후반에 많은 유럽인들이 박해를 피해 미국으로 이민왔다.

☐ **creed** /kriːd/   n. a system of beliefs

(= dogma, credo, faith)

Dongsoo does not eat meat because it is against his religious creed.

동수는 그의 종교관과 일치하지 않기 때문에 육식을 하지 않는다.

☐ **fragmentary** /ˈfræɡmənteri/   adj. characterized as incomplete

(= incomplete, disconnected, fragmented)

n. fragment

The professor said my paper was fragmentary.

교수님은 내 과제가 완전하지 않다고 말씀하셨다.

☐ **sublunary** /sʌ́blunèri/   adj. pertaining to everything on Earth

(= earthly, secular)

He is such an optimist: No sublunary matter worries him.

그는 너무나 낙관적인 사람이다. 하늘 아래 그가 걱정하는 것은 없다.

☐ **negation** /nɪˈɡeɪʃn/   n. opposite

(= contrary, antithesis)

The two sisters were the negation of each other.

그 두 자매는 서로 완전히 반대였다.

☐ **appall** /əˈpɔːl/   v. to horrify

(= shock, disgust, sicken)

adj. appalling

Mother was appalled at the mess we made in the kitchen.

어머니는 우리가 부엌을 어질러 놓은 걸 보고는 깜짝 놀라셨다.

☐ **evangel** /ivǽndʒəl/   n. a doctrine taken as a guide

(= gospel, doctrine)

Walden lived in the woods on his own according to his own evangel of nature.

왈던은 그의 자연을 신봉하는 교리에 의하여 숲속에서 혼자 살았다.

☐ **enfranchisement** /ɪnˈfræntʃaɪzmənt/   n. the right to vote

(= suffrage, empowerment)

In the U.S., women's enfranchisement was achieved nationally in 1920.

미국에서 여성의 투표권 취득은 1920년에 전국적으로 주어졌다.

☐ **agitate** /ˈædʒɪteɪt/   v. to disturb or excite emotionally

(= disturb, stir, rouse)

n. agitation

The news agitated many people.

그 소식은 여러 사람을 불안하게 만들었다.

☐ **lament** /ləˈment/   v. to express grief

(= grieve, mourn, weep)

The entire nation lamented the passing of the great leader.

위대한 지도자의 사망을 전국이 슬퍼하였다.

☐ **proficient** /prəˈfɪʃnt/   adj. very competent

(= capable, skillful, practiced)

n. proficiency

Gary is proficient in four languages.

게리는 4개 국어에 능통하다.

☐ **curator** /ˈkjʊreɪtər/

n. a person in charge of a museum or art collection

(= supervisor, steward, overseer)

Gloria got a job as a curator at the Museum of Vancouver.

글로리아는 밴쿠버 박물관에 큐레이터로 취직하였다.

☐ **herbivorous** /hɜːrˈbɪvərəs/   adj. feeding on plants

(= plant eating)

?. carnivorous

Contrary to common belief, bears are mostly herbivorous.

일반적으로 알려진 것과 달리 곰은 주로 채식을 한다.

☐ **invertebrate** /ɪnˈvɜːrtɪbrət/   adj. relating to creatures without a backbone

The octopus is said to be the most intelligent invertebrate.

문어는 가장 지능이 높은 무척추동물로 알려져 있다.

☐ **devour** /dɪˈvaʊər/   v. to eat up hungrily

(= consume, gulp, wolf)

When Sue saw that her mother made her favorite dish, she devoured it in minutes.

수는 그녀의 어머니가 그녀가 제일 좋아하는 요리를 만든 걸 보고는 몇 분 만에 다 먹어치웠다.

☐ **austere** /ɔːˈstɪr/   adj. without excess or luxury

(= basic, unadorned, plain)

n. austerity

He is said to be extremely rich, but he leads a very austere lifestyle.

그는 매우 돈이 많은 걸로 알려져 있으나, 매우 소박한 인생을 산다.

☐ **obsolescence** /ˌɑːbsəˈlesns/　　　　n. the state of being out of date

(= uselessness, outmodedness, undesirability)

adj. obsolete

Most of the time, computers are discarded more often from obsolescence than from malfunction.

대부분의 경우 사람들이 컴퓨터를 버리는 이유는 작동이 안되서가 아니라 낙후되서 그런 것이다.

☐ **egregious** /ɪˈɡriːdʒiəs/　　　　adj. shocking in a bad way

(= outrageous, shocking, serious)

My decision turned out to be an egregious mistake.

나의 결정이 크나큰 실수였음이 드러났다.

☐ **perpetuate** /pərˈpetʃueɪt/　　　　v. to make something continue forever

(= continue, preserve, prolong)

adj. perpetual

American media perpetuates the image of Muslims as evil.

미국의 미디어는 무슬림들이 악하다는 이미지를 영속시킨다.

☐ **betake** /bɪˈteɪk/　　　　v. to cause to go

(= go, move)

Every Sunday, mother betook herself to the farmers market.

일요일마다 어머니는 파머스 마켓으로 가셨다.

Practice 4.

Fill in the blank with the word that matches the definition provided

01 Raised by parents, who lived a very _____ (without luxury) lifestyle, I cannot understand how some people buy their teenage children expensive cars.

02 Ricky was so hungry that he _____ (eat hungrily) his sandwich before I ate half of mine.

03 Although dogs are not _____ (feeding on plants) by nature, they are known to eat grass when they have indigestion.

04 Having lived in Canada, Russia and Holland, Gary is _____ (skillful) in French, Russian and Dutch.

05 Money is the modern _____ (doctrine as a guide): everyone worships it.

06 We were all _____ (horrified) by the damage the storm caused to our town.

07 The new president's policies were the _____ (opposite) of his predecessor's.

08 Stoicism dictates that all _____ (everything on Earth) enjoyments are vanity.

09 My memory of the event is _____ (incomplete).

10 In lieu of the seriousness of his mistake, Lester _____ (cause to go) himself to his manager's office to explain the situation.

11 American television programs still _____ (to make something continue) the image of Asian people as selfish and good only in math.

12 I could not believe that I could make such a/an _____ (serious) blunder.

13 For a while, vinyl LPs seemed to have reached _____ (state of being out of date), but in the past few years they have made a come-back.

14 Mr. Cramer _____ (expressed grief) the passing of his friend: their friendship lasted 70 years.

15 We were all _____ (disturb emotionally) by the news of a major storm coming.

☐ **admonition** /ˌædməˈnɪʃn/   n. chastisement

(= reprimand, reproach, scolding)

                                                v. admonish

Do not take my admonition lightly!

나의 꾸지람을 가벼이 듣지마라!

☐ **eloquent** /ˈeləkwənt/

adj. characterized to be very expressive verbally

(= expressive, articulate, persuasive)

                                                n. eloquence

The reverend was an eloquent speaker: I decided to be a doctor after listening to one of his speeches about compassion.

목사님은 아주 달변가이다: 나는 동정심에 대한 그의 설교를 듣고는 의사가 되기로 마음 먹었다.

☐ **exponent** /ɪkˈspəʊnənt/   n. an advocate

(= supporter, proponent, champion)

He was raised in a Catholic family but became a staunch exponent of Atheism.

그는 카톨릭 집안에서 자랐지만 완전한 무신론자가 되었다.

☐ **besiege** /bɪˈsiːdʒ/   v. to be surrounded in attack

(= surround, siege, encircle)

The famous performer was besieged by fans as he left the airport.

유명한 연예인이 공항을 빠져나가자 팬들이 그를 둘러쌌다.

☐ **correctitude** /kəréktətjùːd/   n. correctness in behavior

(= correctness, appropriateness, suitability)

Some people say modern emphasis on political correctitude hinders serious discussion about issues of race and gender inequality.

어떤 사람들은 정치적 정당성을 너무 따지는 것이 인종과 성별 불평등에 대한 심각한 대화를 방해한다고 말한다.

☐ **temperament** /ˈtemprəmənt/

n. the mental, physical and emotional traits of a person

(= character, personality, disposition)

I used to hate art classes because I was born with no artistic temperament.

나는 미술적인 재주를 전혀 갖고 태어나지 못해 미술 시간을 싫어한다.

☐ **colloquial** /kəˈloʊkwiəl/   adj. relating to informal speech

(= informal, idiomatic, conversational)

You must try to avoid using colloquial terms when writing an academic paper.

학문적인 글을 쓸 때는 속어적 표현을 쓰지 않도록 조심해야 한다.

☐ **cow** /kaʊ/   v. to frighten with threats

(= intimidate, scare, bully)

Billy cowed his younger sister to give him her candy.

빌리는 여동생에게 강압적으로 사탕을 빼앗았다.

☐ **discomfiture** /dɪsˈkʌmfɪtʃər/   n. confusion

(= embarrassment, confusion, unease)

v. discomfit

Mrs. Harrison's discomfiture grew as the police told her of her son's behavior.

해리슨 부인의 혼란스러움은 경찰이 그녀에게 아들의 행동에 대해 말을 할수록 커져만 갔다.

☐ **abject** /ˈæbdʒekt/   adj. utterly hopeless

(= miserable, wretched, utter)

Mr. San's family emigrated from Cambodia when he was eight and lived in abject poverty, but now he is one of the most successful business people in the state of Washington.

산씨의 가족은 그가 여덟 살 때 캄보디아에서 이민 와 비참한 가난 속에 살았으나, 지금 그는 워싱턴 주에서 가장 성공한 사업가 중 하나이다.

☐ **sling** /slɪŋ/   v. to throw (something like a rock)

(= throw, hurl, chuck)

Jasper slung a rock in the air in frustration.

재스퍼는 좌절감에 허공에다 돌을 던졌다.

☐ **javelin** /ˈdʒævlɪn/   n. a throwing spear

(= spear, lance, harpoon)

Andy's father participated in the 1984 Olympic Games as a javelin thrower.

앤디의 아버지는 1984년 올림픽 때 투창 선수로 참가하였다.

☐ **foreshadow** /fɔːrˈʃædoʊ/   v. to warn of

(= foretell, suggest, predict)

In Asia, the crow is viewed as a bird that brings good luck, but in Europe it is believed to foreshadow death.

아시아에서 까마귀는 길조로 취급되는 반면에 유럽에서는 죽음을 부르는 새로 치부된다.

☐ **retention** /rɪˈtenʃn/   n. keeping possession of

(= holding, retaining, preservation)

                                   v. retain

Retention of all financial records is important.

모든 금융기록을 보유하는 것이 중요하다.

☐ **imprudent** /ɪmˈpruːdnt/   adj. characterized being careless

(= rash, hasty, thoughtless)

                                   n. imprudence

It is imprudent not to check on one's financial status for long periods of time.

자신의 금융상황에 대해 오랫동안 확인하지 않는 것은 매우 위험하다.

☐ **lurch** /lɜːrtʃ/   v. to sway abruptly

(= pitch, stagger, sway)

The bus lurched suddenly causing many people to fall to the floor.

버스가 갑자기 앞으로 휘청하여 많은 승객이 바닥에 넘어졌다.

☐ **levitation** /ˌlevɪˈteɪʃn/   n. rising or floating in the air

(= hovering, floating, flying)

The magnetic levitation train made almost no sound when running.

자기부상열차는 거의 무음으로 운행한다.

☐ **whisk** /wɪsk/   v. to move with a rapid, sweeping stroke

(= carry, whip, bustle)

Jenny has to whisk her kids off to soccer practice as soon as they finish school.

제니는 학교가 끝나자 마자 아이들을 축구 연습장으로 몰고 갔다.

☐ **ramify** /ˈræmɪfaɪ/   v. to divide or spread out in a branch like form

(= branch, split, separate)

Subway lines ramified the entire city.

지하철 선로가 도시에서 사방으로 뻗어나갔다.

☐ **perch** /pɜːrtʃ/   v. to rest on some elevated position

(= sit, alight, balance)

     n. perch

An owl perched on a branch right outside my window.

내 창문 밖의 나뭇가지에 부엉이가 앉아 있었다.

Practice 5.

Fill in the blank with the word that matches the definition provided

01   Despite the popular image of a meditating yogi floating in the air, one cannot achieve _____ (floating in the air) by practicing yoga.

02   Suddenly our train _____ (sway abruptly) forward and began to move.

03   Even in such an economic depression, many companies _____ (move with a rapid stroke) away computer engineering majors as soon as they graduate.

04   The gathering clouds _____ (warned of) a rain storm.

05   When Henry was growing up, his family lived in _____ (utterly hopeless) poverty.

06   Some of the expressions the local people were using were too _____ (related to unformal speech) for me to understand.

07   She is of a calm _____ (character) and never gets excited.

08   As soon as I finished my presentation, I was _____ (attacked from all sides) by questions.

09   Many people were moved by his _____ (verbally expressive) speech.

10   I sat in _____ (confusion) as everyone in the hall reacted to the siren.

11   I made the _____ (careless) decision of agreeing to Tom's plan without thinking it through.

12 The company's employee _____ (keeping possession of) rate is extremely good: 70% of employees have worked in the company for over 5 years.

13 When I walked in the room, I was surprised to see a huge parrot _____ (sit in an elevated position) on a swing.

14 The company was founded as a textile manufacturer 25 years ago but since has _____ (branched out) into several industries.

15 He is a bully, but he does not _____ (frighten with threats) me at all.

Find the correct word

besiege, aggrandize, ornate, perpetuate, indignant, abject, exponent, colloquial, creed, persecution

01 I realized I was getting old when I realized I didn't understand many of the _____ expressions my younger colleagues were using.

02 After my humiliating defeat, all I wanted was to be alone, but my mother _____ me with a barrage of questions the moment I walked in the door.

03 The politician was one of the first _____ of the need for globalization.

04 Hollywood's insistence of casting Asians and Latinos only as gang members or petty criminals _____ negative stereotypes.

05 He is a physicist and I am a theologian: we do not share the same _____, but we do share the quest for the truth.

06 Gennady's parents emigrated from Russia to the west to escape from political _____ in the 1980s.

07 Bill likes to _____ himself by bragging about his rich friends.

08 The dormitory building was quite dull, but some students had decorated their rooms to be quite _____.

09 Henry became _____ when Saul took credit for the term paper they had both written.

10   Penny's plan to become an actress ended in _____ failure, when several movie industry people told her that she had no talent.

devour, foreshadow, inexorable, construe, perch, dismay, imprudent, retention, ramify, austere

11   The underground movement has _____ into the mainstream.

12   It is _____ to jump into a pool before checking the temperature of the water.

13   As we grow older, our mental capability of memory _____ weakens.

14   The CEO's mention of cost reduction _____ either a salary freeze or lay-offs.

15   Although Mr. Harrison was rich beyond most people's imaginations, he taught his children to maintain _____ lifestyles.

16   Having skipped lunch, Randy _____ two servings of meatloaf at dinner.

17   The lifeguard _____ high in his chair making sure that no one was in danger of drowning.

18   After feeling good about her prospects of landing the job, Martha could not hide her _____ at the rejection.

19   Man can do nothing in front of the _____ power of nature.

20   Unfortunately, Robert _____ my criticism as dislike to his work.

ambivalent, agitate, endearing, proficient, underpin, scrawl, discomfit, egregious, appall, revamp

21 Thanks to having spent his formative years in many foreign countries, Jack is _____ in five languages.

22 The news of Paul's traffic accident severely _____ his mother.

23 The principal was _____ that the median score of the seniors who took the Provincial Standardized Test was so low.

24 Henry took over an old automobile service center and _____ it into a very hip cafe.

25 Much of the bystanders' testimony _____ the alibi of the accused man.

26 Mark's textbook was filled with underlined passages and _____ in the margins.

27 Peter felt _____ about leaving for college: he was happy to start a new adventure but was sad to leave his family and friends in his home town.

28 Among his three daughters, Mr. Cranston found his youngest the most _____.

29 The government was clearly _____ by the recent diplomatic mishap.

30 The newspaper editorial called the government's plan to use force against the protestors a/an _____ mistake.

Choose the word that is not a synonym

31 glossy – receptive – amenable

32 nuisance – negation – vexation

33 imply – intimate – lurk

34   bounty – clamor – tumult

35   despoil – underpin – buttress

36   appealing – charming – relishing

37   intellectual – cognitive – commotion

38   persecution – aggrandizement – oppression

39   sublunary – disconnected – fragmentary

40   credo – faith – pittance

41   prone – flat – javelin

42   preach – stump – baffle

43   slumber – rest – temperament

44   savor – relish – substantiate

45   display – candidacy – pageant

46   welter – interpret – construe

47   conducive – candid – favorable

48   prolong – perpetuate – shuffle

49   negation – antithesis – evangel

50   suffrage – enfranchisement – endearment

51   lament – overhaul – grieve

52   flurry – march – procession

53   malicious – monotonous – malevolent

54   treacherous – irksome – deceitful

55   analysis – conjugation – critique

56   unadorned – ornate – austere

57   obsolete – appalling – outmoded

58   varnish – abundance – bounty

59   satiate – quench – broach

60   thaw – doodle – defrost

☐ **locomotion** /ˌləʊkəˈməʊʃn/   n. the power of moving from place to place

(= motion, propulsion, movement)

adj. locomotive

The invention of steam locomotion enabled Britain to become a superpower in the 18th century.

증기기관차의 발명이 영국을 18세기에 강대국으로 변화시켰다.

☐ **incline** /ɪnˈklaɪn/   n. a sloped surface

(= slope, slant, gradient)

The incline became steeper as we climbed up the hill.

우리가 언덕을 올라갈수록 경사가 더 급해졌다.

☐ **erratic** /ɪˈrætɪk/   adj. to be unpredictable

(= unreliable, inconsistent, changeable)

His erratic behavior began to worry those around him.

그의 예측 못 할 행동들이 주변사람에게 걱정을 끼쳤다.

☐ **sanction** /ˈsæŋkʃn/   v. to give approval to

(= approve, endorse, authorize)

n. sanction

Many farmers were miffed that the government sanctioned the import of foreign agricultural goods and showed their dissatisfaction by staging a massive demonstration.

정부가 외국산 농산물의 수입을 허가했다는 소식에 많은 농부들이 화가 났으며 대규모 농성을 조직하여 자신들의 불만을 표출하였다.

☐ **inefficacious** /ˌɪnefɪkéiʃəs/   adj. to be inefficient

(= inefficient, unsuccessful, ineffective)

The government's policy to induce people to quit smoking by raising the prices of cigarettes proved to be inefficacious.

담뱃값을 올림으로써 흡연가들에게 금연을 유도하려 했던 정부의 시책이 효과가 없음이 드러났다.

☐ **constitution** /ˌkɑːnstɪˈtuːʃn/ n. the physical characteristics of a person

(= health, disposition, condition)

The theme park advises people with weak constitutions not to ride on the rollercoasters.

테마파크는 약체질인 사람들은 롤러코스터를 타지 말 것을 권유한다.

☐ **usurp** /juːˈzɜːrp/ v. to take over power by force

(= seize, grab, appropriate)

During the Soviet Era, those who reached the position of General Secretary of the Communist Party served at the post until their natural deaths, except for Nikita Khrushchev, who was usurped by his political rivals.

소비에트 연방 시대에 공산당 서기장의 위치까지 오른 사람은 자연사할 때까지 그 직책을 유지하는 것이 일반적이었으나, 니키타 흐루시체프는 그의 정적에 의해 강제로 퇴위당했다.

☐ **sanity** /ˈsænəti/ n. the soundness of mind

(= reasonableness, sense, reason)

adj. sane

After spending too much time alone, David began to question his sanity.

너무나 혼자서 오랜 시간을 보낸 데이빗은 가끔씩 그가 실성하고 있다고 의심했다.

☐ **elaborate** /ɪˈlæbərət/ adj. to be very complicated

(= intricate, complicated, complex)

Greg drew an elaborate map of how to get to his house from his school.

그렉은 학교에서 그의 집까지 찾아 갈 수 있는 매우 복잡하고 정교한 지도를 그렸다.

☐ **postulate** /ˈpɑːstʃəleɪt/ v. to assume with no proof

(= hypothesize, advance, suggest)

Some ecologist postulate that the Earth is on the verge of massive extinctions of a scale never before experienced.

어떤 환경론자는 지구 역사상 전례 없는 대규모의 멸종위기가 다가오고 있다고 추론한다.

☐ **circadian** /sɜːrˈkeɪdiən/   adj. of the 24 hour cycle of a day
(= daily, 24-hour, quotidian)

Some archeologists imply that the ancient Mayans did not follow the same circadian rhythm as today; it seems that their days rotated around a 60-hour cycle.
어떤 고고학자들은 고대 마야인들이 오늘날과 같은 24시간 주기로 살지 않은 것 같다고 생각하며; 아마도 60시간 주기의 생활을 한 것으로 보인다고 한다.

☐ **abysmal** /əˈbɪzməl/   adj. to be extremely bad
(= terrible, awful, dreadful)

After the abysmal failure of his improvised performances, Jim returned to his old style of rehearsed performances.
그의 즉흥 연주가 완전한 실패로 끝나자, 짐은 다시 옛날의 연습 연주 스타일로 돌아갔다.

☐ **articulate** /ɑːrˈtɪkjuleɪt/   adj. to be very expressive
(= articulate, eloquent, moving)

         n. articulation
The young pianists was very articulate: he moved his audiences with his performances.
어린 피아니스트는 매우 표현을 잘하였다: 그는 연주로 관객을 감동시켰다.

☐ **panacea** /ˌpænəˈsiːə/   n. a remedy for all diseases
(= cure-all, elixir)

Grandfather always starts his day with a cup of ginseng tea: he says that it is the panacea that keeps him healthy.
우리 할아버지는 항상 아침을 인삼차 한 잔으로 시작하신다: 그는 인삼차가 그의 건강을 유지해주는 만병통치약이라고 하신다.

☐ **taut** /tɔːt/   adj. to be tightly drawn
(= tense, nervous, wired)

Both men smiled and exchanged pleasantries, but the taut tension between the two was clearly visible.

두 남자는 서로 인사하고 덕담을 나눴지만, 그 둘 사이의 팽팽한 갈등은 확연히 보였다.

☐ **susceptible** /səˈseptəbl/   adj. yielding readily to

(= vulnerable, liable, prone)

Janet is susceptible to sore throats during the cold months.

추운 계절에 자넷은 목이 잘 쉰다.

☐ **feline** /ˈfiːlaɪn/   adj. pertaining to cats

Her face has feline features.

그녀의 얼굴은 고양이상이다.

☐ **yearning** /ˈjɜːrnɪŋ/   n. a deep desire for something

(= longing, craving, thirst)

After dieting for three days, I developed a yearning for a double cheeseburger.

사흘간 다이어트를 한 나는 갑자기 더블치즈버거가 너무 땡겼다.

☐ **sustenance** /ˈsʌstənəns/   n. something taken sustains health or life

(= nourishment, nutrition, food)

The early settlers of the island found abundant sustenance in the sea.

섬의 초기 정착민들은 바다에서 충분한 식량을 구했다.

☐ **cairn** /kern/

n. a heap of stones set up as a landmark, monument or post

(= landmark, milestone)

Follow this trail and take the path left when you reach a cairn.

이 길을 따라가다가 돌무더기가 나오면 왼쪽 길로 가.

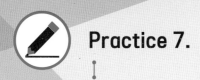

Practice 7.

Fill in the blank with the word that matches the definition provided

01 Cave dwelling life forms have evolved to gather _____ (nourishment) from an environment where no light exists.

02 After barely sleeping for three hours a night for several days, my _____ (of the 24 hour cycle of the day) rhythm is all messed up.

03 Einstein was the first to _____ (assume with no proof) that light can be viewed as a beam of particles as well as a wave.

04 When asked, Horatio will tell a/an _____ (very complicated) story of how he got his name.

05 I have been so busy these past few days that I began to wonder if I could maintain my _____. (soundness of mind)

06 Wild ginseng is considered to be a/an _____ (cure for all diseases) in Eastern medicine.

07 He was an artistic genius and could _____ better with his paintings than with words.

08 My boss said my performance was _____ (very bad) and that if I didn't improve, he would have to fire me.

09 The strings on my new tennis racket were too _____ (tightly drawn) for me.

10 He was born of a sickly _____ (physical characteristics) and has been in and out of hospitals throughout his childhood.

11   The house was built on a steep _____ (slope) so one entered the front door on the first floor and had to walk up two stories to reach the door leading to the backyard.

12   It turned out that Mr. Harrods' push to increase production was not _____ (given approval) by his bosses.

13   I was saddened to learn someone else had _____ (take away by force) my place in her heart.

14   All policies implemented by the government to solve the unemployment problem seems to be _____ (have no effect).

15   After achieving much financial success, Howard developed a/an _____ (deep desire) for spiritual fulfillment.

16   Veterinarians say that large dog breeds, like Great Danes and St. Bernards, are _____ (vulnerable) to joint diseases.

☐ **trot** /trɑːt/   v. to run at a quick steady pace

(= jog, run, sprint)

The horse trotted briefly before it broke into a full gallop.

말이 잠시 빠른 걸음으로 걷다가 전속력으로 달리기 시작했다.

☐ **ephemeral** /ɪˈfemərəl/   adj. passing quickly

(= short-lived, transient, fleeting)

Life is ephemeral, but art is ever-lasting.

인생은 짧고 예술은 영원하다.

☐ **disdain** /dɪsˈdeɪn/   n. ill-feeling

(= scorn, contempt, derision)

         v. disdain

The boy constantly shows disdain for rules.

그 소년은 계속해서 규칙에 거부감을 보인다.

☐ **implication** /ˌɪmplɪˈkeɪʃn/   n. an indirect suggestion or indication

(= inference, allegation, insinuation)

         v. imply

His implication that I was the beneficiary of some great generosity of his family is ludicrous.

내가 마치 그의 가족의 엄청난 관대함의 수혜자인 것처럼 그가 언급하는 것은 웃기는 소리다.

☐ **albeit** /ˌɔːlˈbiːɪt/   conj. even though

(= although, though, even if)

He is improving, albeit slowly.

그는 비록 느리긴하지만 발전하고 있다.

380

□ **bust** /bʌst/   n. a failure

(= failure, crash, collapse)

Economists warned that the housing market is overheated and may go bust soon.

경제학자들은 주택시장이 과열되었고 곧 추락할 것이라고 경고하였다.

□ **inversion** /ɪnˈvɜːrʒn/   n. turning upside down

(= overturn, reversal, upturn)

                     v. invert
                     adj. inversed

The atmosphere at Mark's new office was the inversion of what he was used to.

마크의 새 직장의 분위기는 그가 익숙한 것과 전혀 달랐다.

□ **fiscal** /ˈfɪskl/   adj. related to (usually) government finance

(= monetary, financial)

The problem is that the results of a government's fiscal policies do not show until way after that government has been replaced with a new one, meaning that the new government will get credit for smart policies initiated by the previous one.

문제는 한 정부의 금융정책의 효과가 그 정부가 다음 정부로 대체된 이후에야 나타나기 때문에 그것은 다음 정부가 이전의 정부의 현명한 정책의 덕을 본다는 것이다.

□ **enclave** /ˈenkleɪv/

n. a small area or group enclosed within a larger one

(= area, commune, district)

Most of the students in our school were from rich families, but there was a small enclave of boys from the poorer neighborhoods.

우리 학교의 대부분의 학생들은 돈 많은 가족 출신이나, 몇몇 소년들은 상대적으로 못사는 동네 출신이다.

□ **volition** /vəʊˈlɪʃn/   n. one's free will

(= free-will, choice, option)

After some deliberation, he decided to enter rehab of his own volition because he wanted to overcome his addiction to alcohol.

숙고한 후 그는 자신의 알코올 중독을 이겨내기 위해 자진해서 재활병원에 입원하기로 했다.

☐ **recession** /rɪˈseʃn/   n. an economic downturn

(= depression, slump, decline)

The number of available jobs is getting smaller by the day because of the recession.

불경기에 일자리의 숫자가 점점 줄어들고 있다.

☐ **degradation** /ˌdegrəˈdeɪʃn/   n. the lowering of character or quality

(= squalor, dilapidation, ruin)

Some people say we are witnessing the degradation of democracy.

어떤 사람들은 우리가 현재 민주주의의 퇴보를 목격하고 있다고 말한다.

☐ **udders** /ˈʌdər/

n. the mammary glands of animals like cows or goats

You can tell a female cow apart from a male bull from the cow's udders and the bull's horns

암소에겐 젖이 있고 숫소에게는 뿔이 있어 그 둘을 구분할 수 있다.

☐ **subversion** /səbˈvɜːrʒn/   n. causing the downfall

(= insurrection, rebellion, sedition)

         v. subvert
         adj. subversive

He was sentenced to prison under charges of subversion.

그는 내란선동죄로 투옥되었다.

☐ **subservient** /səbˈsɜːrviənt/   adj. to be obedient

(= submissive, compliant, servile)

         n. subservience

The press was criticized for being subservient to the government.

언론이 정부의 하수인이라는 비판을 받았다.

□ **brevity** /ˈbrevəti/   n. shortness

(= briefness, conciseness, terseness)

                                   adj. brief

When writing, brevity is better than ornamentation.

글을 쓸 때, 만연체보다는 간결체로 쓰는 것이 좋다.

□ **substantiate** /səbˈstænʃieɪt/   v. to provide validation

(= authenticate, verify, corroborate)

He had no one to substantiate his claim.

그에게는 그의 주장을 지지해 줄 사람이 없었다.

□ **perturb** /pərˈtɜːrb/   v. to emotionally disturb

(= trouble, worry, agitate)

The news of the coming storm perturbed those who experienced last year's devastating storm.

작년의 파괴적인 폭풍을 경험한 사람들은 새로운 폭풍이 접근한다는 소식에 불안했다.

□ **mural** /ˈmjʊrəl/   n. a painting on the wall

(= wall painting)

Perhaps the most famous mural is that of the ceiling of the Sistine Chapel in the Vatican.

아마도 가장 유명한 벽화는 바티칸의 시스틴 성당에 있는 천장 벽화일 것이다.

□ **scrutiny** /ˈskruːtəni/   n. watching carefully

(= inspection, examination, analysis)

The artifact was originally thought to be 2,000 years old, but after much scrutiny, archeologists think it's at least 1,000 years older than that.

그 유물은 처음에는 2천 년 이상 된 것으로 추정되었으나, 오랜 관찰 끝에 적어도 천년은 더 오래된 것으로 추정된다.

Practice 8.

Fill in the blank with the word that matches the definition provided

01 One cannot expect a country's _____ (government finance) policies to be effective when such policies are initiated only to gain popularity for the government.

02 David's first business went _____ (failure) after only three months.

03 At first, the experiment results seemed to be inconclusive, but after closer _____ (watching carefully) the researchers realized they discovered something totally unexpected.

04 The church walls were covered with _____ (wall paintings) depicting biblical scenes.

05 Many stories in today's newspaper _____ (emotionally disturbed) me.

06 It took over 30 years for Einstein to _____ (provide validation) his theory through experiment.

07 Many leading educators say that standardized tests have caused the _____ (lowering of quality) of education in recent years.

08 It is important to train for jobs that are relatively unaffected by economic _____. (economic downturns)

09 I am on a diet, so please do not eat ice cream in front of me: I have a weak _____ (free will).

10 When Mr. Huge was in his twenties, he enjoyed _____ (short lived) fame as a singer for a boyband

11   Don't let the _____ (shortness) of the book fool you: it is a profound book.

12   When Dad was a young man, his apartment was a/an _____ (a small area within a larger one) of budding artists, musicians and writers.

13   After much discussion, the two men agreed to cooperate, _____ (although) reluctantly.

14   When Einstein was a boy, he showed a/an _____ (ill-feeling) for learning by memorization and cramming.

15   You don't have to be _____ (obedient) to Donny just because he is two years older than you.

16   You can tell the cow from the bull by its _____ (mammary glands).

Class 09

□ **confide** /kənˈfaɪd/   v. to reveal secrets trustfully

(= disclose, reveal, confess)

n. confidence

Mark has many friends, but he only confides his deepest secrets to two of them: Norman and Piers.

마크는 친구가 여러 명이지만 오로지 두 명, 노먼과 피어스에게만 자기의 가장 깊은 비밀을 이야기 한다.

□ **emulate** /ˈemjuleɪt/   v. to try to equal or excel

(= rival, outdo, compete)

Try as they may, John Lennon's sons will never emulate their father's musical legacy.

시도는 하겠지만 존 레논의 아들들은 아버지의 음악적 유산을 뛰어넘지 못할 것이다.

□ **epitome** /ɪˈpɪtəmi/   n. a perfect example of a characteristic

(= essence, personification, architype)

Mother Teresa was an epitome of Christian benevolence.

테레사 수녀는 기독교 자비의 가장 좋은 본보기이다.

□ **arduous** /ˈɑːrdʒuəs/   adj. requiring much energy

(= laborious, demanding, strenuous)

The hike was long and arduous.

등산은 오래 걸리고 힘들었다.

□ **mockery** /ˈmɑːkəri/   n. a subject of ridicule

(= derision, contempt, disdain)

v. mock

His new hairstyle was the subject of mockery by his friends.

그의 새로운 머리 모양이 친구들로부터 조롱의 대상이 되었다.

□ **veritable** /ˈverɪtəbl/   adj. absolute

(= real, genuine, authentic)

The meal he prepared was a veritable feast.

그가 준비한 식사는 그야말로 만찬이었다.

□ **cohesion** /kəʊˈhiːʒn/   n. the characteristic of sticking together

(= unity, consistency, interconnection)

                                 adj. cohesive

There was no cohesion in the group: everyone was interested in working alone.

그룹인원 간에 아무런 결합력이 없었다: 저마다 혼자 일하고 싶어했다.

□ **predominant** /prɪˈdɑːmɪnənt/   adj. having power or authority over others

(= main, principal, prime)

                                 n. predominance

Dr. Walker is seen as the predominant expert in Cryptozoology.

워커 박사는 미확인 생물연구의 최고 권위자이다.

□ **emphatic** /ɪmˈfætɪk/   adj. being forceful

(= resounding, unequivocal, insistent)

He gave an emphatic "No" to my request.

나의 요청에 그는 노골적으로 "싫어"라고 말했다.

□ **lucrative** /ˈluːkrətɪv/   adj. causing to make much money

(= profitable, productive, rewarding)

After failing several business ventures, Victor finally began a lucrative jewelry business in San Diego.

몇 번의 실패를 한 후 빅터는 마침내 샌디에고에서 보석 사업으로 큰 성공을 거뒀다.

☐ **paramount** /ˈpærəmaʊnt/   adj. to be of great importance

(= supreme, dominant, vital)

It is paramount that I improve my grades this semester.

이번 학기에 내 학점을 올리는 것이 매우 중요하다.

☐ **legible** /ˈledʒəbl/   adj. to be readable

(= intelligible, decipherable, comprehensible)

⇔ illegible

The markings on the stone are thousands of years old but still legible.

천년이 넘었지만 돌에 새겨진 흔적이 무엇인지 알아 볼 수 있었다.

☐ **marginal** /ˈmɑːrdʒɪnl/   adj. pertaining to the margins of something

(= bordering, peripheral, fringe)

n. margin

Climate change is treated as a marginal issue in many developing countries.

많은 개발도상국에서 지구온난화는 큰 문제로 치부하지 않는다.

☐ **plenipotentiary** /ˌplenɪpəˈtenʃieri/

n. a diplomatic agent invested with the authority to negotiate on behalf of his government

(= ambassador, envoy, representative)

Each country sent its plenipotentiary to the conference.

각국이 자신들의 전권대사를 회의에 파견하였다.

☐ **convoke** /kənˈvəʊk/   v. to call together

(= summon, call)

n. convocation

A general shareholders' meeting was convoked.

일반 주주회의가 소집되었다.

□ **sober** /ˈsoʊbər/   adj. the state of not being drunk

(= restrained, abstemious, clear-headed)

                              n. sobriety

It was hard to stay sober at the year-end party.

망년회 파티에서 술에 안 취하기가 어려웠다.

□ **shrivel** /ˈʃrɪvl/   v. to wither with wrinkles

(= wrinkle, shrink, contract)

Even at seventy, Dan's face did not shrivel nor his back stoop.

70세에도 댄은 얼굴에 주름도 없고 등도 전혀 굽지 않았다.

□ **subordinate** /səˈbɔːrdɪnət/   adj. to be lower in rank or importance

(= secondary, lesser, inferior)

For him, making money is subordinate to achieving fame.

그에게 돈을 버는 것은 유명해지는 것보다 덜 중요하다.

□ **reverence** /ˈrevərəns/   n. deep respect

(= respect, admiration, veneration)

Professor Gibbons was held in reverence by the entire faculty and student body of the university.

기본스 교수는 전교의 모든 교수진과 학생들로부터 존경을 받았다.

□ **combatant** /kəmˈbætnt/   n. someone who combats

(= fighter, soldier, belligerent)

Every combatant was willing to die for his country.

모든 병사가 국가를 위해 죽을 각오가 되어 있었다.

Practice 9.

Fill in the blank with the word that matches the definition provided

01 During the American Revolutionary War, Benjamin Franklin was dispatched to the French Court as _____ (diplomatic agent) of the United States.

02 James was disappointed to learn that his hard efforts only resulted in a/an _____ (peripheral) improvement of his grades.

03 Most citizens consider the improvement of the economy to be the a/an _____ (of great importance) issue the country faces.

04 Not many people know that minting coins is a/an _____ (making a lot of money) business for many countries.

05 I was persuaded by his _____ (forceful) reasoning.

06 A democratic government is divided into three branches, so that one branch does not have _____ (having power over) authority over everything.

07 Entering the debate competition, my team members had such looks of determination on their faces that they looked not like debaters, but _____ (fighters).

08 As the speaker stood on the podium, several of his supporters looked at him in _____ (deep respect).

09 Let's not stray into talking about _____ (lower in importance) issues and stay on the main topic.

10 The apples _____ (withered with wrinkles) because they were left outside for too long.

11 The chairman _____ (call together) an emergency meeting of all senior members.

12 The country has very little political or social _____ (characteristic of sticking together) and is divided into a multiplicity of tribes or clans.

13 Amanda is 158cm and her husband Trevor is 198cm: when they stand together he is a/an _____ (absolute) giant compared to her.

14 I will not allow any more of your _____ (subject of ridicule) about my name.

15 The principal heralded Mindy as the _____ (perfect example) of the type of students he wants to attract to the school.

16 Many tennis players try to _____ (try to equal) Roger Federer's winning record but cannot.

17 There are very few people that I _____ (reveal secrets trustfully) in.

☐ **coercive** /kəʊˈɜːrsɪv/   adj. forcing against one's will

(= forced, intimidating, bullying)

         v. coerce

         n. coercion

He is not against using coercive force to get his way.

그는 자기 뜻을 관철시키기 위해 위압적인 행동을 삼가지 않는다.

☐ **alienate** /ˈeɪliəneɪt/

v. to cause to be indifferent, unfriendly or hostile

(= estrange, disaffect, isolate)

He was alienated by his friends for refusing to help them cheat.

그는 친구들이 부정을 저지르는 것에 돕기를 거부했다고 친구들로부터 소외 당했다.

☐ **irrigation** /ˌɪrɪˈɡeɪʃn/   n. the supply of water by artificial means

         v. irrigate

The history of agriculture and irrigation go side by side.

농업과 관개의 역사는 불가분의 관계이다.

☐ **perennial** /pəˈreniəl/   adj. lasting throughout the entire year

(= year-round, recurrent, constant)

Martha planted both seasonal and perennial flowers in her garden.

마사는 정원에 계절 꽃과 다년생 꽃은 같이 심었다.

☐ **compost** /ˈkɑːmpəʊst/

n. decaying organic matter that is used as fertilizer

(= fertilizer, manure)

         v. compost

Many people in Vancouver use food scraps as compost.
밴쿠버의 많은 주민은 음식 찌꺼기로 퇴비를 만든다.

☐ **deploy** /dɪˈplɔɪ/　　　　　　　　v. arrange in a position of readiness
(= position, arrange, install)

　　　　　　　　　　　　　　　　　n. deployment

More than 5,000 troops are deployed along the border.
국경을 따라 5천 명 이상의 병사가 배치되어 있다.

☐ **aggregate** /ˈæɡrɪɡət/　　　　　n. a total or gross amount
(= total, sum, whole)

　　　　　　　　　　　　　　　　　adj. aggregate
　　　　　　　　　　　　　　　　　v. aggregate

The aggregate number of people who visited the exhibition was over 1 million.
전시회를 방문한 사람의 숫자가 통합해서 백만 명이 넘었다.

☐ **chronological** /ˌkrɑːnəˈlɑːdʒɪkl/　adj. in the order of time
(= sequential, consecutive, linear)

　　　　　　　　　　　　　　　　　n. chronology

History is best studied in chronological order.
역사는 시간의 순서에 따라 공부하는 것이 가장 좋다.

☐ **spook** /spuːk/　　　　　　　　v. to scare
(= frighten, startle, alarm)

　　　　　　　　　　　　　　　　　n. spook: a ghost

A strange sound coming from the basement spooked the children.
지하실에서 들리는 이상한 소리가 아이들을 겁에 질리게 했다.

☐ **labyrinthine** /ˌlæbəˈrɪnθɪn/　　adj. to be very complex
(= convoluted, complicated, tangled)

　　　　　　　　　　　　　　　　　n. labyrinth

I had to navigate through labyrinthine corridors to get to Dr. Harris' office.

해리스 박사님의 사무실에 도달하기 위해 나는 꼬불꼬불한 복도를 따라 찾아가야 했다.

☐ **posterior** /pɑːˈstɪriər/　　　　adj. of the rear

(= hinder)

It is believed that the posterior part of the brain regulates the more basic functions of the body, such as breathing and heartbeat.

뇌의 뒷부분이 신체의 더 기초적인 기능, 예를 들어 호흡이나 심장박동 등을 통제한다고 알려져 있다.

☐ **mutable** /ˈmjuːtəbl/　　　　adj. capable of change

(= changeable, alterable, fluctuating)

　　　　　　　　　　　　　　⇔ immutable

Political beliefs are mutable.

정치적인 의견은 바뀔 수 있다.

☐ **protrude** /prəʊˈtruːd/　　　　v. to stick out

(= jut, bulge)

A huge boulder protruded from the side of the hill.

언덕 옆으로 커다란 바위가 툭 튀어나와 있었다.

☐ **insatiable** /ɪnˈseɪʃəbl/　　　　adj. unable to satisfy

(= voracious, greedy, avid)

　　　　　　　　　　　　　　⇔ satiable

Marcus has an insatiable desire to help people.

마커스에게는 남을 돕고 싶어하는 해소할 수 없는 욕망이 있다.

☐ **bloated** /ˈbləʊtɪd/　　　　adj. swollen

(= inflated, expanded, distended)

　　　　　　　　　　　　　　v. bloat

He had a bloated belly after eating so much.

그는 과식한 후 배가 볼록하게 나왔다.

☐ **hail** /heɪl/   v. to acclaim

(= salute, uphold, affirm)

The young boy who saved his dog from drowning was hailed as a hero.

자신의 개가 익사하는 것을 구해 준 소년이 영웅으로 칭송받았다.

☐ **exacerbate** /ɪgˈzæsərbeɪt/   v. to make something worse

(= worsen, aggravate, impair)

The cold night air exacerbated my sore throat.

차가운 밤 공기가 나의 쉰 목을 더욱 악화시켰다.

☐ **presumption** /prɪˈzʌmpʃn/   n. the taking of something for granted

(= supposition, assumption, conjecture)

                                v. presume

It is a presumption that everything you read in the newspaper is the truth.

신문에서 읽는 내용이 모두 사실이라는 것은 선입견이다.

☐ **altruistic** /ˌæltruˈɪstɪk/   adj. characterized of being unselfish

(= humane, philanthropic, noble)

                                n. altruist, altruism

After he retired, he moved to India, set up a hospital and several schools and lived an altruistic life.

그는 은퇴한 후 인디아로 이주해서 병원과 다수의 학교를 설립하고 이타적인 삶을 살았다.

☐ **precipitous** /prɪˈsɪpɪtəs/   adj. extremely steep

(= steep, sheer, abrupt)

                                n. precipice

The monastery was built on a precipitous cliff.

그 수도원은 깎아지른 듯한 낭떠러지에 지어졌다.

Practice 10.

Fill in the blank with the word that matches the definition provided

01 Maria knew that if she intervened now she would only _____ (make worse) the situation.

02 The president was _____ (acclaimed) for expertly handling the foreign relations crisis.

03 Half of Brian's face was _____ (swollen) like a balloon from a bee sting on his cheek.

04 Marlon has a/an _____ (not satisfiable) desire to write. I'm sure he will become a famous writer someday.

05 Both parties agreed that the contract terms were still _____ (able to change).

06 I could recognize the man walking in front of me as William just by his _____ (backside)

07 The United States Navy announced that it will _____ (arrange at a position of readiness) a cutting edge next-generation nuclear submarine by the end of next year.

08 A shortage of electricity has been a/an _____ (lasting throughout the entire year) problem of the region for decades.

09 The ancient people of Angkor were masters of _____ (supply of water): they built a network of water canals that would be difficult to build even now using modern technology.

10 Television programs showing the affluent lifestyles of celebrities have _____ (cause to be indifferent) many ordinary people just trying to get by.

11 The musician had no time to warm up because he spent too much time finding the audition room among the _____ (very complex) corridors.

12 The stock market suffered a/an _____ (extremely steep) drop today that had investors worldwide panicking.

13 In the Italian Renaissance, people of wealth distinguished themselves by their _____ (characterized as unselfish) endeavors.

14 The widespread _____ (the taking of something for granted) that doctors' prognoses are always correct is quite dangerous.

15 The sudden power outage during dinner _____ (scared) all of us.

16 The data were confusing because they were not listed in _____ (in order of time) order.

17 The _____ (total) amount of money we made by the end of the fair was much higher than we had expected.

☐ **ensue** /ɪnˈsuː/   v. to happen right after

(= follow, succeed, proceed)

Once the two men were in the same room, an argument ensued.

그들 둘이 같은 방에 있으면 곧 말다툼이 일어났다.

☐ **malfeasance** /ˌmælˈfiːzns/   n. a wrongful or illegal act by a public official

Several officials from the Mayor's office were involved in malfeasance.

시장실 소속 몇 명의 공무원들이 범법행위에 가담했다.

☐ **substantive** /ˈsʌbstəntɪv/

adj. relating to the essential element of something

(= essential, fundamental, elementary)

The report did not touch upon the substantive issues.

보고서에 핵심 논건에 대한 논의는 없었다.

☐ **deterrent** /dɪˈtɜːrənt/

n. something that discourages or restrains (usually the enemy's) action

(= constraint, prevention, restraint)

Some people say that punishing a person severely as a deterrent to prevent others from committing the same crime is unfair to that person.

어떤 사람들은 다른 사람에게 경고를 주고자, 한 사람을 심하게 체벌하는 것은 그 사람에게 불공평하다고 말한다.

☐ **proliferate** /prəˈlɪfəreɪt/   v. to spread wide

(= multiply, flourish, bourgeon)

       n. proliferation

The virus has proliferated to the entire country.

바이러스는 전국에 스며들었다.

□ **suffice** /səˈfaɪs/   v. to be enough

(= suit, avail, serve)

adj. sufficient

n. sufficiency

Three pairs of clothes will suffice for a week's trip.

일주일간 출장이라 옷 세 벌이면 충분할 것 같다.

□ **demur** /dɪˈmɜːr/   v. to make an objection

(= object, protest, balk)

n. demurral

He did not demur at the accusations.

그는 비난을 거부하지 않았다.

□ **smudge** /smʌdʒ/   v. to mark with dirty smears

(= smear, blot, smirch)

n. smudge

He smudged the windows more as he wiped them with a dirty cloth.

더러운 걸레로 유리를 닦아 유리가 더러워지기만 했다.

□ **fixture** /ˈfɪkstʃər/   n. a fixed object

(= feature, fitting)

The fixtures of this room have hardly changed for twenty years.

방안의 붙박이 장식들이 20년간 하나도 바뀌지 않았다.

□ **gauge** /geɪdʒ/   v. to measure

(= determine, appraise, estimate)

n. gauge

Jeffery tried to gauge his mother's mood before he told her the bad news.

제프리는 나쁜 소식을 전하기 전에 엄마의 기분이 어떤지 가늠해보려 했다.

□ **vestigial** /veˈstɪdʒiəl/   adj. useless

(= nonfunctioning, stunted, degenerated)

n. vestige

A whale's skeleton still bears vestigial leg bones.

고래의 뼈대에는 아직도 퇴보한 다리뼈가 보인다.

□ **jolt** /dʒəʊlt/   v. to roughly shake or push

(= shake, jerk, shove)

n. jolt

I was jolted awake when the train suddenly stopped.

기차가 갑자기 멈춰서 나는 몸이 흔들려 잠에서 깼다.

□ **ombudsman** /ˈɑːmbʌdzmən/

n. an official who investigates and attempts to solve complaints

(= regulator, watchdog)

The ombudsman office at city hall is always full of people with grievances.

시청의 옴부즈만실은 항상 불만사항을 신고하러 온 사람들로 북적인다.

□ **conflate** /kənˈfleɪt/   v. to merge into one

(= merge, combine, amalgamate)

n. conflation

The new theory conflates elements of the older two opposing theories.

새로운 이론은 과거의 두 개 이론의 내용을 한 개로 통합한다.

□ **disseminate** /dɪˈsemɪneɪt/   v. to spread wide

(= distribute, circulate, spread)

Buddhism began in India and disseminated to the rest of Asia.

불교는 인도에서 시작해 나머지 아시아로 넓게 퍼졌다.

□ **slant** /slænt/

n. viewpoint

(= viewpoint, angle, perspective)

v. slant

The media gave a negative slant on the government's push to raise taxes.

미디어에서 주지사가 세금을 올리려는 시도를 부정적인 관점으로 봤다.

□ **contradictory** /ˌkɑːntrəˈdɪktəri/

adj. asserting the opposite

(= inconsistent, contrary, opposing)

v. contradict

n. contradiction

His actions are contradictory to his speech.

그는 행동과 말이 다르다.

□ **furl** /fɜːrl/

v. to roll up neatly

(= roll, curl)

⇔ unfurl

Soldiers furled the flag.

병사들이 깃발을 단정하게 접었다.

□ **defecate** /ˈdefəkeɪt/

v. to dispel waste from the body

(= excrete, evacuate)

All that dog does is eat and defecate.

저 개가 하는 일이란 먹고 싸는 것 밖에 없다.

01 Although Buddhism originated in India, it has _____ (spread far) and prospered in East Asia more than it did in India.

02 Farmers say erecting scarecrows is not an effective _____ (something that prevents) against crows.

03 It was difficult to _____ (measure) whether she was angry or happy.

04 The soldiers _____ (smeared) their faces with dark make up to camouflage themselves in the woods.

05 I did not _____ (object) when Henry offered to treat me to dinner.

06 To check his credentials, one interview shall _____ (be enough).

07 Every morning, the cadets are required to wake at 6 and _____ (roll up neatly) their beddings neatly and store them in the cabinets.

08 The students were confused because they were hearing _____ (opposite) instructions from bursar's office and their counselor.

09 The government implemented many new policies, but after several years, still no _____ (fundamental) improvements have been made.

10 Whenever Robert walks into a room, laughter soon _____ (follows).

11 Mark _____ (roughly shook) me to realize the reality that if I don't do better in the upcoming final exam, I will fail this course.

12   Under the site of the old church, archeologists excavated the traces of a/an _____
     (of which only traces remain) culture that predates Christianity.

13   Many scholars are baffled at how some urban legends could have _____ (spread
     for) so fast through continental America in the late 19th Century.

14   Einstein was never successful in _____ (merging) the two towering theories of
     modern physics: relativity and quantum mechanics.

Find the correct word

substantiate, sanction, articulate, subservient, perturb, brevity, incline, locomotion, postulate, circadian

01 The Board of Directors fired the old CEO because it wanted someone more _____ at the job.

02 Talking much and speaking well are two different things: sometimes _____ is better than verbosity.

03 Because the lighthouse was on top of a steep _____, I was out of breath when I reached it.

04 The two governments decided to _____ a free trade agreement between their countries.

05 I have many thoughts and emotions going through my head, but it's very difficult to _____ them.

06 The sunfish has no tail fin, so it uses its two dorsal fins for _____.

07 When Einstein first _____ his theory of relativity, it was so radical that even he thought that it had to be wrong.

08 Flying to three cities in different time zones within a week has messed up my _____ rhythm.

09   The scientist's theory, which was met with wide spread academic ridicule when it was first published, was _____ fifty years after his death.

10   News of a coming financial crisis has _____ many investors.

coercive, volition, convoke, taut, confide, disdain, imply, emulate, epitome, sustenance

11   The movie begins with a retired commander _____ all his former commando team members, who now work in civilian jobs.

12   When stringing a tennis racket, the more _____ the strings, the more control you have: the looser the strings, the more power you have.

13   Pandas eat almost 70% of their weight of bamboo leaves every day because there is very little _____ in bamboo.

14   A modern capitalist state cannot openly use _____ force to help one class accumulate capital at the expense of others.

15   When the police search intensified, the suspect came to the police station at his own _____.

16   Steve and I are such good friends that there is no secret that I would not _____ to him.

17   It is sad that some people are still treated with _____ because of their race, religion or sexual orientation.

18   Her comments seemed to _____ criticism.

19   It is almost certain that you will fail if you only try to _____ successful people's lives: you must find your own method of success.

20   The actress was now in her 60s but was still considered to be the _____ of beauty.

veritable, inversion, paramount, presumption, lucrative, enclave, mutable, scrutiny, emphatic, deploy

21   My garden had become a/an _____ jungle by the time I came back from vacation.

22   The navy announced that it will _____ a new generation of attack submarines within three years.

23   Einstein's greatest discovery was that time and space are not absolute but _____.

24   James apologized to Jenny for his _____ that she will need his help to complete the project.

25   There has been a worrying _____ of people's values in the last half century: money is preferred over job satisfaction, selfishness overrides courtesy and self-aggrandizement supersedes decency.

26   The luthier's workshop was a/an _____ of poor music students, struggling musicians and out-of-work composers and conductors.

27   Careful _____ of the report reveals many errors.

28   The Polish football team reached the semi-finals yesterday after a/an _____ 5-0 win over the German team.

29   David made a/an _____ living by importing gourmet coffee beans from around the world.

30   The quality of a country's public education must be of _____ importance to any government.

Circle the word that is not a synonym

31 contradictory – veritable – inconsistent

32 slanted – inclined – amalgamated

33 spread – appraise – disseminate

34 suffice – protest – demur

35 substantive – elementary – contradictory

36 useless – mutable – vestigial

37 gauge – smudge – smear

38 deterrent – constraint – retention

39 foreshadow – predict – perch

40 imprudent – abject – wretched

41 discomfiture – sanity – confusion

42 complex – erratic – inconsistent

43 postulate – appropriate – hypothesize

44 dreadful – abysmal – inefficacious

45 craving – endorsement – yearning

46 prone – susceptible – feline

47 fiscal – transient – fleeting

48 enclave – collapse – commune

49 depression – volition – free-will

50 degradation – dilapidation – obsolescence

51 recession – insurrection – subversion

52 brevity – terseness – inversion

53 cohesion – scrutiny – analysis

54 veneration – reverence – epitome

55 unequivocal – disdainful – emphatic

56 sober – abstemious – fringe

57 inferior – constant – perennial

58 tangled – distended – labyrinthine

59 exacerbate – aggravate – hail

60 steep – precipitous – legible

Class 13

□ **testimony** /'testɪməʊni/   n. a declaration of truth or fact

(= statement, declaration, testament)

v. testify

The witness' testimony of the accident was contradictory to the police report.

사고 목격자의 증언과 경찰 보고서와 내용이 달랐다.

□ **infest** /ɪn'fest/   v. to overrun

(= invade, crowd, riddle)

n. infestation

No one must enter the water because the beach is infested with deadly jellyfish.

해수욕장 물속에 위험한 해파리가 득시글거리니 아무도 물속에 들어가서는 안 된다.

□ **posterity** /pɑː'sterəti/   n. future generations

(= descendants, successors, children)

Benjamin Franklin left a legacy to posterity by founding the University of Pennsylvania.

벤자민 프랭클린은 펜실베니아 대학교를 설립하여 후세에 유산을 남겼다.

□ **lisp** /lɪsp/   n. to speak with an impediment
                                      v. lisp

The baby still speaks with a lisp.

아기는 아직도 혀 짧은 소리로 말한다.

□ **prattle** /'prætl/   v. to talk in a baby-like way

(= chatter, blather, gibber)

The children prattled among themselves.

아이들이 자기들끼리 수다를 떨었다.

□ **grievance** /ˈɡriːvəns/   n. a complaint

(= criticism, objection, complaint)

The ombudsman office at city hall is always full of people with grievances.

시청의 옴부즈만실은 항상 불만사항을 신고하러 온 사람들로 북적인다.

□ **interpose** /ˌɪntərˈpəʊz/   v. to cause to intervene

(= interrupt, intervene, meddle)

                                                      n. interposition

I quickly interposed when George and Alex began to argue.

나는 조지와 알렉스가 말다툼하기 시작할 때 급히 끼어들어 말렸다.

□ **perchance** /pərˈtʃæns/   adv. by chance

(= perhaps, possibly)

Perchance, if you're driving downtown, can you give me a lift?

혹시, 시내로 가는 거면 제가 차를 얻어타고 가도 될까요?

□ **inexorable** /ɪnˈeksərəbl/   adj. unstoppable

(= inevitable, relentless, adamant)

The government seems incapable of stopping the inexorable price of gasoline.

끝없이 치솟는 휘발유 가격을 정부가 막을 길이 없어 보인다.

□ **repudiate** /rɪˈpjuːdieɪt/   v. to reject

(= disclaim, deny, disavow)

To the surprise of the jury, the witness repudiated his previous testimony.

배심원들에게 놀랍게도 증인은 그의 과거 증언 내용을 부인했다.

□ **enact** /ɪˈnækt/   v. to make into a law

(= ratify, endorse, decree)

                                                      n. enactment

The bill was enacted into a law.

410

그 안건은 법으로 제정이 되었다.

☐ **doldrums** /ˈdəʊldrəmz/　　　　n. a state of inactivity or stagnation

(= stagnation, boredoms, sluggishness)

The economy has been in the doldrums for years, with no sign of improving.

경제가 수년간 부진했다, 나아질 기미를 보이지 않는 채.

☐ **enumerate** /ɪˈnuːməreɪt/　　　　v. to name one by one as if counting

(= count, tally, itemize)

　　　　　　　　　　　　　　　　　　n. enumeration

Sam's mother enumerated the chores Sam had to do to him.

쌤의 엄마는 쌤이 해야 할 집안 일을 하나씩 나열했다.

☐ **odorous** /ˈəʊdərəs/　　　　adj. emitting an odor

(= scented, smelly, aromatic)

His room was always odorous of cigarette smoke.

그의 방에는 항상 담배 냄새가 났다.

☐ **teem** /tiːm/　　　　v. to be filled with

(= swarm, abound, crowd)

Under a microscope, a drop of water from the pond teemed with life.

연못 물 한 방울을 현미경 밑에서 보면 생명으로 가득찼다는 걸 볼 수 있다.

☐ **deride** /dɪˈraɪd/　　　　v. to laugh at in scorn

(= mock, ridicule, scoff)

　　　　　　　　　　　　　　　　　　n. derision

He was derided for his unorthodox ideas.

그는 그의 비상식적인 아이디어로 조롱을 받았다.

pristine /ˈprɪstiːn/　　　　　adj. having its original purity

(= unpolluted, untouched, primeval)

The beach was pristine and pollution free.

바닷가는 아주 깨끗했고 공해도 없었다.

---

adamant /ˈædəmənt/　　　　adj. refusing to agree or compromise

(= stubborn, intransigent, inflexible)

The workers were adamant in their demands

노동자들은 그들의 요구에 단호했다.

---

geriatric /ˌdʒeriˈætrɪk/　　　adj. relating to old age or old people

(= elderly, old, aged)

Alzheimer's disease is not a geriatric disease: people in their mid-thirties can also contract it.

알츠하이머병은 노인병이 아니다; 삼십대 중반의 사람들도 이 병에 걸린다.

---

infuse /ɪnˈfjuːz/　　　　　　v. to inspire as with feelings or opinions

(= instill, impart, inspire)

　　　　　　　　　　　　　　n. infusion

The new coach infused the team with a fighting spirit.

새 감독이 선수들에게 투지를 심어주었다.

01 The actress was _____ (laughed at in scorn) by the media for her childish remarks.

02 The names of those who died are recorded for _____ (future generations) on a tablet at the back of the church.

03 When put under a microscope, a drop of pond water _____ (is filled with) with living organisms.

04 Gentrification of this area seems to be a/an _____ (unstoppable) trend.

05 It is a secret I'll take to my grave; _____ (by chance) I'll tell you someday.

06 Mom and Dad began to argue so intensely that I had to _____ (intervene).

07 Richard was _____ (refusing to compromise) in this refusal. I don't think he will change his mind.

08 The building was heavily _____ (overrun) with cockroaches

09 The markets of Calcutta are loud, dirty and _____ (emitting a smell) places, but they sell some fantastic foods there.

10 I can't even begin to _____ (name one by one) the grievances I have about the service of this airline.

11 The national assembly is yet to _____ (make into a law) a revised animal cruelty law.

12 The brilliant writer always _____ (imbues or inspires) her novels with humor and yearning.

13 My mother is only 65. Please don't treat her like a/an _____ (relating to old age) patient.

14 With the summer vacationers gone, the beach soon recovered its _____ (having its original purity) state.

15 In a recent press conference, the President _____ (rejected) recent criticism that his government was responsible for mishandling the economic crisis.

Class 14

□ **aloof** /əˈluːf/   adj. to be unenthusiastic about something

(= reticent, distant, supercilious)

While the boys were glued to the television, Martha sat aloof in her chair reading a book.

아이들이 딱 붙어서 텔레비전을 볼 때, 마사는 무신경하게 의자에 앉아 책을 읽고 있었다.

□ **mundane** /mʌnˈdeɪn/   adj. nothing special

(= routine, commonplace, tedious)

Many books characterized as "classical literature" are, in fact, quite mundane.

'전통문학'으로 분류된 많은 책들이 사실 매우 따분하다.

□ **gravitate** /ˈgrævɪteɪt/   v. to be drawn to

(= move, drift, incline)

     n. gravitation

In the 1960s, many folk musicians gravitated to Greenwich Village in New York.

1960년대에 많은 포크 음악인들이 뉴욕의 그린위치 빌리지로 이끌려 모였다.

□ **worship** /ˈwɜːrʃɪp/   v. to feel religious reverence to

(= adore, revere, venerate)

     n. worship

Adam's greatest joy was to take his wife and children to church and worship together.

아담의 가장 큰 즐거움은 아내와 아이들을 데리고 교회에 가서 예배를 드리는 거였다.

□ **monotony** /məˈnɑːtəni/   n. the state of continuous sameness

(= tedium, boredom, dullness)

     adj. monotonous

I have been so busy that I would welcome some monotony in my life.

나는 그간 너무 바빠서 일상이 좀 단조로와지는 것도 좋을 것 같다.

☐ **hedgerow** /ˈhedʒrəʊ/   n. a row of bushes or trees forming a hedge

(= hedge, border, shrubbery)

The hedgerows formed a fence around the garden.

정원 주변으로 생울타리가 둘러쌌다.

☐ **enfeeble** /ɪnˈfiːbl/   v. to make weak

(= weaken, debilitate, fatigue)

The locals were enfeebled by disaster and famine.

현지인들이 자연재해와 기근으로 많이 약해진 상황이었다.

☐ **stupefy** /ˈstuːpɪfaɪ/   v. to overwhelm with amazement

(= overwhelm, amaze, bewilder)

The magician stupefied the audience with his amazing performance.

마술사가 신기한 공연으로 관중을 매료시켰다.

☐ **imperative** /ɪmˈperətɪv/   adj. very important

(= vital, crucial, essential)

It is imperative that I improve my grades this semester.

내가 이번 학기에 학점을 올리는 것이 매우 중요하다.

☐ **alteration** /ˌɔːltəˈreɪʃn/   n. change

(= modification, adjustment, revision)

v. alter

There has been an alteration in our plans.

우리 계획에 변동이 생겼다.

☐ **ominous** /ˈɑːmɪnəs/   adj. foreboding evil

(= portentous, menacing, warning)

Ominous clouds gathered in the sky.

하늘에 암울한 구름이 끼기 시작했다.

☐ **stagnation** /stæɡˈneɪʃn/   n. lack of progress

(= inactivity, torpor, sluggishness)

                         v. stagnate

The economy has been in a state of stagnation for years.

경제가 수년 째 지지부진하고 있다.

☐ **clerical** /ˈklerɪkl/   adj. pertaining to office clerks

(= secretarial, office)

After retiring from boxing, Rocky took a clerical job.

권투에서 은퇴한 후 록키는 사무직 일을 시작했다.

☐ **invasive** /ɪnˈveɪsɪv/   adj. intruding

(= intrusive, interfering, imposing)

                         n. invasion
                         v. invade

Carp is an invasive fish species in Asia: it originated in North America.

잉어는 아시아에서 외래종 생선이다: 원래 북아메리카가 원산지이다.

☐ **squadron** /ˈskwɑːdrən/   n. a group of ships or planes

(= group, team, unit)

A squadron of fighter planes was dispatched to escort the damaged airliner back to safety.

고장난 여객기를 다시 고국으로 안전하게 호위하기 위해 전투기 편대가 급파되었다.

☐ **juvenile** /ˈdʒuːvənl/   adj. related to young people

(= young, childish, immature)

                         n. juvenile

Bob and Norman have continued their juvenile bickering for over thirty years.

밥과 노먼은 삼십년 째 아이들 같이 티격태격 한다.

□ **hierarchy** /ˈhaɪərɑːrki/

n. a system or persons arranged in a graded order

(= strata, rung, pecking order)

adj. hierarchical

Wild wolves form a highly organized hierarchy.

야생 늑대는 매우 엄격한 계층 사회를 이루고 산다.

□ **undulate** /ˈʌndʒəleɪt/   v. to rise and fall like waves

(= roll, ripple)

Low hills undulated for as far as I could see.

눈에 보이는 끝까지 낮은 언덕들이 물결치고 있었다.

□ **conceive** /kənˈsiːv/   v. think of

(= consider, envisage, imagine)

n. concept

It was an idea that I could have never conceived.

나는 절대로 생각해 낼 수 없는 아이디어였다.

□ **preposterous** /prɪˈpɑːstərəs/   adj. not making any sense

(= outrageous, absurd, ridiculous)

The politician claimed that the newspaper story about him was preposterous.

정치인은 신문에 개제된 자기와 관련된 기사가 말도 안 되는 것이라 했다.

01   After decades of _____ (lack of progress), there is a popular groundswell for speedy change and a market economy.

02   When I told my mother I failed calculus, there were five seconds of _____ (foreboding evil) silence before she erupted at me.

03   I was happy to find my Dad's tuxedo would fit me with a little _____ (change).

04   I could never _____ (think of) such an idea in a million years.

05   In Kentucky, we saw miles and miles of fields of wheat _____ (rise and fall like waves) in the breeze.

06   I live a quite _____ (nothing special) life: nothing interesting happens to me.

07   She stood _____ (unenthusiastic) while people around her were enjoying themselves and having a good time.

08   Many Asian conglomerates have a rigid management _____ (order).

09   He is almost 30, but sometimes he still acts _____ (childlike).

10   Harriet is an artist at heart and only works in a/an _____ (pertaining to office clerks) job to pay her bills.

11   Years of toiling as a fireman has _____ (made weak) Mr. Harris.

12 The _____ (the state of continuous sameness) of Professor Guild's voice makes his classes very boring.

13 Harry has such an electrifying personality that people just _____ (are drawn to) towards him.

14 A broad and balanced education is _____ (very important) for raising a strong and confident generation.

15 Richard was _____ (overwhelmed by surprise) when he saw the bill after he and his family had dinner at a fancy restaurant.

16 I saw a/an _____ (not making any sense) article in the newspaper that purported that the economy was improving.

Class 15

☐ **ascertain** /ˌæsərˈteɪn/   v. to find out

(= determine, establish, discover)

The police ascertained the identity of the burglars.

경찰이 절도범들의 신분을 알아내었다.

☐ **detriment** /ˈdetrɪmənt/   n. disadvantage

(= loss, damage, injury)

His contribution was more a detriment than an asset to his group.

그가 참여하여 자기 그룹에 도움 보다는 해악을 더 입혔다.

☐ **fetter** /ˈfetər/   v. to restrain

(= shackle, bind, chain)

n. fetter

We live in a society in which race, gender or religion should not fetter our rights to live with dignity.

우리는 인종, 성별 혹은 종교가 우리의 존엄성을 해칠 염려가 없는 사회에 살고 있다.

☐ **omnipotence** /ɑːmˈnɪpətəns/   n. the ability to be all-powerful

(= supremacy, invincibility, power)

adj. omnipotent

Of all the Greek gods, only Zeus is portrayed to have omnipotence.

모든 그리스 신들 중에 제우스 만이 전지전능한 것으로 묘사되었다.

☐ **temperament** /ˈtemprəmənt/

n. the mental, physical and emotional traits of a person

(= character, personality, disposition)

adj. temperamental

He has a mild temperament: I've never seen him excited or angry.

그는 차분한 성격의 소유자이다: 나는 그가 흥분을 하거나 화를 내는 것을 본 적이 없다.

☐ **constituent** /kənˈstɪtʃuənt/

adj. serving to compose or make up something

(= essential, component, fundamental)

n. constituent

The constituent element of all matter is an atom.

모든 물질을 이루는 기본 원소는 원자이다.

☐ **submerge** /səbˈmɜːrdʒ/   v. to go under water

(= sink, plunge, dip)

A modern nuclear submarine can submerge and not rise above water for three months.

현대 원자력 잠수함은 한 번 잠수하면 삼개월간 수면으로 올라오지 않아도 된다.

☐ **prominent** /ˈprɑːmɪnənt/   adj. noticeable

(= important, well-known, leading)

Several prominent scholars participated in our university's seminar.

우리 대학교의 세미나에 저명한 학자들 여러 명이 참가했다.

☐ **attest** /əˈtest/   v. to testify or bear witness

(= confirm, vindicate, corroborate)

I can attest to his trustworthiness.

내가 그의 신뢰성을 보장할 수 있습니다.

☐ **vernacular** /vərˈnækjələr/   n. colloquial speech

(= dialect, language, lingo)

They spoke in a vernacular that I couldn't understand.

그들은 내가 알아듣지 못하는 방언으로 대화를 하였다.

☐ **empirical** /ɪmˈpɪrɪkl/   adj. resulting from experience

(= observed, experimental, pragmatic)

There is no empirical evidence that aliens from outer space visited Earth.

먼 우주에서 온 외계인들이 지구를 방문했다는 실증적인 증거는 없다.

☐ **analogous** /əˈnæləgəs/   adj. similar

(= equivalent, parallel, comparable)

Some say the diplomatic tension between the major powers is analogous to that before World War II.

어떤 사람들은 현재 강국들 간의 외교적 갈등이 마치 2차 세계대전 이전의 상황과 비슷하다고 한다.

☐ **catalyst** /ˈkætəlɪst/

n. a substance that causes the chemical reaction between two elements to quicken

(= promoter, facilitator, stimulus)

Industrial growth was the catalyst for the sudden increase in population at the end of the 18th century England.

산업 발달이 18세기 후반에 영국의 급격한 인구 성장을 초래했다.

☐ **spawn** /spɔːn/   v. (usually fish or amphibians) to lay eggs

(= reproduce, generate, lay)

n. spawn

Frogs spawn eggs in this pond every year.

해마다 이 연못에 개구리들이 알을 낳는다.

☐ **garner** /ˈgɑːrnər/   v. to bring together

(= gather, collect, harvest)

The young candidate has garnered much support in areas that traditionally back the opposition.

젊은 후보가 전통적으로 상대 진영을 지지하는 지역에서 지지를 많이 모았다.

□ **dispirited** /dɪˈspɪrɪtɪd/   adj. to be disheartened

(= discouraged, demoralized, dejected)

Henry was dispirited because he didn't make it into the tennis team.

헨리는 테니스 팀에 뽑히지 못 해 실망했다.

□ **compulsion** /kəmˈpʌlʃn/

n. forceful pressure to make someone do something

(= force, coercion, pressure)

         adj. compulsory

There is no compulsion on me to help you.

나에게 너를 도와야 하는 강박은 없다.

□ **contend** /kənˈtend/   v. to argue

(= insist, maintain, state)

         n. contention

The senator contended that it was time for the bipartisan bickering to end.

상원의원이 이제는 양당이 티격태격하는 걸 멈출 때라고 했다.

□ **overarching** /ˌəʊvərˈɑːtʃɪŋ/   adj. surrounding or over-covering

(= covering, encompassing)

From the top of the hill, we had an overarching view of the city.

언덕 위에서 우리는 전 도시를 한 눈에 내려다 볼 수 있었다.

□ **convivial** /kənˈvɪviəl/   adj. to be friendly to people

(= pleasant, welcoming, warm)

I was greeted by a convivial man at the gate.

아주 친절한 사람이 나를 문에서 맞이 하였다.

Practice 15.

Fill in the blank with the word that matches the definition provided

01   When I first moved to Scotland, I couldn't understand a word the people were saying, but, ultimately their speech worked its way into my _____ (colloquial) speech.

02   After the humiliating defeat of the First World War, the _____ (disheartened) German people searched for a scapegoat and found one in the Jewish people.

03   By the end of the campaign, the underdog candidate _____ (bring together) enough support for win the election.

04   Salmon hatch in fresh water but spend their adult lives in the ocean, only returning to their native streams to _____ (lay eggs) and die.

05   The only _____ (stimulus) Billy needed to study harder was seeing his cousin Henry, a lawyer, drive up in a shiny new Porsche.

06   The weather patterns are _____ (similar) to those of last year.

07   Einstein's Theory of Relativity initially received much criticism as it was unable to prove using _____ (resulting from experience) evidence.

08   It is difficult to _____ (find out) when and where exactly he was born, since many such records were lost during the war.

09   If you're worried about Janet, I can _____ (confirm) to her capabilities.

10   The first thing you notice when you meet Warren is his _____ (noticeable) nose.

11 Since the issue is too complicated, let's break it up into _____ (component) parts so that we can find a solution more quickly.

12 It is unfair to _____ (restrain) a young man's future for a mistake he made when still a teenager.

13 When we reached the hotel, we were greeted by _____ (friendly) staff that immediately made us feel at home.

14 When setting up his business, Martin had to _____ (argue) with the bureaucracy of city hall when applying for his license.

15 I helped you of my own volition, so there is no need for you to feel any _____ (forceful pressure) of indebtedness to me.

Class 16

☐ **cohort** /ˈkəʊhɔːrt/   n. a group of people with similarities

(= group, gang, unit)

Most photographers have switched to digital photography, but there still remains a small cohort that prefers to use film.

대부분의 사진사들은 디지털 촬영으로 전환했으나, 아직도 필름 카메라를 쓰는 몇몇이 남아있다.

☐ **culinary** /ˈkʌlɪneri/   adj. related to cooking and cuisine

(= cooking, gastronomic)

Chef Jason's culinary skills are highly regarded.

제이슨 요리사의 요리 실력은 매우 높게 인정된다.

☐ **homogenize** /həmádʒənàiz,hou-/   v. to make uniform or similar

(= standardize, regulate, normalize)

Critics of standardized tests say that such tests homogenize students and stifle individuality.

표준화된 시험을 비판하는 사람들은 이런 시험이 학생들을 균일화 하고 개성을 억누른다고 말한다.

☐ **distortion** /dɪˈstɔːrʃn/   n. twisting out of shape

(= alteration, deformation, warp)

     v. distort

His testimony proved to be a distortion of truth.

그의 증언이 사실의 왜곡임이 판명되었다.

☐ **incomprehensible** /ɪnˌkɑːmprɪˈhensəbl/

adj. to be beyond one's understanding

(= unintelligible, inconceivable, perplexing)

     ⇔ comprehensible

His idea for making money by sleeping all day was incomprehensible.

하루종일 자면서 돈을 벌 수 있다는 그의 아이디어는 이해할 수 없는 것이었다.

☐ **scatterbrained** /'skætərbreɪnd/   adj. silly or stupid

(= absentminded, frivolous, silly)

His idea for making money by sleeping all day was scatterbrained.

하루종일 자면서 돈을 벌 수 있다는 그의 아이디어는 바보 같은 것이었다.

☐ **miser** /'maɪzər/

n. one who is reluctant to spend money despite having much

(= scrooge, pinchpenny, cheapskate)

         adj. miserly

A young miser becomes an old philanthropist.

젊은 구두쇠가 나이 든 자선사업가가 되는 법입니다.

☐ **sanctuary** /'sæŋktʃueri/   n. a place of refuge

(= asylum, refuge, shelter)

For Jane, the woods behind her house is a sanctuary: she goes there whenever she needs mental healing.

제인에게 그녀의 집 뒤의 숲은 안식처였다: 그녀는 정신적으로 치유를 받아야 할 필요가 있을 때마다 그곳으로 간다.

☐ **pittance** /'pɪtns/   n. a very meager amount

(= trifle, mothing, peanuts)

Although Michael Jordan is the richest athlete in the world, compared to Bill Gates he has pittance.

마이클 조던이 전 세계에서 돈이 제일 많은 운동선수이긴 하지만, 빌 게이츠와 비교하면 그가 가진 돈은 푼돈에 불과하다.

☐ **aspiration** /ˌæspə'reɪʃn/   n. a strong desire for something

(= ambition, goal, desire)

         v. aspire

Although Harry never told his parents, he had aspirations to become a musician.

해리는 부모님에게는 말 한 적이 없지만, 음악가가 되고 싶은 욕망이 있었다.

☐ **clout** /klaʊt/   n. influence

(= influence, power, weight)

It was obvious that Ned got the job thanks to his father's clout.

네드가 아버지의 도움으로 그 직장을 구한 것이 뻔하다.

☐ **devise** /dɪˈvaɪz/   v. to plan or invent

(= plan, develop, create)

                    n. device

Not after long, the students devised a plan for experimentation.

오래 지나지 않아 학생들은 실험 계획을 고안했다.

☐ **attribution** /ˌætrɪˈbjuːʃn/   n. a designation

(= credit, acknowledgement)

                    v. attribute

There was no attribution to my contribution to the project.

내가 프로젝트에 기여한 것에 대한 아무런 인정이 없었다.

☐ **nomination** /ˌnɑːmɪˈneɪʃn/   n. the appointment to a duty or office

(= recommendation, candidate, nominee)

                    v. nominate

The senator declined his nomination as the head of his party.

상원의원이 당대표로 선출되었지만 사양했다.

☐ **agitation** /ˌædʒɪˈteɪʃn/

n. persistent urging of a social or political cause to the public

(= activism, campaigning, protest)

                    v. agitate

Laborers across the country began an agitation for higher wages and better working conditions.

전국의 노동자들이 임금인상과 노동환경의 개선을 요구하는 시위를 시작했다.

☐ **admirable** /ˈædmərəbl/   adj. highly regarded

(= estimable, commendable, venerable)

v. admire

He did the admirable deed of donating all the money we won in the lottery.

그는 우리가 복권으로 당첨된 모든 돈을 기부하는 존경받을 만한 일을 했다.

☐ **abolition** /ˌæbəˈlɪʃn/   n. elimination

(= ending, eradication, closure)

v. abolish

The abolition of the death penalty is an issue in many countries.

사형제도의 폐지가 많은 국가에서 논쟁의 대상이다.

☐ **reproach** /rɪˈproʊtʃ/   n. an expression of censure

(= criticism, censure, reprimand)

v. reproach

Mark feared his father's reproach more than anything.

마크는 그 무엇보다도 아버지의 꾸지람을 두려워했다.

☐ **dawdle** /ˈdɔːdl/   v. to move lazily

(= dally, linger, lag)

Henry dawdled in the cafeteria even after all his friends left.

헨리는 친구들이 다 떠난 후에도 카페테리아에서 뭉그적댔다.

☐ **retrieve** /rɪˈtriːv/   v. to recover or get back

(= repossess, rescue, reclaim)

n. retrieval

George's dog will retrieve a ball if you throw it in the air.

그레그의 개는 공중에 공을 던지면 달려가서 물어온다.

Practice 16.

Fill in the blank with the word that matches the definition provided

01   Richard _____ (planned) a scheme that I would never have thought of in a
     thousand years.

02   It was clear that global companies use their _____ (influence) to influence
     government policies.

03   Admitting to one's mistakes is a/an _____ (highly regarded) thing to do.

04   The anti-government _____ (activism) began to worry some high officials of the
     government.

05   The _____ (designation) of this sculpture to Rodin has never been proven.

06   Many social activists say that compared to the money countries spend on defense, the
     cost of abolishing world poverty would be _____ (small change).

07   The American landscape has been _____ (made uniform or similar) by malls and fast-
     food restaurants.

08   In the _____ (group of people with similarities) of people aged 21-28, the
     unemployment rate is over 12%.

09   It has been five years since Mr. Han immigrated to the United States, and he now realizes
     that the U.S. is not the _____ (place of refuge) he thought it was.

10   The old man was labelled a/an _____ (someone who doesn't' like to spend money),
     but unbeknownst to most people, he actually donated thousands of dollars each year to
     the local children's hospital.

11 He was known as a brilliant mathematician, but people who meet him in person get the impression that he is slightly _____ (silly or stupid).

12 The politician lambasted the criticizing article about him as a gross _____ (twisting out of shape) of the truth.

13 I have begun to suspect that the reason Kenneth is so involved in volunteering is because he has _____ (a strong desire for something) to run for a public office.

14 The police managed to _____ (get back) all of the stolen jewelry within a matter of hours.

15 Our lunch hour was almost over, but we still _____ (lingered) in the cafeteria.

16 On a naval ship, the commanding officer's behavior and decisions are beyond _____ (an expression of criticism).

□ **corroborate** /kəˈrɑːbəreɪt/   v. to prove the validity of

(= verify, substantiate, confirm)

n. corroboration

Newly found evidence corroborated the accused man's innocence.

혐의를 입은 사람이 무죄라는 것을 입증하는 새로운 증거가 나왔다.

□ **meander** /miˈændər/   v. walking as if having no destination

(= wander, roam, amble)

We spent two days meandering through the old town of the city.

우리는 구 시가지를 이틀동안 돌아다녔다.

□ **threshold** /ˈθreʃhəʊld/   a point of entering or beginning

(= onset, edge, verge)

The misbehaving child began to push my threshold for patience.

그 버릇없는 아이가 나의 인내심의 한계를 시험하고 있었다.

□ **compost** /ˈkɑːmpəʊst/

n. decaying organic matter that is used as fertilizer

(= fertilizer, manure)

v. compost

Many people in Vancouver use food scraps as compost.

밴쿠버에서는 많은 사람들이 음식 찌꺼기를 퇴비로 사용한다.

□ **annihilate** /əˈnaɪəleɪt/   v. to totally destroy

(= obliterate, eradicate, wipe-out)

New evidences corroborate the theory that dinosaurs were annihilated by drastic weather changes triggered after a massive meteor struck the Earth.

공룡이 거대한 운석의 충돌로 야기된 심각한 기후변화의 결과로 멸망했다는 이론을 뒷받침 해주는 새로운 증거가 있다.

□ **embankment** /ɪmˈbæŋkmənt/   n. the ridge along a waterway

(= ridge, dike, levee)

There were rows of cherry blossoms along the embankment.

강가를 따라 벗꽃 나무가 줄지어 서 있었다.

□ **adorn** /əˈdɔːrn/   v. decorate

(= embellish, beautify, garnish)

     n. adornment

The children adorned the Christmas tree with various ornaments.

아이들이 크리스마스 트리를 각종 장식으로 꾸몄다.

□ **scrupulous** /ˈskruːpjələs/   adj. to pay careful attention to

(= painstaking, meticulous, fastidious)

As far as I'm concerned the presentation is ready, but my scrupulous partner Randy is still fiddling with it scrutinizing every petty detail.

나는 우리 프리젠테이션의 준비가 끝났다고 생각하지만, 나의 세심한 파트너 랜디는 아직도 세세한 부분까지 꼼꼼하게 들여다보고 있다.

□ **mumble** /ˈmʌmbl/   v. to speak unclearly

(= mutter, murmur, stammer)

Jacky mumbled something under his breath that I couldn't understand.

잭이 뭔가 내가 못 알아들을 말을 혼자 중얼거렸다.

□ **testimony** /ˈtestɪməʊni/

n. a statement made by a witness in a court of law

(= testament, statement, evidence)

The new witness' testimony proved the accused man's innocence.

증인의 새로운 증언이 혐의를 입은 사람의 무죄를 입증했다.

□ **spherical** /ˈsfɪrɪkl/   adj. ball shaped

(= globular, rotund)

n. sphere

Archeologists found an artifact that was spherical and had unknown markings on it.

고고학자들이 뭔가가 새겨진 구 모양의 유물을 발견했다.

□ **trajectory** /trəˈdʒektəri/   n. a curve made by something in flight

(= route, course, path)

The trajectory of the missile was tracked by radar.

미사일의 궤도를 레이더가 추적하고 있었다.

□ **surmount** /sərˈmaʊnt/   v. to overcome

(= overcome, prevail, conquer)

We surmounted an unbelievably large number of obstacles to achieve this.

이것을 이루기 위해 우리는 말도 못하게 많은 장애물을 뛰어넘어야 했다.

□ **combustible** /kəmˈbʌstəbl/   adj. capable of catching fire

(= flammable, ignitable, inflammable)

n. combustion

Luckily none of the materials were combustible.

다행이 인화성 물질을 하나도 없었다.

□ **sporadic** /spəˈrædɪk/   adj. happening irregularly

(= irregular, intermittent, infrequent)

As the time went by, our meetings became more and more sporadic.

시간이 지나며 우리는 회의를 점점 드물게 했다.

□ **shudder** /ˈʃʌdər/

v. to tremble your body from horror, fear or cold

(= tremble, shake, quake)

n. shudder

I shuddered at the sight of the accident.

사고현장을 목격하고 난 몸을 떨었다.

□ **ponder** /ˈpɑːndər/   v. to think carefully about

(= consider, contemplate, cogitate, ruminate)

Henry pondered deeply before he made his decision to start his own business.

헨리는 자기 사업을 시작하기 전에 깊게 숙고했다.

□ **overawed** /ˌəʊvərˈɔːd/   adj. intimidated

(= scared, impressed, repressed)

Most tennis players are overawed by Roger Federer's tennis skills.

대부분의 테니스 선수들은 로저 페더러의 실력에 경이로와 한다.

□ **fuss** /fʌs/   v. to be anxious

(= fret, nag, bustle)

n. fuss

We have no time to fuss with the details.

지금 사소한 일로 티격태격 할 때가 아니예요.

□ **encounter** /ɪnˈkaʊntər/   v. to come across

(= confront, face, meet)

n. encounter

We encountered a group of sheep on the road.

우리는 길에서 양떼를 만났다.

Practice 17.

Fill in the blank with the word that matches the definition provided

01 The government's plan to finance the project from private investments was a big failure: interested investors were few and _____ (happening irregularly).

02 The artificial flowers that the Gypsy women sold were made from celluloid – a highly _____ (capable of catching on fire) material.

03 When my brother informed us that he was coming home on vacation, mom immediately began to _____ (be anxious) about what to feed him.

04 I was _____ (intimidated) when I met my childhood hero – the famous football player Zinedine Zidane.

05 This is not a matter to decide lightly: take a few days to _____ (think carefully) about your decision.

06 In the Battle of Agincourt, 1415, 5,000 English troops _____ (totally destroyed) over 20,000 French troops.

07 My idea of a good vacation is to go to a city I've never been to, _____ (walk with no destination) the streets until I get hungry, and then find a good restaurant and sample the local cuisine.

08 Although the days are extremely hot, the night winds will make you _____ (tremble).

09 A good tennis player can put a spin on the ball to make it follow a/an _____ (curve made by something in flight) in any direction.

10 Magpies are known to _____ (decorate) their nests with shiny objects, such as spoons and metal trinkets.

11 An Egyptian proverb says, "the only two animals that can _____ (overcome) the pyramids are the eagle and the snail."

12 The Clark are the loudest family that I have ever _____ (come across).

13 A husband's statement that _____ (proves) the alibi of his wife will not stand in a court of law.

14 The two witnesses of the crime scene gave conflicting _____ (statements).

15 While camping with Geoffrey, I noticed that he _____ (speaks unclearly) in his sleep.

16 The nutritionist at the school cafeteria takes _____ (pays careful attention) care so that nutritious and delicious meals are served to students.

Find the most suitable word from the box that fits in the sentence

> **spherical, perchance, surmount, combustible, sporadic, infest, pristine, gravitate, stupefy, fuss, ascertain, doldrums, trajectory, ominous, preposterous**

01 Edam cheeses are small and _____ in shape.

02 Astronomers tracking the _____ of the comet say that it will be visible when it passes by Earth.

03 Everyone experiences hardships in his life, but the difficulties that Louis Milan has _____ to become who he is now are quite incredible.

04 The stacked wood by the river has been drying for months and is most likely highly _____ by now.

05 _____ visits to the dentist is not enough: you must get regular dental check-ups from now on.

06 When Maria discovered that two of her guests were vegetarians, she _____ about what kind of dishes to prepare for them.

07 This is an excellent book: have you read it, _____?

08 The singer had a few hits a decade ago, but since then, his career has been in the _____.

09 To her horror, Lauren discovered that fire ants _____ her kitchen.

10 Darren's antique car was caught in a flood, and it took him over three months to get it back into _____ shape.

11 During economic recessions, many job-seekers _____ towards government jobs: the pay isn't great, but at least there is job security.

12 The news that Jason was charged with battery _____ all of us: he is usually such a mild mannered person.

13 Wilson got a/an _____ feeling when his boss wanted to see him in her office.

14 The premise of the movie was _____, but I guess it is unreasonable to expect reality in super-hero movies.

15 When Mildred _____ the identity of the person who put a dead rat in her locker, she went straight to the principal's office to inform him.

interpose, odorous, vernacular, analogous, dawdle, meander, lisp, mumble, aspiration, clout, scatterbrained, prattle

16 Ever since I began living alone, I noticed that I _____ when at home.

17 Though many people thought Omar was _____, he was actually quite astute.

18 Ulysses Grant, the 18th President of the United States, originally had no political _____ at all.

19 I'm sorry, but I can't help you get a job at my company: I don't have that kind of _____.

20 Helen's mother told Helen not to _____ after school and come straight home.

21 Not having anywhere to go or anyone to meet, I _____ through the mall, window shopping.

22 Paul was able to get rid of his _____ by training with a vocal coach.

23 While on their way to school, the three girls sitting in the back of the bus wouldn't stop _____.

24 When the U.S. announced that it would bomb Iraq, Russia offered to _____.

25 I never realized that freshly cut roses are so _____.

26 He spoke with many pauses so that the translator could convey the message in the _____ of the audience.

27 The principles of the new submarine propellant device is _____ to jet engines in airplanes. The idea is to suck in water from the front and compress it and push it out the back to push the vessel forward.

undulate, adamant, geriatric, convivial, fetter, constituent, garner, compulsion, clerical, attest, homogenize, juvenile, infuse, aloof

28 Do not let other people's opinions _____ you.

29 Caffeine is the active _____ of drinks such as tea and coffee.

30 She is, as her resume _____, very experienced.

31 The writer _____ much interest from the public when one of her books was made into a movie.

32 The shop owner let me try this tennis racket for a week for free. I am under no _____ to pay for it until I am absolutely sure I want it.

33   My business is too small for me to hire a secretary, so I do all the _____ work myself.

34   James, who is in his 40s will never grow up. It seems that the older he gets, the more _____ he becomes.

35   As the music slowly began, the dancers began to _____ to it.

36   Jack was _____ about sticking to his diet.

37   Nurse Chapel says that the stress load from working in the _____ ward is much less than that from working in the children's ward.

38   To _____ children with a sense of morality is not the job of schools alone. It is also the job of parents.

39   I was quite disappointed when my date remained _____ during our entire time together, but later I realized that she was just very shy.

40   The mood at the dinner was relaxed and _____.

41   When West and East Germany unified, the first policy of the government was to _____ the two education systems.

Circle the word that is not a synonym

42   encounter – infuse – confront

43   disseminate - ponder – contemplate

44   embankment – dike – hedgerow

45   slant – threshold – verge

46   substantiate – agitate – corroborate

47   abolition – annihilation – nomination

48   attribute – reproach – accredit

49 distortion – alteration – infusion

50 clout – cohort – gang

51 empirical – observed – undulating

52 stimulus – volition – catalyst

53 omnipotent – ambivalent – supremacy

54 pristine – inexorable – relentless

55 repudiate – riddle – infest

56 devour – wolf – satiate

57 egregious – serious – combustible

58 perpetuate – enumerate – prolong

59 garner – overarch – encompass

60 teem – abound – compost

Class 19

□ **ritual**l /ˈrɪtʃuəl/   n. a formal procedure or tradition

(= custom, ceremony, rite)

adj. ritual

The religious ritual dates back to the pre-Christian era.

이 종교의식은 기독교 시대 이전까지 거슬러 올라간다.

□ **fluorescent** /fləˈresnt/   adj. glowing

(= bright, shining, luminous)

n. fluorescence

The fluorescent vests worn by the cyclists make them visible in the evening.

싸이클 선수들이 입은 형광 조끼들 덕분에 저녁에도 그들이 보인다.

□ **austerity** /ɔːˈsterəti/   n. being without excess or luxury

(= abstinence, scarcity, restriction)

adj. austere

Mr. Bishop has made a lot of money, but he prefers to live a life of austerity.

비숍 씨는 돈을 많이 벌었지만 소박한 삶을 선호한다.

□ **displacement** /dɪsˈpleɪsmənt/

n. the state of being placed where something doesn't belong

(= dislocation, supplanting, shift)

v. displace

Many of the town's people suffered displacement after the devastating hurricane.

파괴적인 폭풍우가 지나간 후 많은 주민들이 집을 잃었다.

- □ **sparse** /spɑːrs/   adj. thinly distributed

  (= thin, meager, scarce)

       n. sparseness

  This part of the country was sparsely populated until the 1980s when the government built a major power plant.

  이 지역은 1980년대에 정부에서 대규모 발전소를 건설하기 전까지는 인구밀도가 매우 낮았다.

- □ **demeanor** /dɪˈmiːnər/   n. a person's manner or appearance

  (= manner, conduct, deportment)

  I could tell from his demeanor that he was a suspicious person.

  그의 행동으로 보아 그가 매우 의심이 많은 사람인 걸 알았다.

- □ **lavish** /ˈlævɪʃ/   adj. luxurious

  (= extravagant, profligate, excessive)

  Henry treated us to a lavish dinner.

  헨리가 우리에게 떡 벌어지는 만찬을 대접했다.

- □ **depict** /dɪˈpɪkt/   v. to describe

  (= portray, show, illustrate)

       n. depiction

  The mural depicts the horror of war.

  그 벽화는 전쟁의 참상을 묘사한다.

- □ **sophisticated** /səˈfɪstɪkeɪtɪd/   adj. reflecting educated taste

  (= urbane, classy, cultured)

       n. sophistication

  I am not sophisticated enough to understand classical music: I prefer hip-hop.

  나는 클래식 음악을 이해할 만큼 수준이 높지 못하다: 나는 힙합이 좋다.

- □ **correlation** /ˌkɔːrəˈleɪʃn/   n. association

  (= connection, relationship, link)

adj. correlated

Scientists were surprised to find that the number of wolves in Yosemite Park has a correlation to the water quality of nearly rivers.

과학자들은 요세미티 공원의 늑대의 수와 주변 강의 수질과 연관이 있다는 걸 알고는 놀랐다.

☐ **trait** /treɪt/   n. a characteristic

(= mannerism, peculiarity, feature)

He had some rather strange traits that I couldn't understand.

그에게 이해하지 못할 다소 이상한 점이 있었다.

☐ **forestall** /fɔːrˈstɔːl/   v. to block from happening

(= prevent, preclude, avert)

It is impossible to forestall all accidents in life.

인생에서 모든 사고를 예방할 수는 없다.

☐ **sly** /slaɪ/   adj. cunning

(= crafty, clever, artful)

The old commander was as sly as a fox.

나이든 사령관이 여우만큼 교활했다.

☐ **pessimistic** /ˌpesɪˈmɪstɪk/   adj. expecting the worst in situations

(= negative, cynical, distrustful)

Based on the news of these days, it is difficult not to have a pessimistic outlook on life.

요즘 뉴스를 보면, 삶에 대한 비관적인 시각을 갖지 않을 수가 없다.

☐ **cast** /kæst/   v. to throw

(= hurl, pitch, toss)

We cast rocks into the water.

우리는 물에 돌을 던졌다.

□ **provoke** /prəˈvoʊk/   v. to give rise to

(= cause, trigger, elicit)

      n. provocation

The government's announcement provoked country-wide demonstrations.

정부의 발표가 전국적인 시위를 부추겼다.

□ **wayward** /ˈweɪwərd/   adj. badly behaved

(= naughty, unruly, disobedient)

Jason treats his parents with great respect as expiation for his wayward days.

제이슨은 과거 막 살던 때에 대한 참회의 마음으로 이제는 부모님께 아주 깍듯하게 대한다.

□ **lurk** /lɜːrk/   v. to lie in wait

(= prowl, loiter, wait)

Jason was surprised to find a snake lurking in his cellar.

제이슨은 창고 안에 뱀이 숨어 있는 걸 보고 놀랐다.

□ **realm** /relm/   n. an area where one dominates

(= kingdom, dominion, territory)

Zeus ruled the heavens, Poseidon the seas, but the underworld was Hades' realm.

제우스는 하늘, 포세이든은 바다를 지배했지만, 지하 세계는 하데스의 왕국이었다.

□ **upheaval** /ʌpˈhiːvl/   n. a strong or violent change (in society)

(= disturbance, turmoil, disorder)

The financial crisis in 1997 caused a huge upheaval to Korean society.

1997년 금융위기가 한국사회에 큰 변혁을 초래했다.

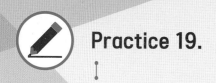
01   Modern technology has made possible devices that only half a century ago belonged in the science fiction _____ (territory).

02   It is expected that all teenagers will go through periods of _____ (badly behaved) activity now and then.

03   The photographer's pictures _____ (illustrate) the lives of ordinary people.

04   Don't try to act _____ (classy). Just be yourself.

05   Sunday lunches with my parents have become a kind of _____ (custom).

06   Matilda called the police because there was a suspicious looking person _____ (prowling) around her house.

07   Changing jobs can be an exciting challenge, but it can also be a time of great emotional _____ (strong violent change).

08   A visit to the Palace of Versailles gave us a glimpse of the _____ (luxurious) lives of French monarchy.

09   The _____ (shining) white lighting made everyone under it look pale.

10   The land was barren, rocky with _____ (thinly distributed) vegetation, so agriculture is almost impossible.

11   Now that I don't make as much money as I used to, I have to live a life of _____ (without luxury).

12 There is no need to be unduly _____ (negative) about the situation.

13 Do not trust his genial demeanor: he is _____ (cunning), devious and manipulative.

14 A large number of riot police were stationed throughout downtown to _____ (block from happening) any violent demonstrations.

☐ **allude** /əˈluːd/   v. to refer to casually or indirectly

(= refer, mention, indicate)

                         n. allusion

Whenever Henry alludes to his wife, he calls her his "ball and chain."

헨리가 집사람 얘기를 할 때 항상 그녀를 "사슬에 쇠뭉치가 달린 족쇄"라고 부른다.

☐ **reconcile** /ˈrekənsaɪl/   v. to bring opposing parties into harmony

(= settle, reunite, resolve)

                         n. reconciliation

Harry and Tonto reconciled their friendship after months of arguing.

해리와 톤토는 수개월간 말다툼을 끝내고 화해를 했다.

☐ **tyranny** /ˈtɪrəni/   n. oppressive authority

(= oppression, dictatorship, autocracy)

                         n. tyrant

Many people moved out of Germany before World War II to escape Nazi tyranny.

많은 사람들이 나찌의 만행을 피해 2차대전이 일어나기 전에 독일에서 도망나왔다.

☐ **consolidate** /kənˈsɑːlɪdeɪt/   v. to combine different pieces into one

(= combine, unite, merge)

                         n. consolidation

We must consolidate our efforts in order to succeed.

우리가 성공하기 위해서는 힘을 합쳐야 합니다.

☐ **solicitude** /səˈlɪsɪtuːd/   n. anxiety

(= concern, sorry, unease)

A mother's solicitude for the well-being of her children is never-ending.

자신의 아이의 행복을 위한 엄마의 걱정은 끝이 없는 것이다.

☐ **tumult** /'tuːmʌlt/   n. huge upheaval

(= uproar, commotion, clamor)

The principal's announcement to cancel the student fair caused a huge tumult among the students.

학교 축제를 취소하겠다는 교장선생님의 발표가 교내에 큰 동요를 일으켰다.

☐ **tranquil** /'træŋkwɪl/   adj. to be peaceful

(= calm, serene, relaxing)

                                    n. tranquility

The sea was tranquil during our cruise.

우리의 항해 동안 바다는 고요했다.

☐ **notwithstanding** /ˌnɑːtwɪθ'stændɪŋ/   adv. nevertheless

(= despite, although, nonetheless)

Notwithstanding his objection, I decided to proceed with my plan.

그의 반대에도 불구하고 나는 나의 계획을 추진하기로 했다.

☐ **inflammatory** /ɪn'flæmətɔːri/   adj. tending to arouse anger

(= provocative, seditious, stirring)

He was notorious for his inflammatory speeches.

그는 선동적인 연설을 하는 걸로 악명이 높았다.

☐ **perilous** /'perələs/   adj. to be very dangerous

(= hazardous, unsafe, risky)

                                    n. peril

It is perilous to travel through the country now: there is a civil war going on.

지금 저 나라를 여행하는 것은 매우 위험한 일이다: 지금 내전이 진행되고 있다.

☐ **procure** /prəˈkjʊr/ v. to obtain

(= acquire, get, buy)

I was in charge of procuring all the equipment we needed.

우리에게 필요한 모든 장비를 구하는 것이 나의 책임이다.

☐ **indignation** /ˌɪndɪɡˈneɪʃn/ n. righteous anger

(= anger, resentment, outrage)

adj. indignant

I could understand his indignation: I, too, have been wrongfully accused of a crime before.

그의 분노가 이해된다: 나 역시도 과거에 범죄를 저질렀다는 누명을 쓴 적이 있다.

☐ **prevail** /prɪˈveɪl/ v. to achieve victory

(= triumph, conquer, win)

I have no doubt that we will prevail.

우리가 승리 할 것이라고 의심하지 않는다.

☐ **abandon** /əˈbændən/ v. to leave completely and finally

(= desert, leave, forsake)

Jeffrey abandoned his long time job to start his own book store.

제프리는 오래 다니던 직장을 그만 두고 자기 서점을 차렸다.

☐ **thrive** /θraɪv/ v. to flourish

(= prosper, succeed, boom)

Several domestic horses escaped and now thrive in the mountains.

몇 마리의 사람들이 키우던 말들이 도망가서 이제는 산 속에서 번식하며 잘 살고 있다.

☐ **stiffen** /ˈstɪfn/ v. to become stiff

(= harden, toughen, solidify)

Henry stiffened in nervousness when the police knocked on his door.

경찰이 그의 문을 두드리자 헨리는 두려움에 몸이 굳었다.

□ **vascular** /ˈvæskjələr/

adj. composed of vessels that convey fluids such as blood or sap.

The human body is basically a huge vascular system.

인간의 몸은 기본적으로 하나의 큰 혈관망이다.

□ **dwell** /dwel/   v. to live

(= reside, live, stay)

Indigenous people of the area dwell in mud huts as there are no trees to provide lumber.

이 지역 원주민들은 목재를 구할 나무가 없어 진흙으로 지은 움막에 산다.

□ **pummel** /ˈpʌml/   v. to hit hard

(= beat, thump, pound)

The two boxers pummeled each other in the ring.

두 권투 선수가 링 위에서 서로에게 강력한 주먹을 날렸다.

□ **impede** /ɪmˈpiːd/   v. to get in the way of

(= obstruct, hinder, hamper)

                     n. impediment

Our progress was impeded by a lack of raw materials.

원자재의 부족으로 인해 우리의 진행이 더뎌졌다.

Practice 20.

Fill in the blank with the word that matches the definition provided

01　Some Papua New Guinean tribes _____ (live) in huts built over 5 meters up in trees to avoid attacks from wild animals.

02　Only a decade ago, it would have been _____ (very dangerous) to walk in this area after dark, but now it is very safe.

03　When in a political debate, it is important not to get agitated by an opponent's _____ (arousing anger) remarks.

04　Thanks to the _____ (concern) of the locals, the refugees were able to get by until government relief arrived.

05　Winslow, who has a crush on Agatha, _____ (become stiff) in nervousness when he saw her walking towards him.

06　Richard adopted three street cats that had been _____ (left completely) when they were kittens.

07　I like movies in which the righteous characters _____ (achieve victory) in the end.

08　The first thing my learning team mates asked me to do was to _____ (obtain) the help of Christie, who had done a similar project last year.

09　The two companies decided to _____ (combine into one) their back-office functions to reduce operating costs.

10　It is very difficult for a working woman to _____ (harmonize) the demands of her job and the desire to be a good mother.

11 The morning lake was calm and _____ (peaceful).

12 Muddy roads _____ (got in the way of) our progress through the country side.

13 When the brothers were young, they used to _____ (hit continuously) each other over everything, but now they are very close.

☐ **telltale** /ˈtelteɪl/   adj. revealing what was not intended to reveal

(= revealing, betraying, informative)

The telltale smell of her perfume proved to me that she had been in my room.

그녀의 독특한 향수 냄새로 그녀가 내 방에 들어왔었다는 걸 알 수 있었다.

☐ **progenitor** /prəʊˈdʒenɪtər/   n. ancestor

(= forerunner, forebear, antecedent)

The progenitors of whales once walked on land.

고래의 조상은 육지에 사는 동물이었다.

☐ **vex** /veks/   v. to irritate

(= irritate, annoy, displease)

     n. vexation

His incessant questions vexed me.

그의 끝없는 질문이 짜증나게 만들었다.

☐ **endorse** /ɪnˈdɔːrs/   v. to give support to

(= support, back, favor)

Michael Jordan endorses Nike sports shoes.

마이클 조던은 나이키 운동화를 보증한다.

☐ **empirical** /ɪmˈpɪrɪkl/   adj. proven from experience or experiment

(= experimental, observed, first-hand)

Despite numerous reports of sightings, there is no empirical evidence that UFOs exist.

많은 목격담이 있음에도 불구하고 미확인비행물체가 존재한다는 실증적 증거는 없다.

□ **conjectural** /kənˈdʒektʃərəl/   adj. hypothetical

(= academic, imaginary, abstract)

                                              n. conjecture

Einstein's Theory of Relativity was considered to be only conjectural until it was proven in 1929.

아인슈타인의 상대성 이론은 1929년 증명되기 전까지는 단지 추측성 이론이라고 생각되었다.

□ **impervious** /ɪmˈpɜːrviəs/   adj. not influenced by

(= unreceptive, unwavering, adamant)

The musician was impervious to the critics' views of his albums.

그 음악가는 자기 음악에 대한 비평가들의 의견에 전혀 신경 쓰지 않았다.

□ **stride** /straɪd/   n. a long step in walking

(= step, walk, pace)

Companies have made huge strides in the field of solar energy recently.

기업들은 최근에 태양광 발전 분야에서 큰 발전을 이뤘다.

□ **prescribe** /prɪˈskraɪb/   v. to order the use of medicine or treatment

(= recommend, suggest, order)

                                              n. prescription

The doctor prescribed antibiotics for my sore throat.

의사 선생님은 내 쉰 목에 항생제를 처방하였다.

□ **commendable** /kəˈmendəbl/   adj. praiseworthy

(= admirable, worthy, laudable)

                                              v. commend

                                              n. commendation

His honorable actions were most commendable.

그의 명예로운 행동은 칭찬을 받아 마땅하다.

□ **fluctuate** /ˈflʌktʃueɪt/   v. to rise and fall

(= vary, swing, waver)

n. fluctuation

The price of gas has fluctuated much in recent months.

최근 몇 달 동안 휘발유 가격이 등락을 거듭했다.

□ **radiate** /ˈreɪdieɪt/   v. to spread from the center

(= spread, diverge, circulate)

The seemingly harmless event radiated to all corners of the world.

이 무해해 보이던 사건이 전 세계 구석구석에 영향을 미쳤다.

□ **sediment** /ˈsedɪmənt/   n. matter that settles to the bottom of a liquid

(= residue, deposit, silt)

Stir the mixture until there are no sediments.

용액을 바닥에 가라앉는 찌꺼기가 없을 때까지 저어 주세요.

□ **foster** /ˈfɑːstər/   v. to promote the development of

(= nurture, promote, raise)

Mr. Cushing fostered an appreciation for hard work in his children.

쿠싱 씨는 자기의 아이들에게 열심히 일하는 것을 중요하게 생각하라는 인식을 심어주었다.

□ **nuisance** /ˈnuːsns/   n. an irritation

(= pain, annoyance, trouble)

The blinking lightbulb was a real nuisance.

깜빡거리는 전구가 진짜 짜증나게 했다.

□ **buttress** /ˈbʌtrəs/

n. an external support built to reinforce a structure

(= support, prop, reinforcement)

v. buttress

Cathedrals built in the Gothic period are often surrounded by buttresses that hold up the weight of the stone walls.

고딕 양식으로 지어진 성당들은 돌벽을 지지하는 부벽으로 둘러싸여 지어질 때가 많았다.

☐ **intricate** /ˈɪntrɪkət/   adj. very complicated

(= complex, elaborate, sophisticated)

n. intricacy

Gary opened the back of his computer to find an intricate maze of wires and circuits.

게리가 그의 컴퓨터 본체의 뒷판을 뜯어내자 복잡하게 얽힌 전선과 회로들이 보였다.

☐ **discard** /dɪˈskɑːrd/   v. to throw away

(= abandon, remove, reject)

Henry discarded his bulky desk top computer and bought a sleek laptop.

헨리는 투박한 데스크탑 컴퓨터를 없애고 날씬한 랩탑을 구매했다.

☐ **seamless** /ˈsiːmləs/   adj. smooth

(= smooth, faultless, flawless)

Gloria thanked the carpenter for doing a seamless job.

글로리아는 흠 잡을 데 없이 일을 해 준 목수에게 감사를 표했다.

☐ **discordant** /dɪsˈkɔːrdənt/   adj. to be incompatible

(= disharmonious, conflicting, disagreeing)

n. discord

He and I have discordant views about many issues.

그와 나는 여러 가지 이슈에 대해 다른 의견을 가지고 있다.

Practice 21.

Fill in the blank with the word that matches the definition provided

01 The meeting's atmosphere was very _____ (incompatible), because several participants had opposing views about a number of issues.

02 If we don't _____ (provide external support) the walls, this house will fall over soon.

03 When I was a boy, my Dad would let me play in his office while he was working, as long as I was not a/an _____ (irritation).

04 It was highly _____ (praiseworthy) for David to donate all his prize money to charity.

05 It is said that Korean doctors _____ (order the use of medicine) antibiotics too often, which said to be harmful for the immune system in the long run.

06 Mark was so tall that I almost had to run alongside him to match his _____ (long steps).

07 While vacationing in Mexico, I noticed how _____ (not influenced by) Martha was to the hot weather: she hardly broke a sweat while the rest of us were soaking.

08 Terry was wearing different clothes and had gotten a new haircut, but once I heard his _____ (revealing) voice, I knew it was him.

09 The President is keen to notch a political triumph that would _____ (promote) freer world trade and faster economic growth.

10 Wait until the _____ (things that settle to the bottom of a liquid) in the mixture settle to the bottom and then scoop out the clear liquid on the top.

11   The movement started in England and _____ (spread from the center) to the whole of Europe.

12   The retiring CEO and the newly elected CEO worked together for several months so that the transition of authority can be _____ (smooth).

13   The plot of Les Miserables is much more _____ (very complicated) than what ordinary people think.

14   The movie was said to be based on a true story, but many scenes were clearly based on _____ (guessed) accounts.

15   I find it hard to _____ (give support to) many of the candidate's opinions.

16   In early spring, the temperature between the lowest and highest point of the day can _____ (rise and fall) by over 15 degrees.

☐ **entropy** /ˈentrəpi/   n. disorder or randomness

(= anarchy, disarray, disorder, chaos)

Many stock analysts will try to persuade you that they can predict financial market trends, but history has proven that the only one true prediction you can make about financial markets is that entropy rules.

대부분의 주식 분석가들은 그들이 미래의 주식시장 추이를 예측할 수 있다고 설득하려 하지만, 역사적으로 보면 자본 시장에 대해 확실히 내릴 수 있는 예측은 무질서가 지배한다는 것 밖에 없다.

☐ **plaudit** /plɔ́:dit/   n. praise

(= approval, acclaim, praise, kudos)

Please join me in my plaudits to Ms Mason, Ms Wright and Mr. Gilmour for their outstanding job in preparing for tonight's event.

저와 함께 오늘 저녁 이벤트를 이렇게 훌륭히 준비해 주신 메이슨 씨, 라이트 양과 길모어 씨에게 칭찬을 보내시죠.

☐ **assailant** /əˈseɪlənt/   n. a person who attacks

(= attacker, assaulter, aggressor)

Despite the dim lighting in the alley, Ruby recognized her assailant as the suspicious man she saw at the bank that afternoon.

골목이 침침했지만 루비는 그녀를 공격한 사람이 낮에 은행에서 봤던 남자라는 걸 알 수 있었다.

☐ **yean** /jíːn/   v. to give birth to

(= bear)

Although there is no way to prove any connection between the two events, I find it most suspicious that our goats have yeaned several deformed goatlings ever since the chemical plant was built in this area.

두 가지 일이 연관되었다는 걸 증명할 길은 없지만, 이 지역에 화학물 공장이 설립된 이후에 우리가 키우는 염소가 기형아를 출산한 사실이 매우 의심스럽다.

☐ **offshoot** /ˈɔːfʃuːt/

n. something that has branched off something else

(= by-product, branch, spin-off, appendage)

The comic strip "Venom" is an offshoot of another one of Marvel Comic's comic strip about possibly the most famous superhero in the world, "Spider-Man."

만화 '베놈'은 마블 코믹스의 아마도 전세계에서 가장 유명한 수퍼히어로에 대한 만화 '스파이더 맨'에서 파생되어 나온 것이다.

☐ **antics** /ˈæntɪks/ n. foolish behavior

(= clowning, mischief, tricks)

In the beginning, his peculiar experiments were received as the naïve antics of a curious but not-very-bright boy.

처음에는 그의 특이한 실험들이 단순히 호기심은 많지만 별로 똑똑하지 못한 아이의 순진한 장난으로 받아들여졌다.

☐ **wangle** /ˈwæŋgl/ v. to obtain by dishonest methods

(= contrive, engineer, fix)

Having spent his entire month's allowance on a new video game, Henry tried to wangle money from his sister.

한 달치 용돈을 새 비디오 게임 구매하는 데 다 써버린 헨리는 누이동생으로부터 돈을 뜯어내려 하였다.

☐ **nitpick** /nítpìk/ v. to find fault in little things

(= criticize, carp, quibble, fuss, finick)

I've decided not to tell him of my decision, as he will likely nitpick about whatever course of action I take.

나는 그에게 내 결정을 말하지 않기로 했다. 왜냐하면 내가 뭐라고 말하건 그는 사사건건 트집을 잡을 거기 때문에.

☐ **duplicitous** /duːˈplɪsɪtəs/   adj. to be dishonest

                                             n. duplicity

(= deceitful, dishonest, disloyal)

People who are unaware of his duplicitous character are easily deceived by his seemingly sincere nature.

그의 위선적인 성격을 모르는 사람들은 그의 외면으로 보기에 진실한 모습에 쉽게 속는다.

☐ **scrumptious** /ˈskrʌmpʃəs/   adj. delicious

(= delicious, delectable, exquisite, appetizing)

The dinner she cooked for her guests was truly scrumptious: everyone was commenting for days about how good the food was.

그녀가 손님들에게 대접한 식사는 정말로 훌륭했다: 모두가 며칠이 지나도록 그날 저녁 음식이 얼마나 맛있었는지에 대해 말했다.

☐ **havoc** /ˈhævək/   n. great destruction

(= devastation, damage, destruction)

Rhea forgot to let Wolfgang, her pet bulldog, out of the living room when she left for work that morning, and later on found that he had wreaked severe havoc on her furniture and carpet that day.

리아는 출근하며 그녀의 반려견인 불독 울프강을 거실에서 나오게 하는 것을 잊어서 나중에 그가 그녀의 가구와 카펫을 엉망으로 만들어 놓은 걸 찾았다.

☐ **woeful** /ˈwəʊfl/   adj. very sad

(= doleful, mournful, wretched, sad)

Everyone cried at Hamil's funeral: it was a woeful event.

모두들 해밀의 장례식에서 울었다: 매우 슬픈 자리였다.

☐ **inculcate** /ɪnˈkʌlkeɪt/   v. to instill by forceful or insistent repetition

(= educate, impart, instill, indoctrinate)

Gloria's father overzealously tried to inculcate a sense of propriety in Gloria.

글로리아의 아버지는 글로리아에게 너무 과하게 예절관을 심어주려고 했다.

☐ **fickle** /ˈfɪkl/　　　　　　　　adj. likely to change

(= erratic, vacillating, capricious)

The weather has been most fickle today: it was brilliant in the morning, but it rained in the early afternoon, and now the rain has turned to sleet.

오늘 날씨가 하루종일 오락가락 하였다: 아침에는 해가 쨍했는데 이른 오후엔 비가 오고 지금은 비가 진눈개비로 변했다.

☐ **maven** /ˈmeɪvn/　　　　　　　n. a specialist

(= expert, connoisseur)

Having been in the same business for over 60 years, Mr. Andrews is considered the top maven in his field.

같은 분야에 60년을 종사한 앤드류스 씨는 자기 분야에서 전문가로 인정 받는다.

☐ **fanfare** /ˈfænfer/　　　　　　n. an ostentatious display

(= flourish, trump)

When it was decided that the Vancouver Canucks were to play in the Stanley Cup finals, the news was met with great fanfare not only by loyal fans but everyone else in the city.

밴쿠버의 카넉스 팀이 스탠리컵 결승에 진출했다는 소식이 알려졌을 때, 팬 뿐만 아니라 전 도시가 대대적인 축하를 했다.

☐ **volition** /vəʊˈlɪʃn/　　　　　　n. an act of willing

(= free-will, choice, option)

He decided to enter rehab of his own volition because he wanted to overcome his addiction to alcohol.

그는 그의 알코올 중독을 벗어나기 위해 자의로 재활병원에 입원하기로 했다.

☐ **munificence** /mjuːˈnɪfɪsns/　　　　n. kindness

(= generosity, bounty, philanthropy, benevolence)

His implication that I was the beneficiary of some great munificence of his family is ridiculous.

내가 그의 가족의 어떤 엄청난 배려로 특혜를 입었다고 한 그의 언급은 웃기는 소리다.

☐ **gnash** /næʃ/   v. to grind teeth together

(= growl, snarl)

If you are disappointed with your test results, I suggest you gnash your teeth and try to do better next time.

만일 시험 결과가 만족스럽지 못하다면 이제부터 어금니 꽉 물고 다음 번엔 더 잘할 수 있도록 노력을 해.

☐ **divine** /dɪˈvaɪn/   adj. relating to God

(= heavenly, spiritual, holy)

I consider it divine intervention that I survived the accident and, therefore, have decided to dedicate my life to doing God's work.

나는 내가 그 사고에서 살아남은 건 하느님의 도움이었다는 걸로 생각하고, 앞으로의 삶을 하느님의 일을 하는데 헌신하기로 했다.

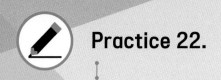

Practice 22.

Fill in the blank with the word that matches the definition provided

01 The newspaper editorial lambasted the government saying that the new tax will wreak _____ (great destruction) among smaller companies.

02 The restaurant was tiny, with only three tables, but the meals served there are simply _____ (very delicious).

03 Jessica is only 12 years old, but she can tell you about fashion trends as if she were a seasoned fashion _____ (specialist).

04 Harrold is quite _____ (liable to change) when choosing a place to eat.

05 The modern education system is criticized for failing to _____ (instill by repetition) students with a love of knowledge.

06 Samuel is brilliant at math and science, but he shows a/an _____ (very sad) lack of knowledge in history and geography.

07 Most people think that post-modernist art is a/an _____ (spin-off) of modernist art, but it's not.

08 The two lambs we took in last year have _____ (gave birth to) several baby lambs, and now we have six.

09 The President revoked one of his primary campaign promises as soon as he was elected: naturally, many people now think he is _____ (dishonest).

10 As far as I could see, our report was done, but Larry continued to _____ (find fault in little things) every word and sentence of it for days.

11   While dining at a café, where my friend Greg works as a waiter, I asked him if he could
     _____ (obtain dishonestly) us some desserts or coffee.

12   The children's rambunctious _____ (foolish behavior) began to annoy Mr. Wilson.

13   Darryl didn't realize he _____ (grinds his teeth) is teeth in his sleep, until he
     married Ola.

14   The children's hospital would not be able to run if not for the great _____ (kindness)
     by supporters in the form of donations.

15   Apple launched the new iPhone with the usual _____ (ostentatious display).

Class 23

□ **incarceration** /ɪnˌkɑːrsəˈreɪʃn/   n. the act of locking in prison

(= imprisonment, confinement, restraint, imprisonment)

The lawyer warned his client that the consequence of perjury will be incarceration.

변호사는 의뢰인에게 위증의 결과는 투옥이라고 경고했다.

□ **indubitable** /ɪnˈduːbɪtəbl/   adj. unable to doubt

(= indisputable, unquestionable)

He locked himself in his workshop vowing not to emerge until he completes what he would call his indubitable masterpiece.

그는 자신의 명실공히 명작을 완성하기 전까지는 나오지 않겠다며 스스로를 작업실에 가뒀다.

□ **ebullient** /ɪˈbʌliənt/   adj. to be very happy

(= jovial, bright, cheery)

The gloomy mood of the meeting turned ebullient when the director announced that the company will be paying a special bonus to each employee this year.

이사가 금년에 직원들에게 특별 상여금을 준다는 발표를 하자 우울했던 회의 분위기가 금방 화기애애해졌다.

□ **lax** /læks/   adj. not strict or severe

(= lenient, tolerant, permissive)

Singaporean laws seem quite draconian at first, but after living in the country for a while one realizes that the law enforcement agencies are quite lax about simple misdemeanors.

싱가포르의 법은 매우 엄격해 보이지만, 이 나라에 몇 년 살아보니 경범죄에 대해서는 법 집행이 그다지 엄격하지 않다는 것을 알 수 있었다.

□ **amorous** /ˈæmərəs/   adj. related to love

(= loving, fond, passionate)

469

She understood that his amorous gestures towards her were genuine, but his childlike antics were so irritating that she could not take him seriously.

그녀는 그의 구애가 진심인 걸 알았지만 그의 아이 같은 장난이 그녀로 하여금 그를 진지하게 받아들이기 힘들게 하였다.

□ **junta** /ˈhʊntə/   n. a small group ruling a country

(= military rule)

All opposition leaders boycotted the elections stating that the military junta will most likely manipulate the results to its advantage if the elections were to proceed.

군사 정권이 선거 결과를 그들에게 유리하게 조작할 가능성이 매우 크기 때문에 모든 야당의 지도자들이 선거를 거부하였다.

□ **doleful** /ˈdəʊlfl/   adj. sad

(= mournful, distressing, dreary, somber)

I could tell immediately that Julie hadn't passed the audition by the doleful expression she had on her face.

줄리의 시무룩한 얼굴을 보고는 그녀가 오디션에 불합격한 것을 금방 알 수 있었다.

□ **derivative** /dɪˈrɪvətɪv/

n. something that has branched off from something else

(= offshoot, by-product)

His newest book was a poor derivative of his earlier masterpiece, with the same plot and historical background, but with less intrigue and suspense.

그의 신작은 그의 초기 명작의 저급한 파생물이었다. 같은 줄거리에 같은 시대적 배경, 그러나 음모와 서스펜스는 적은.

□ **obsolescent** /ˌɑːbsəˈlesnt/   adj. old and out-of-use

(= outdated, antiquated, waning)

Alex tried to sell his old 8mm movie camera on eBay but soon realized no one was interested in such obsolescent cameras anymore.

알렉스는 이베이에 그의 8 밀리미터 무비 카메라를 판매하려 하였으나 이런 낡은 카메라엔 아무도 관심이 없다는 걸 곧 깨달았다.

☐ **guerrilla** /gəˈrɪlə/

n./adj. (pertaining to) a band of soldiers harassing the enemy by surprise raids

(= partisan)

After leaving Cuba, Che Guevara raged a guerilla war in the Bolivian jungle hoping to start a socialist revolution in that country.

쿠바를 떠난 체 게바라는 볼리비아에 사회주의 혁명을 일으키고자 그 나라의 정글에서 게릴라 전투를 진행하였다.

☐ **bromide** /ˈbrəʊmaɪd/

n. a phrase used so often that its meaning has tarnished

(= platitude, cliché, banality)

The coach's usual bromide of "winning isn't everything" did nothing to cheer up the team members after their devastating defeat.

감독님의 판에 박힌 "이기는 게 다가 아니다" 같은 말이 크게 패배한 선수들을 전혀 위로하지 않았다.

☐ **laud** /lɔːd/   v. to praise

(= praise, acclaim, extol)

Nicolas became angry when the professor lauded Bruce's performance only, when the project was handed in under both of their names.

니콜라스는 본인이 공동저자임에도 불구하고 교수님이 브루스만 칭찬을 하여 화가 났다.

☐ **salient** /ˈseɪliənt/   adj. prominent and conspicuous

(= prominent, outstanding, important, marked)

John's presentation left many salient points untouched, and not surprisingly, he faced a barrage of questions from students when he was done.

존은 프리젠테이션에서 몇 가지 중요한 사안에 대해 언급도 하지 않았기 때문에, 놀랍지 않게 그가 끝마치자 다른 학생들로부터 질문 세례를 받았다.

☐ **subversive** /səbˈvɜːrsɪv/

adj. wanting to overthrow the existing government or belief system

(= rebellious, insubordinate)

The book was banned by the government because it was deemed too subversive.

그 책은 내용이 너무 체제 전복적이라는 이유로 정부가 금지하였다.

☐ **waive** /weɪv/　　　　　　　　v. to give up or forego

(= relinquish, renounce, forsake, abandon)

The landlord promised the tenants that he would waive the last month's rent if they agreed to lease the house for two years.

집주인은 세입자들에게 2년 계약을 하면 마지막 달 월세는 빼주겠다고 약속했다.

☐ **reticent** /ˈretɪsnt/　　　　　　adj. shy, disposed to be silent

(= reserved, quiet, restrained)

Don't be bothered by his silence; he is a very reticent man.

그가 조용하다고 신경쓰지 마세요; 그는 매우 과묵한 사람입니다.

☐ **prerogative** /prɪˈrɑːɡətɪv/　　　n. an exclusive right or privilege

(= right, privilege, birthright, authority)

The airline grants gold card members the prerogative to use the airport lounge for free.

항공사는 골드카드 보유 멤버에게 공항 라운지의 무료사용권 혜택을 준다.

☐ **paucity** /ˈpɔːsəti/　　　　　　n. smallness of quantity

(= scarcity, rareness, lack)

We had to change the subject of our report due to the paucity of research material available.

우리는 자료의 부족으로 인해 보고서의 제목을 바꿔야 했다.

☐ **autonomous** /ɔːˈtɑːnəməs/　　adj. self-governing

(= self-ruling, independent, sovereign)

Randy heads the R&D Department, which is a completely autonomous department that reports directly to the CEO, free from any intervention from any of the other business units.

랜디는 완전히 독립적인 부서로서 대표이사에게 직접 보고하고 다른 사업부의 간섭을 전혀 받지 않는 연구개발부서의 책임자다.

□ **herald** /ˈherəld/   v. to signal the coming of

(= signal, proclaim)

In some cultures the crow is seen as a bird that heralds good luck, but in others it is viewed as a messenger of death.

어떤 문화권에서 까마귀는 길조로 여겨지는 반면, 다른 문화권에서는 죽음의 전령이라고 여겨진다.

□ **furtive** /ˈfɜːrtɪv/   adj. done in secret

(= sly, sneaky, surreptitious)

I could tell from their furtive smiles and hushed giggles that the girls were conniving something mischievous.

자기들끼리 몰래 웃고 숨죽이고 낄낄거리는 걸로 봐서는 그 여자아이들이 뭔가 장난거리를 꾸미고 있다는 걸 알 수 있었다.

□ **inclement** /ɪnˈklemənt/   adj. characterized as bad weather

(= stormy, rainy, windy, foul)

After weeks of inclement weather, we finally had a day of sunshine.

몇 주간 날씨가 나빴는데 마침내 해가 나는 날이 왔다.

□ **stifle** /ˈstaɪfl/   v. to suppress the growth of

(= suppress, repress, prevent)

Bureaucracy and favoritism can stifle innovative thinking in a growing company very easily.

발전하는 기업 내에서 요식 체계나 편애는 혁신적 사고를 매우 쉽게 억누를 수 있다.

□ **tantalize** /ˈtæntəlaɪz/   v. to torment or tease

(= tease, torment, entice)

I was vexed at Robin because he tantalized me by giving me one raisin at a time when he knew I was hungry.

나는 로빈이 내가 배가 고픈 줄 알면서도 건포도를 하나씩 주는 짓으로 감질나게 만들어서 짜증이 났다.

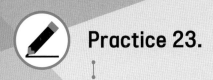

Practice 23.

Fill in the blank with the word that matches the definition provided

01   Ever since the movie "Frozen," the saying "Let it go" has become so _____ (cliché).

02   My computer is 8 years old and _____ (out of date), but as I only used it to browse the internet and send emails, it suits me just fine.

03   For some reason, Glenda sat in a _____ (sad) mood throughout the entire evening.

04   Kate took Harry's professional interest in her work as _____ (related to love) advances.

05   Unfortunately, environmental laws are too _____ (not strict) in Korea.

06   Credit card companies usually _____ (give up) the first year's annual fee to entice new customers.

07   During the tour, our guide pointed out many _____ (prominent) points about the building.

08   In many countries, education is still the _____ (exclusive right) of the rich.

09   All I know about Peter is that he used to be in the military: he is very _____ (silent) about his past.

10   Richard became _____ (very happy) when he received his test results.

11   Although his team lost the match, the coach _____ (praised) each player for doing his best.

474

12   Don't _____ (torment) me: just tell me what's on your mind.

13   The government failed to _____ (suppress the growth of) the public's discontent.

14   If the weather is not _____ (characterized as bad weather) this weekend, we'll go to the park for a picnic.

15   The two girls exchanged _____ (secretive) glances across the dinner table and tried hard not to giggle.

16   Pale lemon forsythia and the pink azaleas _____ (signal the coming of) in spring joyfully.

17   The _____ (smallness of quantity) of information makes it difficult for the police to make an official statement about the case.

Find the most suitable word from the box that fits in the sentence

fickle, offshoot, antics, seamless, reticent, woeful, salient, obsolescent, inculcate, ebullient, depict, discard, provoke, forestall

01 Up to the early 14th century, European artists were only allowed to _____ biblical scenes in their paintings.

02 When cooking clams, remember to _____ any that do not open when heated.

03 The government's announcement _____ a wave of protests.

04 On New Year's Day, mother always hands out to us talismans that are supposed to _____ bad luck during the year.

05 Life can be _____: yesterday's millionaire can be today's pauper.

06 During the 1960s and 1970s, great care was taken to _____ the values of nationhood and family in the elementary school curriculum.

07 When I realized I'd disappointed my parents, I felt _____ for days.

08 Hallabong, a/an _____ of the tangerine, was developed in the South Korean Island of Jeju and has become a very popular fruit in Korea.

09 When they were dating, Gloria found Henry's _____ humorous; now that they are married, she finds them annoying.

10   The 10 year old pianist handled even the most difficult piano pieces _____.

11   She is shy and _____ when you first meet her, but once you get to know her she becomes quite gregarious and raunchy.

12   At the automobile exhibition, representatives of each automaker presented the _____ points of their new models.

13   If you hold on to your _____ electronics for long enough, they become antiques.

14   The entire country fell into a/an _____ mood when their national football team reached the semi-finals of the World Cup Games.

furtive, prerogative, foster, incarceration, prescribe, impervious, tantalize, fanfare, maven, inflammatory, munificence, stifle

15   No amount of hardships could _____ Jim's dream of becoming successful as an actor.

16   As Howard was ranting on about how he was responsible for winning the football game, the other players stole _____ glances at their watches, wanting to go home.

17   As CEO, Mr. Dickens has the _____ to make the strategic decisions for the company.

18   The mayor has tried to _____ civic pride by having a new public library built in the city.

19   Instead of _____ antibiotics, the doctor advised the flu patient to get plenty of rest and drink a lot of fluids.

20   While his wife and daughter were arguing in front of him, Ralph was _____ to the drama and quietly read his book.

21   While waiting for our food to be served, we were _____ by the smell of something delicious coming from the kitchen.

22   New Year's Eve celebrations always involve a lot of _____ and pageantry.

23   I'm no computer _____, but I can probably fix most problems people have with their home computers.

24   The candidate was impervious to the _____ language his opponent used.

25   If the charges against William are proven true, he faces _____.

26   I did not expect such _____ from my former rival.

abandon, prevail, sparse, austerity, wayward, nuisance, telltale, impede, fluorescent, solicitude, upheaval, pummel

27   Don't be a/an _____. Leave so I can concentrate on my work.

28   I could tell that Stephen had arrived by his _____ nasal voice coming from the next room.

29   My recovery from a cold was _____ by my continuous overwork.

30   I decided that the only way to avoid getting beat up by Richard was for me to _____ him first.

31   When our canoe began to draw water and sink, we _____ it and swam towards the shore.

32   Justice _____ over evil.

33 At this time of the morning, the beaches are almost empty with only a/an _____ few people.

34 After the extravagance of the romantic architecture of the late 19th century, early 20th century architecture adopted a sense of _____.

35 These new _____ bulbs emit no heat at all.

36 Thank you for your offer to help. We are touched by your _____.

37 When the previous CEO suddenly left for the job as Vice Chairman at a major competitor and took two Vice Presidents with him, it caused a huge _____ at the company.

38 The leading golfer hit several _____ shots that caused him to drop out of the top ten of the tournament.

Circle the word that is not a synonym

39 platitude – enfranchisement – banality

40 dwell – pummel – pound

41 reinforce – buttress – irritate

42 antecedent – progenitor – posterity

43 lurk – prowl – brawl

44 furtive – sneaky – fickle

45 inclement – herald – signal

46 sovereign – autonomous – indubitable

47 subversive – rebellious – endearing

48 salient – emphatic – prominent

49 admirable – commendable – appalling

50 impervious – unaccepting – contradictory

51 prattle – endorse – support

52 repudiate – tantalize – entice

53 conflate – upheaval – turmoil

54 doleful – treacherous – somber

55 doldrums – entropy – boredom

56 discordant – conflicting – scatterbrained

57 allude – mention – infest

58 demeanor – slant – conduct

59 prevail – protrude – conquer

60 acquire – reconcile – procure

☐ **adulation** /ˌædʒəˈleɪʃn/   n. excessive devotion

(= admiration, exaltation, idolization, adoration)

The more fervent his fans' adulation towards him, the more depressed and empty he felt of his fame.

그의 팬들이 더욱 열성적으로 그에게 열광할수록 그는 그의 인기에 대해 더욱 더 비관하고 공허하게 느꼈다.

☐ **accost** /əˈkɔːst/   v. to boldly approach

(= approach, confront)

It's a good idea to avoid walking down this street after sunset, as you will likely be accosted by beggars and drunks asking for money.

이 거리는 해가 진 다음에는 걸어가지 않는 것이 좋다. 거지와 주정뱅이들이 다가 와서 돈을 요구하는 경우가 많기 때문에.

☐ **diatribe** /ˈdaɪətraɪb/   n. severe criticism

(= attack, tirade, criticism)

Over the years, I've come across numerous diatribes against Euthanasia, but I have to admit it does serve a positive function in certain circumstances.

수년간 나는 안락사에 대한 많은 비판을 들어왔지만, 경우에 따라서는 긍정적인 기능을 한다는 것도 인정해야 한다.

☐ **benediction** /ˌbenɪˈdɪkʃn/   n. a blessing

(= blessing, grace, thanksgiving)

The day before sending her son off to the army, Jessica took Marlon to Father Montgomery and asked for his benediction and prayers to return her son home safely.

아들 말론이 입대하기 전날 제시카는 그를 몽고메리 신부님에게 데려가 아들을 집으로 무사히 돌려 보내달라고 기원하는 축복과 기도를 해달라고 요청하였다.

☐ **neologism** /niˈɑːlədʒɪzəm/   n. a new word or terminology

(= buzz word, new word)

For those of us who are not on the forefront of the newest electronic gadgetry, trying to read an article that reviews the newest computer software is like wading through a dizzy labyrinth of neologisms.

새로운 전자기기기술의 첨단에 있지 않는 우리 같은 사람들에게 최신 컴퓨터 소프트웨어에 대한 기사를 읽는 것은 마치 신조어로 이뤄진 미로를 헤집고 다니는 것 같다.

☐ **enamor** /inǽmər/   v. to fill with love

(= charm, fascinate, captivate, fond)

Ron's plan to enamor Lucy with his charm failed when he accidently spilled a glass of juice in her lap.

랄프가 루시의 환심을 사기 위해 들이던 노력은 그가 그녀의 무릎에 주스를 쏟아 실패로 돌아갔다.

☐ **buffoonery** /bəˈfuːnəri/   n. foolish behavior

(= clowning, jesting, silliness, drollery)

Sandra was in such a lugubrious mood that even my advanced level of buffoonery was unable to uplift her spirits.

산드라는 얼마나 기분이 우울했는지 내가 바보 같은 장난을 본격적으로 했음에도 그녀의 기분이 전혀 나아지지 않았다.

☐ **equanimity** /ˌekwəˈnɪməti/   n. calmness, mental or emotional stability

(= composure, calm, aplomb)

The firemen arrived at the site of the scene with great alacrity and while maintaining equanimity proceeded to evacuate the people from the building.

불이 난 장소에 소방관이 빠른 시간 내에 도착하여 침착하게 건물에서 사람들을 대피시켰다.

☐ **flout** /flaʊt/   v. to treat with disdain

(= scorn, breech, disobey)

The orchestra flouted normal convention and allowed the audience to photograph or record its performances.

오케스트라는 관례를 무시하고 그들의 연주를 관객이 녹음하거나 촬영하는 것을 허락했다.

☐ **panning** /ˈpænɪŋ/   n. extreme criticism

(= criticism)

It is strange how some albums sell better after the receiving nasty pannings from the musical critics.

어떤 앨범들은 비평가의 혹평을 받은 후에 더 잘 팔리는 것은 이상한 일이다.

☐ **guile** /ɡaɪl/   n. artful deception

(= deceit, duplicity, deviousness)

He is reputed to have risen to his current status by guile, rather than hard work.

그는 지금 자리에 오르기 위해 능력을 발휘했다기보다는 권모술수를 이용했다는 평가를 받는다.

☐ **ethereal** /ɪˈθɪriəl/   adj. extremely delicate

(= delicate, frail)

Her ethereal beauty has made many men swoon in the past.

과거에 그녀의 천상의 아름다움을 보고 정신을 잃은 남자들이 한둘이 아니었다.

☐ **swoon** /swuːn/   v. to faint or lose consciousness

(= faint, collapse, pass out)

It was common to see young women swoon at the sight of the singer.

그 가수를 보고 젊은 여자들이 혼절하는 일이 흔했다.

☐ **decimate** /ˈdesɪmeɪt/   v. to drastically reduce the number of

(= devastate, destroy)

The Black Plague was so virulent that in a few short years it decimated the population of medieval Europe severely.

흑사병은 너무나 전염성이 강하여 불과 몇 년 만에 중세 유럽의 인구를 크게 줄였다.

☐ **consternation** /ˌkɑːnstərˈneɪʃn/   n. a feeling of extreme worry

(= dismay, shock, anxiety)

The news of the break up of the Beatles in 1970 threw the entire world into consternation.
1970년에 비틀스가 해산했다는 소식은 전 세계를 큰 실망에 빠뜨렸다.

☐ **doctrinaire** /ˌdɑːktrɪˈner/   adj. to be rigid or inflexible

(= dogmatic, inflexible, unbending)

Ironically, it is the scientific community which one would think to be open to new ideas and to shun convention, that tends to be very doctrinaire and elitist.

아이러니하게도 새로운 아이디어에 더 개방적이고 관례를 따르는 것을 피할 것 같은 과학계가 더 교조적이고 엘리트주의가 팽배하다.

☐ **expunge** /ɪkˈspʌndʒ/   v. to delete or cut out

(= erase, delete, obliterate)

After breaking up with Nora, Brian tried to expunge memories of her from his mind.

노라와 헤어지고 난 후, 브라이언은 기억에서 그녀를 지우고자 노력했다.

☐ **connoisseur** /ˌkɑːnəˈsɜːr/

n. a person who knows much about art, music, food, wine and etc.

(= expert, authority, judge, specialist)

Ken thinks he's become a connoisseur of French cuisine and wines just because he worked as a waiter at his uncle's French Bistro last summer.

케빈은 지난 여름 그의 삼촌의 프랑스 비스트로에서 웨이터로 일했다고 자기가 프랑스 요리와 와인의 전문가인 것처럼 행세한다.

☐ **peg** /peg/   v. to secure

(= fasten, secure, fix)

Our tent collapsed during the night because it wasn't pegged tightly to the ground.

간밤에 우리 텐트는 땅에 단단히 고정하지 않아 넘어졌다.

☐ **fiasco** /fiˈæskəʊ/   n. extreme humiliation

(= flop, debacle, catastrophe)

Our school's marching band has been practicing diligently to not repeat the fiasco of ranking last in the state competition like it did last year.

작년에 주 경합에서 꼴찌한 낭패를 되풀이 하지 않기 위해 우리 학교의 행진밴드는 매우 부지런히 연습 중이다.

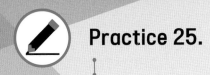

Practice 25.

Fill in the blank with the word that matches the definition provided

01 Percy is one of the best public speakers I know, but he told me that his first ever public speech ended in a/an _____ (huge embarrassment).

02 Inflation in most countries reacts as if it's _____ (secured) to oil prices.

03 When the cable car reached the height of 1,800 meters in less than two minutes, one of the passengers _____ (passed out).

04 Jim's mother has the appearance of a heroine in a Victorian novel - tall, willowy, and _____ (extremely delicate).

05 Many people wondered if the president had enough _____ (artful deception) to ford this political scandal.

06 Who among us would not _____ (treat with disdain) the law if we were sure that there would be no consequences?

07 During his life, Albert Einstein received the _____ (excessive adoration) of the general public, who mostly had no understanding of Einstein's scientific achievements.

08 Owning a ten CD compilation of Beethoven's symphonies does not make you a/an _____ (a specialist in art) of classical music.

09 Mr. Lorne received the news of his termination with _____ (calmness).

10 After looking forward to visiting Paris for years, I find that after my trip I am not much _____ (filled with love) by that city.

486

11   The appearance of the sun after many days of rain was like a/an _____ (blessing).

12   The opposition leader launched into a long _____ (severe criticism) about the current government's mishandlings of many issues.

13   The young clerk boldly _____ the CEO and asked him a sensitive question about the company's future.

14   Hindus bathe in the Ganges river believing that this will _____ (cut out) them of their worldly sins.

15   Second generation immigrants growing up in the U.S. are brought up in a Western society, but many of their parents retain the _____ (dogmatic) beliefs of their home country.

16   To Martha's _____ (extreme worry), when she got home she found that none of her children had returned from school yet.

17   The commanding officer expected his forces to _____ (drastically outnumber) the enemy as they outnumbered them by four to one.

☐ **unfettered** /ʌnˈfetərd/   adj. free from restraint

(= free, loose, tolerant)

Dr. Wiesmeyer was elated at the suggestion to have his own laboratory, where he could conduct his research unfettered by any outside disturbances.

위스마이어 박사는 외부 방해를 전혀 받지 않고 자신의 연구를 진행할 수 있는 자기의 연구실을 갖는다는 말에 매우 기뻐했다.

☐ **amnesty** /ˈæmnəsti/   n. a general pardon for (political) offenses

(= general pardon, mercy, reprieve)

One of the first actions of the new President was to grant an amnesty to political prisoners who were incarcerated for opposing the government in the past.

새로 선출된 대통령이 취임한 후 처음으로 한 행동 중 하나가 과거에 정부에 대항하다가 투옥된 사람들을 사면시키는 것이었다.

☐ **burgeon** /ˈbɜːrdʒən/   v. to grow, to expand

(= grow, thrive, bloom, prosper)

Under his father's guidance, Jack's skills as a stone mason burgeoned every year.

아버지의 지도하에 잭의 석공으로써의 실력이 매년 늘어갔다.

☐ **callous** /ˈkæləs/   adj. not caring about

(= heartless, coldhearted, unsympathetic)

His disregard for other people's feelings and callous refusal to accept excuses make him the most feared manager within the entire company.

타인의 감정을 무시하고 핑계 따위는 노골적으로 거부하는 면이 그를 사내에서 직원들이 가장 두려워하는 관리자로 만든다.

☐ **wail** /weɪl/   v. to cry out in pain or sadness

(= howl, moan, weep)

Tim wailed when he heard that his dog had died in an accident.

팀은 반려견이 사고로 죽었다는 말을 듣고는 슬픔에 울부짖었다.

☐ **immure** /ɪˈmjʊr/   v. to lock up, to imprison

(= imprison, jail, confine, cage)

James immured himself in his room for days after he failed the audition he'd prepared hard for.

제임스는 오랫동안 열심히 준비한 오디션에서 떨어진 후 며칠 동안 방에서 나오지 않았다.

☐ **circumlocution** /ˌsɜːrkəmləˈkjuːʃn/   n. indirectness of speech

(= indirectness, euphemism, redundancy)

When high officials meet, their discussions are usually steeped in circumlocution.

고위관직자들끼리 만나는 자리에서는 대화가 주로 간접적인 표현으로 이루어진다.

☐ **quip** /kwɪp/   v. to joke

(= joke, jest, jibe, banter)

"You look like an overgrown Canary!" quipped John at Laura after she died her hair to a color that was originally intended to be blond, but turned out to be bright yellow.

원래 의도했던 금발이 아니라 샛노랑으로 로라의 머리 색깔이 염색된 것을 보고 "너 거대한 카나리아 같아!"라고 존이 농담했다.

☐ **bequeath** /bɪˈkwiːð/   v. to hand down

(= leave, grant, endow, bestow, entrust)

Many socio-economists believe that the reason for higher savings rates of Asians is that Asians feel more social pressure to bequeath wealth to their children.

많은 사회경제학자들은 아시아인들이 저축률이 높은 이유가 사후에 자식들에게 재산을 남겨야 한다는 사회적 강박을 더 느끼기 때문이라고 한다.

□ **oaf** /əʊf/　　　　　　　　　　n. a fool or dummy

(= lout, brute, fool, jerk)

I may not be the brightest guy in the room, but I'm not an oaf either.

나는 이 방에서 가장 머리 좋은 사람은 아니지만, 그렇다고 바보도 아니다.

□ **infinitesimal** /ˌɪnfɪnɪˈtesɪml/　　　adj. extremely small

(= microscopic, minute, tiny, insignificant)

This snake's venom is an extremely poisonous substances: even an infinitesimal amount in the blood stream can paralyze or kill a full grown adult.

이 뱀의 독은 매우 독성이 강한 성분이다: 아주 미량이 혈관으로 들어가도 성인을 마비시키던지 죽일 수 있다.

□ **lament** /ləˈment/　　　　　　v. to express sorrow

(= mourn, grieve, bemoan, deplore)

Whenever my mother learned of my poor grades, she would exaggeratedly lament about why I had to take after my father's side of the family when it came to brains and intelligence.

내가 성적을 나쁘게 받을 때마다 우리 어머니는 왜 하필 내가 머리와 지능이 친가 쪽을 닮았는지 과장되게 애통해 한다.

□ **hubbub** /ˈhʌbʌb/　　　　　　n. loud confused noise

(= noise, racket, uproar, tumult)

After spending five days in the tranquil lake side bungalow, Cathy was almost nostalgic for the hubbub of the city.

호숫가의 한적한 방갈로에서 닷새를 보낸 후, 캐시는 도시의 시끌적뻑 함이 그리울 정도였다.

□ **preside** /prɪˈzaɪd/　　　　　　v. to occupy a place of authority

(= officiate, moderate, chair)

The judge was famous for presiding over many landmark cases.

그 판사는 여러 건의 역사적인 사건을 판결한 걸로 유명하다.

☐ **archaic** /ɑːrˈkeɪɪk/   adj. old and outdated

(= outdated, antiquated, obsolete)

The first thing I will do with the prize money is buy a new computer because the one I have is so archaic that it needs to be in a museum.

상금으로 제일 먼저 새로운 컴퓨터를 살 것이다, 왜냐하면 지금 쓰고 있는 것이 너무 오래된 것이라 박물관에 들어가야 할 정도라서.

☐ **fastidious** /fæˈstɪdiəs/   adj. taking extreme care of

(= particular, meticulous, fussy, finicky)

Mr. Gibson's writing classes are beneficial because he is very fastidious when he proof reads our essays and makes very detailed suggestions on how we can improve our writing skills.

깁슨 선생님의 작문 시간은 그가 우리의 에세이를 감수할 때 매우 세세하게 봐주시고 어떻게 하면 우리가 작문 실력을 향상시킬지에 대한 아주 구체적인 제안을 해주시기 때문에 매우 유익하다.

☐ **pestilence** /ˈpestɪləns/   n. wide spreading disease
                                       adj. pestilent

(= plague, epidemic, pandemic)

After the flood water had receded, the flood victims had to battle with bad hygiene and pestilence.

범람한 물이 빠져나간 후 피해자들은 나쁜 위생과 질병과 싸워야 했다.

☐ **utilitarian** /juːtɪlɪˈteriən/   adj. being practical and rational

(= pragmatic, practical)

The architect, whose work has been described as functional but lacking elegance, has been criticized for paying too much attention to utilitarian concerns and not enough to aesthetic detail.

작품들이 기능성은 있으나 우아하지 않다는 평가를 받은 건축가가 너무 실용적인 면에만 집중하고 미학적인 면에는 신경쓰지 않는다는 비판을 받았다.

☐ **stature** /ˈstætʃər/   n. degree of development attained

(= prominence, status, eminence, distinction)

The singer is not well known in the U.S. but enjoys iconic stature in his home country.

그 가수는 미국에서는 별로 알려지지 않았지만 그의 고국에서는 유명인사다.

☐ **pious** /ˈpaɪəs/   adj. extremely religious

(= religious, godly, spiritual, devout)

When Mathew was young his dream was to become a priest, and even though he abandoned this dream now, he always lives a pious life.

매튜는 어릴 땐 꿈이 성직자가 되는 거였고, 지금은 그 꿈을 버렸지만 항상 독실한 삶을 살고 있다.

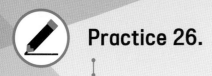

Practice 26.

Fill in the blank with the word that matches the definition provided

01 Thanks to Kelly's hard work, her store's business _____ (grew).

02 Omar was glad that he moved to the top 12th floor, where he had a/an _____ (free from restraint) view of the park and lake.

03 This chemical substance is lethal to humans, even if only a/an _____ (extremely small) amount is ingested.

04 Anthony's father _____ (handed down) Anthony the huge family mansion, but unfortunately Anthony does not make enough money to manage such a large house.

05 I was surprised to find that many of the government departments still used _____ (old and outdated) software.

06 Ricky was asked to _____ (occupy a place of authority) over the meeting.

07 Despite the _____ (loud confusing noise) going on around her, Gloria sat engulfed in her book.

08 Larry was miffed by Greta's _____ (not caring about) answers to his serious questions.

09 The two friends, who hadn't seen each other for over 15 years, _____ (joked) about how each other looked so old.

10 I am tired of your _____ (indirectness of speech): give me a straight answer!

11   Alfred _____ (locked up) himself in his room for days studying for his final exams.

12   Several mourners _____ (cried out loud) as Mr. Lord's coffin was lowered into his grave.

13   When the minister retired, he moved to the country and lived a quiet and _____ (very religious) life.

14   I did not expect a man of Dr. Gibbon's _____ (prominence) to be so humble and easy-going.

15   The new Prime Minister took a/an _____ stance about foreign policy: if he thinks it will benefit his country, he will open a dialogue with any former enemies.

16   Although Mr. Kelly's car is 50 years old, it still runs smoothly because he takes such _____ (very careful) care of it.

☐ **indignation** /ˌɪndɪɡˈneɪʃn/   n. righteous anger

(= resentment, annoyance, fury, offense)

The picture in the newspaper showing the President playing golf on the day of the massive flood aroused public indignation.

신문에 난 큰 홍수가 나던 날 대통령이 골프를 치던 사진에 대중들이 분함을 느꼈다.

☐ **estrangement** /ɪˈstreɪndʒmənt/   n. the state of being unfriendly

     v. to estrange

(= rift, separation, rupture)

The two countries, whose relationship suffered from estrangement during the past two governments, have vowed to renew their friendship and economic cooperation.

지난 두 번의 정권 동안 관계가 소원했던 두 나라가 그들의 우정과 경제적인 협력을 다시 지피기로 했다.

☐ **satiate** /ˈseɪʃieɪt/   v. to satisfy

(= quench, glut, surfeit, sate)

After playing tennis in the sun for two hours, Frank drank two bottles of water to satiate his thirst.

땡볕에서 테니스를 두 시간 친 후에 프랭크는 갈증을 해소하기 위해 물을 두 병이나 마셨다.

☐ **compunction** /kəmˈpʌŋkʃn/   n. second thoughts, hesitation

(= self-reproof, self-reproach, remorse)

Without any compunction, Andy decided to accept the job offer from his current employer's major rival because he felt that he had been overworked and underpaid for long enough.

그가 너무 오랫동안 격무에 시달리며 봉급도 적게 받았다고 생각하기 때문에 앤디는 지금 고용주의 경쟁사인 회사에서 받은 이직 제안을 아무런 거리낌 없이 받아들이기로 했다.

□ **manifestation** /ˌmænɪfeˈsteɪʃn/   n. outward indication

(= sign, symptom, indication)

The low support ratings of the current President is a manifestation of people's dissatisfaction with the government.

현 정권에 대한 국민들의 불만이 대통령의 낮은 지지율로 표현된다.

□ **lethargic** /ləˈθɑːrdʒɪk/   adj. to be listless

(= sluggish, weary, lackluster)

After a hectic week at the office, Jim likes to take it easy on weekends, usually lying by a pool enjoying a lethargic afternoon reading a good book.

일주일간 사무실에서 격무에 시달린 후 짐은 주말에는 수영장 옆에 누워 좋은 책이나 읽으며 한가한 시간을 보내길 좋아한다.

□ **expectorate** /ɪkˈspektəreɪt/   v. to cough up and spit out

(= spit)

I'm sure if you stopped smoking, you would stop expectorating so such.

아마 네가 담배를 끊으면 침을 덜 뱉을 것이 확실해.

□ **cache** /kæʃ/   n. something hidden

(= store, reserve, hoard)

Some historians believe that somewhere in Germany there is a secret vault where the Nazis cached immense amounts of gold before the end of World War II.

어떤 역사학자들은 독일 어딘가에 나치들이 2차 대전이 끝나기 전에 엄청난 양의 금을 숨겨 놓은 비밀 금고가 있다고 믿는다.

□ **titular** /ˈtɪtʃələr/   adj. only in name

(= supposed, so-called)

You can say that Mr. Baxter is the CEO in titular form only: everyone knows that John Riddle, the Executive Director, makes all the important decisions of the company.

백스터 씨는 회사의 명목상의 대표이사일 뿐이다: 전무인 존 리들 씨가 회사의 중요한 결정을 내린다는 건 모든 직원이 아는 사실이다.

□ **modulate** /ˈmɑːdʒəleɪt/   v. to regulate or adjust

(= balance, tone, tune, harmonize)

The financial advisory board holds a senior meeting every month to modulate the government's fiscal policies with the economic status of the country.

금융감독위원회는 매달 고위급 회의를 열어 정부의 금융 정책과 국가의 경제적인 상황이 서로 조화롭도록 조정한다.

□ **equivocal** /ɪˈkwɪvəkl/   adj. of doubtful nature or character

(= ambiguous, uncertain, obscure, suspicious)

The professor gave a rather equivocal answer to Kevin's questions, so we had to stay behind after class to check if everyone understood his meaning in the same way.

교수님이 케빈의 질문에 다소 애매한 대답을 하여서 우리는 수업 후에 남아서 모든 사람이 같은 의미로 이해했는지 확인해야 했다.

□ **impend** /impénd/   v. to approach, to be imminent

(= approach, brew, loom)

Many scientists warn that trajedy impends if we do not deal with global warming now.

많은 과학자들이 우리가 지금 지구온난화를 해결하지 않으면 곧 재앙이 드리닥칠 것이라고 한다.

□ **affix** /əˈfɪks/   v. to attach to

(= attach, stick)

Norbert is waiting for his lawyers to affix the addendum to the contract before he signs it.

노버트는 그가 계약서에 서명하기 전에 그의 변호사들이 계약서에 부록을 첨가하기를 기다린다.

□ **hemorrhage** /ˈhemərɪdʒ/   n. a widespread loss (usually of blood)
(= bleeding)

Gary's father suffered from serious internal hemorrhage resulting from his car accident.

게리의 아버지는 자동차 사고로 야기된 심각한 내출혈로 고생하였다.

□ **fulsome** /ˈfʊlsəm/   adj. insincerely lavish

(= flattering, overgenerous)

The pretentiousness of the candidates was visible when they exchanged fulsome praises of each other after their televised debate.

출마후보들이 텔레비전에 중계되는 토론을 시작하기 전에 서로 본심 없는 덕담을 할 때 그들의 위선이 보였다.

□ **imbroglio** /ɪmˈbrəʊliəʊ/   n. a complicated or difficult situation

(= complication, complexity, quandary)

The imbroglio between the two countries over a territory dispute is over for now, but that doesn't mean the two countries will maintain stable relations soon.

그 두 나라 간의 영토분쟁으로 시작한 난국이 지금은 끝난 것 같아 보이나 앞으로 그들 간의 관계가 안정적일 거라는 뜻은 아니다.

□ **belie** /bɪˈlaɪ/   v. to show that something is a lie or false

(= contradict, disprove, expose, discredit)

The government's claim that the economy is recovering is belied by the high unemployment rate of young people in their twenties and thirties.

2-30대 젊은 층의 높은 실업률이 경제가 호전 중이라는 정부의 발표가 거짓이라는 걸 알려준다.

□ **defractor**   n. a person who disagrees

(= critic)

The President downplayed the oppositions criticism that his policies were regressive as the usual noise his defractors will make no matter what his actions are.

대통령은 그의 정책이 퇴행적이라는 야당의 비판을 그가 무슨 짓을 하건 무조건 반대하는 사람들이 항상 내는 소음이라고 묵살하였다.

□ **flotsam** /ˈflɑːtsəm/   n. floating pieces of stuff

(= debris, refuse, jetsam)

In the mornings, I rummaged through the flotsam on the beach hoping that I would find a message in a bottle.

아침이면 나는 밤새 바닷가에 떠내려온 부유물을 뒤지며 혹시 병 속에 편지가 있는지 살펴보았다.

□ **cogitate** /ˈkɑːdʒɪteɪt/   v. to think carefully about

(= deliberate, ponder, ruminate)

Having had a busy day at work, Harry returned home late in the evening and finally got a chance to sit down and cogitate about his problem.

바쁜 하루를 보낸 해리는 집에 늦게 도착해서야 마침내 그의 고민거리에 대해 곰곰히 생각해 볼 기회를 찾았다.

Practice 27.

Fill in the blank with the word that matches the definition provided

01 Jaime's hypocricy didn't fool me: I could see though his _____ (artificially lavish) congratulations.

02 The first job of the new finance director was to stop the _____ (widespread loss) of cash from the company.

03 Every month a new boy or girl band appears to _____ (satisfy) the global hunger for K-pop.

04 You forgot to _____ (attach) a stamp on the envelope.

05 The professor's _____ (ambiguous) answer to my question only deepened my confusion.

06 Some people are able to _____ (regulate) their voices according to the size of the room in which they speak.

07 He claims he is disposed to our purpose, but his actions _____ (shows something to be false) his claim.

08 The newly elected President will inherit a/an _____ (complicated situation) of domestic and foreign issues.

09 The police have found a/an _____ (something hidden) of automatic weapons in a house in the city centre.

10 Having drunk two glasses of wine at lunch, Bruno felt _____ (listless) and couldn't focus on his work.

11 I spent a few days _____ (thinking carefully) about the problem, but I can't think of any solution.

12 When the flood water receded, there were mountains of _____ (floating pieces of stuff) everywhere in the streets.

13 Mark opened Kevin's refrigerator and began eating out of it without showing any _____ (second-thoughts).

14 Mr. Williams and his son finally reconciled after years of _____ (the state of being unfriendly).

☐ **sierra** /siˈerə/   n. a chain of hills or mountains

(= mountain range)

The average summer temperature for August in this city is over 35 C, but if you travel a short 60 km north to the area just under the sierra, the temperature drops to the mid 25s.

이 도시의 평균 여름 온도는 35도 이상이지만, 북쪽의 산맥 아래로 60km만 이동하면 25도로 떨어진다.

☐ **pariah** /pəˈraɪə/   n. a person others generally despise or avoid

(= outcast, exile, outlaw)

Ever since I decided to stop smoking, most of my former smoking buddies have begun to treat me like a pariah.

내가 담배를 끊은 이후로 과거에 나랑 담배피던 친구들이 나를 왕따시킨다.

☐ **caricature** /ˈkærɪkətʃər/

v. to represent in an exaggerated and funny way

(= parody, mock)

The politician was caricatured as an indecisive amateur in the newspapers, but he was actually a deft tactician and adept decision maker.

그 정치가는 신문에서는 우유부단한 아마추어로 묘사가 되었지만, 사실은 노련한 전략가이자 숙달된 의사결정자이다.

☐ **mollify** /ˈmɑːlɪfaɪ/   v. to soothe or calm

(= placate, pacify, assuage)

No matter how hard she tried to apologize to her mother, Gloria could not mollify her distraught mother.

글로리아가 엄마에게 아무리 용서를 구해도 엄마의 심란한 마음을 달랠 수가 없었다.

☐ **pragmatic** /præɡˈmætɪk/   adj. to be practical and rational

(= utilitarian, sensible, realistic)

Modern politicians must understand that ideological bickering is useless and take a pragmatic approach to solving economic problems and fighting crime.

현대 정치인들은 경제 문제를 해결하고 범죄와 싸우는 데 이상주의적 말다툼은 아무런 도움이 안 되며 실용적인 접근을 해야 한다는 것을 알아야 한다.

☐ **abhor** /əbˈhɔːr/   v. to extremely dislike

(= detest, loath, dislike)

Two things that Yong doesn't like are Western food for breakfast and morning meetings, which means that he will abhor tomorrow's breakfast meeting at the Garden Café.

용이 싫어하는 두 가지는 아침식사로 서양음식을 먹는 것과 아침회의를 하는 것인데, 그렇다면 내일 아침 가든카페에서 진행하는 회의는 혐오할 것이다.

☐ **fumigate** /ˈfjuːmɪɡeɪt/   v. to sterilize with smoke

(= disinfect, cleanse, sterilize)

Our family had to evacuate the house so that exterminators could fumigate the cellar, kitchen and attic, which were infested with cockroaches.

해충퇴치자들이 바퀴벌레가 창궐하는 우리 창고, 부엌, 다락을 훈증 소독하는 동안 우리는 집을 비워야 했다.

☐ **vertigo** /ˈvɜːrtɪɡəʊ/   n. the state of being dizzy

(= dizziness, giddiness)

Bella's low blood pressure sometimes causes her to faint or suffer from vertigo.

벨라는 저혈압으로 가끔씩 혼절을 하거나 어지러움증을 느낀다.

☐ **felicity** /fəˈlɪsəti/   n. the state of being happy

(= ecstasy, bliss, blessedness, joy)

Howard thought he would be bored after he retired, but he has found felicity in a new hobby: carpentry.

하워드는 자신이 은퇴한 후 따분한 인생을 살 거라고 생각했는데 목공이라는 새로운 취미에서 행복을 찾았다.

☐ **efface** /ɪˈfeɪs/   v. to wipe out or do away with

(= eradicate, obliterate, delete, expunge)

Activists trying to eradicate poverty say that the world could entirely efface the hunger problem by employing just a fraction of what countries currently spend on military spending.

가난 퇴치 활동가들은 전 세계가 국방에 쓰는 예산의 아주 일부만 써도 전 세계에서 기아 문제를 해결할 수 있다고 말한다.

☐ **husbandry** /ˈhʌzbəndri/   n. farming

(= agriculture, crop growing)

Martin's family has been in animal husbandry for four generations. Martin is now one of the biggest suppliers of quality meat in all of London.

마틴의 집안은 4대째 목축업에 종사한다. 마틴은 이제 런던에서 가장 큰 품질육 공급자이다.

☐ **inundated** /ˈɪnʌndeɪt/   adj. to be flooded with

(= flooded, swamped, overwhelmed, engulfed)

The torrential rain was the worst in the last two decades, causing most homes in the area to be inundated before authorities could safely evacuate the people.

이십 년 만에 최악의 집중호우로 지역 관계자들이 사람들을 무사히 대피시키기도 전에 대부분의 집들이 물에 잠겼다.

☐ **charlatan** /ˈʃɑːrlətən/

n. someone who pretends to have more knowledge or expertise than he actually has

(= fraud, cheat, fake, quack)

When the soothsayer began to tell me things about me that no one else could ever know, I began to think that maybe she wasn't a charlatan but a genuine medium.

점쟁이가 나 말고는 아무도 알 수 없는 나에 대한 이야기를 하자, 나는 이 사람이 사기꾼이 아니고 정말로 영매일지도 모른다고 생각했다.

☐ **cultivate** /ˈkʌltɪveɪt/   v. to farm, to promote the growth of

(= grow, tend, farm, harvest)

Rice has been cultivated in this region for over 3,000 years.
쌀은 이 지역에서 3,000년 전부터 경작되었다.

☐ **animosity** /ˌænɪˈmɑːsəti/   n. the feeling of ill will

(= hostility, hatred, loathing)

Although the two finally managed to reconcile their differences, it is clear that they will never be friends: the scars from their mutual animosity are too deep.
두 사람은 마침내 화해한 듯 보였지만 그들은 절대로 친구가 되지는 않을 것이다: 서로 간의 적대감이 남긴 상처가 너무 깊었다.

☐ **incarcerate** /ɪnˈkɑːrsəreɪt/   v. to lock up

(= imprison, confine, restrain, immure)

One of the first actions of the new President was to grant an amnesty to political prisoners who were incarcerated for opposing the government in the past.
새로 선출된 대통령이 취임한 후 처음으로 한 행동 중 하나가 과거 정부에 대항하다가 투옥된 사람들을 사면시키는 것이었다.

☐ **vicarious** /vaɪˈkeriəs/   adj. indirect

(= indirect, substitute, surrogate)

Murray gets a vicarious thrill from asking George about his trips to exotic countries.
머레이는 조지에게 그의 이국적인 나라로의 여행에 대하여 물으며 간접적 희열을 느낀다.

☐ **jest** /dʒest/   v. to joke about

(= joke, banter, quip)

I don't believe that Steve would jest about something that serious.
스티브가 그렇게 심각한 내용에 대해 농담을 할 것 같지 않다.

☐ **erudite** /ˈerjədaɪt/   adj. knowledgeable in many fields

(= learned, knowledgeable, scholarly)

The internet has made available such knowledge that in the past was considered within the realm of only an erudite few.

과거엔 박학다식한 사람들만의 영역이었던 지식도 인터넷 덕분에 모든 사람이 나눌 수 있다.

....

☐ **coherent** /kəʊˈhɪrənt/   **adj. logically connected**

(= logical, rational, consistent)

Jack's essay writing style is usually more coherent than this one, which is a careless hodgepodge of inconclusive ramblings.

잭의 문장실력은 보통 밑도 끝도 없는 주절거림을 대강 모아놓은 것 같은 이것보다는 더 논리적이다.

Practice 28.

Fill in the blank with the word that matches the definition provided

01   When the dam broke, water _____ (flooded) the entire valley causing thousands of people to evacuate.

02   I dearly wish that I could _____ (wipe out) the negative memories I have of them.

03   Mrs. O'Keiff, who never had the opportunity to go to college, gets _____ (indirect) joy from asking her granddaughters about their experiences in college.

04   There was an _____ (ill will) between the two countries that went back hundreds of years.

05   I can't believe how, in this day and age, people still are still duped by _____ (frauds) who peddle vitamin tablets as magic elixers.

06   Mom was so upset that it was difficult to _____ (soothe) her.

07   Marilyn Monroe was unfairly _____ (represented in an exaggerated way) as a dumb blond in many movies, but in real life, she was very intelligent and savvy.

08   David was treated like a/an _____ (outcast) for a while by his family because they are deeply Jewish and he married a Catholic girl.

09   Howard was so exhausted that he suffered from _____ (dizziness).

10   When camping for extended periods, during which it is difficult to wash your clothes, you can _____ (sterilize with smoke) your clothes to keep them clean and devoid of unpleasant smells.

11 The reason Percy is such a good athlete is not only because he is physically fit, but also because he _____ (extremely dislikes) to lose.

12 I don't like idealistic people: I prefer _____ (practical) people.

13 After his wife passed away, Mr. Willard thought that he would never find _____ (happiness) in life again until he met Gale.

14 Some people called him a genius, but to me he hardly seemed capable of conducting a/an _____ (logically connected) conversation.

15 Talking with Professor Seth was never dull: he was always _____ (knowledeable in mant forms) and well-informed.

16 I do not _____ (joke) when talking about money.

☐ **proscribe** /prəʊˈskraɪb/　　　　v. to denounce or condemn

(= prohibit, ban, forbid, boycott)

Holland and Belgium are examples of countries where euthanasia is not legally proscribed.
네덜란드와 벨기에는 안락사가 법으로 금지되지 않은 나라다.

☐ **insurrection** /ˌɪnsəˈrekʃn/

n. revolt or resistance against established authority

(= rebellion, riot, coup, uprising)

Such an insurrection would not have been imaginable during his predecessor's time, but Douglas Wolfson was such a miserable leader that his junior officers had no alternative but to confront him directly.
이런 군란은 그의 전임자 시대에는 상상도 할 수 없는 일이었으나, 더글러스 울프슨은 너무나 형편없는 지도자라 그의 부하 장교들이 그를 직접 상대할 수밖에 없었다.

☐ **assuage** /əˈsweɪdʒ/　　　　v. to soothe or calm

(= relieve, ease, mollify, temper, alleviate)

Try as she did, Helen found it hard to assuage her anger at the man who robbed her store.
헬렌은 노력했지만 그녀의 상점을 절도한 남자를 향한 분노를 누그러뜨릴 수 없었다.

☐ **begrudge** /bɪˈɡrʌdʒ/　　　　v. to envy and regard with ill feeling

(= resent, envy)

It is strange that you begrudge his success when everyone knows he put in much more time and effort into his work than you ever did.
그가 당신보다 훨씬 많은 시간과 노력을 투자했다는 것은 누구나 다 아는 사실인데, 당신이 그의 성공을 시셈한다는 것은 매우 이상합니다.

☐ **rupture** /ˈrʌptʃər/   v. to break or burst

(= rift, disruption, schism, split)

Unbeknownst to the common employees, there was an irreconcilable rupture in the relationship between the company's management and its shareholders.

일반직원들은 알지 못했지만 회사의 경영진과 주주들 간의 관계가 고칠 수 없이 망가졌다.

☐ **sated** /ˈseɪtɪd/   adj. to be satisfied fully

(= satiated, satisfied)

I wasn't very hungry, so I felt sated after only a few bites.

나는 별로 배가 고프지 않았기 때문에, 두 입 먹고 배가 불렀다.

☐ **restraint** /rɪˈstreɪnt/   n. constraint in feelings or behavior
                                             v. to restrain

(= self-control, self-discipline)

When Dad came to the police station to fetch me after my friends and I were caught driving in a stolen car, I could tell that he was exercising super-human restraint trying to stay calm.

나와 내 친구들이 훔친 차를 타다가 경찰서에 잡혀 온 후 나를 데리러 경찰서에 오신 아버지를 보고는 그가 평정심을 유지하려고 초인적인 절제력을 발휘하고 계시다는 것을 알았다.

☐ **nauseate** /ˈnɔːzieɪt/   v. to cause to feel nausea

(= sicken, repulse, revolt)

During her entire trip to South Asia, Ana, who has a very weak stomach, was nauseated by the various smells of the local cuisine.

비위가 약한 안나는 남아시아를 여행할 때 지역의 여러 가지 음식 냄새를 역겨워 했다.

☐ **dilatory** /ˈdɪlətɔːri/   adj. slow in action

(= slow, slack, lagging)

Frank is always dilatory about doing his laundry: he will wait until he is down to his last garment before he goes to the Laundromat.

프랭크는 항상 빨래 하는 것에 게으르다: 그는 마지막 옷가지 하나가 남을 때까지 기다렸다가 빨래방에 간다.

□ **helix** /ˈhiːlɪks/   n. a spiral

(= spiral)

The mollusk shell was of the classic helix shape.

그 고둥의 껍질은 전형적인 나선형이다.

□ **stench** /stentʃ/   n. a bad smell

(= stink, smell, stench)

The new tennis court built over the old garbage dump is very nice, but on damp summer days you can still smell a stench emanating from the area.

전에 있던 쓰레기 처리장 위에 지어진 테니스 코트는 매우 좋았으나 습기찬 여름날에는 그 주변에서 쓰레기 악취가 아직도 난다.

□ **benefactor** /ˈbenɪfæktər/

n. a person who extends a benefit to someone else

(= supporter, champion, sponsor)

The hospital operates with funds donated to it by various benefators.

그 병원은 다수의 후원자들의 기부금으로 운영된다.

□ **collaboration** /kəˌlæbəˈreɪʃn/   n. the act or process of working together

(= teamwork, cooperation, partnership)

The finished product of this ensemble's collaboration decidedly exceeds anything that anyone could have achieved individually.

저 모임이 협력해서 얻은 결과물이 한 사람이 혼자서 이룰 수 있는 그 어떤 결과물보다 훌륭했다.

□ **adjacent** /əˈdʒeɪsnt/   adj. located next to

(= adjoining, neighboring, flanking)

Seth was surprised to learn that his room mate and he had actually lived in adjacent apartments years ago when they were toddlers.

세스는 과거에 그와 그의 룸메이트가 유아들이었을 때 서로 옆 아파트에 살았다는 것을 알고는 매우 놀랐다.

☐ **foreboding** /fɔːrˈboʊdɪŋ/

n. a feeling that something bad is going to happen

(= apprehension, premonition)

One look at her grim face and I realized that my dark forebodings had been correct.

그녀의 어두운 얼굴을 보고 나는 나의 불길한 예감이 맞았다는 걸 알았다.

☐ **sordid** /ˈsɔːrdɪd/　　　　adj. very dirty

(= base, degraded, shameful, low)

Sam refused to let his mother wash his jacket even though it was clearly too sordid to wear to school.

샘은 그의 자켓이 학교에 입고 갈 수 없을 정도로 더러움에도 불구하고 엄마가 그 자켓을 빨지 못하게 했다.

☐ **desolate** /ˈdesələt/　　　　adj. barren and devastated

(= bleak, uninhabited, wild, deserted)

The prisoners were transported to a desolate, uninhabitable piece of frozen land devoid of signs of civilization above the arctic circle.

재소자들은 북극한계선 너머 문명의 흔적이라고는 찾아볼 수 없는 황량하고 아무도 살지 않는 동토로 옮겨졌다.

☐ **bustling** /ˈbʌslɪŋ/　　　　adj. teeming with movement

(= busy, active, lively)

Stanley Park is located just minutes away from Vancouver's bustling downtown and is a place where people can enjoy nature's serenity to the fullest.

스탠리 파크는 밴쿠버의 부산한 시내에서 불과 몇 분 떨어져 있지만 시민들이 자연의 평화로움을 즐기기 아주 좋은 장소다.

☐ **protégé** /ˈproʊtəʒeɪ/

n. a person under the patronage of someone else who's interested in this person's career.

(= charge, responsibility)

She displayed such advanced virtuosity for someone her age that, as soon as she entered the conservatoire, she was taken in as the protégé of the great cellist, Arnold Grussardi.

그녀는 그 나이에 맞지 않을 정도의 너무나 앞선 연주기량을 보여서 음악학교에 입학한 후 바로 첼로 거장인 아놀드 그루사르디의 문하생이 되었다.

☐ **decadence**/ˈdekədəns/   n. unrestrained or excessive self–indulgence
(= degeneration, corruption)

Gabrielle decided to indulge in a last night of decadence before going on a diet; she ordered the most rich and sweet desert on the menu.

가브리엘라는 다이어트를 시작하기 전에 하룻밤만 더 타락하기로 했다; 그녀는 메뉴에서 가장 크림이 풍부하고 달콤한 디저트를 시켰다.

01 The government has been criticized for being _____ (slow in action) in dealing with the problem of unemployment.

02 I couldn't fall asleep because of the guy practicing his clarinet in the _____ (located next to) room.

03 Since the unfortunate event, the relationship between the two families has _____ (broken).

04 Though Greg was the older brother, he never _____ (regarded with ill feeling) his younger brother Henry's success.

05 When dad was in such a mood, it took days for mom and us to _____ (soothe) his anger.

06 The newly enacted law _____ (prohibits) smoking in all public areas.

07 I am usually not squeamish about eating exotic foods, but the thought of eating insects _____ (sickened) me.

08 By the 8th century AD, the Roman Empire had fallen into such a state of _____ (unrestrained self-indulgence) that it was doomed to collapse.

09 The _____ (bad smell) of mold and funghi hit our nostrils as soon as we entered the basement.

10 During the debate, Jake showed admirable _____ (self-control) and would not be provoked by his opponent's inflammatory language.

11 After such a big lunch, I was so _____ (satisfied fully) that I had to skip dinner.

12 By 1921, Stalin had firmly positioned himself as _____ (person under patronage) and likely successor of Vladimir Lenin.

13 The café, which was usually quiet at this time of the day, was _____ (teeming) with customers.

14 The Arizona Dessert seems _____ (barren) at first, but when you look closely, it actually teems with life.

15 The cleaning staff was surprised at how _____ (dirty) the hotel rooms were after the students checked out.

16 I don't know why, but thoughts about starting my own business fills me with _____. (feeling that something bad is going to happen)

Find the most suitable word from the box that fits in the sentence

> doctrinaire, decadence, mollify, benefactor, begrudge, diatribe, incarcerate, collaboration, belie, preside, erudite, abhor, efface, burgeon

01 The newly elected President promised that he would _____ government corruption once and for all.

02 Mr. Gaiman is fiercely protective of his privacy: he _____ being asked about his private life.

03 Mrs. Heller was so distraught that I couldn't _____ her no matter how I tried.

04 The business was kicked off thanks to a sizeable loan from a generous _____ - namely, my dad.

05 Kelly _____ Paul for not acknowledging her contribution in the editing and proofreading of his book.

06 When Mr. Wilson talks to his teenage son, he tries hard not to sound _____.

07 With our budget, the ultimate level of _____ was to share one bowl of chocolate ice cream.

08 Albert Einstein was not only brilliant in science, but he was _____ in music, history and politics also.

09   Mr. Bellows was conscripted at the beginning of the war, taken hostage during his first engagement with the enemy and _____ (imprisoned) for the entire duration of the war.

10   The opposition party leaders all launched bitter _____ against the President, accusing him of lying.

11   He feigned ignorance of the subject, but his acute questions _____ a deep knowledge of it.

12   There is no one else but you, who can _____ over the next meeting.

13   The population of the city has _____ by three fold in the last 20 years.

14   The two economists worked in close _____ in putting together this study.

inundate, husbandry, desolate, decimate, expunge, accost, sierra, consternation, foreboding, guile, flout, equanimity, assuage, neologism

15   I wish I could just _____ every memory I have of him from my mind.

16   I felt awkward _____ strangers and asking them questions, but unfortunately it was part of my job.

17   While on my way to Phoenix, Arizona, the view of the _____ from the train was spectacular.

18   The fact that his decision affected the lives of thousands of people caused him great _____.

19   Walruses were once abundant in nature, but unmitigated hunting up to the late 19th century _____ them to the brink of extinction.

20 If not by my intelligence, then by my _____, I will get the job done.

21 Henry nonchalantly _____ the stops sign and crossed the road.

22 The opposing team was much stronger and more experienced than us, so everyone accepted our defeat with _____.

23 Having left the business more than a decade ago, Mr. Bailey did not understand many of the _____ that were used.

24 The once bustling mining town was now empty and _____.

25 The eerie music filled the listeners with a sense of _____.

26 The water pipes ruptured, causing water to _____ our basement.

27 Local farmers have expanded into _____ of value-added crops such as ginseng and mulberry trees.

28 After dad died, I called my mom every other day trying to _____ her loneliness.

cache, fiasco, satiate, estrangement, imbroglio, expectorate, fulsome, archaic, titular, immure, affix, animosity, stature, pestilence

29 Don't forget to _____ the addendum to the main contract.

30 Queen Elizabeth II is the _____ head of state of Canada, Australia and New Zealand.

31 I found a/an _____ of old comic books that I had hidden in the attic when I was 12 and forgotten about.

32 When the lead ballerina hurt her ankle only two weeks before opening night, many of the organizers worried that the ballet might become a/an _____.

33 The two men met and reconciled their differences, forgetting all past _____.

34 When the current President first took office, he inherited perhaps the worst financial _____ in history.

35 He is such a hypocrite – with his patronizing smiles and _____ praises of others.

36 I have a very sore throat: it hurts when I swallow, and I _____ mucus.

37 Drinking sugary sodas will not _____ your thirst – it will only make it worse.

38 After Christian's parents divorced, they remained in _____ for years.

39 For a man of Warren Buffet's _____, he lives an incredibly austere life.

40 Even in this modern age, some areas of the world are still regularly ravaged by famine and _____.

41 The idea that women are weaker than men is now _____.

42 Peter sat in the empty classroom, _____ in his own thoughts.

Circle the word that is not a synonym

43 diatribe – cohort – entourage

44 adulation – admiration – vindication

45 buffoonery – scatterbrain – silliness

46 equanimity – aplomb – benediction

47 ethereal – frail – pristine

48   swoon – lisp – faint

49   protégé – specialist – connoisseur

50   amnesty – mercy – pageant

51   unsympathetic – conducive – callous

52   flurry – stench – disquiet

53   labyrinth – circumlocution – euphemism

54   plenipotentiary – infinitesimal – minute

55   hubbub – fuss – hoard

56   meticulous – fastidious – utilitarian

57   manifestation – proliferation – indication

58   equivocal – ambiguous – adjacent

59   adamant – subservient – compliant

60   substantiate – authenticate – expectorate

61   flotsam – debris – mural

62   bust – pariah – failure

63   fumigate – perturb – disinfect

64   vertigo – panacea – dizziness

65   subversive – vicarious – surrogate

Class 31

☐ **formative** /ˈfɔːrmətɪv/   adj. giving form

(= determining, influential, seminal)

While others her age spent their formative years attending slumber parties and braiding pony tales, Samantha spent her time at her Dad's motor shop learning how to do oil changes and engine tune ups.

그 또래의 다른 여자 아이들이 가치관이 형성되는 나이에 친구집에 가서 밤샘 파티나 하고 서로 머리나 땋아 주고 할 때, 사만다는 아빠의 정비소에서 오일 교환과 엔진 튠업 작업을 배웠다.

☐ **ignoble** /ɪgˈnəʊbl/   adj. dishonorable

(= dishonorable, base, mean, infamous)

A gentleman does not involve himself in ignoble practices.

신사는 비열한 행동에 관여하지 않는다.

☐ **dichotomy** /daɪˈkɑːtəmi/   n. division into two parts

(= division, split, separation, polarity)

Some people say that dividing the political orientation of Americans between Republicans and Democrats is a dichotomy too simple to be valid.

어떤 사람들은 미국의 정치적 성향을 단지 공화당과 민주당으로 나누는 것은 너무 단순한 이분법이라고 한다.

☐ **tantamount** /ˈtæntəmaʊnt/

adj. equivalent in value, amount force, or significance

(= equivalent, equal, same, synonymous)

The state government's decision to reduce the budget for school cafeteria services is tantamount to allowing certain students from poor families to starve.

학교 급식 예산을 줄이겠다는 주정부의 결정은 마치 저소득 가정의 아이들이 굶도록 놔두는 것과 같다.

□ **evict** /ɪˈvɪkt/   v. to expel (a tenant) from a property

(= expel, remove, eject)

The nice thing about having your own parents as your landlords is that they will never evict you no matter how late your rent check is.

부모를 집주인으로 두어서 좋은 점은 집세를 아무리 늦게 내도 집에서 내쫓지 않는 것이다.

□ **spate** /speɪt/   n. a sudden outpouring

(= flood, torrent)

The President's approval rate has decreased significantly as a result of the recent spate of political scandals involving members of the government.

최근 일어난 정부관료와 관련된 몇 차례의 스캔들로 인해 대통령의 지지율이 급락했다.

□ **distraught** /dɪˈstrɔːt/   adj. deeply bothered

(= frantic, wild, desperate, hysterical)

When Jamie didn't return home by midnight, his mother was so distraught that she couldn't sit still.

제이미가 자정이 되도록 집에 오지 않자 그녀의 어머니는 불안감에 가만히 앉아있지를 못했다.

□ **ogle** /ˈoʊɡl/   v. to stare at with greed

(= gaze, stare, leer)

Whenever John walks by a motorcycle dealership, he ogles at the motorcycles.

존은 모터사이클 대리점을 지나칠 때마다 욕심 가득한 눈으로 모터사이클을 쳐다본다.

□ **kowtow** /ˌkaʊˈtaʊ/   v. to be overly servile

(= grovel, bow, kneel)

Richard thinks I should kowtow to him just because his father is on the Board of Directors of my firm.

짐은 자기의 아버지가 우리회사 이사회 멤버라는 이유로 내가 그에게 굽신거려야 한다고 생각한다.

□ **hale** /heɪl/   adj. in good health

(= healthy, robust, vigorous, sound)

Kenneth Jackson, who turned 96 last Friday, says that while he can no longer swim across Kelly Lake, he is still hale and hearty enough to swim 20 laps in his pool every morning.

지난 금요일 96세가 된 케네스 잭슨은 더 이상 켈리호수를 가로질러 수영하지는 못하지만 아직도 아침마다 수영장을 20회 왕복할 정도로 건강하다.

☐ **antagonism** /ænˈtægənɪzəm/　　　n. feeling of dislike

(= hostility, enmity)

The two parties decided to put aside their past antagonisms and work together.

두 당이 과거의 적대감을 버리고 협력하기로 했다.

☐ **malleable** /ˈmæliəbl/　　　adj. easily changing shape, easily influenced

(= impressionable, tractable, pliable)

After fifteen years in the business, Norman is far from the naïve and malleable intern he was when I first met him.

업계에 15년 종사한 노먼은 더 이상 내가 처음 만났을 때의 그 순진하고 귀가 얇은 사람이 아니었다.

☐ **circuitous** /sərˈkjuːɪtəs/　　　adj. indirect

(= indirect, roundabout, meandering)

Andy took a circuitous path home because he didn't want to confront his mother who knew about his exam results.

앤디는 자기 시험성적을 아는 어머니와 마주치기 싫어서 다른 길로 빙 돌아서 집으로 왔다.

☐ **slight** /slaɪt/　　　n. insult

(= snub, affront)

Although Professor Chang's simple query was intended merely to gain more information, the student took it as a slight to her intelligence.

장 교수님의 질문은 단순히 더 많은 정보를 얻고 싶어서 한 것이었는데 왜 그런지 학생은 자신의 지능에 대한 모욕으로 받아들였다.

☐ **gibe** /dʒaɪb/　　　n. mocking words

(= jeer, scoff)

When she was young, Gloria's abnormally long limbs earned her the continuous gibes from

her friends, who used to call her "spider monkey".

글로리아는 어렸을 때 비정상적으로 긴 팔을 가졌다는 이유로 친구들에게 계속해서 "거미 원숭이"라는 놀림을 받았다.

☐ **odious** /ˈəʊdiəs/   adj. causing hatred

(= loathsome, abhorrent, hateful)

Nothing would repulse her more than to see her abductor's odious face again.

그녀를 납치한 사람의 경멸스런 얼굴을 다시 보는 것처럼 그녀에게 혐오감을 주는 일은 없을 것이다.

☐ **discomfit** /dɪsˈkʌmfɪt/   v. to frustrate the plans of

(= mortify, humiliate)

The new coach employed strategies that at first quite discomfited the players.

새로운 코치가 처음에는 선수들을 매우 혼란스럽게 만든 전략을 도입하였다.

☐ **moniker** /ˈmɑːnɪkər/   n. a nickname

(= nickname, alias)

He was such a curmudgeonly fellow that his colleagues hung on him the moniker "the Scroogenator."

그는 얼마나 구두쇠 같은 사람이었는지 동료들이 그에게 "스크루지네이터"라는 별명을 지어 줬다.

☐ **umbrage** /ˈʌmbrɪdʒ/   n. offense or displeasure

(= offense, resentment)

I posed my question out of pure curiosity, but for some reason she took umbrage and walked away without answering.

나는 정말로 궁금해서 질문을 한 것이었는데, 그녀는 왠지 모욕감을 느낀듯 대답도 안하고 가버렸다.

☐ **tirade** /ˈtaɪreɪd/   n. a long outburst of criticism

(= outburst, diatribe, harangue, lecture)

My handing in my report just thirty minutes late was enough to trigger the teaching assistant to launch into a long tirade about the necessity to abide by rules.

내가 과제물을 단지 30분 늦게 제출한 것이 조교가 규칙을 준수해야 하는 이유에 대해 일장연설을 하게끔 만들기에 충분했다.

Practice 31.

Fill in the blank with the word that matches the definition provided

01 Thanks to Martin's humorous _____ (mockings), the awkward meeting atmosphere turned quite genial.

02 When they were young, Norman took advantage of his _____ (easily influenced) sister and got her in trouble all the time.

03 It is difficult to understand the younger generation's _____ (feeling of dislike) towards the older generation these days.

04 After spending a month in the country, I am _____ (in good health) and hearty again.

05 Nick needed to borrow Sally's class notes, so he _____ (was overly servile) to her for days until she lent them to him.

06 Gertie was _____ (deeply disturbed) when she heard that it would rain during the entire duration of her vacation.

07 The sudden _____ (sudden outpouring) of earthquakes in the area made many feel unsafe.

08 The suspicious looking man seemed to hide a dark and _____ (dishonorable) secret.

09 Don't be surprised at the _____ (division into two parts) between what politicians say and what they do.

10 Sam was exposed to all kinds of music in his _____ (determining) years: from Bach to B1A4.

11   Liam finished his hamburger but was still hungry, so he _____ (stare wish greed) at Sheila's French fries.

12   The media launched _____ (long criticisms) against the two major political parties for failing to find a compromise.

13   Millie took _____ (offense) at Bart's intimation that she cheated during the exam.

14   When Milton was in highschool, he was so skinny that he earned the _____ (nickname) "toothpick."

15   The reporter's tricky question about the candidate's finances _____ (confused and embarrassed) him.

16   My first task at my new job was the _____ (causing hatred) one of firing 40 redundant employees.

Class 32

☐ **languish** /ˈlæŋgwɪʃ/   v. to become weak or feeble

(= weaken, fade, suffer, deteriorate)

It is interesting to see that car-sharing is booming while car sales languish.

카 셰어링은 점점 인기가 많아지는데 자동차 판매량은 시들한 것이 흥미롭다.

☐ **impotent** /ˈɪmpətənt/   adj. lacking power

(= powerless, helpless, weak, incapable)

Without the support of the board of directors, the CEO will be impotent to implement any of the policies he views as necessary for the company.

이사회의 지지 없이 대표이사는 그가 회사에 필요하다고 생각하는 정책을 도입할 힘이 없을 것이다.

☐ **lucrative** /ˈluːkrətɪv/   adj. money making

(= profitable, rewarding, fruitful, money-making)

Although Jim's last two business ventures were quite successful, none were as lucrative for him as this one.

짐의 지난 두 번의 사업은 꽤나 성공적이었지만 이번 사업만큼 큰 돈을 버는 사업은 처음이다.

☐ **insurgence** /ɪnsə́ːrdʒəns/   n. an act of revolt

(= rebellion, revolution, resistance, insurrection)

The rebels set up their base camp and began to secretly recruit new troops and prepare for a military insurgence.

반군이 그들의 본부를 설립하고 비밀리에 새로운 병사를 모아 군사반란을 준비했다.

☐ **repute** /rɪˈpjuːt/   n. reputation

(= reputation, standing, fame, distinction)

The journalist's biting commentaries criticizing the waywardness of U.S. foreign policy have earned him quite a repute.

미국의 외교정책의 방향성 결여를 비판한 그의 논평 덕분에 그 기자는 꽤나 명성을 얻었다.

☐ **cloy** /klɔɪ/

v. to become uninteresting through over abundance

(= sicken, disgust, weary)

Initially the local food was delicious, but soon the sweet seasonings began to cloy.

처음에는 현지 음식이 매우 맛있었으나, 자꾸 먹다보니 단맛 나는 양념이 질리기 시작했다.

☐ **rotatory** /róutətɔ́:ri/   adj. spinning

(= pivoting, turning)

The vultures were flying in a rotatory formation, which means they have spotted a dying animal.

독수리들이 빙빙돌며 날기 시작했다. 이것은 그들이 죽어가는 동물을 발견했다는 말이다.

☐ **reek** /ri:k/   v. to emit a bad smell

(= stink, smell, stench)

Seven days after the forest fire was finally put out, the area still reeked of smoke.

산불이 진화된 지 7일이 지났음에도 그 지역에서는 아직도 연기 냄새가 진동했다.

☐ **pedagogic** /ˌpedəˈgɑːdʒɪk/   adj. related to teaching

(= teaching, educational)

At first, the parents were worried of Mr. Rand's unconventional pedagogic skills, but they soon realized that their children were not only enjoying his classes but also learning much from him.

처음에는 란드 선생님의 일반적이지 않은 교습법을 부모님들이 걱정했지만, 곧 아이들이 그의 수업을 좋아할 뿐 아니라 매우 많은 것을 배우고 있다는 것 깨달았다.

☐ **juxtapose** /ˌdʒʌkstəˈpəʊz/   v. to place together side by side

(= adjacent, near, proximate)

The jeweler explained to be me that, although both diamonds were the same size, when juxtaposed in the light, one was clearly brighter than the other.

보석상은 내게, 두 개의 다이아몬드가 크기는 같지만, 서로 병치해서 보면 하나가 다른 것보다 명확하게 더 영롱하다고 설명했다.

☐ **dilettante** /ˌdɪləˈtænti/

n. a person who takes up art or activity for amusement

(= amateur, dabbler)

It's difficult to take his interest in art seriously as he is viewed as a dilettante who suddenly decided to patronize a few minor artists with his new found fortune.

갑자기 떼돈을 벌어 몇 명의 덜 알려진 예술가를 후원하는 그의 예술에 대한 관심을 심각하게 받아들이기가 힘들고 그냥 호사가처럼 보이기만 한다.

☐ **commission** /kəˈmɪʃn/   v. to give an order or official request for

(= appoint, order, contract)

The first thing the dictator did when he seized power was to commission a portrait of himself and ordered to have copies of it hung in every government office and school classroom.

독재자가 정권을 잡은 후 한 최초의 행동이 그의 초상화를 주문해서 모든 정부기관 사무실과 학교교실에 걸도록 하는 것이었다.

☐ **aplomb** /əˈplɑːm/   n. unshakable calmness

(= assurance, composure, self-confidence)

It is during times when others crumble under intense pressure that Nicholas will show the coolest aplomb.

다른 사람들은 압박감에 포기할 때 니콜라스는 아주 냉철한 침착함을 보인다.

☐ **fusillade** /ˈfjuːsəlɑːd/   n. a continuous discharge of fire arms

(= barrage, bombardment)

The movie received a fusillade of favorable reviews from critics and viewers upon its release as a modern day masterpiece.

그 영화는 비평가 및 관객에게 현대 걸작이라고 호평의 집중포화를 맞았다.

□ **obtrusive** /əbˈtruːsɪv/   adj. thrusting forth

(= blatant, flashy, garish)

Please inform Robert that if he regards my presence at the dinner as obtrusive, I would gladly spend my evening somewhere else.

로버트에게 혹시라도 그가 나의 참석이 방해된다고 생각한다면 저는 기꺼이 다른 곳에서 저녁시간을 보내겠다고 전해 주세요.

□ **singe** /sɪndʒ/   v. to burn slightly

(= burn, seer, scorch, blacken)

Everyone laughed when Glenn singed his hair while trying to light a cigarette by the flames from the barbecue pit.

글렌이 바비큐 불에 담뱃불을 붙이다가 머리카락을 태우자 모든 사람이 웃었다.

□ **impugn** /ɪmˈpjuːn/   v. to cast doubt upon

(= charge, accuse, censure)

I must impugn your motives for suddenly offering your friendship, as everyone knows that you and I have never been close.

모든 사람이 당신과 내가 친한 적이 없다는 걸 다 아는데, 갑자기 우정을 권유하는 당신의 저의를 의심할 수밖에 없습니다.

□ **persevere** /ˌpɜːrsəˈvɪr/   v. persist continuously

(= continue, persist, endure)

Despite of the insurmountable obstacles, he persevered up to the last moment and prevailed.

극복하기 힘들어 보이던 장애물에도 불구하고 그는 끝까지 노력해서 성공하였다.

□ **atrocity** /əˈtrɑːsəti/   n. act of extreme cruelty

(= crime, horror, offence, cruelty, brutality)

At the cite of the former Auschwitz Concentration Camp now stands the Auschwitz-Birkenau State Museum, erected as a reminder to posterity of the atrocities that happened there during World War II.

과거 아우슈비츠 수용소가 서 있던 자리에 지금은 제2차 세계대전 중 일어난 잔혹행위를 후세에 알리고자 세워진 아우슈비츠–비르케나우 국가박물관이 서 있다.

☐ **grapple** /ˈɡræpl/   v. to seize in a tight grip

(= deal, tackle, engage)

To everyone's surprise, George grappled with the man holding a gun to the ground.
모든 사람이 조지가 총을 들고 있던 사람을 몸싸움 끝에 바닥으로 쓰러뜨린 것을 보고는 놀랐다.

☐ **brave** /breɪv/   v. to challenge or defy

(= defy, confront, challenge)

We braved through the winter storm for two hours trying to find a motel to spend the night.
한 겨울 폭풍을 두 시간 동안 뚫고 다니며 저녁에 묵을 수 있는 모텔을 찾았다.

01 Kyle's hairstyle and color of clothes were rather _____ (thrusting forth) for the solemn occasion.

02 As soon as my presentation was over, I was faced with a/an _____ (bombardment) of questions.

03 Many people found it hard not to _____ (cast doubt upon) the politician's motives.

04 Remember just to _____ (slightly burn) the meat: don't cook it through.

05 The artist's technique is to _____ (place side by side) bright colors to give a dramatic effect.

06 No matter how hard I tried, my brain could not _____ (seize in a tight grip) the concept of Quantum Physics.

07 The kitchen _____ (emitted a bad smell) of the smell of garlic.

08 The television series was very popular, but soon the use of excessive violence and gore began to _____ (become uninteresting through abundance).

09 Andy's computer gaming skills earned him quite a/an _____ (fame) in school.

10 As a lawyer specialized in environmental cases Rebecca Rolling earned a/an _____ (money making) living suing companies that pollute.

11 Minorities are no longer _____ (lacking power) against oppressions of the ruling classes.

12 We cannot expect _____ (related to teaching) methods developed in the 1970s to still be relevent in the 2010s.

13 Chris performs his hectic tasks with _____ (extreme calmness).

14 The young sculptor got his big break when the city government _____ (gave an official request) him for a new sculpture for the new cityhall building.

15 He says that once an artist acquires material wealth, he is no longer an artist but a/an _____ (someone who does art for amusement)

16 Thousands of people _____ (challenge or defy) the weather to watch the foot ball game live.

□ **bifurcated** /ˈbaɪfərkeɪt/   adj. divided into two parts

(= divided)

The domestic market is more or less bifurcated between two companies, who have almost equal market share.

국내시장은 시장점유율이 비슷한 두 개의 기업에 의해 양분된다.

□ **domicile** /ˈdɑːmɪsaɪl/   n. a place where one lives

(= dwelling, residence, abode, habitation)

Have you changed your domicile recently? The address you've given us doesn't match with our records.

혹시 최근에 이사하셨나요? 당신이 주신 주소가 우리 기록과 일치하지 않습니다.

□ **paraphernalia** /ˌpærəfərˈneɪliə/   n. equipment used for a particular activity

(= equipment, accoutrements)

Howard came to the party dressed as a Crusader decked in medieval military paraphernalia - his head and upper body covered in chainmail, and arms carrying a sword and shield.

하워드는 파티에 십자군 군인의 복장을 입고 장식을 온 몸에 휘감고 왔다 – 그의 머리와 상체는 쇠사슬로 만들어진 갑옷으로 덮여 있었고, 손에는 칼과 방패가 쥐어져 있었다.

□ **oust** /aʊst/   v. to kick out

(= expel, dismiss, exclude, exile, topple)

During the Soviet Era, those who reached the position of General Secretary of the Communist Party served at the post until their natural deaths, except for Nikita Khrushchev, whose political rivals ousted and placed him under house arrest.

소비에트 연방 시대에 공산당 서기장의 위치까지 오른 사람은 자연사할 때까지 그 직책을 유지하는 것이 일반적이었으나, 니키타 흐루시체프는 그의 정적에 의해 강제로 퇴위를 당하고 가택연금 당했다.

☐ **deluge** /ˈdeljuːdʒ/   v. to flood with

(= flood, inundate)

As soon as the personnel ad was posted in the local newspaper, the company was deluged with calls from hopeful applicants.

구인광고가 지역 신문에 개제되자마자 그 회사엔 지원을 희망하는 사람들의 문의전화가 홍수처럼 밀려왔다.

☐ **destitute** /ˈdestɪtuːt/   adj. extremely poor

(= impoverished, penniless)

Mark's father died when Mark was 14, and since then he has been responsible for feeding his destitute family.

마크는 14살 때 아버지를 여읜 후부터 그의 빈곤한 가족을 먹여 살리는 책임을 졌다.

☐ **taunt** /tɔːnt/   v. to provoke in a mocking way

(= insult, gibe, sneer)

When Sam was in grade 5, other kids taunted him for being the smallest in class. Now, in grade 11, he is the tallest kid in his class.

쌤이 5학년이었을 때 반에서 키가 가장 작다고 놀림을 받았다. 지금 11학년에서 그는 반에서 제일 키가 크다.

☐ **indolent** /ˈɪndələnt/   adj. lazy and unmotivated

(= lazy, idle, sluggish)

My boss warned me that although I am quite clever, I am indolent.

우리 상관은 내가 영리하긴 하나 좀 게으르다고 경고했다.

☐ **broach** /brəʊtʃ/   v. to mention or suggest

(= mention, bring up)

It pained him to have to ask his father for a loan because financial matters were a difficult subject for him to broach to someone in his family.

그는 아버지에게 돈을 꿔달라는 이야기를 꺼내기가 괴로웠다. 왜냐하면 가족 간에도 돈 얘기를 꺼내는 건 어려운 일이기 때문이다.

☐ **chagrin** /ʃəˈgrɪn/   n. a feeling of extreme disappointment

(= mortification, disappointment, annoyance, displeasure)

Much to Malcolm's chagrin, Sherry, whom he had a secret crush on, announced she would spend a year in Australia as an exchange student.

그에게 매우 실망스럽게도, 그가 몰래 좋아했던 셰리가 일년간 호주로 교환학생으로 간다고 발표했다.

☐ **syndicate** /ˈsɪndɪkət/   v. to publish simultaneously

(= network, distribute)

At its peak, the Peanuts cartoon was syndicated to over 2,600 newspapers around the world, with a readership of over 750 million and was translated into 21 different languages.

전성기 때 피너츠 만화는 전 세계에 동시에 2,600개의 신문사에 7억 5천만 명의 독자를 가지고 무려 21개 국어로 번역되어 출판되었다.

☐ **culprit** /ˈkʌlprɪt/   n. someone who is guilty of an offense

(= offender, criminal, villain)

The police found the vehicle that the culprit used to escape the crime scene abandoned in an empty car park in a town 80 miles away.

경찰은 범인이 범죄현장에서 도주할 때 탔던 자동차를 80마일 떨어진 도시의 한 주차장에 버려진 상태로 발견하였다.

☐ **reprieve** /rɪˈpriːv/   n. temporary relief

(= pardon, remission, deferment)

With Murray trailing Nadal by two sets, the match was halted due to inclement weather, but for Murray this reprieve proved to be only temporary, as he lost the match within twenty minutes after it had renewed.

머레이가 나달에게 두 세트를 지는 상황에서 테니스 경기는 날씨관계로 지연이 되었으나 머레이에게 이것은 잠시의 구제였다. 왜냐하면 경기가 재개된 후 20분 만에 그가 패배했기 때문이다.

☐ **iconoclast** /aɪˈkɑːnəklæst/   n. a person who rebels against tradition

(= rebel, radical, dissident)

Known as an iconoclast, the architect was famous for designing buildings that looked like upside down beehives.

형식파괴자로 알려진 그 건축가는 마치 뒤집어진 벌집 모양의 건물을 설계하는 것으로 유명했다.

☐ **catharsis** /kəˈθɑːrsɪs/   n. purification of emotions

(= release, cleansing, purging, purification)

I don't know why, but whenever I do badly at an exam, eating a giant meatball sandwich provides a means of catharsis for me.

왜 그런지 모르지만 나는 시험을 망쳤을 때 거대한 미트볼 샌드위치를 먹으면 감정이 정화되는 것을 느낀다.

☐ **aversion** /əˈvɜːrʒn/   n. a strong feeling of dislike

(= repugnance, loathing)

Jake doesn't like heavy rock music; he has an aversion to loud noises.

제이크는 시끄러운 락 음악을 싫어한다; 그는 시끄러운 소리에 거부감이 있다.

☐ **ludicrous** /ˈluːdɪkrəs/   adj. causing ridicule

(= ridiculous, preposterous, incongruous)

In the late 70s, there was a myth that Brazilian killer bees would infest the United States by the 90s, but this turned out to be ludicrous paranoia.

70년대 후반에, 브라질산 살인벌이 90년대 쯤이 되면 미국까지 퍼져 창궐할 거라는 근거없는 믿음이 있었는데, 그것은 단지 바보 같은 피해망상으로 판결났다.

☐ **specimen** /ˈspesɪmən/   n. a sample of a substance

(= sample, example, model)

The scientists who surveyed the remote parts of the jungle brought back many specimens of new flora and fauna.

정글 일대를 수색한 과학자들이 많은 종류의 식물과 동물의 표본을 가져왔다.

☐ **vignette** /vɪnˈjet/   n. a short essay or sketch

(= segment, section)

The movie consisted of several vignettes portraying the everyday life of a typical Victorian family.

영화는 전형적인 빅토리아 시대의 가족에 대한 단막극으로 구성되어 있었다.

....

☐ **timid** /ˈtɪmɪd/　　　　　　　　　adj. lacking in self-assurance

(= shy, fearful, timorous, apprehensive)

In the beginning of his presentation, Luther was vividly timid, but as time went by, he recovered his confidence.

프리젠테이션 초기에 루터는 매우 소심해 하다가 시간이 갈수록 자신감을 되찾았다.

Practice 33.

Fill in the blank with the word that matches the definition provided

01 His column is _____ (publish simultaneously) in more than fifty newspapers and magazines.

02 I have been _____ (lazy) the past few days; I must get back to my studies.

03 Mike _____ (provoke in a mocking way) me, saying that I could never beat him in tennis.

04 Ian was determined to find the _____ (guilty party) that stole his food from the pantry at his office.

05 Albert Einstein was considered a/an _____ (rebel) in his twenties, but by his fifties he turned into a conformist.

06 The government gave the company a year's _____ (temporary relief) to restructure its business.

07 Much to my _____ (extreme disappointment), I wasn't selected to be in my school's tennis team.

08 I have not lived in one _____ (place to live) for over two years for the past ten years.

09 The _____ (extremely poor) refugees had no place to go.

10 Larry saw Sue sitting alone in the cafeteria, but he was too _____ (shy) to go sit with her.

11 As soon as I heard the idea, I put it out of my mind as it was so _____ (causing ridicule).

12 There have been several attempts to _____ (kick out) the current President from power.

13 There is only one shop in the city that sells horse riding _____ (equipment).

14 We sailed the river upstream to the point where it _____ (divides into two).

15 I have a/an _____ (strong dislike) to spicy foods: I prefer milder tasting foods.

16 After a hectic week at his clinic, Dr. Arnold finds _____ (purification of emotions) in his weekend fishing trips.

Class 34

☐ **brittle** /ˈbrɪtl/   adj. breaking easily

(= fragile, delicate, crumbling, frail)

The master realized that by increasing the carbon content of the steel his swords had become stronger but more brittle; small pieces of steel chipped off the blade easily.

장인이 칼을 만들 때 탄소를 더 첨가하면 강철이 더 강해지지만 더 쉽게 부스러진다는 걸 알았다: 칼에서 작은 조각들이 쉽게 부스러져서 떨어져 나갔다.

☐ **glean** /gliːn/   v. to gather bit by bit

(= garner, collect, gather)

After researching the internet for several days, Morgan felt that he had gleaned enough background information on the subject to begin writing his paper.

인터넷에서 며칠간 자료 검색을 한 후 모건은 마침내 과제를 쓰기 시작할 수 있을 만큼 배경 자료를 모은 것으로 생각했다.

☐ **therapeutic** /ˌθerəˈpjuːtɪk/   adj. pertaining to therapy, healing

(= healing, remedial, curative)

I find these morning walks very therapeutic for my nerves: I feel much more relaxed through the day.

나는 이런 아침 산책이 내 신경과민에 매우 치유적이라고 생각한다: 하루 종일 긴장이 덜 된다.

☐ **enmity** /ˈenməti/   n. a feeling of dislike towards another

(= hostility, antagonism)

Since the mid-eighteenth century, there has been much interaction between the cultures of France and Germany despite the frequent enmity between those two countries.

18세기 중반부터 가끔씩의 적대감에도 불구하고 프랑스와 독일 간에는 활발한 문화교류가 있었다.

☐ **lapse** /læps/   n. a slip, error or failure

(= slip, failure, blunder)

The high pitched sound caused a momentary lapse of consciousness in many who had heard it.

그 고음의 소리가 많은 사람들을 잠깐 정신을 잃게 만들었다.

☐ **incantation** /ˌɪnkænˈteɪʃn/

n. the chanting of words that have magical powers

(= spell)

When the magician uttered an incantation and whipped the handkerchief away the dove he had held in his hand was gone.

마술사가 주문을 외우고 들고 있던 손수건을 치우자 손에 들고 있던 비둘기가 사라졌다.

☐ **champion** /ˈtʃæmpiən/   v. to defend or support

(= support, defend, back)

Nelson Mandela had always championed racial equality in South Africa, and in 1993, his accomplishments were commemorated by his winning of the Nobel Peace Prize.

넬슨 만델라는 항상 남아프리카에서 인종 간 평등을 수호했고 1993년에 그의 업적이 그가 노벨평화상을 받으며 기념되었다.

☐ **onerous** /ˈəʊnərəs/   adj. causing hardship

(= taxing, burdensome, laborious)

The shy and inoffensive Haley found it difficult to carry out the onerous task of informing redundant employees that they are being laid off.

소심하고 남에게 나쁜 말 못하는 헤일리는 정리해고되는 직원에게 해직통보를 하는 일을 부담스러워 하고 수행하기 어려워했다.

☐ **semblance** /ˈsembləns/   n. unreal appearance

(= appearance, façade, resemblance)

It has been months since the devastating flood, and for the people who have survived it, life at last has returned to a semblance of normality.

파괴적인 홍수가 지나간 지 수개월이 지났고, 그 고난을 겪은 사람들에게는 삶이 평상과 비슷해지기 시작했다.

☐ **dogged** /ˈdɔːgɪd/   adj. persistent in effort

(= determined, resolute, gritty, persistent)

Through ingenuity and dogged determination the first Chinese immigrants settled down in their new surroundings in Canada.

창의성과 불굴의 투지로 최초의 중국 이민자들은 캐나다의 새로운 환경에 적응했다.

☐ **inglorious** /ɪnˈglɔːriəs/   adj. deserving shame

(= disgraceful, dishonorable, humiliating, ignominious)

Bernard Madoff's legendary career as an investment consultant, which lasted a span of 40 years was shot down in one inglorious scandal.

40년간 계속되었던 버나드 메이도프의 투자 컨설턴트로서의 신화와 같은 커리어는 한 번의 수치스러운 스캔들로 나락으로 떨어졌다.

☐ **eclectic** /ɪˈklektɪk/   adj. drawing from multiple sources

(= diverse, selective, diversified, heterogeneous)

Having lived in Cuba, England and Indonesia, she decorated her house in an eclectic style.

쿠바, 영국과 인도네시아에 살았던 경험이 있는 그녀는 집을 아주 다양한 스타일로 장식하였다.

☐ **nonplussed** /ˌnɑːnˈplʌst/   adj. surprised and confused

(= dumbfounded, flummoxed, baffled)

The room was engulfed in a sudden silence as everyone was nonplussed at the announcement.

모든 사람이 그 발표를 듣고 어리둥절해 하는 바람에 온 방안에 갑자기 적막이 흘렀다.

☐ **hedonist** /ˈhedənɪst/

n. someone who pursues pleasure and self-gratification

(= Epicurean, bon vivant)

The current depression has hedonists cutting back on spas and beauty salons, helping consumer goods companies to sell more beauty products to be applied at home.

최근 불경기로 쾌락주의자들이 스파와 미용실에 가는 횟수를 줄이는 바람에 생활용품 생산업체들이 집에서 사용할 수 있는 상품들을 더 많이 판매하게 되었다.

□ **émigré** /'emɪgreɪ/

n. a person who is forced to leave his country for political reasons

(= expatriate, exile, emigrant)

After the collapse of the Soviet Union in 1991, the Russian émigré Alexandr Solzhenitsyn returned to his home country after 20 years of exile.

1991년 소련의 붕괴 이후 알렉산더 솔제니친은 20년간의 추방자 생활을 끝내고 고국으로 돌아갈 수 있었다.

□ **buoyant** /'bɔɪənt/   adj. tending to float

(= floating, vivacious, bouncy, lively)

He had a robust, buoyant character that was quite infectious as every time he entered a room filled with people the atmosphere turned jovial in no time.

그는 매우 원기왕성하고 자신감에 가득찬 성격의 소유자였으며 그가 사람이 있는 방 안에 들어오면 금방 분위기가 쾌활해졌다.

□ **underpinning(s)** /ˌʌndərˈpɪnɪŋ/   n. a foundation or basis

(= foundation, groundwork, reinforcement)

At the time no one could have suspected that those playful afternoons of kicking around the ball in the mud with his friends would become the underpinnings of the success he had later in his life as a soccer player.

그 당시에 그가 진흙탕에서 오후마다 친구들과 공놀이를 한 것이 나중에 그가 축구선수가 되었을 때 이룩한 성공의 기초가 될 것이란 걸 아무도 예측할 수 없었을 것이다.

□ **tawdry** /'tɔːdri/   adj. showy and cheap

(= garish, gaudy, flashy)

The first time it was performed in 1921, the play was regarded to be so tawdry that the theater was forced to stop it after only two performances.

1921년에 초연되었을 때 그 연극은 너무나 유치하다는 평가를 받아 극장이 2회만에 상연을 끝내야 했다.

□ **loathe** /ləʊð/　　　　　　　　　　　　v. to extremely hate

(= hate, dislike, detest, abhor)

While most western people would loathe the idea of having one's marriage prearranged without having any say in the affair, the practice of arranged marriages is still prevalent in many countries.

서양인들의 입장에서 누군가가 미리 정한 나의 결혼에 내가 한 마디도 참견할 수 없다면 혐오하겠지만 이러한 정혼 풍습은 아직도 많은 나라에서 행해지고 있다.

□ **foist** /fɔɪst/　　　　　　　　　　　　v. to force upon

(= impose, finagle)

He exaggerated the fact that he and I were from the same hometown to foist an insurance contract on me that I didn't need.

그는 나와 동향 출신이라는 사실은 강조하면서 내게 필요 없는 보험계약을 억지로 떠안기려 하였다.

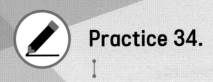

Practice 34.

Fill in the blank with the word that matches the definition provided

01 The football team achieved the _____ (deserving shame) record of having lost the most consecutive games during this season.

02 The reporter continued to ask biting questions with _____ (persistent effort) persistence.

03 At age 50, Albert Einstein had to flee from Germany and arrive in the U.S. as a/an _____ (exile).

04 The speaker seemed to be _____ (surprised and confused) by my question.

05 She had a wide and _____ (drawing from many sources) collection of paintings, statues and sculptures.

06 While travelling in Calcutta, I was accosted everyday by street vendors trying to _____ (force upon) their goods on me.

07 "Abracadabra" is perhaps the most famous _____ (magical words) ever.

08 Please excuse my _____ (error) of the tongue: I did not mean to sound disrespectful.

09 Mr. Heller insists on doing all housework because he finds it _____ (pertaining to therapy).

10 If you read a book each month, after ten years, you will have read more than 100 books and _____ (gathered slowly) an immense amount of knowledge.

11 In the beginning, rubber was not considered to be a suitable industrial material because it melted in the heat and became _____ (breaking easily) in the cold.

12 He was wearing _____ (showy and cheap) chains around his neck.

13 The _____ (basis) of good journalism is a devotion to objectivity and impartiality.

14 When I saw the oil tanker up close, I couldn't believe that such a huge vessel could be _____ (floating on water).

15 After the great period of celebration had died down, our lives returned to some _____ (resemblance) of normality.

16 I was responsible for the _____ (burdensome) task of cleaning up after the party.

17 For his entire life, Mahatma Gandhi _____ (supported) non-violent resistence.

I

Find the most suitable word from the box that fits in the sentence

destitute, enmity, iconoclast, brave, fusillade, therapeutic, odious, oust, hedonist, reprieve, culprit, brittle, vignette

01 The temperature in Kuala Lumpur was 34C, but we still _____ the heat to see the sights and try the street food.

02 Helen agreed to adopt a cat as long as Mark did all the _____ chores such as cleaning the litter box and vacuuming the hair.

03 There was a bloody power struggle, and the younger brother finally _____ his older brother, who had been King.

04 In modern times, one needs money to be a/an _____.

05 The Olympic Gold medalists received a/an _____ of congratulatory messages.

06 After four hours of morning training, the athletes get an hour's _____ for lunch and a break and then return for another three hours of afternoon training.

07 Using modern day DNA testing technology, scientists have found out who was the _____ of Prince Rudolf of Saxony's murder in 1623.

08 When Prince Siddhartha Gautama, who later became the Buddha, left his palace for the first time at 26, he witnessed for the first time in his life _____ and sick people.

09 Don't express _____ towards your parents: they only want what is best for you.

10 Glass is too _____ a material to make Christmas ornaments from.

11 The movie consisted not of one continuous story but of five loosely related _____.

12 Bernie Sanders' image as a/an _____ is what made him so popular to the younger generation, who were tired of established politics.

13 Yoga is supposed to be _____ for the mind as well as the body, but, unfortunately, modern people only seem to focus on its physical aspects.

lucrative, insurgence, tantamount, ignoble, nonplussed, dogged, bifurcated, specimen, eclectic, catharsis, slight, circuitous

14 During the past half century, only half of the country's regime changes were results of peaceful elections. The rest were all _____.

15 Don't take my criticism as a/an _____. I'm only trying to help you.

16 I couldn't afford to buy a ticket for a direct flight, so I took a/an _____ route.

17 Saul makes a/an _____ living playing saxophone on a cruise ship.

18 In Jack's company, the CEO Ken Koh's orders are _____ to law.

19 Is an honorable war better than a/an _____ peace?

20 I was _____ to see Richard, who I thought was still in Europe, walk in my office door.

21 She says her house is decorated with _____ art. I think it's just filled with a hodgepodge of junk.

22 Richard has come this far only through _____ determination.

23 Follow this road and take the left route when it _____.

24 The deep water exploration team gathered many _____ of living organisms from below 3,000m that they had never seen before.

25 Some Korean foods are so spicy that many foreigners can barely sample a taste. But many Koreans experience _____ when eating such spicy foods.

malleable, aplomb, kowtow, domicile, juxtapose, evict, impugn, lapse, repute, foist, tawdry, discomfit, rotatory, grapple, atrocity

26 In the minds of modern-day Americans, Benjamin Franklin is inseparably linked with the city of Philadelphia, but actually, his _____ was in Boston until he was seventeen.

27 I was young and _____ and therefore made many mistakes, some of which I am quite ashamed now.

28 Janet Taylor, the first woman Police Chief of the city, was praised for her professionalism and _____ in handling the difficult situation.

29 There is no need to _____ to me. I have no authority to hire you.

30 The police had to come and forcefully _____ the protesting students, who had occupied the Dean's Office.

31 When you _____ the current diplomatic situation of the Far East with that of the late 19th Century, there are many similarities.

32 The honey extractor uses _____ motion to create centrifugal force which extracts honey out of the combs.

33 Lawrence Braggs earned international _____ when he won the Nobel Prize for Physics at only 25.

34 The police officer caught up to the running man, _____ him and pulled him to the ground.

35 Some of the darkest _____ in human history have happened in the name of religion and patriotism.

36 Overly proud people refuse to admit their mistakes — and sometimes even deny the fact that they make them — because they feel that it would _____ their image.

37 In a short _____ of memory, I forgot his name.

38 I do not enjoy the company of overly religious people who try to _____ their religion on me.

39 She was wearing a necklace made of huge beads that looked too _____ to be real jewels.

40 Angela was _____ when Julie, her five year old daughter, burped loudly in front of the guests.

Circle the word that is not a synonym.

41 brave – defy – perturb

42 slight – moniker – snub

43 ignominious – immured – ignoble

44 antagonism – indignance – enmity

4 subservient – impotent – languished

46 spate – ogle – gaze

47 tirade – diatribe – fuss

48 odious – abhorrent – inexorable

49 prattle – sicken – cloy

50 languish – fade – postulate

51 interpose – impugn – doubt

52 pedagogic – educational – gastronomic

53 loath – detest – impose

54 distraught – vivacious – buoyant

55 nonplussed – scatterbrained – dumbfounded

Class 36

□ **aboriginal** /ˌæbəˈrɪdʒənl/   adj. native

(= indigenous, native)

Many towns in Australia derive their names from aboriginal words.

호주의 여러 도시들은 원주민 언어에서 유래된 도시명을 가진다.

□ **imbue** /ɪmˈbjuː/   v. to inspire, as in feelings or images

(= instill, fill, permeate)

The artist's repeated use of pale colors and amorphous forms intended to imbue his paintings with a sense of ambiguity.

그 예술가가 창백한 색과 무정형의 형태를 반복해서 쓰는 이유는 그의 작품들에 모호함이 깃들게 하기 위한 것이다.

□ **nomadic** /nəʊˈmædɪk/   adj. roaming around, not staying on one place

(= itinerant, traveling, roaming)

Many Mongolian tribes still continue the nomadic lifestyles of their ancestors, roaming the deserts endlessly in search of fodder for their herds.

몽고의 많은 부락들이 아직도 그들의 조상들이 했던, 가축에게 먹일 풀을 찾아 사막을 헤매는 유목민과 같은 생활을 한다.

□ **languor** /ˈlæŋɡər/   n. characteristic of having no energy

(= laziness, sleepiness, torpor, lethargy)

With the kids at school, wife out shopping, and even the dog at the vet, I could lie back on my sofa and doze off in a delightful languor for several hours.

아이들은 학교에 가고, 아내는 장 보러갔고, 반려견 마저 동물병원에 보낸 후, 나는 소파에 길게 누워 몇 시간 동안 달콤한 나태함을 보낼 수 있었다.

☐ **vivacious** /vɪˈveɪʃəs/   adj. to be full with energy

(= lively, spirited, bubbly)

All three of his daughters were quite convivial, but Anna, the second, is particularly vivacious.

그의 세 딸 모두 명랑했지만 둘째인 안나가 특히 유쾌하였다.

☐ **postulate** /ˈpɑːstʃəleɪt/   v. to make an educated assumption

(= assume, hypothesize, suggest, claim)

Some ecologist postulate that the Earth is on the verge of massive extinctions of a scale never before experienced.

어떤 환경론자는 지구 역사상 전례없는 대규모의 멸종위기가 다가오고 있다고 추론한다.

☐ **brigand** /ˈbrɪɡənd/   n. a robber or burglar

(= bandit, outlaw, gangster, desperado)

The documentary was about a medieval English thief and his band of brigands who are thought to be the origins of the legend surrounding "Robin Hood and His Merry Men."

다큐멘터리는 로빈 훗과 그의 무법자들의 전설의 유래가 된 중세 영국의 한 도둑과 그의 도적 떼에 관한 것이었다.

☐ **vacuous** /ˈvækjuəs/   adj. lacking of intelligence

(= blank, stupid, dim)

Many scientific theories that were later proven to be true were accepted as vacuous initially.

최초에 말도 안 되는 것으로 받아들여진 많은 과학 이론들이 후에 사실로 증명되었다.

☐ **disposition** /ˌdɪspəˈzɪʃn/   n. state of mind regarding something

(= character, nature, spirit)

Although aging brings about profound physiological changes, it doesn't often alter an individual's disposition.

나이를 먹음에 따라 신체적으로는 큰 변화가 일어나나 사람의 성격이 바뀌는 경우는 별로 없다.

□ **congeal** /kənˈdʒiːl/

adj. to change from a soft fluid state to a rigid or solid state

(= clot, coagulate, gel)

You must eat this soup while its hot: it will congeal when it gets cold.

스프가 뜨거울 때 먹어야 돼: 식으면 엉겨.

□ **consummate** /ˈkɑːnsəmət/　　　　v. to complete or perfect

(= complete, achieve, accomplished)

Having worked together many times before, the two men consummated their business deal with no difficulties.

과거에 수차례 같이 일한 경험이 있는 두 사람은 어려움 없이 그들의 사업 거래를 성사시켰다.

□ **slink** /slɪŋk/

v. to move in a slow, careful manner (from fear, shame or cowardice)

(= creep)

Kevin's plans to slink through the back door and creep up to his room backfired when Cooper, his pet dog, barked at him when he tried to pry open the door silently.

뒷문으로 몰래 들어와 자기 방으로 살금살금 올라가려고 했던 케빈의 계획은 그가 조용히 문을 열려고 할 때 그의 반려견인 쿠퍼가 짖는 바람에 실패로 끝났다.

□ **stupor** /ˈstuːpər/　　　　n. state of unconsciousness

(= daze, numbness, unconsciousness, trance)

We were most worried when Frank did not awake from his stupor for several minutes after he fell off his motorcycle.

프랭크가 모터사이클에서 떨어진 후 몇 분간 정신을 잃고 깨어나지 않았을 때 우리는 매우 걱정했다.

□ **dexterous** /ˈdekstrəs/　　　　adj. skillful in the use of hands or body

(= deft, nimble, agile)

Harvey must be an extremely dexterous baker to bake and decorate such an extravagant cake.

이렇게 화려한 케이크를 굽고 장식할 수 있는 하비는 아마 매우 손재주가 좋은 제빵사인가 보다.

☐ **monolithic** /ˌmɑːnəˈlɪθɪk/　　　　　adj. extremely big, large and slow to change

(= gigantic, enormous)

Many government institutions are monolithic – so pitted with bureaucracy that it is almost impossible for them to change.

많은 정부기관들은 거대한 바위 같다 – 너무나도 관료주의에 익숙해서 변화가 거의 불가능하다.

☐ **intersperse** /ˌɪntərˈspɜːrs/　　　　　v. to scatter here and there

(= nest, interlard)

To ensure that his classes were not unnecessarily tedious, Dr. Hunter always interspersed his lectures with jokes, funny anecdotes and interesting trivia.

그의 강의가 필요 이상으로 따분하지 않게 하기 위해서 헌터 박사는 강의 중간중간에 농담, 재미있는 이야기, 그리고 흥미로운 잡상식을 섞어 넣는다.

☐ **affront** /əˈfrʌnt/　　　　　v. to insult

(= offend, insult)

During the world cup games many fans fashioned the national flag into interesting items of clothing, and this affronted some, who said that such people did not show the proper respect to a national symbol.

월드컵 동안에 많은 팬들이 국기를 개조해서 다양한 옷으로 만들어 입자 어떤 사람들은 국가의 상징에 적합한 존경심을 보이지 않는다며 모욕적이라고 했다.

☐ **florid** /ˈflɔːrɪd/　　　　　adj. colorful and fancy

(= ornate, extravagant, fancy)

He was a born orator; he could rouse a docile group of farmers into a violent crowd of protestors with his florid speeches.

그는 타고난 달변가였다: 그는 화려한 말솜씨로 온순한 농부들을 폭력적인 시위대로 바꿀 수 있었다.

---

absolve /əbˈzɑːlv/　　　　　v. to forgive a sin

(= pardon, forgive)

After World War II, many of the German scientists interrogated by allied forces claimed innocence, stating that they were forced to commit crimes under military orders, but this was not enough to absolve them from their crimes against humanity

2차 대전이 끝난 후 많은 독일의 과학자들은 그들이 그저 군의 명령을 받들다가 죄를 저질렀을 뿐이라며 무죄를 주장했지만 이것은 그들이 인류에 저지른 범죄를 용서 받기에는 부족한 핑계였다.

☐ **corporeal** /kɔːrˈpɔːriəl/   adj. of the nature of the physical body

(= physical, material, bodily)

After spending a lifetime amassing huge wealth, Stanley suddenly realized that material wealth only satisfies his corporeal needs, and he is still spiritually needy.

평생동안 물질적 풍요로움을 모았던 스탠리는 갑자기 물질적 부유함은 육체적인 요구만 만족시킬 뿐 그는 아직도 정신적으로는 부족하다는 걸 깨달았다.

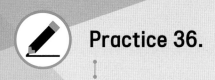

Practice 36.

Fill in the blank with the word that matches the definition provided

01 I noticed Percy _____ (moving slowly and carefuly) in school all day, trying to avoid running into Marta.

02 It took the two parties less than two weeks to _____ (complete) their cooperation agreement.

03 When you store this broth in the refrigerator, it will _____ (solidify) into a jelly-like form.

04 Please don't be _____ (insulted) by not being invited to my wedding, but it will be a small ceremony with only family members participating.

05 The road between the two villages are dangerous, as _____ (burglars) often hijack passing cars.

06 Oliver is such an optimistic guy: No amount of hardships can dampen his cheerful _____ (character).

07 Although Phylia explained the theory to Ethan three times, he still stared back at her in a/an _____ (lacking intelligence) expression.

08 My father has passed away: his _____ (physical) presence is gone, but he lives on in my heart.

09 In the middle ages, overly pious people would whip themselves or wear vests made of thorns to _____ (forgive a sin) themselves.

10 Dad's soothing voice used to _____ (inspire a feeling) such a feeling of security in me when I was young.

11 Now that Youtube is an incorporated company, it must make profits, and that is why most of the videos are _____ (scattered here and there) with advertisements.

12 I thought the dress Laura wore to the funeral was too _____ (colorful and fancy) and inappropriate for the occasion.

13 The researchers were excited that the experiment results conformed with those they _____ (made an educated assumption).

14 At the shop, we were helped by a particularly _____ (full of energy) sales clerk.

15 Mr. Boggart decided to end his _____ (wandering around) lifestyle and settle down in San Diego, California.

16 I am not _____ (having skilled hands) : in fact, I am quite clumsy at times.

17 At the Christmas dinner, I ate so much that afterwards, I fell into a/an _____ (state of unconsciousness).

☐ **protagonist** /prəˈtægənɪst/   n. the main character

(= character, hero)

The boy, for the sole reason of being at the wrong place at the wrong time, became the unlikely protagonist in a gruesome drama that would span for 15 years.

소년은, 순전히 잘못된 시간에 잘못된 장소에 있었다는 이유로, 15년간 지속된 끔찍한 드라마 같은 사건의 우연한 주인공이 되었다.

☐ **proximity** /prɑːkˈsɪməti/   n. nearness

(= closeness, vicinity)

Unlike some of my friends who attend colleges thousand miles away from home, I attend one that is in close proximity to my home.

집에서 몇 천 마일 떨어져 있는 대학을 다니는 내 친구들과 달리 나는 바로 우리집에서 얼마 안 떨어진 대학에 다닌다.

☐ **connive** /kəˈnaɪv/   v. to cooperate secretly

(= conspire, scheme, plot)

I could tell from their sideway glances and giggles that the girls were conniving something mischievous, but I couldn't imagine what it was.

자기들끼리 몰래 웃고 숙덕이고 낄낄거리는 걸로 봐서는 여자아이들이 뭔가 장난거리를 몰래 꾸미고 있다는 걸 알 수 있었다.

☐ **dogma** /ˈdɔːgmə/   n. established belief, opinion or principle

(= creed, doctrine)

Efforts to improve the living standards in one's community must be dictated by pragmatic common sense, not some political dogma.

지역사회의 생활 수준을 향상시키기 위한 노력은 정치적 독단이 아닌 실용주의적인 상식에 의해 결정해야 한다.

□ **sleuth** /sluːθ/   n. a detective

(= inspector, detective)

Every generation has its favorite detective character, but perhaps the most famous sleuth of all time is Sherlock Holms.

각 세대마다 인기있는 탐정 캐릭터가 있지만 아마도 역사상 가장 유명한 탐정은 셜록 홈즈일 것이다.

□ **stigma** /ˈstɪgmə/   n. a mark of disgrace

(= disgrace, dishonor)

In some Asian countries, there is still a stigma attached to interracial marriages.

어떤 아시아 국가에서는 아직도 국제결혼과 관련된 오명 같은 것이 있다.

□ **prolific** /prəˈlɪfɪk/   adj. producing much

(= productive, fertile, copious, creative)

Asimov was one of the most prolific writers of all time, having written or edited more than 500 books and an estimated 9,000 letters and postcards.

500여 권의 책을 집필 혹은 편집하고 무려 9,000장의 편지와 엽서를 쓴 아시모프는 역사상 가장 다작한 작가 중의 하나였다.

□ **languid** /ˈlæŋgwɪd/   adj. having no strength or energy

(= relaxed, leisurely, indolent, lethargic)

Too tired to even speak, Mr. Rutherford sent the boy away with a languid wave of his hand.

말할 힘조차 남아있지 않던 러더포드씨는 힘없는 손짓으로 소년에게 돌아가라고 했다.

□ **admonish** /ədˈmɑːnɪʃ/   v. to scold

(= reprimand, scold, reprove)

My Dad never admonishes me about my grades, but whenever I do something he considers to be rude, he will scold me very sternly.

우리 아버지는 성적문제로 나를 나무란 적은 없지만, 내가 뭔가 예의에 어긋나는 행동을 하면 아주 심하게 꾸지람을 하신다.

☐ **inane** /ɪˈneɪn/   adj. lacking sense

(= ridiculous, idiotic, frivolous)

Rather than using their lunch meeting to discuss work, the two employees wasted time talking about inane subjects.

두 직원은 점심시간에 업무에 대한 상의를 하기보다는 별 거 아닌 이야기를 하다가 다 보냈다.

☐ **heresy** /ˈherəsi/

n. a thought or belief that is considered to be opposed to established theory

(= sacrilege, profanation)

In medieval Europe, non-Christians were burned at the stake for heresy.

중세 유럽에서 비기독교인들은 이단으로 화형했다.

☐ **faction** /ˈfækʃn/

n. an organized group of people within a larger group

(= section, party, bloc)

With rival factions continuously bickering for more power, it seems that the time when people's welfare will be the main preoccupation of politicians in this country is still far off.

라이벌 정당끼리 서로 권력을 차지하기 위해 툭탁거리는 이 마당에 국민들의 복지가 정치인들의 주관심사가 될 날은 아직도 먼 것 같다.

☐ **gaffe** /ɡæf/

n. a careless mistake (especially made during an important event)

(= slip)

Robert made the gaffe of mispronouncing the Mayor's name when he introduced her to the audience at her inauguration ceremony.

로버트는 주지사님 취임 행사에서 주지사를 소개할 때 그녀의 이름을 잘못 발음하는 경솔한 실수를 했다.

☐ **stereotype** /ˈsteriətaɪp/   n. a set form or convention

(= typecast, label, pigeonhole)

If you are from the South, Jon will stereotype you as a racist, die-hard Christian and hillbilly.

당신이 만일 남부에서 왔다면 존은 당신이 전형적인 인종차별 주의자에 골수 기독교에 촌뜨기라고 여길 것이다.

□ **homogeneity** /ˌhəʊməʊdʒəˈniːəti/

n. cultural, social, biological or other similarities within a group

(= uniformity, similarity, correspondence)

Korea is a country where ethnic homogeneity is regarded as a virtue, so James' half-American background was always viewed as a blemish when he was young.

한국은 순수민족성이 중요하다고 여겨지는 나라라서 제임스의 반 미국인이라는 배경이 그가 어렸을 때 항상 흠으로 여겨졌다.

□ **conceited** /kənˈsiːtɪd/

adj. thinking that your own opinion is more important than others'

(= vain, smug, arrogant)

Despite being a lady of high social status, she was never haughty or conceited in speech or action.

그녀는 상류사회의 귀부인임에도 불구하고, 말이나 행동에서 거만하거나 자만하지 않는다.

□ **debilitate** /dɪˈbɪliteɪt/   v. to severely weaken

(= weaken, exhaust, incapacitate, enfeeble)

The recent scandal that exposed his family's involvement in illegal financial activities had debilitated the incumbent president's chances of being reelected for a second term.

그의 가족이 불법 금융거래에 연관이 되었다는 스캔들이 현직 대통령의 재선 가능성을 극도로 낮춰 놓았다.

□ **diktat** /dɪkˈtæt/   n. an authoritative statement

(= decree)

Local school teachers went on strike to protest diktats from the Ministry of Education that they believe are harmful.

교육부의 강권이 해롭다고 믿는 교사들이 농성을 시작했다.

☐ **phonetic** /fə'netɪk/   adj. related to speech or sound

Westerners find it particularly difficult to learn to read and write Mandarin Chinese, because the language is made up not of a phonetic alphabet but of hieroglyphs.

중국어가 표음문자가 아닌 상형문자로 이뤄져 있기 때문에 서양인들에게는 특히 배우기가 어렵다.

☐ **stoic** /'stəʊɪk/

adj. to be impassive and not show one's emotion

(= impassive, unemotional)

Even with a bleeding knee, Andy remained stoic and continued to play football.

무릎에서 피가 남에도 불구하고 앤디는 아무런 내색없이 계속해서 축구를 했다.

01 In Europe, the _____ (typecast) of the English is that they have terrible food, of the French, that they don't wash often and of the Belgians, that they are not very bright.

02 I chose the apartment for its _____ (closeness) to the subway station and shopping district.

03 The police matched that the _____ (related to speech) signatures of the recorded voice with those of the suspect.

04 If you think your work is more important than mine, you are _____ (arrogant).

05 In the late 19th century, Korea restricted foreigners from entering the country in the fear that they will contaminate the cultural and ethnic _____ (uniformity) of the country.

06 In Issac Newton's day, it was considered scientific _____ (sacrilege) to doubt the teachings of Aristoteles.

07 I would like to apologize for the intolerable _____ (mistake) I committed.

08 In Canadian politics, the Green Party, which pushes environmental agenda into the forefront of political debate, is no longer a small _____ (a groups within a larger group) but one of the three major opposition parties.

09 The government's _____ (authoritative statement) to ban all imports of items made of ivory has met with much approval.

10 Replacing the basketball team's coach this closely to the tournament will _____ (seerrely weaken) the morale of the team.

11   The _____ (not showing emotion) little boy had a bleeding nose and a blackened eye, but he didn't cry.

12   The director cancelled the weekly meeting, calling it useless and _____ (lacking sense).

13   The principal asked the student if she had helped _____ (cooperate secretly) the theft of the exam answers.

14   During his 25 year career, Isaac Asimov wrote more than 500 books. He was one of the most _____ (producing much) authors in history.

☐ **proficient** /prəˈfɪʃnt/   adj. to be skillful at something

(= adept, dexterous, skillful)

Sam did not understand a single word of English when he first immigrated to Canada, but in two short years he became remarkably proficient in the language.

쌤이 캐나다로 이민갔을 때 영어를 한 마디도 못 알아들었지만 불과 2년 만에 놀라울 정도로 유창해졌다.

☐ **nascent** /ˈneɪsnt/   adj. young and new

(= budding, embryonic, blossoming)

It is too early to say at this nascent stage of development whether this product will be well received by the market.

이 상품의 시장 반응이 좋을 지는 아직 개발단계의 초기라서 말하기는 이르다.

☐ **drab** /dræb/   adj. dull or lacking in spirit

(= dull, plain, dingy)

On a rainy day, the usually vibrant Vancouver skyline turns drab and dreary.

보통 때는 선명한 밴쿠버의 스카이 라인이 비가 오면 침침해진다.

☐ **augment** /ɔːɡˈment/   v. to enlarge in size, number or strength

(= expand, enhance, boost)

Starbuck's wished to augment its profits in Asia by introducing beverages that Asians could identify with, such as its Green Tea Latte, and Chai Tea Latte.

스타벅스는 아시아에서 이익을 창출하기 위해 아시아인들에게 익숙한 그린 티 라떼나 차이 티 라떼 같은 음료를 출시하였다.

☐ **frivolity** /frɪˈvɑːləti/

n. the quality of being self-indulgent and irresponsible

(= flippancy, folly, jest, trifling)

My father always said that my reading so many super-hero comics was an act of frivolity, but reading such comics is what encouraged me to become a scientist.

우리 아버지는 내가 항상 수퍼히어로 만화책만 읽는 것은 바보 같은 행동이라고 하였지만, 그런 만화를 읽은 것이 내가 과학자가 되게 한 계기가 되었다.

☐ **terrain** /təˈreɪn/   n. the physical character of a piece of land

(= ground, country, land)

It was interesting how we entered into a totally different terrain once we passed the state border.

주 경계를 지나가자마자 완전히 다른 지형이 나타났다는 것이 매우 흥미로웠다.

☐ **abrasive** /əˈbreɪsɪv/   adj. prone to argue

(= harsh, rude, argumentative)

The readers were puzzled at the politician's abrasive description of the peace movement in his recent memoirs because only two years previously, he had actively participated in rallies organized by this very movement.

그 정치인의 회고록을 읽는 독자들이 그가 그 평화움직임을 매우 비판적으로 묘사한 것이 의외라고 생각하는 이유는 불과 2년 전에 그가 그 움직임이 주선한 평화시위에 활동적으로 참가했기 때문이다.

☐ **gruesome** /ˈɡruːsəm/   adj. causing great horror

(= horrific, shocking, terrible)

The black wasp then displays a rather gruesome form of parasitic behavior to the tarantula; it lays its eggs within the paralyzed body of the giant spider, which will be devoured alive when these eggs hatch.

검은말벌은 그 후 타란툴라 거미에게 꽤나 끔직한 기생 행위를 한다: 그는 마비시킨 거대 거미의 몸에 알을 낳고, 그 알이 깨면 아직 살아있는 거미를 애벌레들이 먹어치운다.

☐ **levy** /ˈlevi/   v. to impose a tax

(= impose, charge, tax, gather)

The state government's decision to levy a new harmonized sales tax has created a furor among residents of British Columbia.

주정부가 새로운 조화 판매세를 도입하기로 한 결정이 브리티시 컬럼비아 주민들을 화나게 만들었다.

□ **penury** /ˈpenjəri/   n. extreme poverty

(= indigence, destitution, poverty)

After spending most of my childhood in relevant affluence, he was terrified of the prospect of living in penury.

유년기를 상대적인 부유함 속에 보낸 그에게 가난하게 살 수 있다는 전망이 너무 무서웠다.

□ **flux** /flʌks/   n. a state of constant change

(= instability, change, transition)

Korea is a fascinating country that has been in a flux for the past 60 years.

한국은 지난 60년간 격동기를 보낸 아주 환상적인 나라이다.

□ **quarantine** /ˈkwɔːrəntiːn/   n./v. enforced isolation

(= isolation, segregation, solitude)

In medieval times, because there was no cure for the black plague, those afflicted with the disease were quarantined in a building that was sealed off from the outside meaning that even those who survive the deadly epidemic would eventually die of starvation.

중세시대에는 흑사병을 치료할 수 있는 방법이 없었기 때문에 그 병에 걸린 사람들을 건물에 가두고는 밖에서 닫아버렸다. 그 말은 누군가가 그 병으로 죽지 않고 살아나도 결국엔 굶어 죽을 수밖엔 없었다는 것이다.

□ **wee** /wiː/   adj. very small

(= little, small, minute, tiny)

Grandma claims that taking a wee amount of whiskey before she goes to bed always helps her to sleep better.

할머니는 잠자리에 들기 전에 아주 작은 양의 위스키를 마시면 잠이 잘 온다고 하신다.

□ **soliloquy** /səˈlɪləkwi/   n. the act of talking as if alone

(= monologue)

The ground breaking play has five main characters, who never share the stage together, but in stead occupy the stage one after another to deliver soliloquies, and only after the audience sits through all five will they understand the plot.

그 파격적인 연극은 주인공이 다섯인데, 그들 모두가 같이 무대에 올라오는 경우는 없고 한 사람씩 올라와서 독백을 하는데 관객이 다섯 사람의 독백을 다 들어야만 줄거리를 이해할 수 있다.

☐ **timorous** /ˈtɪmərəs/   adj. to be shy and uncertain of oneself

(= nervous, timid, afraid)

When a man is pushed too far, even the most servile and timorous man will find the courage to stand up against his oppressor.

누군가를 지나치게 압박하면 아무리 온순하고 내성적인 사람이라도 그를 박해하는 사람에 대항할 수 있는 용기를 낸다.

☐ **accoutrements** /əˈkuːtrəmənts/   n. special equipment (usually of a soldier)

(= paraphernalia, fittings, array)

Having never faced this enemy in battle before, the men did not understand what the purpose of the various accoutrements of the enemy troupes were.

상대편 적과 한번도 전장에서 싸워보지 못했기 때문에 병사들은 상대군이 가지고 있는 장비의 용도가 뭔지 알지 못했다.

☐ **credo** /ˈkriːdəʊ/   n. a formula of belief

(= philosophy, principals, beliefs)

Travis Higgins was fired because his actions of taking kick backs from suppliers went totally against his company's credo of "reliability, innovation and harmony."

트래비스 히긴스는 공급자로부터 뇌물을 받은 것이 회사 사훈인 신뢰, 혁신, 인화를 완전히 저버리는 행동이었기 때문에 해고당했다.

☐ **indigence** /índidʒəns/   n. poverty

(= penury, destitution)

Fifty years ago, Korea was a country of extreme indigence: however, now it is the 10th largest economy in the world.

50년 전만해도 한국은 아주 가난한 나라였다: 하지만 지금은 전 세계에서 10번째로 큰 경제규모를 가졌다.

☐ **spawn** /spɔːn/

v. to give birth to (especially fish or amphibians)

(= produce, generate)

Little did he suspect that his journey across Canada would make Terry Fox a hero, and that it would spawn numerous marathons and running events to help increase cancer awareness.

테리 폭스는 그가 캐나다를 가로질러 달린 여정이 그를 영웅으로 만들 줄 전혀 몰랐으며, 암 인식을 높이는데 도움을 줄 많은 마라톤과 달리기 이벤트를 생기게 만들 줄 몰랐다.

☐ **apathy** /ˈæpəθi/   n. absence of passion or emotion

(= indifference, inertia, stoicism)

The professor's droning voice and lecture's boring topic drummed Michael into a state of apathy.

교수의 졸림을 유발하는 목소리와 따분한 강의가 마이클을 멍한 상태로 만들었다.

Practice 38.

Fill in the blank with the word that matches the definition provided

01 Sally refused to watch the _____ (causing great horror) movie that Tod picked and instead, picked a comedy.

02 My boss, Mr. Harrington, is such a/an _____ (argumentative) man that I am afraid to ask him a question in the fear that he will get angry at me.

03 Sometimes, it is important for parents to show _____ (absence of emotion) and let children solve their own problems.

04 Grandfather says that the corner grocery has been on the same spot since he was a/an _____ (small) boy.

05 Einstein's theories posit that there is no absolute time, space or speed, as everything in the universe is in a constant state of _____. (constant state of change)

06 The government has set up a special office that will review the methodology of how to _____ (impose a tax) taxes on crypto-currencies.

07 I suggest not taking your dog with you on your trip to England, because they force you to keep your dog in _____ (forced isolation) for up to six weeks.

08 My wordkay was entirely too serious, so I'm going to meet up with a few buddies to enjoy some _____ (the quality of being irresponsible) this evening.

09 My current job pays too little: I will have to find a second job to _____ (enlarge in size) my income.

10 Although Marissa saw her favorite actor dining at the café, she was too _____ (shy and afraid) to approach him to ask for an autograph.

11 Matilda, who usually wears vibrant colored clothes, was wearing a very _____ (dull colored) coat today.

12 Kenneth's business is still too _____ (young) to tell if it will be a success, but from what I've seen so far, it was great potential.

13 The _____ (poverty) we witnessed in some parts of West Virginia was beyond what we imagined exists in the United States.

14 The soldiers were busy checking their _____ (special equipment) before they set out on a reconnaissance mission.

15 The _____ (character of land) of the hiking track was relatively flat, making it an easy walk for us.

16 Hamlet's lines, "to be or not to be" are probably the most famous _____ (talking as if alone) in history.

Class 39

☐ **desultory** /'desəltɔːri/   adj. lacking in consistency

(= random, irregular, inconsistent, erratic)

No one likes to pair up with Omar for a lab project because he works in such a desultory way that it's very confusing for his partner to focus on one subject.

누구도 오마와 함께 실험실 프로젝트를 하는 것을 좋아하지 않는다. 왜냐하면 그는 너무나도 순서 없이 일을 하기 때문에 그의 파트너가 되면 한 가지 일에 집중하기가 어렵다.

☐ **collateral** /kə'lætərəl/   adj. accompanying

(= related, secondary, subordinate, ancillary)

The reading requirements for the course was immense; there was a main text book, a supplementary text book, and a list of over 12 books of collateral reading.

그 강의의 필수 독서량이 매우 많았다; 주 교재, 부 교재가 있고 참고교재가 12권이나 있었다.

☐ **castigate** /'kæstɪgeɪt/

v. to reprove or rebuke severely, especially in a formal way

(= reprimand, chastise, scold)

I expected that my boss would be upset at my mistake, but I never imagined that he would so completely castigate me.

나는 내 실수로 보스가 뭐라고 한마디할지는 예상을 했지만 그렇게까지 호되게 꾸지람을 할지는 상상도 하지 못했다.

☐ **mock** /mɑːk/   v. to ridicule

(= ridicule, scoff, scorn, sneer)

Randolph mocked Betty for her naïveté of thinking that politicians are motivated more by conscience than by money.

랜돌프는 베티가 정치인들이 돈이 아닌 양심에 의해 동화된다는 생각을 한다는 것에 그녀가 순진하다며 놀렸다.

□ **sacrosanctity** n. holiness, extreme sacredness
adj. sacrosanct

(= sacredness, sanctification)

The sacrosanctity of the newly constructed temple was tragically violated by the vandal's offensive graffiti.

새로 지은 사원의 성스러움이 공공기물 파손자의 모욕적인 낙서에 의해 더럽혀졌다.

□ **clandestine** /klænˈdestɪn/ adj. characterized by secrecy or concealment

(= secret, private, hidden, concealed)

Anne Frank's family hid in the attic of their house, which they could enter through a clandestine entrance that was unnoticeable behind a bookshelf.

안네 프랑크의 가족은 그들 집의 책장 뒤에 안 보이는 비밀 문을 통해 출입이 가능한 다락방에 숨었다.

□ **atrophy** /ˈætrəfi/ v. to degenerate or decline from disuse
n. atrophy

(= shrink, deteriorate, wither, degenerate, shrivel)

Scientists say that the prehistoric ancestors of modern whales were four legged mammals, whose limbs atrophied as they adapted to life underwater.

과학자들은 현재 고래들의 고대 선조들은 네 발 달린 동물이었으나 그들이 수중 생활에 적응하면서 다리가 퇴화하였다고 한다.

□ **catapult** /ˈkætəpʌlt/ v. to thrust or move quickly or suddenly

(= sling, throw, cast)

After twenty years of obscurity, the actor was catapulted into fame by one memorable role he played in the hit movie and now he was recognized everywhere he went.

20년간의 무명생활 끝에 그 배우는 히트 친 영화에서 맡은 한 개의 인상적인 역할로 벼락 인기를 얻었으며 이제는 가는 곳마다 사람들이 알아본다.

□ **pageantry** /ˈpædʒəntri/ n. spectacular display or empty display

(= spectacle, splendor, pomp, display)

The inauguration ceremony was held in all the pomp and pageantry that was expected of

such an event.

취임행사가 이런 행사들이 개최된다고 하면 기대하는 수준의 화려함과 과시 속에 치뤄졌다.

☐ **cohesive** /kəʊˈhiːsɪv/   adj. tending to stick together

(= sticking, grouping)

The professor's feedback to Gene's report was that despite the amount of research and thought that went into the report, all the facts were fragmented and did not form a cohesive whole.

진의 과제물에 대한 교수님의 지적은 많은 연구와 사고가 들인 것이긴 하나 모든 팩트들이 하나의 결론으로 통합되지 못하고 다들 동떨어져 있다는 것이었다.

☐ **auspice** /ˈɔːspis/   n. patronage or sponsorship

(= support, backing, sponsorship, patronage)

As he was from a poor Romanian family background, Victor would not have been able to finance his medical education if it not were for the auspices of the Anatoli Shteinberg Foundation, an organization set up to assist medical students from East European countries.

가난한 루마니아 집안 출신인 빅터는 동유럽 출신의 의대생들을 지원하는 단체인 아나톨리 슈타인베르그 재단의 후원이 아니었으면 그의 의대진학 등록금을 구하지 못했을 것이다.

☐ **palpable** /ˈpælpəbl/   adj. capable of being touched or felt

(= tangible, real, material, substantial, concrete)

The influence of the post-modernist author Kurt Vonegut Jr.'s writing style is palpable in many satirical authors of today.

포스트모더니즘 작가인 커트 보네컷 2세의 작문 스타일의 영향은 오늘날 풍자작가들의 글에서 쉽게 찾아볼 수 있다.

☐ **serenity** /səˈrenəti/   n. quietness and peacefulness

(= tranquility, calmness, peacefulness)

Stanley Park is located just minutes away from Vancouver's bustling downtown and is a place where people can enjoy nature's serenity to the fullest.

스탠리 파크는 밴쿠버의 부산한 시내에서 불과 몇 분 떨어져있지만 시민들이 자연의 평화로움을 즐기기 아주 좋은 장소다.

☐ **hapless** /ˈhæpləs/   adj. unlucky

(= unfortunate, miserable, wretched)

The people who lost their homes in the incident were hapless victims of administrative incompetence and beaurocracy.

그 사건으로 집을 잃은 사람들은 행정적 무능함과 관료주의의 운 나쁜 희생자들이었다.

☐ **emasculate** /ɪˈmæskjuleɪt/   v. to draw the strength away from

(= weaken, enfeeble)

By early 1943, the French resistance movement had done enough damage to seriously emasculate the occupying Nazi forces within France.

1943년 초에 들어와서 프랑스의 레지스탕스 움직임은 점령 중인 나찌 세력을 심각하게 약화시킬 만큼 피해를 줬다.

☐ **akimbo** /əˈkɪmbəu/   adv/adj. with hands raised to one's hips

When I saw my mother standing akimbo with a stern expression on her face, I knew that I was in trouble.

우리 엄마가 허리에 손을 얹고 화가 난 얼굴로 서 있는 것을 보고 나는 뭔가 잘못한 일이 있구나라고 생각했다.

☐ **derisible** /dirízəbl/   adj. deserving mockery or ridicule

(= ridiculous)

John laughs at me and calls it a derisible excuse when I tell him that I can't go bowling with him because I have to help my son with homework, but this is because he doesn't have children of his own and doesn't understand responsibilities of a parent.

존은 내가 아들 숙제를 도와야 한다고 같이 볼링을 치러가지 못한다고 말하면 말도 안 되는 핑계라고 웃는데 그것은 그가 아이가 없어서 부모로서의 책임을 모르기 때문이다.

☐ **humus** /ˈhjuːməs/

n. upper soil containing decomposing organic matter, which improves fertility

(= upper soil)

The soil is dry and parched, containing almost no humus at all; in other words a most barren patch of land.

땅은 마르고 갈라졌으며 상토가 전혀 없었다: 다시 말하면 매우 척박한 땅덩어리라는 말이다.

☐ **pervious** /pə́:rviəs/   adj. able to be penetrated

(= penetrable, absorbent)

Burned skin is treated with artificial skin that is made of a pervious material that let's air and moisture pass through to allow the damaged skin to breath and perspire.

화상 치료를 위해 쓰는 인공피부는 공기와 습기가 통과하는 재질로 만들어져 다친 피부가 호흡하고 땀도 흘릴 수 있게 해준다.

☐ **stanza** /ˈstænzə/   n. a few rhyming lines of a poem

(= verse, stave)

The homework is for everyone to write a humorous stanza about a character from Shakespeare.

숙제는 셰익스피어의 작품에 나오는 인물 한 사람을 골라 재미있는 싯구를 몇 줄 써 오는 것이었다.

Practice 39.

Fill in the blank with the word that matches the definition provided

01 The boys could easily leave and enter the boarding house through a/an _____ (secret) entrance that lead into the basement.

02 The coach _____ (severely rebuked) the players, not for losing, but for not trying their best.

03 Aaron was offered a very good position at the firm, with many _____ (accompanying) benefits.

04 As a man grows older, his mind becomes less _____ (able to be penetrated) to new ideas.

05 Dad says he used to dunk basketballs easily, but that skill has _____ (declined from disuse) with age.

06 The new community center was set up under the _____ (patronage) of the regional government.

07 At the moment, I only have a/an _____ (inconsistent) pile of random writings. It will take a while until it takes on the semblance of a real book.

08 The years had _____ (weakened) the man, but he still had the signature twinkle in his eyes.

09 The _____ (unfortunate) passengers had to spend the night at the airport until the snowstorm blew over.

10 I planted the plants in deep _____ (upper soil), and then watered and sprayed them with a garlic solution to deter bugs.

11 It is hard to believe that some people pay attention the claims of that _____ (deserving mockery) quack on latenight television, who peddles some strange herbal tea as a cure for all ailments.

12 When his bicycle hit a rock, Dave was _____ (thrust suddenly) into the air and fell hard on his back.

13 People are sick of politicians' empty promises – they want _____ (tangible) change.

Find the most suitable word from the box that fits in the sentence

protagonist, corporeal, spawn, indigence, timorous, gaffe, monolithic, admonish, connive, apathy, absolve, affront, dogma

01 Most of the young generation feel only _____ towards politics.

02 My boss laughed at my _____ at the reception and told me not to worry about it.

03 In the scientific age, should religious _____ be taken verbatim?

04 Many frogs come to this pond to _____ in the spring.

05 _____ must not be a hindrance to receiving medical care. This is why medicare is free for all citizens in many countries.

06 Many citizens have criticized the government for taking a/an _____ approach to solving the unemployment problem.

07 Up close, the Stalin Towers in Moscow are _____. One cannot fathom the size of these buildings until one stands in front of them.

08 A good leader _____ his subordinates privately, but praises them openly.

09 If we do not take everyday measures, such as recycling and reusing, we are all _____ in the crime of destroying our planet.

10 Interestingly, the _____ of the movie is a mute, so he has no dialogue.

11 Hinduism teaches that our _____ bodies are only vessels that carry our souls, and when we die our souls remain intact.

12 Michael asked Helen to _____ his misbehavior by offering to buy her dessert.

13 How dare you _____ my favorite football team by saying that they are not the best team in the league?

> **vivacious, nomadic, stoic, stigma, heresy, inane, diktat, conceited, aboriginal, imbue, nascent, quarantine, sleuth, stereotype, penury, frivolity**

14 Only two decades ago, there was a/an _____ attached to being divorced, but nowadays, it is no longer so.

15 The movie "Mr. Holmes" is about the famous _____ in his old age, suffering from dementia.

16 A/an _____ by nature, William finds it hard to express his emotions to his loved ones.

17 The CEO issued a/an _____ to all employees that a strict dress code must be adhered to from now on.

18 Please excuse me for sounding _____, but I think I have a better idea than yours.

19 Mr. Hwang does not fit the _____ of a Korean father – obstinate, imperious and unemotional.

20 Mr. Laverty found felicity in his new wife, charming and _____, and fifteen years his junior.

21 The tribe led _____ lives, wandering the desert of Inner Mongolia.

22 Most of the _____ languages of the native people of Canada are in danger of disappearing.

23 In some tribes, the hunters drink the blood of the animals they kill, believing that this _____ them with the strength and speed of the animal.

24 Doctors and nurses returning from the area will be _____ for three days to ensure safety.

25 His lifelong struggle with _____ finally ended when he sold his patent for more than USD2 million.

26 The Victorian novel, "Vanity Fair" is filled with humor, but there is a serious message embedded under the _____.

27 In Korea, movements to enact animal rights laws are only in their _____ stage.

28 In Brazil, to speak badly of football is considered to be _____.

29 The movie's plot was so _____ that I stopped watching it.

---

hapless, akimbo, prolific, dexterous, serenity, pageantry, clandestine, castigate, congeal, catapult, vacuous, intersperse, emasculate

30 When the police asked to enter the house, Dad stood _____ refusing to let them in.

31 The movie producer produced twelve movies in seven years. He is becoming one of the most _____ producers in the industry.

32 The pianist was now in his 80s, but his fingers were still as _____ as they were when he was in his 20s.

33 The three day electronics fair was _____ with presentations, discussions, and product demonstrations.

34 By the end of the first half, our team had racked up enough points to totally _____ the other team.

35 At the end of World War II, the allies were faced with the problem of how to help the millions of _____ victims of the war.

36 A morning kayak ride on the lake provides a sense of _____ few people experience.

37 The popularity of the new single _____ the band to the top of the charts.

38 The meeting of the two world leaders happened without any pomp or _____. They dove immediately into a serious discussion as soon as they met.

39 Last night there was a/an _____ meeting between the company's management and majority shareholders. I think there will be an important announcement today.

40 I am not happy because I was _____ for something that was not my responsibility.

41 Blood _____ under Norman's nose, where Kevin struck him.

42 Professor Gibson could tell by the _____ expressions of the students' faces that nobody understood him.

Circle the word that is not a synonym.

43 hapless – wretched – perturbed

44 opine – ogle – harangue

45 proximity – vicinity – disposition

46 tangible – admirable – palpable

47 plain – smug – drab

48 faction – cohort – doldrums

49 dexterous – languid – indolent

50 patronage – auspice – sacredness

51 desultory – ancillary – collateral

52 creep – meander – slink

53 vignette – stanza – verse

54 beliefs – credo – epitome

55 indigence – testimony – penury

Ted Chung
유학/SAT/ACT 필수 Vocabulary

| The Bodacious Book of |

Voluminous Vocabulary

Series 2-Real

(From Past SAT/ACT Tests)

-Answers -

01 pageant   n. 야외극, 행사
많은 학생들은 교내 장기자랑 대회가 학부모
회 의장의 딸 매리 앤더슨의 많지만 평이한 장
기를 뽐낼 수 있는 행사라고 생각하고 비웃었다.

02 agitated
v. 뒤흔들다, 휘젓다, 마음을 어지럽히다
아버지와 형 아니의 말싸움은 어머니의 마음
을 어지럽혔다.

03 construed   v. 해석하다
러시아 대통령은 북해에서 영국, 프랑스와 독
일이 합동 군사훈련을 진행하면 러시아 연방에
대한 적대행위로 해석될 것이라고 경고했다.

04 relished   v. 즐기다
나는 다니엘이 내가 한 잘못으로 혼난 점을 즐
겼다.

05 ambivalent
adj. 엇갈리는, 양가적인
윌리엄은 아버지 따라 의사가 되는 길에 대해
엇갈린 감정을 가졌다: 가족의 대를 이을 수
있어 좋았지만, 항상 아버지와 비교될 것 같아
걱정됐다.

06 engendered   v. 낳다, 초래하다
정부 발표는 대중적 토론을 초래했다.

07 endearing   adj. 사랑스러운
그 사람한테서 사랑스러운 면을 아예 찾을 수
없었다.

08 scrawled
v. 어색하게 쓰다, 휘갈겨 쓰다
교수님이 칠판에 휘갈겨 쓴 내용을 읽을 수 있
는 학생은 많지 않았다.

09 substantiate   v. 입증하다
경찰은 용의자의 주장을 입증할 증거를 찾지
못했다.

10 flurry
n. 혼란, 갑작스러운 소란
길고양이의 출현이 아이들이 있는 놀이터에
갑작스러운 소란을 불러일으켰다.

11 pervasive
adj. 스며드는, 만연하는
아프리카 드럼 소리가 그 아티스트의 음악에
스며들어 있었다.

12 procession   n. 행진, 행렬
런던에 여행을 갔을 때 왕족들의 행렬을 볼 흔
치않은 기회가 있었다.

13 conducive   adj. ~에 좋은
힐리 박사는 강의를 할 때 즐거우면서도 교화
적으로 하려고 한다; 그는 재미있어하는 학생
이 배우는 데 더 좋은 환경에 놓여 있다고 생
각한다.

14 candor   n. 솔직함
나는 그가 나의 질문에 완전히 솔직하게 답변
했다고 믿는다.

15 receptive   adj. 수용적인
너는 건설적 비판에 대해 조금 더 수용적일 수
있도록 노력하면 좋을 것 같아.

01 malignity   n. 악의, 앙심
제임스가 나를 배신할 때 처음으로 앙심이 어떤 느낌인지 확실하게 알았다.

02 tumult   n. 소란, 소동
길고양이가 나타나자 유치원의 놀이터에 잠시 소란이 일어났다.

03 intimated   v. 넌지시 알리다
교수님은 끄덕이고 웃으면서 해리엇에게 문제를 잘 풀고 있다고 넌지시 알렸다.

04 nuisance   n. 골칫거리
짐은 집청소 하는 것이 골칫거리라고 생각하지만, 나는 일종의 치료가 되는 것처럼 기분이 좋아진다.

05 thaw   v. 녹다
3월 말인데 아직도 서리가 녹기를 기다리고 있는 게 믿기지 않는다.

06 satiated   v. 충분히 만족한
믹은 지난 생물 수업에서 개구리 해부를 하며 그의 소름끼치는 환상을 충분히 만족시켜키며 즐거워했다.

07 broach   v. 꺼내다
앨리스를 만날 때, 아들의 사고 얘기 꺼내지 않도록 조심해.

08 irksome   adj. 짜증나는, 귀찮은
그 불쾌한 학생의 귀찮은 질문들이 교수님을 짜증나게 하기 시작했다.

09 baffled
v. 완전히 당황하게 만들다
책의 결말은 나를 완전히 당황하게 했다; 이야기가 그렇게 끝날 줄 몰랐다.

10 prowling
v. 살금살금 돌아다니다
야영지 경계선을 넘어가지 마: 야생 동물들이 근처 지역에서 살금살금 돌아다니고 있으니까.

11 trifling   adj. 하찮은, 사소한
난 너무 바쁘니까 사소한 일로 귀찮게 하지 마.

12 fetish   n. 집착
헨리에타는 한국에 이사 오고 나서부터 매운 음식에 대한 집착이 생겼다.

13 opine   v. 의견을 밝히다
뱁스 이모가 해당 주제에 대한 의견을 밝히고 싶어하는 것을 느꼈다.

14 prone   idiom. 수평의
탁자를 만들 때 상판이 완전 수평인 것을 꼭 확인해.

15 despoiled   v. 빼앗다
파리의 날씨가 영하까지 내려가는 바람에 그 도시를 방문 할 기회를 빼앗겼다.

Class 03

01 reverberated   v. 울리다
그녀의 키는 150cm이고 나뭇가지처럼 말랐지만, 목소리는 콘서트 홀 전체를 울렸다.

02 underpinned   v. 뒷받침하다
피고인은 고소인의 주장이 사실에 뒷받침되어 있지 않다고 주장했다.

03 cognitive   adj. 인식의, 인지적
아이가 다섯 살 때 글자를 읽도록 가르쳐주는 것은 아이의 인지 능력을 발전시키기에 좋다고 증명되었다.

04 welter   n. 엄청난 양
카일의 뇌에는 유용하기도 하고 쓸모없기도 한 엄청난 양의 정보가 저장되어 있다.

05 brawl   n. 패싸움, 주먹다짐
말싸움이 패싸움으로 악화되기까지 얼마 안 걸렸다.

06 aggrandized   v. 크게 하다, 확대하다
마크의 아버지는 거의 업계 최초로 인터넷 마케팅을 도입하면서 가족 사업을 확대했다.

07 allude   v. 암시하다, 넌지시 말하다
나단을 만날 때, 키 얘기 꺼내지 마: 그 주제에 매우 예민한 사람이야.

08 dismay   n. 실망, 경악
금융위기에 관한 뉴스는 많은 사람을 경악하게 했다.

09 malicious   adj. 악의적인
정치인은 신문이 본인에 대한 악의적인 거짓말을 퍼뜨리고 있다고 비판했다.

10 inexorable   adj. 멈출 수 없는
케이팝의 인기는 멈출 수 없는 것 같다.

11 slumber   n. 잠
아기는 새벽 두 시에 열이 드디어 내려가 깊은 잠에 빠졌다.

12 ornate   adj. 화려하게 장식된
그녀의 방안은 화려하게 장식되었다.

13 revamped   v. 개조하다, 개편하다
우리는 옛날 영화 스튜디오를 인수하여 실내 놀이공원으로 개조했다.

14 treacherous   adj. 기만적인, 신뢰할 수 없는
아무도 제임스가 그렇게 기만적인 사람일 줄 몰랐다: 그를 믿었던 모든 사람을 배신했다.

15 indignation   n. 분개
교통비의 갑작스러운 인상은 시민의 분개를 초래했다.

01 austere   adj. 꾸밈없는, 소박한
나는 매우 소박한 부모님 아래서 자라서 그런지 청소년인 자녀들에게 비싼 차를 선물하는 몇몇 부모들이 이해가 안 된다.

02 devoured   v. 집어삼키듯 먹다
리키는 너무 배고파서 내가 내 샌드위치의 반을 채 먹기도 전에 이미 자기 샌드위치를 집어삼키듯 다 먹었다.

03 herbivorous   adj. 초식성의
개는 선천적으로 초식성 동물이 아니지만, 소화불량일 때 풀을 먹기로 알려져 있다.

04 proficient   adj. 능숙한
캐나다, 러시아와 네덜란드에서 산 경험이 있는 개리는 프랑스어, 러시아어와 네덜란드어에 능숙하다.

05 evangel   n. 복음
돈이 현대의 복음이다: 모두가 숭배한다.

06 appalled   adj. 끔찍한 충격을 받은
우리 모두 폭풍이 우리 마을에 입힌 피해에 끔찍한 충격을 받았다.

07 negation   n. 반대
새로운 대통령의 정책은 전임자와 반대였다.

08 sublunary   adj. 달 아래의, 지구상에 있는
스토아 철학은 달 아래의 모든 즐거움이 헛되었다고 구술한다.

09 fragmentary   adj. 단편적인, 부분적인
나는 그 행사 때 일어난 일에 대해 기억이 띄엄띄엄 난다.

10 betook   v. 가게 하다, 가다
그가 저지른 실수의 심각성을 고려해서 레스터는 그의 관리자의 사무실로 가서 상황을 설명했다.

11 perpetuate   v. 영구화하다, 영속시키다
미국의 텔레비전 프로그램들은 여전히 아시아인들의 이미지를 이기적이고 수학만 잘하는 사람들로 영속시키고 있다.

12 egregious   adj. 심각한, 지독한, 극심하게 나쁜
나는 내가 이렇게 심각한 실수를 할 것이라고는 상상도 못했다.

13 obsolescence   n. 구식이 된, 진부화, 노후화
한동안, LP 레코드판은 구식이 되어 아무도 사용하지 않는 것처럼 보였지만, 지난 몇 년 동안 다시 유행을 타기 시작했다.

14 lamented   v. 애통하다, 애도, 애가
크라머 씨는 친구가 사망하자 애통해했다: 그들의 친분은 70년 동안 지속되었기 때문이다.

15 agitated   v. 뒤흔들다, 휘젓다, 마음을 어지럽히다
우리는 모두 큰 폭풍이 온다는 뉴스에 마음이 어지러웠다.

Class 05

Answers

01 levitation   n. 공중부양
공중에 떠 있는 명상하는 요기에 대한 고정적 이미지와 달리 요가를 한다고 공중부양을 할 수는 없다.

02 lurched   v. 휘청하다
갑자기 기차가 앞으로 휘청하면서 움직이기 시작했다.

03 whisked
v. 휘젓다, 재빨리 가져가다
이렇게 심각한 경제 불경기에서도 컴퓨터공학 전공자들은 졸업하자마자 기업에서 재빨리 데려간다.

04 foreshadowed
v. 전조가 되다, 조짐을 나타내다
다가오는 먹구름들이 폭풍우의 조짐을 나타냈다.

05 abject   adj. 극도로 비참한
헨리가 어렸을 때 그의 가족은 극도로 비참한 가난 속에서 생활했다.

06 colloquial
adj. 구어의, 일상적인 대화체의
주민들이 사용하는 몇몇 표현들은 내가 이해하기에는 너무 생소한 구어체였다.

07 temperament   n. 기질
그녀는 차분한 기질이 있어 흥분하지 않는다.

08 besieged   v. 포위하다, 둘러싸다
발표를 끝내자마자, 질문 세례로 둘러싸였다.

09 eloquent   adj. 유창한
많은 사람들은 그의 유창한 연설로 감동을 받았다.

10 discomfiture   n. 당황
복도에 있는 모든 사람들이 사이렌에 반응을 할 때 나는 당황해서 앉아만 있었다.

11 imprudent   adj. 경솔한
나는 톰의 계획에 대해 충분히 생각하지 않은 채 경솔하게 수락했다.

12 retention   n. 보유, 유지
회사의 직원 유지율은 굉장히 좋다: 5년 이상 일한 직원이 70%나 된다.

13 perched
v. ~에 앉아 있는, 위치한
내가 방에 들어갔을 때, 엄청 큰 앵무새가 작은 그네에 앉아 있어 놀랐다.

14 ramified
v. 가지를 내다, 분기하다
회사는 25년 전에 섬유제조업체로 설립되었지만 시간이 지나면서 각종 업계로 다변화하였다.

15 cow
v. 겁을 주다, 위협하다
그는 불량배이지만, 나에게 전혀 위협적이지 않다.

01 colloquial adj. 구어의, 일상적인 대화체의
나는 직장 후배들이 사용하는 구어체 표현들이 이해가 안 되자 늙고 있다는 사실을 실감했다.

02 besieged v. 포위하다, 둘러싸다
부끄러운 패배 이후, 혼자만 있고 싶었는데 집에 들어가자마자 엄마가 질문 세례로 나를 포위했다.

03 exponents n. 주창자
그 정치인은 세계화의 선두적인 주창자 중 한 명이었다.

04 perpetuates v. 영구화하다, 영속시키다
할리우드에서 아시아인과 라틴계 사람을 갱에 속해있는 사람, 또는 하찮은 범죄자로만 캐스팅하는 고집은 부정적인 고정관념을 영구화하기만 한다.

05 creed n. 신조
그는 물리학자고 나는 신학자다: 우리는 같은 신조를 공유하고 있지는 않지만 진실을 위한 탐구를 공통적으로 추구한다.

06 persecution n. 박해, 학대
게나디의 부모님은 정치적 박해를 피하기 위해 1980년대에 러시아에서 서구로 이민을 갔다.

07 aggrandize v. 크게 하다, 확대하다
빌은 돈 많은 인맥을 자랑하면서 본인을 더 대단한 사람으로 보이게 하기를 즐긴다.

08 ornate adj. 화려하게 장식된
기숙사 건물은 꽤 칙칙했지만, 몇몇 학생들은 방안을 꾸며 화려하게 장식했다.

09 indignant adj. 분개한
헨리는 사울이 둘이 같이 쓴 보고서에 대한 공을 모두 본인의 것으로 돌리자 분개했다.

10 abject adj. 극도로 비참한
패니가 여배우가 되려고 한 계획은 몇몇 영화 업계 종사자들에게서 재능이 없다는 말을 들으면서 극도로 비참하게 무너졌다.

11 ramified v. 분기하다, 가지를 내다
그 지하 운동은 메인스트림으로 가지를 뻗쳤다.

12 imprudent adj. 경솔한, 현명하지 못한
물의 온도를 확인하지 않고 수영장에 뛰어드는 것은 현명하지 못한 행동이다.

13 retention n. 보유, 유지
우리는 나이가 들면서 기억을 유지하는 능력이 서서히 저하된다.

14 foreshadowed v. 전조가 되다, 조짐을 나타내다
최고 경영자의 비용 절감에 대한 언급은 연봉 동결, 또는 정리 해고의 조짐을 나타냈다.

15 austere adj. 꾸밈없는, 소박한
해리슨 씨는 대부분 사람들의 상상 이상으로 부유했지만, 그는 자녀들에게 소박한 생활습관을 유지하라고 가르쳤다.

16 devoured v. 집어삼키듯 먹다
점심을 못 먹은 랜디는 저녁때 미트로프 2인분을 집어삼키듯 먹었다.

17 perched v. ~에 앉아 있는, 위치한
구조원은 아무도 물에 빠지지 않는지 확인하기 위해 의자에 높이 앉아 있었다.

18 dismay n. 실망, 경악
취업 성공에 대한 기대를 해서 그런지 마사는 불합격 소식을 받고 실망을 금치 못했다.

19 inexorable adj. 멈출 수 없는, 막지 못하는

인간은 자연의 멈출 수 없는 힘 앞에서 아무것도 할 수 없다.

20 construed   v. 해석하다
불행하게도 로버트는 나의 지적을 그의 일에 대한 반감으로 해석했다.

21 proficient   adj. 능숙한
해외 여러 나라에서 살고 자라서 그런지 잭은 5개국어를 능숙하게 구사할 줄 안다.

22 agitated   v. 뒤흔들다, 휘젓다, 마음을 어지럽히다
폴의 교통사고 소식은 그의 어머니의 마음을 심하게 어지럽혔다.

23 appalled   v. 끔찍한 충격을 주다
교장선생님은 전국연합학력평가를 본 고등학교 3학년 학생들의 점수의 중앙값이 너무 낮아 충격을 받았다.

24 revamped   v. 개조하다, 개편하다
헨리는 낡은 자동차 정비소를 인수하여 힙한 카페로 개조했다.

25 underpins   v. 뒷받침하다
대부분의 목격자 증언은 피의자의 알리바이를 뒷받침한다.

26 scrawls   n. 낙서, 휘갈겨 쓴 흔적
마크의 교과서에 문단에는 밑줄, 여백에는 낙서로 가득했다.

27 ambivalent   adj. 동시에 기쁘면서 슬픈, 엇갈리는, 양가적인
피터는 대학교에 입학하기 위해 떠나면서 기쁘면서도 슬픈 감정을 느꼈다: 새로운 모험을 시작할 수 있어 기뻤지만 가족과 친구들이 있는 고향을 떠나야 해서 슬펐다.

28 endearing   adj. 사랑스러운
크랜스턴 씨는 자신의 세 딸 중 막내가 가장 사랑스럽다고 생각했다.

29 discomfited   v. 당황하다
정부는 최근 외교적 사고에 의해 당황한 기색이 역력했다.

30 egregious   adj. 지독한, 극심하게 나쁜
신문 사설은 정부에서 시위자들을 상대로 폭력을 쓸 계획을 극심하게 나쁜 실수라고 했다.

31 화려한, 윤이 나는 – 수용적인 – 말을 잘 듣는

32 골칫거리 – 부정, 반대 – 짜증, 성가신 것

33 암시하다 – 넌지시 알리다 – 숨어 있다

34 풍부함 – 시끄러운 외침 – 소란, 소동

35 빼앗다 – 뒷받침하다 – 지지하다

36 매력적인 – 매력적인 – 즐기는

37 지적인 – 인지의, 인식의 – 소란, 소동

38 박해, 학대 – 권력 강화, 지위 확대 – 학대, 탄압

39 달 아래의 – 연결되지 않은 – 부분적인, 단편적인

40 신조 – 믿음, 신앙 – 아주 적은 돈, 박봉

41 하기 쉬운 – 평탄한 – 투창, 창

42 설교하다 – 쩔쩔매게 하다 – 완전히 당황하게 만들다

43 잠 – 휴식 – 기질

44 즐기다 – 즐기다 – 입증하다

45 전시하다 – 입후보 – 야외극, 행사

46 엄청난 양 – 설명하다, 이해하다 – ~을 이해하다

47 ~에 좋은 – 솔직한 – 호의적인

48 연장하다 – 영속시키다 – 발을 끌며 걷다, 이리저리 움직이다

49 정반대, 부정 – 반대, 대조 – 복음

50 투표권 – 참정권 부여 – 애정을 담은 말

51 애통하다 – 점검하다 – 비통해하다

52 혼란, 갑작스러운 소란 – 행진 – 행진

53 악의적인 – 단조로운 – 악의적인

54 기만적인 – 짜증나는 – 기만적인

55 분석 연구 – 활용, 결합 – 평론, 비평

56 아무런 장식이 없는 – 화려하게 장식된 – 꾸밈없는

57 더 이상 쓸모가 없는 – 끔찍한 – 구형의, 더 이상 쓸모없는

58 광택제 – 풍부 – 풍부함

59 실컷 만족시키다 – 끄다, 충족하다 – 꺼내다

60 녹다 – 끄적거리다 – 해동하다

01 sustenance

n. 자양분, 생명을 건강하게 유지시켜 주는 것, 식량

동굴에서의 생존하는 생물들은 빛이 없는 환
경에서도 자양분을 취할 수 있도록 진화했다.

02 circadian

adj. 24시간을 주기로 생활하는, 생물학적 주기의

며칠 동안 3시간씩도 못 잤더니 24시간을 하
루로 사는 주기가 완전히 망가졌다.

03 postulate

v. 상정하다, 증거 없이 추정하다

아인슈타인은 빛이 파동인 동시에 입자로 볼
수도 있다고 처음 상정했다.

04 elaborate

adj. 복잡한

질문을 하면 호라시오는 그의 이름을 어떻게
가지게 됐는지에 관한 복잡한 이야기를 해줄
것이다.

05 sanity

n. 온전한 정신

지난 며칠간 너무 바빠서 온전한 정신을 유지
할 수 있을지 궁금해지기 시작했다.

06 panacea

n. 만병통치약

산삼은 동양 의학에서 만병통치약으로 여겨
진다.

07 articulate

adj. 분명히 표현하다

그는 예술계 천재였고 말보다 작품으로 표현
을 더 잘했다.

08 abysmal

adj. 최악의

내 상사는 내 성과를 최악이라고, 앞으로 나아
진 모습을 보이지 않으면 해고를 할 수밖에 없
을 것이라고 하였다.

09 taut

adj. 팽팽한

내 테니스 채의 줄이 내 기준으로 너무 팽팽
했다.

10 constitution

n. 체질

그는 약한 체질을 가지고 태어나서 어린 시절
부터 병원을 자주 드나들었다.

11 incline

n. 경사

집은 경사가 심한 지역에 세워져 1층 입구로
들어오는 사람들은 뒷마당으로 가려면 2층을
걸어 올라가야 했다.

12 sanctioned

v. 허가, 승인

해로드 씨의 생산 증가를 위한 제안은 상사들
로부터 허가를 받지 못한 것으로 드러났다.

13 usurped

v. 빼앗다

나는 그녀의 마음속 내 자리를 다른 사람에게
빼앗김을 깨닫고 매우 슬펐다.

14 inefficacious

adj. 효력이 없는

정부가 실업 문제를 해결하기 위해 도입한 모
든 정책은 효력이 없는 것 같다.

15 yearning

n. 갈망

경제적으로 성공을 한 이후, 하워드는 정신적
성취에 대한 갈망이 생겼다.

16 susceptible

adj. 민감한, 예민한

수의사들은 그레이트데인이나 세인트버나드와
같은 큰 종의 개는 관절병에 민감하다고 한다.

01 fiscal   adj. 국가 재정의
한 국가의 재정 정책들이 정부의 인기를 상승시키기 위한 수단으로만 쓰이니 당연히 효과적일 것이라는 기대를 못한다.

02 bust   n. 실패, 망하다
데이빗의 첫 사업은 석 달 만에 망했다.

03 scrutiny
n. 정밀 조사, 철저한 검토
처음에는 실험 결과가 아무런 결과를 도출하지 못한 것처럼 보였으나, 철저한 검토 이후 연구자들은 아예 예상하지 못한 결과를 발견했다.

04 murals   n. 벽화
교회의 벽들은 성경에 나오는 내용을 기반으로 한 벽화로 덮였다.

05 perturbed
v. 혼란된, 동요된, 불안한
오늘 신문의 많은 이야기들은 나를 혼란스럽게 했다.

06 substantiate   v. 입증하다
아인슈타인이 이론을 실험을 통해 입증하기까지 30년이 넘게 걸렸다.

07 degradation   n. 비하, 저하
많은 선도적인 교육자들은 표준화된 시험들이 최근 몇 년 교육의 질을 저하시켰다고 말한다.

08 recessions   n. 불경기, 불황
경제 불경기에 상대적으로 영향을 받지 않는 직업을 위한 교육을 실시하는 건 중요하다.

09 volition   n. 자유 의지
다이어트 중이라, 제발 내 앞에서 아이스크림 먹지 마: 나는 의지가 약한 사람이야.

10 ephemeral
adj. 수명이 짧은, 단명하는
휴즈 씨는 20대 때 남성 밴드의 가수로 짧은 기간 인기를 즐긴 바가 있다.

11 brevity   n. 간결성, 짧음
책의 간결성에 속지 마라: 정말 엄청난 책이야.

12 enclave
n. 소수 민족 거주지, 큰 지역 속 작은 공간, 아지트
아버지가 젊은 시절 살았던 아파트는 신예 예술가, 음악가와 작가들의 아지트였다.

13 albeit   conj. 비록…일지라도
오랜 토의 이후 두 남성은 비록 망설여졌지만 서로 협조하기로 했다.

14 disdain   n. 업신여김, 무시
아인슈타인은 어렸을 때, 암기와 벼락치기를 통한 배움을 업신여겼다.

15 subservient   adj. 굴종하는
도니가 너보다 두 살 많다고 무조건 굴종해야 하는 건 아니야.

16 udders   n. 젖통
소의 젖통으로 황소와 구분할 수 있어.

01 plenipotentiary   n. 전권 대사
미국 독립 전쟁 동안 벤자민 프랭클린은 미국의 전권 대사로 프랑스 법원에 파견되었다.

02 marginal   adj. 주변부의, 미미한
제임스는 그가 열심히 노력했음이 성적에는 미미한 영향만 미쳤다는 사실을 알고 실망했다.

03 paramount
adj. 다른 무엇보다 중요한
대부분의 국민들은 경제 성장이 국가의 무엇보다 중요한 문제라고 생각한다.

04 lucrative   adj. 수익성이 좋은
많은 나라에서 주화사업이 수익성이 좋은 사업이라는 걸 아는 사람은 많지 않다.

05 emphatic
adj. 강조하는, 강한, 확실한
나는 그가 강조하는 논리에 설득당했다.

06 predominant   adj. 우세한, 지배적인
민주주의적 정부는 세 부분으로 분리되어 한 지사가 지배적인 권한을 가지지 않도록 되어 있다.

07 combatants   n. 전투원
토론 대회에 들어설 때 팀원들의 얼굴에 묻어난 투지는 토론자가 아닌 전투원의 모습을 보였다.

08 reverence   n. 숭배
강연자가 연단에 서자, 몇몇 지지자들은 그를 숭배하는 눈빛으로 바라보았다.

09 subordinate   adj. 부차적인, 하급자
부차적인 이슈들에 대해 얘기하면서 새지 말고 주요 논의사항에 대한 얘기만 하자.

10 shriveled   v. 쪼글쪼글해지다
사과들을 밖에 너무 오랫동안 둬서 쪼글쪼글해졌다.

11 convoked   v. 소집하다
회장은 긴급회의를 위해 모든 임원들을 소집했다.

12 cohesion   n. 결합, 응집력
이 나라는 정치적, 사회적 응집력이 거의 없고 다수의 부족, 집단 등으로 나뉘어 있다.

13 veritable
adj. 진정한, 굉장한, 엄청난
아만다는 키가 158cm이고 그녀의 남편인 트레버는 198cm이다: 둘이 같이 서 있을 때 트레버는 아만다 옆에서 엄청난 거인 같다.

14 mockery   n. 조롱
더 이상 내 이름에 대한 조롱은 받아들이지 않을 거야.

15 epitome
n. 훌륭한 본보기, 대명사, 전형
교장 선생님은 민디를 그가 원하는 본교의 학생의 훌륭한 본보기라고 지명했다.

16 emulate   v. 모방하다
많은 테니스 선수는 로저 페더러의 우승 기록을 모방하고자 노력했지만 실패한다.

17 confide   v. 털어놓다, 신뢰하다
내가 신뢰하는 사람은 많지 않다.

01 exacerbate   v. 악화시키다
마리아는 지금 개입하면 상황을 악화시키기만 할 것을 알았다.

02 hailed
v. 만세, 환호하며 맞이하다, 크게 칭찬을 듣다.
대통령은 대외 문제를 전문가답게 잘 해결하여 국민의 칭찬을 받았다.

03 bloated   adj. 부은
브라이언의 볼을 벌에 쏘인 바람에 얼굴의 반이 풍선처럼 부었다.

04 insatiable
adj. 채울 수 없는, 만족할 줄 모르는
말론은 글에 대한 채울 수 없는 갈망이 있다. 언젠가 엄청난 작가가 될 것이 분명하다.

05 mutable   adj. 변할 수 있는
두 당 모두 계약 조항들이 변할 수 있다고 동의했다.

06 posterior   adj. 뒤의
내 앞에서 걷고 있는 사람의 뒷모습만 봐도 윌리엄인 걸 알 수 있었다.

07 deploy   v. 배치하다
미국의 해군은 내년 후반기를 목표로 최첨단 원자력 잠수함을 배치하겠다고 발표했다.

08 perennial   adj. 지속되는
전력 부족은 지역에서 몇십 년간 지속되고 있는 문제다.

09 irrigation   n. 관개
고대 앙코르의 주민들은 관개 전문가들이었다: 현대 기술을 사용해도 만들기 어려운 수로망을 지었다.

10 alienated
v. 소원하게 만들다, 소외감을 느끼게 하다
연예인의 부유한 삶을 보여주는 텔레비전 프로그램들은 근근히 살아가는 사람들에게 소외감을 느끼게 했다.

11 labyrinthine   adj. 복잡한
그 음악가는 복잡한 복도 사이 오디션 방을 찾느라 몸을 풀 시간이 없었다.

12 precipitous   adj. 가파른
오늘 주식 시장은 가파른 하락세를 보여 전 세계의 투자자들을 겁에 질리게 했다.

13 altruistic   adj. 이타적인
이탈리아 르네상스 때 부유한 사람들은 이타적인 노력들로 다른 사람들과의 차이를 보였다.

14 presumption   n. 추정, 넘겨짚음
의사의 진단이 항상 맞다는 대중적인 추정은 매우 위험한 생각이다.

15 spooked   v. 겁먹은
저녁때의 갑작스러운 정전은 우리를 겁먹게 했다.

16 chronological
adj. 시간순, 연대순의, 발생 순서대로 된
데이터가 시간순으로 정렬이 되지 않아 헷갈렸다.

17 aggregate   n. 총, 합계
행사 막바지에 번 총액은 예상보다 훨씬 높았다.

01 proliferated   v. 급증하다, 확산되다
불교는 인도에서 유래됐지만, 크게 확산되면서 인도보다 동아시아에서 훨씬 번창했다.

02 deterrent   n. 제지하는 것
농부들은 허수아비를 세우는 것은 까마귀를 제지하는 수단으로 효율적이지 않다고 한다.

03 gauge   v. 측정기, 판단하다
그녀가 화난 건지 즐거운 건지 판단하기 어려웠다.

04 smudged   v. 마구 바르다, 더럽히다
군인들은 숲 속에서 위장을 하기 위해 얼굴에 위장 크림을 마구 발랐다.

05 demur   v. 이의를 제기하다
헨리가 나에게 저녁 초대를 할 때 나는 이의를 제기하지 않았다.

06 suffice   v. 충분하다
그의 자격을 검토하기 위해서는 면접 한 번으로 충분하다.

07 furl   v. 접다
간부 후보생들은 매일 새벽 여섯 시에 기상하여 침구를 접고 보관함에 넣어야 한다.

08 contradictory   adj. 모순되는
학생들은 회계 담당자와 학생 지도자 사이 모순되는 지시를 받아 혼란스러웠다.

09 substantive   adj. 실질적인
정부는 많은 새로운 정책을 도입했지만, 몇 년이 지난 후에도 실질적인 변화는 없었다.

10 ensues   v. 뒤따르다
로버트가 들어서는 방마다 웃음소리가 곧 뒤따른다.

11 jolted   v. 갑자기 거칠게 움직이다
마크가 나를 갑자기 거칠게 흔들면서 기말고사 때 더 잘하지 않으면 이 수업에서 낙제할 것을 깨닫게 했다.

12 vestigial   adj. 남아 있는
옛날 교회가 있던 곳에서 고고학자들은 기독교 이전의 문화의 남아 있는 흔적을 발견했다.

13 disseminated   v. 퍼뜨리다, 퍼지다
많은 학자들은 도시 괴담이 19세기 후반 빠른 속도로 미국 대륙 내에서 퍼진 사실에 놀란다.

14 conflating   v. 융합하다
아인슈타인은 현대 물리학의 두 대단히 뛰어난 이론: 상대성 이론과 양자역학을 융합시키는 데에 성공한 적이 없다.

01 subservient
adj. 순순히 말을 잘 듣는, 굴종하는
이사회는 일에 조금 더 순순히 말을 잘 듣는 사람을 원했기 때문에 전 CEO를 해고했다.

02 brevity   n. 간결성, 짧음
말이 많은 것과 말을 잘하는 것은 다르다: 간결성이 수다보다 좋은 순간들도 있다.

03 incline   n. 경사
등대가 경사가 심한 언덕 위에 지어져 있어서 그곳에 도달할 때 나는 숨이 턱에 와 닿았다.

04 sanction   v. 허가, 승인
두 정부는 나라들 사이 자유무역협정을 승인하기로 결정했다.

05 articulate   adj. 분명히 표현하다
머릿속에서는 생각과 감정이 많지만, 분명히 표현하기 너무 어렵다.

06 locomotion   n. 추진력, 운동, 이동
개복치는 꼬리지느러미가 없기 때문에 추진력을 얻기 위해 두 등지느러미를 사용한다.

07 postulated
v. 상정하다, 증거 없이 추정하다
아인슈타인이 처음 상대성 이론을 상정했을 때, 너무 파격적이어서 본인도 틀렸다고 생각했다.

08 circadian
adj. 24시간을 하루의 주기로 생활하는, 생물학적 주기의, 신체적 주기
일주일 동안 세 개의 각기 다른 시간대의 도시에 방문했더니 신체적 주기가 망가졌다.

09 substantiated   v. 입증하다
과학자의 이론은 처음 게재됐을 때 학계에서 조롱거리로 퍼졌었지만, 그가 죽고 50년이 지난 후 입증되었다.

10 perturbed
v. 혼란된, 동요된, 불안한
다가오는 경제 위기 소식이 많은 투자자들을 불안하게 했다.

11 convoking   v. 소집하다
영화는 은퇴한 지휘관이 민간인으로서 일을 하고 있는 이전 특공대 팀원들을 소집하면서 시작한다.

12 taut   adj. 팽팽한
테니스 채에 줄을 달 때, 줄이 팽팽할수록 콘트롤을 하기가 쉽고, 줄이 느슨할수록 더 많은 파워를 얻을 수 있다.

13 sustenance
n. 자양분, 생명을 건강하게 유지시켜 주는 것; 식량
판다는 대나무에서 얻을 수 있는 양분이 적기 때문에 매일 대나무 잎을 본인 무게의 70%만큼 먹는다.

14 coercive   adj. 강압적인
현대의 자본주의 국가에서 한 계층이 다른 사람들을 희생하며 자본을 더욱 얻기 위해 강압적인 힘을 쓰면 안 된다.

15 volition   n. 자유 의지
경찰 조사가 더욱 강화되었을 때, 용의자는 본인의 의지로 경찰서에 갔다.

16 confide   v. 털어놓다, 신뢰하다
나는 스티브에게 털어놓지 못할 비밀이 없을 정도로 그와 친하다.

17 disdain   n. 업신여김, 무시
인종, 종교나 성적 기호 때문에 여전히 무시당하는 사람이 있는 것이 참 슬프다.

18 imply
v. 암시하다, 넌지시 나타내다
그녀의 평가에 비난이 암시된 듯했다.

19 emulate   v. 모방하다
성공한 사람들의 인생을 모방하면 아마 무조건 실패할 것이다: 본인만의 성공 방법을 찾아야 한다.

20 epitome　　　　n. 대명사, 전형
여배우는 현재 60대지만 여전히 아름다움의
대명사로 여겨진다.

21 veritable
adj. 진정한, 굉장한, 엄청난
휴가에서 돌아오니 내 정원이 엄청난 정글이
되었다.

22 deploy　　　　　　v. 배치하다
해군은 3년 이내에 신세대 공격 잠수함을 배
치하겠다고 공지했다.

23 mutable　　　　adj. 변할 수 있는
아인슈타인의 위대한 발견은 시간과 공간이
절대적이지 않고 변할 수 있다는 사실이었다.

24 presumption
n. 넘겨짚음, 추정, 건방짐
제임스는 제니가 프로젝트를 완성하려면 그의
도움이 필요할 것이라고 넘겨짚은 점에 대해
사과했다.

25 inversion　　　　n. 역전, 자리바꿈
지난 50년 동안 사람들의 가치관의 걱정스러
운 역전이 있었다: 직업 만족도보다 돈, 공손
함보다 이기심이 중요시되고 있고, 자기확대가
품위를 대신하고 있다.

26 enclave
n. 소수 민족 거주지, 큰 지역 속 작은 공간, 아지트
현악기 제작자의 작업실은 가난한 음악 전공
생들, 음악가들과 일을 찾지 못하는 작곡가들
과 지휘자들의 아지트였다.

27 scrutiny
n. 정밀 조사, 철저한 검토
보고서의 철저한 검토 해 보니 많은 오류가 발
견되었다.

28 emphatic
adj. 강조하는, 강한, 확실한
폴란드의 축구 선수단은 어제 독일 팀을 확실
한 5–0으로 승리하며 준결승에 진출했다.

29 lucrative　　　　adj. 수익성이 좋은
데이빗은 전 세계에서 고급 커피빈을 수입하
면서 수익성이 좋은 사업을 했다.

30 paramount
adj. 다른 무엇보다 중요한
한 나라의 공교육의 질은 그 어느 정부에게 그
무엇보다 더 중요해야 한다.

31 모순되는 – 진정한 – 내용이 다른

32 비스듬한 – ~쪽으로 기울다, 경사 – 합치다

33 확산 – 살피다 – 퍼뜨리다

34 충분하다 – 시위, 이의를 제기하다 – 이의를
제기하다

35 실질적인 – 초보의, 근본적인 – 모순되는

36 소용없는 – 변할 수 있는 – 남아 있는

37 측정기, 치수 – 번지게 하다 – 더럽히다, 마
구 바르다

38 제지하는 것 – 제약, 제한 – 보유, 정체

39 전조가 되다 – 예측하다 – 앉아 있다, 높은
지위

40 경솔한 – 극도로 비참한 – 비참한

41 실패, 당황 – 온전한 정신 – 혼란

42 복잡한 – 불규칙한 – 내용이 다른, 부합하지
않는

43 상정하다 – 책정하다 – 가설을 세우다

44 끔찍한 – 최악의 – 효력 없는

45 갈망 – 지지, 보증 – 갈망

46 하기 쉬운, 경향이 있는 – 할 수 있는 – 고양
이 같은

47 국가 재정의 – 일시적인 – 순식간의

48 아지트 – 무너지다 – 공동체, 최소 행정 구역

49 우울증 – 자유 의지 – 자유 의지

50 비하, 저하 – 황폐, 무너짐 – 진부화

51 불경기 – 반란 사태 – 전복, 파괴

52 간결성 – 간결성 – 역전

53 응집력 – 정밀 조사 – 분석 연구

54 존경 – 숭배 – 대명사

55 명백한 – 업신여기는 – 확실한

56 술 취하지 않은, 진지한 – 자제하는 – 술, 둘
레를 형성하다

57 하위의 – 끊임없는 – 지속되는

58 헝클어진 – 넓어진 – 복잡한, 엉클어진

59 악화시키다 – 악화시키다 – 만세, 환호하며
맞이하다

60 가파른 – 가파른 – 읽을 수 있는, 또렷한

Class 13 Answers

01 derided   v. 조롱하다
여배우는 유치한 발언 때문에 미디어로부터
조롱당했다.

02 posterity   n. 후세
돌아가신 분들의 이름은 후세를 위해 교회 뒤
쪽 한 태블릿에 기록되어 있다.

03 teems
v. 풍부하다, 가득 차다
현미경 아래에 둔 연못수 한 방울은 생명체로
가득 차 있다.

04 inexorable   adj. 멈출 수 없는
이 지역에서 발생하고 있는 젠트리피케이션은
멈출 수 없는 현상 같다.

05 perchance   adv. 아마 어쩌면
이것은 묘에 묻힐 때까지 지킬 비밀이야; 아마
어쩌면 어느 날 말해줄 수도 있어.

06 interpose   v. 끼어들다, 중재하다
부모님은 너무 세게 다투기 시작하셔서 끼어
들 수밖에 없었다.

07 adamant
adj. 요지부동의, 단호한
리처드는 이 거절에 대해 단호했다. 생각을 바
꾸지 않을 것 같다.

08 infested   v. 들끓다, 우글거리다
건물 내부에 바퀴벌레가 우글거렸다.

09 odorous   adj. 냄새가 나는
캘커타의 시장은 시끄럽고, 더럽고 냄새가 나
는 곳들이지만, 굉장히 맛있는 음식을 팔기도
한다.

10 enumerate   v. 열거하다
이 항공사의 서비스에 대한 불만사항이 너무
많아 열거할 힘도 없다.

11 enact   v. 제정하다
국회에서 수정된 동물학대 관련 법률을 제정
하기까지 아직 멀었다.

12 infuses   v. 불어넣다
그 훌륭한 작가는 항상 유머와 갈망을 작품에
불어넣는다.

13 geriatric   adj. 늙은이, 노인의
저희 어머니는 65세밖에 안됐습니다. 노인처
럼 대하지 말아주세요.

14 pristine
adj. 완전 새것 같은, 자연 그대로의
여름 관광객들이 가자, 해수욕장은 빠르게 자
연 그대로의 모습을 찾았다.

15 repudiated   v. 거부하다
최근 기자회견에서 대통령은 정부가 경제위기
를 잘못 처리했다는 비난을 전면 거부했다.

01 stagnation   n. 침체, 부진
몇십 년간의 부진 이후, 빠른 변화와 시장 경제를 위한 대중적 고조가 존재한다.

02 ominous   adj. 불길한
엄마에게 미적분학 과목에 낙제했다고 말씀드렸을 때, 엄마는 5초간의 불길한 침묵 후 나에게 폭발적으로 분노하셨다.

03 alteration   n. 변화, 고침
아빠의 턱시도를 약간 고치면 나한테 맞을 것 같아서 기뻤다.

04 conceive   v. 상상하다
나는 그런 아이디어를 절대 상상도 하지 못할 것같다.

05 undulate   v. 파도 모양을 이루다
켄터키에서 우리는 몇 마일을 걸친 밀밭이 바람에 파도 모양을 이뤄 요동치는 것을 보았다.

06 mundane   adj. 일상적인, 재미없는
나는 재미없는 일상을 보낸다: 딱히 흥미진진한 일을 경험하지는 않는다.

07 aloof   adj. 냉담한
주변 사람들이 즐기며 좋은 시간을 보내는 동안 그녀는 혼자 냉담하게 서 있었다.

08 hierarchy   n. 계층, 체계
많은 아시아의 대기업들은 엄격한 경영 관리 체계가 있다.

09 juvenile   adj. 유치한
그는 거의 30세가 되었지만, 가끔 여전히 유치하게 행동한다.

10 clerical   adj. 사무직의
해리엇은 천성적으로는 예술가이나, 월세와 관리비 등을 내기 위해 사무직에서 일하고 있다.

11 enfeebled   v. 약화시키다
오랫동안 소방관으로 힘들게 일한 경험은 해리스 씨의 건강을 약화시켰다.

12 monotony   n. 단조로움
길드 박사의 단조로운 목소리는 강의를 매우 지루하게 한다.

13 gravitate   v. 끌리다
해리의 짜릿한 성격은 사람을 그에게 끌리게 한다.

14 imperative   adj. 긴요한, 반드시 해야 하는
포괄적이고 균형 잡힌 교육은 강하고 자신감 넘치는 세대를 키우기 위해 긴요하다.

15 stupefied   v. 깜짝 놀라게 하다, 충격을 주다
리처드는 패밀리 레스토랑에서 가족들과 식사를 한 이후 영수증을 보자 깜짝 놀랐다.

16 preposterous   adj. 말도 안 되는
경제 상황이 나아지고 있다는 말도 안 되는 기사를 신문에서 봤다.

01 vernacular n. 말, 구어
스코틀랜드에 처음 이사 갔을 때, 사람들이 무슨 말을 하는지 아예 못 알아들었지만 그들의 말을 서서히 나도 사용하기 시작했다.

02 dispirited
adj. 의기소침한, 낙심한
세계 1차 대전에서의 굴욕적인 패배 이후, 낙심한 독일 사람들은 희생양을 찾기 시작했고 결국 유대인들에게서 찾았다.

03 garnered v. 얻다
초기에 상대적으로 약했던 후보자는 선거운동 기간 말미에 선거를 이기기 위한 지지를 충분히 얻었다.

04 spawn v. 알을 낳다
연어는 담수에서 부화하지만 다 자랐을 때는 바닷물에서 생활을 하고, 알을 낳기 위해 고유 하천으로 돌아가 죽는다.

05 catalyst n. 촉매, 기폭제
빌리가 공부를 열심히 하기 위해 필요했던 유일한 촉매는 변호사인 사촌 헨리가 포르쉐를 운전하며 오는 모습을 보는 것이었다.

06 analogous adj. 유사한
기후 패턴은 작년과 유사했다.

07 empirical
adj. 경험에 의거한, 실험에 의거한
아인슈타인의 상대성 이론은 초기에 실험에 의거한 증거로 증명을 하지 못하여 많은 지적을 받았다.

08 ascertain v. 알아내다
전쟁 동안 관련 자료들이 많이 없어져서 그가 언제 어디서 태어났는지 알아내기 어렵다.

09 attest v. 증명하다
자넷의 능력에 대해 걱정이라면 내가 그녀의 역량을 보증할 수 있다.

10 prominent
adj. 눈에 잘 띄는, 두드러진
워렌을 처음 만날 때 그의 두드러진 코부터 보인다.

11 constituent
adj. 구성 성분, 을 구성하는
문제가 너무 복잡하니, 해결책에 더 빠르게 도달할 수 있도록 구성하는 부분으로 나누자.

12 fetter v. 구속하다
남자가 아직 청소년일 때 저지른 실수 때문에 그의 미래를 구속하는 것은 불공평하다.

13 convivial adj. 명랑한, 유쾌한
호텔에 도착했을 때, 유쾌한 직원들이 환영해주며 바로 집처럼 편안하게 해주었다.

14 contend v. 다투다
사업 초기 단계에 마틴은 허가를 신청할 때 시청의 관료와 다퉈야 했다.

15 compulsion n. 강요, 부담감
나의 자의로 도와줬으니, 나한테 신세를 져서 갚아야 한다는 부담감을 안 느꼈으면 좋겠어.

Class 16

01 devised   v. 창안하다, 고안하다
리처드는 내가 상상도 하지 못할 계획을 고안했다.

02 clout   n. 영향력
세계적인 기업들이 그들의 영향력을 이용해 정부 정책을 바꾸려고 하는 것이 명백하다.

03 admirable
adj. 존경을 살만한, 감탄스러운, 훌륭한
본인이 저지른 실수를 인정하는 것은 매우 존경을 살만한 일이다.

04 agitation   n. 불안, 시위
반국가 시위는 정부의 고관들을 걱정시키기 시작했다.

05 attribution
n. 속성, 권능, 귀착시킴
이 조각이 로댕의 작품이라는 사실은 증명된 적이 없다.

06 pittance   n. 아주 적은 돈, 박봉
많은 사회 운동가들은 국가들이 방어를 위해 소비하는 돈에 비해 세계의 빈곤을 없애기 위한 필요한 돈이 더 적다고 주장한다.

07 homogenized
v. 균질화하다, 통일하다
미국의 전경은 쇼핑몰과 패스트푸드 식당으로 통일되었다.

08 cohort   n. 집단, 지지자
21-28세 집단 중 실업률은 12%가 넘는다.

09 sanctuary
n. 보호구역, 안식처, 피난처
한 씨가 미국으로 이민간 지 5년이 지났고, 이제서야 미국이 본인이 생각했던 안식처가 아님을 깨달았다.

10 miser   n. 구두쇠
아저씨는 구두쇠라고 불렸지만, 그는 많은 사람들이 모르게 매년 지역 어린이 병원에 수천 달러씩 기부했다.

11 scatterbrained
adj. 정신이 산만한 사람
그는 훌륭한 수학자로 유명했지만, 실제 그를 만나는 사람들은 정신이 산만한 사람이라는 인상을 받는다.

12 distortion
n. 찌그러진 상태, 왜곡된 이야기
정치인은 본인에 대한 비평을 적은 기사를 진실을 왜곡한 이야기라고 비난했다.

13 aspirations   n. 포부, 염원
케네스가 봉사를 꾸준히 하는 이유가 추후에 공직자로 출마할 포부가 있기 때문이라는 의심이 들기 시작했다.

14 retrieve   v. 되찾아오다
경찰은 훔쳐진 보석들을 몇 시간 만에 되찾았다.

15 dawdled
v. 꾸물거리다, 머물렀다
점심시간이 거의 끝났지만, 우리는 식당에 머물렀다.

16 reproach   n. 비난
해군함정에서 함장의 행동과 결정은 비난 대상으로 삼으면 안된다.

Class 17 Answers

01 sporadic   adj. 산발적인
민간 투자로 프로젝트를 지원할 정부의 계획은 큰 실패로 드러났다: 관심을 보인 투자자는 많지 않았고 산발적이었기 때문이다.

02 combustible
adj. 불이 잘 붙는, 인화성의
집시 여성들이 판 조화들은 불이 잘 붙는 물질인 셀룰로이드로 만들어졌다.

03 fuss   v. 호들갑, 법석을 떨다
형이 휴가 때 집에 온다고 하자, 엄마는 곧바로 뭘 먹여야 할지 호들갑을 떠셨다.

04 overawed   adj. 위압하다
어린 시절 롤모델이었던 유명한 축구선수 지네딘 지단을 만났을 때 위압감을 느꼈다.

05 ponder   v. 곰곰이 생각하다
이것은 가볍게 결정할 문제가 아니야: 며칠 동안 곰곰이 생각하고 결정해.

06 annihilated
v. 전멸시키다, 완파하다
1415년 아쟁쿠르 전투에서 5천 명의 영국 군대는 2만 명이 넘는 프랑스 군대를 전멸시켰다.

07 meander   v. 거닐다
내가 생각하는 좋은 여행은 한 번도 가본 적 없는 도시에 가서 배고플 때까지 길거리를 거닐다가, 좋은 식당을 찾아서 지역 음식을 맛보는 것이다.

08 shudder   v. 몸을 떨다
날이 매우 덥지만, 밤바람은 너의 몸을 떨리게 할 거야.

09 trajectory   n. 탄도, 궤적
실력 좋은 테니스 선수는 공에 스핀을 넣어 원하는 방향으로 궤적을 그리게 할 수 있다.

10 adorn   v. 꾸미다, 장식하다
까치는 둥지를 숟가락이나 금속 장신구 등 반짝이는 물건으로 장식하는 동물로 알려져 있다.

11 surmount
v. 극복하다, 의 위에 얹히다
한 이집트 속담에 따르면, "피라미드의 정사에 오를 수 있는 유일한 두 동물은 독수리와 달팽이다".

12 encountered
v. 맞닥뜨리다, 접하다, 만나다
클락 가정은 내가 만난 가장 시끄러운 가족이다.

13 corroborates   v. 확증하다
남편이 아내의 알리바이를 확증하는 발언은 법정에서 효력이 없을 것이다.

14 testimonies   n. 증언
사건 현장의 두 목격자는 상충하는 증언을 했다.

15 mumbles   v. 중얼거리다
제프리와 캠핑을 했을 때, 그가 잠결에 중얼거린다는 사실을 알게 됐다.

16 scrupulous   adj. 세심한, 꼼꼼한
학교 식당의 영양사는 학생들에게 영양가 있으면서 맛있는 식사를 제공할 수 있도록 세심하게 신경을 쓴다.

Class 18

01 spherical · adj. 구 모양의
에담 치즈는 작고 동그란 공 모양을 가진다.

02 trajectory · n. 탄도, 궤적
그 혜성의 궤적을 추적하는 천문학자들은 혜성이 지구를 지나칠 때 지구에서 볼 수 있을 것이라고 한다.

03 surmounted
v. 극복하다, 의 위에 얹히다
누구나 인생의 어려움을 겪지만, 루이 밀란이 그가 오늘의 그가 되기까지 극복한 어려움은 꽤나 엄청나다.

04 combustible · adj. 불이 잘 붙는
강변 옆에 쌓여있는 목재는 몇 달 동안 마르고 있어서 아마 지금 불이 엄청 잘 붙는 상태일 것이다.

05 sporadic · adj. 산발적인
치과에 산발적으로 다녀오는 것은 충분하지 않다: 너는 앞으로 정기적인 검사를 해야 한다.

06 fussed
v. 호들갑, 법석을 떨다
마리아는 손님 중 두 명이 채식주의자임을 발견했을 때, 어떤 음식을 준비해야 할지 호들갑을 떨었다.

07 perchance · adv. 아마 어쩌면
이 책은 훌륭하다: 혹시 읽었어?

08 doldrums · n. 부진, 침체
그 가수는 몇십 년 전에 히트곡 몇 개를 발매했지만, 그 이후부터 그의 커리어는 침체기를 들어섰다.

09 infested
v. 들끓다, 우글거리다
경악스럽게도 로렌의 부엌은 불개미로 우글거렸다.

10 pristine
adj. 완전 새것 같은, 자연 그대로의
대런의 골동품 차는 홍수 중에 침수되어, 그 이후 다시 새것처럼 복원하기까지 3개월이 걸렸다.

11 gravitate · v. 끌리다
경제 불황기동안 많은 구직자들은 공직에 끌린다: 연봉이 높진 않지만 안정성이 보장되기 때문이다.

12 stupefied
v. 깜짝 놀라게 하다, 충격을 주다
제이슨이 폭력 혐의를 받았을 때 우리는 모두 깜짝 놀랐다: 그는 원래 온화한 사람이기 때문이다.

13 ominous · adj. 불길한
윌슨은 그의 상사가 사무실에서 윌슨을 보자고 했을 때 불길한 기운이 엄습했다.

14 preposterous · adj. 말도 안 되는
영화의 전제는 말이 안 됐지만, 히어로 영화에서 현실적인 내용을 기대하는 것 자체가 불합리한 것 같다.

15 ascertained · v. 알아내다
밀드레드가 그녀의 라커에 죽은 쥐를 넣은 사람의 정체를 알아내자, 바로 교장선생님의 사무실에 가서 보고했다.

16 mumble · v. 중얼거리다
자취를 시작한 뒤, 혼자 중얼거리는 내 모습을 발견했다.

17 scatterbrained
adj. 정신이 산만한 사람
많은 사람들은 오마가 정신이 산만한 사람이라고 생각했지만, 그는 사실 꽤 예리했다.

18 aspirations · n. 포부, 염원
미국의 18대 대통령인 율리시스 그랜드는 원래 정치와 관련한 포부가 아예 없었다.

19 clout   n. 영향력

미안하지만, 우리 회사에서는 일자리를 줄 수 없을 것 같아: 내게 그럴만한 영향력이 없어.

20 dawdle

v. 꾸물거리다, 머물렀다

헬렌의 어머니는 헬렌에게 학교 끝나고 꾸물거리지 말고 바로 집에 오라고 하셨다.

21 meandered   v. 거닐다

갈 데도 없고 만날 사람도 없는 나는 백화점에서 거닐며 윈도우 쇼핑을 했다.

22 lisp   n. 허짤배기소리

폴은 보컬 코치와 훈련을 하며 허짤배기소리를 없앨 수 있었다.

23 prattling

v. 지껄이다, 수다를 떨다

학교 가는 길에 버스 뒤쪽에 앉아 있던 세 여자들은 수다를 멈추지 않았다.

24 interpose   v. 끼어들다, 중재하다

미국은 이라크에 폭탄을 떨어뜨리겠다고 발표했을 때, 러시아는 중재하겠다고 했다.

25 odorous   adj. 냄새가 나는

갓 자른 장미가 이렇게 냄새가 날 줄 몰랐다.

26 vernacular   n. 말, 구어

그는 통역가가 관객이 이해하기 쉽게 말을 의역할 수 있도록 여러 번 멈추면서 말을 이어갔다. .

27 analogous   adj. 유사한

잠수함 추진 장치의 원리는 비행기의 제트 엔진과 유사하다. 앞에서 물을 빨아 압축시키고, 뒤로 내뿜으면서 선박을 앞으로 가게 하는 것이다.

28 fetter   v. 구속하다

다른 사람들의 의견이 너를 구속하게 하지 마.

29 constituent

adj. 구성 성분, 을 구성하는

카페인은 차와 커피 같은 음료수의 주요 구성 성분이다.

30 attests   v. 증명하다

그녀는 이력서가 증명하듯 굉장한 경력을 가졌다.

31 garnered   v. 얻다

그 작가는 그가 쓴 책 한 권이 영화로 제작되자 대중으로부터 많은 관심을 얻었다.

32 compulsion   n. 강요

가게 주인은 이 테니스 채를 일주일동안 무료로 쓰게 해주셨다. 나는 완전히 쓸 의향이 있지 않은 이상 억지로 구매할 마음이 없다.

33 clerical   adj. 사무직의

내 사업은 비서를 고용하기에는 너무 작아서 내가 사무적인 일을 다 한다.

34 juvenile   adj. 유치한

현재 40대인 제임스는 절대 성숙해지지 않을 것이다. 그는 나이가 들수록 더 유치해지기만 하는 것 같다.

35 undulate

v. 파도 모양을 이루다

음악이 서서히 재생되자, 댄서들은 그에 맞게 파도 모양을 만드는 동작을 하였다.

36 adamant

adj. 요지부동의, 단호한

잭은 그의 식단을 지키기 위한 단호한 태도를 보였다.

37 geriatric   adj. 늙은이, 노인의

채플 간호사님은 노인 병동에서 일하면서 받는 스트레스는 아동 병동에서 일하면서 받는 스트레스보다 훨씬 적다고 말했다.

38 infuse   v. 불어넣다

아이들에게 도덕에 대한 감각을 불어넣는 것은 학교만의 일이 아니다. 부모님도 같은 일을 해야 한다.

39 aloof   adj. 냉담한

데이트 상대가 데이트 내내 냉담해서 꽤나 실망스러웠지만, 나중에 그녀가 그냥 부끄러움을 많이 타는 사람인 것을 알게 됐다.

40 convivial   adj. 명랑한, 유쾌한
저녁 식사의 분위기는 편안하고 유쾌했다.

41 homogenize
v. 균질화하다, 통일하다
서독일과 동독일이 통일했을 때, 정부의 첫 정
책은 두 교육 체계를 통일시키는 것이었다.

42 맞닥뜨리다 – 불어넣다 – 맞서다

43 퍼뜨리다 – 곰곰이 생각하다 – 심사숙고하다

44 둑 – 둑 – 생울타리

45 기울어지다 – 문턱, 한계점 – 맨 끝, 한계

46 입증하다 – 뒤흔들다 – 확증하다

47 폐지 – 전멸 – 임명

48 결과로 보다 – 비난 – 간주하다

49 찌그러뜨림, 왜곡 – 변화, 고침 – 주입

50 영향력 – 집단 – 조직, 무리

51 실증적인 – 관찰된 – 물결 모양의

52 자극제 – 자유 의지 – 촉매, 기폭제

53 전능한 – 반대 감정이 병존하는 – 우위, 패권

54 완전 새것 같은 – 멈출 수 없는 – 수그러들
지 않는

55 거부하다 – 창궐하다 – 우글거리다

56 집어삼키다 – 게걸스레 먹다 – 실컷 만족시
키다

57 지독한 – 심각한 – 불이 잘 붙는

58 영속시키다 – 열거하다 – 연장시키다

59 얻다 – 지배하다 – 아우르다, 에워싸다

60 쏟아지다 – 풍부하다 – 퇴비, 두엄

Class 19

01 realm   n. 영역
현대 기술은 50년 전까지만 해도 공상 과학의 영역으로 여겨졌던 기기를 만들 수 있게 했다.

02 wayward   adj. 다루기 힘든
모든 청소년들은 사춘기 때 힘든 시기를 한 번쯤은 겪을 것으로 예상된다.

03 depict   v. 그리다
그 사진가의 사진은 일반인들의 인생을 그린다.

04 sophisticated
adj. 세련된, 교양 있는
세련된 척하지 마. 그냥 너만의 모습을 보여줘.

05 ritual   n. 의례
부모님과 일요일마다 먹는 점심은 일종의 의례가 되어버렸다.

06 lurking
v. 잠복하는, 숨어 있는
마틸다는 집 근처에서 잠복하는 사람이 있는 것 같아 경찰에 신고했다.

07 upheaval   n. 격변, 대변동
이직은 신나는 도전이 될 수 있지만, 굉장한 감정적 격변의 시기일 수도 있다.

08 lavish   adj. 풍성한, 호화로운
베르사유 궁전에 방문하면서 프랑스 군주의 호화로운 삶을 잠시나마 느낄 수 있었다.

09 fluorescent   adj. 형광성의, 선명한
선명한 흰 조명이 모든 사람을 창백해 보이게 했다.

10 sparse   adj. 드문, 희박한
땅은 황량하고 초목이 드문 바위투성이여서 농업이 거의 불가능하다.

11 austerity   n. 검소함
나는 이전만큼 돈을 많이 벌고 있지 않아서 검소한 일상생활을 보내야 한다.

12 pessimistic   adj. 비관적인
지금 상황에 대해서 지나치게 비관적일 필요는 없다.

13 sly   adj. 교활한, 음흉한
그의 착해 보이는 행실을 믿지 마: 그는 사실 음흉하고, 정직하지 못하고 교활해.

14 forestall   v. 미연에 방지하다
많은 폭동 진압 경찰들이 폭력적인 시위를 미연에 방지하기 위해 시내 곳곳에 배치되었다.

01 dwell   v. 살다
몇몇 파푸아 뉴기니 부족들은 야생 동물에게
공격당하지 않으려고 나무 위 5미터 이상 높
이에 지은 오두막에 산다.

02 perilous   adj. 아주 위험한
10년 전까지만 해도, 해지고 이 지역은 걸어다
니기 조차도 매우 위험했지만, 지금은 굉장히
안전하다.

03 inflammatory
adj. 강한 분노를 유발하는
정치적 토론 중일 때, 상대의 강한 분노를 유
발하는 발언에 뒤흔들리지 않는 것이 중요하다.

04 solicitude   n. 배려
주민들의 배려 덕분에 난민들은 정부 구호품
이 도착하기 전까지 잘 버틸 수 있었다.

05 stiffened   v. 뻣뻣해지다
아가타에게 마음이 있는 윈슬로우는 그녀가
그를 향해 걸어오고 있는 것을 보자 긴장해 몸
이 뻣뻣해졌다.

06 abandoned   v. 버려지다, 유기된
리처드는 새끼일 때 유기된 길고양이 세 마리
를 입양했다.

07 prevail   v. 승리하다
나는 정의로운 캐릭터들이 마지막에 승리하는
영화를 좋아한다.

08 procure   v. 구하다
팀원들이 나에게 요청한 첫 번째 일은 작년에
비슷한 프로젝트를 수행한 크리스티의 도움을
구하는 것이었다.

09 consolidate   v. 통합하다
두 회사는 비영업 부서들을 통합해서 운영 비
용을 줄이기로 결정했다.

10 reconcile   v. 조화시키다
직장을 다니는 여성들은 직장에서 업무적으로
요구되는 것과 좋은 어머니가 되도록 요구되
는 것들을 조화시키기 매우 어렵다.

11 tranquil   adj. 평온한
아침의 호수는 잔잔하고 평온했다.

12 impeded   v. 지연시키다
진흙으로 덥힌 길바닥은 시골길을 지나가기에
어렵게 만들었다.

13 pummel   v. 계속 치다
형제는 어렸을 때, 걸핏하면 서로를 주먹으로
때리곤 하였으나, 지금은 매우 친하다.

01 discordant

adj. 조화를 이루지 못하는, 불협화

몇몇 참여자들이 논의사항에 반대되는 의견을 가지는 바람에 회의의 분위기는 별로 조화롭지 못했다.

02 buttress

v. 지지하다, 외부지지

벽을 지지하지 않으면, 이 집은 곧 무너질 것이다.

03 nuisance

n. 귀찮은 존재, 골칫거리, 방해되는 것

어렸을 때, 아버지가 사무실에서 일하실 때 내가 귀찮게 굴지 않는 조건으로 옆에서 놀 수 있게 해주셨다.

04 commendable

adj. 칭찬받을 만한

데이빗이 얻은 상금을 모두 기부한 사실은 매우 칭찬받을 만했다.

05 prescribe

v. 처방하다

한국 의사들은 장기적으로 면역 체계에 해로운 항생제를 너무 자주 처방한다고 알려져 있다.

06 strides

n. 큰 걸음

마크는 키가 너무 커서 그의 옆에서 거의 달려야 그의 큰 보폭을 맞출 수 있었다.

07 impervious

adj. ~에 영향받지 않는

멕시코에서 휴가를 보내는 동안, 마사가 더위에 영향받지 않는 모습을 봤다: 다른 사람들다 땀에 젖어있을 때 혼자 땀 한 방울도 흘리지 않았다.

08 telltale

adj. 숨길 수 없는

테리는 옷도 다르게 입었고 머리카락도 새로 잘랐지만, 숨길 수 없는 그의 목소리를 들었을 때 테리임을 알았다.

09 foster

v. 조성하다

대통령은 더욱 자유로운 세계 무역과 빠른 경제성장을 조성할 수 있는 정치적 승리를 거두려고 노력하고 있다.

10 sediments

n. 침전물

침전물이 바닥까지 내려갈 때까지 기다린 뒤에 위의 투명한 액체를 떠라.

11 radiated

v. 퍼지다

그 운동은 영국에서 시작된 후 유럽 전체로 퍼졌다.

12 seamless

adj. 아주 매끄러운, 연결한 자국이 보이지 않는

은퇴하는 회장과 새로 선출된 회장은 매끄러운 인수인계를 위해 몇 달 동안 함께 일을 했다.

13 intricate

adj. 복잡한

레미제라블의 줄거리는 사람들이 일반적으로 생각하는 것보다 훨씬 복잡하다.

14 conjectural

adj. 추측의

영화는 실제 이야기를 기반으로 제작되었다고 발표됐지만, 많은 장면은 추측된 이야기로 만들어진 것이 분명했다.

15 endorse

v. 지지하다

나는 후보자의 대부분 의견들을 지지하기 어렵다.

16 fluctuate

v. 변동을 거듭하다

이른 봄에는 하루의 일교차가 15도 이상 변동될 수 있다.

01 havoc   n. 큰 혼란
신문 사설은 정부를 신랄하게 비난하며 새로운 조세 제도는 중소기업의 큰 혼란을 불러일으킬 것이라고 했다.

02 scrumptious   adj. 아주 맛있는
테이블이 세 개밖에 없는 매우 작은 음식점이었지만, 제공되는 식사는 굉장히 맛있었다.

03 maven   n. 전문가
제시카는 12살밖에 안 됐지만, 노련한 패션 전문가만큼 패션 트렌드에 대해 설명할 수 있었다.

04 fickle   adj. 변덕스러운
해럴드는 식사를 할 음식점을 고를 때 꽤 변덕스럽다.

05 inculcate   v. 심어주다
현대 교육 체제는 학생들에게 지식에 대한 열의를 심어주는 데에 실패하고 있다는 비평을 받고 있다.

06 woeful   adj. 한심한, 몹시 슬픈
사무엘은 수학과 과학 능력이 뛰어나지만, 역사와 지리에 한심한 지식 부족을 보인다.

07 offshoot   n. 파생물
대부분의 사람들은 포스트모더니즘 예술이 모더니즘 예술의 파생물이라고 생각하지만, 사실 아니다.

08 yeaned   v. (양, 염소가) 낳다
작년에 입양한 두 마리의 양 새끼 양을 여럿 낳아서 이제 여섯 마리가 됐다.

09 duplicitous   adj. 불성실한, 사기의
대통령은 캠페인의 주요 공약 하나를 당선되자마자 폐지시켰다: 당연히 많은 사람들이 그를 사기꾼으로 여긴다.

10 nitpick   v. 별것 아닌 트집을 잡다
내가 생각했을 때 보고서를 완성된 것 같았지만, 래리는 며칠 동안 모든 단어와 문장에서 별 것 아닌 트집을 잡았다.

11 wangle   v. (부정하게) 얻어 내다
친구 그렉이 웨이터로 근무하는 카페에서 식사를 하면서 혹시 디저트나 커피를 몰래 얻어낼 수 있는지 물어봤다.

12 antics   n. 익살스러운 짓
아이의 난폭하고 익살스러운 행동은 윌슨 씨를 짜증나게 하기 시작했다.

13 gnashes   v. 이를 갈다
대럴은 올라와 결혼하기 전까지 자기가 잠결에 이를 가는 줄 몰랐다.

14 munificence   n. 아낌없이 줌, 관유
아동 병원은 지지자들이 아낌없이 후원하지 않았으면 운영하지 못했을 것이다.

15 fanfare   n. 대대적인 축하, 팡파르
애플은 그 어느 때와 같은 팡파르를 울리며 새로운 아이폰을 출시했다.

01 bromide
n. 클리쉐, 식상한 표현, 고정관념
'겨울왕국'이 나온 이후, 'let it go'라는 표현은
식상한 표현이 되었다.

02 obsolescent
adj. 쇠퇴해 가는, 시대에 뒤져
내 컴퓨터는 8년이 되었고 시대에 뒤처졌지만,
인터넷 검색과 이메일 전송으로만 사용하기
때문에 괜찮다.

03 doleful
adj. 슬픈, 애절한
이유는 모르겠지만, 글렌다는 저녁 내내 슬픈
모습으로 앉아있었다.

04 amorous
adj. 애정 있는, 사랑과 관련 있는
케이트는 해리가 그녀의 업무에 대한 전문적
관심을 보이는 것을 자기에게 이성적인 관심
이 있는 것으로 해석했다.

05 lax
adj. 느슨한
불행하게도, 한국의 환경법은 너무 느슨하다.

06 waive
v. 면제해주다, 포기하다
신용카드 회사들은 새로운 고객을 유입하기
위해 첫해의 수수료를 면제해 준다.

07 salient
adj. 핵심적인, 가장 두드러진
투어 도중에 우리의 가이드는 건물에 대한 많
은 핵심요점을 설명했다.

08 prerogative
n. 특권, 특혜
많은 나라에서 교육은 여전히 부유층의 특권
이다.

09 reticent
adj. 말을 잘 안 하는
내가 피터에 대해 아는 것은 그가 군인이었다
는 사실뿐이다: 그는 그의 과거에 대해 말을
잘 안한다.

10 ebullient
adj. 혈기 왕성한, 기쁜
리처드는 시험 결과를 받고 기뻐했다.

11 lauded
v. 칭찬하다
그의 팀은 대결에서 패배했지만, 코치는 각 선
수에게 최선을 다했다고 칭찬했다.

12 tantalize
v. 감질나게 하다
나를 감질나게 하지 마: 그냥 무슨 생각하고
있는지 말해줘.

13 stifle
v. 억누르다
정부는 대중의 불만을 억누르는 데에 실패했다.

14 inclement
adj. 좋지 못한
이번 주말에 날씨가 괜찮으면, 공원으로 소풍
가자.

15 furtive
adj. 은밀한
두 여자들은 식사 자리에서 서로를 은밀하게
쳐다보며 웃음을 참으려고 노력했다.

16 herald
v. 예고하다, 알리다
옅은 레몬색 개나리와 분홍색 진달래는 봄을
즐거이 예고한다.

17 paucity
n. 소량, 부족
그 사건에 대한 정보의 부족이 경찰로 하여금
사건에 대해 공식적인 발표를 하는 데에 어려
움을 준다.

01 depict   v. 그리다
14세기 초까지 유럽 아티스트들은 작품에 성경 속 장면만 그릴 수 있었다.

02 discard   v. 버리다
조개 요리를 할 때, 열을 가했음에도 열리지 않는 조개는 버려야 한다는 것을 기억해라.

03 provoked   v. 유발하다
정부 발표는 많은 시위를 유발했다.

04 forestall   v. 미연에 방지하다
새해 첫날, 어머니는 항상 우리에게 1년동안 불운을 미연에 방지하는 부적을 나눠준다.

05 fickle   adj. 변덕스러운
인생은 변덕스러울 수 있다: 어제의 억만장자는 오늘의 거지가 될 수 있는 법이다.

06 inculcate   v. 심어주다
1960년대와 1970년대에는 초등학교 교육과정에 학생들에게 국민의식과 가족에 대한 가치관을 심어주기 위한 세심한 노력들이 있었다.

07 woeful
adj. 한심한, 몹시 슬픈
부모님을 실망시켰다는 사실을 깨달았을 때, 며칠 동안 몹시 슬펐다.

08 offshoot   n. 파생물
귤의 파생물인 한라봉은 대한민국 남쪽에 있는 제주도에서 자라기 시작했고 국내에서 매우 인기 있는 과일이 되었다.

09 antics   n. 익살스러운 짓
연애할 때 글로리아는 헨리의 익살스러운 짓들이 웃겼지만, 결혼한 이후부터는 짜증나기 시작했다.

10 seamlessly   adj. 아주 매끄러운
10살인 피아니스트는 가장 어려운 피아노 연주곡도 매끄럽게 연주했다.

11 reticent   adj. 말을 잘 안 하는
그녀는 처음 만날 때 수줍음을 많이 타고 말을 잘 안하지만, 알면 알수록 꽤 사교적이고 선정적으로 변한다.

12 salient
adj. 핵심적인, 가장 두드러진
자동차 전시에서 각 자동차 회사의 대표는 회사의 새로운 모델에 대한 가장 핵심적인 요점들을 소개했다.

13 obsolescent
adj. 쇠퇴해 가는, 시대에 뒤져
쇠퇴해 가는 전자기기를 오랫동안 보관하고 있다 보면 언젠가 골동품이 될 것이다.

14 ebullient
adj. 혈기 왕성한, 기쁜
전국은 축구 대표팀이 월드컵에서 준결승에 진출했을 때 기쁜 분위기를 즐겼다.

15 stifle   v. 억누르다
그 어떤 어려움도 짐의 배우로서 성공하는 꿈을 억누를 수 없었다.

16 furtive   adj. 은밀한
하워드가 축구 게임을 이기는 데에 본인이 가장 많은 기여를 했다고 주장하고 있을 때, 다른 선수들은 시계를 은밀하게 보면서 집에 가고 싶어했다.

17 prerogative   n. 특권, 특혜
회장으로서 디킨스 씨는 기업의 전략적 결정을 내릴 수 있는 특권을 가지고 있다.

18 foster   v. 조성하다
시장은 도시에 새로운 공립 도서관을 지어 시민의 자랑거리를 조성하고자 했다.

19 prescribing   v. 처방하는
의사는 항생제를 처방하지 않고 환자에게 충분히 쉬고 액체를 많이 마시라고 조언했다.

20 impervious

adj. ~에 영향받지 않는

아내와 딸이 랄프의 앞에서 싸우는 동안 그는 전혀 영향받지 않고 조용히 책만 읽었다.

21 tantalized

v. 감질나게 하다

음식이 나오기를 기다리면서 부엌에서 나는 좋은 냄새가 우리를 감질나게 했다.

22 fanfare

n. 대대적인 축하, 팡파르

새해 전날의 축제는 항상 큰 팡파르와 화려한 행사를 포함한다.

23 maven

n. 전문가

나는 컴퓨터 전문가가 아니지만, 사람들이 집에서 겪는 대부분의 컴퓨터 문제들을 아마 해결할 수 있을 것이다.

24 inflammatory

adj. 강한 분노를 유발하는

후보자는 상대방이 사용한 강한 분노를 유발하는 언어에 흔들리지 않았다.

25 incarceration

n. 감금, 투옥

윌리엄이 받고 있는 혐의가 사실로 드러나면, 그는 투옥당할 것이다.

26 munificence

n. 관대함, 아낌없이 줌, 관유

나는 나의 과거 라이벌이 그 정도의 관대함을 보일 거라고 예상하지 못했다.

27 nuisance

n. 귀찮은 것, 골칫거리, 방해되는 것

귀찮게 좀 굴지 마. 업무에 집중할 수 있게 나가.

28 telltale

adj. 숨길 수 없는

옆방에서 들려오는 숨길 수 없는 콧소리로 스티븐이 도착했다고 알았다.

29 impeded

v. 지연시키다

감기 회복은 계속되는 과로로 지연되었다.

30 pummel

v. 계속 치다

리처드한테 얻어맞지 않는 유일한 방법은 내가 먼저 그를 치는 것이라고 생각했다.

31 abandoned

v. 버려지다, 유기된

카누 안에 물이 들어와 가라앉기 시작하자, 버리고 해안 쪽으로 수영했다.

32 prevails

v. 승리하다

정의가 악을 상대로 승리한다.

33 sparse

adj. 드문, 희박한

아침 이 시간대에 해변가는 거의 비어 있고 몇몇 사람들만 있다.

34 austerity

n. 검소함

19세기 후반 낭만주의 시대의 화려함 이후, 20세기 초반의 건축물은 일종의 검소함을 보였다.

35 fluorescent

adj. 형광성의, 선명한

이 새로운 형광등은 열이 아예 안 난다.

36 solicitude

n. 배려

도와주겠다고 제안해줘서 감사합니다. 당신의 배려에 감동 받았습니다.

37 upheaval

n. 격변, 대변동

이전 대표이사가 큰 경쟁사에서 부회장직을 맡고자 퇴사하고 두 명의 부사장을 같이 데려갔을 때, 회사에 엄청난 격변을 일으켰다.

38 wayward

adj. 잘못된 방향으로 가는, 다루기 힘든

선두에 있던 골프선수가 몇 개의 공을 엉뚱한 방향으로 쳐 대회 상위 10위에서 떨어졌다.

39 평범 – 참정권 부여 – 평범

40 살다 – 계속 치다 – 치다

41 강화하다 – 지지하다 – 짜증나게 하다

42 선행 사건 – 창시자 – 후세

43. 숨어 있다, 잠복 – 은밀하게 돌아다니다 – 싸움을 벌이다

44 은밀한 – 교활한 – 변덕스러운

45 날씨가 좋지 못한 – 예고하다 – 신호를 보내다

46 자주적인 – 자주적인 – 확실한

47 전복적, 파괴적 – 반항적인 – 사랑스러운

48 가장 중요한 – 강조하는 – 중요한

49 감탄스러운 – 칭찬받을 만한 – 끔찍한

50 ～에 영향받지 않는 – 받아들일 수 없는 – 모순된

51 수다를 떤다 – 지지하다 – 지지하다

52 거부하다 – 감질나게 하다 – 유혹하다, 유도하다

53 융합하다 – 격변 – 혼란

54 슬픈, 우울한 – 기만적인 – 어두침침한

55 침체, 부진 – 예측 불허 – 지루함, 따분함

56 조화를 이루지 못하는 – 서로 싸우는 – 정신이 산만한

57 넌지시 말하다 – 말하다 – 우글거리다

58 품행, 태도 – 기울어지다 – 행동

59 승리하다 – 튀어나오다 – 정복하다

60 습득하다 – 조화시키다 – 구하다

01 fiasco   n. 낭패
퍼시는 내가 아는 사람 중에 연설을 제일 잘하는 사람 중 한 명인데, 그는 그가 한 첫 연설이 낭패로 끝났다고 말해줬다.

02 pegged   v. 고정하다
많은 나라의 물가상승은 유가에 고정되어 있는 것처럼 움직인다.

03 swooned   v. 황홀해 하다, 기절하다
케이블카가 2분도 안 돼서 1800미터를 올라갔을 때, 승객 중 한 명이 기절했다.

04 ethereal   adj. 지극히 가볍고 여린, 천상의
짐의 어머니는 빅토리아 시대 소설의 여주인공 같은 모습을 지닌다 – 키가 크고, 호리호리하고, 천상의 모습이다.

05 guile   n. 간교한 속임수
많은 사람들은 대통령이 이러한 정치적 스캔들을 무사히 헤쳐 나갈 할 능력이 있을지 궁금해했다.

06 flout   v. 무시하다, 어기다
아무런 책임도 질 필요가 없다는 것이 보장되면 누가 법을 어기지 않겠나?

07 adulation   n. 열렬한 사랑, 과찬
알베르트 아인슈타인은 살아 있는 동안에도 대부분이 그의 과학적 성취를 이해하지 못하는 대중의 열렬한 사랑을 받았다.

08 connoisseur   n. 감정가, 박사
베토벤 교향곡을 담은 CD 열 개를 보유한다고 해서 클래식 음악의 박사가 되지는 않는다.

09 equanimity   n. 침착, 평정
론 씨는 그의 해고 소식을 침착하게 받아들였다.

10 enamored   v. 매혹된, 사랑에 빠진
나는 몇 년 동안 파리를 방문할 기대를 했으나, 막상 파리를 여행한 후 그 도시에 그닥 매료되지 않았다.

11 benediction   n. 축복
며칠 동안 비 온 이후 해가 보이자 축복받은 것만 같았다.

12 diatribe   n. 비판
야당의 지도자는 현재 정부의 잘못된 문제해결방식 대한 긴 비판을 했다.

13 accosted   v. 다가가 말을 걸다
젊은 사원은 당당하게 회장에게 다가가 말을 걸어 기업의 미래에 대해 민감한 질문을 했다.

14 expunge   v. 지우다
힌두교 신자들은 갠지스 강에서 목욕을 하며 세속적인 죄를 지울 수 있다고 믿는다.

15 doctrinaire   adj. 교조적인
미국에서 자라는 이민 2세들은 서구적인 사회에서 자라지만, 그들의 부모들은 대부분 고향의 교조적인 가치관을 유지한다.

16 consternation   n. 실망
마사는 집에 왔을 때 아이들은 아직 학교에서 집에 오지 않아서 실망했다..

17 decimate   v. 대량으로 죽이다, 심하게 훼손하다
사령관은 아군이 적군보다 4배 이상 수가 많으므로 그의 군대가 적에게 심각한 타격을 줄 수 있을 것으로 예상했다.

01 burgeoned
v. 급성장하다, 부어오르다
켈리의 노력 덕분에 가게의 사업이 급성장했다.

02 unfettered
adj. ~을 자유롭게 하다, 해방하다
오마는 공원과 호수를 자유롭게 볼 수 있는 12층으로 이사 가서 기뻤다.

03 infinitesimal   adj. 극소의
이 화학물질은 극소량만 먹어도 인간에게 치명적이다.

04 bequeathed   v. 남기다
앤서니의 아버지는 앤서니에게 그의 가족이 대대로 살던 거대한 저택을 남겼지만, 불행하게도 앤서니는 그 집을 관리하기에 충분한 돈을 벌지 못했다.

05 archaic   adj. 낡은
많은 정부 부서들이 여전히 낡은 소프트웨어를 사용한다는 사실에 놀랐다.

06 preside   v. 주재하다
리키는 회의를 주재해달라는 요청을 받았다.

07 hubbub   n. 왁자지껄한 소리
글로리아 주변의 왁자지껄한 소리가 났음에도 불구하고, 그녀는 책에 몰입해 있었다.

08 callous   adj. 냉담한
래리는 그레타가 그의 진지한 질문에 대해 보인 냉담한 태도에 약간 화가 났다.

09 quipped
v. 재담을 하다, 농담 따먹기를 하다
15년 동안 서로 만나지 못한 두 친구는 서로 나이 들어 보인다고 재담을 했다.

10 circumlocution   n. 에둘러 말하기
네가 계속 에둘러 말하는 것이 너무 지쳐: 똑바로 된 대답을 해줘!

11 immured   v. 가두다
알프레드는 기말고사 공부를 하고자 자의로 본인 스스로를 방안에 가뒀다.

12 wailed   v. 통곡하다
몇몇 문상객들은 로드 씨의 관이 무덤으로 낮춰지자 통곡했다.

13 pious   adj. 독실한
장관이 은퇴한 후, 그는 시골로 이사하여 조용하고 독실한 삶을 살았다.

14 stature   n. 위상
기본 박사 정도의 위상을 가진 사람이 이렇게 겸손하고 태평할 것이라고 예상하지 못했다.

15 utilitarian   adj. 실용적인
새로운 국무총리는 해외 정책에 대한 실용적인 태도를 취했다: 그가 국가에 이득이 된다고 예상하면, 이전 적들과 기꺼이 대화를 시작할 생각이다.

16 fastidious   adj. 세심한
켈리 씨의 차가 50년이 되었지만, 그만큼 세심한 관리를 해와서 여전히 잘 굴러간다.

Class 27  Answers

01 fulsome adj. 인위적으로 과장된, 지나친
제이미의 위선은 나를 속이지 못했다: 그의 인위적으로 과장된 찬사 너머 본심을 볼 수 있었다.

02 hemorrhage n. 대출혈, 자산 손실
새로운 재무 담당 이사의 첫 업무는 회사의 자산 손실을 막는 것이었다.

03 satiate v. 실컷 만족시키다
매달 새로운 여자, 혹은 남자 아이돌 그룹이 데뷔하여 케이팝에 대한 전 세계적인 갈망을 실컷 만족시키는 듯하다.

04 affix v. 부착하다, 붙이다
너는 봉투에 우표를 부착하는 것을 잊어버렸어.

05 equivocal adj. 모호한
내 질문에 대한 교수님의 모호한 답변은 나를 더 헷갈리게 했다.

06 modulate v. 조절하다
어떤 사람들은 말을 하는 방의 크기에 따라 목소리 크기를 조절할 수 있다.

07 belie v. 거짓임을 보여주다
그는 우리의 목적을 생각하고 있다고 하지만, 그의 행동은 그 주장이 거짓임을 보여준다.

08 imbroglio n. 난국
새로 당선된 대통령은 국내, 해외 문제의 난국을 물려받게 할 것이다.

09 cache n. 은닉처
경찰은 도시 중심에 위치한 한 집에 자동발사 무기를 보관하고 있는 은닉처를 발견했다.

10 lethargic adj. 무기력한
점심때 와인을 두 잔 마신 브루노는 무기력했고 업무에 집중을 못했다.

11 cogitating v. 심사숙고하여
나는 며칠 동안 문제에 대해 심사숙고했으나, 해결책이 떠오르질 않는다.

12 flotsam n. 표류물, 부유물, 부랑자
홍수 물이 빠졌을 때, 길거리에 엄청난 양의 표류물이 산처럼 쌓여있었다.

13 compunction n. 죄책감
마크는 케빈의 냉장고를 열어 죄책감 없이 먹기 시작했다.

14 estrangement n. 소원해짐
윌리엄스 씨와 그의 아들은 소원해지고 몇 년이 지난 후 드디어 화해했다.

01 inundated   adj. 침수시키다
댐이 무너지자, 물이 계곡 전체를 침수시켜 수천 명을 대피시켰다.

02 efface   v. 지우다, 없애다
내가 가지고 있는 그들에 대한 안 좋은 기억들을 진심으로 없애고 싶다.

03 vicarious   adj. 대리의
대학교에 재학할 기회가 없었던 오키프 부인은 손녀들의 대학 생활에 대해 물어보면서 대리 만족을 느낀다.

04 animosity   n. 반감, 적대감
그 두 국가 간에 수백 년간 지속되어 온 적대감이 존재했다.

05 charlatans   n. 사기꾼
아직도 오늘 같은 시대에 사람들이 비타민을 마법의 묘약이라고 하는 사기꾼들한테 속는다는 것이 믿기지 않는다.

06 mollify   v. 달래다
어머니가 너무 속상해하셔서 달래기 어려웠다.

07 caricatured   v. 과장하여 표현하다, 왜곡하다
마를린 먼로는 많은 영화에서 멍청한 금발 여자로 부당하게 왜곡되어 표현되었지만, 실제로 매우 똑똑하고 상식이 통하는 사람이었다.

08 pariah   n. 버림받은 사람
데이빗은 가톨릭 신자와 결혼해서 유대인 가족들에게 한동안 버림받은 사람처럼 대해졌다.

09 vertigo   n. 어지러움
하워드는 너무 피곤해 어지러움으로 고생했다.

10 fumigate   v. 연기로 소독하다, 훈연하다
긴 기간 동안 캠핑을 하며 빨래를 하기 어려울 때 옷을 연기를 씌워 소독하면 깨끗하게 하고 악취를 없앨 수도 있다.

11 abhors   v. 혐오하다
퍼시가 좋은 선수인 이유는 신체적으로 건강할 뿐만 아니라, 패배를 혐오하기 때문이다.

12 pragmatics   adj. 실용적인
나는 이상주의자를 안 좋아한다: 실용적인 사람을 선호한다.

13 felicity   n. 더할 나위 없는 행복
아내가 사망한 후, 윌러드 씨는 게일을 만나기 전까지는 인생에 다시는 더할 나위 없는 행복을 느끼지 못할 것만 같았다.

14 coherent   adj. 일관성 있는, 논리정연한
누구는 그를 천재라고 했지만, 나한테는 논리정연한 대화조차 진행하는 데에 어려움을 느끼는 사람 같았다.

15 erudite   adj. 박식한
세스 박사와의 대화는 지루한 적이 없었다: 그는 항상 박식했고 최근의 사정에 정통했다.

16 jest   v. 농담하다
나는 돈 관련 이야기를 할 때 절대 농담하지 않는다.

01 dilatory   adj. 느린, 지체시키는
정부는 실업 문제 해결에 늑장을 부린다는 비난을 받고 있다.

02 adjacent
adj. 인접한, 가까운, 옆의
옆방에서 클라리넷 연습하는 남자 때문에 잠들지 못했다.

03 ruptured   v. 파열시키다
불상사 이후, 두 가정의 사이가 파열되었다.

04 begrudged   v. 못마땅해하다
그렉이 형이었지만, 동생 헨리의 성공을 못마땅해 한 적은 없다.

05 assuage   v. 누그러뜨리다
아버지가 화났을 때, 어머니와 우리가 그의 분노를 누그러뜨리기까지 며칠이나 걸렸다.

06 proscribes   v. 금하다
새로 발의된 법안은 모든 공공 영역에서 흡연을 금한다.

07 nauseated   v. 역겹게 하다
나는 보통 이국적인 음식을 먹는 것에 대해 비위가 약하지는 않지만, 곤충을 먹을 생각을 하자 역겨워졌다.

08 decadence   n. 타락, 퇴폐, 사치
기원후 8세기가 되자 로마 제국은 너무 심각한 타락 상태에 접어들어 붕괴될 운명이었다.

09 stench   n. 악취
지하실에 들어가자마자 곰팡이의 악취를 맡을 수 있었다.

10 restraint   n. 자제
토론을 하는 동안, 제이크는 감탄스러울 정도로 자제 능력을 보였고 상대방의 선동적인 발언들에 화나지 않았다.

11 sated   adj. 채워진
점심 때 과식한 이후, 배가 너무 불러서 저녁을 먹지 않았다.

12 protégé   n. 후배
1921년까지 스탈린은 자신을 블라디미르 레닌의 후배이자 후임자 후보로 입지를 굳건하게 했다.

13 bustling   adj. 북적거리는
보통 이 시간에 조용했던 카페는 손님으로 북적거렸다.

14 desolate   adj. 황량한
애리조나 사막은 처음에 황량해보이지만, 자세하게 보면 사실 생명체로 가득하다.

15 sordid   adj. 몹시 지저분한
청소부는 학생들이 체크아웃한 이후 호텔 방이 얼마나 지저분한지 보고 놀랐다.

16 foreboding   n. (불길한) 예감
이유를 모르겠지만, 나는 내 사업을 시작한다고 생각하면 불길한 예감이 들었다.

01 efface   v. 지우다, 없애다
새로 당선된 대통령은 정부 부패를 완전히 없애겠다고 약속했다.

02 abhors   v. 혐오하다
게이맨 씨는 그의 사생활에 대해 굉장히 보호적이다: 그는 그의 사생활에 대한 질문을 혐오한다.

03 mollify   v. 달래다
헬러 부인이 제정신이 아닐 정도로 흥분한 상태라 아무리 노력해도 달랠 수가 없었다.

04 benfactor   n. 후원자
사업은 관대한 후원자의 꽤 큰 액수의 대출로 시작될 수 있었다.

05 begrudged   v. 못마땅해하다
켈리는 폴이 책을 쓰는 과정에서 그녀가 수정, 퇴고에 참여했다는 사실을 인정하지 않아 못마땅해했다.

06 doctrinaire   adj. 교조적인, 가르치려고 드는
윌슨 씨는 사춘기인 아들에게 얘기할 때, 너무 교조적으로 보이지 않도록 신경을 쓴다.

07 decadence   n. 타락, 퇴폐, 사치
우리 예산으로 누릴 수 있던 최대의 사치는 초콜릿 아이스크림을 한 그릇을 나눠먹는 것이었다.

08 erudite   adj. 박식한
알베르트 아인슈타인은 과학에서만 훌륭하지 않았고, 음악, 역사와 정치에도 박식했다.

09 incarcerated   v. 감금, 투옥
벨로스 씨는 전쟁 초기에 소집을 당했고, 적들과 처음 싸울 때 인질로 잡혀 전쟁 내내 감금되었었다.

10 diatribes   n. 비판
상대당은 대통령을 상대로 그가 거짓말을 했다고 주장하며 격렬한 비판을 했다.

11 belied   v. 거짓임을 보여주다
그는 그 주제에 대해 아무것도 모르는 척을 했지만, 날카로운 질문을 하며 그의 무지함이 거짓임을 보였다.

12 preside   v. 주재하다
다음 회의를 주재할 사람이 너 말고 아무도 없어.

13 burgeoned   v. 급성장하다
그 도시의 인구는 지난 20년 동안 세 배로 급성장했다.

14 collaboration   n. 공동 작업, 협력
두 경제학자들은 공동 작업을 통해 이 연구를 만들었다.

15 expunge   v. 지우다
나는 머릿속에서 그에 대한 모든 기억을 지우고 싶다.

16 accosting   v. 다가가 말을 걸다
나는 모르는 사람에게 다가가 말을 걸고 질문을 하는 것이 어색했지만, 불행하게도 내 직업의 일부뿐이었다.

17 sierra   n. 산맥
애리조나의 피닉스로 가는 길에 기차에서 본 산맥은 굉장했다.

18 consternation   n. 실망
그의 결정이 수천 명의 인생에 영향을 미쳤다는 사실이 그에게 큰 실망을 안겼다.

19 decimated   v. 대량으로 죽이다, 심하게 훼손하다
바다코끼리들은 한 때 자연에 풍부했지만, 19세기 후반까지의 마구잡이로 사냥하여 멸종의 위기까지 갔다.

20 guile   n. 간교한 속임수
내 지능으로 부족하다면, 간교한 속임수를 써서라도 그 일을 성공시킬 것이다.

21	flouted	v. 무시하다, 어기다

21 flouted   v. 무시하다, 어기다
헨리는 아무렇지 않게 정지 신호를 무시하고 길을 건넜다.

22 equanimity   n. 침착, 평정
상대 팀은 우리보다 훨씬 강하고 경험있었기에, 모두가 우리의 패배를 침착하게 받아들였다.

23 neologisms   n. 신조어
10년 전에 업계를 떠난 베일리 씨는 현재 그 업계에서 사용되고 있는 대부분의 신조어를 이해하지 못했다.

24 desolate   adj. 황량한
한때 북적거렸던 광업 도시는 이제 공허하고 황량했다.

25 foreboding   n. (불길한) 예감
으스스한 음악은 청취자들에게 불길한 예감을 가지게 했다.

26 inundate   adj. 침수시키다
배수관이 파열되어 우리 지하실을 침수시켰다.

27 husbandry   n. 농사
지역 농부들은 인삼과 뽕나무 등 부가가치의 작물의 농사로 확장했다.

28 assuage   v. 누그러뜨리다
아버지가 돌아가신 후, 나는 매일 어머니에게 전화를 드려 어머니의 외로움을 누그러뜨리려고 했다.

29 affix   v. 부착하다, 붙이다
부록을 주 계약서에 부착해야 하는 것 잊지 마.

30 titular   adj. 명목상의, 명의뿐인
엘리자베스 2세 여왕은 캐나다, 호주와 뉴질랜드의 명목상의 국가 원수다.

31 cache   n. 은닉처, 캐시
나는 12살 때 다락방에 숨겨두어 잊어버린 옛 만화책 보따리를 찾았다.

32 fiasco   n. 낭패
수석 발레리나가 공연 첫날의 2주 전 발목을 다치자 많은 주최자들은 공연이 낭패가 될까 봐 걱정했다.

33 animosities   n. 반감, 적대감
두 남자는 만나서 이전의 적대감을 잊고 서로의 차이점을 받아들이며 화해했다.

34 imbroglio   n. 난국
현재 대통령이 처음 당선되었을 때, 역대급으로 심각한 경제적 난국을 물려받았다.

35 fulsome   adj. 지나친
그 사람은 위선자다 – 잘난 체하는 미소와 다른 사람에 대한 지나친 칭찬으로 드러난다.

36 expectorate   v. 침/가래를 뱉다
목에 인후염이 너무 심하다: 삼킬 때 아프고, 가래로 점액을 뱉는다.

37 satiate   v. 충분히 만족한
설탕 가득한 탄산음료를 마시는 것은 갈증을 충분히 만족시키지 못하고, 오히려 더욱 심각하게 할 것이다.

38 estrangement   n. 소원해짐
크리스천의 부모님은 이혼한 후 몇 년 동안 여전히 소원했다.

39 stature   n. 위상
워렌 버핏은 그 정도의 위상을 가진 사람 치고는 굉장히 소박한 삶을 산다.

40 pestilence   n. 악성 전염병
요즘 같은 시대에도 우리 세계의 몇몇 지역들은 여전히 기근과 악성 전염병으로 황폐하다.

41 archaic   adj. 낡은
여성이 남성보다 약하다는 생각은 이제 낡은 생각이다.

42 immured   v. 가두다
피터는 아무도 없는 교실에 앉아 본인의 생각에 빠졌다.

43 비판 – 집단 – 수행단

44 과찬 – 감탄 – 옹호

45 익살 – 정신이 산만한 사람 – 어리석음

46 침착 – 침착함 – 축복

47 지극히 가볍고 여린 – 약한 – 완전 새 것 같은

48 황홀해 하다, 기절하다 – 혀짤배기소리 – 기절하다

49 후배 – 전문가 – 박사, 감정가

50 사면 – 자비 – 야외극

51 인정 없는, 매정한 – ∼에 좋은 – 냉담한

52 혼란 – 악취 – 불안

53 미로 – 에둘러 말하기 – 완곡 어구

54 전권 대사 – 극소의 – 극히 작은

55 왁자지껄한 소리 – 호들갑 – 비축물

56 꼼꼼한 – 꼼꼼한 – 실용적인

57 징후 – 급증, 확산 – 표시

58 모호한 – 애매모호한 – 인접한

59 요지부동의 – 굴종하는 – 따르는

60 입증하다 – 진짜임을 증명하다 – 하여 가래를 뱉다

61 표류물 – 잔해 – 벽화

62 (사업이) 망하다 – 버림받은 사람 – 실패

63 소독하다 – 동요하게 하다 – 소독하다

64 어지러움 – 만병통치약 – 현기증

65 파괴적 – 대리의 – 대리의

01 gibes   n. 조롱거리, 웃음거리
마틴의 재미있는 웃음거리 덕분에 어색한 회의 분위기는 꽤 친근하게 변했다.

02 malleable
adj. 남의 말에 잘 속는, 영향을 잘 받는
어렸을 때 노먼은 자기 말에 쉽게 속는 여동생을 이용해 그녀를 항상 곤경에 빠지게 했다.

03 antagonism   n. 적대감
요즘 젊은 세대가 윗세대에 대해 가지는 적대감을 이해하기 어렵다.

04 hale   adj. 건강한
시골에서 한 달 동안 지냈더니 다시 건강하고 원기 왕성해졌다.

05 kowtowed   v. 굽실거리다
닉은 샐리의 수업 필기 공책를 빌려야 해서 샐리가 빌려줄 때까지 며칠 동안 그녀에게 굽실거렸다.

06 distraught
adj. 완전히 제정신이 아닌, 심란한
거티는 휴가 기간 동안 계속 비 온다는 소식을 듣고 매우 심란해했다.

07 spate   n. 빈발
지역의 갑작스러운 지진의 빈발이 많은 사람들을 불안하게 했다.

08 ignoble   adj. 비열한, 야비한
그 의심스러운 남자는 어둡고 야비한 비밀을 지키고 있는 것만 같았다.

09 dichotomy   n. 양분, 이분
정치인들이 말하는 바와 행동하는 바가 다른 것에 놀라지 마.

10 formative
adj. 형성에 중요한, 자라는 과정의
샘은 크면서 바흐부터 B1A4까지 다양한 장르의 음악에 노출되었다.

11 ogled
v. 추파를 던지다, 욕심 있게 바라보다
리암은 햄버거를 다 먹었는데도 여전히 배가 고파서 실라의 감자튀김을 욕심 있게 바라보았다.

12 tirades   n. 비난
미디어에서 두 주요 정치당은 협의점에 도달하지 못했다고 비난했다.

13 umbrage   n. 불쾌, 분개
밀리는 바트가 그녀가 시험에서 부정 행위를 저질렀다고 암시하자 불쾌함을 느꼈다.

14 moniker   n. 이름, 별명
밀튼이 고등학교를 다니는 동안 너무 말라서 '이쑤시개'라는 별명을 가졌었다.

15 discomfited   v. 혼란스럽게 만들다
후보자 재정상황에 대한 기자의 어려운 질문은 후보자를 당황스럽게 했다.

16 odious   adj. 끔찍한
새로운 직장에서의 첫 업무는 40명의 업무가 중복되는 직원을 해고하는 끔찍한 일이었다.

01 obtrusive adj. (보기 싫게) 눈에 띄는, 두드러지는
카일의 헤어스타일과 옷의 색깔은 이런 엄숙한 행사에서 보기 싫게 두드러졌다.

02 fusillade n. 연속 사격, 빗발치는 것, 세례
발표가 끝나자마자, 질문이 끊임없이 빗발쳤다.

03 impugn v. 의문을 제기하다
많은 사람들은 정치인의 의도가 순수한지 의심을 제기하지 않을 수 없었다.

04 singe v. (표면을) 불에 그을리다, 태우다
고기를 겉이 살짝 탈 때까지만 익혀: 완전히 속 까지 익히지 마.

05 juxtapose v. 병치하다, 나란히 하다
그 예술가의 기술은 밝은 색깔을 서로 나란히 칠하여 더욱 극적인 효과를 주는 것이다.

06 grapple v. 격투 끝에 붙잡다
아무리 열심히 노력해도, 나의 뇌로는 양자물리학의 개념을 이해하기 힘들었다.

07 reeked v. 지독한 악취를 풍기다
부엌은 마늘 냄새로 악취를 풍겼다.

08 cloy v. 물리다, 질리다
드라마 시리즈는 매우 인기 있었지만, 지나친 폭력과 피의 사용으로 시청자들을 질리게 했다.

09 repute n. 명성
앤디의 컴퓨터 게임 실력은 그를 학교에서 꽤 명성을 얻게 했다.

10 lucrative adj. 수익성이 좋은
환경 관련 사건을 전문적으로 다루는 변호사로서 레베카 롤링은 환경오염에 기여하는 기업을 고소하면서 돈을 꽤 잘 벌었다.

11 impotent adj. 무력한
소수자들은 더 이상 지배계층의 억압에 무력하지 않다.

12 pedagogic adj. 교육학적
1970년대에 개발된 교육적 체계가 2010년대에 여전히 유의미하다고 생각하면 안 된다.

13 aplomb n. 침착함
크리스는 정신 없는 업무를 침착하게 수행한다.

14 commissioned v. 공식적으로 의뢰하다
젊은 조각가는 시 정부가 그에게 새로운 시청 건물을 위한 조각품을 공식적으로 의뢰하면서 큰 기회를 잡았다.

15 dilettante n. 호사가
그는 예술가가 물질적인 부를 얻게 된다면 더 이상 예술가가 아닌 호사가라고 한다.

16 braved v. 용감히 대면하다
수천 명이 악천후에 맞서 꿋꿋이 직접 축구 게임을 관전하려고 한다.

01 syndicated
v. (기사, 사진, 텔레비전 프로그램 등을 여러 신문사 등에) 팔다
그의 칼럼은 50개가 넘는 신문기사와 잡지에 팔리고 있다.

02 indolent adj. 게으른, 나태한
나는 지난 며칠 동안 게을렀다; 다시 공부를 시작해야겠다.

03 taunted v. 조롱하다, 비웃다
마이크는 내가 그를 테니스로 절대 이길 수 없다고 조롱했다.

04 culprit n. 범인
이안은 사물의 식료품 저장실에서 그의 음식을 훔친 범인을 찾겠다고 결심했다.

05 iconoclast n. 우상 파괴자
알베르트 아인슈타인은 20대 시절 우상 파괴자로 여겨졌지만, 50대에 접어들었을 때 순응주의자로 변했다.

06 reprieve
n. 집행 유예, 징수 유예, 잠깐의 휴식
정부는 기업에게 1년의 징수 유예를 주어 기업 구조 조정을 하게 했다.

07 chagrin n. 원통함, 분함
분하게도, 나는 우리 학교 테니스팀에 선발되지 못했다.

08 domicile n. 거주지
지난 10년 동안 2년 이상 한 거주지에 머문 적이 없다.

09 destitute adj. 극빈한, 빈곤한
극빈한 난민들은 갈 곳이 없었다.

10 timid
adj. 소심한, 용기가 없는
래리는 수가 혼자 식당에 앉아 있는 것을 봤지만, 같이 앉을 용기가 없었다.

11 ludicrous adj. 터무니없는
그 말을 듣자, 나는 너무 터무니없는 이야기여서 바로 잊었다.

12 oust v. 몰아내다
현재 대통령을 권력에서 몰아낼 몇 번의 시도가 있었다.

13 paraphernalia n. 용품
이 도시에서 승마용품을 파는 가게는 딱 한 군데밖에 없다.

14 bifurcates adj. 두 갈래로 나뉘다
강 상류에서 물줄기가 두 갈래로 나뉘는 지점까지 배를 탔다.

15 aversion
n. 아주 싫어함, 혐오감
나는 매운 음식에 대한 혐오가 있다: 간이 싱거운 음식을 선호한다.

16 catharsis n. 카타르시스, 정화
진료소에서 정신없는 한 주를 보낸 아놀드 박사는 주말에는 낚시로 카타르시스를 느낀다.

01 inglorious   adj. 수치스러운
축구팀은 이번 시즌 동안 최다 연속 패배를 한 수치스러운 기록을 세웠다.

02 dogged   adj. 끈덕진
기자는 날카로운 질문을 끈덕지게 계속 하였다.

03 émigré   n. 망명자
50세에 알베르트 아인슈타인은 독일에서 도망을 가 망명자로 미국에 도착했다.

04 nonplussed
adj. 몹시 놀라 어쩔 줄 모르는
연설자는 내 질문에 몹시 놀라 어쩔 줄 몰라 하였다.

05 eclectic   adj. 다방면에 걸친
그녀는 포괄적이고 다방면에 걸친 그림, 조각상과 조각품을 수집했다.

06 foist
v. 떠맡기다, 속여서 팔다, 요구하다
캘커타에서 여행하는 동안, 상품을 속여서 팔려는 행상들이 매일 나한테 접근을 했다.

07 incantation   n. 주문
'아브라카다브라'는 아마 가장 잘 알려진 주문일 것이다.

08 lapse   n. 실수
제 말실수를 용서해주세요: 무례한 말을 할 의도는 없었습니다.

09 therapeutic
adj. 긴장을 푸는 데 도움이 되는, 치료법의
헬러 씨는 집안일이 긴장을 푸는 데 도움이 된다고 느껴 스스로 다 하려고 하신다.

10 gleaned   v. 조금씩 모으다
한 달에 책 한 권을 읽으면, 10년 뒤 100권 이상의 책을 읽어 많은 지식을 조금씩 모은 자신을 발견할 것이다.

11 brittle   adj. 잘 부스러지는
고무는 처음에 더위에 녹고 추위에 잘 부스러져 좋은 산업용 물질로 여겨지지 않았다.

12 tawdry
adj. 번쩍거리는, 저속한
그는 목에 싸구려로 보이는 체인을 둘렀다.

13 underpinnings   n. 기초, 토대
좋은 저널리즘의 기초는 객관성과 공정성을 추구함에 있다.

14 buoyant   adj. 떠 있는
유조선을 가까이서 봤을 때, 그렇게 큰 선박이 떠 있을 수 있다는 것이 믿기지 않았다.

15 semblance   n. 닮음, 비슷함
축배의 기간이 지난 후, 우리 일상은 정상과 비슷하게 돌아갔다.

16 onerous   adj. 아주 힘든
나는 파티가 끝난 후 아주 힘든 청소 업무를 맡았다.

17 championed   v. 옹호하다
마하트마 간디는 평생 무저항주의를 옹호했다.

01 braved   v. 용감히 대면하다
콸라룸푸르의 기온은 34도씨였지만, 더위에 용감히 대면하며 관광을 하고 길거리 음식을 먹었다.

02 odious   adj. 끔찍한
헬렌은 마크가 똥통을 치우고 털을 진공청소기로 미는 끔찍한 일을 하는 조건 하에 고양이 입양에 동의했다.

03 ousted   v. 몰아내다
피 튀기는 권력 투쟁이 있었고, 결과적으로 남동생이 왕이었던 형을 몰아냈다.

04 hedonist   n. 쾌락주의자
현대 시대에 쾌락주의자가 되려면 돈이 있어야 한다.

05 fusillade   n. 연속 사격, 빗발치는 것, 세례
올림픽 금메달리스트들은 축하 세례를 받았다.

06 reprieve   n. 집행 유예, 징수 유예, 잠깐의 휴식
네 시간의 아침 훈련 이후, 선수들은 한 시간의 점심 및 휴식 시간이 주어지고 다시 세 시간의 오후 훈련을 한다.

07 culprit   n. 범인
현대 DNA 실험 기술을 사용하여 과학자들은 1623년에 일어난 작센 공국 루돌프 공자 살인 사건의 범인을 찾았다.

08 destitute   adj. 극빈한, 빈곤한
부처가 된 싯다르타 왕자는 26살 때 처음 궁전을 떠나 인생에서 처음으로 빈곤하고 아픈 사람을 봤다.

09 enmity   n. 원한, 증오, 적대감
부모님에게 적대감을 보이지 마라: 부모님들은 단지 너한테 가장 좋은 것만 주기를 원한다.

10 brittle   adj. 잘 부러지는
유리로 크리스마스 장식을 만들기에는 너무 잘 부러지는 재료이다.

11 vignettes   n. 삽화
영화는 하나의 연결되는 이야기가 아닌 약간의 관계가 있는 다섯 개의 삽화로 구성되어 있다.

12 iconoclast   n. 우상 파괴자
버니 샌더스의 우상 파괴자로서의 이미지가 기성 정치에 지친 젊은이들 사이의 인기 비결이다.

13 therapeutic   adj. 긴장을 푸는 데 도움이 되는, 치료법의
요가는 몸뿐만 아니라 정신의 긴장을 푸는 데 도움이 되는 운동이지만, 요즘 사람들은 요가의 신체적 요소에만 집중을 하는 것 같다.

14 insurgences   n. 반란, 폭동
지난 50년간 나라의 제도 변경의 반만 평화로운 선거의 결과로 발생했다. 나머지는 모두 반란에 의한 결과였다.

15 slight   n. 모욕
내 지적을 모욕으로 받아들이지 마. 도와주고 싶어서 하는 말이야.

16 circuitous   adj. 빙 돌아가는, 우회하는
직항 비행기표를 구할 돈이 없어서 몇 군데 우회하는 노선을 택했다.

17 lucrative   adj. 수익성이 좋은
사울은 유람선에서 색소폰을 불며 많은 돈을 벌고 있다.

18 tantamount   adj. ~에 버금가는
잭이 일하는 회사에서 대표이사 켄 고씨의 지시는 곧 법과 같다.

19 ignoble   adj. 비열한, 야비한
명예로운 전쟁이 야비한 평화보다 나은가?

20 nonplussed

adj. 몹시 놀라 어쩔 줄 모르는

아직 유럽에 있는 줄 알았던 리처드가 사무실로 들어오자 나는 몹시 놀라 어쩔 줄 몰랐다.

21 eclectic

adj. 절충적인, 여기저기서 가져온, 다방면에 걸친

그녀는 그녀의 집에 다방면의 분야에서 가져온 예술작품들이 있다고 했다. 내가 보기엔 그냥 쓰레기가 뒤죽박죽 있는 것 같았다.

22 dogged   adj. 끈덕진

리처드가 이렇게 멀리 올 수 있었던 이유는 오로지 끈덕진 투지 때문이다.

23 bifurcates   adj. 두 갈래로 나뉘다

이 길을 쭉 가다가 두 갈래로 나뉠 때 왼쪽으로 가세요.

24 specimens   n. 견본, 샘플

심해 탐사팀은 이전에 본 적 없는 생명체 견본을 수면 아래 3000미터에서 모았다.

25 catharsis   n. 카타르시스, 정화

어떤 한국 음식은 너무 매워서 외국인들이 제대로 맛보지도 못할 정도다. 그러나 많은 한국인들은 이러한 매운 음식을 먹을 때 일종의 카타르시스를 느낀다.

26 domicile   n. 거주지

현대 미국인들은 벤자민 프랭클린이 필라델피아 시와 불가분의 관계가 있다고 생각하지만, 그는 사실 17살 때까지 보스턴에서 거주했다.

27 malleable

adj. 남의 말해 잘 속는, 영향을 잘 받는

나는 어리고 남의 말에 잘 속아 실수를 했고, 그중 지금 생각해도 꽤나 부끄러운 실수가 몇 개 있다.

28 aplomb   n. 침착함

이 도시의 첫 여성 경찰서장 자넷 테일러는 어려움을 대처하는 전문성과 침착함으로 많은 칭찬을 받았다.

29 kowtow   v. 굽실거리다

나한테 굽실거릴 필요는 없어. 나는 너를 고용할 권한이 없거든.

30 evict   v. 쫓아내다

경찰은 학교에 와서 학과장 사무실을 차지하며 시위하는 학생들을 강제로 쫓아내야 했다.

31 juxtapose

v. 병치하다, 나란히 하다

현재 극동 지역의 외교적 상황을 19세기 후반의 상황과 나란히 비교해보면 많은 공통점을 찾을 수 있다.

32 rotatory   adj. 회전하는

꿀 추출 장치는 원심력을 위한 회전 운동으로 꿀을 벌집에서 추출한다.

33 repute   n. 명성

로렌스 브랙스는 25살에 노벨 물리학상을 수상하여 국제적 명성을 얻었다.

34 grappled   v. 격투 끝에 붙잡다

경찰은 도망가는 남자를 따라잡고 격투 끝에 붙잡아 바닥에 쓰러뜨렸다.

35 atrocities

n. 잔혹 행위, 극악, 참극

인류 역사 속 가장 잔혹한 행위들은 종교와 애국심으로 발생했다.

36 impugn

v. 의문을 제기하다, 공격하다

자만심이 넘치는 사람들은 실수를 인정하지 않고, 가끔은 실수를 했다는 사실조차 거부한다 – 이는 모두 본인의 이미지가 공격을 받을 수 있다는 생각이 들어서다.

37 lapse   n. 실수

나는 잠깐 깜빡하여 그의 이름을 잊어버렸다.

38 foist

v. 떠맡기다, 속여서 팔다, 요구하다

나는 신앙심이 지나치게 깊어 자신의 종교를 나에게 강요하는 사람과 같이 있는 것을 즐기지 않는다.

39 tawdry

adj. 번쩍거리는, 저속한

그녀는 큰 구슬로 만든 목걸이를 하고 있었는데 진짜라고 하기에는 너무 저속해 보였다.

40 discomfited   v. 당황

안젤라는 그녀의 다섯 살짜리 딸 줄리가 손님들 앞에서 크게 트림하자 당황했다.

41 용감하게 뚫고 나아가다 – 반항하는 – 동요하게 하다

42 모욕 – 이름 – 모욕하다

43 수치스러운 – 가두다 – 비열한

44 적대감 – 분개함 – 적대감

45 굴종하는 – 무력한 – 시들해지다

46 빈발, 침 등을 뱉다 – 탐욕스럽게 주시하다 – 응시하다

47 장황한 비난 – 비판 – 호들갑

48 끔찍한 – 혐오스러운 – 멈출 수 없는

49 수다를 떨다 – 역겹게 만들다 – 물리다, 질리다

50 약화되다 – 서서히 사라지다 – 상정하다

54 덧붙이다 – 의문을 제기하다 – 의심하다

52 교수법의 – 교육적인 – 미식의

53 ～하기를 꺼리는 – 혐오하다 – 강요하다

54 (슬픔, 흥분에) 완전히 제정신이 아닌 – 명랑한 – 성격이 쾌활한

55 몹시 놀라 어쩔 줄 모르는 – 정신이 산만한 사람 – 말을 잇지 못하는

01 slinking
v. 살금살금 돌아다니다, 느리고 조심스럽게 움직이다
퍼시가 학교에서 하루종일 살그머니 움직이며 말타와 마주치지 않도록 노력하는 것이 보였다.

02 consummate   v. 완성하다
두 정당이 업무협정을 완성하기까지 2주 채 걸리지 않았다.

03 congeal   v. 굳다
육수를 냉장고에 보관하면 젤리처럼 굳을 것이다.

04 affronted
v. 모욕하다, 상처를 주다
네가 결혼식에 초대받지 못해서 상처받지 않았으면 좋겠어, 가족과 친척들만 오는 작은 식일 거야.

05 brigands   n. 도둑
두 마을 사이의 길은 도둑들이 지나가는 차를 훔치는 경우가 잦아서 위험하다.

06 disposition   n. 기질, 성향
올리버는 매우 긍정적인 사람이다: 그 어떤 어려움도 그의 발랄한 성향을 꺾지 못한다.

07 vacuous   adj. 멍청한
필리아가 이던에게 그 이론을 세 번이나 설명했지만, 그는 여전히 이해를 못하고 멍청한 표정으로 그녀를 바라봤다.

08 corporeal
adj. 신체의, 물질적인
아버지가 돌아가셨다: 그의 신체적 모습은 이제 볼 수 없지만, 이제 내 마음속에 사실 것이다.

09 absolve   v. 용서하다
중세에 많이 독실한 사람들은 용서받기 위해 스스로 채찍질하거나 가시로 만든 조끼를 입곤 했다.

10 imbue   v. 가득 채우다
내가 어렸을 때 아버지가 나를 달래는 목소리는 내게 안정감을 가득 채워주곤 했다.

11 interspersed   v. 배치하다, 산재되다
이제 유튜브가 법인회사다 보니, 수익을 창출해야 하고, 그래서 대부분의 영상에 광고가 삽입되어 있다.

12 florid   adj. 화려한
나는 로라가 장례식에 입고 간 드레스가 지나치게 화려해서 상황에 부적절하다고 생각했다.

13 postulated   v. 상정하다, 예상하다
연구자들은 실험 결과가 상정한 바와 맞아서 기뻤다.

14 vivacious   adj. 명랑한, 쾌활한
가게에서 우리는 특히 쾌활한 판매 사원으로부터 도움을 받았다.

15 nomadic   adj. 유목의, 방랑의
보가트 씨는 방랑 생활을 끝내고 캘리포니아의 샌디에고 시에 정착하기로 마음을 먹었다.

16 dexterous
adj. 손재주가 좋은, 솜씨 좋은
나는 손재주가 좋지 않다: 사실 꽤 어설프다.

17 stupor   n. 인사불성, 혼미
크리스마스 식사 자리에서 너무 많이 먹어서 그 이후 약간 혼미한 상태였다.

01 stereotype   n. 고정관념
유럽에서 영국은 음식이 맛 없고, 프랑스인들은 잘 안 씻고, 벨기에 사람들은 똑똑하지 않다는 고정관념이 있다.

02 proximity   n. 가까움
나는 이 아파트가 지하철과 쇼핑 지역과 가까워서 입주하기로 결정했다.

03 phonetic   adj. 음성의
경찰들은 용의자의 목소리와 녹음된 음성이 일치한다고 발견했다.

04 conceited   adj. 자만하는
너의 업무가 내 업무보다 중요하다고 생각하면 그건 자만하는 것이다.

05 homogeneity   n. 균질성, 동질성
19세기 후반에 한국은 외국인들이 나라의 문화적, 민족적 동질성을 위협할까 봐 그들의 입국을 막았다.

06 heresy   n. 이단, 신성 모독
아이작 뉴턴이 살아 있던 시절 아리스토텔레스의 가르침을 거부하는 것은 신성 모독으로 여겨졌다.

07 gaffe   n. 실수
제가 범한 용서할 수 없는 실수에 대해 사과를 드리고 싶습니다.

08 faction   n. 파벌
캐나다 정치계에서 환경적 의제를 정치 토론에서도 다룰 수 있도록 미는 녹색당은 더 이상 작은 파벌이 아니라 삼대 야당 중 하나다.

09 diktat   n. 강권
정부의 상아로 만든 물건의 수입을 금지하는 강권은 찬성을 많이 받았다.

10 debilitate   v. 약화시키다
대회가 얼마 안 남은 이 시점에서 농구 팀의 코치를 교체하는 것은 팀의 사기를 약화시킬 것이다.

11 stoic   adj. 극기적인, 감정을 쉽게 나타내지 않는, 참을성이 많은
참을성이 많은 남자아이는 코피가 나고 눈에 멍이 들어도 울지 않았다.

12 inane   adj. 어리석은
그 이사는 쓸모없고 어리석다고 주간 회의를 취소했다.

13 connive   v. (나쁜 일을) 묵인하다
교장 선생님은 학생에게 시험 답안지를 훔친 사건에 대해 묵인했는지 물어봤다.

14 prolific   adj. 다작하는
25년의 작가 생활 동안 아이작 아시모프는 500권이 넘는 책을 썼다. 그는 역사 속 가장 다작한 작가들 중 한 명이었다.

01 gruesome   adj. 섬뜩한
샐리는 토드가 고른 공포 영화 보기를 거부하고 대신 코미디 영화를 골랐다.

02 abrasive   adj. 거슬리는, 거친
우리 상사 해링턴 씨는 매우 거친 분이셔서 나한테 화를 내실까 봐 질문을 드리기 무섭다.

03 apathy   n. 무관심
가끔 부모님들은 아이들에게 무관심을 보여 문제를 스스로 해결하도록 해야 한다.

04 wee   adj. 아주 작은
할아버지는 길 구석에 있는 구멍가게가 할아버지가 작은 아이였을 때부터 저 위치에 있었다고 말씀하셨다.

05 flux   n. 끊임없는 변화
아인슈타인의 이론은 은하계의 모든 것이 끊임없는 변화를 겪고 있어 절대적인 시간, 공간과 속도가 있지 않다고 한다.

06 levy   v. 부과하다
정부는 가상화폐에 세금을 부과하는 방법론을 검토하는 특별한 부서를 만들었다.

07 quarantine   n. 격리
강아지를 영국에 데려가면 최대 6주 동안 격리해야 해서 안 데려가는 게 좋을 것 같아.

08 frivolity   n. 오두방정, 경망
오늘 하루종일 너무 심각한 업무만 했더니, 친구 몇 명과 만나서 저녁에 오두방정 조금 떨어야 할 것 같아.

09 augment   v. 늘리다, 증가시키다
현재 직장에서 받는 돈이 너무 적어서, 수입을 늘릴 수 있는 직업을 하나 더 찾아야겠어.

10 timorous   adj. 겁이 많은, 소심한
마리사는 가장 좋아하는 배우가 카페에서 식사하는 것을 봤지만, 사인을 부탁하기에는 너무 소심했다.

11 drab   adj. 생기 없는, 칙칙한
평소에 쨍한 색깔의 옷을 자주 입는 마틸다는 오늘 칙칙한 색깔의 코트를 입었다.

12 nascent   adj. 초기의
케네스의 사업은 성공 여부를 판단하기에는 아직 초기 단계지만, 지금까지 봐온 바로는 잠재력이 크다.

13 indigence   n. 빈곤, 극빈
우리가 웨스트버지니아 주의 일부 지역에서 목격한 빈곤은 미국에 존재할 거라고 예상한 바보다 훨씬 심각했다.

14 accoutrements   n. 장비
군인들은 정찰임무로 떠나기 전에 바쁘게 장비를 확인하고 있었다.

15 terrain   n. 지역, 지형
등산로의 지형이 상대적으로 평평해서 쉽게 걸을 수 있었다.

16 soliloquy   n. 독백
햄릿의 '죽느냐 사느냐'는 아마 역사 속 가장 유명한 독백일 것이다.

Class 39

01 clandestine   adj. 은밀한, 비밀
그 남자들은 지하실로 통하는 비밀 입구를 통해 기숙사를 쉽게 들락날락할 수 있었다.

02 castigated   v. 혹평하다
코치는 선수들이 패배해서가 아닌 최선을 다하지 않아서 혹평을 했다.

03 collateral
adj. 부수적인, 이차적인
애런은 회사에서 많은 부수적인 혜택과 함께 매우 좋은 자리를 제안받았다.

04 pervious
adj. 통과시키는, 받아들이는
남자는 나이가 들면서 새로운 아이디어를 수용하기 힘들어진다.

05 atrophied
v. (사용하지 않으며) 위축되다
아버지는 원래 농구 덩크슛을 쉽게 성공시켰지만 나이가 들면서 그 실력이 위축됐다고 말씀하셨다.

06 auspices   n. 찬조, 후원
새로운 지역 센터는 지역 정부의 후원으로 세워졌다.

07 desultory
adj. 두서없는, 종잡을 수 없는
현재 시점에서 나는 종잡을 수 없는 글만 많이 썼다. 정리된 책의 형태를 띠기까지 아직 시간이 필요하다.

08 emasculated
v. 무력화시키다, 무력하게 만들다
시간은 그 남자를 무력하게 만들었지만, 특유의 눈빛은 여전했다.

09 hapless   adj. 불행한
불행한 승객들은 눈보라가 지날 때까지 공항에서 밤을 새야 했다.

10 humus   n. 부엽토
깊은 부엽토에 식물을 심었고, 벌레를 없애기 위해 마늘 용액으로 물을 주고 뿌렸다.

11 derisible
adj. 웃음거리가 되는, 조롱거리인
사람들이 밤늦게 텔레비전에서 이상한 허브차를 만병통치약이라고 주장하는 저 웃음거리인 사람의 주장을 새겨듣는다는 것이 믿기지 않는다.

12 catapulted   v. 내던지다
자전거가 돌과 부딪치자 데이브는 공중으로 내던져 등으로 바닥에 떨어졌다.

13 palpable   adj. 감지할 수 있는
사람들은 정치인의 가식적인 약속에 지쳤다 – 그들은 감지할 수 있는 변화를 원한다.

Class 40

01 apathy   n. 무관심
젊은 세대들은 대부분 정치에 무관심하다.

02 gaffe   n. 실수
나의 상사는 내가 행사에서 범한 실수에 웃으
며 걱정하지 말라고 하셨다.

03 dogma   n. 신조
과학의 시대에 종교적 신조는 말 그대로 받아
들여져야 할까?

04 spawn   v. 알을 낳다
많은 개구리들은 봄에 이 연못으로 와 알을 낳
는다.

05 indigence   n. 빈곤, 극빈
빈곤은 의료 진단의 걸림돌이 되면 안 된다.
그래서 많은 나라에서 의료 서비스는 모든 국
민에게 무료다.

06 timorous   adj. 겁이 많은, 소심한
많은 국민들은 정부가 실업 문제를 해결하기
위해 소심한 접근을 했다고 지적한다.

07 monolithic   adj. 엄청 큰, 하나로 된
가까이서 보면 모스크바의 스탈린 타워들은
말도 못하게 크다. 바로 앞에 서 있기 전까지
는 건물의 크기를 쉽게 체감할 수 없다.

08 admonishes   v. 꾸짖다, 충고하다
좋은 리더는 후배들을 남몰래 충고하지만, 공
개 선상에서 칭찬한다.

09 conniving   v. 묵인하다
분리수거와 재활용 등을 일상적으로 하지 않
으면 환경 파괴에 묵인하는 것이다.

10 protagonist   n. 주인공
흥미롭게도 영화의 주인공은 말을 못하기 때
문에 대사가 없다.

11 corporeal   adj. 신체의, 물질적인
힌두교에서는 인간의 신체는 영혼을 담는 그
릇일 뿐이기 때문에 우리가 죽은 후에도 영혼
은 여전히 살아있다고 한다.

12 absolve   v. 용서하다
마이클은 헬렌에게 디저트를 사주면서 용서를
빌었다.

13 affront   v. 모욕하다, 상처를 주다
네가 어떻게 내가 제일 좋아하는 축구팀이 리
그에서 제일 잘하는 팀이 아니라고 모욕할 수
있어?

14 stigma   n. 오명, 낙인
20년 전까지만 해도 이혼과 관련된 낙인이 존
재했지만, 요즘은 그렇지 않다.

15 sleuth   n. 탐정
'Mr. Holmes'라는 영화는 치매로 고생하는 유
명한 탐정의 노년을 다룬다.

16 stoic   adj. 감정표현을 쉽게 하지 않는, 극기적인
본래 감정표현을 잘 하지 않는 사람인 만큼 윌
리엄은 사랑하는 사람들에게 마음을 표현하는
데에 어려움을 겪는다.

17 diktat   n. 강권
대표이사는 앞으로 무조건 따라야 하는 엄격
한 복장 규정을 강권했다.

18 conceited   adj. 자만하는
자만하는 것처럼 들린다면 죄송하지만, 더 나
은 아이디어가 있습니다.

19 stereotype   n. 고정관념
황 씨는 전형적인 '한국인 아버지'상 – 고집
세고 고압적이고 감정을 잘 드러내지 않는 –
하고 다르다.

20 vivacious   adj. 명랑한, 쾌활한
래버티 씨는 매력적이고, 쾌활하고 15살 어린 새 아내를 통해 행복을 느꼈다.

21 nomadic   adj. 유목의, 방랑의
그 종족은 내몽골의 사막을 거니는 유목 인생을 살았다.

22 aboriginal   adj. 원주민의
캐나다 원주민의 고유 언어들이 대부분 사라질 위기에 처해있다.

23 imbues   v. 가득 채우다
몇몇 종족에서 사냥하는 사람들은 죽은 동물의 힘과 속도를 얻을 수 있다는 믿음에 사냥한 동물의 피를 마신다.

24 quarantined   n. 격리
그 지역에서 돌아오는 의사와 간호사는 안전을 보장하기 위해 사흘간 격리해야 할 것이다.

25 penury   n. 극빈
그의 극빈으로 고생하는 일상은 특허를 200만 불에 팔면서 끝났다.

26 frivolity   n. 오두방정, 경망
'Vanity Fair'라는 빅토리아 소설은 유머로 가득하지만, 그 경망함 아래 진지한 메시지가 담겨있다.

27 nascent   adj. 초기의
한국에서 동물보호법을 도입하려는 움직임들은 여전히 초기 단계에 있다.

28 heresy   n. 이단, 신성 모독
브라질에서 축구에 대해 안 좋게 말하는 것은 신성 모독으로 여겨진다.

29 inane
adj. 바보 같은, 어리석은
영화의 줄거리가 너무 바보 같아 보다가 그만뒀다.

30 akimbo
adj. 양손으로 허리를 짚고
경찰이 집에 들어와도 되는지 물어봤을 때, 아버지는 양손으로 허리를 짚고 거절했다.

31 prolific   adj. 다작하는
그 영화 제작자는 7년동안 영화를 12편 제작했다. 그는 업계에서 가장 다작을 하는 제작자 중 한 명으로 거듭나고 있다.

32 dexterous
adj. 손재주가 좋은, 솜씨 좋은
그 피아니스트는 현재 80대지만, 20대였을 때만큼 손가락이 잘 움직인다.

33 interspersed   v. 배치하다, 산재되다
사흘 동안 지속된 전자 전시회는, 프리젠테이션, 토론회와 제품 발표회로 산재되었다.

34 emasculate
v. 무력화시키다, 무력하게 만들다
전반부가 끝날 때 즈음에, 우리 팀은 상대팀을 완전히 무력하게 만들 정도로 점수를 많이 땄다.

35 hapless   adj. 불행한
세계 2차 대전이 끝날 때, 연합군은 전쟁의 수백만 명의 불행한 피해자들을 어떻게 도울지에 대한 문제를 직면했다.

36 serenity   n. 고요함
아침에 호수에서 카약을 타는 것은 많은 사람이 경험하지 못하는 고요함을 제공해준다.

37 catapulted
v. 내던지다, 앞으로 밀어내다
신곡의 인기는 가수를 차트 최상위권으로 내던졌다.

38 pageantry   n. 화려한 행사
두 세계 지도자들의 만남은 보여주기식 화려한 행사 없이 이뤄졌다. 그들은 만나자마자 진지한 회의를 했다.

39 clandestine   adj. 은밀한, 비밀
어젯밤 회사 경영진과 대주주들의 비밀 회의가 있었다. 오늘 중대발표가 있을 것 같다.

40 castigated   v. 혹평하다
내 책임이 아니었던 사항에 대해 혹평을 받아서 속상하다.

41 congealed   adj. 굳다

노만의 코 밑에 케빈에게 맞은 부위에 피가 굳었다.

42 vacuous   adj. 멍청한

깁슨 박사는 학생들의 멍청한 표정들로 보아 아무도 그를 이해하지 못했다고 깨달았다.

43 불행한 – 가련한 – 동요하게 하다

44 의견을 밝히다 – 추파를 던지다 – 열변을 토하다

45 가까움 – 부근 – 기질

46 분명히 실재하는 – 감탄스러운 – 뚜렷한

47 평범한 – 우쭐해 하는 – 재미없는

48 파벌 – 집단 – 침울

49 솜씨 좋은 – 힘없는 – 나태한

50 후원, 지원 – 찬조, 후원 – 신성성

51 두서없는 – 보조적인, 부수적인 – 부수적인

52 살금살금 움직이다 – 거닐다 – 살금살금 움직이다

53 삽화 – 연 – 연, 절

54 신념 – 신조 – 대명사

55 극심한 곤궁, 극빈 – 증거, 증언 – 극빈

The Bodacious Book of
Voluminous Vocabulary

발 행 2021년 9월 30일 초판 1쇄
지은이 정태훈
펴낸이 최영민
출판등록 제406-2015-31호
펴낸곳 헤몬
전화 031-8071-0088
팩스 031-942-8688
주소 경기 파주시 신촌로 16
이메일 hermonh@naver.com

ISBN 979-11-91188-49-3 (13740)

• 헤르몬하우스는 피앤피북의 임프린트입니다.
• 책값은 뒤표지에 있습니다. 잘못된 책은 구입하신 곳에서 교환해드립니다.